PIZZA CITY, USA

PIZZA CITY, USA

101 Reasons Why Chicago Is America's Greatest Pizza Town

Steve Dolinsky

Foreword by Grant Achatz

NORTHWESTERN UNIVERSITY PRESS
EVANSTON, ILLINOIS

Northwestern University Press
www.nupress.northwestern.edu

Photographs by Steve Dolinsky, unless otherwise noted.

Printed in Canada

10   9   8   7   6   5   4   3   2   1

Library of Congress Cataloging-in-Publication Data

Names: Dolinsky, Steve, author.
Title: Pizza City, USA : 101 reasons why Chicago is America's greatest pizza
    town / Steve Dolinsky.
Other titles: 101 reasons why Chicago is America's greatest pizza town |
    One hundred one reasons why Chicago is America's greatest pizza town
Description: Evanston, Illinois : Northwestern University Press, 2018.
Identifiers: LCCN 2018004071 | ISBN 9780810137745 (pbk. : alk. paper) |
    ISBN 9780810137752 (ebook)
Subjects: LCSH: Pizza—Illinois—Chicago. | Pizzerias—Illinois—
    Chicago. | Chicago (Ill.)—Social life and customs.
Classification: LCC TX909.2.I32 C453 2018 | DDC 338.4764182480977311—
    dc23
LC record available at https://lccn.loc.gov/2018004071

For Neil and Dad, who showed me what
a strong work ethic looks like.

What I wouldn't give to have a pizza
with you both now.

CONTENTS

Grant Achatz

Throughout my career as a chef, I have been asked many times what my favorite foods are and what I eat at home. Inevitably, my answer is always the same: pizza.

Typically, people expect me to wax poetic about trips to Rome visiting tiny artisan pizzerias, where one person makes the pie, painstakingly following methods and recipes passed down from earlier generations. They think I will emotionally describe a *pizzaiolo* who has apprenticed for years, learning the craft much like a sushi master, in some hidden, unknown corridor, where you had to know someone to get in. All of this is absolutely true—I do love experiencing that, and I make it a point to visit at least one pizza place in each city I travel to.

But with pizza there is so much more.

Chefs find pizza's bandwidth impressive. Not only are there a tremendous number of styles to explore, but each of those styles has variations and twists based on the maker—the region they come from, their purpose, their creativity, and the ingredients available to them. Throughout my travels around the world, I have found pizza everywhere. It can go from a high-end art form and something considered very exclusive, to a readily accessible snack, intended solely to satiate hunger in a dire moment of need.

Way before pizza became the gastronomic addiction and obsession it is today, it was a big part of my life growing up in Michigan. "Pizza Day" at school was a huge deal. And every Friday night I would have my neighborhood friends over for a sleepover. Video games and movies would merely serve as a backdrop to the much-anticipated pizza. It was, as many Americans know it, "Pizza Night." Were these pizzas beautifully handcrafted objects of food art? You might expect me to say no, but the answer is a resounding yes, for a different reason. Pizza was fulfilling a social usefulness. It was something to look forward to, bringing people together, and to my twelve-year old palate, it was simply delicious. To this day, one of my favorite pizza experiences is making it at home with my two sons, getting to watch them pick out the toppings, and then the inevitable, impatient cracking open of the oven door, to see if the crust has blistered and the cheese is bubbling.

When I moved to Chicago in 2001, my preconception of the pizza here was solely deep-dish. Having never experienced a true deep-dish pizza, I blindly held the same opinion as many do from around the country: "Deep-dish is not pizza, it is a casserole." After living here for seventeen years and getting to experience—and appreciate—some delicious versions, my response is now: "So is a calzone a pizza? Open your mind." The other false impression outsiders have is that deep-dish is the only

Pizza as interpreted by Alinea

 # INTRODUCTION

Americans sure do love pizza. According to a study by *PMQ Pizza Magazine*, we, as a nation, spent more than $38 billion on this beloved combo of crust, sauce, and toppings in 2015 alone. That's a lot of dough, and—not surprisingly—when it comes to assessing pizza quality, it really is all about the dough. Say what you will about the merits of San Marzano tomatoes, *fior di latte* versus mozzarella *di bufala*, or sausage made in-house versus the local butcher's recipe. When it comes to assessing pizza quality, the dough is what stands out, or, alternatively, dooms an otherwise well-intentioned pie. It is, after all, the basis for everything and the one thing that a pizza lover experiences with each and every bite.

Just as each pie must have a solid foundation in order to stand out, each city that considers itself a "pizza town" must have a solid variety of pizza offerings in order to cut the mustard. In this way, Chicago has a special connection to pizza. I say it's the city with the most pizza variety in the country. Just Google "Chicago pizzerias" and you'll get more than four hundred thousand results. As for varieties, I tallied ten distinctive types in my research: tavern-style, thin, New York-style, artisan, Neapolitan, deep-dish, stuffed, Sicilian, Roman, and Detroit-style.

In New York City, slice joints are ubiquitous—it seems there's one on every corner. This led Colin Hagendorf to write the book *Slice Harvester: A Memoir in Pizza*, for which the author spent two years tasting a slice of cheese pizza from every slice joint in the city. NYC also has Neapolitan joints, serving this subcategory of artisan pies, and several places that offer charred-and-blistered New York-style pizza, slightly thicker in the middle than the typical slice. There are also a number of heftier, Sicilian-style joints and a handful now boasting Detroit-style. But in terms of options, there just aren't that many outside of the greasy, foldable slices that every food blogger and celebrity seems to think warrant an Instagram homage. How can I be so sure? I visited fifty well-regarded places in the five boroughs over the course of ten months (all listed at pizzacityusa .com) so believe me, I'm sure.

Pizza aficionados in other regions of the United States also seem to think their cities deserve recognition, when in fact they typically offer one-note experiences. In New Haven, Connecticut, home to Yale University, you'll find two of the most famous coal ovens in America, Sally's Apizza and Frank Pepe Pizzeria Napoletana. Both establishments produce enormous pies, the size of semitrailer hubcaps, with the requisite misshapen edges, blistered tops, and signature sauces. However, that's the end of the story.

In St. Louis, Imo's offers the original St. Louis-style pizza—thin and crispy, topped with Provel cheese—but that's about it. Phoenix is the birthplace of the legendary Pizzeria Bianco, but outside of Chris Bianco's gem of a shop near the Science Museum downtown, his artisan pies remain an anomaly in the city.

When I tell people I'm from Chicago and that I'm a food writer, their first questions usually hover around hot dogs and deep-dish pizza. They're often surprised when I tell them that yes, deep-dish was created in Chicago, but people who live in Chicago tend not to eat it as much as the tourists do. It's kind of like how New Yorkers rarely go to Times Square and stand outside of the *Good Morning America* studios, hoping to be on TV.

In fact, walk into any neighborhood pizza joint, be it a family-run place in a bar or a local chain with multiple locations, and ask them what they're known for. I'll bet it's a Chicago-style thin pizza, also known as tavern-style, rather than deep-dish.

That's why I always laugh when New York City–based media talk about Chicago-style pizza. They come here for a day or two, talk to the out-of-state rubes waiting for an hour in the cold outside famous deep-dish pizza restaurants, and then proceed to dump all over the city by mocking the use of a knife and fork to eat pizza. They don't have a clue. Many locals actually agree with Jon Stewart's rant about deep-dish on *The Daily Show*: "This is not pizza, this is tomato soup in a bread bowl!" (I actually believe he was referring to stuffed pizza, because this depiction hardly describes the city's best deep-dish, but I digress.)

The true pizza landscape in Chicago is far more diverse than the deep-dish stereotypes suggest. Though our unique regional style is notable and is often quite delicious when done right, as are the regional styles in St. Louis and New York, it's hard to argue with Chicago's range of offerings. I've had plenty of opportunities as a professional food reporter to assess and, if you'll forgive me, *chew* on it, and the pies discussed in this book are all the evidence I need to say that Chicago truly deserves the title "Pizza City, USA."

Call it hubris or just plain crazy, but over the course of two months, I managed to sample pizzas from a staggering seventy-six different locations throughout Chicagoland (referring to the combination of city and suburbs, including the five collar counties, that form a contiguous border around the city proper). Originally embarking on this pizza project for a special series of reports for my employer, ABC7 Eyewitness News, I considered it a once-in-a-lifetime quest, unparalleled in Chicago's illustrious pizza history and unlikely ever to be eclipsed, at least in terms of thoroughness. I figured my efforts would be celebrated, like those of a soldier returning victorious from the battlefield.

What I didn't expect was the massive quantity of impassioned responses I got from readers, viewers, and social media followers. "You forgot about Phil's," they reminded me, "not the one in Bridgeport, but Oak Lawn." "Any list without Pudgy's isn't a proper list at all," another naysayer scolded. That's when I knew I had only scratched the surface.

Earlier that year, I had embarked on an Italian beef quest, targeting thirty-one locations throughout Chicagoland, figuring that was a large enough sample to rank them all. I did the same thing with Vietnamese pho, visiting every joint in the city and slurping from at least thirty-one bowls of the heady, rich beef broth with rice noodles.

But pizza is different, as I quickly discovered. Chicagoland offers multiple styles of pizza—tavern-style, thin crust, deep-dish, etc.—not to mention the recent wave of Neapolitan-style options, with these skilled *pizzaiolos* all trying to outdo each other. I knew that if I was going to produce a proper accounting of Chicago's pizza landscape for this book, I needed to eat a lot more pizza than I had for my original quest. My editor and I settled on a sample of 101 pizzas—just enough to get the lay of the land while (hopefully) limiting my weight gain.

I ended up trying a lot more than that (180 actually), since not every pizza made the final cut. Many were great; some were overrated. All of them pushed up the number on my scale. Taken together, the pizzas that I tried offer a complete picture of the unparalleled pizza scene in Chicago, and if I weren't still so full I'd happily eat each of them again.

PIZZA BASICS

CHAPTER 1

What Is Chicago-Style Pizza?

The City of Big Shoulders is a city of neighborhoods—seventy-seven to be exact. Each neighborhood has its own flavor. Bridgeport, home to the Daley political machine and more than a few judges, is traditionally Irish. Bronzeville was the gateway for the Great Migration and continues to remain African American. Logan Square is where you'll find skinny jeans and tattoos on your friendly barista, while Rogers Park still qualifies as the city's unofficial port-of-entry for the Indian and Pakistani diasporas (though my friends at Patel Bros., a marketplace for fine Indian ingredients, would argue it's now suburban Schaumburg). The neighborhoods are what make Chicago so wonderfully diverse—a multicolored quilt of different languages, cultures, and tastes. But when it comes to pizza, the city seems to be divided into only two camps along a dual axis: North vs. South and Deep vs. Thin.

North vs. South

Long before the Cubs won the World Series, the city had an identity crisis split roughly along Madison Street, the official "0" point on the North–South grid system that Daniel Burnham devised over a century ago. Streets to the north of Madison belong to the Cubs, while streets to the south are White Sox territory.

Mayor Richard M. Daley and President Barack Obama are proud Sox fans. (The Cubs wisely presented the latter with an away jersey, which says only "Chicago" on the front, at their White House ceremony—in case the

President didn't care to wear the home jersey, which screams "Cubs" across the chest.) On the other hand, Mayor Rahm Emanuel is often spotted in North Side restaurants, and his love for Cubbie blue runs deep.

How does pizza figure into this divide? For one thing, South Side pizza joints tend to make their sauces sweeter. Just look at Palermo's on Ninety-Fifth or Triano's on South Archer. They fess up to using sugar in their tomato sauces. On the extreme side, there's Arrenello's Pizza in Tinley Park, where the sauce is sweeter than a Hershey's Kiss. If you like that sort of thing, I recommend crumbled Sprinkles Cupcakes as an extra topping. A sweeter tomato sauce is definitely a characteristic you rarely see on the North Side.

Chicago also has more pizza chains loyal to their neighborhoods than you might think. North Side legends include Lou Malnati's, Giordano's, and Rosati's. (There are actually two Rosati's, the result of a family feud that split the chain in two; they're mostly in the suburbs.) But did you know about Waldo Cooney's and Barraco's (South and Southwest Sides), or Parlor Pizza and Chicago's Pizza on the North Side? Each of these companies has multiple locations, making our cheese-and-sausage-covered landscape even more nuanced than I previously thought.

The South and Southwest Sides also tend to have more restaurants that double as Italian beef operations, and thus offer giardiniera, the optional pizza topping that consists of an oil-slicked, spicy relish of celery, sport peppers, cauliflower, and carrots. You won't see that option in New York City, and if you come across it in Chicago, get it. The crunchy, spicy condiment is a perfect foil for the rich, cheesy, salty toppings that typically inhabit a thin pie.

Regional North vs. South differences, however, tend to be malleable. For example, several notable North Side chains, such as Giordano's, were actually born on the South Side. Known for its stuffed pies rather than standard deep-dish, Giordano's is now the official pizza at Wrigley Field—a reality that probably says more about the size of Giordano's venture capital–backed checkbook than the unique quality of their pies. It's a similar story with Home Run Inn, which has a place in many North Side grocery store frozen food sections, but was born on Thirty-First Street, in the shadow of Comiskey Park.

Deep vs. Thin

While pizza flavors and sauces may separate North and South Side Chicagoans, pizza style is not really a differentiating factor. As I mentioned earlier, it's mostly tourists and late-night talk show hosts who think Chicago is a deep-dish pizza town. They make jokes about how we swim in pools of sauce atop double layers of dough and use a knife and fork to eat a simple slice of pepperoni.

Ed Levine, the NYC-based founder of the website seriouseats.com, authored a pizza book several years ago, and in it he referred to deep-dish as a "cheese casserole." I don't disagree. But what I do take issue with is that Levine claims Chicagoans eat deep-dish every chance we get. This couldn't be further from the truth. Deep-dish may have been created here, but it's simply one of the ten distinct styles of pizza we offer. The only time you'll see a local eating deep-dish is when one of their out-of-town friends or relatives comes to visit and insists they go wait in line somewhere for a ridiculously long time to order one.

"Chicago is a good neighborhood town and it's also a good tavern town," said Tim Samuelson, cultural historian at the Chicago Cultural Center. "The corner tavern is the great gathering place in each community. The [square-cut] pizza wound up being a staple of many classic Chicago taverns. It works out well and it's tasty. You can hold it in one hand and hold your drink in the other, which also marks the big difference [with] New York pizza, where you have to do this elaborate folding—and you still wind up with part of the pizza in your lap."

According to a 2016 Harris Poll on preferences for half a dozen different pizza styles, 15 percent of Americans prefer deep-dish while twice that number prefer thin crust. There's a reason our tavern-style (Chicago-style thin) and thins take up the most space in this book. It's what we eat when we want pizza. As I visited restaurants anonymously, asking the person behind the counter which style of pizza they were known for or which was the most popular (many places in and around Chicago offer multiple styles), the majority said "thin." I dare you to eat a slice of deep-dish (or two) and not feel like taking a nap immediately afterward. It's like an afghan for your stomach. Don't get me started on stuffed. While several places offer it on their menus, only a handful consider it their specialty; even fewer do it well enough to warrant a return visit.

Though the dichotomy between deep-dish and thin crust pizzas is one that has more to do with Chicago's reputation than its reality, the fact that these two drastically different foods have thrived within the same city speaks to Chicago's pizza prowess. Each side has its staunch defenders, and—though it's already clear where my own loyalties lie—Chicago could not be Pizza City, USA, without these two distinctive styles, as well as the eight others that complete the picture.

CHAPTER 2

Methodology for the 101

Who made me the expert on pizza? I get this question frequently, and I'm happy to make my case here. Let's forget, for a moment, my professional credentials. I could probably just say I've been covering food professionally in Chicago full-time since 1995, and leave it at that. I've also eaten pizzas at some of the touchstones in America—Bianco (Phoenix), Frank Pepe's (New Haven), A16 & Delfina (San Francisco), Mozza (Los Angeles), and Lucali (NYC). But the thing that truly qualifies me more than anyone else is the fact that I wasn't born in Chicago.

Stay with me.

One of the unfortunate things pizza does is it creates bias. Midway through my research, I diagnosed a common ailment that affects thousands of people, which most likely includes you or someone you know. That malady is the Pizza I Grew Up Eating (PIGUE) Syndrome. The result of countless birthday parties, special events, and high school sleepovers, PIGUE somehow attaches itself to the frontal cortex. Few of us have fully developed palates when we're young (although I'm guessing Andrew Zimmern and Anthony Bourdain ate foie gras as teenagers), so it's difficult to assess food accurately in your preteen and teenage years.

The pizza I had as a kid in St. Cloud, Minnesota, was Shakey's. It was our go-to destination after Little League games (followed by Dairy Queen), and it served as a de facto birthday headquarters for me and many of my friends. Do I think Shakey's has the best pizza in the world? Of course not—it's chain food mediocrity along the lines of Pizza Hut, Domino's, and Little Caesar's. I'm wise enough to know that there are plenty of pizzas out there far superior to the processed-cheese-and-sweet-tomato-sauce-on-cardboard that defined my childhood pizza eating experience.

PIGUE Syndrome, however, hits Chicagoans especially hard. I can now tell where someone is from based solely on the kind of pizza they love. You like Armand's? I'm guessing you grew up near Elmwood Park. More of an Aurelio's person? Even if you don't insist it comes out of the "old" oven, there's a pretty good chance you grew up in Homewood or Flossmoor. Still think Barnaby's has the best thin crust in the world? Here's some news for you: not only are you from the North Shore but that cornmeal crust is a myth—they only sprinkle cornmeal (as many other smart places do) underneath the pizza to keep the crust from sticking to the bottom of the oven.

And the list goes on. A cult-like pocket of eaters on the Northwest Side is loyal to Trattoria Porretta. Some crazy Norridge devotees swear by Villa Napoli, although after my visit there with Fooditor founder and *Chicago Reader* contributor Michael Gebert, I'm not sure why. Down in Palos Heights there's a faction that truly believed Anemone Caffé (no longer open) made an authentic Neapolitan pizza, which is like saying the Bears are fielding one of the NFL's top teams right now. The loyalty and stubbornness was truly puzzling, especially after I took two bites.

But I get it. PIGUE affects everyone, and it doesn't matter if the dough is tough or flavorless, the mozzarella is part-skim from a giant bag, or the sausage comes in frozen. No one—not even a professional eater who attempts to judge on an even playing field—is going to change their mind. Which leads me back to my thesis on why I'm the most qualified person to tackle this subject.

I didn't grow up here but I've lived in Chicago for twenty-five years. I have no childhood memories in any of these legendary joints, but I moved here in my twenties, just as my palate started to grow up, and shortly thereafter began eating professionally. I became wise enough to know the difference between a place that made its own gyros (Parthenon) and one that didn't, despite its outsized reputation (sorry, Chuck Wagon). I still had plenty to learn, of course, and still do, but I like to think I don't carry biases around like those misguided souls who still think Gene & Jude's makes the best hot dogs. (Don't get me wrong. I respect their longevity, but it's hard to argue on their behalf when they still sell size 10s, aka "meat pencils," with only a fraction of the holy seven condiments.)

Here's the rub: unlike other homegrown "experts," I'm not afraid to call it like I see it, and I can recognize the effects of PIGUE. Honesty is always the most refreshing aspect of my quest. I don't feel inhibited, as most would, knocking more than a few reputation coasters off their tomato-and-cheese-fortified pedestals (looking at you, Art of Pizza).

I know there are several styles of pizza in Chicago, but I didn't want to define them until I recognized regular patterns. Ultimately I came up with ten pizza categories, including an all-new one: artisan. I'll explain more about my categories at the beginning of each chapter. Some restaurants are featured in more than one category; for example, Paulie Gee's has two notable styles: artisan and Detroit.

I also wanted to give everyone a fair shake, which means that just because one pizza place has a special pie, say an 'nduja (a spicy, spreadable pork salumi from Italy) with fresh ricotta and arugula, and another place keeps things pretty basic, it wouldn't be fair to judge them side-by-side. The one with killer toppings would be far superior, even if the crust or sauce wasn't. So for consistency, I decided to place a standard order: half pepperoni and half sausage. If the pizza place specialized in a Neapolitan-style with a fancier wood-burning oven and listed a Margherita, then that's what I'd order as a baseline, judging just the crust, tomato sauce, and mozzarella (but mostly crust).

I made a point to call ahead before visiting each establishment to ask what their specialty was, to ensure I was trying the proper pizza at each place. In several instances, menus listed multiple styles—thin, extra thin, double-dough, deep-dish, and stuffed—so I'd ask the person at the counter or my server what the restaurant was known for. A few times the server offered up a personal favorite from the menu, which didn't influence me at all. Sometimes a restaurant ended up in more than one category, such as thin crust *and* by-the-slice or New York-style.

I wanted this quest to be a snapshot in time. One of my colleagues asked why I felt compelled to return to places I'd already frequented, like Lou's. "Why not just use a picture you already have on file?" Because that wouldn't be fair. If you're going to make a list with any credibility, you need to visit the places in question within the same time frame. What if the cook has left after twenty years and a bunch of teenagers are now in charge? Don't you think that might change the quality and consistency? Burt's Place in Morton Grove, a precursor to Burt's later establishment, Pequod's, is a good example. It had been a few years since I visited the original Burt's Place—and since that visit, the spot had been temporarily closed "due to health reasons." So there was no way I could include my older review in a modern pizza roundup. Sadly, Burt passed away a few months after my initial quest was completed; new owners took over, re-creating his original recipes. I had a chance to visit in early 2017, after the grand reopening and during the second wave of tasting for this book. It was pretty good, but not quite as special as I had initially remembered.

Another parameter, at least during the first round of tasting, was to concentrate on pizza places—restaurants that devoted more than 50 percent of their food business to pizza. This did two things: it kept me from going insane on a never-ending treadmill of pizzas, and it whittled down the contenders considerably. But as I restarted the tasting process in 2017, I realized that it would be a disservice not to include restaurants like Quartino and Piccolo Sogno—among others—where they have pizza ovens and churn out very good pies, even if the pizzas make up a small percentage of the menu.

Scoring was pretty simple. Points were awarded for crust, sauce, sausage and pepperoni quality, application and mouthfeel of cheese(s), and overall taste—with crust weighing most heavily in the equation. The ratio was certainly a factor: the term I came up with is Optimal Bite Ratio (OBR). If the crust was good but overwhelmed by too much cheese, then points were deducted. Conversely, that didn't mean I wanted a mouthful of bare baked gluten in every bite.

Finally, I always visited anonymously, without warning, and oftentimes alone, although on occasion I went with a friend or relative who was game. I always paid with my own credit card (essentially spending my book advance on pizzas) and after leaving, I posted a picture and some commentary on Instagram, where I post both @stevedolinsky as well as @pizzacityusa. If you're curious about where I ate in New York City, check out #StevesNYCPizza.

CHAPTER 3

Glossary of Pizza Terminology

Some of the following terms are industry standards. Others I created myself after realizing there were no other words to describe what I intended to say. It's a short list, but if you scan it quickly you'll gain a better understanding of my descriptions of individual places and pizzas.

"00" The type of Italian flour usually used by hardcore *pizzaiolos* when making a Neapolitan pizza.

beehive Refers to the shape of the brick wood-burning oven that is typically the focal point for a serious pizza operation. This includes a large igloo-shaped bottom where the wood burns and the pizzas cook, as well as a long, slender vent to guide smoke out of the building.

***bufala* (BOO-fah-la)** Fresh mozzarella made from buffalo's milk. When true mozzarella is made in the Italian style, it usually calls for this kind of milk. Domestic producers in the United States often substitute *fior di latte*, or cow's milk.

char The blackened spots that dot a pizza, usually from excessive hot spots in the oven. Charring is typically more prevalent on Neapolitan pies.

char dome A small dome, anywhere from a half-inch to an inch or so in diameter, which appears on the surface of artisan and Neapolitan pizzas. Char domes are blackened and filled with air pockets.

cheese lava The runny, oozing mass of mozzarella that typically spills out of an overstuffed deep-dish, or (more likely) a stuffed pizza, when a slice is moved to a plate.

cheese pull   Think of the Instagram-worthy shot of the mozzarella pulling away from the slice as you remove it from the main pie. Some pulls are flaccid and runny; others sturdy and majestic. Either way, a decent pull means the kitchen isn't skimping on mozzarella. Too much cheese pull, however, might mean an imbalance when it comes to OBR.

cornicione (**core-nitch-ee-OH-nay**)   The outer lip, or puffy perimeter, of a Neapolitan pizza. The *cornicione* should be slightly misshapen and jagged but also chewy and filled with tiny air pockets.

docker   Also referred to as a dough docker or roller docker, this handheld tool has a small cylinder at the end (think of a mini-steamroller like you'd see smoothing out blacktop) that has small squat pins or spikes on it. Bakers roll it across their doughs before baking to get rid of air pockets and prevent undesired rising or blistering in the middle of the pizza.

doming   The act of using a pizza peel to raise a pizza in a wood-burning oven up to the highest point of the dome and where the hottest temperatures are. This quickly sears and bakes the top of the pizza, creating a little extra char and caramelization.

fermentation   The process of letting the dough rest to allow the yeast and bacteria inside the dough to convert carbohydrates to carbon dioxide, which causes gas bubbles to form. This has a leavening effect on dough and the process causes a strong aromatic sensation that is usually pleasing.

fior di latte (**fee-OR de LAH-tay**)   Fresh mozzarella made from pasteurized or unpasteurized cow's milk rather than water buffalo milk (*bufala*), which is what a Neapolitan purist would typically use. It's usually less expensive than *bufala* and more widely used in America.

leavening   During fermentation, gas bubbles expand inside the dough, making it increase in size.

leopard spotting   The tiny black char spots that line the perimeter of a nicely fermented Neapolitan or artisan pizza.

lip   The outer ring, or perimeter, of the pizza, frequently referred to as the "heel." Also known as a *cornicione* when talking about a Neapolitan pie.

Optimal Bite Ratio (OBR)   My term for the perfect combination of dough, cheese, sauce, and toppings in each bite. Balance is key, either elevating a pie to the 101, or sinking it into the realm of forgettable pizzas.

peel The long-handled tool, usually with a metal or wooden head slightly wider than a pizza, used to move the pizza in and out of the oven as well as to reposition it while baking, which ensures even cooking.

PIGUE Syndrome "Pizza I Grew Up Eating" is an affliction, a crippling bias that forces normally sane people to support the notion that the pizza they grew up with is somehow the best on the planet.

pizzaiolo A person responsible for making pizza—from the dough to the sauce and on through the baking process. The word is usually used to refer to a person with extensive training who has mastered the Neapolitan pie.

proofing Term used by bakers for the final rise of shaped dough before baking. It refers to a specific resting period within the fermentation process.

San Marzano The tomato variety of choice not only for Neapolitan aficionados but also for many artisan cooks and *pizzaiolos*.

sheeter A machine with two opposing rollers that you can set to a certain thickness. It is used to pass balls of dough through, pressing them out into flat, wide sheets. While convenient and good for eliminating any chance that an inexperienced cook will mess up a dough by hand-tossing or rolling out with a pin, sheeters tend to force all of the air out of the dough, resulting in a tougher crust.

undercarriage The area beneath the pizza that you usually can't see, unless you lift up a slice. It's the only part of the pizza that's in direct contact with the oven's surface.

Vera Pizza Napoletana (VPN) A governing body based in Italy, which bestows its VPN designation to *pizzaiolos* and restaurants that abide by a number of strict guidelines regarding the type of flour, tomatoes, and cheese, as well as the length of fermentation, type and temperature of the oven, and other quality controls.

PIZZA STYLES

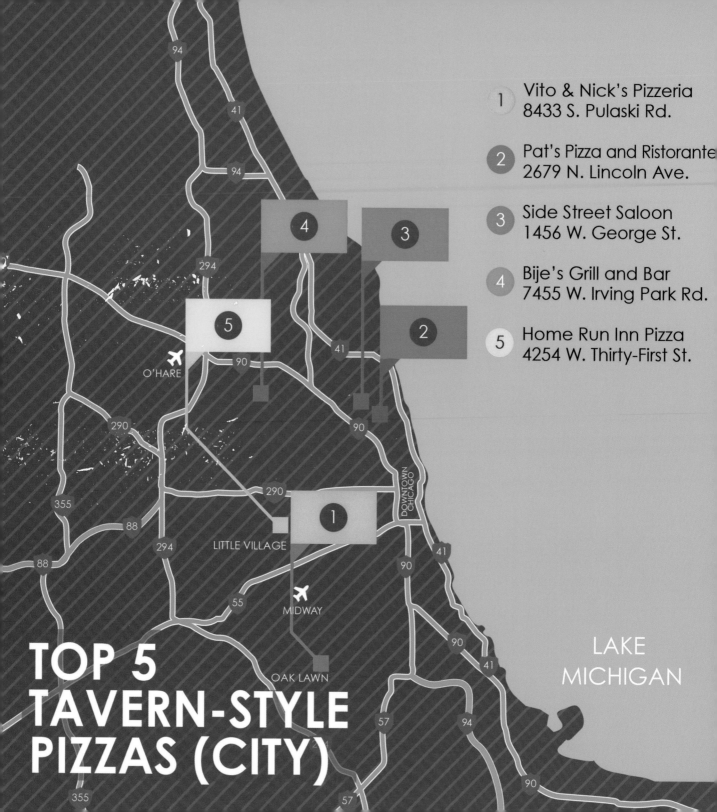

TOP 5 TAVERN-STYLE PIZZAS (CITY)

1. Vito & Nick's Pizzeria
   8433 S. Pulaski Rd.

2. Pat's Pizza and Ristorante
   2679 N. Lincoln Ave.

3. Side Street Saloon
   1456 W. George St.

4. Bije's Grill and Bar
   7455 W. Irving Park Rd.

5. Home Run Inn Pizza
   4254 W. Thirty-First St.

LAKE MICHIGAN

DOWNTOWN CHICAGO
O'HARE
MIDWAY
LITTLE VILLAGE
OAK LAWN

CHAPTER 4

Tavern-Style (Chicago-Style Thin)

Ask diehard Chicagoans how they define "Chicago pizza" and they'll respond with a unanimous "thin" rather than "thick." So why is it that out-of-towners think Chicago is a deep-dish town? Blame it on the media, I guess, and those giant Giordano's billboards. Maybe it's because Pizzeria Uno debuted here in 1943 or because tourists come in droves to see, taste, and poke around what they think makes Chicago famous. But no amount of advertising or tourism hype can change the fact that Chicagoans like their pizza thin.

Maybe a little history can explain this great pizza misconception. Chicago is the city that works, and immigrants who originally built the roads, bridges, and skyscrapers loved to end the workday at the neighborhood tavern for a beer. Intuitive bar owners realized they could make ultra-thin pizzas for cheap, cut their pies into tiny squares (known as the "party cut"), and then pass the bite-sized snacks around the bar.

The goal was to get something salty into the customers' mouths, so they'd order more beer. The plan worked. This practice also launched the Chicago tavern-style pizza, also known as Chicago-style thin, which shows up at legendary places like Marie's, Vito & Nick's, and Pat's, not to mention suburban haunts like Barnaby's and Armand's.

In line with this backstory, Chicago historian Tim Samuelson says that one of the reasons thin, square-cut pizzas came about was because "you can pop the whole piece in your mouth at once. The corners—you've got a lot of nice pieces in there. That built-in crusty handle is missing from the middle. But you rarely see a pizza platter with any remaining pizza going back to the kitchen."

In other words, those middle pieces have no crust on their borders; they're flabby and cheesy all the way around. The pie's corner pieces have actual hard crust on the sides—your "crusty handle"—which makes it easier to hold a pizza slice.

There are entire swaths of the city that claim true Chicago pizza is thin and not a thick casserole. Also, as I explained in this book's introduction, my eating research led me to actually identify five different categories of thin pizza in Chicago: thin, Chicago-style thin (or tavern-style), Neapolitan, New York-style slices, and artisan. After all my research, I theorize that tavern-style is what Chicagoans mean by "thin."

To find the best tavern-style pizza in Chicago proper as well as in the Chicago suburbs, I first came up with a list of contenders. Before visiting each establishment, I called ahead to determine whether the restaurant's specialty was indeed thin crust, tavern-style. When I arrived, I ordered a small half-sausage, half-pepperoni.

I'll list all of the tavern-styles in the city alphabetically, starring those that made the top five. Then I'll do the same thing with the suburbs. The accompanying maps roughly show their locations.

City

There are actually two Bricks pizza places on Lincoln Avenue in the city. There's Bricks Chicago in Lincoln Park and Big Bricks farther north in Lake View, with both establishments owned by the same person, but each with different offerings.

Big Bricks has a smoker that churns out respectable ribs, pork, and brisket, including the pride of Kansas City, burnt ends. The bar has a number of impressive beers. It feels a little like a Wisconsin hunting lodge where the local VFW goes to meet on Tuesdays.

The menu special on the night I visited was a remarkable Reuben sandwich made with smoked corned beef, Thousand Island dressing, and homemade sauerkraut. It was absolutely delicious. So was the pizza.

A true tavern-style pie, this one combines whole wheat flour with high-gluten flour, which gives the crust another level of flavor I have rarely, if ever, come across in Chicago. Properly crispy-crunchy on the undercarriage, this pie features sausage from Bartlett-based Greco and Sons, Inc., that is a tad spicier than normal and just barely coated with a lacy, caramelized afghan of whole milk and low-moisture mozzarella. About a quarter-inch of the lip is unprotected from any sauce or cheese, which some might find to be distinctly lacking sauce. I disagree. Whereas this crispy edge is sometimes left behind on the plate in a pile of what look like tiny bones as a sort of *fuck you* to the inferior cook, signifying that the only edible part of the pizza is the area that's covered by sauce, cheese, and meat, that's

Big Bricks
3832 N. Lincoln Avenue
773-525-5022
www.bigbrickschicago.com
Ordered: small half-sausage, half-pepperoni

Bricks Chicago
1909 N. Lincoln Avenue
312-255-0851
www.brickschicagopizza.com

not the case here. The addition of whole wheat gives it some nuttiness, and the fact that Big Bricks figured out the OBR (the perfect combination of dough, cheese, sauce, and toppings in each bite) mightily contributes to the pleasure of crushing one of these pies.

Design aside, regulars seem to come for Bije's Chicago-style thin pizza (or get it to go, as I saw several make their way out the door with pizza boxes). That's not a surprise, really. Owner Carl Quilici's father, Armando, was one of the original owners of Gino's East downtown; yet despite having that deep-dish pedigree, Carl has devoted his kitchen to thin crust ever since he opened in the Belmont Heights neighborhood in 1995.

The pies are typical Chicago-style thin with an even smaller square cut than usual. Whole milk mozzarella blankets generous hunks of fennel-laced sausage, bought from Chicago's Anichini Brothers, Inc. Even though the cheese is ample, it's cooked to the perfect doneness. No need to ask for "well-done" here, as you must at so many places in order to get a properly cooked pie. The edges and bottom are super crispy, with barely a half-inch of open real estate around the perimeter before the sauce and cheese begin to intrude.

I think the crust lacks flavor, but when combined with the homemade tomato sauce—as intense and flavorful as anything in town—plus the proper proportion of cheese, each bite is a pleasure, even the ones with pepperoni buried beneath the cheese, which makes it impossible for the spicy circles to crisp up.

★ **Bije's Grill and Bar**
7455 W. Irving Park Road
773-625-9700
www.bijespizza.com
Ordered: small half-sausage,
  half-pepperoni

It's easy to miss Bije's (pronounced Bee Gee's) as you cruise down Irving Park Road on your way to or from Harlem Avenue, but it's worth keeping an eye out. There's convenient free parking on the side of the building and, despite its forlorn facade, the interior delivers typical Chicago neighborhood-bar conviviality. All six TVs were tuned to the Sox game, and the décor leans toward the Bears-Blackhawks-Bulls theme. A significant bar runs almost the entire length of the main dining room, which is adorned with actual green-and-white Chicago street signs as well as an enormous moose head.

Size can be deceiving. Borelli's medium, which is the smallest option available, could easily feed four or five hungry people. Big seems to be a theme here, as this Ravenswood neighborhood favorite offers plenty of large tables for groups and parties as well as a nice-sized stage for live music. The artwork is limited to a giant Italian flag and some oil paintings. The music on the stereo is pure '70s rock—the soundtrack to my childhood.

Owner Mark Borelli comes naturally to the restaurant biz—his grandparents ran a diner near the United Center that burned down in the '68 riots—and he says his pies follow the recipe he's been making since he was twelve. That means typical tavern-style, with an über-thin, cracker-like crust as the foundation of this square-cut pie.

The crust has an almost saltine-like quality, making an audible crunch when you bite into it. The whole milk mozzarella topping is pretty average, although the sausage has a nice kick to it, with notes of fennel, oregano, and garlic. There wasn't too much sauce beneath a generous cheese layer, but I have a feeling regulars don't mind.

Since the crust on its own doesn't have much flavor, Borelli's runs the sauce, cheese, and toppings all the way to the edge of the pie, leaving barely any naked perimeter, which I'm not complaining about.

Borelli's
2124 W. Lawrence Avenue
773-275-1700
www.borellipizza.com
Ordered: medium half-sausage,
    half-pepperoni

Touting "Pizza & Pierogi," and with a giant signboard listing the number of Polish vodkas they carry, this South Loop neighborhood joint clearly has more than just pizza on the menu. A number of sandwiches and salads also star here, although their Polish ingredients—like smoked kielbasa and sauerkraut—can also be used as pizza toppings. Flo & Santos typically has a "farmer's market" pizza as a special, but, as per my pizza quest rules, I opted for their half-sausage (Italian rather than Polish), half-pepperoni pie.

The crust here is classic tavern-style, which I'd define as a supremely thin layer of dough that's just enough to hold the toppings. I would have preferred a slightly crisper crust, as there was no crunch, just chew. Whole milk mozzarella is generously applied, though a tad too heavily in the center, where it overwhelms the ingredients. The ingredients themselves are tasty, especially the generous crumbles of sausage. The sauce is pleasant, but not necessarily remarkable—kind of like a Bruno Mars hit that's great the first time you hear it but doesn't get stuck in your head.

Overall, it's a tasty pizza that I'd have no problem crushing with a hungry friend. It doesn't make my top five in the tavern-style category, but if you want a place to watch a game, eat some pizza, and drink a nice craft beer, there are few better options in the area. And if your crazy uncle from the burbs doesn't feel like pizza, he'll be content with the hearty menu's other plentiful options.

Flo & Santos
1310 S. Wabash Avenue
312-566-9817
www.floandsantos.com
Ordered: 12-inch half-sausage,
   half-pepperoni

At first I was extremely pessimistic about this one—one of the most expensive pizzas in Chicago—especially considering that it's from a mini-chain with nine locations in the region and a massive frozen pizza line. They also sponsor the White Sox, and anytime there's a pizza at a stadium, it's usually not of the greatest quality. Choosing to visit Home Run Inn Pizza's original location, which launched in 1947, I figured the pizza might have a chance of rising above mediocrity—despite the high price tag. It did.

The main dining room is a collection of Everywhere, USA: a big screen, a small bar with neon beer ads, and a long brick wall. The row of Tiffany lamps hovering over the wooden booths is a nice touch, right out of the 1970s Chicago neighborhood pizzeria design playbook.

My pizza arrived resting on a proprietary pan, which features a series of protruding, stubby dimples that elevate the pizza to allow airflow underneath and prevent the bottom from getting soft or soggy.

Even though this pizza is classified as "thin," there is a slightly raised lip—the result of pinching the dough before baking, like the crimping that pie bakers do with their crusts—that gives it a slightly elevated perimeter. I loved the crunch, both on the sides and from underneath. As I bit into the lip, the dough had an almost malty character.

This is pizza to be eaten while drinking beers. And despite the raised edge, make no mistake, the interior is as thin as can be. Generously applied homemade sausage is assertive without being overwhelming. The mozzarella and tomato sauce combine in a very pleasant way. The result is not too sweet, not too acidic.

OK, so I was wrong about this going in, and I'm glad to see that having nine locations doesn't necessarily mean skimping on quality.

✳ **Home Run Inn Pizza**
Chicago locations include:
4254 W. Thirty-First Street
773-247-9696
10900 S. Western Avenue
773-432-9696
6221 S. Archer Avenue
773-581-9696
3215 N. Sheffield Avenue
773-756-5576
www.homeruninnpizza.com
Home Run Inn Pizza includes five
    suburban locations: Berwyn,
    Bolingbrook, Darien, Hillside,
    and Melrose Park.
Ordered: small half-sausage,
    half-pepperoni

This neighborhood throwback has been slinging pasta, panini, and broasted chicken since 1947. The Logan Square location, where I went, has dramatic wallpaper depicting images from the Italian countryside and the requisite trio of TVs tuned to whatever game is on. The menu is massive, and their pizza section is also—if you'll forgive the pun—pretty deep.

In addition to their famous thin and crispy, they also make deep-dish, New York-style, and an assortment of gourmet pizzas with ingredient combinations like gorgonzola and candied walnuts or Thai chicken with peanut sauce. They also have a gluten-free pizza. My server suggested the thin and crispy since that's what they've been doing for more than sixty years.

The pie came served on a tray with a few dozen holes punched out of it; the air circulation promotes a crispy bottom, and indeed, after ten minutes, the pieces retained a bit of their texture. You can see just how even the browning is underneath each piece—even the ones in the middle. Their sausage with its hint of fennel is just barely perceptible, as each little jagged knob is tucked beneath a lacy blanket of mozzarella.

The cheese, in fact, is quite generous, and I'm not sure they need that much. On the pepperoni side, the discs are placed on top of the cheese, which allows them to crisp up ever so slightly. The tomato sauce is quite thick by tavern-style standards, but no matter, the OBR is intact and each bite is a pleasure.

Marcello's
2475 N. Milwaukee Avenue
773-252-2620
www.marcellos.com
Marcello's includes one suburban location in Northbrook.
Ordered: small (12-inch) half-sausage, half pepperoni

Marie's Pizza & Liquors
4127 W. Lawrence Avenue
773-685-5030
www.mariespizzachicago.com
Ordered: medium half-sausage,
    half-pepperoni

Talk about a throwback. You almost expect the ghost of Studs Terkel to belly up next to Nelson Algren at the bar. The vintage mirrors reflect the Chicago skyline, and the decorative ceiling lights over the bar cast shadows on red vinyl booths that would be right at home in a *Mad Men* revival—if Matthew Weiner had grown up near Pulaski and Lawrence.

The pizza is all about its thin crust, which many of my readers matter-of-factly say is the best in town. I take exception.

My pizza arrived nicely well done, so there were no puddles of grease, and they use a top-notch sausage—you could see the fennel seeds. But like most tavern-style pies, the dough is simply a sturdy vehicle for transporting the cheese, sauce, and meat to your pie hole. In fact, the crust is so sturdy that it didn't absorb anything—not the sauce, not the cheese, and certainly not the fat rendered from the sausage. This is the difference between long fermented, hand-tossed, and hand-formed pizza vs. the short-cut, mechanically formed pies you see in most bars. Sure, the place has a nostalgic ambiance (there's a reason they've been in business for seventy-five years, causing more than a few PIGUE memories), and their pie even tastes pretty darn good with a few beers, but I'm not sure it changed my life.

Obbie's Pizza
6654 W. Archer Avenue
773-586-2828
Ordered: small half-sausage,
   half-pepperoni

Cruising down Archer Avenue, the long, diagonal commercial street that runs through the city's Southwest Side, parallel to the Stevenson Expressway, you see plenty of Mexican taquerias and Polish restaurants. But then there's Obbie's pizza joint, which several of my readers hail as a neighborhood favorite and a must-visit for this book. So I went.

When I called ahead and asked to eat in, my request got a good laugh, since Obbie's is carryout only, like many Southwest Side establishments. When I walked in to pick up my carryout, I saw five guys completely focused—like pastry chefs assembling wedding cakes—rolling out dough, topping large discs with tomato sauce, filling pans with homemade sausage, and checking on pizzas in the enormous rotating deck ovens. All the while, the phone kept ringing, people kept streaming in and out—and it was only 5 P.M. on a Thursday.

I took my small pie outside to the car, opened up the tailgate, plopped it down, and tore the paper bag off—revealing a bubbly, cheesy sphere embedded with nice little irregular balls of sausage and thin, slightly spicy pepperoni. The warm, wonderful smell of cheese, tomato sauce, and yeast rose from the pie in a puff of steam.

The pie's undercarriage, with that telltale sign of slightly black-ened corn flour, gives it a nice texture. The crust, however, is a tad too soft, with absolutely no chew here. I think you'll have an even soggier bottom if you eat the pie after a ten- or fifteen-minute drive back home. The only remedy is to eat it as soon as it comes out of the oven, but I'm not sure how practical that is. How much fun is it to eat in your car? Although, if you're really hungry, and you're in the neighborhood, there's no shame in devouring one of these pies.

The legend that is Pat's has always been about its thin crust. When the pie arrives at your table on a stainless-steel disc, you can tell immediately how thin it is. Almost caramelized on the edge, the pizza is nicely browned and blackened all over its undercarriage. In an interesting architectural note, the sausage side is covered with cheese while the pepperonis rest above the cheese on their side.

The cheese is baked well—nice and golden—but there is so much that it can easily dominate the entire pie.

The sauce is hardly notable, but I like how it goes all the way to the edge. The crust is where Pat's excels: so perfectly crispy, almost like eating a salty cracker dipped in cheesy tomato sauce. You can actually hear when you bite into the crust, which is rare among thin crust competitors.

★ **Pat's Pizza and Ristorante**
2679 N. Lincoln Avenue
773-248-0168
www.patspizza.info
Ordered: 12-inch half-sausage,
    half-pepperoni
Thin and pan options available in
    12-inch, 14-inch, and 16-inch.

Pat's

628 S. Clark Street

312-427-2320

Ordered: personal (8-inch)
half-sausage, half-pepperoni

Pan and stuffed options
available in 12-inch and 14-inch.
Thin options available in
12-inch, 14-inch, and 16-inch.

Yes, there is a family connection with the Pat's in Lake View, but Pat's in the South Loop has very different recipes, and it is certainly smaller in terms of space.

As the story goes, brothers Nick (North Side) and Sam (South Side) both named their respective joints after their dad, Pat. The North Side site used to be located at Sheffield and Belmont, but moved to North Lincoln a few years ago. The South Side location, having been in the Loop for most of the '80s and '90s, moved to its current small, mostly take-out spot in the South Loop in '97. Both locations present ambitious menus—ribs, chicken, shrimp—but you come to the South Side joint for the pizza.

Its crust is über-thin, like any self-respecting thin—barely thicker than a Keebler cracker—and square-cut. (The personal pizza is wedge cut, however, since it's so small). The crust rests for barely two hours. The undercarriage has large, evenly spread brown spotting, and the sauce (made in-house) is pleasant without being as sweet as at some other South Side joints. Toppings and sauce go all the way to the edge, so nothing's left naked.

They make the excellent coarse, fennel-jammed sausage in-house. The juicy and meaty pepperoni has an excellent kick to it, and it's baked on top of the cheese to release some of the fat while baking. Pat's combines whole milk and part-skim mozzarella, which adds plenty of richness, but they wisely hold back on covering their delicate pies with too much cheese, realizing how crucial a great ratio is to total pizza enjoyment.

Salerno's Pizza of Chicago
1201 W. Grand Avenue
312-666-3444
www.salernospizza.com
Salerno's Pizza includes three
    suburban location: Bolingbrook,
    Oak Park, and Lyons.
Ordered: 12-inch half-sausage,
    half-pepperoni
Thin and regular pizzas available
    in 8-inch, 10-inch, 12-inch,
    14-inch, and 16-inch.

This family-friendly restaurant in West Town has been around since 1966—they have a few other locations in the suburbs, too. Pizzas take about twenty-five minutes but are worth the wait. Normally, smaller pizzas are cut into wedges, but if you get a 12-inch or larger pie, it's cut into squares, tavern-style.

The crust here differs from many of the usual tavern-style pizzas in that it has dimension and some cracker-like qualities. In other words, it's not one solid mass throughout, and you can actually chew it. The crust perfectly absorbs the zesty tomato sauce and cheesy topping, which, incidentally, covers the entire pizza like a yellow shield. The pepperoni has a slight bite to it, but the mild, homemade sausage is the star. Even though I had tasted six pizzas previous to this one—on the very same day—I still managed to eat a full three pieces, which says a lot.

★ **Side Street Saloon**
1456 W. George Street
773-327-1127
www.sidestreetsaloon.com
Ordered: small half-sausage,
   half-pepperoni

f you win the lottery, do they pay you all at once, or do you get it in installments?" asked an older gentleman sitting at the bar one afternoon at the Side Street Saloon. The afternoon news was on one TV, ESPN on the other, and with the exception of the elderly gent, the bartender, and my friend and me, the place was empty.

There are, of course, dozens, if not hundreds, of neighborhood taverns like this, and it's what makes Chicago so damn wonderful. Sure, you're in a big city (in Lake View, to be exact), but when walking into a joint like this in the middle of the day, you might just as well be in Kenosha or Escanaba. Tempting as the pool table was, my friend Gina and I opted simply to settle in for a small pizza (our third of the day).

When our pie hit the table, I was reminded of both Northbrook's Barnaby's (crimped edges) as well as Pizano's (tender, butter crust). Turning to the toppings, I'd say that the sausage was pleasant, while the pepperoni was slightly greasy, as it sat in a pool of barely underdone melted cheese.

On the other hand, Gina liked both toppings, and I could easily see polishing off the pie as I played pool or watched TV, contemplating the machinations of the Illinois Lottery system on a quiet Tuesday afternoon.

★ **Vito & Nick's Pizzeria**
8433 S. Pulaski Road
773-735-2050
www.vitoandnicks.com
Ordered: large half-sausage,
    half-pepperoni
Food and jukebox are cash only.
Small pies available.

There's a reason Vito & Nick's has been in business since 1932, and it's not just the nostalgia on the walls. PBR and Old Style are on tap, the vinyl booths are still turquoise, and the Formica tabletops have the worn patina of a faded era—definitely pre–*Mad Men*. Families in Hawks T-shirts, grandparents celebrating birthdays, and countless softball teams have made Vito & Nick's their go-to pizza joint for generations, and I can see why.

In 1923, Vito and Mary Barraco opened their first tavern, located downtown at Congress and Polk, and then, in 1932, they opened a new location at 80th and Halsted, calling it Vito's Tavern. Seven years later, Vito moved the tavern to 79th and Carpenter, so there was space for more tables, a bar, and an expanded menu, which at that point included Italian sausage and beef sandwiches.

Their son Nick joined the business in 1945 and a year later, Nick, Vito, and Mary began making pizzas. Vito's granddaughter, Rose George, is the matriarch in charge today, greeting many of the regulars by name.

The pizza crust is ultra-thin, still bearing the blistered burn marks from the hot spots in the giant, industrial-strength Blodgett ovens. There is a thin sheath of seasoning scattered across the bottom edge, too, redolent of black pepper and oregano. The harmony (yes, I said harmony) between the mozzarella, chunky sausage (made outside, but to their specs), and the zesty tomato sauce makes this pie a pleasure to eat; thankfully, they haven't gotten lazy like so many others who simply pile on the cheese and call it a day. This is pizza with balance (think OBR), not overkill, and since it's so thin, you could easily polish off a large and a few PBRs with a friend and still have change left for the jukebox.

Note for pizza historians: Rose is quick to point out that the business is not related to Barraco's, a well-known mini-chain on Chicago's South and Southwest Sides. According to Rose, her grandfather sponsored his nephew (also named Vito Barraco) to emigrate from Italy in the 1940s. He worked at Vito & Nick's and learned the business. Years later, the younger Vito and his wife, Pauline, left to open their own place—Barraco's Pizza—on Ninety-Fifth Street in Evergreen Park. The company went on to open several more pizza establishments. See page 36.

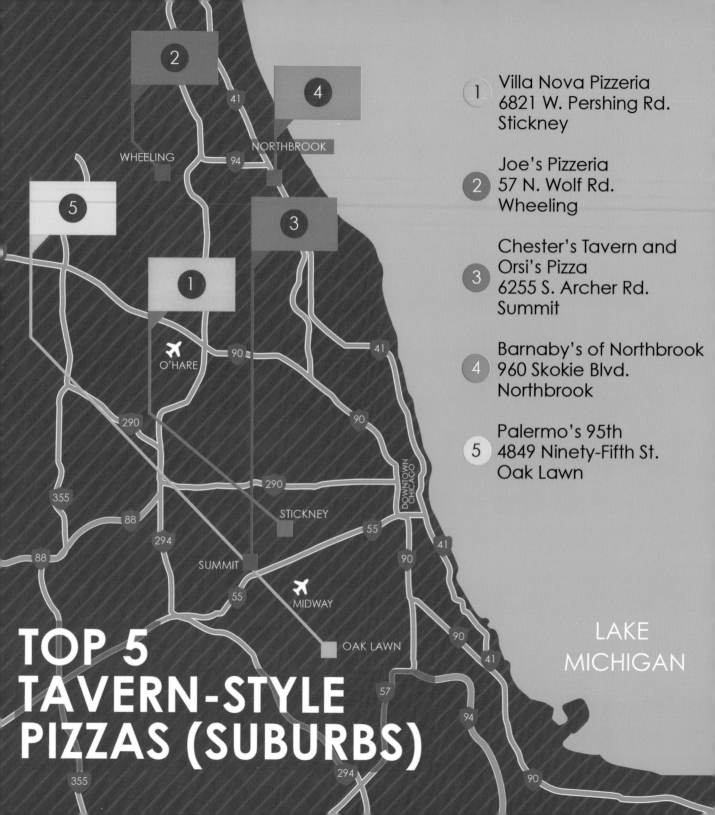

TOP 5 TAVERN-STYLE PIZZAS (SUBURBS)

1 Villa Nova Pizzeria
6821 W. Pershing Rd.
Stickney

2 Joe's Pizzeria
57 N. Wolf Rd.
Wheeling

3 Chester's Tavern and
Orsi's Pizza
6255 S. Archer Rd.
Summit

4 Barnaby's of Northbrook
960 Skokie Blvd.
Northbrook

5 Palermo's 95th
4849 Ninety-Fifth St.
Oak Lawn

LAKE MICHIGAN

WHEELING

NORTHBROOK

O'HARE

STICKNEY

SUMMIT

MIDWAY

OAK LAWN

DOWNTOWN CHICAGO

Suburbs

One note on suburban thin crust ordering: whether it's tavern-style or traditional thin, I noticed on several occasions that the pizzas were slightly underdone on the top—not raw, per se, but in need of a bit more time in the oven to get the top layer slightly more browned. Several readers, followers on Instagram, and even pizza employees working the phone reminded me that I should have ordered my pizzas "well-done."

This argument carries little weight with me, and I think it speaks to the lack of talent or experience in the kitchen. C'mon folks. This isn't a steak we're ordering; it's a pizza. Why should someone have to order it well-done? How about just baking the pizza until it's at its optimal doneness? If I've never been to your place before, and if the person on the phone doesn't even ask me how I want the pizza done, then how in the world would I know that the level of doneness was an option? Just bake the fucking pizza right every time, and we'll all be better off for it.

Armand's Pizzeria
105 W. First Street
Elmhurst, Illinois
630-782-5800
www.armandspizzeria.com
"Armand's Pizza & Pasta" is the
    name in suburban locations:
    Elmhurst, Elmwood Park,
    Arlington Heights, Lombard,
    LaGrange, and Edison Park.
They also have two city locations:
    1416 S. Michigan Avenue and
    4159 N. Western Avenue.
Ordered: small half-sausage,
    half-pepperoni

This family favorite was a mainstay in Elmwood Park on Grand Avenue for decades. In 1956, the owners took over the Victory Tap and started serving pizza. The original space on Grand closed several years ago, but over the past few years it has reopened and expanded with a few satellites.

One of the locations, Armand's Victory Tap in the Yorktown Mall, is a throwback and a nod to its Victory Tap roots. So when I asked the manager of the Elmhurst location what style of thin they had, he replied "thin."

Really, though, it's more of a tavern-style pizza, with a super-thin, cracker-like crust that borders on crunchy—thanks to the handfuls of cornmeal tossed onto the base of the oven deck, which prevents the crust from sticking to the bottom of the undercarriage, much like at Barnaby's.

The sausage is mild and the pepperoni assertive. The cheese is slightly browned in spots on the top, and when biting into a square-cut slice, you get a hint of yeasty earthiness along with the slightest amount of sweetness from the tomato sauce, which is applied as thinly and delicately as a watercolor artist brushing a canvas.

Talk about PIGUE (Pizza I Grew Up Eating) Syndrome. After I posted a picture following my unannounced visit to Barnaby's, my Facebook and Instagram lit up with breathless melancholy. "I went there all throughout high school" and "Been going there for twenty years" came the reactions to my nattily crimped, thin, tavern-style pizza photo post.

No question it's a good pie. (Although despite North Shore myth, they do not make a cornmeal crust. They simply use cornmeal—as many other places do—beneath the pizza to keep it from sticking to the oven deck.) And everyone who grew up within five miles of the original Barnaby's, located in Northbrook, claims it to be the center of the pizza universe. So to get the true Barnaby's experience, I headed to the Northbrook mother ship. Filbert's root beer and Green River soda—both a source of nostalgia for Chicagoans of a certain age—wouldn't color my opinion.

Getting down to my pizza, the sausage side (covered in cheese) was respectable—much more so than the other side, with its weak, mass-produced pepperoni (placed on top of the cheese). The crust is what you're coming here for: thin, crispy, and when you take a bite the sound is actually audible.

That's a pretty good sign. I saw some air pockets in the cutaway section of the pie, indicating there might be some fermentation or at least a decent period of resting for the dough. The sauce is innocuous, like a song by Ed Sheeran. I didn't hate it; I didn't love it; I don't really remember it.

Is this the best thin crust in the region? Definitely not. Is it worth a detour if you're heading down the Edens Expressway and feel the urge to devour a pizza? Sure. There's a reason generations of families have been coming here since 1969.

✳ **Barnaby's of Northbrook**
960 Skokie Boulevard
Northbrook, Illinois
847-498-3900
www.barnabysofnorthbrook.com

There are Barnaby's locations in Niles and Des Plaines, but they are unrelated to the original in Northbrook.
Ordered: small half-sausage, half-pepperoni

Barraco's

5740 W. 87th Street

Burbank, Illinois

708-636-9594

www.barracos.com

Barraco's has five suburban
    locations—Burbank, Crestwood,
    Evergreen Park, Orland Hills,
    and Orland Park—plus two in
    the city.

Ordered: small half-sausage,
    half-pepperoni

The original Barraco's came about after Vito Barraco and his wife, Pauline, left Vito's uncle's place—Vito & Nick's. There is no connection between the two businesses.

Barraco's is a family-run group of pizzerias that slowly added stores around the South and Southwest suburbs over the years. They offer quite a few pizza styles (thin, deep, Sicilian, and stuffed), but when asked on the phone what they specialize in, the kind woman on the line didn't hesitate: thin. Of course, this being the Southwest Side, thin really means Chicago-style thin, which, as we know by now, is the same as tavern-style.

The Burbank location, like a few of the others, is delivery and carryout only, so I did what I always do when faced with one of these to-go operations: I tailgate. During a steady snowfall, I tore into this steaming, beautifully burnished pie.

The undercarriage maintains a gentle, brownish hue, while the top aspires to greatness as the tangy sauce and cheese nearly overflow beyond the crisp, crunchy edges. Whole milk mozzarella serves as an insulator and dairy shield for the juicy, flavorful knobs of sausage, courtesy of Chicago-based Peoria Packing Butcher Shop. The pepperoni side is generous—although I'm rarely a fan of places that bury the discs beneath the cheese, since they tend to steam there and not really render off any of their fat, which prevents them from becoming crispy spheres. No matter, the slices have plenty of flavor, a nice OBR, and that telltale tavern-style thickness, which is to say not much thicker than a few sheets of printer paper.

Sure, I would have preferred a bit more crunch underneath, but the flavor combo of the sauce, cheese, and toppings more than make up for any lack of cracker-like crunchiness.

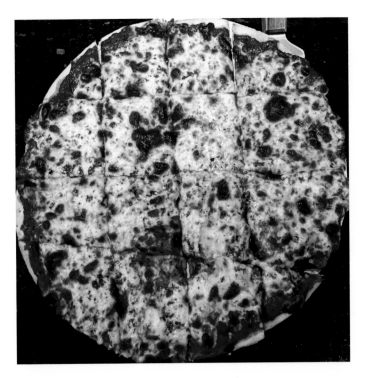

Just parking your car on busy Archer Avenue in this tiny, industrial suburb along the Stevenson Expressway can be daunting. Cars park up on the curb, since so many semis use the road as a bypass. Look both ways before crossing. It's mostly Mexican panaderias and taco shops now, but Chester's Tavern defies the trend and has remained staunchly Italian, serving cheap beer and good pizza in one of the oldest buildings in town.

Don't let the front bar, beaten and worn from years of people propping their elbows on it, scare you away. The overall décor is dark, a bit dingy, and on the night I visited, had more video poker machines than patrons.

Dick Orsi took over the place about thirty years ago and added a pizza menu. Apparently, he and Evel Knievel were friends, so the daredevil hung out here when he was in town.

The pizzas are as textbook tavern-style as you can get: a thin and crispy crust, rolled out on a mechanical sheeter just before assembly; a thickish tomato sauce, imbued with oregano, basil, and a hint of sugar (another anomaly of the South and Southwest Sides); plus generous applications of the local Battaglia's fennel sausage and mild pepperoni, all adequately blanketed beneath a layer of part-skim mozzarella that somehow manages to taste like a domestic burrata—that rich and dreamy semisoft cheese made from mozzarella and cream.

The key here: a great OBR of crust-to-sauce-to-toppings that have been cooked just to the precipice of charred. The top is evenly browned—what some folks would call well done—and a free side-car of the oily, spicy Italian relish giardiniera is right out of a Chicago food lover's fantasy. (Pretty much every joint in town that has Italian beef and pizza on their menu will offer this condiment as a topping.) Add a spoonful or two to your square slice and savor some history from the city's often-neglected, rarely touted Southwest Side.

✷ **Chester's Tavern and Orsi's Pizza**
6255 S. Archer Road
Summit, Illinois
708-458-1117
Ordered: small half-sausage,
    half-pepperoni
Sizes include 8-inch, 12-inch,
    14-inch, and 16-inch.

Fasano's Pizza
8351 Roberts Road
Justice, Illinois
708-598-6971
www.fasanospizza.com
Ordered: small half-sausage,
   half-pepperoni

Like many of its Southwest Side brethren, Fasano's offers a fairly large menu of chicken dishes, sandwiches, and Italian entrees—all for either delivery or carryout. There is nowhere to sit, unless you're a delivery driver, and when I first arrived to pick up my pizza, I noticed cars double-parked in the small front lot. Several of the vehicles had people sitting inside, eating their dinner, ready to pull away if need be to let someone in or out. The business has been around since 1972, and even though they specialize in thin, or more accurately, tavern-style,

they've also added a deep-dish and a double-dough version; the latter features extra thick side walls, perhaps to contain any threat of cheese lava that might ooze out from the center.

One of their more recent business decisions was to move production of their homemade sausage out-of-house to a packer on the South Side, but it doesn't seem to have diminished the quality. It's still loaded with fennel, salt, and pepper, and manages to rise above the blend of whole milk and part-skim mozzarella that envelops the pie. The pepperoni doesn't

fare as well, limping beneath the somewhat heavy coating of cheese.

The sauce, however, brings everything into balance, playing both a supporting role and, after a few bites, taking the lead, much like a Tour de France racer suddenly appearing in the yellow jersey. They begin with Modesto, California–based Stanislaus Food Products tomatoes, but puree the tomatoes in-house with their own spice blend (no garlic).

The crust, meanwhile, is barely browned underneath, providing a decent chew while also maintaining the über-crispness that's a hallmark of pies on the South and Southwest Sides.

Many of Fasano's contemporaries—like Fox's in Beverly—stem from the legendary Bernie & Betty's, where tavern-style was celebrated in the 1950s. Fortunately, like those fellow Chicago pizza slingers who keep an Italian beef sandwich on the menu for good measure, Fasano's does likewise, which means they offer up giardiniera and some thinly sliced roast beef as optional toppings for their pizzas.

Since 1947, this casual restaurant, located along a busy stretch of South Harlem Avenue, has attracted fans from Tinley Park and surrounding suburbs for its simple but well-executed thin crust. Like a true tavern-style, the pieces are square-cut, and the dough is as thin as a business card, with an audible crunch as you bite into it.

They make their sausage in-house—a point of pride—and it's stellar, loaded with more fennel than most, but still on the mild side. Unfortunately, the pepperoni is buried beneath the top layer of cheese (a rare trifecta of whole milk and skim mozzarella with provolone), rendering the discs somewhat flaccid. Had they topped the pie with the generously scattered pepperoni, the discs would likely have crisped up in the heat and possibly gotten a bit crunchy as they baked in the giant, black Blodgett ovens.

Some parts of my pie were pretty charred, adding another note of complexity. Combine that with the undercarriage—a tan bottom that contains tiny craters and ridges—and a super tomato-y sauce that is somewhat reduced to help thicken it, and you have a PIGUE Syndrome pizza that is, in this case at least, nothing to be ashamed of.

Joe's Italian Villa
12207 S. Harlem Avenue
Palos Heights, Illinois
708-361-1431
www.joesitalianvilla.com
Ordered: small half-sausage,
    half-pepperoni
Sizes include 10-inch, 12-inch,
    14-inch, 16-inch, and 18-inch.
Deep-dish and stuffed options
    available in 10-inch, 12-inch,
    and 14-inch.

Since 1966, Joe's has served its ultra-thin pizzas on the North Shore and beyond. Not related to the Joe's on Higgins or Joe's Italian Villa in Palos, this neon-lit beacon does a brisk carryout business, but also has a few high-backed wooden booths if you want to eat in. As I waited for my pie, I was entertained by the big screen, by the comically small bar with four taps and two stools, and by a guy playing video poker in the corner. (What is it with the video poker machines in suburban pizza joints?)

The menu checks off several boxes—pasta, ribs, chicken, and one dessert option, cannoli—but fans come here for the tavern-style pies, which rely on sausage from Fontanini (based in McCook, Illinois) and Battaglia pepperoni, both submerged ever so slightly beneath an even layer of part-skim mozzarella.

Cornmeal is used to prevent pies from sticking to the giant, rotating deck oven, but the key is really the resting time for the dough. While a day is minimum, Joe's tries to let the dough rest two to three days for optimal flavor.

The slightly thickened, oregano-flecked tomato sauce is spread all the way to the edge—leaving very little unmolested space. Nicely browned spots on the top give the pie character and depth, and I could practically smell the fennel in the sausage before biting into one of the jagged pieces. Despite the fact that the pepperoni is placed beneath the cheese, it wasn't completely soggy and limp, like at a lot of other places. Had I not had two additional spots to hit that particular night, I could easily have crushed the pie and been content to call it a night.

★ Joe's Pizzeria
57 N. Wolf Road
Wheeling, Illinois
847-537-8110
www.joespizzausa.com
Ordered: small half-sausage, half-pepperoni
Sizes include 12-inch, 14-inch, and 16-inch.

La Rosa
4012 Golf Road
Skokie, Illinois
847-674-7540
www.larosapizzainskokie.com
Ordered: 12-inch half-sausage,
 half-pepperoni
Pan and stuffed also available.

This no-frills joint on Golf Road, just a mile or so east of Old Orchard Mall, has been hand-tossing pies and baking them in its big, beautiful green Faulds rotating deck oven since 1957. It's carryout or delivery only, as there is no dining room. Long before there was a Lou's down the road in Lincolnwood, generations of Skokie pizza lovers made La Rosa their go-to for thin, square-cut pies. Located in a dingy strip mall between a True Discount Cigarettes & Food Mart and a dry cleaner, they produce one helluva pizza.

Classic tavern-style is the way to go here. The bottom crust is thin enough to hold the toppings, which for my pie included an extremely generous layering of Greco sausage and chewy discs of pepperoni that were slightly crisped in the oven. Part-skim mozzarella adds a good amount of richness without competing against the fairly mild sausage. The ratio seems right here, with no particular ingredient dominating any other.

Like any self-respecting joint that also makes Italian beef sandwiches, they offer giardiniera and sliced beef as optional toppings. #OnlyinChicago

★ **Palermo's 95th**
4849 Ninety-Fifth Street
Oak Lawn, Illinois
708-425-6262
www.palermos95th.com
Ordered: small "thin and crispy,"
    half-sausage, half-pepperoni
Regular thin, deep-dish, and
    stuffed also available.

For more than thirty-five years, Palermo's has been a South Side institution, serving the same local families, watching their children grow up and then go on to college. Lasagna, pasta, and pizza are its calling cards. Popping in unnoticed on a Wednesday afternoon, I found the brick-arched dining room with grapevine wallpaper pretty quiet. Tony Bennett crooned on the speakers, serenading the families and nearby hospital workers on their lunch breaks.

My server said without a doubt "thin and crispy" was their specialty, so that's what I ordered, with the usual toppings. Fifteen minutes later, he placed a beautifully crisp, square-cut pizza in front of me, set on top of a cooling rack that rested over the pizza pan. Elevating the pizza, just like the Japanese tonkatsu houses do for their breaded-and-fried pork cutlets, keeps that bottom crust crisp.

I don't think I've ever seen tomato sauce so red. It is almost like tomato paste, as thick as something out of a jar. And like the sauce at so many other South Side joints, it has a hint of sweetness (definitely a regional differentiation within Chicagoland). Sausage is cut into large, amorphous hunks, tucked beneath a substantial (but not overwhelming) layer of oregano-flecked cheese. I ate about three pieces, including a good edge slice, so I could really taste the cracker-thin crust.

It's very different from Vito & Nick's, but worth a try. I hesitate to call it tavern-style, since it's served in a proper restaurant with a wine list and uniformed waiters, but there's no denying Palermo's 95th's square-cut, thin, light-as-a-cracker crisp crust—a true hallmark of tavern-style, aka Chicago-style thin.

have no idea if there is a connection between Villanova University in Philadelphia and this Stickney legend, which has been specializing in thin, tavern-style pies since 1955. What I do know—after experiencing more than my fair share of slightly underdone pizzas on this quest—is that you have to order your pie "well done," otherwise the bottom dough remains a tad too soggy and underdone. (Why can't the kitchens of these places—such as Pizza Castle, Aurelio's, Beggars, etc.—just bake the pies long enough so that there doesn't need to be a special order?)

Oh, but that edge! That glorious, crispy, cracker-like edge . . . it's a remarkable thing, especially when the rest of the pie is topped with beautifully melted mozzarella and literal meatballs of sausage, all formed by hand, dusted with oregano, and placed as meticulously as a jeweler would set a diamond. The sauce—like that at many of the South and Southwest Side joints—leans a bit sweeter and darker, but I don't think that would turn off a purist from elsewhere. This is what Chicago pizza was a half century ago and remains in many pockets of the city today.

Update: Since I initially wrote about this place, the owner has emailed to let me know that he re-trained the staff to simply bake the pizzas for the appropriate amount of time and thus prevent first-timers from getting an underdone pie. I would still ask when ordering.

★ **Villa Nova Pizzeria**
6821 W. Pershing Road
Stickney, Illinois
708-788-2944
www.pizzastickney.com
Villa Nova also has locations in Lockport and New Buffalo, Mich., and Chesterton, Ind.
Ordered: small half-sausage, half-pepperoni
Sizes include 12-inch, 14-inch, and 16-inch.

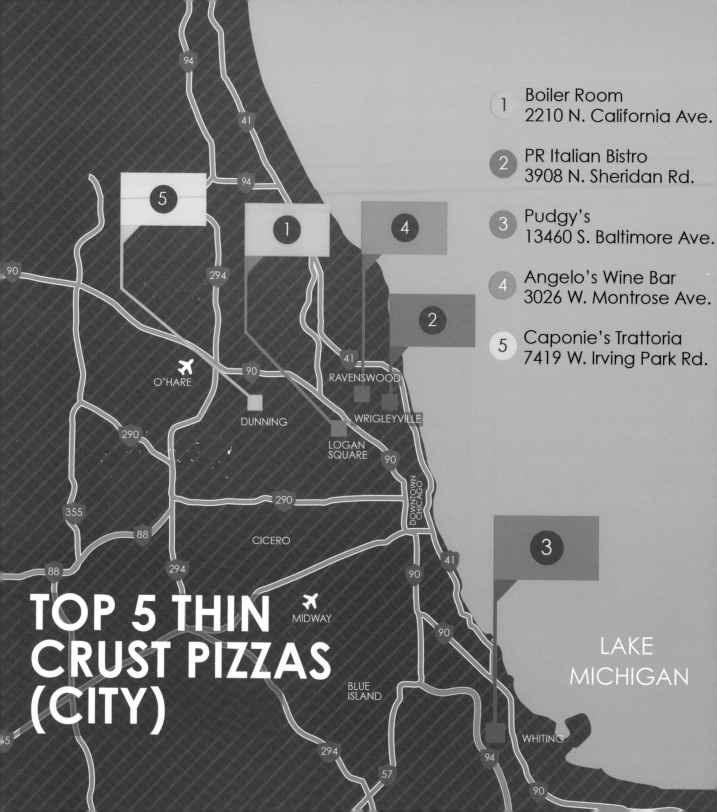

TOP 5 THIN CRUST PIZZAS (CITY)

1 Boiler Room
2210 N. California Ave.

2 PR Italian Bistro
3908 N. Sheridan Rd.

3 Pudgy's
13460 S. Baltimore Ave.

4 Angelo's Wine Bar
3026 W. Montrose Ave.

5 Caponie's Trattoria
7419 W. Irving Park Rd.

LAKE MICHIGAN

O'HARE
DUNNING
RAVENSWOOD
WRIGLEYVILLE
LOGAN SQUARE
DOWNTOWN CHICAGO
CICERO
MIDWAY
BLUE ISLAND
WHITING

CHAPTER 5

Thin

I realize a lot of people will think I'm splitting hairs here, but there truly is a difference between thin and tavern-style (Chicago-style thin). Whereas the latter is always cracker-thin with an audible crunch and square-cut, allowing for easy eating with one hand while the other nurses a beer, the former is simply a thin crust. Not deep, not done in a pan, and certainly not the width of a saltine. These pies tend to have a little more chew to them, are often cut into wedges, which allows for folding in half from the wide side (like they do in New York City), and tend to have a bit more fermentation in the dough, since there is a more pleasant chew rather than a crispy crunch.

I also love these pies, and they allow for more pizza consumption, as opposed to the knife-and-fork variety. There were enough locations to warrant both a city and a suburban roundup (presented alphabetically, of course). My top five in each section are starred and appear on an accompanying map.

Paulie Gee's Logan Square

Angelo's has been in business since 1962, but clearly they've undergone a renovation. Including those on the giant U-shaped bar and recycled wood walls, I counted eleven big-screen TVs. (All three of the dining room walls are covered with screens, making the dining room feel a little bit like a scene from *Black Mirror*.)

Pizza options range from the creative (breakfast pizza with garlic cream, bacon, poached egg, and sausage) to gourmet (figs and prosciutto). They even go Chicago-style with some Italian beef and giardiniera. But since they offered a Margherita, which is my baseline in lieu of a sausage-pepperoni option, I opted for that.

The biggest difference with their Margherita, which you notice right away, is that it arrives with a giant sphere of creamy burrata, the size of a baseball, in the center of the pie and a network of smaller fresh mozzarella blobs extending from the center to the edges. The

✴ **Angelo's Wine Bar**
3026 W. Montrose Avenue
773-539-0111
www.angeloswinebar.com
Ordered: burrata Margherita (half-sausage,
    half-pepperoni was not an option)

oozing cheese serves as a counter-point to the crispy crust.

While the casual observer might think their Margherita adheres to the traditional Italian Neapolitan style, it's really just a fancy thin. A generous chiffonade of fresh basil, blobs of Wisconsin mozzarella, and a shower of halved cherry tomatoes make it feel like a caprese salad rests atop the standard-issue crust. The pie's outer lip, or *cornicione*, is tight, but I like that it is brushed with olive oil just before serving, giving it a sheen and a bit of extra flavor.

The sauce is laid on fairly thick for a pizza of this style, and I thought the crust was a bit lacking. Perhaps they could add some salt to give it another dimension, while letting it rest a little longer to develop some character. But overall the crispy pieces and even cooking, combined with the thoughtfully applied sauce and toppings (OBR in effect here), lend themselves to a flavorful pie.

★ Boiler Room
2210 N. California Avenue
773-276-5625
www.boilerroomlogansquare.com
Ordered: half-sausage,
   half pepperoni
Whole pies come in one size—
   between 18 and 20 inches in
   diameter. There is also a pretty
   brisk by-the-slice program.
   All food is cash only.

From the fine folks who brought you Simone's in Pilsen, the Boiler Room delivers a recycled DIY aesthetic, complete with old *Twilight Zone* episodes on screen behind the bar. But their pizza puts this program front-and-center. Take a quick look to your left as you enter. You'll see the pizza guys tossing their dough for a ton of pies that will eventually be sold by the slice.

I visited the Boiler Room with a friend, so we weren't interested in slices and opted for my usual: a half-sausage, half-pepperoni whole pie. There are plenty of other whack-a-doodle options here, including Thai cream-cheese sauce, curry, serranos, beet bruschetta . . . but for this stop, we stuck to the half-and-half rule.

My friend and I literally let out an audible gasp when our server placed a comically large 20-inch pizza in front of us. Even if we hadn't been planning to try other pizzas on this day, there would have been plenty to bring home.

Aside from its scene-stealing size, the pizza is a beauty. On the pepperoni side, wide circles cover every possible bit of real estate, looking like a map from Dubai's Urban Planning Department. On the other side, crumbled, beautifully seasoned sausage complements the melted cheese. Beneath it all, a delicate, cornmeal-flecked dough maintains a crispy edge, unlike, say, the pies at Piece in Wicker Park, which has a superior oven, but clearly not a better dough recipe. This is OBR at its finest among the thin crust cool kids.

This tiny deli is popular with River North and Loop workers during the day for lunch—particularly because you can get in and out quickly. The décor is Italian Village cliché, complete with red-and-white-checkered tablecloths and pictures of local sports heroes. In the shadow of both the Trump Hotel and the Wrigley Building, it can be a little hard to spot, but it's just a minute or two off Michigan Avenue, so it's well suited for visitors and tourists.

The pies seem to reach for Neapolitan categorization, with their blobs of fresh, creamy *fior di latte* mozzarella and giant basil leaves, but the crust is far from textbook. It's definitely more crispy than chewy—the result of very little fermentation and probably a drier dough. The bottom is nicely charred and a couple bulbous air pockets peek out at the top, but in the end, it's a thin pie and not a Neapolitan.

The sauce is pleasant but not memorable, like the guy at Abt who sold you that TV. If you're walking along North Michigan Avenue and you get a sudden pizza craving, it's certainly worth a stop. I waited all of six minutes for my pizza to hit the table. At the very least, peruse the large gelato case on the way out.

Bongiorno's Cucina Italiana & Pizzeria
405 N. Wabash Avenue
312-755-1255
www.bongiornoschicago.com
Ordered: small (10-inch) Margherita pizza

★ **Caponie's Trattoria**

7419 W. Irving Park Road

773-804-9024

www.caponiespizza.com

Ordered: small Margherita; and
    half-sausage, half pepperoni

Deep-dish and stuffed options
    available in 12-inch, 14-inch,
    16-inch, and 18-inch sizes.

I'm sure if there was some sort of organization against Italian American stereotyping, it would take issue with Caponie's interior decorator. The Belmont Heights trattoria has more pictures of mobsters than you would see on an Untouchables Tour. Tony, Fredo, Michael—they're all up on the walls, led, of course, by a big black-and-white of Alphonse Capone himself at the entrance. The other notable piece of equipment here is the large, wood-burning oven at the back of the dining room and across from the bar.

Caponie's specializes in thin crust, but there is a notable difference between my baseline Margherita Napoletana and the eatery's other thin crust options, so I did the extremely rare thing and ordered two pizzas here.

The Margherita is uniformly thin, with barely any *cornicione*, and the chew is nonexistent— more cracker than real crust, with hardly any black spots on the undercarriage. Topped with a fair amount of plum tomato sauce and generous blobs of fresh mozzarella, it was sprinkled, inexplicably, with dried basil (!).

Their traditional sausage and pepperoni pizza, my second order, offers a much more interesting dough—slightly blistered, yeasty, and chewy, with a decent amount of heft and a fair number of air pockets inside the edge. Why didn't they use this same dough for their Margherita? I couldn't quite understand my server, but it has something to do with them cutting the dough in half to make an ultra-thin pizza, which makes no sense.

Their OBR of crust-to-cheese is spot-on and both the sausage and pepperoni present great flavor. I managed to eat two slices, despite my one-slice rule (admittedly, often flouted).

Now, if they could only use their thin pizza dough (and fresh basil) for their Margherita, they'd be onto something a little more special.

Note: Best to call ahead; they typically don't open until 5 P.M.

I visited the Seventy-First Street location, directly across from the Bryn Mawr Metra station and a chop suey joint and next to a neighborhood food mart. They apparently do a brisk late-night business, as they have a bulletproof window inside the foyer, before you get to the main room. I say "main room" and not "dining room" because there really is no décor to speak of, let alone a table. The only place to sit (if you want to eat in) is the wide ledge along the front window, which is exactly where I ate.

It's actually a lot like most of the fast food restaurants on the South Side, with their odd signs regarding customer service and refunds. I noticed a big sign next to the order counter saying, "No Cash Refunds—Exchanges only. Un-eaten portion must be returned for credit." Huh?

My small half-and-half was pretty good. I guess I shouldn't be surprised since the place has been in business since 1951 (the current owners have had it since '67), and they still make their sausage in-house—it's a fennel-lover's dream. Pieces are large and misshapen, gathering and clinging to the moz-zarella that is generously spread over the square-cut thin crust.

The sauce doesn't have much flavor, and in fact they go pretty easy on it.

But I love how the bottom crust, and especially the edge, has both crispiness and crunch. A gentle shower of oregano is dusted over the top, but they'll give you more seasonings in a disposable packet if you like.

They realize that most of their customer base gets these addictive pies to go, so portability is crucial. For example, from 11 A.M. to 4 P.M., you can get a quick slice for just $2.75.

Italian Fiesta Pizzeria
1919 E. Seventy-First Street
773-684-2222
8058 S. Halsted Street
773-684-2222
4659 S. Lake Park Avenue
773-684-2222
www.italianfiestapizzeria.com
Italian Fiesta Pizzeria also has
    two suburban locations:
    Dolton and New Lenox.
Ordered: small half-sausage,
    half-pepperoni

Served on a wooden pizza peel, PR Italian Bistro's pizza presents a beautifully crisp edge that continues underneath the pizza, resulting in extremely delicious bites. The fennel-laced sausage is a pleasure to eat, roughly crumbled and buried beneath a perfectly respectable layer of mozzarella, which is nicely browned in splotches.

My pizza lacked any discernible amount of sauce, however, which might have helped it a bit. Each bite is basically crispy dough, cheese, and sausage or pepperoni, contributing to an OBR that every pizza joint should aspire to. I also like how the pepperoni slices were placed on top of the pie, so the discs could render some of their fat in the oven and remain crisp on top.

izzeria Serio makes a very big deal about their brick oven, since I guess they want you to know they are serious about their pizza—even though the oven is gas-fired, not wood-fired.

They describe their pizza as "NeapolAmerican East Coast" style. I actually think it's more of a Margherita, and in fact, it holds up pretty well. When removed from the pie, a slice is relatively stiff, not wet, like most traditional Neapolitan pies, and despite a slightly sweeter-than-normal sauce, there is decent char and chew with lots of nice little air pockets in the dough, indicating either a fair amount of fermentation, a wetter-than-normal dough, or both.

The sausage-pepperoni version I ordered was loaded with oregano on top (ease up, guys), but I was really struck by how good the chew is on this version. While it is soft enough to enjoy, there is also a decent amount of crispiness on the outer rim, giving it a pleasant textural contrast. Who says you need wood to make a good pizza?

Pizzeria Serio
1708 W. Belmont Avenue
773-525-0600
www.pizzeriaserio.com
Ordered: small Margherita;
  and small half-sausage,
  half-pepperoni

Bob Zajac knew things were going south when, as a delivery driver for Pudgy's in 1995, his bosses went through a divorce. "I could see they were cutting corners—using some lesser product," he said. The couple had only been in business for about a year, and as the divorce progressed, the business suffered. Zajac eventually bought Pudgy's and has been the only owner since.

Weekend visitors to Chicago probably aren't going to make the drive to Hegewisch, near the Ford auto assembly plant right next to the Indiana border, just for pizza. But I can see why generations of Southeast Side regulars have made Pudgy's their go-to.

Like so many other pizza joints in the city, it's mostly take-out, with just one table (seats four) jammed into the front corner of the restaurant. When I say restaurant, I really mean house, because you're walking into a building that clearly used to be someone's residence, and from the looks of it, there's still someone living upstairs. The wood-paneled walls—right out of my 1970s childhood basement in Minnesota—have a worn patina, the result of years of absorbing heat and smoke from the four giant Blodgett deck ovens in the middle of the room.

Up near the front, a guy uses a simple wooden pastry roller to hand-roll the pizza dough, which has been resting overnight. A thickish layer of tomato puree and paste is seasoned with salt and oregano and then spread thinly across the diameter. Mini balls of sausage (from Russo Wholesale Meats, Inc., in Alsip) are scattered, along with thin pepperoni discs. Both meats are buried well beneath a combo layer of part-skim and whole milk mozzarella.

Sauce and cheese are spread all the way to the edges of the lip, which leaves very little room to taste the crust naked. Doesn't really matter. Even though the undercarriage may be a tad too blond for me (there is no char), the ultra-thin slices do have quite a bit of flavor, thanks in part to the vibrant tomato sauce that keeps me coming back for more.

★ **Pudgy's**
13460 S. Baltimore Avenue
773-646-4199
www. hegewisch.net/pudgys
Ordered: small half-sausage,
  half-pepperoni

Roots Handmade Pizza
1924 W. Chicago Avenue
773-645-4949
2200 W. Lawrence Avenue
773-433-5959
www.rootspizza.com
Ordered: small half-sausage,
  half pepperoni

I'd be willing to bet I'm the only food writer in town who has actually logged time in the Quad Cities (Bettendorf and Davenport, Iowa, on one side of the Mississippi River; Moline and Rock Island, Illinois, on the other). Today it's often referred to as the Quint Cities, since East Moline has become its own little fiefdom thanks to John Deere HQ, but I digress. I lived there in the early '90s, doing my TV news reporter thing, and while I have fond memories of devouring the matzo ball soup at the Duck City Bistro and then standing in line for a cold, creamy treat at Whitey's Ice Cream (both in Davenport), I don't really recall a distinctive local pizza style.

Roots is sort of a sports bar meets neighborhood hang, with large booths, TVs, and a kitchen claiming to serve Quad City–style pizza. The unique, standout element is the dark roasted malt used in the dough. Other Quad City–style hallmarks allegedly include hand-tossing the dough, using a thin sauce and top quality ingredients (they make their own sausage), and cutting the pies with scissors (one of only two joints in Chicagoland that do so as far as I know; the other being Coda di Volpe). But honestly, the most unique element is their malted dough.

When you first encounter a Roots pizza, there's the aroma of oregano anchored in a lake of thick, melted cheese, rather like so many boats on Lake Geneva. Slightly spicy crumbled sausage (a tad spicier than most) rests beneath it all and, underneath, light and dark cornmeal flecks make it look like an everything bagel. In fact, if you bite the outer crust, where there isn't any cheese or sauce, the dough tastes like a crispy bagel or pretzel.

Like Freddy's, it's one of the thicker thin pizzas in Chicago, with a puffy outer ring. The problem is that when the outer rim gets a little overdone, as mine was, it tastes like burnt bagel. Again, that might be what they're going for in Rock Island, Bettendorf, or Moline, but if I'm walking along Chicago and Damen, I'd rather head up the street to Craft for a different interpretation.

However, Roots Handmade Pizza's newer location in Lincoln Square satisfies a gaping hole in quality pizza coverage, so I'd be more inclined to stop in if I were roaming around that neighborhood.

Like pretty much every pizza joint on the Southwest Side, seating is at a minimum at Triano's, which has been slinging pies (and some seriously good Italian beef) since 1984. I had a choice of one of four stools at a V-shaped counter, the other option being to tailgate. The owner, Anthony, is right out of central casting, complete with Hawks cap and gold chain, and he'll happily answer any questions about his beloved pizza.

The square-cut pies aren't quite thin enough to qualify as tavern-style, but it is remarkable how the OBR (Optimal Bite Ratio) remains intact, despite the generous layer of whole milk mozzarella, house-made sausage chunks, and slightly sweetened sauce (very much a South Side thing). Each bite has a nice crunch and light crispiness to it. The fact that the pepperoni rests on top of the cheese while baking (rendering off fat and making each disc a bit crispy) is enhanced by the fact that they dust the top with oregano and Romano cheese.

While they admittedly use a little bit of sugar in the sauce, which also contains a tomato puree and some crushed tomatoes, I didn't find it to be too cloying (looking at you, Arrenello's). Even with cheese and sauce spread all the way to the outer edges, each piece of every pie still maintains its integrity, with a remarkable chew that encourages eating a few more slices than you probably intended to.

For the record, they sell a lot of jumbo slices ($5) in the summertime, when they set up a picnic table on the side of the building and also sell hot dogs and Italian ice.

Triano's Pizza
6758 W. Archer Avenue
773-229-1444
www.trianospizza.com
Ordered: small half-sausage, half-pepperoni
Sizes include 10-inch, 12-inch, 14-inch, 16-inch, 18-inch, and 20-inch; slices available upon request.

Pudgy's

TOP 5 THIN CRUST PIZZAS (SUBURBS)

1 **Freddy's Pizza**
1600 S. Sixty-First Ave.
Cicero

2 **La Bella Pasteria**
1103 South Blvd.
Oak Park

3 **Penguino's Pizza**
141 W. Dundee Rd.
Buffalo Grove

4 **Bricks Wood Fired
Pizza & Cafe**
1763 Freedom Dr.
Naperville

5 **Aurelio's Pizza**
18162 Harwood Ave.
Homewood

LAKE
MICHIGAN

Suburbs

Since 1959, families have been piling into this soaring, barn-like structure, hung with Tiffany lamps and old photos of Homewood VIPs. Located a few yards from the Metra line, the restaurant has its charms. My former colleague at ABC7—Ben Bradley—is a proud local boy, always touting Aurelio's alleged superiority when I saw him in the hallways around the office. There are forty-two locations—mostly in the suburbs, downstate, and even a few in Florida, Georgia, and Las Vegas—but I knew that I would have to visit the mother ship in Homewood in order to make the most accurate assessment.

I ordered my usual—half-sausage, half-pepperoni—and I remembered to ask about using the "old oven," a reference to the stone deck oven vs. the quicker conveyor belt oven that Ben said makes the difference. About ten minutes later, I was served a small circular pie on a wire cooling rack.

The old oven gives the pie a nice even golden-brown hue across the entire bottom. However, the tiny, blueberry-sized sausage balls on top leave me unimpressed. Since the company is so big, they can't make the sausage in-house anymore, so they purchase it from a sausage supplier. (Progress and efficiency doesn't always bode well for pizza quality. See Connie's at the United Center and Lollapalooza, or Imo's in St. Louis.) Sadly, there is hardly any detectable flavor in that sausage—nary a whisper of fennel or even a note of garlic.

There is a slightly raised ridge on the outer rim of the pizza, which holds in the well-done baked cheese crisp, reminding me a little bit of Pequod's. A bit of dried oregano is scattered over the top.

Aurelio's is one of the best examples of PIGUE, meaning that the best pizza in the world is the one you grew up eating. I can imagine generations of Little League teams, dance recitals, and birthdays here, with everyone gobbling up this thin crust and logging some of their fondest memories in life. But come here as an unbiased eater seeking some really good pizza, and you might leave a little less satisfied. Of course, there are forty-two locations, so what the hell do I know.

★ **Aurelio's Pizza**
18162 Harwood Avenue
Homewood, Illinois
708-798-8050
www.aureliospizza.com
Aurelio's has a total of forty-two locations, with thirty-two in Chicagoland.
Ordered: 10-inch half-sausage, half-pepperoni

★ Bricks Wood Fired Pizza & Cafe
1763 Freedom Drive
Naperville, Illinois
630-799-6860
www.brickswoodfiredpizza.com
Bricks Wood Fired Pizza & Café
    also has locations in Lombard,
    Mount Prospect, Wheaton, and
    West Dundee.
Ordered: 12-inch Neapolitan

This mini-chain has roots in the Western suburbs, and it's extremely convenient if you suddenly get the urge for a pizza while cruising down Interstate 88 or shopping in the nearby malls. During lunch, office workers pop in to grab a fast, fairly tasty pizza, made to order and then baked in an enormous, round, wood-burning oven made of copper. The pizza certainly aspires to be a true Neapolitan, and it looks like one, but it's really more of a Neapolitan-ish thin crust.

That crust—a nice, light crust, with not much of an outer lip—is mottled, with blackened bits of char underneath. There are fairly decent splotches of fresh mozzarella, and the middle isn't wet like a lot of Neapolitan-style pizzas. Unlike traditionalists, the chefs at Bricks scatter a chiffonade of basil around the surface, rather than placing four giant leaves down.

The sauce, however, is a mild disappointment. Underseasoned to the point where I almost asked for a salt shaker, it tastes nothing like the vibrant, bursting-with-acidity tomato sauces I've had at places like Freddy's and Pizza Barra. Here's hoping it was an off-day, because your options in Wheaton, Lombard, and West Dundee aren't exactly unlimited.

There are several types of pizzas offered at Freddy's, including their legendary Sicilian-style, which is listed in chapter 10. But in terms of thin, they offer a few types, like a rectangular sheet of Margherita and a more standard round pizza. I got one of each.

The Margherita is affordable, typically sold by the slice, and you should know that a full sheet will feed a small army of hungry teenagers. It's a different dough than the one they use for their Sicilian, and the key is fermentation—at least a day and a half. Baked in a giant Blodgett deck oven, the pizza emerges charred on the edges and bubbling in the middle, with more *fior di latte* cheese than most delis have in their entire cheese section. Basil is sprinkled liberally, and the sauce is obviously homemade.

I like this pizza. It's not really a classic VPN or D.O.P. Neapolitan, but the owners—who try to visit a part of Italy every summer, and have been to Naples—say that locals sometimes don't want one of those soggy and wet pizzas, preferring something with more heft. This one certainly delivers.

Same goes for their thin pizza, which would beat most other thins in town. The slices are puffy and generous, and the toppings are solid, but still, the bottom crust retains crispness. One reason you find yourself reaching for another piece is the slight tanginess and sourness that comes from a long fermentation as well as a solid OBR. There

are also some interesting little air pockets here, which lend the pizza even more character and chew.

Do yourself a favor and save room for the gelato. Trust me.

Note: VPN is a designation awarded to qualifying pizzerias by the Naples-based Associazione Verace Pizza Napoletana, also called Vera Pizza Napoletana. D.O.P. stands for *Denominazione di Origine Protetta*, a guarantee that the cheese meets certain explicit standards related to production and aging.

★ **Freddy's Pizza**
1600 S. Sixty-First Avenue
Cicero, Illinois
(708) 863-9289
www.freddyspizza.com
Ordered: Margherita; small
  half-sausage, half-pepperoni

This neighborhood trattoria, wedged into an 1891 storefront in the historic Pleasant District of Oak Park, near the famed block loaded with Frank Lloyd Wright homes, does a serviceable job with its casual Italian fare. A chalkboard lists the day's specials, and since most of the tables were taken during my weeknight visit, I sat at the cozy four-seat bar, waiting for my half-and-half. They also offer "Entree Pizzas" (think chicken marsala or Sicilian eggplant on pizza dough) as well as a pan or a double-dough version.

After about twenty minutes, my ten-inch pie emerged looking as though there were two differ-ent cheeses, since the sausage side is visibly a whiter shade than the pepperoni side. In fact, the cheese is all the same—whole milk mozzarella—and I love how they place the thin discs of pepperoni on top, rather than underneath the cheese.

The undercarriage has a nice even brown color while those hand-torn pieces of sausage still retain their fennel kick, even though they're buried beneath cheese. The sauce has a slight

sweetness—not offensive, mind you, just maybe not for everyone. The crust, however, saves it, with a dough that is supple, on the verge of flaky, with just a hint of salt, and an ever-so-slight crunch. Its outer edges are just barely browned, and a whisper of oregano across the top pulls everything together.

✴ **La Bella Pasteria**
1103 South Boulevard
Oak Park, Illinois
708-524-0044
www.labellapasteria.com
Ordered: small half-sausage,
    half-pepperoni

★ **Penguino's Pizza**
141 W. Dundee Road
Buffalo Grove, Illinois
847-459-0002
www.penguinospizzeria.com
Ordered: small half-sausage,
  half pepperoni
Deep-dish and pan options
  available in sizes 12-inch,
  14-inch, and 16-inch.

This mostly take-out and delivery joint in a sleepy strip mall, next to a dance studio, lives a lonely existence. Since it has just two tables and an odd rack to sell company T-shirts, I don't imagine many people spend a lot of time dining in. Like many suburban operations, Penguino's offers a few styles of pizza, but when pressed, the owner says it is the thin they are most known for.

The tomato sauce is on the thickish side, with pretty good flavor and not too much sweetness. While the crust seems a bit limp, and maybe lacking the crunch I was hoping for, the toppings save this pie. The combo of the pepperoni and the sausage, along with the appropriate amount of mozzarella, adds a wonderful richness to this pizza. I found myself going for the edges, where the dough had a chance to maintain its crispness.

This is a respectable pizza for taking home and planting in front of the TV to watch the game—or anything else for that matter.

Rosangela's Pizzeria
2807 1/2 W. Ninety-Fifth Street
Evergreen Park, Illinois
708-422-2041
www.allmenus.com/il/worth
  /220692-rosangelas/menu/
Ordered: small half-sausage,
  half-pepperoni

Since 1955, this family-run restaurant in Evergreen Park has been the pizza source for countless birthdays, post–Little League games, and celebrations. The large dining room houses the requisite photos from Italy and antique light fixtures. They do quite a bit of non-pizza business here, along the lines of Italian beef, sausage, and meatball sandwiches. But the pizza is worth a stop.

Cut into squares, like its tavern-style brethren, it's a tad too thick on top to be classified as tavern-style. The gentle blanket of skim and part-skim mozzarella just barely covers the hand-pinched knobs of sausage, made by Russo. There is even browning across the top, sealing in that wonderful, homemade sauce, which I could easily see going into a pasta dish or on a meatball sandwich.

I enjoyed biting into the thin crust, especially near the edges, where it's lightly seasoned and just the slightest bit flaky, like a saltine. There is an audible crunch, even as you work your way to the center. One might argue that this crust is considered Chicago-style thin, aka tavern-style, but my impression was that it's not as paper-thin as other category leaders, such as Vito & Nick's or Villa Nova.

A whisper of dried oregano across the entire pizza surface skims over the ultra-thin and crispy discs of pepperoni, which are two notches spicier than most of the pepperoni I've tried in the city.

Pizzeria Bebu

TOP 5 ARTISAN PIZZAS

1. Robert's Pizza Company
   411 E. Illinois St.

2. LaBarra
   3011 Butterfield Rd.
   Oak Brook

3. Pizzeria Bebu
   1521 N. Fremont St.

4. Stella Barra Pizzeria
   1954 N. Halsted St.

5. Coalfire
   1321 W. Grand Ave.

UPTOWN

LINCOLN PARK

OLD TOWN

WEST TOWN

NEAR WEST SIDE

STREETERVILLE

DOWNTOWN CHICAGO

LAKE MICHIGAN

OAK BROOK
20 Miles
West of Downtown

CHAPTER 6

Artisan

Chicago's pizza makers, or if you want to get technical, *pizzaiolos*, usually come in one of two breeds. There are the teenage cooks who are trained to add ladles of sauce to a dough that's been run through a sheeter and then apply handfuls of shredded mozzarella and toppings. The only skills required when it comes to baking are placing the pizza into the oven, setting a timer, and removing it when it's done.

The other type of pizza maker is the salty, old, I've-been-here-for-years cook who dons a company T-shirt, and maybe a sauce-splotched paper hat, and who has the burns and scars from a decade or more of honest service. It's almost always a guy; he keeps his head down, in silence, as he either rolls out or hand-tosses the dough, then works like a surgeon to add the sauce and toppings before getting everything into the oven. He has not only memorized where the hot spots are in the oven, he has an internal timer that knows the status of each of his pizzas and is able to keep track of them without the aid of pen or paper.

The thing these two cooks have in common? Their lack of passion as it relates to the dough-making process. It's usually an afterthought, something that was made a few hours ago, or maybe the night before, and must be rolled out as quickly as possible to get it topped, baked, and sent out to the customer.

Enter the pizza artisan.

Guys like Chris Bianco (Pizzeria Bianco, in Phoenix of all places) started making every pie themselves using local ingredients and handmade sausage. Then master bread bakers like LA's Nancy Silverton (La Brea Bread) proved you could spend a lot of time mastering a pizza dough, adding the best cheeses and vegetables before baking it off in a wood-fired oven, as Silverton does at her Pizzeria Mozza. These chefs realized people would pay a premium for pies of a higher caliber, and thus ambitious cooks began treating pizza like any other artisan bread. The dough is, after all, the most important component, so why not devote extra time to its care and assembly?

Customers have responded, and in Chicago, at least, there has been a nascent movement toward an actual artisan pizza category. Years ago, the lucky few will remember the quirky, iconic Great Lake. Owners Nick Lessins and Lydia Esparza had their Byzantine rules and Soup Nazi rigidity (*No parties over four! Sorry, Beyonce and Jay-Z, wait outside!*). And there was their minimalist menu, but oh, what Nick could do with dough. I remember seeing a restaurant guest inexplicably break into applause after eating a few pieces.

After Alan Richman deemed Great Lake the best pizza in the country for *GQ*, the lines became impossible and as Yogi Berra famously said, "It's so popular no one goes there anymore." A landlord dispute forced them to close, and they never reopened.

But no matter, there are several committed artisan chefs working in Chicago today, giving their ultra-wet doughs up to three days of rest to properly ferment and develop plenty of air pockets inside, which results in extra flavor, character, and a more pleasant chew. Bread bakers refer to this as "open crumb structure." They don't over-handle the dough, treating each sphere as gently and tenderly as they would give a newborn a bath. They meticulously source (or more likely, make) their sausage, and they know most of the farmers who grow the produce for their toppings. Some even have impressive wine lists.

In short, I'm talking about restaurants with very talented cooks in the back who use only the finest ingredients they can get and also happen to make pizzas for a living

There are not enough artisan options in the city and suburbs to justify two separate divisions, as in previous chapters, so the following represent mostly city locations, with a few suburban spots mixed in. There is only one "Top 5" map, at the beginning of the chapter.

Since my deadline, a few other notable artisan spots have cropped up, and I'm sorry they're not in the book. One in particular—Grateful Bites Pizza Shoppe in sleepy Winnetka. Who does a three-day cold ferment on the North Shore?! Regardless, I've added some of these other notable pizzas on our website: pizzacityusa.com.

The Allis
113 N. Green Street (inside the
    Soho House)
312-521-8000
www.theallis.com
Ordered: burrata with capers
    and olives

Pizza East sadly closed about a year after the Soho House opened—I always liked their Neapolitan pies, riddled with char and leopard spots—but you can still find a great pizza in this private club that remains open to the public.

The Allis has always been the lobby-level hangout for afternoon tea and coffee during the day, but today it has taken over the now-closed pizza and antipasto restaurant on the second level, changing up the pizza recipe in the process.

The new management hasn't done anything with the original beloved wood-burning ovens, which reach temps well over 800 degrees.

They have, however, tweaked the recipe for the dough. It's still Italian Le 5 Stagioni flour, a high-protein flour for long rising, along with fresh yeast and a sourdough starter, but the dough has less moisture than its predecessor, and instead of a standard three-day rest, the optimal time is now anywhere from four to six days. That longer fermentation results in a crust that is simply divine.

To make their sauce, they strain plum tomatoes with olive oil and garlic, then cook that liquid down to concentrate it, adding fresh oregano, olive oil, and salt to finish. There are only a handful of options on the pizza menu (all 10-inch), each one sounding more attractive than the last—but there is no baseline Margherita, so I ordered the simplest option, featuring briny capers, chopped olives, and four large balls of creamy-rich burrata, all sprinkled with dried oregano.

The dough is remarkable. While the *cornicione* is actually about half the size of a typical Neapolitan, the middle retains its shape, texture, and best of all, crunch, much like the version at Pizzeria Bebu. There are quite a few air pockets within the lip (itself a hazy golden brown), and the bottom has the most beautifully charred undercarriage. There are leopard spots here, but they're subdued. The perimeter is evenly salted with Maldon sea salt, a premium all-natural seasoning, and kissed with olive oil before baking, resulting in a wedge that has full flavor in every single bite. While it didn't make my top five list, I would certainly consider this an honorable mention.

Most times, especially with movies, the sophomore effort falls flat, but in the case of this pizza rebirth, like *Lord of the Rings*, they've managed to improve their fortunes.

✷ **LaBarra**
3011 Butterfield Road
Oak Brook, Illinois
630-861-6177
www.labarraristorante.com
LaBarra also has a suburban location in
   Riverside. The same owners own Labriola
   in Oak Brook and off of Michigan Avenue,
   but they do not have a coal oven there,
   and thus, do not make the same type of
   artisan pie described here.
Ordered: Dante Margherita pizza
Chicago-thin options available in 10-inch,
   12-inch, 14-inch, and 16-inch.

Rich Labriola knows dough. The guy built his eponymous bakery, sold it, and has since moved on to licensing UCLA's Stan's Donuts, which is quickly gobbling up retail space around the city. His original namesake—Labriola Chicago—has kept humming along in a semi-fancy Oak Brook strip mall, and just a few years ago, he opened a branch off Michigan Avenue, which has suffered through a bit of an identity crisis. What started out as two restaurants there—one more upscale in back, another deli and sandwich joint in the front—has morphed into a Stan's Donuts satellite, as well as a pizza outpost for Chicago-style thin and outstanding deep-dish. But a few years after opening the café in Oak Brook (which offers only Neapolitan-style),

he took over a nearby space in an adjacent mall, opening LaBarra, a true suburban pizza temple.

His massive Oak Brook restaurant offers three types of pizza: Chicago-style thin, pan (deep-dish), and their signature pie, which is a coal-fired artisan pie that emerges from the brick ovens with some of the most beautiful *cornicione*s in the tri-state area. (The same menu is available at Rich's suburban Riverside location, but they use a deck oven, which allows for more consistency with the dough.)

As much as I like Coalfire downtown, *this* is the kind of dough I want putting up a fight in the blistering oven heat. The result is a great open crumb along the lip, lots of air pockets, plenty of olive oil–kissed blistering around the

top, and a puffiness that allows for a good, hearty chew. Once baked, the middle is still as thin as can be, supporting any number of artisan toppings, roasted vegetables, or even 'nduja.

Their basic Margherita-style isn't a Margherita at all (although I had them make me one, just for comparison's sake). It's called a Dante, and it has some of the freshest organic Bianco di Napoli tomatoes spread across the middle, seasoned with a bit of fresh marjoram. The giant blobs of cheese are really a blend of a few sheep's milk cheeses (I find them a little too barnyard-y), but that crust . . . oh that crust. Definitely a pizza you'll be devouring no matter what's on top.

Max & Leo's Artisan Pizza
1500 N. Clybourn Avenue
312-973-4920
www.kingsbowlamerica.com
   /lincoln-park/max-and-leos
Ordered: Margherita

The location isn't ideal—tucked away in the New City Complex, near the parking deck, inside the King's Bowling Alley, with no external signage. But their coal-fired oven does most of the heavy lifting on the menu, including the chicken wings that come in a few tempting flavors, including honey habanero and garlic rosemary. There are about a dozen pizzas here, some with caramelized vegetables, others with meatballs and grilled chicken, but all are available as either an "uno" (for one) or "due" (for two).

My Margherita arrived four minutes after I ordered it, boasting a few nice air pocket domes across the top, which the sauce didn't cover, and an undercarriage mottled black and tan. It's a really crispy pie, and the slices are relatively wide and eminently foldable.

A pretty chiffonade of basil is scattered across the top, almost to the edges. At the lip—which is just chewy enough but maybe lacking enough salt—there is a slightly raised edge, not as much as on a traditional Neapolitan, but high enough to contain some air pockets. The taste, without any sauce or cheese on it, reminds me of a baguette in terms of its yeastiness.

There is a lot of sauce here, and its application is haphazard, as if the cook was doing it blindfolded. He simply tosses it on the dough, Jackson Pollack–style, dotting it and then leaving a few spots bare, which tend to puff up into mini-domes.

They place Romano cheese at the bottom, as well as appropriate blobs of whole milk mozzarella from Grande Cheese Company in Fond du Lac, Wisconsin.

If you can get over the fact that you're in a completely manufactured city mall where most of the food is pretty average, you'll do fine; that is, if you can find the joint.

What started in Greenpoint, Brooklyn, and has spread to a half-dozen other locations, including Columbus, Baltimore, and Miami, now has a location in the heart of hipster paradise, aka Chicago's Logan Square. Goofy names aside (Mo Cheeks, Ricotta Be Kiddin' Me, Brian DeParma, etc.), Paulie Gee's intense wood-burning ovens churn out seriously blistered pies with nice leopard spotting throughout the *cornicione* and more than a dozen options for fancy-pants pizzas. The key is the three-day cold fermentation that results in dough with incredible chew and complexity.

The sweet Italian fennel sausage is a favorite, but so is anything with pickled cherry peppers, fresh mozz, or Berkshire guanciale (cured pork cheek). The beer list is vast, matching the pizza quality in terms of variety and depth.

Paulie Gee's Logan Square
2451 N. Milwaukee Avenue
773-360-1072
www.pauliegee.com
Ordered: "Keep it Simple Stupid" with fennel sausage

ony Priolo's Piccolo Sogno (Italian for "little dream") has always been one of my favorites for Italian in the city, since everything—including the breadsticks—is made in-house. At lunchtime, expect to see plenty of suits and shiny cufflinks while Loop office workers travel a few blocks west for handmade pastas. (The parking lot is a big plus, too.) The crystal chandeliers and white tablecloths, along with exposed brick and deep-blue walls, make this a slightly more elegant option for pizza eating, but no less comfortable.

With the house olive oil bottle standing sentinel, my pizza arrives, and it is majestic, hiding a few well-placed basil leaves and lots of *fior di latte* mozzarella, which is combined with a buffalo milk starter. Priolo uses a little bit of the previous day's dough to add complexity and lift. Once the dough is made, it rests overnight.

The ultra-thin center is not typically Neapolitan, in that it's not all wet. That's just fine with me. As I pick up a slice, it holds its shape, despite the generous application of San Marzano–based sauce.

I thought the undercarriage could have had some more charring, but that's a minor quibble. This is an "Italian-style" pizza as Priolo calls it, and it does its country of origin proud.

Piccolo Sogno
464 N. Halsted Street
312-421-0077
www.piccolosognorestaurant.com
Ordered: Margherita

TODD ROSENBERG

ocated in a former barbecue joint, this husband-and-wife café dispenses with the heavy, cliché-driven Italian-American entrées and sticks to the basics: antipasto, pasta, pizza, and panini. The cozy bar holds a massive Simonelli espresso machine and features five stools. During the day, large windows fill the space with gentle light. It sits, almost hidden, near the busy intersection of Elston, California, and Belmont, and the free parking in back is a big plus.

The pizza menu lists nine specialties, including some really creative ones such as a housemade fennel sausage with castelvetrano olives, black truffle purée, and stracciatella cheese. I may have to go back to try the whipped ricotta with roasted garlic, mozzarella, and pepperoncino. Either way, I'm definitely going back. Here's why.

The dough gets an overnight rest and two separate periods to rise (proof). That's part of the reason the crust has so much integrity—but the dough recipe itself is another reason. Even after the pies bake, they maintain their wonderful structure, despite the relatively heavy toppings of San Marzano tomato sauce and cheese.

On the Margherita, enormous pools of *fior di latte* rest among the gargantuan basil leaves, and when you remove a wedge from the pie it doesn't budge (much like at Pizzeria Bebu). There are extremely small air pockets lining the lip, along with some mild charring, but the use of a dough docker helps to punch out air pockets in the middle, keeping the center über-thin. Underneath, the bottom has a few interesting craters with random charring and brown spots. They also brush the perimeter of each pizza with a little bit of herb oil just before baking, which results in a barely greenish hue at the furthest edges (no, it's not pesto). Just before serving, they sprinkle a bit of Parmigiano-Reggiano over the top, adding some complex saltiness.

This pizza doesn't need chili flakes or oregano or anything shaken from a cheese container to enhance it. The kitchen does all the heavy lifting. Why would you mess with it?

Pisolino
2755 W. Belmont Street
773-293-6025
www.pisolinochicago.com
Ordered: Margherita pizza

★ Pizzeria Bebu
1521 N. Fremont Street
312-280-6000
www.bebu.pizza
Ordered: Margherita pizza

Pizzerias are typically the kinds of places you expect to have a beer or a glass of wine with dinner—although you probably don't expect to see a '78 Mt. Eden Cabernet, for $200 a bottle, on the wine list. But Zach Smith is trying to change your idea of what a pizza joint can be.

A veteran of the Gold Coast's Nico Osteria, he and his partner, Jeff Lutzow, created a hidden gem among the caverns of unidentifiable apartment and light industrial buildings just south of North Avenue and near a massive Whole Foods store. Up until Bebu opened, the only other pizza option in the neighborhood was Sono Wood Fired, across from the gleaming white Apple Store on North Avenue, but there really is no comparison between the two. I say walk the extra two blocks for a seat at Bebu.

The restaurant doesn't look like much from the outside. Tucked into a long, narrow room at the base of a micro-apartment building with floor-to-ceiling windows, it could just as well be a furniture store. But from the looks of it, the neighbors are excited to have some artisan pies in the 'hood. Servers stand sentinel, in "Feed Me Pizza" T-shirts, waiting to take your order and happily guide you through the wine list.

The dough gets a gentle two-day rest before being shaped and tossed into a gas-fired, brick-lined oven, kept right around 700 degrees. The pizzas take six to eight minutes to bake.

A trio caddy of dried oregano, chili flakes, and grated parm arrive at your table just in case you want to doctor up your pie—but it's unnecessary. These are truly transcendent pizzas, achieving what few artisan or Neapolitan pies can: an ultra-thin middle that manages to stay firm, upright, and impossibly crispy.

The Margherita has a nice lip with an even char on the undercarriage. Five large basil leaves top off the pie, along with a half-dozen amorphous blobs of fresh mozzarella. Unlike those of many shops in town, Pizzeria Bebu's tomato sauce is more generous (I guess when you know that your bottom crust can hold its own—and hold things up—you feel more confident adding liquid or sauce on top of the crust).

My only quibble: I thought the dough could have used a bit more salt for balance, but that's not enough to keep me from coming back here again and again. Next time, I'm getting the "Sausage & Broccoli Rabe," with its generous knobs of fresh ricotta and housemade Italian sausage.

Pizzeria DeVille
404 N. Milwaukee Avenue
Libertyville, Illinois
847-367-4992
www.pizzeriadeville.com
Ordered: 13-inch Margherita;
    and 13-inch half-sausage,
    half-soppressata
A 12-inch, gluten-free crust is
    available

I've been to this place once before, during lunch, but was told that they don't make anything using their wood-burning oven until dinner. Naturally, I had to go back. And yes, the dinner lineup is impressive: homemade sausage (excellent, by the way), soppressata, whipped ricotta . . . the usual artisan lineup of goodies, but one that is rarely, if ever, found in the far northwest burbs. They offer well over a dozen specialty pies, with crazy toppings like meatballs, corned beef, and pastrami—if you like that sort of thing. Sometimes less is more.

I started with a Margherita (called the Queen's Pizza*), featuring *fior di latte*, fresh tomato sauce, and basil. The key, of course, is that dough, and it emerges from the wood-burning oven beautifully charred and knobby, with an impressive undercarriage of blackened but not overdone crust. There is a nice chew to the edge. Perhaps not as salty as it could be, but still definitely craveable to the point where I ate almost three pieces.

I also tried a half-sausage, half-soppressata, and sadly, this recipe is drowning in cheese. (My server insisted it was the same *fior di latte* as in the Margherita, but I find that hard to fathom, as it would have jacked up the food cost by 100 percent.) The cheese obliterates this pie, which is a shame considering the quality of the sausage and soppressata hidden beneath the milky blanket.

Regardless, this is a must-visit if you're in the area. You'll have a hard time finding wood-burning ovens this far north in Chicagoland, especially one that produces pies of this caliber.

Note: The Queen in this case was the Queen consort of Italy from 1878 to 1900, Margherita of Savoy. On June 11, 1889, as a way to honor her, the Neapolitan pizza maker Raffaele Esposito created the "Pizza Margherita," a pizza garnished with tomatoes, mozzarella, and basil, to represent the national colors of Italy on the Italian flag.

With a veteran like John Coletta manning the kitchen, you know that this Italian restaurant in River North isn't just going to serve average pizza. He's going to take it to the ultimate level, using as many housemade ingredients as he can.

The restaurant is lively at night, with TVs showing old black-and-white Italian films and purposefully dim lighting. Subway tiles and wooden floors lend an air of urban rusticity, as if you're dining in a curated West Village bistro that had the budget for an interior designer.

Surprisingly, there isn't a wood-burning oven. It's a gas-fired, man-made, stone hearth from Italy that gets up to 700 degrees. That said, the guy still manages to churn out some impressive pies. There's an entire side of the menu dedicated to Neapolitan pizza, ranging in price from $10 for a simple Bianca with no tomato sauce or Marinara with no cheese, all the way up to $16 for elaborate pizzas featuring housemade duck prosciutto and wild arugula or smoked provolone with spinach, speck, and Grana Padano cheese.

My Margherita arrived with the largest basil leaves I'd ever seen (no small feat in the middle of winter). Beneath the leaves, housemade *fior di latte* is almost completely incorporated into the San Marzano tomato sauce, and there is cheese complexity, thanks to a shower of Parmesan, I'm sure.

A very small *cornicione* indicates a shorter resting time for the dough, yet there are ample air pockets and a very good chew. The edge stays crispy, and each slice is a pleasure.

I visited after a long day of trying other pizzas, but somehow managed to fit in a taste of the smoked provolone pizza as well as a unique pizza version with homemade ricotta, roasted cherry tomatoes, and a rich, melted cheese fonduta instead of tomato sauce. Too full from the antipasti? *Mangia!*

Quartino
626 N. State Street
312-698-5000
www.quartinochicago.com
Ordered: 12-inch Margherita

Reno
2607 N. Milwaukee Avenue
773-697-4234
www.renochicago.com
Ordered: "Reno" with half-
sausage, half-pepperoni

On a rainy, dreary Wednesday night in Logan Square, the hipsters are jammed into booths, music playing loudly, for Reno's $20-for-two-pizzas-and-PBR night.

The focal point here is the wood-burning oven, which also finishes off Montreal-style bagels for the morning crowd. But at night, nearly every table has a large (14-inch) pizza on it, and I can see why. They offer about a dozen creative pizza options, including "Fancy Nancy" with burrata and truffle oil, and "Hog" with pork carnitas and cotija cheese.

I opt to go baseline, with a "Reno" (fresh domestic mozzarella, a chiffonade of basil, and a base of Valorosa tomatoes) and add-ons of sausage and pepperoni.

The housemade fennel sausage is the standout here. It's crumbled onto the pie in generous handfuls and packs a mouthful of fatty-rich flavor with the barest whisper of anise. Even the pepperoni—sourced from elsewhere—is sliced a shade thicker and contains the slightest amount of chili heat, just as a sort of wake-up call. The naked lip, about a half-inch wide, is softer than on most artisan pies, but I like seeing a pair of char domes on one side, indicating some texture and extraordinary heat from the oven, which hovers around 800 degrees. The undercarriage is also suitably charred, but the slices are so thin that they flop beneath the weight of just about any topping. You can fold them if you prefer, since the outer lip is soft and chewy and folds easily. Take that, NYC.

★ **Robert's Pizza Company**
411 E. Illinois Street
(no phone number at press time)
robertspizzacompany.com
Ordered: Basic fresh mozz
    with tomato sauce; and
    half-sausage, half-pepperoni

No matter how good a pizza in Naperville or Libertyville or Northbrook is, tourists won't likely make the schlep to the burbs, even for a pizza. For this reason alone, Robert Garvey had an advantage for the first year of business: his namesake joint was conveniently located in Streeterville, just a quick cab ride from most of the hotels downtown. Sadly, a partner dispute temporarily closed the restaurant in 2017.

At press time, he had just signed a lease a few blocks away, so I opted to keep the website, which will reveal the new phone number once he gets that hooked up.

Wherever it is, go. His pizzas are pretty amazing. Consider the fact that he's spent the past twenty years with an obsession. He says he had a slice-a-day habit in New York. That led to five years of almost daily baking experimentation to come up with his ideal pizza. Like any good pie, it's all about the dough. It's a cold rise in a refrigerator for three days, and then he gives it a long time to proof when it comes out of the cooler.

Garvey handles the dough like it's a precious stone or treasured relic, careful not to overwork it. He uses his fingers rather than a roller to put a little bit of air in the crust, which gives it a nice, light chew in the finished product. The sauce is homemade, sausage is carefully sourced, and additional toppings include Brussels sprouts with bacon, a seafood version with clams and shrimp, and Peking duck with hoisin. After about ten minutes in a gas-fired oven, the pizzas emerge beautifully crisp on the edge. A wire rack beneath elevates the pies, preventing them from getting soggy and maintaining a crisp bottom crust.

It's all part of the plan to create the perfect slice. "The middle is kind of a nice, soft chew; then it moves to a nice crunchy chew, then you finish with that nice big heel, which is a terrific finish to the slice," he explained.

I couldn't agree more. And good news for celiacs: Robert's Pizza Company has a gluten-free option (although I can't attest to its quality).

★ **Stella Barra Pizzeria**
1954 N. Halsted Street
773-634-4101
www.stellabarra.com
Ordered: Margherita pizza

With locations in Hollywood, Santa Monica, and Bethesda, Maryland, this Lincoln Park sibling to Summer House Santa Monica is part of the Lettuce Entertain You empire. Chef Jeff Mahin oversees the menus at both restaurants, and has created a pretty lovely lineup of pies that take a farmers' market approach. Alongside the home-made sausage and fresh mozzarel-la, you'll also spot fennel pollen, fresh ricotta, and peppery arugula, plus an outstanding mushroom pie with truffle oil, but I digress.

The star here is the crust, and I can't overstate its importance. Too many pizza fans rave with misguided loyalty about places that have crusts so substandard I wouldn't serve them at a six-year-old's birthday party, and I'm sure those same fans will berate me for touting a pizza joint in Lincoln

Park that has leather couches and hand-crafted cocktails. But if you consider yourself a pizza lover, you have to give this crust a try.

It's everything I want in a chew: salty, slightly textured (is that corn-meal on the bottom?), and with an enormous *cornicione* revealing air pockets the size of edamame beans. Mahin says his dough gets a lot of rest and time to develop its signature flavor.

The middle of the pizza is also impressive, with a sturdiness despite its shallow depth, which is only a millimeter or two, that holds up under the fresh mozzarella and tomato sauce. For the record, that sauce has more intensity than

most, as if the kitchen first reduced it before adding it to the pie.

My only complaint: not enough cheese. Believe me, I've bemoaned the overkill on many pizzas in town, where they rely too heavily on cheese (Milano's in Beverly is one), but Stella was a little weak with the fresh mozzarella and needs to bump it up a tad.

That said, even after taste-testing a few other pizzas on the day I visited Stella Barra, I still managed to eat an entire slice—a compliment to the person who did the baking. My recommendation? Get thyself to the corner of Halsted and Armitage and dive into one of Chicago's best artisan pizzas.

Grateful Bites Pizza Shoppe, Winnetka

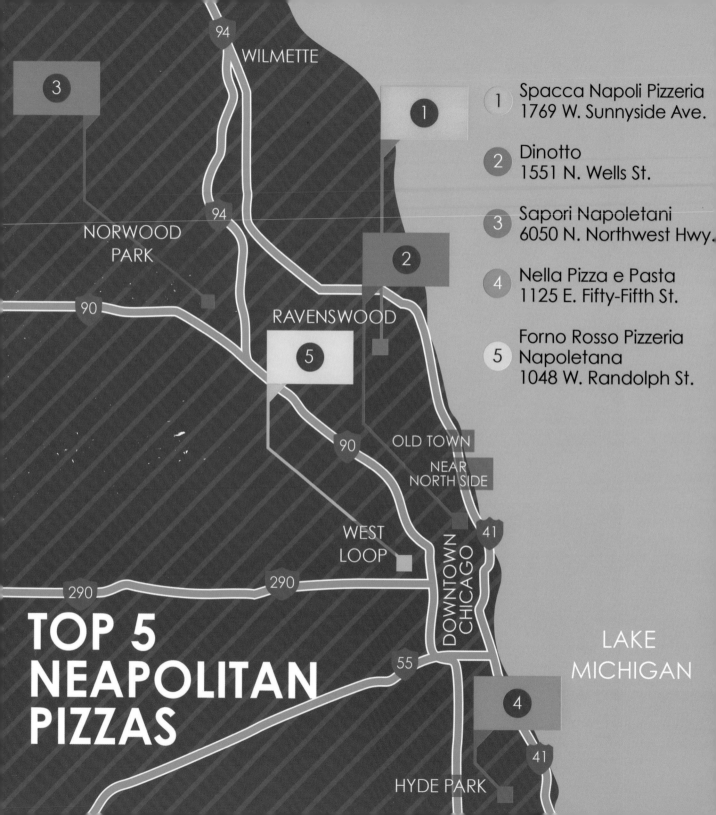

TOP 5 NEAPOLITAN PIZZAS

1. Spacca Napoli Pizzeria
1769 W. Sunnyside Ave.

2. Dinotto
1551 N. Wells St.

3. Sapori Napoletani
6050 N. Northwest Hwy.

4. Nella Pizza e Pasta
1125 E. Fifty-Fifth St.

5. Forno Rosso Pizzeria Napoletana
1048 W. Randolph St.

WILMETTE

NORWOOD PARK

RAVENSWOOD

OLD TOWN

NEAR NORTH SIDE

WEST LOOP

DOWNTOWN CHICAGO

LAKE MICHIGAN

HYDE PARK

CHAPTER 7

Neapolitan

It's not exactly a secret society like Skull and Bones, but the fraternity of *pizzaiolos* who ply their trade beneath the mantle of Neapolitan pizza do refer to each other with reverence. In Chicago, Jonathan Goldsmith is the high priest of Neapolitan pizza at Spacca Napoli. A pioneer in his trade, he's the "dough whisperer," managing to transform flour and water into one of the city's most heavenly chews. Some of his former employees have opened their own Neapolitan pizza joints (a sort of Rick Bayless effect for the beehive oven set), assembling faithful re-creations, doming them just before serving, and in the process, expanding the Neapolitan-style pizza landscape.

What is a Neapolitan? In short, it's a pizza style originating from—you guessed it—Naples, Italy. There is actually an international governing body, the Vera Pizza Napoletana (VPN), which attempts to preserve this tradition and ensure that *pizzaiolos* and restaurants claiming to serve the real thing abide by certain rules. There is also an Association of Neapolitan Pizza Makers and, like the VPN, their goal is to make sure anyone claiming to sell a Neapolitan pizza is upholding tradition.

In short, these *pizzaiolos* must use "00" flour, which is highly refined. The water must have a certain pH level; sea salt and compressed solid yeast must be used; and there are rules regarding how many times the dough should rise and for how long. In addition, San Marzano tomatoes must be used for the sauce. Even the type of oven used to bake the pies is specified with somber authority. In this quote from their official guidelines, the Association of Neapolitan Pizza Makers describes what a pizza should look and taste like when it emerges from the oven:

The consistency of the pizza should be soft, elastic, and easy to manipulate and fold. The center should be particularly soft to the touch and the taste and appearance of the pizza must be evidenced by the red color of the tomato. For the Pizza Marinara, the green of the oregano and the white of the garlic must be homogeneously spread, while, in the case of the Pizza Margherita, the white of the mozzarella should appear in evenly spread patches, in contrast with the green of the basil leaves, slightly darkened by the cooking process. The crust should possess the flavor of well-baked bread. The slightly acidic flavor of the densely enriched tomatoes, mixed with the characteristic aroma of the oregano, garlic or basil ensures that the pizza, as it comes out from the oven, delivers its characteristic aroma of a fresh and fragrant typical Mediterranean product.

Several pizza makers in town claim to make a Neapolitan, but many fall short. Unfortunately, there aren't enough Neapolitan specialists to warrant a "Top 5" list for both the city and the burbs, so the map shows my top five for the entire Chicagoland region.

You can't really call Acanto a pizza joint. That would be like calling Smoque BBQ a mac 'n' cheese joint. Sure, the restaurant has two pizzas on the menu—the basic Margherita and a sausage version for two bucks more—but it's really a semi-classy Italian restaurant, with a dynamic menu featuring homemade pasta, 'nduja and burrata, and a well-chosen wine list.

The younger, more sophisticated sibling to the boisterous Gage next door, Acanto's Michigan Avenue address brings lots of walk-ins and tourists, since it sits directly across from Jaume Plensa's Crown Fountain at Millennium Park. The room is warm, with its large Oriental rug and dim mood lighting directed at a wall of empty liquor and wine bottles. It all makes for easy conversation.

For some reason, my pie took longer than it should have (I have a feeling the host recognized me and may have gone down to tell the kitchen), since we waited about fifteen to twenty minutes. But the wait was worth it.

The pie arrives perfectly blistered and charred, with lots of leopard spotting on the elevated *cornicione*. The chew is magnifi-

cent, and while there isn't much sauce to speak of, the enormous blobs of fresh mozzarella manage to stay on the pizza rather than slink away. I also thought there was ample salt in each bite—a sign that the kitchen *pizzaiolo* knows what's up.

Acanto
18 S. Michigan Avenue
312-578-0763
www.acantochicago.com
Ordered: Margherita pizza

Antica Pizzeria
5663 N. Clark Street
773-944-1492
Ordered: Margherita pizza

This Andersonville restaurant underwent a minor remodeling shortly before I visited—adding a bar and fixing the tin ceiling— but the wood-burning oven in the middle of the restaurant is still the centerpiece. I opted for a basic Margherita, my standard barometer in any Neapolitan joint, and I like this pie's chew, redolent with luscious tomato sauce and large, wide swaths of fresh mozzarella. However, the crust—especially the outer rim, or *cornicione*—is somewhat tough, and I couldn't see any leopard spotting on the perimeter or the undercarriage. The overall effect is tight and dense, and a far cry from the fluffy, puffy, air pocket–filled wonders at Forno Rosso and Spacca Napoli.

I don't dislike this pizza; I am just disappointed. But certainly, if you are in the neighborhood and craving some zesty tomato sauce and springy fresh mozz with a smattering of basil shards, all presented on a sturdy and serviceable crust, then by all means, be my guest.

This River North stalwart is one of the best places for a business lunch or romantic dinner. Like John Stamos, the restaurant seems to be ageless and still looks good, with its exposed wooden beams and giant bar at the back of the dining room. Proprietor Jack Weiss and his wife are usually on the floor, checking on regulars and making sure everything is running smoothly. Their renowned and massive antipasto bar is still located up front—all the better to tempt you—in case you feel like something other than one of their six pizzas.

Chef Federico Comacchio has a deft hand, whether it be forming pasta or hand-stretching his dough, which rests for a minimum of three days. He offers some Italian specialties, like a *diavola* (spicy salami) and *verdure* (eggplant, zucchini, and olives), but tasting his Margherita is just as much a pleasure.

It's very nearly a VPN-certified pie, and it should be, with its "00" flour, hand-crushed and milled San Marzano tomatoes, and *fior di latte* cheese that's generously placed around the pie. The result looks much like a tomato sky full of clouds. There is wonderful charring along the *cornicione*, thanks to that 800-degree wood-burning oven, while the undercarriage has a similar look. The chew is splendid. There is a subtle sweetness that comes from the tomatoes and a tanginess from the dough, which is perfectly seasoned with salt. Basil is an afterthought, with a few micro threads scattered about and a lone leaf or two plopped in the middle, but when you have the complexity of that dough, with its attendant air pockets and addictive chew, a few herbs are beside the point.

Bottom line, even the dudes in suits at lunch can't resist the allure of this pizza.

Coco Pazzo
300 W. Hubbard Street
312-836-0900
www.cocopazzochicago.com
Ordered: Margherita pizza

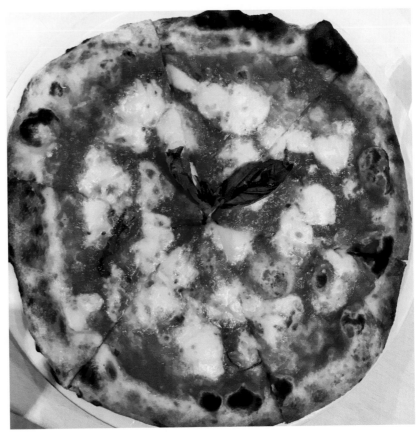

illy Lawless has always, it seems, had a pretty good idea about what his customers want. On Michigan Avenue, he masters the gastropub concept at The Gage, serving food that doesn't play dumb for the masses. Next door to The Gage, at Acanto, he's created an Italian lounge with stellar cocktails and a better-than-expected Neapolitan pizza (also on my 101 list). At Coda di Volpe on Southport, he's struck a balance between an approachable neighborhood restaurant and a River North vibe.

Coda di Volpe patrons are two-deep at the bar on the Friday I decide to go check it out. High-backed booths, not unlike something from The Pump Room, line the middle of the dining room. The glorious pizza oven is impossible to miss, sitting next to a wall of chopped wood no less than eight feet tall. Like the Hope Diamond, its white-and-gray-tiled shell is proudly displayed (and guarded) behind a phalanx of cooks, all scurrying around, shifting and transferring blistered pies into and out of the oven's mouth.

There are just eight options on the menu, and these are the only pizzas in Chicago that come with your very own set of kitchen shears, with which you are left to cut the pie as you wish. Preserving the integrity of the pizza, in its whole form, is something a lot of *pizzaiolos* would probably like to do, rather than cut it prematurely. This small detail speaks volumes.

The kitchen also understands OBR, as it manages to add just the right amount of tangy *fior di latte* and tomato sauce (which might be a tad too thin for some) without overwhelming the delicate, thin slices.

A pizza with high ambitions must have an impressive *cornicione*, and this one is no different. It's speckled and blistered with a generous amount of char (both on top and underneath), giving each bite a pleasant chew with the slightest hint of tang—a result of letting the dough rest enough to kick-start fermentation. Another plus is the appropriate seasoning and salt usage, so that the naked pieces of the lip that are left over actually retain flavor.

I can't wait to go back and try the versions with pesto, roasted mushrooms, and fennel sausage.

Coda di Volpe
3335 N. Southport Avenue
773-687-8568
www.cdvolpe.com
Ordered: Margherita pizza
Upgrade to mozzarella *di bufala* is available.

Davanti Enoteca
1359 W. Taylor Street
312-226-5500
www.davantienoteca.com
Davanti Enoteca also has
   one suburban location,
   in Western Springs.
Ordered: D.O.C.

This restaurant—a creation of Francesca's Restaurant Group—is the brainchild of Scott Harris, who divides his time between Chicago and San Diego, where there are two additional Davantis. The menu lists just a handful of pizzas, all fired in an igloo-style brick oven that's gas-fired to about 550 degrees. Each order is presented with a trio of sidecars containing oregano, salt, and chili flakes, so you can customize your pizza.

The dough rests overnight—about twelve hours—and as much as I would have loved to try the creations with wild mushrooms, braised leeks, and taleggio cheese, or the soppressata, with its spicy pepperoni, mozzarella, and chili oil, I stuck to the basics for the sake of my quest: a Margherita, or in this case, the restaurant's "D.O.C." For the record, D.O.C. stands for *Denominazione d'Origine Controllata*, a certification that signifies a controlled designation of origin and is a quality assurance label usually seen on Italian wines.

The ultra-thin undercarriage just barely holds up the ingredients and the light amount of sauce. A small *cornicione* fails to reach the height of the city's more grand Neapolitan houses, although it maintains a nice chew and plenty of salt content.

The kitchen is definitely generous with the fresh mozz, and while some slices were charred underneath, others could have used another twenty seconds on the oven's deck to turn them from pale blond to black. Likewise, some slices had just enough sauce coverage while others seemed lacking, which results in a few dough-only bites.

★ **Dinotto**
1551 N. Wells Street
312-202-0302
www.dinotto.com
Ordered: Margherita pizza

Thank you, Reenie O'Brien King! Although I got dozens of recommendations via Facebook and Instagram during round one of my pizza crawl to check out Dinotto, King convinced me to give them a try. "Their long presence in the neighborhood [since 1989], charming hospitality, and red-tiled wood-burning oven from Naples are part of the reason why, quite often, my family uses the restaurant as our own dining room table," she wrote. "Their housemade mozzarella tops my favorite pizza in Chicago . . . it's always delicious." After such high praise, how could I not check out their Neapolitan?

First, the beautiful red-tiled, wood-burning oven sits in the back of the open kitchen, like a new Ferrari that the owners get to take for a spin every few minutes. The pizzas emerge from the oven nicely blistered throughout, with a wonderful chew. The pies manage to balance the amount of *fior di latte* mozzarella with a zippy, brightly acidic tomato sauce that I couldn't stop eating. More important, the texture of the triangular slices were spot-on—the middles were appreciably wet (like any self-respecting Neapolitan should be), but not to the point of soupiness, like Spacca Napoli in the early days.

I had already eaten a few slices of pizza prior to my visit here on this particular day, but I had no problem eating half of my Margherita. Would I like a little bit more fermentation so that the edges attain more stature and heft, with the accompanying air pockets? Sure. But I wouldn't let that stop me from eating another pizza here.

This chain of Italian marketplaces, now with five locations in the United States and a gondola load across the globe, opened its gigantic, two-level ode to all things Italian in River North a few years ago. Boasting a larger footprint than the New York City original in the Flatiron District, there are several stations and restaurants to choose from inside the massive sixty-thousand-square-foot behemoth. Naturally, I visited La Pizza & La Pasta up on Eataly's second floor.

The Margherita, cooked in a wood-burning oven, looks as if the *pizzaiolo* was in a hurry. Not only is the interior edge of the dough slightly wet and chewy, but also one section of the pie actually lacks tomato sauce. Don't get me wrong, I love the fresh mozz and chewing the crust is a pleasure (they now offer a few optional doughs, such as rustic and gluten-free), but there are highs and lows here.

Eataly actually outsources the pizza making to a Napoli-based company called Rossopomodoro, which sends trainers to Chicago to supervise the *pizzaiolos*. When ticket counts run high and the noise level increases, sometimes the staff is harried. But they need to slow down and take their time, because if they're going to carry the mantle of Eataly's owners, they need to improve the quality control. The pizza here can be very good, but the *pizzaiolos* need to remember that consistency is as important as anything else.

Eataly
43 E. Ohio Street
312-521-8700
www.eataly.com/us_en/stores
/chicago
Ordered: Margherita pizza

Elio Bartolotta takes an old-school approach to making his pizza—the same way he learned as a kid in Sicily and then later in New York City. He begins by chopping wood out back behind his store (located in an Addison strip mall). The wood is usually a mix of hickory, oak, and maple. Once he gets his custom-made, wood-burning brick oven up to temperature, he sets to work on his pizza. The options run the gamut, like they do in most Neapolitan joints, including arugula- or prosciutto-topped pies, some without sauce (white), and some with extra shavings of Pecorino Romano. As I've done throughout this quest, however, I ordered a Margherita.

The dough is obviously the most critical, and Bartolotta lets his rest about a day. Hand-stretching it like the guys who showed him how, he ladles on a crushed tomato sauce derived from San Marzanos and adds a generous handful or three of fresh mozzarella—even *bufala* mozz, if the customer asks. Then his creation goes into the oven, where he works it with a long peel, moving it in and out and around the hot spots, finally doming the pie just before removing it and serving it uncut, to preserve its integrity.

While I would prefer a slightly larger, puffier, and chewier *cornicione*, this pie still manages to produce a good chew and slightly crispy edge. The middle is riddled with that wonderfully rich and creamy mozzarella, while the sauce doesn't overwhelm the bite. Basil is an afterthought—there are just a few shards scattered like sprinkles on a cupcake—but it still somehow manages to suffuse the pie with ample aroma.

Elio Pizza on Fire
445 W. Lake Street
Addison, Illinois
630-628-0088
www.eliopizzaonfire.com
Ordered: Margherita pizza

✱ **Forno Rosso Pizzeria Napoletana**
1048 W. Randolph Street
312-243-6000
www.fornorossopizzeria.com
The original location is on the western edge of the city:
   3719 N. Harlem Avenue
   773-716-3000
Ordered: Margherita pizza

Nick Nitti has been a student of Neapolitan pizza for some time, and when I interviewed him a few years ago for ABC7, I recall him telling me how he looked up to (and visited) gurus like Chris Bianco, in Phoenix, before deciding to open his own place in the Dunning neighborhood on Chicago's Northwest Side. (His newer location, on West Randolph, is much more convenient for Neapolitan-loving pizza fans near downtown.)

The *cornicione* here is majestic. Slightly charred from the heat of his wood-burning, beehive brick oven, it arrives amply blistered, covered in generous blobs of fresh mozzarella and a half dozen fresh basil leaves. The tomato sauce is simple, fresh, and evenly applied, contributing to slices that hold their shape when lifted.

The bottom crust has a decent amount of char and the perimeter is soft yet chewy. Take a look inside that crust and you'll see air pockets, revealing a decent amount of fermentation. This is a crust you want to finish off.

One note: this is a fragile creation. Don't get it to go, or you'll miss the entire experience. Eat it as soon as it hits your table!

Napolita Pizzeria & Wine Bar
1126 Central Avenue
Wilmette, Illinois
224-215-0305
www.napolitapizza.com
Ordered: Margherita pizza

Located on the same block as the Wilmette movie theater and the beloved Chuck Wagon Gyros, this relatively new addition to the sleepy North Shore community's downtown district is making pies that are probably better than they need to be. Kid-friendly is a given here—there are as many sippy cups as Negroni cocktails—but they're not dumbing down the pizzas.

Just take a look at the majestic wood-burning oven in the corner, and keep your eye on the *piz-zaiolo* through the sneeze-guard glass. Watch the way he forms the dough, the quality of his toppings (San Marzano tomatoes and fresh mozzarella, of course), and the heat of the wood-burning oven—all signs that Napolita is striving to reach the coveted VPN designation, known as Vera Pizza Napoletana.

The Margherita, with its basil leaves and fresh mozzarella, emerges nicely blistered. So does a sausage version with peppers and caramelized onions. It's cooked incredibly quickly, resulting in a very light crust that's slightly chewy but crisp.

They also offer bianco, or white, pizzas, featuring a base of fonduta rather than the usual tomato sauce. Think cheese sauce cooked with garlic, white wine, and various cheeses. Had I allowed an honorable mention for this category, this would have made the cut.

The plan is to eventually get that VPN certification, but with or without it, the owners say their goal is to have Napolitas all over the North Shore at some point.

Panino's Pizza
3702 N. Broadway Street
(entrance on Waveland Avenue)
773-472-6200
www.paninospizzeria.com
They also have locations in
  Evanston and Park Ridge.
Ordered: Margherita pizza
Several specialty pies available,
  including ones with burrata
  and buffalo mozzarella.

Each of Panino's suburban locations is a stand-alone restaurant and pizzeria. But the city location is really two different restaurants within one. On the Broadway side (facing a strip mall), it's a standard-issue thin, deep-dish, and by-the-slice joint, with pies baked in electric ovens. On the Waveland side, a completely different personality emerges. Here, it's Panino's Pizzaiolo, a reference to the fact that they are putting their Neapolitan hats on, and indeed,

the giant red-tiled, wood-burning oven in the back has "MASTER PIZZAIOLO" spelled out in white tiles, indicating they take the pizzas a tad more seriously here.

The key is their mother starter, a strain of yeast that is recycled and reused, integrated and fed with more water and flour, then kneaded and aged—left to ferment and develop serious air pockets within the dough.

After the pizza—topped with healthy blobs of fresh mozzarella, zesty tomato sauce with a few basil leaves, and a drizzle of olive oil—is scorched and baked in the Italian-made oven, it emerges with beautifully charred edges as well as blackened splotches above and below. There is a great chew, with wonderful texture, and a homey, misshapen *cornicione*.

My only complaint is that there is not enough salt in the dough, because after you work your way to the edge and get past the last bits of cheese and sauce, the resulting plain crust just doesn't have the same craveability as versions from Spacca Napoli, Forno Rosso, or even Stella Barra. That said, it's still one hell of a delicious pizza that I'd have no problem crushing on my own.

Pizza Art Café
4658 N. Rockwell Street
773-539-0645
www.pizzaartcafe.com
Ordered: Margherita pizza

This quaint neighborhood café, on the border of Ravenswood and Lincoln Square, sits directly next to the Rockwell CTA Brown Line stop, at a point in the city where the train rides along at grade level so that, during rush hour, the security gates are constantly rising and falling.

Once you step inside Pizza Art Café, notice the handmade pizza oven just to your left and behind the bar. It's wood-fired, of course, and the insulated bricks bring the internal temperature up to around 800 degrees. The pizza menu lists thirteen vegetarian options, seventeen with meat (they're particularly proud of their house-smoked meat), and another five with seafood.

The Margherita, which takes about four minutes to reach your table, arrives with a slightly puffy edge and a respectable amount of leopard spotting. It has a nice, easy chew and a fair number of tiny air pockets within, indicating some fermentation. The top of the pie is dominated by fresh mozzarella—not a bad thing, but also not very Neapolitan. Rather than the balanced splotches I was expecting, this pie has a little too much cheese for my taste, but cheese lovers will appreciate the kitchen's generous hand. You can always ask them to back off, I guess. Oregano flecks and a half dozen or so enormous basil leaves cover the pizza, making it a pleasure to eat—even though the tomato sauce might be a tad too thick for some.

✴ **Nella Pizza e Pasta**
1125 E. Fifty-Fifth Street
773-643-0603
www.nellachicago.com
Ordered: Margherita pizza

Naples native Nella Grassano enchanted Chicagoans with her deft touch while working as the *pizzaiola* for Jonathan Goldsmith at Spacca Napoli between 2000 and 2010. The duo famously parted ways, with Grassano first going to work for Scott Harris's Francesca empire, then later opening her own place on a congested stretch of Fullerton with historically very little foot traffic.

In late 2017, a dispute with her landlord (and some wooing from the University of Chicago) led her to a much larger space at the base of a new dorm on Fifty-Fifth Street in Hyde Park. Her skills, honed over a lifetime of trial and error, have been rewarded and praised by several local critics, and rightly so. What a pleasure it is devouring Nella's Margherita. I'm sure the ones topped with arugula or prosciutto are equally enjoyable, but whatever you order, just inhaling the smell of the "00" flour, baked to exact specs in the wood-burning oven, and biting into the textbook delicious *cornicione* delivers one of the city's best Neapolitan-style pie experiences . . . *mmm.*

The Margheritas are nicely charred and I love how the middle is just thick enough to withstand the blobs of mozzarella and fresh tomato sauce. Rather than falling over limp at the first touch, the pieces actually hold their shape as I bring each bite to my mouth.

And that chew! One of the hallmarks of a great pizza—and a compliment to the *pizzaiola*—is being able to thoroughly enjoy the entire slice, from the point all the way to the edge.

✴ Sapori Napoletani
6050 N. Northwest Highway
773-628-7894
www.saporinapoletani.com
Ordered: Margherita pizza

It's tough to spot Sapori, which is situated directly in the middle of a tidy strip mall that runs along busy Northwest Highway (which is really just a city street, despite the name). After passing an engraving and embossing shop as well as a transmission repair and a dentist's office, you'll finally find Sapori.

Here, Antonio Vitiello, a Naples native who lived there for twenty-five years, plies his trade, making every pizza and firing each one himself. Vitiello even built his own large, beehive oven; wood-fired, of course, it gets up to about 700 degrees, turning the crusts into blistered beauties. San Marzano tomatoes, *fior di latte* cheese, and a few large basil leaves come together so well here, and despite the fact that he adds a bit more cheese than the usual suspects in town (creating a slight pool of liquid in the center), his version—hewing more closely to the Naples original—is still complex and not overwhelmed by any one ingredient.

He lets the dough rest at least a day, but more often forty-eight hours. With more than a dozen options on the menu, I was tempted to try something else, maybe a daily special with mozzarella, potato, and rosemary, or a fantastic-sounding pizza with caciocavallo cheese and spicy soppressata. Considering how perfect his *cornicione* is, with its occasional blister domes and misshapen edges, I know I'll be back to try more.

★ **Spacca Napoli Pizzeria**
1769 W. Sunnyside Avenue
773-878-2420
www.spaccanapolipizzeria
.com
Ordered: Margherita pizza

So much has been said about Jonathan Goldsmith's Ravenswood pizzeria. Most comments are glowing, of course, since he lectures on the subject of pizza making at trade shows and conventions, travels to Italy regularly, and has made the art and tradition of Neapolitan pizza his mission since he opened on a quiet stretch of Sunnyside in 2006. If children dreamed of becoming a Neapolitan *pizzaiolo* when they grew up, like some kids fantasize about playing in the NBA or NFL, they'd have posters of Goldsmith up on their walls, elbow-deep in flour or poised at the mouth of his oven, peel in hand, ready to turn or dome a pie.

All of the hallmarks for a fine Neapolitan are here: "00" flour; the *fior di latte* cheese, which is oozing, creamy-sweet, and placed haphazardly about the hand-formed spheres; and the San Marzano tomatoes, crushed into part-sweet, part-acidic oblivion. The telltale crust—puffy and blistered—has a remarkable chew that comes from a long fermentation.

Early on, when Spacca Napoli first opened, I felt that the pie centers were too thin and too wet (I know true Neapolitans adore this tomato-cheese puddle), and while I enjoyed the *cornicione*, I rarely praised the interior. Things have changed (perhaps the recipe has been tweaked), and those droopy interiors are a thing of the past. The dough these days is a little bit more structured, and the other dozen or so pizzas all feature top-quality ingredients, such as arugula, prosciutto, sausage, and rapini, a green cruciferous vegetable.

Is this Chicago's best Neapolitan pizza? Probably. Like a slowly aged Barolo wine or a twenty-month wheel of Parmigiano-Reggiano, Goldsmith's Neapolitan know-how only gets better with age.

1. Jimmy's Pizza Café
5159 N. Lincoln Ave.

2. D'Amato's Bakery
1124 W. Grand Ave.

3. Gigio's Pizzeria
4643 N. Broadway St.

4. Dante's Pizzeria
3028 W. Armitage Ave.

5. Dimo's Pizza
1615 N. Damen Ave.

EDGEWATER

UPTOWN

LOGAN SQUARE

LINCOLN PARK

TOP 5 PIZZAS BY-THE-SLICE

LAKE MICHIGAN

DOWNTOWN CHICAGO

CHAPTER 8

By-the-Slice (New York-Style)

In this mostly thin-pizza chapter, we turn to a category not particularly well represented in Chicago: the slice (or as some people in the city might say, "da slice"). When people talk about NYC-style pizza, they are typically referring to pizza by-the-slice. You've seen those enormous blobs of cheese, ringed with dough, in the front cases behind sneeze guards, manned by spatula-wielding young men and women who dispatch orders with lightning speed. Once you order, they whisk the room temperature slices into hot ovens to crisp them up, bringing the cheese and toppings back from the dead. After a minute or two, they'll summarily toss your order onto a paper plate (or two) before handing it over.

The lip and the tip of the gargantuan wedges usually hang over the edge of the flimsy plate, they're so large. To eat, you must grab the pizza by the edge, fold it with the same hand (three fingers!), and then tackle it from the center tip while working your way out.

As I mentioned in the introduction, the by-the-slice subject has been mined extensively, especially in *The Slice Harvester*, by Colin Atrophy Hagendorf, a book about one man's quest to try every slice joint in Manhattan. Since bars—and let's face it, people—are so prevalent in NYC, slice joints can survive in close proximity, within yards of each other, or just across the street. NY Pizza Suprema, A Slice of New York, and Rosario's are a few popular spots, not to mention Carmine's Original and Joe's, two of the more critically acclaimed joints. I know people who've waited over an hour for a taste of DiFara in Brooklyn. As I embarked on a noble quest to visit fifty pizzerias in the five boroughs to gain a better understanding of NYC-style pizza, I realized there really are only a few styles there: Sicilian, slice, artisan, Neapolitan, and grandma—a sort of Sicilian baked in a sheet pan that's not quite as high, but always served in rectangles.

Chicago doesn't quite have the population crush that could handle hundreds of by-the-slice joints, which tend to be located near late-night spots and bars, or on blocks convenient for millennials who just want something quick and inexpensive on their way home from the train. Needless to say, I didn't find many by-the-slice spots in the suburbs, but the city does have several that I feel warrant a review.

I've had quite a few slices in New York City after dark—Sal & Carmine's, Giardini's, and Artichoke, to name a few—and my memories of them are pretty sad: usually limp, greasy wedges of cheese-soaked cardboard, about as appetizing as a day-old baguette dunked in congealed pork fat. This was stoner food, or at the very least, a snack for people who were so inebriated that they wouldn't know pizza from shoe leather. I'm happy to say that in Chicago, we have higher standards when it comes to pizza slices, and in a sort of Darwinian survival of the fittest, if the pizza sucks, it's not going to be around long.

All of the following places are located within the city.

Boiler Room
2210 N. California Avenue
773-276-5625
wwwboilerroomlogansquare.com
Ordered: pepperoni slice

This pizza is one of my top five in the thin category, and I also have no hesitation recommending their by-the-slice offerings. Some of these go well beyond the predictable sausage, pepperoni, and vegetable, and the crust here is really something special. As you peer in through the front window, you can see the pizza guys tossing their dough to get ready to make a ton of pies that will eventually be sold by the slice.

Some of their wacky flavors include Thai cream cheese sauce, curry, serranos, and beet bruschetta. I, however, ordered a basic slice of sausage, with well-seasoned crumbles covering much of the generous wedge. The slices are hefty but not unwieldy. They've let the dough rest enough to build gluten and strength, while not compromising on the topping quality.

Beneath every slice is a delicate, cornmeal-flecked dough that maintains a crispy edge, unlike the crust at a lot of other so-so slice joints. This is OBR at its finest among the thin crust cool kids.

Note: They also offer a PB & J Special all day, every day—a slice of pizza, a PBR tall boy, and a shot of Jameson.

I realize some of the best dining occurs in unlikely places, which is why I tried to be optimistic when I approached the mini strip mall near the Stevenson Expressway and noticed Brandi tucked in among a liquor store, a currency exchange, and a payday advance storefront. The dining room won't win any awards in *Metropolitan Home*—it's simply two tables and another eight wooden seats at a high counter.

There are two types of slices to choose from in the front case: deep and thin. When I asked the woman behind the counter what their specialty was, she waffled between the two, and then came out in favor of the thin. "It's about 60 to 40 ordering thin over deep," she told me. I tried a deep-dish anyway. My mistake. The tasteless dough and cheese overload did nothing to elevate this slice into recommended territory.

Thin slices arrive unceremoniously on a sheet of wax paper, but heated up properly and with steam still rising ever so gently. However, my slice looks more like a sail, with one of the sides much longer than the other.

Across the top is a layer of mozzarella, applied a bit thicker than normal and with an evenly mottled char. The generous pieces of sausage—courtesy of Battaglia—are rugged and large, although lacking any discernible spices save for a bit of garlic.

But that undercarriage! It's a nice, crispy base providing a decent crunch, a respectable chew, and an evenly browned base.

The sauce is about as remarkable as Billy Joel's backup singers. They certainly contribute to the overall experience, but I'd never pay to see them on their own. It's pretty well baked into the crust, and seems to get lost beneath that cheesy cap. Bottom line: if you find yourself in the neighborhood, a quick stop to Brandi's isn't going to kill you, but I'm not sure I'd go out of my way for a slice.

Brandi Pizza & Wings
3170 S. Ashland Avenue
773-847-5888
www.brandipizza.com
Ordered: sausage slice

✳ **D'Amato's Bakery**
1124 W. Grand Avenue
312-733-5456
www.damatosbakerychicago.com
Ordered: sausage slice

Y ou can't miss the "cash only" sign directly behind the cashier at this legendary West Town bakery. Generations have come here for the fantastic, crusty loaves baked in their coal-fired oven (grandfathered in after city regulations changed). Patrons also flock here for the excellent sandwiches and round focaccias, the latter embedded with black olives, artichokes, and plump tomatoes. Look further down the case for the blackened rectangular sheet pans and you'll find a treasure trove of Sicilian gold: large rectangular slices of colorful pizzas, topped with all manner of onions, tomatoes, pepperoni, and anchovies.

The sausage slices are clearly the most popular, as they consume most of the real estate. By Chicago standards, the sausage balls are mini (and sourced from elsewhere; they wouldn't disclose the producer). But no matter; you could put

jawbreakers in their place and I'd still happily devour these slices.

D'Amato's takes a different approach to their assembly. While still raw, the dough is embedded with both cheese and sauce (redolent with the plumpest, ripest tomatoes), and then left to rise a second time. This Sicilian tradition of adding toppings and cheese before the dough is fully proofed is still carried on at places like Buddy's in Detroit. Finally, it goes into the oven, where the cheese-sauce-topping mixture literally bakes into the soft, supple dough.

And that dough is what you come for. The undercarriage looks like the surface of the moon, with tiny craters and ridges that provide

extra crunch and a caramelized texture, while the top is pillow-soft, as light as cotton candy but with a sturdy density that holds up the cheese and sauce so well. The edges are also what you need to try, with their blackened and charred exterior. It's a perfect crispy counterbalance to the softer interior. For that reason, make sure you ask for a corner or an edge piece.

I'm very disciplined when it comes to eating pizzas. Lord knows I've had more than most people in Chicago, and when I'm doing a crawl of three or four places in one day, I usually take just one to three bites, depending on quality. But in this case, I ate the whole damn slice. I dare you not to finish yours.

and garlic sauce, I opted instead for a humbler slice with sausage.

These mammoth pieces dwarf anything from the East Coast, and in many ways are superior to them. Let's begin with the lip, which is at least an inch wide and brushed with garlic butter, parmesan, and herbs, packing a lot more flavor than you'll find at 99 percent of the by-the-slice joints in Chicago. Then there's the dough itself, slightly crispy with a number of air pockets. My slice offered two pockets that looked like the United Center from 35,000 feet above—the result of at least a twenty-four-hour rest before baking in one of Dante's numerous Blodgett ovens.

Dante's Pizzeria uses a home-made tomato sauce that is applied cold and raw, and then cooks in the oven. The owner emphasizes that there is no sugar in the sauce; any sweetness comes from the quality of the tomatoes they're using. The knobs of sausage are pretty generous and somewhat mild. (The sausage comes from the same supplier who handles the orders for Aurelio's.)

A well-charred undercarriage and an excellent dough-to-topping ratio make this chewy, blistered mega-slice great any time of the day—although I can see why it would taste even better to late-night by-the-slicers.

★ **Dante's Pizzeria**
3028 W. Armitage Avenue
773-342-0002
2825 N. Milwaukee Avenue
773-384-8888
www.danteschicago.com
Ordered: sausage slice

The Palmer Square joint on Armitage is a bit more of a dive than the one on Milwaukee Avenue, but still, it has its charms. With an in-your-face attitude, the BYOB café offers both enormous 20-inch specialty pies and gigantic, Fred Flintstone–sized slices. As much as I was curious about the Charon option, with its shrimp, prosciutto, pineapple, and jalapeños, and the Minotaur, with Italian beef, giardiniera, provolone, mozzarella,

★ **Dimo's Pizza**
1615 N. Damen Avenue
773-525-4580
3463 N. Clark Street
773-525-4580
www.dimospizza.com
Ordered: pepperoni slice

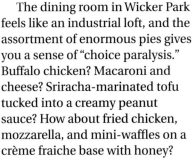

With both locations in bar-dense areas (Wicker Park and Wrigleyville) and signs out front advertising their PBR Tall Boy nights along with delivery until 2:00 or 3:00 A.M. on weekends, Dimo's typical demographic is probably a little younger than I am.

The dining room in Wicker Park feels like an industrial loft, and the assortment of enormous pies gives you a sense of "choice paralysis." Buffalo chicken? Macaroni and cheese? Sriracha-marinated tofu tucked into a creamy peanut sauce? How about fried chicken, mozzarella, and mini-waffles on a crème fraiche base with honey?

Sticking to my baseline plan of either sausage or pepperoni—so I can better assess the crust and chew—my slice of pepperoni wasn't all that bad. Incidentally, they get their pepperoni from the well-regarded Ezzo Sausage Company in Columbus, Ohio.

Heated up in their Bakers Pride oven for just a few minutes, the slices emerge slightly crispy. The middle of the slice is super-thin, just enough to hold up the generous sauce and cheese, while the lip is a bit more substantial. I love how the undercarriage is evenly charred throughout and the pepperoni on top maintains a nice kick. I think Dimo's is also a bit more generous with the sauce than most.

This quick-service joint, nestled among a slew of bars in River North, knows its audience. Sure, a few office workers stop in when the sun is out, picking up a sub or a slice to go, but with a closing time of 4:00 A.M., Dough Bros. isn't focused on sober diners. With just five tables and a half-dozen gargantuan pies up front behind the glass case, this is alcohol-soaking food.

My large slice of sausage pizza arrives, heated up nicely after a few minutes in their deck oven, and it's served cafeteria-style, atop black-and-white checkered paper sitting on a paper plate. It has an appealing aroma and a significantly thick lip, but when I try to fold it in half, New York-style, for easier eating, it falls apart.

The top is slightly greasy, which is odd since there was no pepperoni, but the homemade sausage pieces have a very pleasant aroma and chew. Same for the crust, which is ultra-thin in the middle and tapers off from the lip, where it's just a lot of dough that needs seasoning. There is an audible crunch when biting into the slice, even though much of it is buried beneath cheese.

The sauce is pleasant (though there isn't much to speak of), and I like how some of the spots on top of the pizza slice have a little bit of browning from hot spots in the oven. Since some of that cheese is from the well-regarded Grande Cheese Company, it tastes that much better.

Dough Bros. Pizzeria & Sub Shop
400 N. State Street
312-600-9078
www.doughbrospizza.com
Ordered: sausage slice

Georgio's Gourmet Pizza
11 W. Division Street
312-255-0999
www.georgiosondivisionchicago
 .com
Ordered: sausage slice
Full pizzas available in 12-inch,
 16-inch, and 18-inch.

Georgio's—embedded within the Division Street bars that Rob Lowe and Jim Belushi made famous in *About Last Night* back in the '80s—still draws a young, boisterous crowd, although most of it is imported from the suburbs. And for the record, the "gourmet" reference in this joint's name isn't just for marketing purposes. They offer several unique pizza flavors, including chicken fajita, eggplant parmesan, pesto tortellini, and black bean, chicken, and rice.

These generous made-to-order slices—heated up in a tidy Bakers Pride oven—are tasty, with a nice, crunchy crust and an easily foldable spine. Smaller bits of mildly seasoned sausage are present and the mozzarella has a nice pull to it. A slightly sweet sauce serves as a base for the rich, salty toppings.

The late-night hours (until 4:00 or 5:00 A.M. on weekends) mean that the pizza probably doesn't have to be all that good—the crowd is probably slightly inebri-ated and not so discerning. Most of the eating is done either standing next to a high counter or at one of the few stools facing out onto Division Street.

There are certainly slices of a higher caliber elsewhere in the city, but for sheer convenience after a night of drinking and carrying on, there's nothing wrong with a solid slice from Georgio's.

★ **Gigio's Pizzeria**
4643 N. Broadway Street
773-271-2273
www.gigiospizzachicago.com
There are unrelated Gigio's
  in suburban Evanston and
  Des Plaines.
Ordered: sausage slice

This dive (and that's a generous assessment) sits across from the renovated Wilson Avenue CTA station and next to some random businesses that never seem to keep their leases for very long. There are a few tables here, along with a high counter at the window overlooking Broadway. Other than that, the interior design is limited to some garage-sale quality, Italian-themed prints.

Décor isn't likely a top priority, since Gigio's is a late-night mainstay for the after-show crowds coming from the Green Mill or the Aragon—so the pizzas probably don't need to be that good. Especially when the guy in front of me in line, a shaggy-looking fellow who could use a shower, wants his fried chicken wings "extra hot."

The slices, however, exceed expectations. Gigio's also makes whole pies, but clearly they do most of their business by heating up slices in their enormous rotating deck oven.

Ruddy knobs of homemade sausage, laced with plenty of fennel, stand sentinel among the even spread of mozzarella and zesty tomato sauce, all of which rest on a cushioned bed of firm crust that's still pliable enough to bend in half, NYC-style. There is a slight char on the lip, supplying additional crunch. The bottom manages to maintain its crispness (it's a hand-tossed dough), and even though it's served on flimsy paper plates, this is not throwaway pizza meant only to fill your stomach on an alcohol-laced evening. It's solid, respectable pizza that fits firmly into the canon of quality late-night munchies. Just don't ask for a glass with your can of pop. It's not that kind of joint.

This is one of the best deals in town. A café with little more than a handful of tables and some Intelligentsia coffee, they manage to crank out just a few simple items and do them extremely well: New Orleans-style beignets covered in powdered sugar, calzones, chicken wings, garlic knots (essentially dough topped with Parmesan and basil, served with a side of marinara), and by-the-slice pizza options. They hold six large pies in the front glass case. You choose your slice and they pop it into a small Bakers Pride oven that heats your selection up in about two minutes.

The slices are generous—easily enough for one—and somehow maintain their crispiness. The undercarriage is almost universally blackened, and there's an audible crunch when you bite into it. The slices claim to be New York-style (yes, you can fold them), but they seem to have more heft and substance than those I've had in New York. And there is certainly a welcome lack of grease from inferior cheese. In fact, the Grande mozzarella is divine, and with the large crumbles of spicy Fontanini sausage embedded within, Jimmy's Pizza Café devises an excellent ratio of dough-to-toppings. (FYI, they use Black Angus for their meatballs.) They also offer specials. On the day I visited Jimmy's,

the menu featured an eggplant pizza and a chicken-and-bacon pizza.

Regardless of flavor, the dough is almost bread-like in appearance and texture, sort of like ciabatta (an Italian white bread), with a slightly raised edge and a few air pockets, indicating that they let the dough rest and ferment a bit. The tomato sauce is zesty without being overpowering; it plays a nice supporting role.

★ **Jimmy's Pizza Café**
5159 N. Lincoln Avenue
773-293-6992
www.facebook.com/jimmys
    pizzacafe
Ordered: sausage slice
Whole pies are available in
    16-inch and 20-inch.

Hidden along a busy stretch of Chicago Avenue in Noble Square, where you're more likely to stumble into a mom-and-pop Cuban joint or a dive bar, Paula & Monica's prides itself on its range of slices. They come in regular, medium, and jumbo, and are available either thin or deep. They also have a few specialty pizzas, including a Hawaiian (pineapple, ham, and barbecue sauce), a BLT, and a "meat lovers" version with ground beef, bacon, sausage, and pepperoni (BYO Lipitor). I got there right when they opened on a quiet Wednesday, ordering a medium sausage slice.

The slices here, presented on an industrial tin plate, have quite a bit of heft, making a fold nearly impossible. I just wish they paid more attention to the ratio of cheese to sausage. Only six pieces of well-seasoned, housemade sausage (a combo of beef and pork) grace each slice, leaving a lot of cheese real estate untouched. I'm not advocating for a sausage Frisbee, like the pucks you see at Malnati's, but a more even distribution would be appreciated. However, as sparingly applied as the sausage is, there's an excellent mouthfeel and plenty of fennel in each crumbly bite. Here's hoping the *pizzaiolo* on duty next time isn't as stingy with it.

As for the crust, it's pretty good—even better, I imagine, late at night. There is a nice chew in the lip, but it's not as impressive in the middle and on toward the point, where the cheese is overwhelming.

Paula & Monica's Pizzeria
1518 W. Chicago Avenue
312-929-3615
www.paulaandmonicaspizzeria
.com
Ordered: medium sausage slice

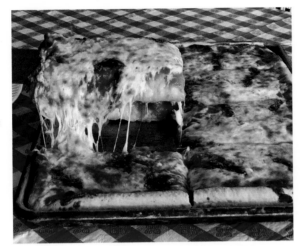

Sicilia Bakery
5939 W. Lawrence
    Avenue
773-545-4464
chicagosbakery.com
Ordered: sausage
    slice

There are few throwbacks as old and durable as Sicilia Bakery. Located in Jefferson Park, the fifty-year-old neighborhood staple has seen a number of changes. When it first opened, the neighborhood had a much larger Italian concentration. But many of them moved west in the '70s, to towns like Elmwood Park, giving way to a large wave of Polish immigration that descended on the Northwest Side in the '80s and '90s, from small towns all over Poland. As you head west on Lawrence Avenue, the Polish-run hair salons, bakeries, and travel agencies are hard to miss. In fact, on the two-block stretch just east of Austin (5800 and 5900 W. Lawrence), there are three completely different bakeries, each catering to a different customer base. Sandy's is for the Serbians, Delightful Pastries is predominantly Polish, and Sicilia is obviously Italian.

Sicilia knows exactly what it peddles: flavors from the old country. There's the pastry case filled with sfogliatelle, cannoli, and biscotti—all as authentic as they come. On the opposite side of the pastry case is a full deli where you can assemble your own sandwich or go with an Italian beef or meatball sub. And up near the front register, look for the case of focaccia and Sicilian pan pizza.

There are usually two puffy discs of focaccia (black olive and artichoke are the most common) as well as a half-dozen sheet pans filled with Sicilian-style pizza. With pans only $12 and slices just $2, you can afford to experiment. Beyond the usual trifecta of sausage, cheese, and pepperoni, Sicilia also has a bacon cheddar as well as a solid veggie pizza. If we were in New York, we'd call these grandma slices for sure.

My sausage slice didn't look all that promising at first, but after being heated up, I saw immediately why this place is so beloved. That undercarriage (I'm probably the only wack job who looks underneath a pizza as much as I look at what's on top) has all the signposts I want to see: an uneven, almost crater-like surface, several potholes and ridges, and a completely blond color. On the top, a beautifully golden layer of part-skim mozzarella gently covers half-inch-sized balls of housemade sausage embedded with fennel seeds.

The homemade tomato sauce is as red as a fire engine, and its natural sweetness is a pleasure—but not as pleasurable as that crust. Typically, Sicilian slices tend to be about a half-inch high, but my slice's middle section is barely thicker than your average thin crust. When you bite into it, there is the slightest, faintest crunch, playing the harmonizing backup beneath the soft, chewy melody.

The sides—slightly higher than the middle as a result of being pushed up against the edge of the baking pan—have ample crunch as well. The dough has a buttery-rich flavor, akin to Pizano's or Lou's, yet is completely blond and not charred at all.

I can't wait to go back for a different flavor, and if I need to bring something to a party, I've got the perfect $12 solution.

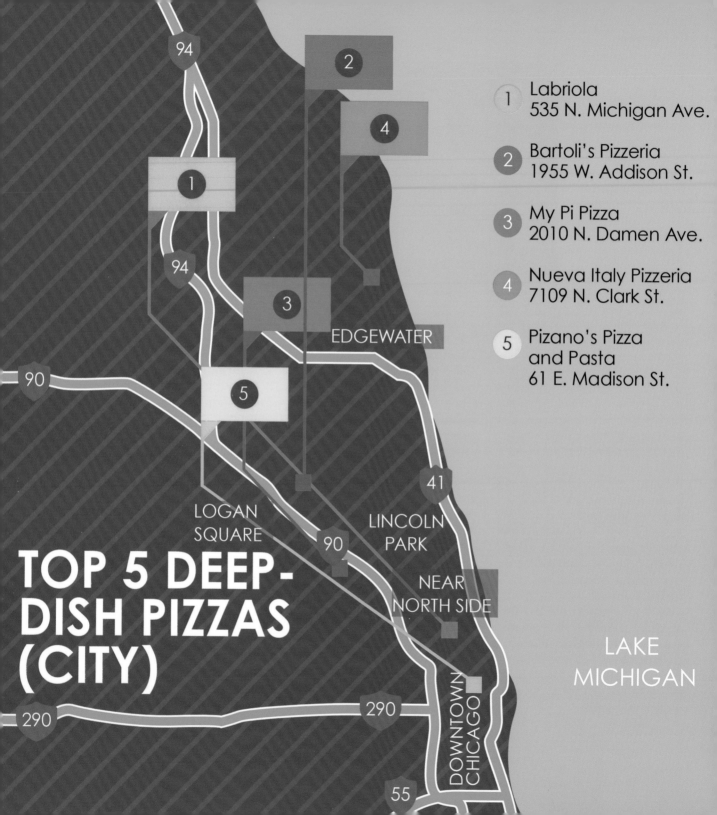

TOP 5 DEEP-DISH PIZZAS (CITY)

1 Labriola
535 N. Michigan Ave.

2 Bartoli's Pizzeria
1955 W. Addison St.

3 My Pi Pizza
2010 N. Damen Ave.

4 Nueva Italy Pizzeria
7109 N. Clark St.

5 Pizano's Pizza
and Pasta
61 E. Madison St.

EDGEWATER

LOGAN
SQUARE

LINCOLN
PARK

NEAR
NORTH SIDE

DOWNTOWN
CHICAGO

LAKE
MICHIGAN

94

94

90

90

41

290

290

55

CHAPTER 9

Deep-Dish and Pan

Ike Sewell was an industrious fellow and no question a great marketer. He worked for Fleischmann's Distilling, while his friend Ric Riccardo owned a popular hot spot on Rush Street. In the early 1940s, the two friends bought a bar together, and, according to Chicago historian Tim Samuelson, went on to create the deep-dish pizza as we know it today.

The creation, which would eventually send shockwaves through the traditional pizza establishment, was inspired by generosity. Sewell and Riccardo wanted to offer GIs returning from World War II something more substantive than the usual thin crust offerings in town. Sewell and Riccardo's kitchen staff created a thicker-crust pizza that needed to be baked in a high-sided circular pan from thirty to forty-five minutes. The recipe reverse-engineered a traditional pizza pie, placing cheese on the bottom layer of dough, adding toppings, and finally ladling on the tomato sauce. Once the two men opened Pizzeria Due a block away in 1955, they changed the name of their original bar to Pizzeria Uno.

But when it comes to assigning credit where credit is due, Samuelson begs to differ with the often-told traditional story about deep-dish's evolution. "I take every opportunity to remind folks that Ike Sewell really didn't come up with what's served at Pizzeria Uno," he said. "It was Ric Riccardo all the way. Ike was a great guy and early partner. But develop the actual pizza? Ain't so—even if there's a bronze plaque saying this at Wabash and Ohio. If Ike was alive to speak for himself, he'd readily agree. All of the other stories are a big lumbering freight train of fake history." One reason Samuelson knows this to be true is a conversation he had with Chicago literary lion Studs Terkel, just two weeks before he died.

The author, historian, and Pulitzer Prize–winner told him, "Ric invented the fucking pizza for God's sake." Another possibility is that deep-dish as we know it today was created by either Adolpho "Rudy" Malnati Sr. or Alice May Redmond, both of whom worked in the kitchen at Uno's from the early days.

With Uno and Due offering the only deep-dish pizza anywhere in the country at the time, they maintained a monopoly on this pizza style for at least twenty years in Chicago.

Riccardo died in 1954 and never saw what his creation led to—a much bigger enterprise that began when a Boston-based Kentucky Fried Chicken franchise owner convinced Sewell to franchise Uno's in 1979. The Uno's corporation eventually established itself in Boston, where it remains today, overseeing some 150 locations worldwide.

As the Uno's franchise grew, its original name morphed into the more universally accepted Uno Pizzeria & Grill. Sewell passed away in 1990, but both Pizzerias Uno and Due, as well as the Uno Pizzeria & Grill franchise are going strong today.

To put it bluntly, though, the company that made deep-dish famous (and continues to promote it around the world) hasn't been a Chicago company for decades. And yet, if you randomly ask visitors walking down Michigan Avenue where they're going for dinner, I'll bet you more than 75 percent will tell you either Giordano's, Gino's East, Uno's, or Due's. I'll go one further. Ask anyone standing outside one of these four businesses on a Friday or Saturday night where they're from and my guess is not one of them will hail from Chicago— Hinsdale, maybe, but not the city. Being so close to the majority of the city's hotels has its benefits.

This is not to say that deep-dish or its close relative, pan pizza, can't be an enjoyable, albeit occasional, indulgence. Classic deep-dish usually begins with a circular steel pan, greased with corn or vegetable oil. A pliable, somewhat oily dough is smashed into the pan, until it covers both the bottom and interior walls. Some restaurants will make a butter crust, which emerges from the oven with an almost pastry-like crispness. As much as I find myself putting it down, I do still love the buttery crust at Pizano's and Lou's. I can appreciate the boulders of fennel-laced sausage and hunks of juicy tomatoes at LaBarra. I can easily polish off two thick slices from Bartoli's, even though I know it's like eating the equivalent of a block of mozzarella. There is a delicious harmony between the brightly acidic, charred, and naturally sweet tomatoes and the rich layer of Wisconsin mozzarella that rest

above a buttery, short-dough crust from the likes of Pequod's or Labriola. I dare any naysayer to take two bites and proclaim otherwise.

There is some argument about the differences between pan and deep-dish. I think they're one and the same. To me, pan implies baking in a rectangular pan—what some might refer to as Sicilian, or, if you live in New York, grandma style. In Detroit, they make their pizzas in a high-sided square pan, which is technically deep-dish. In Chicago, the hair-splitters might point out the dough recipe is slightly different between pan and deep; one could argue a deep has more crispness and richness in the dough—a direct result of the butter or oil—while pan implies a broad spectrum of doughs. The bottom-up architecture, however, should remain the same: dough, then cheese, then toppings, and finally, sauce.

Having several homegrown businesses all laser-focused on making deep-dish is one of Chicago's unique characteristics. It makes the city a true Pizza City, because it shows that, while we have plenty of the styles that are well known in New York, we also have styles that are homegrown. Sure, you can find deep-dish at an Uno's franchise anywhere in the country, but that's about as unique as a Burger King or Arby's. A friend from New York City, who works for the prestigious James Beard Foundation (and has eaten in some of the best restaurants in the world), asked me where to get deep-dish when he's in Chicago, since it's something he cannot find at home. It's not an unusual request. Professional food reporters and critics I know, who come to town for two to three days of concentrated, focused grazing, often sheepishly ask me where to go to try a deep-dish, knowing it's like asking a friend in Philly where to grab a cheesesteak.

I have local friends and colleagues, too, who will order a deep-dish pizza—in a moment of laziness or if the thought of Grubhub seems overwhelming. It's just sometimes easier to go the deep-dish route, mainly because there are so many convenient locations not more than ten minutes from most downtown businesses and hotels. If you live in one of the neighborhoods, however, chances are your deep-dish will come from Lou Malnati's, since they're about as ubiquitous as Walgreen's. But when people ask me for deep-dish recommendations, I usually send them to some of the off-the-beaten-path locations, like one of the places listed in this chapter.

City

Here's the thing about deep-dish. Each person really only needs about one slice, so don't feel any shame ordering a small pizza for four or five people. Also, at Bartoli's and most similarly established places, expect a thirty- to forty-minute baking time (we called ahead), but often the wait is worth it.

Brian Tondryk's grandfather, Fred Bartoli, was partners with Sam Levine at the very first Gino's East. They had originally hired Alice May Redmond, a former cook at Uno's, to make the deep-dish at their store, just off Michigan Avenue. In my opinion, Gino's no longer belongs to the upper echelon of deep-pie slingers. As I've done with Uno's, I would again blame corporate bean counters. Tondryk had missed the flavors of his childhood, and spent the better part of a year trying to re-create and rebuild that original recipe. His efforts paid off.

Bartoli's bakes one of my favorite pies in the city. High sides show heft, but it's only about a quarter-inch thick at the bottom—where a gooey, melted mozzarella layer supports huge pieces of impressively meaty, well-seasoned sausage. There are enormous hunks of juicy tomatoes, blistered from the oven and exploding with acidity and sweetness. The highlight is the buttery-crispy crust, which is reminiscent of the crust at Lou's and Pizano's.

Even though my pizza quest took me to several places on this particular day, I had no problem polishing off a full slice here.

✱ **Bartoli's Pizzeria**
1955 W. Addison Street
773-248-0455
www.bartolispizza.com
Ordered: 12-inch half-sausage, half-pepperoni
Also available in 14-inch.

With pizzas for sale in the United Center, at Taste of Chicago, and at Lollapalooza, Connie's is familiar to many Chicagoans, albeit their deep-dish version. That's the style they typically sell outside of the restaurant and at special events. It's also what they ship all over the United States. But when you dine in their massive Bridgeport restaurant, with its soaring ceilings and decorative industrial belt system that looks like a gear factory from the dawn of the Industrial Age, you see a few differences right away.

Since 1963, the brand has been known for its "Original Pan" pizza. The same dough is used for their deep-dish, with the same bottom crust thickness, but the deep-dish version has higher sides and thus more crust to eat through. That means that the "Original Pan"—while technically cooked in the same black deep-dish pan that everything else is baked in—is just slightly shorter on the edges. It makes a difference. With less dough to chew through, the OBR is better on the "Original Pan."

Both the "Original Pan" and deep-dish are served on special metal pizza pans that have holes cut into them, allowing for air circulation below, which keeps the evenly tanned, slightly dimpled undercarriage crisp and prevents sogginess.

Fontanini Italian Meats produces Connie's sausage of choice, while the restaurant uses a simple

Connie's Pizza
2373 S. Archer Avenue
312-266-6437
Connie's Pizza at McCormick Place
2301 S. Lake Shore Drive
www.conniespizza.com

Ordered: small half-sausage, half-pepperoni original pan
Deep-dish, thin, stuffed, Sicilian, and gluten-free pies also available.
"Original Pan" available in 7-inch, 10-inch, and 14-inch.

Wisconsin part-skim mozzarella to present a cheesy blanket of sorts. They do make their sauce in-house, adding touches of sugar, basil, and oregano as they see fit.

The thing about the crust here, on both the "Original Pan" and deep-dish, is that while the outside is a tad crispy, the inside resembles a focaccia, with tiny air pockets and

a fluffy chew. Depending on how busy the restaurant is, pies emerge with a decent browning on the top—the result of even baking. The paprika-laced pepperoni is mild but intriguing; however, the fact that it's buried beneath a healthy layer of cheese prevents it from ever crisping up, if you like that sort of thing.

Since 1965, Gulliver's has been the pizza place for families in West Rogers Park who didn't want to schlep downtown for deep-dish. (Lou Malnati's didn't open until 1971.) You might be tempted to ask, "Is this an antique store or a pizza joint?" since Tiffany lamps, stained glass, and more bronze and metal statues than you can possibly count are scattered among the multiple dining rooms.

On the day I visited Gulliver's, a pair of cops sat at a table eating their personal pan pizzas while a group of regulars chatted up their waitress, who's been with Gulliver's for almost thirty years. As for my order, I went with a deep-dish pizza. Despite the joint's press clippings for stuffed pizza, they're really known for their deep-dish.

When the pizza arrives at the table, the servers take the liberty of serving the first piece with a metal spatula. The slices come out easily, and the outer crust only rises about halfway in the pan—not nearly as high as at some of the other places in town, like Pizza Italia or Louisa's. The crust is pleasant, with a slight crunch that's almost like a well-done focaccia. But I found the tomato sauce and large pieces of sausage—courtesy of Battaglia—to be almost too mild for my palate.

Even with a decent shower of oregano, this is a pan pizza for beginners. If you have an aunt or mother-in-law always complaining about how spicy everything is, this is the pizza for her. You'll most likely want to keep the red chili flakes nearby. The pepperoni, funny enough, did have a good little kick to it, which helped.

Gulliver's Pizza & Pub
2727 W. Howard Street
773-338-2166
630-691-1888
www.gulliverspizza.com
Gulliver's has a suburban location in Oakbrook Terrace.
Ordered: small deep-dish, half-sausage, half-pepperoni
Stuffed pizza is also available.

★ **Labriola**
535 N. Michigan Avenue
312-955-3100
www.labriolacafe.com/chicago
Labriola has a café and bakery
   in Oak Brook, but they do
   not serve deep-dish, only
   Neapolitan-style.
Ordered: 12-inch Russo sausage
Deep-dish pizzas are available in
   12-inch and 14-inch.
Thin pizzas are available in
   10-inch, 12-inch, 14-inch, and
   16-inch.

Rich Labriola's downtown location, just off Michigan Avenue, has struggled with its identity ever since it opened. After going through countless tweaks and menu exorcisms, he has opened pizza concepts in the suburbs (LaBarra) and still maintains the original Labriola Café in Oak Brook (although they only make Neapolitan pizzas at that location). His Michigan Avenue location is well within the tourist strike zone, which means deep-dish is a must. Sit at a table during lunch on any given day, and I'll bet 80 percent of the tables are ordering one.

As my 12-inch deep-dish with sausage is placed in front of me, I like what I see: generous, chunky icebergs of fresh tomato lightly seasoned with fresh herbs; fragrant, juicy, jagged-edged pieces of sausage (from Russo in suburban Alsip) nestle within melted mozzarella; and then—the best surprise of all.

As I lift out my first piece, I see that outer edge, just like at Pequod's—a caramelized, darkened, thin layer of cheese, clinging to the perimeter, all the way around. Underneath, I notice how firm the dough is; as I cut into it with my knife, I realize it is actually crispy all the way around, and so I pick up the rest of my piece with my hands, and summarily devour it. The ratio! Unlike Pequod's, they figured out the OBR!

I bet it was hard for Labriola to temper his ambition in a high-profile restaurant with his name on it. After burning through some chefs and a lot of sleepless nights—forever trying to figure out if tourists *really* wanted extruded pasta and handmade cavatelli—turns out all they want is a good pizza. Here, in the shadow of the soon-to-be former Tribune Tower and across the street from a gigantic Nordstrom's, he and his staff have cracked the code: they offer a deep-dish pizza that both tourists and picky locals like me actually crave.

★ My Pi Pizza
2010 N. Damen Avenue
773-394-6900
www.mypiepizza.com
Ordered: small half-sausage,
   half-pepperoni

Since 1971, My Pi has been serving deep-dish pizzas, but for several years I think they dropped off the radar. Now sharing a space with Lil' Guys Sandwiches in a Bucktown strip mall featuring an L.A. Tan salon, My Pi serves thin or deep slices as well as whole pies.

The construction of the deep is a bit different: the dough is an even thickness across the bottom and then rises up on the sides a good one- to one-and-a-half inches. Cheese covers the bottom layer, insulating the crust from becoming soggy as a result of rendered sausage fat or tomato juices. Then comes the sausage or pepperoni, and finally, the tomatoes. But unlike the thin tomato sauces elsewhere, this topping is a forest of tomato chunks, roasted and slightly blistered, that release their sweetness as they combine with oregano and a hint of garlic.

Even after visiting several other pizza places on this particular day, I had a hard time stopping after one slice. This is a wonderful pie that I think pizza lovers can agree on, and unlike a lot of deep pizzas, those at My Pi get the OBR right.

★ **Nueva Italy Pizzeria**
7109 N. Clark Street
773-770-8296
www.nuevaitalypizzamenu.com
Ordered: small deep-dish half-
    sausage, half-pepperoni

Y**ou** can get a thin pizza at this Rogers Park take-out joint (that's apparently what *Chicago* magazine prefers), but Nueva acknowledges that they are best known for their butter crust deep-dish.

Located in a gritty stretch of Clark Street, a few blocks south of Evanston and tucked among Mexican grocery stores, Nigerian restaurants, and discount shops, Nueva is mostly take-out and delivery. The stack of white carry-out boxes, piled all the way to the ceiling behind the front counter, is a pretty good indicator. Yet, even though they lay claim to only three tables, the woman working the counter couldn't have been nicer when my party of four showed up on a Friday night and wanted to eat in. She put two tables together, fetched us plates, silverware, and water, and then took our order for a nine-inch pizza, which would yield only four pieces. (We had to hit three other places that night.)

What arrived was truly among the better deep-dish pies in the city. The butter crust is excellent, not unlike Lou's or Pizano's, with a flaky-rich crust on the outside, plenty of tiny air pockets inside, and the overall texture of a good focaccia. The outside lip is narrow and relatively squat, about two inches high—not insurmountable and not so thick as to throw off the OBR.

Large pieces of Greco sausage rest on the bottom layer of part-skim mozzarella and mix with the large, heaping chunks of fresh tomato that are scattered about like cumulus clouds covering most of the pepperoni and sausage. The undercarriage is wonderfully crisp, which is somewhat surprising since they serve the pizza on a flat plate set on top of a dimpled tray. Usually the pizza is placed directly on the dimpled risers to allow for airflow beneath it, thus yielding a crispier bottom. But look closer under the hood and check out those tiny holes, allowing for airflow into the nooks and crannies.

That's the difference between Nueva and so many other wannabe deep-dish joints. This is a dough that's rested a bit, gone through a little fermentation—and, upon hitting a hot deck oven for thirty minutes—reveals itself to have more character than the factory pies coming out of Uno's or Due's downtown.

pened in 1970 by the legendary Burt Katz, Pequod's ownership may have changed hands over the years, but the caramelized mozzarella crust hasn't changed a bit. This pizza's edge is close to two inches high, but up along the perimeter, in the upper quarter or so, is a blackened rim of mozzarella cheese that is tossed into the cast-iron pans at some point during the baking process. It's lacy and delicate, almost like a cheese crisp, but it does little to mitigate the overwhelming presence of the dough.

Here's where I will most certainly disagree with Pequod's devotees—and there appear to be thousands of them. In fact, the night I was there, a solid twenty people were sitting on benches outside with pagers, waiting for tables. What many first-timers don't realize is that the crust shouldn't overwhelm the pie, and in Pequod's case, it often does.

Do I like the thick tomato sauce, the slightly spicy, jagged-edged sausages well seasoned with oregano, and the melted mozzarella? Of course I do. But after one slice—no, actually, after two-thirds of my slice—I felt bloated, like a duck in Hudson Valley with an engorged liver. If you were to cut off the top layer of cheese, topping, and sauce, you would be left with a ridiculous amount of soft dough that could double as muffuletta housing at the Central Grocery in New Orleans.

I see why it takes thirty to forty minutes to bake these pizzas. What they're really doing is baking a giant loaf of bread beneath what is really a pretty good pizza topping. But when the kitchen is actually paying attention to the ratio, and not too busy cranking out pies for tourists, they have the potential to make some of the city's very best deep-dish. An honorable mention for sure, but not quite "Top 5" material.

Pequod's Pizza
2207 N. Clybourn Avenue
773-327-1512
Pequod's also has a location in
   suburban Morton Grove.
847-470-9161
www.pequodspizza.com
Ordered: small half-sausage,
   half-pepperoni
Pan pizzas come in four sizes:
   personal, small, medium,
   and large.

Rudy Malnati Sr. was one of the early cooks at Pizzeria Uno in the '40s. He and his wife, Marie, held onto their secret recipe for years. Their son, Lou, opened his own place in Lincolnwood in 1971, and today Lou's sons Marc and Rick run the empire. But Malnati Sr. also had a second wife, Donna Marie, and *their* son, Rudy Jr. (Lou's half-brother) eventually opened Pizano's in 1991.

Pizano's pizza has the distinctive, buttery, pastry-like dough that's become a hallmark at Malnati's, and here it's just as addictive. Like a good pan pizza, the sides are high but the middle is relatively thin. There's a layer of mozzarella directly above the crust, as insulation, and then giant pancakes of homemade sausage on top of that. Finally, there's a thin layer of fresh roasted tomatoes flecked with fresh oregano. This is probably as close to what the original Pizzeria Uno was doing seventy years ago, before the brand and the recipe were sold and commoditized.

It may not be the most original deep-dish, but for historians and purists, it's as close to the original version as you can get.

✶ **Pizano's Pizza and Pasta**
61 E. Madison Street
312-236-1777
www.pizanoschicago.com
There are five Chicagoland locations.
Ordered: 10-inch half-sausage, half-pepperoni
Sizes include 10-inch, 12-inch, and 14-inch.

TOP 5 DEEP-DISH PIZZAS (SUBURBS)

1. LaBarra
3011 Butterfield Rd.
Oak Brook

2. Louisa's Pizza
and Pasta
14025 Cicero Ave.
Crestwood

3. Pizza Italia
218 S. Milwaukee Ave.
Libertyville

4. Old World Pizza
7230 W. North Ave.
Elmwood Park

5. Lou Malnati's Pizzeria
6649 N. Lincoln Ave.
Lincolnwood

LAKE MICHIGAN

Suburbs

There are few personalities left in Chicago's pizza world. Most of the founders of the great places have passed away. Burt Katz was one of the few remaining founders, still going strong in the early part of this decade. He launched a trio of important pizzerias in Chicago. First there was Gulliver's in 1965, followed by Pequod's in 1971 (which eventually included a Lincoln Park branch), and then in 1989, he opened his namesake.

Located across the street from a dingy apartment building, Burt's Place looks a little like a log cabin. Inside, wood paneling right out of my 1970s childhood lines the walls, while restored brown vinyl booths keep the atmosphere casual and comfy. It feels a little like being in a Wisconsin supper club, but without the old-fashioneds and relish trays.

When Burt's Place first opened, there were certain rules you had to abide by. You couldn't just walk in; you had to call and preorder your pizza. Whoever took your order gave you a time to arrive and eat it or pick it up to go. The same rules hold true under the new ownership.

Katz tended to be media-shy, only doing a handful of TV interviews during his entire career. He did, however, earn a trifecta of recognition for Burt's Place—featured by Anthony Bourdain on the Travel Channel; in the local restaurant review series *Check, Please*; and, most notably, on the cover of *Saveur* magazine's Chicago issue. The notoriety helped catapult his little store onto the serious pizza-seekers' must-visit list.

In September 2015, the restaurant closed due to Burt's health. Not much information was released. Jerry Petrow, who was a futures trader at the time, snail-mailed a letter to Katz about buying his business. While several people were talking to Katz about the same thing, Petrow's letter prompted Katz to respond. The two reached an agreement just over two months later, in December 2015.

For the first four months of 2016, Petrow and his partner, John Munao, frequently met with Katz in the hospital, bringing him dough samples and trying to absorb as much as they could about his philosophy and recipes. Katz passed away in April 2016.

Petrow and Munao did a thorough cleaning of the Morton Grove space and remodeled to add

Burt's Place
8541 Ferris Avenue
Morton Grove, Illinois
847-965-7997
www.facebook.com/burtspizza
Ordered: small sausage

The topping starts with whole milk mozzarella that's pushed into the dough, then the entire pizza is covered with a chunky, vibrant, oregano-seasoned mess of tomato sauce.

As it emerges from the oven, the highest points of the tomato pieces are charred black, adding depth and subtle sweetness. Rather than embedding sausage pieces, four discs are placed on top, one on each quadrant. Finally, the top is well seasoned with Pecorino Romano and oregano.

The day I visited Burt's Place, it was 70 degrees outside—a freak occurrence for Chicago in March—and the host informed me that the unseasonably warm weather had affected their dough's second rise, which impacted the proofing and caused parts of the dough to be almost too active. Indeed, half of my pizza seemed too high with too much dough while the other half was perfect in regards to OBR.

Granted, they had only been open for a few weeks—so I cut them some slack. But the chew, the crispness of the bottom crust, and the airiness of the dough were enough to keep me going back for a second slice. The chunky, charred tomato topping reminded me of LaBarra and Bartoli's, and that saved the day. I only wish that the caramelized cheese perimeter was better. But since it tasted more like carbonized ash than mozzarella, it didn't make my top five. Alas . . .

a small bar, reopening as Burt's Place in March 2017.

The pizza today is not as good as I remember it from 2009, but it's still remarkable. Think of it as the love child of a Sicilian slice and a deep-dish pie. The dough is made at 5:00 A.M. each day, then allowed to proof and rise twice before service begins at 4:30 P.M. The dough is appropriately light and airy, but also somewhat dense. The bottom crust has a significant bit of crispiness and the outer edge a blackened, caramelized (some would say carbonized) mozzarella border. (I think LaBarra and Union Squared do this much better.)

This neighborhood joint, tucked along a quiet street in the even quieter suburb of Lake Forest, sits across the street from the Metra train tracks, and I imagine legions of commuters have picked up pizzas to go here since the place opened in 1980.

Ferentino's checks off all of the Chicago-style boxes: Italian beef, sausage, and meatball sandwiches, plus some salads and low-carb options if that's your thing. The pizzas dominate, however, and there are myriad ways with which you can indulge your love of cheese, tomato, and toppings: thin, gluten-free, Roma-style, pan, and stuffed.

My choice, the small deep-dish, is darn good. The crust is wonderfully crisp on both the sides and bottom—thanks to a dimpled pan that elevates the pie to allow for air circulation and to prevent sogginess. The sauce isn't too thick, and it's redolent with oregano—although I felt it could use a bit more salt. The fennel-laced sausage (from Joseph's Finest Meats in the city) is sublime, and the ratio of dough-to-cheese-to-fillings was spot-on, most likely a result of that bottom crust not creeping up as high as the sides. Fans of Malnati's will appreciate the OBR.

Ferentino's
842 N. Western Avenue
Lake Forest, Illinois
847-295-8888
825 S. Waukegan Road
Lake Forest, Illinois
847-615-1000
www.ferentinos.pizza
The Waukegan Road location is closed on Sundays.
Ordered: small deep-dish half-sausage, half-pepperoni

✳ **LaBarra**
3011 Butterfield Road
Oak Brook, Illinois
630-861-6177
2 E. Burlington Street
Riverside, Illinois
708-887-7700
www.labarraristorante.com
Ordered: 12-inch Russo sausage
Deep-dish pizzas available in 12-
    inch and 14-inch.
Thin pizzas available in 10-inch,
    12-inch, 14-inch, and 16-inch.
An artisan pie is also available.

In 2015, Rich Labriola took over a vacant space in Oak Brook to set up his pizza fantasyland. He recruited a chef from downtown with a good reputation, and they tried to come up with something truly unique. LaBarra is as big as its ambitions. The restaurant offers three types of pizza: Chicago-style thin, deep-dish, and their signature coal-fired artisan pie, which emerges from the brick ovens with some of the most beautiful *cornicione*s in the tri-state area. While I love their artisan pie—it's in my "best artisan pie" category—it's the deep-dish that purists will really love.

I never saw it coming. Hit like a quarterback on the blind side by Singletary on the blitz, my 12-inch deep-dish with sausage is placed in front of me, and I like what I see: generous, chunky icebergs of fresh tomato, lightly seasoned with fresh herbs; jagged-edged pieces of sausage, fragrant and juicy, tucked within melted mozzarella; and then the best surprise of all—as I lift out my first piece, I see that outer edge, just like Pequod's. There's a caramelized, darkened, thin layer of cheese clinging to the perimeter, all the way around. This dough is so firm you don't need a knife and fork. In fact, I dare you to simply use your hands. The other benefit here is the OBR—Labriola spent countless hours trying to get that balance right.

It seems strange to say it, but out in a quiet Oak Brook mall, next to a corporate plaza, overlooking a man-made lake, an Italian guy has cracked the code—after a lot of trial and error, no doubt—and is creating the best deep-dish in Chicagoland, now available in two suburban locations and another off Michigan Avenue.

HUGE GALDONES

★ Lou Malnati's Pizzeria
6649 N. Lincoln Avenue
Lincolnwood, Illinois
847-673-0800
www.loumalnatis.com
Located almost everywhere, with many locations
  in the city and one in nearly every suburb.
Ordered: personal Buttercrust™ and a small pan
  half-sausage, half-pepperoni
Pan pizza is available in personal, small, medium,
  and large.

A visit to the first Lou's, which opened more than forty years ago and has been the site of countless birthdays and post-game Little League celebrations, is like going home again—if you grew up nearby. Not unlike a visit to Hackney's or Vito & Nick's or Charlie Beinlich's, there is a large amount of nostalgia served up with the house special: deep-dish pizza.

Lou Malnati worked at Pizzeria Uno in the '60s and left to open his namesake along a stretch of Lincoln Avenue in Lincolnwood in 1971. In the decades since, his offspring have stretched the brand into nearly every Chicagoland nook and cranny. They've also set up a nationwide shipping apparatus, so your homesick cousins in California can get their deep-dish fix anytime, thanks to FedEx.

I met my brother-in-law for lunch on the day set aside for this pizzeria, since he's a huge fan, and we ordered both the standard deep-dish plus a personal pizza featuring Malnati's trademarked Buttercrust™ for an extra seventy-five cents.

Both versions arrive with a crispy-edged crust about two inches high on the outside and a tad shorter on the interior. That crust is sturdy, holding up the layer of Wisconsin mozzarella, lean sausage, and chunky tomato sauce.

In fact, like very few pizzerias in the region, Lou's understands OBR. Each bite is a perfect blend of cheese-to-crust-to-topping-to-sauce. And that sauce, a rough mix of chunky California tomatoes sprinkled with grated Pecorino Romano and seasoned with oregano, offers excellent acidity to balance the rich, melted cheese.

I'm not a fan of the lean sausage disc, however, that covers the entire bottom, as it tends toward the bland side. (I still prefer the old-school, handmade style of breaking off sausage pieces and spreading them around the pie.) The pepperoni definitely has a stronger spice profile than most, offering a good contrast to the oozing mozzarella.

As for that Buttercrust™, it's pretty tasty—but it's overkill. The fatty, melted mozzarella provides plenty of richness already, and adding a buttery crust just gilds the lily. There's nothing wrong with the regular crust, but in both cases, we noted how the whole pizza changed character after about ten minutes at the table. I'm guessing most customers aren't going to let their pizzas sit that long, since these slices are somewhat addictive.

✳ **Louisa's Pizza and Pasta**
14025 Cicero Avenue
Crestwood, Illinois
708-371-0950
Ordered: small half-sausage,
    half-pepperoni

Louise Benash was a waitress in the '70s at the original Pizzeria Due, and even worked with some guy named Lou Malnati, who was busy back in the kitchen making Chicago's original deep-dish pizza. She opened her namesake bar and pizza joint in 1980, and after she passed away, left the business to her daughter, Linda.

The family still runs the business, making the same deep-dish pie as they have the past thirty-five years. Figure forty-five minutes at least for baking, and you typically need to ask if you want the pizza cut into slices. These pies come in the same industrial, blackened, stainless-steel pan you see in every deep-dish joint.

At the bottom and up along the sides, a sturdy, slightly rich, buttery crust holds in the bottom layer of mozzarella, extra-large hunks of cooked Anichini Brothers sausage in the middle layer, and the top layer of bright-and-chunky tomato sauce. The result covers everything except the outermost ring of crust.

The high edge is slightly browned in spots, yielding to a fork, but somehow riding that beautiful middle ground between crispy exterior and softened, cheese-riddled interior.

Even after visiting two pizzerias earlier that same day, I polished off a full slice. I dare you to try to eat just one—assuming you haven't had a few pizzas beforehand.

Maybe it was the four Sopranos posters, or the one of Sinatra, but I had a sinking feeling that the clichés were going to continue onto the plate as I walked into this local landmark, which has served Elmwood Park since '63. Thankfully, I was wrong.

If you try to find Old World Pizza online, it can be a little confusing—they're aligned with a company called Fat Ricky's, with locations in Tinley Park, Shorewood, Romeoville, and Plainfield. I called to ask what they specialize in and was told thin and deep—with an emphasis on deep. That's what I ordered.

I was told it would be about forty-five minutes until my pie would be done, so I took my time driving over and pulled into the quiet strip mall just a few minutes before my deep-dish was ready.

This pizza has a sturdy two-inch-high outer crust, but inside, where the toppings reside, the crust is only about a quarter-inch thick—much like Malnati's. Cheese is, of course, the first layer, and then comes some nicely seasoned sausage that's separated into large, jagged pieces. Their beautifully seasoned tomato sauce rests above it all, in splotches rather than a uniform coating, making the top of the pizza look like a map of the world. The "continents" are made of tomatoes and sausage, garnished lightly with Romano cheese and swimming in an ocean of mozzarella.

You don't need a fork and knife here, since the slices are sturdy enough to hold with one hand. The crust has plenty of flavor, and I'll bet you there aren't any crust fragments left on your plate, as there would be at several lesser pizza joints. This is a pizza you're going to have a hard time putting down, especially if you like Malnati's style.

✴ **Old World Pizza**
7230 W. North Avenue
Elmwood Park, Illinois
708-456-3000
www.originaloldworldpizza.com
Ordered: small half-sausage,
    half-pepperoni

didn't expect much from this mostly carryout joint, which is located in a strip mall along busy Milwaukee Avenue. The problem, I thought, was that they offer so many types of pizza—and that's often a clue that they don't really do anything well. I did call ahead, since their deep-dish pies take about forty minutes to bake, but I still arrived early. That meant waiting in their small, eight-table dining room. Turns out the wait is worth it.

High-sided, like all deep-dish pizzas, the crust has a wonderful crispness to it, as well as richness from the butter in the dough. Greco & Son's sausage is formed into pretty small pieces and the mozzarella (part-skim and whole milk) is gooey but not overpowering. The tomato sauce is vibrant red and slightly acidic, while the addition of chunky tomatoes on top adds some wonderful bites, bursting with natural sweetness. Their pies also get a healthy shower of grated Parmesan before being served.

Pizza Italia's version of pan is slightly different from deep. The architecture for the pan (from the bottom crust up) goes: dough, sauce, ingredients, cheese—then into the oven. The build on their deep-dish goes: dough, cheese, ingredients, sauce, some chunks of tomatoes—then into the oven.

This is typically how the big boys do it at Lou's and Bartoli's. That cheese at the bottom insulates the dough and protects it from getting too soggy.

I could have easily eaten two pieces here, but stuck with one, since I had to run to a few more joints that day. By the way, this pizza reheats wonderfully in the oven.

★ **Pizza Italia**
218 S. Milwaukee Avenue
Libertyville, Illinois
847-281-8404
www.mypizzaitalialibertyville.com
Ordered: 10-inch deep-dish
    half-sausage, half-pepperoni
Pan, thin, butter crust, hand-
    tossed, and gluten-free pizzas
    are also available.

Oven at Coalfire

CHAPTER 10

Stuffed, Sicilian, Roman, and Detroit-Style

Stuffed pizza is not a category most people crave. On top of that, the name is misleading. Stuffed. Does that imply there is cheese or sauce jammed into the outer crust? It's true that some places do this, wrapping and crimping the outer edge to contain those ingredients. (I believe Pizza Hut sells millions of these cheese-and-sauce-jammed pies across the country.) Does it mean something is hidden in the bottom crust, ready to ooze out when you cut into it? No, the only oozing occurs when these slices are lifted and removed from the main body of the pizza. That's because of the stuffed construction, which from bottom to top goes like this: dough, cheese (lots of it), toppings, another extra-thin layer of crust, and finally a lake of tomato sauce.

Stuffed pies need at least forty-five minutes to bake—and then must live up to the mockery inflicted by haters everywhere who say these are essentially cheese casseroles. I'm convinced these are the pizzas Chicago is mocked and ridiculed for. A cheese lava flow is typical when moving a slice of stuffed from the mother ship to your plate. The thought of an OBR is almost nonexistent with these pizzas. Overkill is king. Better to have a giant slice that requires a chainsaw to cut into than have any sort of nuanced, balanced bite.

As for Sicilian pizzas, the second category in this chapter, here in Chicago they're mostly found in a few Sicilian bakeries tucked beside Polish and Italian delis in the city's North and Northwest Sides. In neighborhoods such as Jefferson Park and towns like Franklin Park, these bakeries often serve the same lineup of goods: cookies, sandwiches, and pizza. But the pizzas tend to be made in large trays and with a different dough than

Union Squared, Evanston

the usual thins you're accustomed to. New York City tends to do Sicilian-style quite well.

D'Amato's in West Town (one of my top five by-the-slice spots in the city) is a perfect example of Sicilian pizza excellence. The top layer of the dough is embedded with cheese and sauce that almost permeate the core. The dough itself is light and fluffy—like a focaccia—with the tiniest air pockets and a firm texture. Toppings like anchovies are not uncommon. The large, rectangular slices (Sicilian-style pizza is baked in a rectangular pan) are great reheated in the oven and eaten right there.

Those rectangular pans are also displayed front and center inside Bonci, one of the most exciting new pizza places in Chicago. Gabriele Bonci partnered with an American investor to bring his unique Roman-style pizza *al taglio* (translation: pizza by the slice in rectangular pans) to the masses. I find it interesting that they didn't open their first and only United States branch of the popular Roman pizzeria in New York City, but I'm certainly pleased they're in Chicago. Incidentally, when referring to "Roman-style," there are technically two types of pizza in play, which I learned after emailing Union Square Hospitality Group CEO (and Rome aficionado) Danny Meyer. One is cracker-thin and round, much like what you'd find at Martina in New York City or at Pizzeria Via Stato in Chicago. The other style is a denser, slightly thicker (Sicilian) style of pizza that is cut to order and weighed in front of you, since you're paying by the pound. Places like Alice and Bonci in Rome are known for this style.

Bonci's pizzas are recognized for their beguiling dough, which manages to be soft, chewy, light, airy, and crispy all at once. Sliced with scissors and then weighed, the pizza is available in a number of seasonal flavors, such as roasted pumpkin atop supple burrata or sheep's milk ricotta studded with thinly sliced zucchini. Since you choose how much of each flavor you want cut off and weighed, you can try a few without breaking the bank. I wouldn't call the pizzas Sicilian or even focaccia-like, as those doughs tend to be more dense and spongy. Bonci has introduced Chicago (and for that matter, America) to true Roman-style pizzas, adding yet another feather to the city's sauce-laden cap.

Another vaguely Sicilian-esque style of pizza hails from Michigan, and it's known as Detroit-style—the fourth and final category in this chapter. This style was virtually unknown in Chicago until Jet's arrived in Naperville (the chain has since opened stores all over the region). In just the past few years, places like Union Squared have opened in Evanston and at the Revival Food Hall in the Loop, while Paulie Gee's Logan Square added

Detroit-style to their regular menu. Transplanted Detroiters have also tried re-creating the style they grew up with, opening Longacre in Uptown and Fat Chris's in Andersonville. Who knows, maybe Detroit-style will become an acceptable alternative to deep, Sicilian, or tavern-style.

Buddy's, with its eleven locations throughout metro Detroit, is the standard-bearer everyone emulates. They set the bar for this square pizza when it was created there in 1946, just three years after Uno's created deep-dish in Chicago. With its cheesy, baked-on perimeter (not unlike those at Pequod's or LaBarra) and the focaccia-esque texture that a Sicilian pie is known for, the rectangular or square Detroit-style pie is constructed a bit differently than the pizzas you might be used to seeing. If you're in New York City, Emmy Squared makes my favorite version. The unique thing about the Detroit-style is that the dough typically is left to proof for at least a day, oftentimes with some cheese and pepperoni (it's always pepperoni) pushed into the top. When an order comes in, more brick cheese is scattered across the top, pushed all the way to the edges, while just a racing stripe or two of thick tomato sauce is draped across the top. The pizzas emerge with a blackened, crispy cheese perimeter and a height of no less than two inches.

So in our final chapter, let's celebrate these wonderful innovators, some of whom are trying to carry on a tradition while others are hoping to set a new standard—and perhaps create a viable category for yet another style of pizza that makes Chicago's pizza scene noteworthy.

Stuffed

Angelo's Stuffed
4850 S. Pulaski Road
773-927-9355
www.angelosstuffedpizza.com
Ordered: 10-inch half-sausage,
    half-pepperoni
Thin and stuffed pizzas available
    in 8-inch, 10-inch, 12-inch,
    14-inch, and 16-inch.

Since 1992, this Archer Heights family favorite has been located next door to Zaragoza—one of my all-time favorite joints, where they honor the goat in all its glory, especially in their *birrieria*, a spicy Mexican stew. I must have completely missed Angelo's Stuffed the last time I was in this Southwest Side neighborhood. By the way, it's a convenient stop if you're flying into or out of Midway, and it's best to call ahead with your order, since their stuffed pies take anywhere from forty-five minutes to an hour, depending on how busy they are.

The room has the requisite four TVs, all tuned to whatever Bulls or Blackhawks game is on, and the menu is probably too ambitious for its own good. With "stuffed" in your title, why offer fried appetizers, pastas, burgers, and entrees like chicken Parmesan?

Regardless, my majestic pie arrives showered in Romano cheese and dried parsley; the cheese pull (a combo of low-moisture and whole milk mozzarella) is impressive. Unlike most other stuffed versions, this one doesn't ooze a river of cheese lava.

Just above that bottom crust, and nestled among the cheese, are large icebergs of Battaglia sausage on one side and mild pepperoni discs on the other side. Both could use more assertive seasoning, as the majority of the pie consists of dough and cheese.

The outer perimeter of crust—at least two to three inches high—has a nice, even browning, like a retiree in Boca, and the chew is pleasant, although I would have liked mine baked just another six to eight minutes.

The homemade sauce is the star here. It rests above that top layer of dough, and it's good enough to serve with pasta or meatballs—vibrant, with bright acidity and a freshness that only comes from a product made in-house, each day.

Clearly, things have changed in the fifteen-plus years since The Art of Pizza was voted the #1 deep-dish by the *Chicago Tribune*. (Is there a statute of limitations on a ranking or review?) Many of my readers and followers recommended I give them a try, so I did, but I was surprised when my server said that they are actually better known for their stuffed pies, rather than their deep-dish.

In addition to the stuffed pizza, I also tried a slice of deep-dish sausage, but with both of them, all I could think of was cheese bread, which some people apparently love. In both cases, tiny, dime-sized balls of sausage are sparingly arranged beneath a cap of mozzarella as thick as the blacktop in my alley.

The crust? It is a light tan color with a very average chew—more crumbly than chewy—and not nearly as memorable as the crusts from Bartoli's or My Pi. The semi-chunky tomato sauce, flecked with dried oregano, provided tangy acidity with an intense hit of herbs.

Like Mike Tyson in his tattoo phase, time has not been kind to this former heavyweight pizza champion. Still, if you're looking for a decent stuffed option on the city's North Side, you could do a lot worse.

The Art of Pizza
3033 N. Ashland Avenue
773-327-5600
727 S. State Street
312-877-5335
www.artofpizzachicago.com
Ordered: 10-inch half-sausage, half-pepperoni
Thin and deep-dish available in 10-inch, 12-inch, and 14-inch.

The Suparossa Hospitality Group owns and manages about a dozen concepts in Chicagoland, including an adorable gelateria, a couple of Pete's Pizzas, and a more "upscale" gastropub called Legno, where I was served an under-cooked Neapolitan Margherita, which the cook told me afterward was my fault—since I should have ordered "well-done" to get the authentic experience. Really? Since when did you need to specify the doneness of a Neapolitan?

Directly behind Legno is a carryout and delivery-only branch of Suparossa. While waiting for my check after Legno's Neapolitan di-saster, I called Suparossa to place an order for a stuffed pie, which I had been told they're known for. Though I find the excess of dough unnecessary (it makes the top and bottom of the pizza look more heavily fortified than a castle in *Game of Thrones*), I begrudgingly tried it for the sake of the quest.

But this recipe—created in the late 1950s—has a lot more appeal than the usual stuffed cheese casseroles I've tried around the region. Yes, there are those high sides holding a potential lava flow of whole milk mozzarella, but once you bite into it, there is actu-ally some flakiness, not the usual wet cardboard. The top layer is as thin as the *Trib*'s sports section, holding up a lake of fresh, vibrant tomato sauce that I'd be happy to have mingling with some pasta.

Buried beneath are some of the juiciest, most flavorful boulders of sausage—made in-house.

The standard construction for a stuffed pizza, from the bottom crust up, goes like this: cheese, ingredients, top layer of thin dough, and sauce. But that sauce, which the owners readily admit has sugar in addition to the oregano and other proprietary spices, somehow manages not to overwhelm. It adds a lovely sweet acidity to the richness from the cheese and the meats.

This is a one-slice-per-person endeavor; knife and fork recom-mended. It's the scourge of East Coast pizza snobs who laugh at Chicago through their greasy, flaccid, yeast-crusted glasses, but for a certain segment of the popula-tion, it's truly a thing of beauty that reminds them of their childhood on the city's Northwest Side.

Suparossa
4256 N. Central Avenue
773-736-5828 (carryout and delivery only)
www.suparossa.com
Suparossa also has two suburban locations:
    Harwood Heights (Cucina Bragio) and Woodridge.
Ordered: small half-sausage, half-pepperoni
Also available in 9-inch, 10-inch, 12-inch, and 14-inch.

Sicilian

D'Amato's
1124 W. Grand Avenue
312-733-5456
www.damatosbakerychicago
.com
Ordered: sausage slice

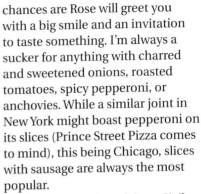

Having already expounded upon the glorious merits of this West Town bakery's by-the-slice pizza, I felt it necessary to reiterate them here, since this slice is, after all, a Sicilian original.

Rosanna D'Amato's grandparents, Nick and Rosa, came to Chicago from Bari, Italy. In 1961, they purchased a bakery in West Town called "Italian and French," which had a coal-fired oven built in 1912. It's been in the family ever since. Their son, Victor, grew up in the business with his brothers. Today, Victor mans the wholesale bakery across the street, while Rosanna oversees the retail bakery, which sells pastries, dynamite sub sandwiches, and pizzas that come sixteen slices to a tray.

As you enter the tiny store, chances are Rose will greet you with a big smile and an invitation to taste something. I'm always a sucker for anything with charred and sweetened onions, roasted tomatoes, spicy pepperoni, or anchovies. While a similar joint in New York might boast pepperoni on its slices (Prince Street Pizza comes to mind), this being Chicago, slices with sausage are always the most popular.

The construction of these Sicilian pies is quite a bit different from the standard Chicago pizza architecture. While still raw, the dough is embedded with both cheese and sauce, redolent with the plumpest, ripest tomatoes, and then left to rise a second time. This pre-embedding and proofing is not that different from the Sicilian tradition born in Detroit, which led to places like Buddy's and Cloverleaf.

The dough is the basis for one of the most remarkable pizzas in town. Its undercarriage contains dozens of tiny craters and ridges, providing extra crunch and a caramelized texture. I could just eat this bottom layer and forget the rest. But you can't, of course, since the top is pillow-soft, as light as a cotton ball but with a sturdy density that holds up the cheese. The edges are also what you need to try—their blackened and charred exterior provides the perfect crispy counter balance to the softer interior. For that reason alone, make sure you ask for a corner or edge piece.

Freddy's Pizza
1600 S. Sixty-First Avenue,
Cicero, Illinois
708-863-9289
www.freddyspizza.com
Ordered: full pan half-sausage, half-pepperoni

Honestly, a slice for $3 would have been plenty, but I ordered a half pan of half-sausage, half-pepperoni anyway, just to see how they sell these Sicilian beauties. (They sold me a full pan, so be sure you're clear when ordering.)

I made it past one slice. That was it. Like hitting a wall at the eighteenth mile of a marathon, I was on a particularly long pizza tasting jag through the Western suburbs on this day, and although I had just tried a slice of their Margherita and a slice of their thin (also included in this book), I felt it necessary to get the pizza this legendary grocery store is known for: Sicilian.

From the tradition of neighborhood bakeries—like the Sicilian Bakery on Cumberland—Freddy's Sicilian pizza is really more about the crust than the toppings. Sure, the giant crumbles of sausage and discs of pepperoni are nice and the sauce is pleasant, but when you look at the side of a slice, you see about 80 percent bread, 20 percent topping.

Granted, if you're on a budget, a full pan for $19 easily feeds thirteen to fourteen hungry people, so the economics are great. In terms of pizza satisfaction, some fans will definitely think there is a problem with this much bread beneath the top layer, but regardless, it's bread with a whole lotta flavor.

There are few throwbacks as old—and as durable—as Sicilia Bakery. Located in Jefferson Park, the fifty-year-old neighborhood staple has weathered the demographic changes in the area, continuing to adapt while still offering its original lineup of Italian classics.

Sicilia re-creates flavors from the old country. There's the pastry case filled with *sfogliatelle*, cannoli, and biscotti—all as authentic as they come. On the opposite side of the pastry case is a full deli, where you can assemble your own or go with an Italian beef or meatball sub. And up near the front register, look for the case of focaccia and Sicilian pan pizza.

With pans only $12 and slices just $2, you can afford to experiment. There's usually a trifecta of sausage, cheese, and pepperoni on hand. My sausage slice didn't look all that promising at first, but after it was heated up for a few minutes, I saw immediately why this place is so beloved. That undercarriage has all of the indicators I want to see, beginning with an uneven, almost crater-like surface hiding several potholes and ridges, completely blond in color. On the top, a beautifully golden layer of part-skim mozzarella gently covers tiny balls of housemade sausage embedded with fennel seeds.

Their tomato sauce is bright red, with a lovely, natural sweet-

ness. Typically, Sicilian slices tend to be about a half-inch high, but my slice's middle section is barely thicker than your average thin crust. New Yorkers would call it a grandma slice. When you bite into it, there is the slightest, faintest crunch.

The sides—slightly higher than the middle, as a result of being pushed up against the edge of the baking pan—have ample crunch as well.

I can't wait to go back for a different flavor, and if I need to bring something to a party, I've got the perfect $12 solution.

Sicilia Bakery
5939 W. Lawrence Avenue
773-545-4464
www.facebook.com/siciliabakery.com
Ordered: sausage slice

Roman

Bonci
161 N. Sangamon Street
248-705-0402
1566 N. Damen Ave.
872-829-3144
https://bonciusa.com
Ordered: several small slices
of various flavors, priced
per pound

SPICY EGGPLANT 10.99/lb

Forty-year-old Gabriele Bonci looks like he could wrestle a crocodile. As wide as a linebacker, bald, and tattooed, he sports a short-sleeved chef's coat and speaks in rapid-fire Italian to his young cooks. They all race around the narrow West Loop kitchen, filling orders and answering questions from customers. I witnessed this scene only two days after the highly anticipated pizzeria opened and just one day before Gabriele had to go back to Rome, where he began his pizza business in 2003.

Bonci partnered with a former P. F. Chang's executive to bring his concept to the United States. Why Chicago? "We wanted to get to an area where people were food savvy, where they understood food and were willing to try new things," said Rick Tasman, whose company—Bonci USA—has the rights to open more stores outside Italy. "We weren't trying to redefine what pizza is for Chicagoans, but we wanted people to try it. We liked the urban area and the good foot traffic," he said. "With the

[Morgan Street Green Line] train stop and the young people here, it's the perfect location."

The Roman style of pizza is something Chicagoans have only seen elsewhere. Maybe they were on vacation in Europe and tried it; perhaps they saw Anthony Bourdain feature Mr. Bonci on his TV show. There really is nothing even close to what Bonci does in Chicago, even if you count Pizza Metro in Wicker Park, which claims to be Roman but is really just a good thin pizza (featured in chapter 5). Bonci makes pizza *al taglio*, referring to the sturdy rectangular trays the pizzas bake in, which also help to evenly distribute heat.

Besides the shape, the other important point of difference is the crust's texture. It somehow maintains an impossibly crispy, light bottom crust—showcasing browned spots and uneven surfaces on the outside. That delicate undercarriage supports a fluffy, pockmarked interior, as light and airy as an artisan bread that's been left to ferment for days.

Calling it simply focaccia or Sicilian doesn't do it justice. Those pizzas have a density and sponginess that Bonci's pizzas manage to avoid. Tasman says the secret is Bonci's dough, which contains a blend of Italian "00" flour as well as whole grain and minimally pro-

cessed organic flour. There are two separate fermentations of at least twenty-four hours each, which build structure and complexity. Baked in imported Italian handmade Castelli ovens with terra cotta decks, the pizzas bake at 575 degrees. But due to the ovens' special construction, the heat is controlled on both the deck *and* the ceiling. Dough this delicate doesn't need a blast furnace; it needs to be coaxed to life.

Bonci really gets creative with his toppings. Using as many local sources as he can (for example, 'nduja from 'Nduja Artisans and cheese, olive oil, and cured meats from local suppliers), he thinks seasonally about what goes on top. If it's summer, you'll see thinly sliced zucchini with tiny blobs of fresh ricotta and black pepper; fall means pureed pumpkin; spring offers ramps and young garlic.

You'll never see pepperoni, since that's an American invention. "Ask for pepperoni in Italy and you'll get green peppers," says Tasman. They're more likely to pair up fresh, peppery arugula or seasonal mushrooms with 'nduja—my favorite spreadable, spicy Calabrian sausage—often referred to as "pork butter." Several of Bonci's pizzas don't even contain cheese, which will take Chicagoans some getting used to.

The other aspect of the *al taglio* style of pizza is how it's ordered. You're paying by the pound, so simply tell your friendly cook how much you'd like by making a sign with your thumb and forefinger. They'll position their kitchen shears along the rectangular pizza, ask if that's sufficient, cut across the width of the tray, and then weigh it for you. This allows you to try several styles without committing to enormous slices. The slices are then reheated, cut into small squares, and served. I was able to try four different flavors on my first visit, including the strangely addictive mozzarella and potato, and got out of there for $15. Bonci has more than a thousand flavors in his portfolio but will most likely rotate about fifty of them on the Chicago menu. I, for one, hope to try them all.

Pizza Metro
1707 W. Division Street
773-278-1753
www.pizzametro.com
Ordered: small half-sausage, half-pepperoni
Sizes include small, medium, large, and slices.

This West Town pizza shop claims to specialize in Roman-style pizza, which could mean one of two things: a thin, crispy pie like the ones at Pizzeria Via Stato, or a rectangular one, like PR Italian Bistro, though not as focaccia-esque as Bonci. You wouldn't be completely wrong referring to it as tavern-style, since they're cut into thin, square pieces. Since the shop specializes in pies with toppings such as potato and rosemary, or simply anchovy, they certainly look and taste more like Roman pizzas than ones born in Chicago.

There are a few seats at the counter, and it took all of thirteen minutes to get my small, which was really the perfect size for one relatively hungry person. The crust is seriously thin, almost creeping into tavern-style territory, and the crumbled sausage, buried beneath a snowdrift of cheese, certainly had me coming back for extra slices. The pepperoni is standard stuff, but I liked how simple yet tasty this pizza was, especially how good the OBR of toppings-to-cheese-to-crust.

Not a bad option if you're nearby at one of the bars or just shopping along Division Street and craving a snack.

izzeria Via Stato, next door to its sibling, Osteria Via Stato, is easy to miss as you walk down State Street on your way to a River North bar or club. But this little pizza joint does quite a bit with a simple electric oven. They bill their pizzas as "cracker-thin, Roman-style." But instead of cutting them into wedges, they make them a little bit more Chicago-style, by employing a square cut. These tavern pizzas, as they're listed on the menu, have a serious chef behind them, who also creates the menu at the Osteria. Consider the stellar options with mushroom, sausage, and vegetables, as well as a couple of white pizzas and a pizza of the month. (The special pizza when I was there included the cruciferous green rapini, goat cheese, home-made sausage, and caramelized onions. Sounds pretty good to me.)

Their pie size is a bit smaller, about ten inches, which is perfect for one hungry person or a great snack to share. Even though I had taste-tested a few slices from other places before arriving at Pizzeria Via Stato's, I almost polished off their entire Margherita. It was that good, with its juicy, naturally sweet San Marzano tomatoes, an ultra-thin, cracker-like crispy crust that prevents you from getting too full, plus a generous garnish of torn basil and a drizzle of olive oil.

The edges have a wonderfully rough, misshapen border to them, with all kinds of air pockets scattered about. I even appreciated the ventilated tray that the pizza was served on, preventing the middle and undercarriage from getting soggy.

Pizzeria Via Stato
620 N. State Street
312-642-8450
www.osteriaviastato.com/pizzeria
Ordered: Margherita pizza
(half-sausage, half-pepperoni not an option)

Detroit-Style

Nick Milazzo and his two brothers grew up about twenty minutes north of Lansing, Michigan. So while Buddy's is certainly a part of their childhood PIGUE, the former schoolteacher says he wanted to offer a Detroit-style that didn't taste exactly the same as the other recent players in town.

Their no-frills Andersonville restaurant has the requisite Chicago interior design elements: TV, Cubs shirt, W flag, and Blues Brothers painting. They do offer a hand-tossed pie, but it's the Detroit versions you'll want to seek out here. A small is more than enough for two people, as the slices tend to be bulkier than the other Detroit versions in town. I actually found the pizza to be on the excessively bready side, the bottom two-thirds of the slice overwhelming the cheese, topping, and sauce. After I shared my opinion of the bite ratio, Milazzo explained to me their elaborate system of preparation.

Since they have two conveyor belt ovens set to different times, they can't just load up the square pies all at once. First, they par-bake the dough that has been rested and proofed overnight (this might be part of the problem). That process takes a little more than six minutes.

Then toppings and cheese (brick, of course) are placed on top, with the cheese pushed all the way to the edges; then another six minutes in the oven. Finally, two giant stripes of thick, bright red tomato sauce are painted across the top, while some shredded mozzarella is added just to hold the toppings in place. The pizza gets a final six minutes and forty-five seconds in the oven. I asked if they press any cheese or toppings into the pies before the initial proofing, like they do at Buddy's. They do not.

The pies emerge with a gorgeous mahogany perimeter and undercarriage, as burnished and deep-hued as a Coach bag. Served on a dimpled pan that elevates the pizza and allows for airflow underneath, the bottom maintains its crispness. Sausage and pepperoni are pretty basic. I actually thought the pepperoni was a tad too thin. If you like Jet's and lean more toward the dough-forward side of pizza, then you'll love this version. I think if they can cut that crust elevation in half, they'd have a pretty outstanding pizza. It's all about the OBR, baby.

Fat Chris's Pizza and Such
1706 W. Foster Avenue
773-944-5444
www.fatchrispizza.com
Ordered: Small (four-slice)
	Detroit half-sausage,
	half-pepperoni

Jet's Pizza
4112 Dempster Street
Skokie, Illinois
224-534-7151
www.jetspizza.com
There are twenty-three locations
   throughout Illinois.
Ordered: small deep-dish
   half-sausage, half-pepperoni

I've driven by a Jet's Pizza so many times that the chain is almost invisible to me—like a Little Caesar's or Domino's. The franchise has been around since 1978, and a few friends from the Detroit area told me that Jet's pizza was worth a try (thanks, Jason) after I had posted a picture of the stellar Detroit-style pizza from Union Squared, located inside the Revival Food Hall in the Loop.

What is Detroit-style? It seems to be a focaccia-type dough, riddled with tiny air pockets and heated until it rises at least an inch or two, and with an almost caramelized, crispy exterior. At Union Squared, they add some cheese to the outer perimeter, giving it a wonderful, flavorful chew and texture (kind of like Pequod's). But at Jet's, they omit the outer cheese layer and call their pizzas "deep-dish." They also allow you to "flavorize" your crust. If you choose the more traditional, circular shape, think poppy seed, sesame seed, Parmesan, or "turbo" (butter, garlic, Romano).

The Skokie branch, where I ate, is pretty spartan in terms of décor—just a counter and a long red bench like you'd see in a public park. The perfectly square, small deep-dish arrives half covered in an addictively delicious pepperoni and half with a generous topping of quite small, misshapen pieces of ground, fennel-flecked sausage. The cheese application is generous, but not overwhelming, and the sauce has some nice flavor to it, hidden as it is between the high dough and caramelized cheese.

The dough is denser than focaccia, and certainly just as high, but it doesn't take away from or overwhelm the ingredients on top of the dough.

If you like deep-dish, and don't feel like using a knife and fork to get it into your mouth, this dough-centric pizza is for you.

Longacre Pizza Squared
1309 W. Wilson Avenue
773-293-7413
www.longacrechicago.com
Ordered: slice of Chicago craft
    pepperoni and slice of sausage

Andy Kalish was born in Detroit and grew up in suburban Southfield, so Joe Louis Arena, the Tigers, Flames, and Detroit-style pizza are in his DNA. After running a catering business in Chicago and on the North Shore for many years, he opened Longacre and a vegan café in 2017, right next door to each other. "Inspired by the 313" says their website, and with that area code, and the legendary Buddy's as inspiration, Kalish has managed to create pies worthy of a visit, even if there are a few ratio issues to work out.

The ten- by fourteen-inch pans are made from automotive sheet metal, and are purposefully deep, to ensure large slices. Pans cost around $20 (yielding four slices) but a slice is the way to go; each one could probably feed two moderately hungry people. Flavors range from dime-sized pepperoni, sourced from the excellent 'Nduja Artisans, to homemade sausage, a red velvet vegan, chicken sausage, and Zabiha Halal beef sausage.

After mixing up their dough, they'll let it rest about forty-eight hours, par-baking it for just six or seven minutes in their gas-fired ovens. They then wrap the dough and let it continue to rest another day. Once they assemble their pies—and by assembly, I mean the addition of Wisconsin brick cheese and white cheddar, then the toppings—they're baked at 500 degrees for about twenty to thirty minutes. Canned San Marzano tomato sauce is gently heated, then carefully drawn in a diagonal sash across the top of the pizza *after* it comes out of the oven. In a very non-Detroit flourish, Kalish adds a final garnish of shredded fresh basil and large, thin wisps of Parmesan to give his pizzas a bit more flavor.

The key to a Detroit-style pizza is that cheesy, caramelized perimeter, where the brick and cheddar have spilled over the side edges and transformed into a blackened crisp, thanks to the blazing hot sheet pan's interior border. The undercarriage is slightly misshapen, revealing a gorgeous, golden brown surface that retains its crispiness. I would have like a slightly better OBR here—I thought the focaccia-like dough tended to overwhelm the rest of the ingredients, but I can see how homesick Detroiters would take to this pizza instantly, along with the requisite Vernors sodas that remind them of home.

Paulie Gee's Logan Square
2451 N. Milwaukee Avenue
773-360-1072
www.pauliegee.com
Ordered: Paulie's "Prohibited
   Pepperoni"

I already included Paulie Gee's Logan Square in this book's artisan pizza chapter, as they make truly remarkable artisan pies. But the local owner has some leeway from what the Brooklyn mother ship allows, and the result is a Detroit-style pizza that also deserves recognition.

What started in Greenpoint, Brooklyn, and has spread to a half-dozen other locations, including Columbus, Baltimore, and Miami, now has a location in that heart of hipster paradise, Logan Square.

Goofy pie names aside ("Mo Cheeks," "Ricotta Be Kiddin' Me," "Brian DeParma," etc.), the intense, wood-burning ovens churn out seriously blistered pies with nice leopard spotting. The key is the three-day cold fermentation that results in dough with incredible chew and complexity.

Formerly available only three days each week, "Logan Squares"—an homage to Buddy's in Detroit—are now sold every day. There are usually four options, and supplies are limited. You'll never see pepperoni on a standard, circular pizza from any of the Paulie Gee's locations in the country (Brooklyn HQ doesn't allow it). But since these are squares, the Chicago franchise owner is able to get away with it through a geometric loophole. White cheddar, mozzarella, and tiny pepperoni discs are topped with cold tomato sauce, which lends a beguiling contrast to the hot slice, and a bit of Pecorino Romano is sprinkled on top of each red tomato river. That caramelized cheese perimeter also lends some texture and crunch to this angular pizza, which is wisely served on top of a cooling rack, allowing for an even airflow on all sides and keeping the undercarriage crisp.

There are more than a dozen great dining options inside the Revival Food Hall, located in the epicenter of the Loop, in the former Chicago Public Schools' headquarters. Open from breakfast through dinner, you can grab your share of fried chicken, pastries, tacos, and smoked brisket. But the Hall's only pizza place happens to specialize in Detroit-style pizza, which delivers a thicker, focaccia-like dough inspired by Sicily.

Union offers two choices: a whole pie (serves three to four) or a personal pie. They offer plenty of special pies among the whole options, including broccoli and potato, burrata Margherita, and barbecued chicken. The personal options are more basic: sausage, mushroom, and pepperoni. Also called quarter pies, these giant, rectangular slices are plenty hefty.

My sausage arrives with large pieces of green pepper embedded in a red lake of zesty tomato sauce resting on a soft pillow of mozzarella. The highlight is the caramelized border—consisting of a brick and mozzarella cheese combo. It all lends nice color and texture to each bite. The fennel-heavy sausage comes from the well-regarded Joseph's Finest Meats on the city's Northwest Side.

Union Squared's owner models the pies after Buddy's and Cloverleaf in Detroit. I've been to both, and after tasting Union's thick, delicious pieces of cheesy, caramelized pleasure, I would not hesitate to make the drive to the Motor City once again, or even to Evanston.

Union Squared
125 S. Clark Street (inside Revival
  Food Hall)
773-770-6168
www.unionpizza.com
1307 Chicago Avenue
Evanston, Illinois
224-714-3100
There is also a Union Pizzeria in
  Evanston (same owners) but
  it offers no Detroit-style pizza,
  only Neapolitan.
Ordered: personal pie, sausage

CHAPTER 11

Overrated

Many of the best-known pizza places have benefited from outsized profiles in gossip magazines or too many celebrity mentions in those same glossy mags—like when Tina Fey, Conan O'Brien, or Jeff Garlin, who all lived here for a time, recall their beer-and-pizza-fueled all-nighters in between improv sets. I've also noticed a strange willingness on the part of food writers and local media types to give these icons a pass. I suppose they feel as if it would be like piling on the Bulls or Sox if they're having a bad year.

The only problem as it relates to the downtown-friendly deep-dish houses, however, is that they've all been bad pretty much since the '70s—and it's still the same today. At Giordano's, the manager couldn't care less that the dough is underdone and the sauce tastes like it comes out of a jar; people waiting for tables get top priority. At Uno's, the sauce is some-what better, but the OBR is a joke, and the crust tastes like a mouthful of bread sticks you might eat at Olive Garden.

Over the past fifteen years, we've seen the emergence of places like Pizano's, which has helped, but there still isn't that much competition—at least near the River North and downtown tourist core. There are places that opened in several Chicago neighborhoods, such as Bartoli's and My Pi, that present exceptional deep-dish options, but many of the best deep-dish versions happen to exist in the suburbs. And the few Chicago-proper pizzerias that I do recommend truly offer something unlike what you'll find downtown, with an OBR (Optimal Bite Ratio) and a memorable crust.

Meanwhile, neighborhood favorites with multiple locations, like Leona's and Chicago's Pizza, just seem to have run out of steam. Crusts are rushed, toppings are *meh*, and the teenagers charged with manning the ovens just don't have the same emotional investment or critical eye as guys like Brian Tondryk at Bartoli's or Richard Aronson at My Pi.

So, if your favorite place isn't listed among my 101, there's a pretty good chance it's listed below. I took pictures of just about every one as proof that I was there. Too much cheese, undercooked or tough dough, a greasy top layer, flavorless sauce, or a dry, cardboard-like crust are all typical culprits here. Also, places that don't get the OBR right might fall into this category. I'm not saying these pizzas are bad; I'm just saying they're unremarkable—not memorable. I've broken them into two camps—thin and thick—and indicated whether or not they were in the city. If your neighborhood favorite is listed here, I'm sorry; I tried, but I didn't like.

Note: I didn't visit Bake 425, which has five suburban locations, because they specialize in selling prepared, uncooked pizzas that you take home to bake yourself (remember Homemade Pizza Co.?).

Thin—City

Apart Pizza Co.
Avanti Caffé
Bar Siena
Café Luigi
Candlelite
Capri's
Chicago's Pizza
Fox's Restaurant & Pub
Happy Camper
Italian Pizza Kitchen
Joe's Pizza
Knead
La Crosta
Lark
Legno
Leona's
The Local Pizzeria
Macello
Mama Luna's
Michael's Original Pizza & Tavern
Nick's Pizza & Pub
ORD Pizzeria
Parlor Pizza Bar
Pete's
Phil's
Piece Brewery & Pizzeria
Pi-Hi
Pizza Castle
Pranzi
Punky's
Sono Wood Fired
The Stop Along
Tony's Italian Deli & Subs
Trattoria Porretta
Uprising Wood Fired Pizza Co.
Via Carducci
Villa Napoli
Villa Rosa
Village Pizza
Waldo Cooney's Pizza

Thin—Suburbs

Bacci (Elmhurst)
Baldinetti's (Hinsdale)
The Big Tomato (Schaumburg)
Big Tomato Pizzeria (Wilmette)
Bill's Pizza & Pub (Mundelein)
Cassano's (Naperville)
Chesdan's (Homer Glen)
DiLeo's (Elmhurst)
Fiammé (Naperville)
Gianni's Ristorante and Pizzeria
    (Franklin Park)
Grand Stand Pizza (Franklin Park)
Jimmy's Place (Forest Park)
Judy's Pizzeria (Highland Park)
Olive Theory (Downers Grove)
Parker's Restaurant & Bar
    (Downers Grove)
The Pizza Factory (Barrington)
Pizza Palace (Elmhurst)
Pizzeria Antica (Bloomingdale)
Roberto's (Elmhurst)
Rosati's Chicago Pizza
    (rosatispizza.com) 24 locations
Rosati's Authentic Chicago Pizza
    (myrosatis.com) 78 locations
Slice Factory (Oak Lawn plus four
    other suburban locations)
Union Pizza (Evanston)

Thick—City

Bacino's
Chicago Pizza & Oven Grinder Co.
Milano's Pizza & Specialties
Medici
Nancy's
Papa Joe's
Phil's Pizza D'Oro
The Original Pizzeria Uno
    (referred to nationally as
    Uno Pizzeria and Grill or
    Uno Chicago Grill)
Sicilian Bakery
Tano's

Thick—Suburbs

Arrenello's (Tinley Park and
    Glenwood)
Beggars Pizza (Oak Lawn)
Edwardo's Natural Pizza
    (Oak Park)
Gino's East (Five suburban
    locations plus one in Chicago)
Giordano's (18 locations in
    Chicago; 34 in suburbs)
Phil's (Oak Lawn)
Piero's (Highland Park and
    Northbrook)
Tortorice's (three suburban
    locations)
Wa-Pa-Ghetti's (Wheeling)

ACKNOWLEDGMENTS

This immense task would not have been possible without a lot of support from so many people. First of all, I couldn't have done this without the undying, unified support from my family—Amy, Max, and Madeline. Thank you for putting up with more pizza than most families consume in a year, over the course of many weeks in a row, and then going back out to try some more with me after a full night of deep, thin, and tavern-style the night before. There were a few weeks there where I felt like a horrible parent, just feeding my kids leftover pizza every night, but your enthusiastic support and encouragement erased much of my guilt.

Thanks, also, to all of my friends who so bravely came along for the ride: Asha, Lin Brehmer, Mike Gebert, Dan Kuruna, Virginia, Kristine, Vince and Dr. Lyle, Andres and Mabel, Eli and Nicole, Paul and Andrea, Neal and Amy McKnight, Doug and Stacy Meyer, Gina and Jay, Todd Rosenberg, John Roth, Coop, the Mankowskis, John Burks, Andrew, Susie, and the magnificent Hattie Dordek, whose discerning palate and keen eye for OBR was mightily impressive for a three year-old.

Big thanks, also, to Kristine Sherred for tracking down Tim Samuelson at the Chicago Cultural Center, for mapping out the 101, and just generally being very willing to do whatever I asked regarding research and quote grabbing. Same goes for Lynnea Domienik, who came through with some last-minute edits and fact-checks.

A million thanks to Todd Rosenberg, fellow Badger and visionary, who brilliantly laid out the cover shot with the help of Amy Andrews, our talented food stylist. I'm also in constant awe of how Gina Hutchings, from LunarMedia.net in Chicago, can translate an idea in my head and make it

161

look perfect; her "Top 5" maps saved the day. And enormous thanks and gratitude to my copy editor, Donna Shryer, who knows more about the minutiae of the *Chicago Manual of Style* than I could ever dream of. Her eye was sharper than a pizza cutter and her probing questions made me reflect on the fact that not everyone is a pizza savant.

Thanks also to Anne Gendler, Jill Petty, and Madison Jacobs at Northwestern University Press for supporting this project with such gusto and shepherding me through the process. To Marianne Jankowski at Northwestern University Press, a huge thanks for creating the mouthwatering interiors and cover design of the book. Your art direction was both inspired and appreciated. Also Jennifer Graves, my News Director at ABC 7—and to some extent, GM John Idler and his predecessor, Emily Barr—for being the only local TV news executives in Chicago (if not the country) to devote so much airtime to food coverage. They've given me the freedom to cover whatever I find interesting in Chicagoland, and certainly pizza is a part of our shared experience.

Finally, thanks to my neighborhood CorePower Yoga. The number one question I get while tackling a subject like this, whether it's pho, Italian beef, or, in this case, pizza, is "How do you keep the weight off while doing all of that eating?" I tend to be very good about portions, but I also have to exercise. The sixty-minute yoga sculpt classes were lifesavers. Thanks to Monica, Audrey, Reyna, Danielle, Antonio, Chelsea, and all of the other great teachers in Bucktown who kept me on pace, burning calories and keeping my metabolism up so I could confidently go out for one of my three-a-days with confidence and eat more pizza.

INDEX

About the Cover

In the painting *King George III Statue, 1776,* American artist William Walcutt (1819–1882) depicts the toppling of the monument in New York City that occurred on July 9, 1776. The Declaration of Independence had been read aloud a few days earlier and revolutionary feeling ran high. Walcutt, who moved to the city from Ohio as very young man—when old people still remembered the dramatic events— imagined the scene as one in which all types of people participated with gusto, happy to be part of changing the world as they knew it.

OF THE PEOPLE

OF THE PEOPLE

A History of the United States

WITH SOURCES

FIFTH EDITION

VOLUME I

To 1877

Michael McGerr
Camilla Townsend
Karen M. Dunak
Mark Summers
Jan Ellen Lewis

New York   Oxford
Oxford Unviersity Press

Oxford University Press is a department of the University of Oxford.
It furthers the University's objective of excellence in research, scholarship,
and education by publishing worldwide. Oxford is a registered trademark of
Oxford University Press in the UK and certain other countries.

Published in the United States of America by Oxford University Press
198 Madison Avenue, New York, NY 10016, United States of America.

For titles covered by Section 112 of the US Higher Education
Opportunity Act, please visit www.oup.com/us/he for the latest
information about pricing and alternate formats.

Library of Congress Cataloging-in-Publication Data

Names: McGerr, Michael E., author. | Townsend, Camilla, 1965- author. |
  Dunak, Karen M., author. | Summers, Mark (History professor), author. |
  Lewis, Jan, 1949-2018, author.
Title: Of the people : a history of the United States with sources /
  Michael McGerr, Camilla Townsend, Karen M. Dunak, Mark Summers, Jan
  Ellen Lewis.
Other titles: History of the United States with sources
Description: Fifth edition. | New York : Oxford University Press, [2022] |
  Includes bibliographical references and index. | Contents: Volume 1. To
  1877—Volume 2. Since 1865. | Summary: "A higher education history
  text for United States history courses"—Provided by publisher.
Identifiers: LCCN 2021006879 (print) | LCCN 2021006880 (ebook) | ISBN
  9780197585955 (v. 1 ; paperback) | ISBN 9780197585962 | ISBN
  9780197586150 (v. 2 ; paperback) | ISBN 9780197586167 | ISBN
  9780197585986 (v. 1 ; epub) | ISBN 9780197585979 (v. 1 ; pdf) | ISBN
  9780197586181 (v. 2 ; epub) | ISBN 9780197586174 (v. 2 ; pdf)
Subjects: LCSH: United States—History—Textbooks. | United
  States—History—Sources.
Classification: LCC E178.1 .M455 2022 (print) | LCC E178.1 (ebook) | DDC
  973—dc23
LC record available at https://lccn.loc.gov/2021006879
LC ebook record available at https://lccn.loc.gov/2021006880

9 8 7 6 5 4 3 2 1
Printed in Mexico by Quad/Mexico

Jan Ellen Lewis
1949–2018
Historian, Teacher, Friend

Brief Contents

Contents

CHAPTER 1

Worlds in Motion, 1450–1550   2

CHAPTER 2

Colonial Outposts, 1550–1650   34

CHAPTER 3

The English Come to Stay, 1600–1660   64

CHAPTER 4

Continental Empires, 1660–1720   94

CHAPTER 5

The Eighteenth-Century World,
1700–1775   130

CHAPTER 6

Conflict in the Empire, 1713–1774   164

CHAPTER 7

Creating a New Nation, 1775–1788   196

CHAPTER 12

Manifest Destiny, 1836–1848   378

American Portrait: Joe, an Enslaved Man at the Alamo   380

CHAPTER 13

The Politics of Slavery, 1848–1860   408

CHAPTER 14

A War for Union and Emancipation,
1861–1865 442

CHAPTER 15

Reconstructing a Nation, 1865–1877   482

Maps

America in the World

New Primary Sources

All versions of the text now include end-of-chapter primary source documents, both textual and visual, designed to reinforce students' understanding of the material by drawing connections among topics and thinking critically. Nearly all chapters in the fifth edition include at least one new source document:

DIGITAL LEARNING RESOURCES FOR
OF THE PEOPLE

Oxford University Press offers instructors and students digital learning resources that increase student engagement and optimize the classroom teaching experience

Oxford Insight

Developed with a foundation in learning science, Oxford Insight courseware enables instructors to deliver a personalized and engaging learning experience that empowers students by actively engaging them in course content. Oxford Insight delivers high quality content within powerful, data-driven courseware designed to optimize student success. To learn more, and to book a demo of Oxford Insight Courseware, go to https://pages.oup.com/he/us/oxfordinsight.

Oxford Learning Link (OLL) and Oxford Learning Link Direct (OLLD)

This online resource center www.learninglink.oup.com is available to adopters of *Of the People*, offers a wealth of teaching resources, including a test-item file, a computerized test bank, an instructor's resource manual, quizzes, PowerPoint slides, videos, and primary sources. Oxford Learning Link Direct (OLLD) makes OUP's digital learning resources for *Of the People* available to adopters within their institution's own LMS via a one-time course integration.

Sources for *Of the People*

Edited by Maxwell Johnson, this two-volume sourcebook includes five to six primary sources per chapter, both textual and visual. Chapter introductions, document headnotes, and study questions provide learning support. The sourcebooks are also available as eBooks.

Mapping and Coloring Book of US History

This two-volume workbook includes approximately 80 outline maps that provide opportunities for students to deepen their understanding of geography through quizzes, coloring exercises, and other activities. *The Mapping and Coloring Book of US History* is free when bundled with *Of the People*.

E-Books

Digital versions of *Of the People* are available at many popular distributors, including Chegg, RedShelf, and VitalSource.

Other Oxford Titles of Interest for the US History Classroom

Oxford University Press publishes a vast array of titles in American history. The following list is just a small selection of books that pair particularly well with *Of the People: A History of the United States*, Fifth Edition. Any of these books can be

Jason Parker
Texas A&M University

Burton W. Peretti
Western Connecticut State University

Jim Piecuch
Kennesaw State University

John Putman
San Diego State University

R. J. Rockefeller
Loyola College of Maryland

Herbert Sloan
Barnard College, Columbia University

Vincent L. Toscano
Nova Southeastern University

William E. Weeks
San Diego State University

Timothy L. Wood
Southwest Baptist University

Jason Young
SUNY–Buffalo

Expert Reviewers of the Concise Second Edition

Hedrick Alixopulos
Santa Rosa Junior College

Guy Alain Aronoff
Humboldt State University

Melissa Estes Blair
Warren Wilson College

Amanda Bruce
Nassau Community College

Jonathan Chu
University of Massachusetts–Boston

Paul G. E. Clemens
Rutgers University

Martha Anne Fielder
Cedar Valley College

Tim Hacsi
University of Massachusetts–Boston

Matthew Isham
Pennsylvania State University

Ross A. Kennedy
Illinois State University

Eve Kornfeld
San Diego State University

Peggy Lambert
Lone Star College–Kingwood

Shelly L. Lemons
St. Louis Community College

Carolyn Herbst Lewis
Louisiana State University

Catherine M. Lewis
Kennesaw State University

Daniel K. Lewis
California State Polytechnic University

Scott P. Marler
University of Memphis

Laura McCall
Metropolitan State College of Denver

Stephen P. McGrath
Central Connecticut State University

Vincent P. Mikkelsen
Florida State University

Julie Nicoletta
University of Washington–Tacoma

Caitlin Stewart
Eastern Connecticut State University

Thomas Summerhill
Michigan State University

David Tegeder
Santa Fe College

Eric H. Walther
University of Houston

William E. Weeks
University of San Diego

Kenneth B. White
Modesto Junior College

Julie Winch
University of Massachusetts–Boston

Mary Montgomery Wolf
University of Georgia

Kyle F. Zelner
University of Southern Mississippi

Expert Reviewers of the Concise First Edition

Hedrick Alixopulos
Santa Rosa Junior College

Guy Alain Aronoff
Humboldt State University

Melissa Estes Blair
Warren Wilson College

Amanda Bruce
Nassau Community College

Jonathan Chu
University of Massachusetts–Boston

Paul G. E. Clemens
Rutgers University

Martha Anne Fielder
Cedar Valley College

Tim Hacsi
University of Massachusetts–Boston

Matthew Isham
Pennsylvania State University

Ross A. Kennedy
Illinois State University

Eve Kornfeld
San Diego State University

Peggy Lambert
Lone Star College–Kingwood

Shelly L. Lemons
St. Louis Community College

Carolyn Herbst Lewis
Louisiana State University

Catherine M. Lewis
Kennesaw State University

Daniel K. Lewis
California State Polytechnic University

Scott P. Marler
University of Memphis

Laura McCall
Metropolitan State College of Denver

Stephen P. McGrath
Central Connecticut State University

Vincent P. Mikkelsen
Florida State University

Julie Nicoletta
University of Washington–Tacoma

Caitlin Stewart
Eastern Connecticut State University

Thomas Summerhill
Michigan State University

David Tegeder
Santa Fe College

Eric H. Walther
University of Houston

William E. Weeks
University of San Diego

Kenneth B. White
Modesto Junior College

Julie Winch
University of Massachusetts–Boston

Mary Montgomery Wolf
University of Georgia

Kyle F. Zelner
University of Southern Mississippi

About the Authors

Michael McGerr is the Paul V. McNutt Professor of History and Chair of the Department of History at Indiana University–Bloomington. He is the author of *The Decline of Popular Politics: The American North, 1865–1928* (1986) and *A Fierce Discontent: The Rise and Fall of the Progressive Movement, 1870–1920* (2003), both from Oxford University Press. He is writing *"The Public Be Damned": The Kingdom and the Dream of the Vanderbilts*. The recipient of a fellowship from the National Endowment for the Humanities, Professor McGerr has won numerous teaching awards at Indiana, where his courses include the US Survey; War in Modern American History; Rock, Hip Hop, and Revolution; The Rich; The Sixties; and American Pleasure. He has previously taught at Yale University and the Massachusetts Institute of Technology. He received his BA, MA, and PhD from Yale.

Camilla Townsend is Distinguished Professor of History at Rutgers University—New Brunswick. She is the author of six books, among them *Fifth Sun: A New History of the Aztecs* (2019), *Annals of Native America* (2016), *Malintzin's Choices: An Indian Woman in the Conquest of Mexico* (2006), and *Pocahontas and the Powhatan Dilemma* (2004). She is also the editor of *American Indian History: A Documentary Reader* (2010). Her books have won numerous prizes, including the 2020 Cundill Prize for *Fifth Sun*. The recipient of fellowships from the National Endowment for the Humanities and the John Simon Guggenheim Memorial Foundation, she has also won awards at Rutgers and at Colgate, where she used to teach. Her courses cover the colonial history of the Americas as well as Native American history, early and modern. She received her BA from Bryn Mawr and her PhD from Rutgers.

Karen M. Dunak is Associate Professor of History and Chair of the Department of History at Muskingum University in New Concord, Ohio. She is the author of *As Long as We Both Shall Love: The White Wedding in Postwar America* (2013), published by New York University Press. She currently is working on a book about media representations of and responses to Jacqueline Kennedy Onassis. Her courses include the US Survey, Women in US History, Gender and Sexuality in US History, and various topics related to modern US history. She earned her BA from American University and her PhD from Indiana University.

Mark Summers is the Thomas D. Clark Professor of History at the University of Kentucky–Lexington. In addition to various articles, he has written *Railroads, Reconstruction, and the Gospel of Prosperity* (1984), *The Plundering Generation* (1988), *The Era of Good Stealings* (1993), *The Press Gang* (1994), *The Gilded Age; or, The Hazard of New Functions* (1997), *Rum, Romanism and Rebellion* (2000), *Party Games* (2004), and *A Dangerous Stir* (2009). At present, he has just completed a book about a Tammany politician, *Big Tim and the Tiger*. He is now writing a survey of Reconstruction and a book about 1868. He teaches the American history survey (both halves), the Gilded Age, the Progressive Era, the Age of Jackson, Civil War and Reconstruction, the British Empire (both halves), the Old West (both halves), a history of political cartooning, and various graduate courses. He earned his BA from Yale and his PhD from the University of California–Berkeley.

Jan Ellen Lewis was Professor of History and Dean of the Faculty of Arts and Sciences, Rutgers University–Newark. She also taught in the history PhD program at Rutgers, New Brunswick, and was a visiting professor of history at Princeton. A specialist in colonial and early national history, she wrote *The Pursuit of Happiness: Family and Values in Jefferson's Virginia* (1983) as well as numerous articles and reviews. She coedited *An Emotional History of the United States* (1998), *Sally Hemings and Thomas Jefferson: History, Memory, and Civic Culture* (1999), and *The Revolution of 1800: Democracy, Race, and the New Republic* (2002). She served as president of the Society of Historians of the Early American Republic, as chair of the New Jersey Historical Commission, and on the editorial board of the *American Historical Review*. An elected member of the Society of American Historians and the American Antiquarian Society, she received her AB from Bryn Mawr College and MAs and PhD from the University of Michigan.

OF THE PEOPLE

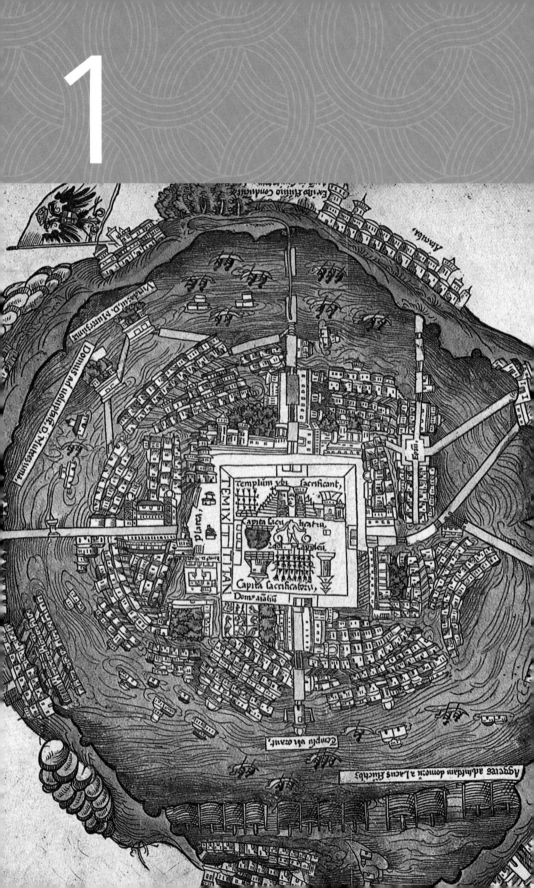

Worlds in Motion
1450–1550

< Tenochtitlan, the capital of the Aztecs

3

Malinche, Cultural Translator

When the Native American woman who would later be known as La **Malinche** was a little girl, she listened to the poems and histories of her people on starlit evenings. Her father was a nobleman from Coatzacoalcos, on the Gulf of Mexico; his people had lived there for generations in adobe houses built around communal courtyards. Her mother, though, was lowborn, maybe even a captive concubine, and this made the child vulnerable. Trouble came when she was still young. The powerful Aztecs from the Central Valley of Mexico were expanding their dominion, and she was either taken in battle or, more likely, given away as a preemptive peace offering to the invaders. Then the Aztecs sold her to the Mayas, and she lived with them for years as a slave.

When strangers from across the sea came on huge canoes with cloth sails, the Mayas attacked them—and lost the battle. Once again, the girl was given away as a peace offering. This time, she found herself among the newly arrived Spaniards, who baptized her "Marina." The Indians heard the name as "Malina" (as they had no "r") and called her "Malintzin" to convey respect. The Spaniards heard "Malinchi" or "Malinche" (as they had no "tz" sound), and so we still call her today. We will never know what her mother had once named her. She had become someone different, and she soon discovered her potential importance to her new captors. Her native language was Nahuatl, the same tongue spoken by the Aztecs, and by now she also spoke the coastal Mayan dialect. The Spaniards had with them one Jerónimo de Aguilar, who had lived for years among the Mayas as a shipwreck victim and also spoke their language. In a perfect translation chain, **Hernando Cortés** spoke to Aguilar, who spoke to Malinche, who in turn spoke to the Aztecs. She was a gifted young woman and learned Spanish quickly, soon becoming the only translator needed.

Malinche told the Spaniards about the Aztec capital where Moctezuma ruled, and she helped to guide them there. She had no reason to protect the Aztec people; after all, they had threatened her own family and caused her enslavement. And she had every reason to work cooperatively with the newcomers. If she did, they would treat her well. If not, they would use her as a sexual slave. She also soon saw that the Spanish were brutal on the battlefield and learned that there were many thousands more of them ready to come. Often she advised indigenous villages that they passed to make peace with the strangers rather than fight them. She said, quite rightly, that they could be useful friends but would make dangerous enemies. When they reached the Aztec capital, she translated adroitly between Cortés and Moctezuma, refusing to be intimidated, and helped Cortés determine what to do at each stage.

Hernando Cortés probably would not have been able to bring down the Aztecs without the help of Malinche. And yet if he had failed, some other Spaniard almost certainly would eventually have found some other captive woman to act as translator and mediator, for the domineering Aztecs had many enemies.

Like many people who have been forced to become **cultural mediators**, Malinche survived as best she could. She bore a son by Cortés, and when, after the conquest, she demanded a Spanish husband for her own protection, he saw her married to one of his lieutenants. She later bore her husband a daughter. A strong young woman, she lived through the initial onslaught of European diseases, but after a decade of exposure to various novel viruses, she at length succumbed to one of them. Malinche died before she was 30, but not before she had helped her children enter the Spanish world on a firm footing, with wealth and position. She knew by then that the New World she had helped to create was proving dangerous to indigenous people, even those who befriended the Spaniards. As she lay dying, she may have had fears for the future, but she could not have had any real regrets about the past, for at the time, she had had very few options. She had done the best she could in an extraordinarily difficult situation.

THE WORLDS OF INDIAN PEOPLES

For most of human history, there were no people in the Americas. Archaeologists have found that modern humankind (*Homo sapiens*) originated in Africa about 400,000 years ago. In a sense, all people alive today are ultimately African, as we are all descended from those early humans. Some of them migrated northward and eventually populated Europe and Asia. Mutations occurred along the way, yielding populations who looked different but still had almost all of their genetic material—and their natures and abilities—in common.

Great Migrations

In the last Ice Age, arctic glaciers expanded so extensively that the world's sea level dropped, perhaps by as much as 350 feet. This phenomenon created a land bridge (called **Beringia**) between Siberia in Asia and Alaska in America. Humans hunting mammoths and other big game traveled along the new corridor into America. Linguistic evidence indicates that there were three great waves of migration. Archaeologists argue fiercely about when the first one occurred. Most agree it was about 12,000 BCE, but there are a few sites that may suggest otherwise. The Monte Verde site in Chile—where a child's footprint next to a hearth has been forever preserved—seems to have been inhabited a thousand years earlier, for example. Eventually, about 9000 BCE, the ice melted, the sea level rose, and the land bridge disappeared, closing off the Old World from what would later be called the New.

The people living in the Americas, known now as Paleo-Indians, at first remained what they had been—hunter-gatherers who moved in small groups of no more than about 25, generally choosing their spouses from other bands whom they met in passing.

Because of the end of the Ice Age, the climate began to shift, yielding distinct changes in lifestyle. At the start of the Archaic period (approximately 8000 BCE), most of the large mammals that were hunted for food went extinct. Overhunting may have contributed to their disappearance, but climactic shifts probably explain the demise of species like the woolly mammoth. The men learned to hunt and trap smaller species, and the women foraged more determinedly for edible and useful plants. They moved through their environment in seasonal cycles, making satisfying and productive lives for themselves for many generations. By the time of Columbus's voyage, there were hundreds of indigenous groups in the Americas.

The Emergence of Farming

As temperatures rose and more species of plants appeared, people around the world began to experiment with planting the seeds of their favorite types. They continued to follow the game as they always had, but then returned to the same place months later to harvest what they had planted. In some places, the available plants proved so rich in protein—containing the amino acids necessary to support life—that human populations gradually ceased to be nomadic hunter-gatherers and became full-time farmers instead. In other places, the available plants were not nutritious enough to enable a major change in lifestyle. In Southwest Asia, for example, in the area traditionally known as "the Fertile Crescent," located between the Tigris and the Euphrates Rivers, wheat, barley, and peas were all native to the region, and all were protein-rich. Not surprisingly, humans' early efforts to domesticate plants in this part of the world led relatively rapidly to the adoption of farming as a full-time occupation by about 8000 BCE. In New Guinea, to take a contrary example, the native plants included bananas and sugarcane, both delicious but not rich in protein. People planted them occasionally, but they continued their hunting-and-gathering lifestyle.

In the Americas, there were also very few plant species rich in the amino acids needed to synthesize protein. The ancestor of today's corn, which first appeared in what is today Mexico, was an exception to some extent, but the kernels at that time were extremely tiny, and they were missing some key amino acids. During the Archaic period (8000 BCE–2000 BCE), a number of groups did experiment with growing it (as well as squash and other plants). However, it took many generations of selective planting to create the ears of corn we know today. It took people even longer to discover that if they ate corn together with beans, they were left as well-nourished as if they had eaten meat. (The beans provided the amino acids missing from corn: together, they form a complete protein.) Once these breakthroughs had occurred, more societies adopted full-time agriculture.

The Cradle of the Americas

Mesoamerica, the area stretching from the Rio Grande to today's Panama, has been called "the Cradle of the Americas" because it was here that the hemisphere's first technologically advanced civilizations emerged. They appeared wherever corn became the centerpiece of a farming culture, beginning in about 2000 BCE. In every part of the ancient world, numerous technological innovations followed the advent of full-time farming. A sedentary lifestyle in which only a portion of the population was engaged in full-time food production enabled the emergence of such things as complex architecture, large ceramics, forges, irrigation techniques, and detailed recordkeeping. Mesoamerica was no exception.

By about 200 CE, two distinct zones of Mesoamerican culture had emerged. In the **Yucatan Peninsula**, the Classic Mayan civilizations flourished. The central basin of Mexico saw a succession of prominent states, beginning with the city of Teotihuacan—the breathtaking ruins of which still stand—and ending with the Aztec Empire, dominant when the Europeans arrived. We know a great deal about the Mayas and Aztecs because they had their own pictoglyphic writing traditions, and they wrote down more about their culture when they learned the Roman alphabet from Spanish priests in the sixteenth century. In reading these individuals' writings, sometimes we stumble eerily into a moment from the past. One day in about the year 800, for example, a skilled Mayan artisan crafted a cup for drinking hot chocolate as a gift for a young prince. In the midst of the complicated paintings on the cup, which had religious and astronomical significance, he composed a poem in glyphic writing. He ended it by connecting the earthly world to the divine world, honoring both a powerful prince and a creator god: "He who gave the open space its place/who gave Jaguar Night his place/was the Black-Faced Lord, the Star-Faced Lord."

Scholars studying the writings and other remains of ancient Mesoamerican peoples have helped dispel some of the myths about them. Like people everywhere, they could be gentle and had senses of humor, but they were also competitive and often fought for dominance. They sometimes sacrificed prisoners of war to the gods, but they were not inherently more violent than other humans; they did *not* routinely sacrifice thousands of people at a time, as was once believed. In general, victors in political power struggles preferred that outsiders choose to ally with them rather than be destroyed. The more scholars learn about individual ethnic groups in the pre-Columbian period, the clearer it becomes that they were nearly all based on alliances formed between disparate groups in a more remote past. As bands grew to become chiefdoms—and in some cases, actual states—they governed themselves successfully by allowing the different subunits to have a voice in the increasingly complex polity. Constituent groups negotiated with each other and rotated between them the duties of going to war, for example, or working on a temple. In some regards, Mesoamerican native cultures thus constituted the hemisphere's first democracies although they were ruled by chiefs.

The Northern World Takes Shape

In the pre-Columbian period, North America was peripheral to Mesoamerica. Due to the centrality of farming in Mesoamerica, the population there was many millions strong (scholars debate the exact number), while the population of all of North America was about 1 million. Because a desert covered northern Mexico, the culture centered on corn did not travel northward as easily as comparable crops had once traveled from the Fertile Crescent throughout Europe and Asia. But ancient Mesoamerican migrants and traders did eventually spread their valuable

American Landscape
Tenochtitlan

When the European conquistadors arrived at the lake that lay at the very center of the Central Valley of Mexico, they spied an extraordinary island city: "When we saw all those villages built in the water, . . . and the straight and level causeway leading to the City of Mexico, we were astounded. These great pyramids and buildings rising from the water, all made of stone, seemed like an enchanted vision."

The city, called **Tenochtitlan** (Te-noch-TEE-tlan), was less than one hundred years old, but the farming culture of the central valley had existed for many centuries. The region's reputation for wealth had gradually drawn nomads down from what is today the American Southwest. The Mexica (pronounced Me-SHEE-ka), the last group to arrive, had found it difficult to carve out a space for themselves. But in the mid-1300s, they discovered the island at the center of the great lake and saw that it had no inhabitants. This was because it was swampy, reedy territory, unfit for the valley's corn-and-bean agriculture. The Mexica made the best of the situation: they learned to harvest the lake's edible algae, fish, and wild birds, and they hired themselves out as mercenaries to other tribes when they needed to earn a little something on the side and trade for corn to make tortillas. They even found that the location had a distinct advantage: a huge market grew up on the north side of the island, as it was easily accessible by canoe from all the surrounding villages built on the shores of the lake. Their power grew.

In the 1420s, a brilliant Mexica nobleman named Itzcoatl (Eetz-CO-wat) or "Obsidian Snake" forged an alliance with some other noblemen in surrounding towns, and together, they brought down the region's most powerful city state. Then Tenochtitlan replaced it, taking up its kingpin status. The city's leaders became brilliant military strategists, and Tenochtitlan soon was the single most powerful entity in all of Mesoamerica.

In the center of the city, builders gradually turned the simple temple dedicated to the people's protector god into a huge and imposing pyramid, and next to it they built another one for the rain god. They painted these with lime, so that they shimmered white in the sunlight, and added colorful decorations. The high chief's compound, built around a massive courtyard where people sang and danced, housed a library of pictographic scrolls, used to maintain records of the tribute owed by conquered states. Just outside, a zoological garden showed off the exotic birds and animals collected throughout the realm, wherever Mexica power extended.

All around the central precinct lived more ordinary people in highly commodities, largely through canoe travel along the coasts and eventually even across the Gulf of Mexico.

Beginning as early as 100 CE, small villages began to be established in what we call the American Southwest following the Mexican model. The Anasazi, the Mogollon, and the Hohokam cultures all experimented with agriculture and built houses around courtyards. Later, the climate and their nomadic enemies caused

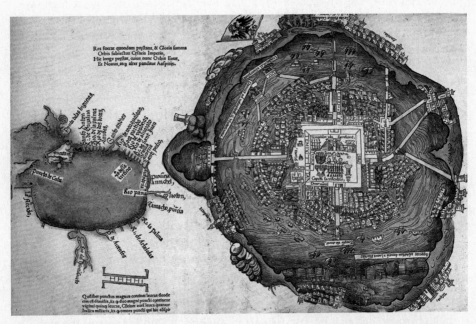

Tenochtitlan This 1524 engraving of Tenochtitlan was drawn by a European, but it accurately captures the layout of the Aztec city.

organized neighborhoods. They rotated among them the duties of repairing the streets and pyramids, and the causeways and aqueducts linking the city to the shore. Boys mostly learned the artisan trades of their fathers, but when they were young teens, they went to schools where they all learned to be warriors as well, able to be called upon whenever the city needed to make another conquest. Girls also went to school, in their case to learn to spin, weave, sew, and embroider.

At the edges of the island, people planted *chinampas*, aquatic hanging gardens: basket-like structures were filled with silt and submerged, and food plants were carefully tended there. But no matter how hard the chinampa farmers worked, they could not feed the 50,000 or more people who lived on the island. Tenochtitlan relied on forcing some conquered people to pay them tribute in foodstuffs, as well as on enticing local peoples to come voluntarily to trade food for artisan crafts at the huge lakeshore market. The city was a finely tuned organism that was working very well when the Europeans made their appearance.

most of them to return to hunting and gathering for a time. The Anasazi, however, persistently circled back to planting corn and eventually built their remarkable cliff dwellings and the towns of **Chaco Canyon**, among them the 800-room complex at Pueblo Bonito. This extraordinary architectural wonder seems to have been built largely for ceremonial purposes; thousands of people working over generations were dedicated to its construction.

Meanwhile, the Mississippi River had long functioned as a great highway for the exchange of goods and ideas. Once corn reached the mouth of the river, it was not long before it spread northward. We call the style of culture that traveled up the artery of the river "Mississippian." Mississippian sites, ranging from about 800 CE to 1500 CE, included the region's more ancient funerary mounds, as well as Mexican-style ball courts next to grand pyramids, central courtyards, and, of course, corn farming. **Cahokia**, a city-state located near the point where the Missouri River runs into the Mississippi, rose to become the greatest power in the region for a time, exacting tribute from surrounding villages. In the eleventh century, the town boasted about 10,000 people. After that, its power declined and its people abandoned the site; perhaps the powerful lords had made too many enemies, or perhaps a terrible drought struck, or both.

Even as Cahokia saw its demise, however, Mississippian culture spread into the American Southeast, and corn also traveled up the Ohio River to the Great Lakes, to the ancestors of the Iroquoian peoples. By the time the Europeans met the cultures of the Eastern Woodlands, many of them had been part-time farmers for a few hundred years, although they also continued to rely on hunting deer and gathering wild plants. Those groups who farmed most successfully saw their populations rise relative to their neighbors. The Iroquoian peoples in particular translated this into political power by resolving their internal differences through democratic discussion and presenting a united face to the world. It seems that at least a century before the Europeans arrived, the leader Deganawidah helped them found the entity later known as the League of Five Nations. Women, whose work in agriculture was deemed highly important, had a voice in the selection of chiefs.

Some parts of North America were not subject to the influence of Mexican culture and corn. The peoples of the far north, relatively few in number, survived through expert hunting. The Great Plains were largely uninhabited, for in a world

Image of Community of Cahokia The community at Cahokia, at eye level, as envisioned by a modern-day graphic artist. The town was surrounded by a stockade, which enclosed the mounds, plazas, temples, and homes.

without horses, their vastness and aridity seemed impenetrable, except for a few people who piled their goods onto a chamois pulled by dogs. A few corn farmers nestled around the edges of the prairies, and sometimes enterprising men drove roaming herds of buffalo over cliffs to harvest the meat. Many of these people lived in villages of earthen lodges. Farther west, along the coast of California and in the Pacific Northwest, large numbers of people lived by fishing and processing acorns. They built lodges and totem poles out of wood and painted them with bright colors. On the Columbia Plateau, a great annual trade fair centered on the buying and selling of dried salmon. Even here, although the people had not become farmers, some Mexican influence was felt. Travelers brought luxury goods to trade, like turquoise jewelry, which had come from the lands to the south.

These northwestern fisher peoples would be among the last to come face-to-face with Europeans. The newcomers were approaching from the south and east.

THE WORLDS OF CHRISTOPHER COLUMBUS

In the world into which Christopher Columbus was born, Europe was peripheral. Great overland trade caravans and the sea routes of the Indian Ocean connected the known world. The Middle Eastern merchants at the center formed the hub (see Map 1–1). The goods of China were in greatest demand. Europeans constituted the least powerful element of the world's trade system. Princes and merchants there longed to be able to compete with other players on the world stage, and some desperately sought ways of doing so.

The *Reconquista*

Middle Eastern economic power had spurred the spread of the Islamic faith after its inception in the seventh century. By the year 711, most of the **Iberian Peninsula** (today's Spain and Portugal) had fallen to Muslim conquerors of Arab and Berber descent (called "Moors" by Christians). The new authorities were generally tolerant of those they had vanquished and allowed Christian and Jewish subjects to coexist peacefully alongside Muslims. Toward the end of the eleventh century, however, dissatisfied descendants of the ousted ruling families began a concerted effort toward reconquest, or *reconquista*. In 1085, Alfonso VI of Castile retook Toledo. "Inspired by God's grace," he wrote triumphantly, "I moved an army against this city, where my ancestors once reigned in power and wealth, deeming it acceptable in the sight of the Lord." Over the course of the next four centuries, other Christian princes followed Alfonso's lead. In these years, warfare shaped all aspects of Iberian society. The priests who proclaimed the *reconquista* a holy struggle against the Moorish infidel and the soldiers who waged such wars were elevated to positions of prestige. The surest path to wealth and honor lay in plunder and conquest.

By the time the Italian-born Christopher Columbus arrived in Spain in 1485, the Muslim rulers had been ejected from the entire peninsula, except Granada. The 1469 marriage of Isabel, princess of Castile, and her cousin Ferdinand, prince of Aragon, had unified the heart of what would soon be the nation of Spain. Although Isabel was only 18 when she married (and her husband a year younger), she had already shown herself to be a woman of boldness and determination, and

Tlaxcalan codex (a pictorial account painted on bark or paper) illustrates the ceremony. In the picture, Cortés sits on a chair, his officers behind him. In front of him is the Tlaxcalan leader, also backed up by his nobles. Malintzin stands addressing the Tlaxcalan women, who include elegantly dressed nobles, intended to be accepted as wives for Spanish leaders. The group also includes the daughters of lesser nobles, as well as some commoners intended as slaves.

Several decades later, the names and fates of some of the elite women were still remembered by both sides. Tecuiluatzin, a daughter of Xicotencatl, an important Tlaxcalan chief, was renamed doña Luisa and became the mistress of Pedro de Alvarado, second in command after Cortés. She accompanied him to Guatemala, and although they were not married, their children entered the higher ranks of Spanish society in the New World. Many of the first generation of elite *mestizo* (or mixed) sons, including Malinche's son by Cortés, were brought up in their fathers' households and even sent to Spain for their education, while the daughters generally found prominent husbands.

This state of affairs did not last, however. Indigenous women continued to bear children by European men, but once there were more Spanish women in the colonies, fewer such women ended up married, and fewer of the children received places of honor when they reached adulthood. Nevertheless, many of the relationships between the Spaniards and Native American women were consensual. The women had few options, given the devastation in their communities, and their cultures had instilled the idea that true strength lay in survival, rather than choosing death over compromise. The mestizo population grew larger every year.

TIME LINE

▼**ca. 12,000** BCE
Indian peoples arrive in North America

▼**711** CE
Moors invade Iberian Peninsula

▼**1275–1292**
Marco Polo travels in Asia

▼**1434**
Portuguese arrive at West Coast of Africa

▼**1492**
Spanish complete the *reconquista*, evicting Moors from Spain

Jews expelled from Spain
Columbus's first voyage to America

▼**1493**
Columbus's second voyage

▼**1494**
Treaty of Tordesillas divides New World between Spain and Portugal

▼**1496**
Spanish complete conquest of Canary Islands

▼**1497**
John Cabot arrives in North America

▼**1498**
Columbus's third voyage to America, reaches South American coast

▼**1500**
Portuguese arrive in Brazil

▼**1504**
Columbus's fourth voyage to America ends

▼**1508**
Spanish conquer Puerto Rico

CONCLUSION

Within a half century after Columbus's arrival in the New World, both the world he had come from and the one he had reached had been transformed into a new, global political economy (see Map 1–5). Thanks to the decision made by Queen Isabel, Spain dominated exploration, colonization, and exploitation of the New World. The wealth that Spain extracted from her colonies encouraged rival nations to enter into overseas ventures. Eventually France, England, the Netherlands, Sweden, and Russia all established New World colonies. Because Spain (along with Portugal, which claimed Brazil) had such a head start, rival nations would have to settle for the lands Spain left unclaimed.

In the wake of the unprecedented wealth gained in the Americas, a new global economy was established, linking the Old and New Worlds. Gold and silver extracted from its empire sustained Spain's rise to power, and the plantation crops of the New World made many Europeans wealthy. Thus, the divergence in the power of the two hemispheres grew wider, and Europe's power also grew relative to Asia's.

Native Americans faced enslavement or were given out in *encomienda*. As the native population was depleted and the morality of enslaving native populations was questioned, Europeans turned to the African slave trade. Suffering in the Americas was therefore intense, and yet at the same time, the people who survived learned to carry on with their lives. Ways of life stemming from multiple traditions unfolded, and cultures evolved in creative ways. The young girl named Malinche, it turned out, had been pointing the way.

▼**1513**
Spanish *Requerimiento* promises freedom to all Indians who accept Spanish authority
Spanish conquer Cuba
Ponce de León reaches Florida
The Laws of Burgos attempt to regulate working conditions of Indians

▼**1518**
Spanish introduce smallpox to New World

▼**1519**
Cortés lands on Yucatan coast

▼**1519–1522**
Ferdinand Magellan's crew sails around the world

▼**1521**
Tenochtitlan falls to the Spanish
Ponce de León returns to Florida

▼**1526**
Ayllón explores South Carolina coast and

establishes fort in Georgia

▼**1528**
Narváez explores Florida

▼**1539–1543**
De Soto and his party explore Southeast, arriving at Mississippi, devastating the Indians and their land

▼**1540–1542**
Coronado explores Southwest

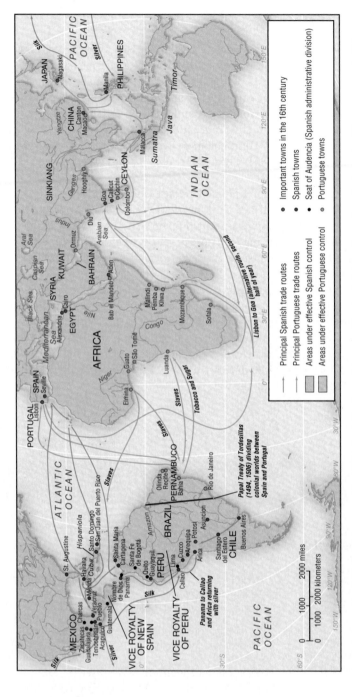

Map 1-5   A New Global Economy By 1600, both Spain and Portugal had established empires that reached from one end of the globe to the other.

WHO, WHAT, WHERE

Beringia   5

Cahokia   10

Chaco Canyon   9

Columbian Exchange   27

Cortés, Hernando   4

cultural mediator   5

encomienda   17

Hispaniola   17

Iberian Peninsula   11

Malinche (Malintzin, doña Marina)   4

Mesoamerica   6

Mexica   23

Moctezuma II   20

political economy   17

Ponce de León, Juan   19

the *Requerimiento*   18

Tenochtitlan   8

Tlaxcala   23

Yucatan Peninsula   7

REVIEW QUESTIONS

1. Describe the development of indigenous civilizations in Central and North America from Archaic times until 1500. What were the major forces of change within these early populations?

2. What were the forces that led European countries, and particularly Spain, to explore the New World?

3. What was the impact of European conquest on the population and environment of the New World?

CRITICAL-THINKING QUESTIONS

1. Compare older ways of explaining the conquest (such as Moctezuma's supposed belief that Hernando Cortés was a god) with scholars' more recent explanations. What beliefs about Native Americans does each set of explanations reflect?

2. How would Native American men and women have experienced conquest differently?

3. Compare Spain's treatment of Muslims and Jews in Spain following the *reconquista* with the country's later treatment of conquered Native Americans in the New World. Do you think these groups received similar or different treatment? Why?

SUGGESTED READINGS

Diamond, Jared. Guns, Germs and Steel: The Fates of Human Societies. New York: Norton, 1997.

Lockhart, James, ed. We People Here: Nahuatl Accounts of the Conquest of Mexico. Los Angeles: University of California Press, 1993.

Richter, Daniel K. Before the Revolution: America's Ancient Pasts. Cambridge, MA: Harvard University Press, 2011.

Tedlock, Dennis. 2000 Years of Mayan Literature. Berkeley: University of California Press, 2011.

Wey-Gómez, Nicolas. Tropics of Empire: Why Columbus Sailed South to the Indies. Cambridge, MA: MIT Press, 2008.

For further review materials and resource information, please visit www.oup.com/us/ofthepeople

CHAPTER 1:   WORLDS IN MOTION, 1450–1550
Primary Sources

1.1   AZTEC SONGS

The Nahuas began to arrive in central Mexico in the 900s. They migrated from what is today Arizona and New Mexico and settled among people who had been farmers for at least two millennia. One of the last groups to arrive, the Mexica, had risen to great power by the time the Spanish came, ruling over hundreds of other city states. We know them now as the Aztecs. They had a remarkable literary culture, including poetry, songs, histories, and prayers. However, it was an oral culture and would probably be lost to us today were it not for the efforts of Christian missionaries. In the 1560s, forty years after the Spanish conquest, a Franciscan named Bernardino de Sahagún orchestrated a project in which Nahuatl-speaking assistants wrote down the lyrics of songs that had been popular for generations. One surprising revelation is that the Aztecs lamented the need for violence.

Tlaocoya in noyollo nicuicanitl nicnotlamatia
Yehua ça ye yn xochitly, Çan ye in cuicatli,
ica nitlacocoa in tlalticpac.
Yn ma çan oc huel nemohua on in tlalticpac . . .

I, the singer, suffer and grieve.
With flower- song [songs of war]
I'm inflicting wounds on earth.
Let there be more living here on earth . . .

Çan ye tonmotlatia in chicomoztoc mizquitl yhcaca
quauhtlin tzatia ocelotl chocac
Yn titlauhquecholin ye tonpatlantinemia ixtlahuatl ytic
Quenomanican ohuaya ohuaya

You hid yourself [you died] at the Seven Caves, where the mesquite plant grows.
The eagle called, the jaguar cried,
And you, a red swan, flew away from the battlefield
To the place unknown.

Source: Cantares Mexicanos, Biblioteca Nacional, Mexico City. Translations are our own.

1.2   VISUAL DOCUMENTS: CHACO CULTURE NATIONAL HISTORICAL PARK, PUEBLO BONITO

The corn that sustained Mesoamerican civilization eventually spread outward through long-distance trade. For example, in the San Juan River basin and especially in Chaco Canyon in the northwestern corner of today's New Mexico, people experimented with agriculture from the ninth to the eleventh century, adopting it for a few generations and then, when times were tougher, breaking into small nomadic groups. They built impressive stone-and-wood villages organized around *kivas*, large communal ceremonial chambers. The largest of these sites is now called Pueblo Bonito. Archaeologists have confirmed that the people who lived there were well aware of their history. A small original construction became the ceremonial heart of the large village, which was built around it several generations later. There the people concentrated their burials, reliquaries, and precious goods, which included products brought from as far away as Mexico. At the town's height, as many as a thousand people lived there.

Source: Getty Images/DEA/SIOEN/Contributor and Getty Images/Education Images/Contributor.

1.3   KING FERNANDO AND QUEEN ISABELLA OF SPAIN, "GRANADA CAPITULATIONS" (1492)

In 1492, King Fernando and Queen Isabella of Spain defeated the last Muslim kingdom on the Iberian Peninsula, freeing them to turn their attention to international trade. They signed a business contract with a Genoese explorer named Christopher Columbus, who believed he could reach Asia by sailing west. They promised him a percentage of all the profits, and later, at his request, they also agreed that he could govern any territories he might conquer. They were all imagining he might conquer territories on the outskirts of Asia. This document, called the "Granada Capitulations," was signed April 30, 1492.

Sir Fernando and Lady Isabel, by the grace of God king and queen of Castile, Leon, Aragon, Sicily, Granada, Toledo, Valencia, Galicia, the Balearics, Seville, Sardinia, Cordoba, Corsica, Murcia, Jaen, the Algarve, Algeziras, Gibraltar and the Canary Islands, count and countess of Barcelona, lords of Vizcaya and Molina, dukes of Athens and Neopatria, counts of Roussillon and Cerdagne, marquises of Oristano and Goceano.

Because you, Christopher Columbus, are going at our command with some of our ships and personnel to discover and acquire certain islands and mainland in the Ocean Sea, and it is hoped that, with the help of God, some of the islands and mainland in the Ocean Sea will be discovered and acquired by your command and expertise, it is just and reasonable that you should be remunerated for placing yourself in danger for our service.

Wanting to honor and bestow favor for these reasons, it is our grace and wish that you, Christopher Columbus, after having discovered and acquired these islands and mainland in the Ocean Sea, will be our admiral of the islands and mainland that you discover and acquire and will be our admiral, viceroy and governor of them. You will be empowered from that time forward to call yourself Sir Christopher Columbus, and thus your sons and successors in this office and post may entitle themselves sir, admiral, viceroy and governor of them.

You and your proxies will have the authority to exercise the office of admiral together with the offices of viceroy and governor of the islands and mainland that you discover and acquire. You will have the power to hear and dispose of all the lawsuits and case, civil and criminal, related to the offices of admiral, viceroy, and governor, as you determine according to the law, and as the admirals of our kingdoms are accustomed to administer it. You and your proxies will have the power to punish and penalize delinquents as well as exercising the offices of admiral, viceroy, and governor in all matters pertaining to these offices. You will enjoy and benefit from the fees and salaries attached, belonging and corresponding to these offices, just as your high admiral enjoys and is accustomed to them in the admiralty of our kingdoms....

Source: Granada Capitulations, Granada, April 30, 1492, as translated in Geoffrey Symcox and Blair Sullivan, eds., *Christopher Columbus and the Enterprise of the Indies* (Boston: Bedford, 2005), pp. 60–61.

1.4   AZTEC PRIESTS, STATEMENT TO THE FRANCISCAN FRIARS (1520s)

In 1524, three years after the conquest of Tenochtitlan, a group of 12 Franciscan friars representing the 12 apostles arrived in Mexico. They orchestrated a series of official meetings with high-ranking Aztec political leaders and priests. On several of these occasions, the Europeans took notes. Years later, in the 1560s, another Franciscan rewrote these notes as though the exchange he was recording had occurred on a single occasion, though he was really creating a composite picture. Here is a direct translation from the Nahuatl of what he claimed the Aztec priests said after having listened for several hours to the messages of the Christians. Notice that what has truly angered them is not so much the idea of a new god as the demand that they abandon the old.

You say that we do not recognize the being who is everywhere, lord of heaven and earth. You say our gods are not true gods. The new words that you utter are what confuse us; due to them we feel foreboding. Our makers [our ancestors] who came to live on earth never uttered such words. They gave us *their* laws, their ways of doing things. They believed in the gods, served them and honored them. They are the ones who taught us everything, the gods' being served and respected. Before them we eat earth [kiss the ground]; we bleed; we pay our debts to the gods, offer incense, make sacrifice. . . . indeed, we live by the grace of those gods. They rightly made us out of the time, the place where it was still dark. . . . They give us what we go to sleep with, what we get up with [our daily sustenance], all that is drunk, all that is eaten, the produce, corn, beans, green maize, chia. We beg from them the water, the rain, so that things grow upon the earth.

The gods are happy in their prosperity, in what they have, always and forever. Everything sprouts and turns green in their home. What kind of place is the land of Tlaloc [the rain god]? Never is there any famine there, nor any illness, nor suffering. And they [the gods] give people virility, bravery, success in the hunt, [bejeweled] lip rings, blankets, breeches, cloaks, flowers, tobacco, jade, feathers and gold.

Since time immemorial they have been addressed, prayed to, taken as gods. It has been a very long time that they have been revered, since once upon a time in Tula, in Huapalcalco, Xochitlapan, Tlamohuanchan, in Teotihuacan, the home of the night. These gods are the ones who established the mats and thrones [that is, inherited chieftainships], who gave people nobility, and kingship, renown and respect.

Will we be the ones to destroy the ancient traditions of the Chichimeca, the Tolteca, the Colhuaca, the Tepaneca? [No!][1] It is our opinion that there is life, that people are born, people are nurtured, people grow up, [only] by the gods' being called upon, prayed to. Alas, o our lords, beware lest you make the common people do something bad. How will the poor old men, the poor old women, forget or erase their upbringing, their education? May the gods not be angry with us. Let us not move towards their anger. And let us not agitate the commoners, raise a riot, lest they rebel for this reason, because of our saying to them: address the gods no longer, pray to them no longer. Look quietly, calmly, o our lords, at what is needed. Our hearts cannot be at ease as long as we cannot understand each other. We do not admit as true [what you say]. We will cause you pain. Here are the towns, the rulers and kings who carry the world. It is enough that we have lost political power, that it

---

[1] Nahuatl texts are full of rhetorical questions, the answer to which is always meant to be a resounding "No!"

was taken from us, that we were made to abandon the mats and thrones. We will not budge; we will just end [this conversation]. Do to us whatever you want. This is all with which we return, we answer, your breath, your words, o our lords.

Source: Miguel León Portilla, ed., *Coloquios y doctrina cristiana* (Mexico City: UNAM, 1986). This edition provides a facsimile of the original document; we have translated from the original Nahuatl into English.

1.5   ALVAR NÚÑEZ CABEZA DE VACA, DESCRIBING NORTH AMERICA (1535)

In 1528, a Spanish exploratory expedition wrecked off the coast of Florida. The survivors met with a hostile Indian population and eventually fled from them in rafts that they built. Ultimately, only four men survived—three Spaniards and one North African, who had been a slave. They lived for years along the coast of what is today Texas, where they gained a reputation as healers among the local people. In 1535, they wandered into Spanish settlements in northern Mexico and re-entered European society. One of them, Alvar Núñez Cabeza de Vaca, wrote a long narrative about his experiences among people who had never seen a white man—or a black man—before.

The Indians from the Island of Malhado . . . are warlike people, and they have as much cunning to protect themselves from their enemies as they would have if they had been raised in Italy and in continuous war. When they are in a place where their enemies can attack them, they set up their houses at the edge of the most rugged woods and of the greatest density they find there. And next to it they make a trench and sleep in it. All the warriors are covered with light brush, and they make their arrows. And they are so well covered and hidden that even if their heads are uncovered, they are not seen. And they make a very narrow path and enter into the middle of the woods. And there they make a place for their women and children to sleep. And when night comes, they light fires in their houses, so that if there should be spies, they would believe that they are in them. And before dawn, they again light the same fires, and if by chance their enemies come to attack the houses themselves, those who are in the trench surprise them and from the trenches do them much harm without those outside seeing them or being able to find them. . . . While I was with the ones of Aguenes, they not being warned, their enemies came at midnight and attacked them and killed three of them and wounded many others, with the result that they fled from their houses forward through the woods. And as soon as they perceived that the others had gone, they returned to them. And they gathered up all the arrows that the others had shot at them, and as secretly as they could, they followed them and were near their houses that night without being perceived. And in the early morning they attacked them and they killed five of them and injured many others, and made them flee and leave their houses and their bows with all their possessions . . . The manner in which they fight is low to the ground. And while they are shooting their arrows, they go stalking and leaping about from place to place, avoiding the arrows of their enemies, so much so that in such places they manage to suffer very little harm. The Indians are more likely to make fun of crossbows and harquebuses [than to fear them] because these weapons are ineffective against them in the flat, open areas where they roam free. They are good for enclosed areas and wetlands, but in all other areas, horses are what must be used to defeat them, and are what the Indians universally fear. Whoever might have to fight against them should be advised to prevent them from perceiving weakness or greed for what the [Indians] have. And as long as war lasts, they must treat them very badly, because if they know that their enemy has fear or some sort of greed [that may affect their decisions] they are people who know how to recognize the times in which to ... take advantage of the fear [or greed] of their enemies.

Source: Rolena Adorno and Patrick Charles Pautz, eds., *The Narrative of Cabeza de Vaca* (Lincoln: University of Nebraska Press, 2003), pp. 127–129.

precious metals, and, most important, sedentary farming peoples who were already accustomed to a political hierarchy and to paying tribute to others. The northern European nations could not afford expeditions comparable to that of Columbus when it became clear that the North American world was very different from New Spain in these key regards.

Northern European nations learned what they knew of the North American world by sponsoring small, economical expeditions designed to establish trade and seek a sea route to Asia. Would-be explorers sold their services to the highest bidder. John Cabot, who sailed for England, was, like Columbus, born in Genoa, Italy. (His real name was Giovanni Caboto.) Before coming to England, he had spent time in Muslim Arabia, Spain, and Portugal, apparently looking for sponsors for a voyage to Asia. He found them in the English port city of Bristol, from whence he sailed in 1497. He landed in Newfoundland and claimed the territory for England.

Soon both England and France sent fishing expeditions to the waters off Newfoundland (see Map 2–1). The population of northwestern Europe exploded in the sixteenth and seventeenth centuries, creating an increased demand for fish, and fishing expeditions to Newfoundland were relatively inexpensive to sustain.

The French colony of **New France**, planted in the St. Lawrence River region of Canada, grew out of the French fishing ventures off Newfoundland. Although early French explorers discovered neither gold nor a Northwest Passage to Asia, French fishermen found that the Indians were willing to trade beaver pelts at prices so low that a man could make a fortune in a few months' time.

The Huge Geographical Barrier

At first, North America seemed little more than an obstacle on the way to Asia. In 1522, Ferdinand Magellan's expedition had completed the first round-the-world voyage for Spain, proving finally that one could get to the East by heading west. Other nations then became interested in finding a way through, rather than around, North America. Two years after Magellan's voyage, the Italian Giovanni da Verrazano sailed on behalf of France. He explored the coast from South Carolina to Maine and was the first European to see New York Harbor. To Europeans, however, all that Verrazano had discovered was a huge barrier between Europe and Asia.

On that "huge barrier" of North America lived Indians, some wary and some friendly. Unfamiliar with Indian customs, Europeans often could not distinguish hospitality from malice. When Algonquian Indians attempted to dry out one of Verrazano's sailors, who had almost drowned, by setting him near a campfire, Verrazano feared that they "wanted to roast him for food." In the early years of exploration, survival often depended on local Indians, yet because the Europeans were looking either for treasure or for a Northwest Passage and were not necessarily thoughtful students of human nature, they tended to see cultural differences rather than similarities.

Between 1534 and 1542, King François I of France financed **Jacques Cartier** to make three expeditions to seek a route through North America and to look out for any riches along the way. All three came to naught. On their second trip, the French sailed up the St. Lawrence River as far as the town of Hochelaga (near present-day Montréal). The Iroquoian speakers there told of a wealthy land to the west. Although the Indians may have been trying to deceive the French, it is possible that the shiny

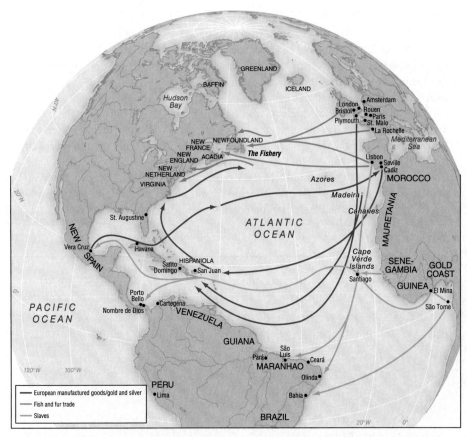

Map 2–1 North Atlantic Trade Routes at the End of the Sixteenth Century Hundreds of entrepreneurs from England, France, and Portugal sent ships to fish off the coast of Newfoundland to feed the growing population of Europe. The fur trade grew out of the Newfoundland fishing enterprise when fishermen who built winter shelters on the shore began trading with local Algonquian Indians (green lines). At the same time, European cities sent food, cloth, and manufactured goods to New Spain, in return for gold and silver (red lines). After 1580, the Portuguese began transporting slaves from Africa to sell in Brazil and New Spain (yellow lines).
Source: D. W. Meinig, *The Shaping of America* (New Haven, CT: Yale University Press, 1986), vol. 1, p. 56.

metal they spoke of was the copper that the Hurons to the west mined and traded. The winter was brutal. Even with food and care from the Indians, at the end of the winter almost a quarter of the party was dead. The French found that their survival depended on the native peoples.

Later expeditions fared as badly. The region was cold and remote. The French quarreled with their Indian hosts and fought among themselves. Because their early attempts at finding easy riches failed, the French were in effect demonstrating that European profits in North America would have to rest on exploration, conquest of the natives, and colonization. Needless to say, this principle of European colonialism was gradually established without the consent of the Indians who inhabited the land.

Spanish Outposts

Throughout the sixteenth century, European nations jockeyed for power on their own continent. Because most of these nations were at war with each other, North America was often a low priority. But when the fighting in Europe abated, the Europeans looked across the Atlantic in hopes of gaining an advantage over a rival nation or finding a new source of wealth.

Soon the French and English, who found no gold or jewels along the coast, discovered an easier source of wealth—stealing from the Spanish. Every season, Spanish ships laden with treasure from Mexico and South America moved out of the Caribbean into the Atlantic and north along the coast until they caught the trade winds home. By the middle of the sixteenth century, French ships were lying in wait off Florida or the Carolinas. Because it was cheaper than exploration, preying on Spanish ships became a national policy.

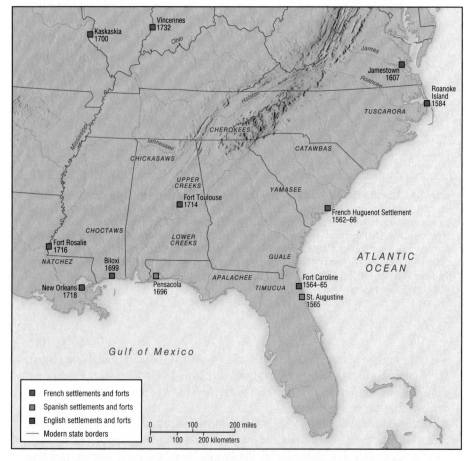

Map 2-2   European Colonization of the Southeast Beginning in the second half of the sixteenth century, the French, Spanish, and English established settlements in the Southeast.
Source: Charles Hudson, *The Southeastern Indians* (Knoxville: University of Tennessee Press, 1976), pp. 430–431.

To prevent these costly acts of piracy, King Philip II established a series of forts along both coasts of Florida. At the same time, a group of Huguenots (French Protestants) established a colony, Fort Caroline, near present-day Georgia. For the new commander of the Spanish forts, Pedro Menéndez de Avilés, the task was to destroy the French settlement. On a September morning in 1565, 500 Spanish soldiers surprised the French at Fort Caroline. Although the French surrendered and begged for mercy, they were slaughtered. The religious and nationalist conflicts of Europe had been transplanted to North America (see Map 2–2).

One of the forts established by the Spaniards, **St. Augustine**, settled in 1565, is the oldest continuously inhabited city of European origin in the United States. Most of Menéndez's ambitious plans for Spanish settlements, however, were undermined by local Indians whom the Spanish alienated. After attacks by the Orista Indians in 1576 and by England's **Francis Drake** a decade later, the Spanish abandoned all of their Florida forts except St. Augustine. They faced the reality that this was not a territory either of silver mines or of sedentary Indians who could easily be given out in *encomienda*. Spanish dreams of an empire in this part of North America had been reduced to a small coastal garrison designed to protect the far richer territories to the south. Although the Spanish would later establish other missions in Florida, their presence was peripheral to Spain's American empire.

NEW FRANCE: AN OUTPOST IN GLOBAL POLITICS AND ECONOMICS

The Spanish had given up hopes of an empire along the southeast coast of North America, but they had at least succeeded in scaring off the French from there. After the massacre at Fort Caroline, the French once again turned their focus to the St. Lawrence River. By the beginning of the seventeenth century, the French had discovered the beaver trade. The pelts found a ready market in Europe, where they were turned into felt hats. A trade that began almost as an accident on fishing expeditions soon became the basis for the French empire in modern Canada. The French were drawing the Indians into a global economy, a process that dramatically changed not only the world of the North Americans but that of the Europeans as well.

The Five Nations of Iroquois and the Political Landscape

The French intruded on a region where warfare among Indian tribes had recently been widespread. At least a century previously, five Iroquoian-speaking tribes living in today's New York State (see Map 2–3) had ended a period of feuding among themselves by establishing a league called the **Five Nations**. The members of this alliance were bound to keep peace among themselves and to coordinate a common defense against outsiders. Their new policy, combined with a relatively dense population due to their practicing agriculture for part of the year, easily rendered them the dominant political entity in the region. They made war against the Algonquian-speaking tribes living primarily to the north of the St. Lawrence, but they also attacked other Iroquoian-speaking groups and may even have annihilated some, such as the Hochelegans. The Hurons, for example, although speakers of an Iroquoian language, were the avowed enemies of the Five Nations when the French

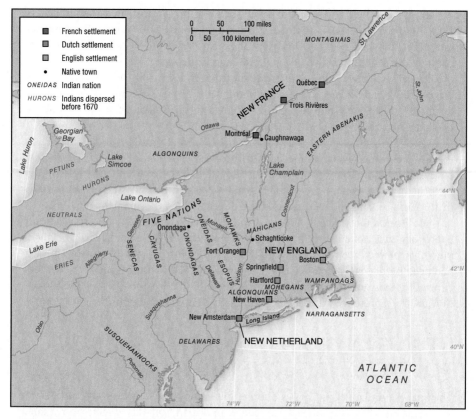

Map 2–3   The Iroquois Region in the Middle of the Seventeenth Century By the middle of the seventeenth century, the French, Dutch, and English had all established trading posts on the fringe of the Iroquois homeland. In the Beaver Wars (ca. 1648–1660), discussed later in the chapter, the Iroquois lashed out at their neighbors, dispersing several Huron tribes.
Source: Matthew Dennis, *Cultivating a Landscape of Peace* (Ithaca, NY: Cornell University Press, 1993), p. 16.

arrived. Such schisms would have serious consequences indeed when the Europeans became a factor in the political landscape.

However, despite the endemic warfare, we must not imagine a world of unending violence. Casualties tended to be light, which was not the case in European wars. Most often, the goal was not to kill as many of the enemy as possible, but to take young women and children captive so that they might be adopted to replace deceased clan members. Furthermore, these wars focused violence outward. The cruelty that Indians practiced on their enemies shocked Europeans, but unlike in European society, violence or even crime within a clan or extended family was virtually unknown.

Champlain Encounters the Hurons

After Cartier's last voyage in 1541, the French waited more than half a century before again attempting to plant a settlement in Canada. They were preoccupied with a brutal civil war. In 1594, Henry of Navarre, a Huguenot, emerged the victor, converted to Catholicism, and in 1598 issued the Edict of Nantes, which granted limited religious toleration to the Huguenots. The French could once again look to North America.

The French had continued to fish off Newfoundland, sending ships to the mainland to trade for beaver pelts. The French Crown now realized that extending commerce with the Indians could increase its power and wealth. Several early efforts to establish a permanent trading settlement failed, but in 1608, **Samuel de Champlain** and a small band retraced Cartier's route up the St. Lawrence River and established a post at Québec (see Map 2–4). Champlain, after several attempts, finally established the first French foothold in Canada, created a trading network along the St. Lawrence River, and learned how to live among people with a culture different from his own.

As the French government provided them with little support, Champlain's party depended on the aid of their Montagnais Indian hosts (an Algonquian-speaking tribe). To survive in New France, they had to adapt to Indian customs and assist their Indian benefactors in wars against their enemy. Killing the enemy in warfare was relatively easy for an experienced soldier such as Champlain. Indian forms of torture, however, seemed barbaric, not because Europeans did not engage

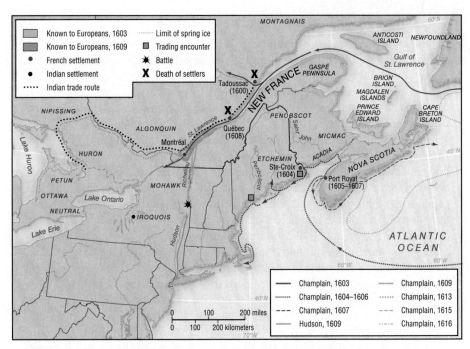

Map 2–4   French Exploration and Settlement, 1603–1616 Between 1603 and 1616, Samuel de Champlain and other French explorers made numerous trips up the St. Lawrence River and along the New England coast as far south as Cape Cod. They established several settlements, and they traded with local Indians and fought with them as well.

in torture—it was even a part of courtroom protocol to accept evidence elicited under torture—but because Europeans usually did not practice it against other soldiers.

Over the next several years, Champlain established a widespread fur trade in the region, linking the French and the Indians in a transformed transatlantic economy. Peasants were brought to New France in 1614 to raise food for the traders; Jesuits were sent to convert the Native Americans. The missionaries were more successful than the peasants. The persistence and adaptability of the missionaries and their ability to make Catholicism meaningful to Native Americans, as well as their encouragement of trading relationships, eventually gained them many converts.

After Champlain's original trade monopoly expired, his group competed with other Frenchmen in the fur trade. The French government was too busy with conflicts at home and abroad to support any of these outposts. To maintain a competitive edge, each summer Champlain pushed farther up the St. Lawrence River from his base at Québec to intercept the Indian tribes who were bringing pelts to the east. Each winter he also sent some of his men to live among the western Hurons and Algonquians to learn their languages and customs. These Indians already traded widely in corn, fish, nets, **wampum**, and other items. As French traders and Huron and Algonquian hunters created a trade network, each group became dependent on the others.

Creating a Middle Ground in New France

Indians and French traders accommodated each other's cultural practices. Together they created a **middle ground** neither fully European nor fully Indian, but rather a new world built from two different traditions. A middle ground came into being in other places in America as well, whenever Europeans and Indians needed each other and, at least for the present, could not achieve what they wanted through the use of force.

As the French drew the Native Americans into a global trade network, the Indians began to hunt more beaver than they needed for themselves, depleting the beaver population. Some historians believe that the introduction of European goods and commerce destroyed Native American cultures from within by making them dependent on those goods and inducing them to abandon their own crafts. Others have pointed out that the trade had different meanings for the French and for the Indians. For the French, trade was important for its cash value; for the Indians, trade goods were important both for the practical uses to which they could be put and for their symbolic value in religious ceremonies.

A métis (or mixed) culture soon emerged. Traders and priests learned to sleep on the cold ground without complaint and to eat Indian foods such as sagamité, a sort of cornmeal mush in which a small animal had been boiled. Many French traders found Indian wives. Most Native Americans accepted the taking of more than one wife, so they were not troubled if the French also had wives at home. Moreover, the Hurons were accustomed to adopting members of different ethnic groups, and the French were not averse to racial mixing. Both the Indians and the French believed mixed marriages strengthened trading and military alliances.

Struggles For Democracy

The Settlers and the Indians Learn to Compromise

Should we speak of democracy when people are forced to negotiate because no individual or group has enough power to force all others to acquiesce to their will? That is far from our usual understanding of democracy, in which formalized institutions guarantee that different voices will be heard. Nevertheless, the lack of extreme power on the part of any one group in early America may have helped engender our modern democracy. Europeans maintained outposts of empire; they were far, both literally and figuratively, from being at the center of empire, and as a result they learned to compromise. In the fur-trading regions of Canada, for example, negotiated settlement was the norm for many decades.

Never was this clearer than in the case of murder. Among the Native Americans, if someone was murdered by a fellow tribal member or ally, the killer and his people could atone for the death by offering gifts to the bereaved family or by presenting them with a captive to be adopted. (If someone was killed by an enemy tribe, it was tantamount to a declaration of war.) Among the French, a murder was resolved not by the killer and the kinfolk, but by the state. And the state demanded as punishment the death of the killer.

In the hunting season of 1682–1683, tensions percolated in the Keewenaw Peninsula of today's **Lake Superior**. The local Algonkian-speaking Sault Chippewas were embittered because disease had been running rampant, recent Iroquois attacks had gone unavenged by their French allies, and the French were beginning to trade directly with the Siouan peoples to the west, eliminating the need for the

French and Indian Traders *Voyageurs at Dawn* by Frances Anne Hopkins was not painted until the nineteenth century, but it conveys the interdependence of early French traders and their Native American partners.

continued

Hudson, soldiers such as Sir Francis Drake and Samuel de Champlain, the poor dragooned into sailing for Roanoke and left there to die, and Huron women who married French traders: all of them left their mark on the New World, even before the English planted their first permanent colonies in North America.

WHO, WHAT, WHERE

REVIEW QUESTIONS

1. What were the key European objectives in exploring North America in this period? To what extent did England, France, and the Netherlands achieve their objectives?

2. What do we know about the precontact history of the Five Nations of Iroquois? How did this history affect the world of colonial America? How did the European colonial ventures affect the Iroquois?

3. What was the middle ground, and how was it created?

CRITICAL-THINKING QUESTIONS

1. What were the ramifications of the northern Europeans failing to find cities equivalent to Tenochtitlan anywhere in North America?

2. Did the English, French, and Dutch have profoundly different attitudes toward the Indians at the outset? If the English had been the ones to spearhead the beaver trade, do you think that English traders and trappers might have married Huron women?

3. Early on, the Dutch faced the need to democratize their colony to some extent. Did other colonies of the era face a similar need? Why or why not?

SUGGESTED READINGS

Hoffman, Paul. *A New Andalusia and a Way to the Orient: The American Southeast During the Sixteenth Century*. Baton Rouge: Louisiana State University Press, 1990.

Kupperman, Karen. *Roanoke: The Abandoned Colony*. Lanham, MD: Rowman & Littlefield, 2007.

Quinn, David. *North America from Earliest Discovery to First Settlements*. New York: Harper & Row, 1977.

Shorto, Russell. *The Island at the Center of the World*. New York: Doubleday, 2004.

Trigger, Bruce. *Natives and Newcomers: Canada's "Heroic Age" Reconsidered*. Kingston, ON: McGill-Queen's University Press, 1985.

For further review materials and resource information, please visit www.oup.com/us/ofthepeople

CHAPTER 2: COLONIAL OUTPOSTS, 1550–1650
Primary Sources

2.1 LETTER FROM FRAY PEDRO DE FERIA TO PHILLIP II, KING OF SPAIN, ABOUT PAQUIQUINEO (1563)

Paquiquineo, a Native American boy, was kidnapped from the Chesapeake by Spanish explorers in 1561. He and a companion were taken to Spain, where they met the king. Paquiquineo refused to convert to Christianity and begged the monarch to send him home. His wish was granted, but he was sent first to Mexico; from there he was to be taken to the northern territories. While in Mexico, he became a Christian and was baptized "don Luis de Velasco," in honor of the viceroy. The following letter offers insight into his frustrating experiences among his captors. It was written by the head of the Dominican order in Mexico City soon after Paquiquineo had been left to his keeping. The friar was alight with zeal: he had in his hands a young man whom he believed would be a perfect intermediary in a major effort to proselytize in the northern territories.

Your Holy Royal Majesty:

In the last fleet there came to New Spain two Indians whom Captain Antonio Velázquez brought before Your Majesty, and whom Your Majesty ordered Captain Pedro Menéndez to return to their homeland as they were not baptized at the time they left the kingdom [of Spain]. As soon as they arrived in this city they got so sick and arrived at such a point that it was not thought they would escape death. For that reason, having learned of their desire to be baptized, as they had asked for it more than once, they were given the sacrament of baptism. Our Lord was moved to give them back their health. The religious [brothers] of this your Convent of Santo Domingo begged your Viceroy to keep them here among us so we might instruct them in the things of our holy Catholic Faith and also so that they would become tied by affection to the friars. It was done, and thus they have been and still are among us, and have been treated like sons and taught the things of our faith. Seeing that they are now Christians and members of the church, and that if they were returned to their land alone without ministers who could keep them from straying from the faith and from Christian law, and if they were to return to their rites and idolatries and thus lose their souls, then their baptism would have caused them to be damned. Permitting all of that to happen would seem to be a great inhumanity, even a grave offense against our Lord, and a disservice to Your Majesty. It is believed that your desire to return them to their land depended on their being pagans, as they were when they left you. Considering as well the fine presence and capacity of this Indian, and what he tells us of his land, that it is well populated with peaceful people, and believing as we do that Our Lord has arranged all of this business and sent this Indian so that he may be the means of saving all of that land, your viceroy, with the zeal of a true Christian and a Catholic and a vassal of Your Majesty . . . communicated with the Provincial and other leading men of our Dominican Order what we might do assuming we received the permission of Your majesty so that the excellent opportunity we had been offered by means of the conversion of this Indian would not be lost. Thus the Order offered to send religious brothers on this project. . . . And to be more effective your Viceroy, desirous of being of service to Our Lord and to Your Majesty, offered to pay expenses himself . . . There then arrived the moment to deal with the captain [of the royal convoy] Pedro Menéndez about the necessary measures for the execution of this business . . . Because he did not have the necessary orders, or because Our Lord ordered it otherwise, wanting the expedition to be better guided by Your Majesty's hands, he denied the departure of the religious . . .

The Archbishop[1] then ordered Pedro Menéndez not to return the Indians to their homelands since no ministers would go with them. If he wanted to bring them back to Spain to go before Your Majesty, of course he could do that. The Indians were at full liberty to go to Spain and even encouraged to do so, but they said that if they were not going to return to their land, they preferred to stay here than to go all the way to Spain. Thus they remained here and are still among us, who take care to teach them the doctrine and all that is appropriate. Your Viceroy takes a special interest in them and oversees their good treatment . . .

Understanding the desire that exists on the part of the Order to serve Our Lord and Your Majesty and the opportunity that exists just now to save those people [of the northern territory] and the misfortune it would be if this opportunity were lost, it seems Your Majesty was well served. Those people are peaceful, and it is believed that they would be even more so if this Indian were to go there and give an account of what he has seen and the benefits he has received. No more than forty or fifty men would have to go with the religious, in one ship, which would be able to pacify the people there. . . . May Our Lord keep the holy person of Your Majesty and augment your territories for his service . . . Mexico City, February 13, 1563.

Fray Pedro de Feria

Source: Archivo General de Indios, Seville, Spain. Record Group Mexico, vol. 280, February 1563. Our own translation.

2.2 RICHARD HAKLUYT, EXCERPT FROM *THE PRINCIPAL NAVIGATIONS, VOYAGES, TRAFFIQUES, AND DISCOVERIES OF THE ENGLISH NATION* (1589–1600)

Toward the end of Queen Elizabeth I's reign, two cousins, both named Richard Hakluyt, became involved in the project of advancing English explorations and conquests overseas. The elder Hakluyt became known to merchants and geographers for his immense collection of letters and documents related to English interactions abroad, and the younger eventually published the collection in three volumes in 1598, 1599, and 1600. The latter Hakluyt conceived of his project as showing the way to young Englishmen who also wished to pursue exploration and conquest. The original spelling has been retained in the case of this document in order to show how differently the English language of earlier centuries reads.

"A brief relation of two sundry voyages made by the worshipful M. William Haukins [Hawkins] of Plimmouth, father to Sir John Haukins knight, late treasurer to her Majesties Navie, in the yeere 1530 and 1532"

Olde M. William Haukins of Plimmouth, a man for his wisedome, valure, experience, and skill in sea causes much esteemed, and beloved of K. Henry the 8, and being one of

---

[1]The Archbishop at the time was a Dominican. He was a friend of the Provincial of the Order and strongly in favor of any plan that would help the Dominicans gain influence in the New World.

might be. They hurried out together, and saw with astonishment the phenomenon which now appeared to their sight, but could not agree upon what it was; some believed it to be an uncommonly large fish or animal, while others were of opinion it must be a very big house floating on the sea. At length the spectators concluded that this wonderful object was moving towards the land, and that it must be an animal or something else that had life in it; it would therefore be proper to inform all the Indians on the inhabited island of what they had seen, and put them on their guard. Accordingly they sent off a number of runners and watermen to carry the news to their scattered chiefs, that they might send off in every direction for the warriors, with a message that they should come on immediately. These arriving in numbers, and having themselves viewed the strange appearance, and observing that it was actually moving towards the entrance of the river or bay; concluded it to be a remarkably large house in which the Mannitto (the Great or Supreme Being) himself was present, and that he probably was coming to visit them. By this time the chiefs were assembled at York island, and deliberating in what manner they should receive their Mannitto on his arrival. Every measure was taken to be well provided with plenty of meat for a sacrifice. The women were desired to prepare the best victuals. All the idols or images were examined and put in order, and a grand dance was supposed not only to be an agreeable entertainment for the Great Being, but it was believed that it might, with the addition of a sacrifice, contribute to appease him if he was angry with them. The conjurers were also set to work, to determine what this phenomenon portended, and what the possible result of it might be. To these and to the chiefs and wise men of the nations, men, women and children were looking up for advice and protection. Distracted between hope and fear, they were at a loss what to do; a dance, however, commenced in great confusion. While in this situation, fresh runners arrived declaring it to be a large house of various colors, and crowded with living creatures. It appears now to be certain, that it is the great Mannitto, bringing them some kind of game, such as he had not given them before, but other runners soon after arriving declare that it is positively full of human beings, of quite a different color from that of the Indians, and dressed differently from them; that in particular one of them was dressed entirely in red who must be the Mannitto himself. They are hailed from the vessel in a language they do not understand yet they shout or yell in return by way of answer, according to the custom of their country; many are for running off to the woods, but are pressed by others to stay, in order not to give offence to their visitor, who might find them out and destroy them. The house, some say large canoe, at last stops, and a canoe of a smaller size comes on shore with the red man, and some others in it; some stay with his canoe to guard it. The chiefs and wise men, assembled in council, form themselves into a large circle, towards which the man in red clothes approaches with two others. He salutes after their manner. They are lost in admiration [stunned surprise]; the dress, the manners, the whole appearance of the unknown strangers is to them a subject of wonder; but they are particularly struck with him who wore the red coat all glittering with gold lace,[2] which they could in no manner account for. He, surely, must be the great Mannitto, but why should he have a white skin? Meanwhile, a large *Hackhack* [gourd] is brought by one of his servants, from which an unknown substance is poured out into a small cup or glass, and handed to the supposed Mannitto. He drinks—has the glass filled again, and hands it to the chief standing next to him. The chief receives it, but only smells the contents and passes it on to the next chief, who does the same. The glass or cup thus passes through the circle, without the liquor being tasted by any one, and is upon the point of being returned to the red clothed Mannitto, when one of the Indians, a brave man and a great warrior,

---

[2]Note that this is not really how the Dutch officers dressed in 1609. It is, however, how British officers dressed in the eighteenth century, when the story was recorded.

suddenly jumps up and harangues the assembly on the impropriety of returning the cup with its contents. It was handed to them, says he, by the Mannitto, that they should drink out of it, as he himself had done. To follow his example would be pleasing to him; but to return what he had given them might provoke his wrath, and bring destruction on them. And since the orator believed it for the good of that nation that the contents offered them should be drunk, an as no one else would do it, he would drink it himself, let the consequence be what it might; it was better for one man to die, than that a whole nation should be destroyed. He then took the glass, and bidding the assembly a solemn farewell, at once drank up its whole contents. Every eye was fixed on the resolute chief, to see what the effect the unknown liquor would produce. He soon began to stagger, and at last fell prostrate on the ground. His companions now bemoan his fate, he falls into a sound sleep, and they think he has expired. He wakes again, jumps up and declares, that he has enjoyed the most delicious sensations, and that he never before felt himself so happy as after he had drunk the cup. He asks for more, his wish is granted; the whole assembly then imitate him, and all become intoxicated.

After this general intoxication had ceased, for they say that while it lasted the whites had confined themselves to their vessel, the man with the red clothes returned again, and distributed presents among them, consisting of beads, axes, hoes, and stockings such as the white people wear. They soon became familiar with each other, and began to converse by signs. The Dutch made them understand that they would not stay here, that they would return home again, but would pay them another visit the next year, when they would bring them more presents and stay with them awhile; but as they could not live without eating, they should want a little land of them to sow seeds, in order to raise herbs and vegetables to put into their broth. They went away as they had said, and returned in the following season, when both parties were much rejoiced to see each other; but the whites laughed at the Indians, seeing that they knew not the use of the axes and hoes they had given them the year before; for they had these hanging to their waists as ornaments, and the stockings were made use of as tobacco pouches. The whites now put the handles to the former for them, and cut trees down before their eyes, hoed up the ground, and put the stockings on their legs. Here, they say, a general laughter ensued among the Indians, that they had remained ignorant of the use of such valuable implement, and had born the weight of such heavy metal hanging to their necks, for such a length of time. They took every white man they saw for an inferior mannitto attendant upon the Supreme Deity who shone superior in the red and laced clothes. As the whites became daily more familiar with the Indians, they at last proposed to stay with them, and asked only for so much ground for a garden lot, as, they said the hide of a bullock would cover or encompass, which hide was spread before them. The Indians readily granted this apparently reasonable request; but the whites then took a knife, and beginning at one end of the hide, cut it up to a long rope, not thicker than a child's finger, so that by the time the whole was cut up, it made an great heap; they then took the rope at one end, and drew it gently along, carefully avoiding its breaking. It was drawn out into a circular form, and being closed at its ends encompassed a large piece of ground. The Indians were surprised at the superior wit of the whites, but did not wish to contend with them about a little land, as they had still enough themselves. The white and red men lived contentedly together for a long time, though the former from time to time asked for more land, which was readily obtained, and thus they gradually proceeded higher up the mahicannittuck [Hudson River], until the Indians began to believe that they would soon want all their country, which in the end proved true.

Source: John Heckewelder, *An Account of the history, manners, and customs of the Indian nations, who once inhabited Pennsylvania and neighboring states* (Philadelphia: Historical Society of Pennsylvania, 1876 [1819]), pp. 71–75 and 321–322.

The English Come to Stay
1600–1660

< **Elizabeth Paddy Wensley, ca. 1670**

65

The Predicament of Pocahontas, Alias Rebecca

Because Pocahontas was the subject of a 1995 animated Disney movie, many people do not realize that she was a real girl who lived during difficult times. Born in the 1590s in what is today **Virginia**, **Pocahontas** was the daughter of **Powhatan**, paramount chief of at least 20 tribes, but she herself held no special status. In her world, although men ruled, power passed through the female line. (A chief was thus succeeded by his sister's son, not his own son.) Pocahontas's mother was unimportant (she may even have been a prisoner of war), so Pocahontas was not marked to rule or even to marry a chief. As a child, Pocahontas would have worked alongside other children to protect the village's crops from hungry animals and birds.

When the girl was about 10 years old, events occurred that would eventually lead to immense change for her people. In 1607, the Jamestown colonists arrived and built a permanent fort. Despite the trade opportunities, many of Powhatan's people did not want them there, and some skirmishing occurred. Eventually, an Englishman named John Smith, president of the struggling colony, came upriver to try to trade for corn, and some relatives of Powhatan kidnapped him and brought him to the high chief. Through sign language, he attempted to communicate his desire for trade. For the next several weeks, he was left in the company of young Pocahontas; they tried to teach each other something of their two languages. When Powhatan felt confident that he had made a friend and trade partner of the Englishman, he had him escorted back to the fort. Later he sent advisers to visit, and they took Pocahontas along to translate. In the report that Smith sent back home, he said nothing about Powhatan ever having tried to kill him, or about Pocahontas having rescued him. That was a story he told 17 years later, when all the principals were dead. (In his writings of later years, Smith elaborated on the theme of beautiful young women having rescued him from death everywhere he went.)

Smith returned to England shortly after his sojourn with the Indians ended. Battles escalated between the hungry English colonists—who wanted the Indians to pay them tribute—and the Indians—who had no intention of doing so. Eventually, it was learned that Pocahontas was visiting a village on the Potomac. She was kidnapped and brought to Jamestown, where she was held prisoner for a year.

The English wanted the Indians to agree to pay tribute, or at least to offer a significant ransom. Powhatan, however, could not afford to do that for a politically insignificant child. In the meantime, the colonists taught Pocahontas English and attempted to convert her to Christianity, hoping she could at least be an effective go-between. Pocahontas does seem to have learned English quite easily, but she steadfastly refused to convert to Christianity.

One day in 1613, in frustration, the English took her aboard a war ship and went up the James River, approaching her father's village, training their guns on the shore. They wanted Powhatan to fear for his daughter's life and the lives of his people. At this juncture, a young man named John Rolfe, who had apparently been one of Pocahontas's English teachers, asked the English colonial governor for permission to marry the girl. Messengers were dispatched to Powhatan, who immediately consented to the marriage. In his world, the daughters of noblemen often had to marry the enemy in an effort to broker peace.

Pocahontas faced a difficult future as a prisoner-wife, though it was a familiar fate for indigenous women. She agreed and found the strength to do what she was expected to do. She took her husband's god as her god and became a Christian. Three days later, she went through the marriage ceremony. When it came time to choose her baptismal name of Rebecca, the English were startled to learn that "Pocahontas" was not her real name, but a childhood nickname. Her real name was Matoaka.

Pocahontas continued to protect her own customs and sense of what was right even after the marriage. She did not always do what Christians thought she should do. John Rolfe appeared to be very happy with her, but he wrote in frustration that the Indians "doe runn headlong, yea with joy, into destruction and perpetuall damnation."

In the spring of 1616, Pocahontas and her husband and young son, Thomas, were asked to travel to England to help rescue the Virginia Company from financial disaster. Several of Powhatan's highest-ranking advisers accompanied them, so as to glean needed information about these strangers. Pocahontas worked to establish confidence in the venture. But she also insisted, through her husband, that her people be well compensated for their land. Her experience of England had been enough to convince her that negotiated settlements were the most they could hope for; they could not win wars against Renaissance technology. For the first time, she understood the magnitude of her people's predicament. In 1617, just as they were about to sail for home, Pocahontas succumbed to a European lung ailment and died. She was no more than 21 years old.

THE FIRST CHESAPEAKE COLONIES

When Queen Elizabeth died in 1603, she was succeeded by her Scottish cousin, King James I, who immediately signed a treaty with Spain ending decades of warfare. With peace established, all those who had lived off privateering and warfare had to look for another source of income. They joined with old advocates of colonization to establish new colonies in North America. In 1606, James granted charters to two groups of English merchants and military men, one in London and the other in **Plymouth**. The Plymouth group would colonize the northern coast, and the Londoners the Chesapeake region. Each operation was chartered as a private company, which would raise money from shareholders and finance, populate, and regulate its colonies.

Founding Virginia

In 1606, the Plymouth-based company deposited some settlers at the mouth of the Kennebec River in today's Maine, but the climate defeated them within a season. The Virginia Company (named in honor of the recently deceased, never-married queen) had wealthy London backers and met with greater success. Just before Christmas in 1606, it sent out three ships under Captain Christopher Newport, a one-legged veteran Atlantic explorer. When the ships arrived at Virginia on April 26, 1607, the colonists learned that they were to be governed by a council of seven men. Unfortunately, two of them, Edward Maria Wingfield, an arrogant gentleman and investor in the company, and **Captain John Smith**, the equally arrogant but considerably more capable soldier of fortune, despised each other. By the end of the summer, another council member had been executed because he was supposedly a double agent for the Spanish. The early history of Jamestown was marked by internal wrangling. External conflict soon developed as well, as the colonists antagonized their Indian hosts. Almost everything that could go wrong did.

The experience of Roanoke notwithstanding, the English still hoped to find a land like Mexico, filled with gold and other less glamorous raw materials. Whatever limited manufacturing was needed could be performed either by English criminals, sent over to work as their punishment, or by indentured servants, English men and women from the lowest ranks of society who agreed to work for a set period to pay their transportation expenses. The colonists expected to trade with the local Indians, who would be the primary suppliers of food.

The Virginia Company planned to get the colony up and running within seven years. During that period, all colonists would work for the Company, which would give them food and shelter. At the end of that time, they would receive grants of land. The Company evidently thought the colony would need a great deal of direction, for about one-third of the original settlers were gentlemen, that is, members of the

The Fort at Jamestown
This nineteenth-century engraving of Jamestown in 1607 shows the difficulties of unloading goods from a ship in the earliest days of settlement.

elite, a proportion of the colony's population that was six times higher than it was in England.

The Company also sent skilled laborers, many with skills of little use in the colony, such as tailors, goldsmiths, and a perfumer. Some were thought necessary to support the gentlemen. Others were to work the gold and precious gems colonists hoped to find. Farmers and ordinary laborers, on the other hand, were in short supply, for it was assumed that the Indians would fill these roles.

Starving Times

Poor planning and bad luck placed the colonists on swampy ground with bad water. The salty water of the James River could be poisonous, and in summer it became a breeding ground for typhoid and dysentery. Some historians have argued that these diseases left the survivors too weak to plant food, whereas others note that many of the healthy seemed to prefer prospecting for gold. The colonists depended on the resentful Powhatan Indians for food, and the resulting malnutrition made the effects of disease worse. These factors, along with skirmishes with the Powhatans, led to appallingly high mortality rates. By September 1607, half of the more than 100 original colonists were dead, and by the following spring only 38 were still alive. Although the Company sent over more colonists, they continued to die off at extraordinary rates. As late as 1616, the English population was only 350, although more than five times that number had emigrated from England (see Table 3–1).

Troubled Relations with the Powhatans

In Virginia, the English encountered the powerful paramount chieftaincy of the Powhatan Indians. Originally a small tribe of Algonquian-speaking Indians like many others in the region, the Powhatans had attained great power when, through a series of politically motivated marriages, a young chief of theirs had inherited the rulerships of several other tribes, some through his mother and some through his father. This man, called Powhatan in honor of his people, took his larger-than-usual force of warriors and made a series of strategic attacks, then followed up by taking a wife from each of numerous chiefly families in the area. At the time of the arrival of the English, Powhatan's chieftaincy included about 20,000 Indians, divided into about three dozen tribes.

Powhatan hoped to use the English to buttress his power by trading for metal goods and textiles, but he recognized that the strangers might constitute a threat. In his negotiations first with Smith and then with others, he attempted to tie the English into his world as his vassals. But of course the English hoped for the inverse. At one point, the English put a fake crown on the kneeling Powhatan's head, imitating the ceremonies in which feudal princes pledged allegiance to a king. The Indians, however, remained unmoved by the ceremony.

With his large force, Lord De La Warr immediately set out to subjugate the Indians. He ordered Powhatan to return all English captives taken in prior skirmishes. When Powhatan refused, De La Warr ordered an attack on an Indian village. The English killed about 75 inhabitants, burned the town and its cornfields, and captured the wife of a chieftain and her children. As the English sailed back

Table 3–1 English Population of Virginia, 1607–1640

Population in Virginia Colony	Immigration to Virginia Colony
104 (April 1607)	104 (April 1607)
38 (January 1608)	
	120 (January 1608, 1st supply)
130 (September 1608)	
	70 (September 1608, 2nd supply)
200 (late September 1608)	
100 (Spring 1609)	
	300 (Fall 1609, 3rd supply)
	540 (1610)
450 (April 1611)	
	660 (1611)
682 (January 1612)	
350 (January 1613)	
	45 (1613–1616)
351 (1616)	
600 (December 1618)	
	900 (1618–1620)
887 (March 1620)	
	1,051 (1620–1621)
943 (March 1621)	
	1,580 (1621–1622)
1,240 (March 1622)	
	1,935 (1622–1623)
1,241 (April 1623)	
	1,646 (1623–1624)
1,275 (February 1624)	
1,210 (1625)	
	9,000 (1625–1634)
4,914 (1634)	
	6,000 (1635–1640)
8,100 (1640)	total: 23,951

Source: Data from Carville Earle, *Geographical Inquiry and American Historical Problems* (Stanford, CA: Stanford University Press, 1992), and Virginia Bernhard, "Men, Women, and Children at Jamestown: Population and Gender in Early Virginia, 1607–1610," *Journal of Southern History* 58 (1992).

Note: Although about 24,000 men and women immigrated to Virginia between 1607 and 1640, in 1640 the population stood at only 8,100. Most of the inhabitants fell victim to disease, although the Indian uprising of 1622 took 347 lives.

to Jamestown, they threw the children overboard and shot them as they swam in the water. So opened the First **Anglo-Powhatan War**, the first of three conflicts between 1610 and 1646. Eventually, a brief peace was ushered in when Pocahontas married John Rolfe, but it could not last.

Toward a New Economic Order and the Rise of Democracy

The tide finally turned against the Powhatans, not because of a failure in diplomacy or the politics of marriage, but because the English finally found a way to make money in Virginia. Pocahontas's husband, John Rolfe, developed a strain of tobacco that found a ready market in England. It transformed the colony almost overnight. Within three years, Virginia was shipping 50,000 pounds of tobacco to England per year. Suddenly Virginia experienced an economic boom. By 1619, a man working by himself was making £200 in one crop, and a man with six indentured servants could make £1,000, money only the nobility was accustomed to. Once fortunes this large could be made, the race to Virginia was on.

Powhatan and English Dwellings
These are reconstructions of typical Powhatan Indian and English homes, ca. 1607. Both are dark and small.

All that was needed to make money in Virginia was land and people to work it. In 1616, the Virginia Company, which had land but no money, offered land as dividends to its stockholders. Those already living in Virginia were given land, and anyone who came over (or brought another person over) was to be granted 50 acres a head (called a **headright**). The Company was moving toward private enterprise, away from the corporate, company-directed economy of the early years. The leadership of the colony also gave itself grants, laying the basis for its own wealth and power. It was far easier to obtain land in Virginia than in England.

To attract settlers, the Company replaced martial law with common law, guaranteeing colonists all the rights of the English people. The colonists were also granted greater rights to self-government than were enjoyed by those who lived in England. The first elected representative government in the New World, the Virginia House of Burgesses (renamed the General Assembly after the American Revolution), met in Jamestown on July 30, 1619.

These inducements attracted 3,500 settlers to Virginia in three years, three times as many as had come in the preceding 10 years. By accident more than planning, Virginia had found the formula for a successful English colony. It was one that all other colonies generally followed: offering colonists greater opportunities to make money and greater rights of self-government than they had at home. These changes came too late, however, to rescue the Virginia Company, which went bankrupt in 1624. King James I dissolved the Company and turned Virginia into a **royal colony** under his control.

Toward the Destruction of the Powhatans

As the new colonists spread out, establishing private plantations, English settlers claimed all the Indians' prime farmland on both sides of the James River and began to move up its tributaries (see Map 3–1). At the same time, the Powhatans became increasingly dependent on English goods such as metal tools. Moreover, as the English population began to grow its own food, it had less need of Indian food, the only significant commodity the Indians had to trade. The Indians slowly accumulated a debt to the English and lost their economic independence.

After Powhatan died, his more militant brother, Opechancanough, decided to get rid of the English. He wanted to convince them to go home or at least to limit their spreading. On the morning of March 22, 1622, in an extraordinarily well-planned attack, the Indians struck at most of the plantations along the James River, killing about one-quarter of the colonists. The Second Anglo-Powhatan War, which continued for another 10 years, had begun. This war marked a turning point in English policy. Although some of the English recognized that the Indian attack had been caused by their "own perfidiouse dealing," most decided that the Indians were untrustworthy and incapable of being converted to the English way of life. Therefore, a policy of extermination was justified. Some were almost happy that the Indians had attacked; John Smith concluded that the massacre "will be good for the Plantation, because now we have just cause to destroy them by all meanes possible." Until this point, the English had claimed only land that the Indians were not currently farming. Now they seized territory the Indians had just cleared and planted. In only 15 years' time, the English and Indians in Virginia had become implacable enemies.

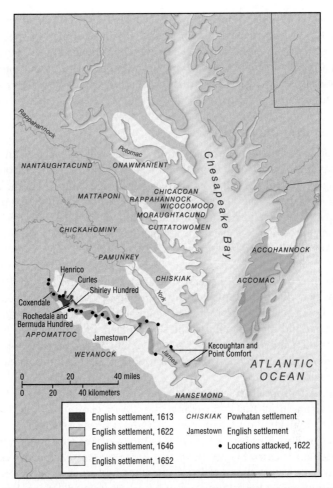

Map 3-1   English Encroachments on Indian Land, 1613–1652 After John Rolfe's development of a marketable strain of tobacco, the English spread out through the Chesapeake region, encroaching steadily on Indian land. Tobacco planters preferred land along the rivers, for casks filled with tobacco bound for England were more easily transported by ship.

Source: Frederic Gleach, *Powhatan's World and Colonial Virginia* (Lincoln: University of Nebraska Press, 1997), and James Horn, *Adapting to a New World: English Society in the Seventeenth-Century Chesapeake* (Chapel Hill: University of North Carolina Press, 1994).

Indian resistance only made the English more determined to stay, and with the tobacco economy booming, settlers poured into Virginia. They spread across the Chesapeake to the Eastern Shore and north to the Potomac River. The aged Opechancanough, determined to make one final push, struck again on April 18, 1644, killing about 400 and taking many prisoners.

The Third Anglo-Powhatan War ended, however, in the Indians' total defeat two years later. Opechancanough was killed. The English took complete possession of the land between the James and York Rivers. Henceforth, no Indian was allowed to enter this territory unless he was bringing a message from a chief. Any English person who sheltered an Indian without permission was to be put to death. The land north of the York River was set aside for the Indians, making it the first American Indian reservation. Soon, English settlers moved into that region, too. It was not the last time that the English settlers would break a treaty with the Indians.

A New Colony in Maryland

Virginia's original plan to make money from trading with the local Indians was not entirely forgotten. When tobacco prices dipped in the 1620s, trade became attractive once again. By the late 1620s, an outpost had been established at the northern end of the Chesapeake Bay to obtain beaver furs from the Susquehannocks. Sir George Calvert, the first Lord Baltimore and a Catholic, saw the commercial potential of this region and in 1632 persuaded King Charles I, a Catholic sympathizer, to grant him the land north of the Potomac and south of the Delaware that was "not yet cultivated and planted." This territory became **Maryland**, the first **proprietary colony**, that is, a colony owned literally by an individual and his heirs. (Virginia was originally a **charter colony**, held by a group of private shareholders. Unlike royal colonies, in charter and proprietary colonies the English Crown turned over both financing and management to the shareholders or proprietors.) Maryland, named after the Catholic queen of England, remained the hereditary possession of the Calvert family until the American Revolution, although the majority of the settlers were not Catholics.

As the first proprietary colony, Maryland established a pattern for subsequent proprietorships. The proprietor had extensive powers to grant land and make laws by himself, but perhaps because Calvert knew he would have to compete for settlers with Virginia, which had a representative government, he agreed to a representative assembly. In 1649, that assembly passed the Act of Toleration, which said that no one would be "compelled to the beliefe or exercise of any other Religion against his or her consent." Even though religious toleration was extended only to Christians, Maryland was among the most tolerant places in the world. Moreover, this right was extended to women as well as men. (This experiment in religious toleration faced a crisis, however, in 1689, when Coode's Rebellion overthrew the proprietor, making Maryland temporarily a royal colony and, in 1702, establishing the Anglican Church. In 1715, the Calvert family was restored to power. See Chapter 4 for more on the effects of England's "Glorious Revolution" in America.)

Although Maryland's population increased slowly, the familiar political economy emerged quickly. As in Virginia, attracting colonists required greater opportunities and freedoms—of self-government and of religion—than they enjoyed in England. Even during the conflict with the Powhatan Confederacy, the booming tobacco economy drew settlers to Virginia and, after about 1650, to Maryland as well. Although they had separate governments, Virginia and Maryland had similar political economies, based on tobacco. The defeat of the Indians made more land available for cultivation; the colonies needed only people to work it.

THE ECONOMY BASED ON SLAVERY EMERGES

Chesapeake society in the first half of the seventeenth century was shaped by four forces: weak government, the market for tobacco, the availability of land, and the need for labor. Because government was weak, the forces of plantation agriculture were unchecked, and the profit motive operated without restraint. Those who could take advantage of these opportunities—male and female both—profited wildly, whereas the poor, both white and African, were without defense. In this environment an economy based on slavery took root.

The Insatiable Demand for Cheap Labor

Once the crises of the early years had passed, the Chesapeake's greatest problem was securing laborers to produce tobacco. As soon as John Rolfe brought in his first successful crop, the Virginia governor began pressing England to send him its poor. The Virginia Company also encouraged the emigration of women, for the young colony was primarily male. No matter how many colonists came, however, the demand for labor always outstripped the supply. By 1660, 50,000 Britons, mostly single men in their 20s, had migrated to the Chesapeake, but the population was still only a little over 35,000. Because of disease and malnutrition, the death rate remained extraordinarily high. It did not help that most of the colonists came from impoverished backgrounds and arrived alone and friendless to face a harsh new situation.

The profits from tobacco were so great and the risk of death so high that landowners squeezed out every penny of profit as quickly as they could. Those with land and servants to work it could become rich overnight. Colonial officials, including members of the legislature, discovered a variety of ways to make themselves wealthy. Great wealth, however, could be achieved only by the labor of others, and the demand for labor was almost insatiable. Perhaps 90 percent of those who migrated to the Chesapeake in the seventeenth century came as servants, and half died before completing their term of service. In England, servants had some basic protections, but in Virginia, working conditions were deadly brutal. In 1623, Richard Frethorne, a young Virginia servant "with weeping tears" wrote to his parents in England, "We must work early and late for a mess of water gruel and a mouthful of bread and beef."

Servants might be beaten so severely that they died, or they might find their indentures (the contract that bound them to service for a period of usually seven years) sold from one master to another. They found little protection from the courts. They were not, in fact, enslaved people. They would become free if they outlived their period of indenture; they retained all of the rights of English people, and their servitude was not hereditary. But they were far worse off than servants in England.

Some colonists tried to resolve the problem of the labor shortage by purchasing Indian slaves who had been captured by other Indians in wars farther west, but there were not nearly enough of these to meet the demand (see Chapter 4).

The Origins of African Slavery in the Chesapeake

Other New World plantation societies in which labor was in short supply had already turned to African slavery, so it was probably only a matter of time until the Chesapeake did as well. Historians do not know precisely when slavery was first practiced on a widespread basis in the Chesapeake, but Africans first arrived in Virginia in 1619, when a Dutch ship sailing off course sold its cargo of "twenty Negars" to the Virginians. As long as life expectancy was low, it was generally more profitable for a planter to purchase an indentured servant for a period of seven years than an enslaved person for life. Not until life expectancy improved toward the end of the seventeenth century were significant numbers of African slaves imported into the Chesapeake.

All the English plantation colonies followed the same pattern in making the transition from white servitude to African slavery. The transition was quick in some places and slow in others; in Virginia, it took about three-quarters of a century. The primary factors dictating how readily English colonists adopted African slavery were the need for plantation laborers and the availability of African slaves at a good price. If there was any discussion about the justice of slavery, the English claimed that slavery was an appropriate punishment for certain crimes and for prisoners taken in just wars. No white people were ever enslaved in the English colonies, however. It was a practice reserved for "strangers," primarily foreigners of a non-Christian religion. At first, some of the Africans who ended up in the colonies were those who came as the domestic servants of well-to-do colonists, not as chattel slaves. In addition, some buyers in the early years allowed Africans to earn their freedom as did English indentured servants. Still, all the British colonies eventually practiced permanent chattel slavery, and it became critical to plantation economies. African slaves were even brought back to the British Islands, and by the middle of the eighteenth century, 2 percent of London's population was African.

Even before they had substantial contact with African people, the English and other northern Europeans probably harbored prejudice against dark-skinned people. By the second half of the sixteenth century, the English were depicting Africans in derogatory terms, saying that Africans were unattractive, with "dispositions most savage and brutish," a "people of beastly living" who "contract no matrimonie, neither have respect to chastity." Northern Europeans considered African women particularly monstrous, sexually promiscuous, and neglectful of their children. Although these views were not explicitly used to justify slavery, they formed the basis for the racism that would develop along with the slave system.

During the first half of the seventeenth century, African slavery and white and African servitude existed side by side. The Chesapeake was a society with slaves, but it was still not a slave society. The first clear evidence of permanent and generalized enslavement of Africans in the Chesapeake dates to 1639, when the Maryland Assembly passed a law guaranteeing "all the Inhabitants of this Province being Christians (Slaves excepted)" all the rights and liberties of "any natural born subject of England." The first Virginia law recognizing slavery, passed in 1661, said that any English servant who ran away with an African would have to serve additional time not only for himself but for the African as well. Such Africans were clearly already understood to be slaves for life and hence were incapable of serving any additional time.

Such laws reveal the great familiarity that existed between white and Black servants. Slaves and white servants worked together, enjoyed leisure together, had sexual relations with each other, and ran away together. As late as 1680, most of the plantation laborers were still white indentured servants. There is no evidence that they were kept separate from Africans by law or inclination.

As long as the Black population remained small, the color line was blurry. Not until late in the seventeenth century were laws passed that restricted free African Americans. In fact, in 1660, Anthony Johnson, an African who had arrived in Virginia as a servant in 1621, owned both land and African slaves. In the 40 years that he had been in Virginia, slavery had become institutionalized and recognized by the law, but laws separating the races had yet to be enacted.

Gender and the Social Order in the Chesapeake

The founders of England's colonies hoped to replicate the social order they had known at home. As early as 1619, the Virginia Company began to bring single women to the colony to become brides of the unmarried planters. As in England, it was expected that men would perform all the "outside" labor, including planting, farming, and tending large farm animals. Women would do all the "inside" work, including preserving and preparing food, spinning and weaving, making and repairing clothing, and gardening. In English society, a farmer's wife was not simply a man's sexual partner and companion; she was also the mistress of a successful household economy. Both men and women were vital to the society the English wanted to create in the Chesapeake.

However, the powerful tobacco economy transformed both the economy and society of the New World. With profits from tobacco so high, women went directly into the tobacco fields instead of the kitchen. Children were in the fields as soon as they could work. Only when a man became wealthy did he hire a servant—often a woman—to replace his wife in the fields. As a result, for many years, Virginia society lacked the "comforts of home" that women produced, such as prepared food, homemade clothing, and even soap. Tobacco was everything.

Colonial society also weakened patriarchal controls. Chesapeake governments tried—but failed—to control immigrant women, insisting, for example, that a woman receive government permission before marrying and prosecuting for slander women who spoke out against the government or their neighbors. But colonial government was relatively weak, and women, far from their own fathers, found themselves unexpectedly free from traditional restrictions.

Although women without the protection of fathers were vulnerable in seventeenth-century plantation societies, in a world where men outnumbered women three or four to one, women were often in a position of relative power. Local governments struggled to impose order by prosecuting women for adultery, fornication, and giving birth to illegitimate children. The public, however, was more tolerant of sexual misconduct than government officials were. The first generation of women to immigrate to the Chesapeake region married relatively late—in their mid-20s or later. As a result, they had relatively few children, and it was many decades before

America In The World
The English Enter the Slave Trade

By the sixteenth century, slavery did not exist in England, and its people prided themselves on their "free air." History books in the Anglo-American world have tended to blame the Portuguese and the Spanish for initiating the African slave trade and the Dutch merchants for developing it. Yet by the eighteenth century, British shipping dominated the trade, and English merchants made immense profits from it. Slavery eventually took root everywhere in the Americas, including the English colonies. English traders entered the business as soon as it was feasible to do so, and their actions sped the rise of slavery in the Americas, which in turn encouraged the trade.

In 1562, John Hawkins, from a wealthy seafaring family in Plymouth, decided to break into the Portuguese slave trade. He seized hundreds of Africans, as well as valuable trade goods, from Portuguese ships along the Guinea coast of West Africa and took them to Santo Domingo on Hispaniola to sell. Even after paying the necessary bribes to Spanish officials—as trade with England was illegal—the profits were enormous. Queen Elizabeth I, who had been against the slave trade, began to pay attention, and she later invested Crown resources. On his second voyage, Hawkins experimented with attacking African villages himself, but he found the costs to be high: in one incident, he seized 10 Africans but lost 7 crew members. Hawkins eventually learned that Africans could be his allies in the trade. An emissary from an African king approached him with a proposition: help the king defeat his enemies and share in the slaves taken as booty. Hawkins agreed and ended up with hundreds

Chesapeake society reproduced itself naturally. Perhaps half of all children born in the colony died in infancy, and one marriage partner was also likely to die within seven years of marriage. At least until 1680 or so, to be a widow, widower, or orphan was the normal state of affairs. Widows who inherited their husband's possessions were powerful and in demand on the marriage market. Children, however, often lost their inheritances to a stepparent.

A BIBLE COMMONWEALTH IN THE NEW ENGLAND WILDERNESS

In 1620, 13 years after the founding of the Virginia Colony, England planted another permanent colony at Plymouth; 9 years after that, it planted one at Massachusetts Bay. In many ways the Virginia and Massachusetts colonies could not have been more different. The primary impetus behind the Massachusetts settlement was religious. Both the Pilgrims at Plymouth and the much more numerous **Puritans** at Massachusetts Bay sought to escape persecution and to establish new communities based on God's law as they understood it. The Puritans and Pilgrims were middle of captives. It was the beginning of a hideous guns-for-slaves cycle that would eventually cripple Africa. For Hawkins, ironically, the voyage ended badly. The Spaniards in the Caribbean, having been punished for their prior illegal dealings with him, refused his merchandise. Then they attacked his fleet off the coast of Veracruz, Mexico, and killed and imprisoned nearly all his men. Hawkins himself barely made it home to England.

It was the lack of a ready legal market in the New World that made the business impossible for the time being. In the first half of the seventeenth century, however, that situation changed as the English established colonies on the mainland of North America and on certain Caribbean islands. In 1630, wealthy Puritans established the colony they hoped would make England rich on Providence Island, off the coast of Nicaragua. The investors had in mind the widespread production of cash crops that grew readily in tropical climates. After only four years, the investors abandoned the importation of indentured English servants and filled the land with Africans—whom enthusiastic captains found they could buy along the Central American coast. After the Pequots lost a war with the New Englanders, Pequot prisoners were also sold on Providence Island. One man wrote with abhorrence of the turn of events; his Puritan brethren were unmoved. Only the constant rebellions frightened them, so they took steps to curb the total number relative to the number of English. Yet by the time the Spanish navy destroyed the colony in 1641, there were more than 380 enslaved Africans and fewer than 350 English settlers.

From 1640 on, the numbers of enslaved Africans grew in Barbados and other English island colonies, and after the 1660s in the Chesapeake as well. As soon as they were available cheaply enough, slaves became widespread wherever cash crops could grow— even in a Puritan colony. The English slave trade had blossomed.

class, and their ventures were well financed and capably planned for the benefit of the settlers. The environment was much more healthful than that of the Chesapeake, and the population reproduced itself rapidly. Relations with the Indians were better than in the Chesapeake. Nonetheless, despite the colonies' differences, the Puritan movement was in fact originally a product of the same growth of national states in Europe and the expansion of commerce that led to the European exploration of the New World and the foundation of **Jamestown**. Furthermore, the Puritans themselves often demonstrated the same tendencies as other Englishmen.

The English Origins of the Puritan Movement

In Europe during the sixteenth century, ordinary people and powerful monarchs had vastly different reasons for abandoning the Roman Catholic Church in favor of one of the new Protestant churches. In England, these differing motives led to 130 years of conflict, including a revolution and massive religious persecution. In the 1530s, Henry VIII established his own state religion, the Church of England, for political rather than for pious reasons. After many years of marriage to Catherine of Aragon, Henry still did not have a male heir. With one of Catherine's

Struggles For Democracy
The First African Arrivals Exercise Some Rights

One day in 1654, an African American family living on Virginia's Eastern Shore met on their plantation for a family conference. They were all free; in fact, they themselves owned a few slaves. One of these enslaved people, a man named John Casor, had recently complained that he was really an indentured servant and should have been given his liberty by now. A court investigator reported that "Anthony Johnson's son-in-law, his wife and his own two sons persuaded the old Negro Anthony Johnson to set the said John Casor free."

To modern readers, the Johnson family saga seems a remarkable one. Anthony Johnson arrived as an enslaved person in Virginia in 1621, aboard one of the first ships to bring Africans to the new colony. The following year, the plantation where he worked was attacked by the Powhatan Indians in the uprising of 1622, but Johnson managed to escape death. That same year, he married another newly arrived African named Mary. They went on to spend forty years together and had at least four surviving children. Within a few years, they found a way to gain their freedom—probably by being allowed to raise their own cattle on the side and keep the proceeds. After he was free, Johnson put the money he made into buying slaves and indentured servants, and eventually was able to claim 250 acres of land under the headright system (through which colonists were given 50 acres for each

ladies-in-waiting, Anne Boleyn, already pregnant, Henry pressed the pope for an annulment of his marriage. In 1533, the pope refused the annulment, and Henry removed the Catholic Church as the established religion of England, replacing it with his own Church of England. He confiscated Catholic Church lands, which he redistributed to members of the English nobility in return for their loyalty. In one move, Henry eliminated a powerful political rival, the Roman Catholic Church, and consolidated his rule over his nobility.

Replacing the Catholic Church did not bring stability, however. Henry's successors alternated between Protestantism and Catholicism. Under the reign of Catherine's daughter Mary, hundreds of Protestants left the country to avoid persecution. When Mary's Protestant sister, Elizabeth, ascended the throne, these exiles returned, having picked up the Calvinist doctrine of predestination on the Continent. John Calvin, the Swiss Protestant reformer, insisted that even before people were born, God foreordained "to some eternal life and to some eternal damnation." Although the Church of England adopted Calvin's doctrine of predestination, the Church never held to it thoroughly enough or followed through on other reforms well enough to please those who called themselves Puritans. And because the monarch viewed challenges to the state religion as challenges to the state itself, religious dissenters were frequently persecuted.

person they brought into the colony). Then in 1653, the Johnson family experienced catastrophe: a fire on their plantation left them nearly destitute. Fortunately, however, they had gained their community's respect and liking over the years, and the court allowed them tax relief for a significant period so they might put themselves back on their feet. And they did indeed collect themselves.

Anthony Johnson found a way to empower himself. Within a few decades, however, it became impossible for any Black man in Virginia, no matter how enterprising, to achieve what he achieved. An extraordinary legal constriction of the rights of Africans occurred. From the time of their first arrival, Africans had generally been viewed as slaves for life, unlike indentured servants; nevertheless, the lines of demarcation were at first somewhat fuzzy. Many Africans were freed by their masters after years of service or were encouraged to buy themselves, and once they were free, no laws forbade them from participating in community activities like anyone else. In the 1660s, as the colony became more dependent on plantation agriculture and slave labor, this began to change. The Virginia Assembly gradually passed laws disfranchising the region's Black population on multiple levels. Most of the laws applied to enslaved people only and came to be called "the slave code." But free Blacks were not immune. By the 1690s, any enslaved person who became a freedman was required to leave Virginia within six months. And in 1705, people of African descent living in the colony were specifically prohibited from holding office or giving grand jury testimony. For people of African descent, the Virginia Assembly, rather than being an entity that enabled them to voice their concerns, was the instrument that destroyed their hard-won freedoms. By then, the Johnson family had moved away.

What Did the Puritans Believe?

Like all Christians, Puritans believed that humanity was guilty of the original sin committed by Adam and Eve when they disobeyed God in the Garden of Eden. They believed that God's son, Jesus Christ, had given his life to pay (or atone) for the original sin and that, as a consequence, all truly faithful Christians would be forgiven their sins and admitted to heaven after they died. Unlike other Christians, Calvinists insisted there was nothing that people could do to guarantee that God, by an act of "grace," would grant them the faith that would save them from hell.

Protestants rejected the hierarchy of the Catholic Church, maintaining that the relationship between God and humanity should be direct and unmediated. Because every person had direct access to the word of God through the Bible, Protestants promoted literacy and translated the Bible into modern languages.

As Calvinists, Puritans wanted to "purify" the Church of England of all remnants of Catholicism, including rituals and priestly hierarchy. Furthermore, Anglicans (members of the established Church of England) had come to think that Catholics were partly right—that believing Christians *could* earn their way to heaven by good works, a doctrine the Puritans labeled **Arminianism**. Puritans, in contrast, continued to insist that salvation was the free gift of God and that human beings could not force God's hand. Individuals could only prepare for grace by reading and studying the Bible, so that they understood God's plan, and by attempting to live the best lives they could. Because they could never be certain of salvation, Puritans always lived with anxiety.

Puritanism contained a powerful tension between intellect and emotion. On the one hand, Puritanism was a highly rational religion, requiring all of its followers to study the Bible and listen to long sermons on fine points of theology. As a result, Puritans, male and female, were highly literate. On the other hand, Puritans believed that no amount of book learning could get a person into heaven, and that grace was as much a matter of the heart as of the mind. The Puritan movement always struggled to contain this tension, as some of its believers embraced a more fully rational religion and others abandoned book learning for emotion.

Puritans believed that church membership was only for those who could demonstrate that they were saved. As they were persecuted for their faith, they came to believe that, like the Israelites of old, they were God's chosen people—that they had a covenant or agreement with God, and that if they did his will, he would make them prosper.

The Puritans first attempted to reform the Church of England. Once they saw that the Church would resist more reformation and was moving further from the Calvinist principle of predestination, some Puritans began to make other plans.

The Pilgrim Colony at Plymouth

The first Puritan colony in North America was established in 1620 at Plymouth, by a group of Puritans known as the Pilgrims, "Separatists" who had given up hope of reforming the Church of England. The Pilgrims had already moved to Holland, thinking its **Calvinism** would offer a better home. It was hard for the Pilgrims to fit themselves into Holland's economy, however, and they found their children seduced by "the manifold temptations of the place."

By 1620 the Pilgrims were ready to accept the Virginia Company of London's offer of land in America for any English people who would pay their own way. With the colony at Jamestown foundering and the Company looking for other opportunities, it filled two ships, the *Mayflower* and the *Speedwell*, with the Pilgrims from Holland, other interested Puritans, and a large number of non-Puritans also willing to pay their own way.

The leaking *Speedwell* had to turn back, but the *Mayflower* arrived at Plymouth, Massachusetts, in November 1620, far north of its destination and outside the jurisdiction of the Virginia Company. Because the Pilgrims had landed in territory that had no legal claim and no lawful government, 41 of the adult men on board signed a document known as the Mayflower Compact. The men bound themselves into a "Civil Body Politic" to make laws and govern the colony and also to recognize the authority of the governor. Although the compact provided a legal basis for joint government and to a large extent allowed for self-determination on the part of the people, it was by no means a wholly democratic document. By design, it excluded those who were not "Saints," or Puritans, from the body politic. Some of the non-Puritans (called "Strangers") had been talking about mutiny, so the Pilgrims wanted to make their power secure.

Only 1 of the 102 passengers had died en route, but only half of the party survived the harsh first winter. Years later the second governor, William Bradford, remembered the Pilgrims' ordeals. The Indians, he complained, were "savage barbarians . . . readier to fill their sides full of arrows than otherwise." And their new home was "a hideous and desolate wilderness, full of wild beasts and wild men."

In fact, the Plymouth Colony would never have survived had it not been for the assistance of friendly Indians. Like the French in New France and unlike the English at Jamestown, the Pilgrims established diplomatic relations both because they were good diplomats and because the local Indians desperately needed foreign allies. Before the Pilgrims' arrival, Plymouth Bay had been inhabited by as many as 2,000 people. Then European fishermen and traders introduced some fatal disease—possibly viral hepatitis—which was carried along the trading network and killed 90 percent of the local population. Indians "died in heapes as they lay in their houses," their villages filled with the bones of the unburied dead. So recently had Patuxet and Pokanoket Indians inhabited the region that the Pilgrims were able to supplement their meager supplies by rummaging Indian graves, homes, and stores of grain.

The world was vastly changed for Native Americans who survived. Tisquantum, or Squanto, had spent the plague years in Europe, having been kidnapped by an exploring Englishman (see Chapter 2). He had only recently made his way back and found that his tribe had almost entirely disappeared. The once-powerful Pokanokets, led by Massasoit, were now paying tribute to the Narragansetts, who had escaped the deadly disease. Squanto persuaded Massasoit that the English might be allies against the Narragansetts. Thus, in the spring of 1621, Squanto offered his assistance to the Pilgrims and showed them how to grow corn.

From the Indian perspective, this assistance was a diplomatic initiative, enabling a treaty between the Pokanokets and the Pilgrims. It worked for the English, too, however. By the time Squanto died in 1622, he had helped secure the future of the Pilgrims' Plymouth Colony. Plymouth remained a separate colony until 1691, when it was absorbed into the larger, more influential **Massachusetts Bay** Colony. Plymouth demonstrated that New England could be inhabited by Europeans and that effective diplomatic relations with local Indians were critical for a colony's survival.

The Puritan Colony at Massachusetts Bay

In England, increasing numbers of people considered themselves Puritans and yet were not Separatists, like the Pilgrims. Many dreamed of founding colonies, but they wanted to serve as models to other Englishmen, not sever themselves from them. In February 1630, an English Puritan noted in his diary that the faithful had recently sent off ships to New England as well as to a place near Mexico. He was referring to Providence Island, off the coast of Nicaragua. Many Puritans were wealthy landowners and merchants who could not bear to think that the great wealth of the Americas should go mostly to Spain. They wanted an English colony in the tropics and so found an uninhabited island upon which to establish a plantation economy. They first envisioned a labor force of **indentured servants**, as in the Chesapeake, but rapidly moved to African slavery, with only one Puritan voicing serious opposition. In 1641, the Spanish navy destroyed the fledgling colony.

In the meantime, friends and relatives of the Providence Island Puritans had remained focused on New England and the transport of Puritan settler families. In 1629, the Massachusetts Bay Company, a group of London merchants, had received a charter from King Charles I to establish a colony. The investors in the joint-stock company would have full rights to a swath of land reaching from Massachusetts Bay west across the entire continent. Along with Puritans looking for a new home where they could govern themselves, the company included some who hoped to turn a profit from trade. By the end of the year 1630, Boston and 10 other towns had been founded. By the early 1640s, between 20,000 and 25,000 Britons (not all of them Puritans) had migrated to the Puritan colonies of Plymouth, Massachusetts Bay, Connecticut, Rhode Island, and New Hampshire. Although fewer than half as many migrated to New England as to the Chesapeake region, by 1660 both had populations of a similar size—around 35,000.

New England was able to catch up and keep pace with the Chesapeake for three reasons. First, New England was a much more healthful region. Long, cold winters killed the mosquitoes that carried fatal diseases, and the water supply was good. Second, Puritans migrated as families. Ninety percent came as part of a family group, a pattern almost exactly the reverse of that in the Chesapeake. In such circumstances, the population soon reproduced itself. Third, most of the settlers were not desperate; they had resources to help them make the transition. Most were prosperous members of the middle range of society. Many of the men were professionals—craftsmen, doctors, lawyers, and ministers—people who profited from the changing English economy of the late sixteenth and early seventeenth centuries. Again, the contrast with the Chesapeake was dramatic. There, the vast majority of migrants were people with few skills and dim prospects.

Elizabeth Paddy Wensley Far from the grim Massachusetts settler we imagine, Elizabeth Paddy Wensley dressed stylishly by the standards of the 1670s. A mother of five, she was married to the wealthy Boston merchant John Wensley.

The New England Way

The Puritans of Massachusetts Bay Colony were men and women with a mission. Their first governor, John Winthrop, set out the vision of a Bible **commonwealth** in a sermon he preached aboard the *Arbella* in the spring of 1630, before the ship even docked. God, Winthrop said, had entered into a covenant with the Puritans, just as they had entered into a covenant with one another. Together they had taken enormous risks and begun an extraordinary experiment to see whether they could establish a society based on the word of God: "We shall be as a city upon a hill, the eyes of all people are upon us. So that if we shall deal falsely with our God in this work we have undertaken, and so cause Him to withdraw his present help from us, we shall be made a story and a by-word through the world." This broad vision shaped the development of New England's society.

This communal vision made early New Englanders relatively cohesive. Each town was created by a grant of land by the Massachusetts General Court (the name given to the legislature) to a group of citizens. The settlers in turn entered into a covenant with one another to establish a government and distribute the land they held collectively. This was not a modern democracy, for Puritans believed in hierarchy, and their vision was more communal than individualist. Nonetheless, there was considerably more economic equality and cohesion than in most parts of the world.

At first, the new towns divided up only a portion of the land that they held, reserving the rest for newcomers and the children of the original founders. The land was distributed unequally, according to social status and family size (see Table 3–2). Although New England society was relatively egalitarian, with only a small gap between the richest and poorest, the Puritans set out to create a social hierarchy. The rich and powerful were supposed to take care of the poor, and Puritan towns did assist all those who could not care for themselves. Each town administered itself through a town meeting, a periodic gathering of the adult male property owners to attend to the town's business. In the past, historians pointed to the democratic elements in the town meeting as the source of American democracy. More recently, historians have emphasized undemocratic elements. Participation was restricted to adult male property holders, who were only 35 percent of the adult residents, once women are considered. In addition, the habit of deference to the powerful, prosperous, and educated was so strong that a small group of influential men tended to govern each town. Moreover, Puritans abhorred conflict, so great social pressure was used to ensure harmony and limit dissent. If democracy means the right to disagree and majority rule in open elections, then the New England town meeting was not fully democratic. However, even with all these restrictions, the New England town meeting was far more democratic than any form of government in England at the time, where the vast majority of men, not to mention women, were excluded from political participation.

Changing the Landscape to Fit the Economic Needs of the Commonwealth

The Puritans' corporate social vision was generally compatible with a capitalist political economy. Although land was distributed to towns, once those towns transferred parcels of the land to individual farmers, the farmers were free to leave it to their heirs, to sell it to whomever they pleased, and to buy more land from

Table 3–2 Distribution of Land in Rowley, Massachusetts, 1639–ca. 1642

Acres	No. of Grants
Over 250	0
201–250	1
151–200	1
101–150	0
51–100	7
21–50	22
20 or less	63
No record	1
Total	95

Source: David Grayson Allen, In *English Ways: The Movement of Societies and the Transferal of English Local Law and Custom to Massachusetts Bay in the Seventeenth Century* (Chapel Hill: University of North Carolina Press, 1981), p. 32.

Note: Between 1639 and 1642, the town of Rowley, Massachusetts, distributed a little over 2,000 acres to 95 families—an average of just 23 acres per family—even though the grant to the town was for many thousand acres. Although most grants were for fewer than 20 acres, some families received considerably more. The founders of Rowley wanted to re-create the hierarchical social order they had known in England.

others. Any improvements on the land (from clearing away trees to building homes, fences, dams, or mills) remained the property of the owners. These practices followed English law.

The contrast with Indian patterns of land use was dramatic. Indians held their land communally, not individually. The entire group had to consent to its sale. At first, when Indians "sold" land to the Puritans, they thought that they were giving them the right to use the land only and to share the land with them. They might allow the Puritans to build a village, plant, and hunt, while they retained similar rights over the same parcel of land, including the right to allow it to be used by several groups of Europeans at once.

The Puritans' notion of exclusive land rights was a cornerstone of their political economy. Because a man could profit from the improvements made on his land and pass those improvements on to his heirs, he had incentives to make them. Moreover, not only the land but its products became commodities to be sold. Thus, like other European colonists, the Puritans turned their Indian neighbors into commercial hunters. For centuries, the Indians had taken only as many beaver as they needed, but now that they found themselves fenced out of their former lands, they could no longer live part of the year by farming and became more committed to hunting. Overhunting led to the disappearance of beaver in the region.

The Puritans themselves cleared the forests of trees. They found a ready market for timber in England, as New England's trees were much taller and straighter than any known in Europe. The English navy came to depend on New England for its masts. Although the bounty of the land had seemed limitless, by 1800 much of southern New England had been stripped of its forests and native wildlife.

Prosperity did not come to Massachusetts immediately. For the first decade, the colony maintained a favorable balance of trade with England only by sending back the money that new immigrants brought with them in return for goods from the mother country. New England's cold climate made it impossible to develop a cash crop such as tobacco. In the 1640s and 1650s, the government encouraged local manufacturing (to cut down on imports) and export of raw materials. Through government policy and individual initiative, New Englanders eventually made great profits from selling timber, wood products, and fish and by acting as merchants. In the meantime, successful family farms were the mainstay of the local economy.

The Puritan Family

Like most early-modern western Europeans, Puritans thought of the family as the society in microcosm, or "a little Church, and a little commonwealth." There was no sharp distinction between home and the wider world. Although Harvard College was founded in 1636 (to train ministers) and the Massachusetts General Court established a system of public education in 1647, most early instruction and virtually all vocational teaching took place at home. Parents were required to teach their children to read the Bible.

The family was also the center of the Puritans' economy. Farmers, of course, worked at home, as did almost all craftsmen. Women also performed tasks critical to the survival of the family. Although tasks were assigned by gender, in the absence of her husband a woman could assume his responsibilities, selling the products he had made or even fighting off Indians. The family, like society, was a hierarchy, with the husband at the top and his wife as his "deputy."

Puritans lived in fear of lawlessness, and they used the family as an instrument of order. Puritans considered excessive affection and particularly excessive maternal love a danger. Children were subjected to strict discipline not out of cruelty but from deep religious convictions. Considering that Puritan women bore on average eight or nine children and that families were confined in small houses over long New England winters, this harmony was probably necessary for survival.

Despite the importance of control, Puritan households were hardly prisons. If Puritans believed that men were the natural heads of the household and that women bore particular responsibility for Eve's original sin, they also believed that both were equally capable of God's grace. Puritans distrusted the passion of love, which could lead to impulsiveness and disorder. They had great respect, however, for the natural affection that grew over the course of marriage and encouraged playfulness when it helped rather than impeded social harmony.

So successful were the early Puritans in establishing tight-knit communities that only two years after their great migration to America had begun, Reverend Thomas Welde could write proudly back to England, "Here I find three great blessings, peace, plenty, and health. . . . I profess if I might have my wish in what part of the world to dwell I know no other place on the whole globe of the earth where I would be rather than here."

DISSENSION IN THE PURITAN RANKS

Yet not everyone lived in such bliss. The Puritan movement embodied tensions that created individual and social turmoil. Puritans had difficulty balancing emotion and intellect, the individual and the community, spiritual equality and social hierarchy, and anxiety over salvation and the satisfaction of thinking oneself a member of a chosen people. The Puritans also had no mechanisms for handling dissent, which they interpreted as a replay of original sin. The migration to a strange land, populated by people they thought of as savages, as well as the pressure of thinking that the whole world was watching them, only increased the Puritans' desire to maintain a strict order.

Roger Williams and Toleration

The Massachusetts Bay Colony was only a year old when trouble appeared in the person of **Roger Williams**, a brilliant and obstinate young minister. No sooner had he landed than he announced that he was really a Separatist and would not accept appointment at a church unless it repudiated its ties to the Church of England. Massachusetts Bay was already walking a fine line between outward obedience to the laws of England and inner rejection of the English way of life, and an explicit repudiation of the established church was thought to be an act of political suicide.

Without a church of his own, Williams began preaching to those who would listen. Saying that the king had no right to grant land owned by the Indians, he questioned the validity of the Massachusetts charter and argued for strict separation of church and state, as well as strict separation of the converted and the unconverted. Williams went so far as to advocate religious toleration, with each congregation or sect governing itself completely free from state interference.

These doctrines were heresy to both Puritan church and state. In 1635, when Williams violated an order to stop preaching his unorthodox views, the magistrates decided to ship him immediately to England, where he might be imprisoned or even executed. **John Winthrop** warned Williams of his fate, giving him time to sneak away to Narragansett Bay, outside the jurisdiction of Massachusetts Bay. Williams and some followers established the new colony of Rhode Island, which was chartered in 1644. The colony, which became a refuge for dissenters of all sorts, was referred to by Massachusetts Puritans as "the sewer of New England."

Anne Hutchinson and the Equality of Believers

One of Puritanism's many tensions concerned the position of women. By insisting on the equality of all true believers before God and the importance of marriage, Protestantism and especially its Puritan branch undermined the starkly negative image of women that prevailed in sixteenth-century Europe. When Puritan ministers preached that women and men were both "joynt Heirs of salvation" and that women, rather than being a "necessary evil," were in fact "a necessary good," they were directly criticizing both the Catholic legacy and common folk belief.

Puritanism extended women respect, but it also insisted they be subordinate to men. In their hierarchical society, woman's position was clearly beneath that of man. Puritanism struggled to find the balance between women's spiritual equality and their earthly subordination: although most Puritan women deferred to male authority, others seized the opportunity that Puritanism seemed to offer. Without exception, the Puritan authorities put them back in their place.

Anne Hutchinson was just over 40 when she, her husband, and their 12 children followed the Reverend John Cotton to Massachusetts Bay. Cotton was a popular preacher who placed particular emphasis on the doctrine of predestination. Hutchinson pushed that doctrine to its logical, if unsettling, conclusion. She claimed that she had experienced several direct revelations, one telling her to follow Cotton to Boston. At informal Bible discussion meetings at her Boston home, which even the new governor attended, Hutchinson challenged the Puritan doctrine of "preparation": if God had truly chosen those whom he would save, it was unnecessary for Puritans to prepare themselves for saving grace by leading sin-free lives. Nor was good behavior a reliable sign of salvation. Hutchinson did not favor sin; she simply believed her neighbors were wrong in thinking that good works would save them. She accused them of the heresy of Arminianism. By claiming that the Holy Spirit spoke directly to her, Hutchinson opened herself to charges of another heresy, **antinomianism**.

Hutchinson's views were so popular that many residents—possibly a majority—became her followers. Once she accused certain ministers of being unconverted, the colony leaders mounted a campaign against her and her allies. In 1637, they moved the site of the election for governor outside Boston, where her strength was greatest, so that John Winthrop could win. Then, after her most prominent ally among the ministers had been banished, Hutchinson was put on trial for slandering the ministry, convicted, and ordered to leave the colony. Followed by 80 other families, she and her family found temporary refuge in Roger Williams's Rhode Island. (She later moved to New Netherland, where she was killed in an Indian war.) The fact that Hutchinson's ideas came from a woman made them even more dangerous to the Massachusetts leadership. John Winthrop suggested that she might be a witch. Without any evidence at all of sexual misconduct, ministers asserted that Hutchinson and her female followers were driven by lust and that unless they were punished, it would lead to communal living, open sex, and the repudiation of marriage.

It is sometimes asserted that Puritans came to New England in search of religious freedom, but they never would have made that claim. They wanted the liberty to follow their own religion but actively denied that opportunity to others. Puritans insisted on their right to keep out nonbelievers. "No man hath right to come into us," John Winthrop wrote, "without our consent."

Puritan Indian Policy and the Pequot War

The Puritan dissidents were all critical of the Puritans' Indian policy. Roger Williams insisted on purchasing land from the Indians instead of simply seizing it, and the men in the Hutchinson family refused to fight in the **Pequot War** of 1637. The Puritans had been fortunate in settling in a region in which the Indian population had recently been decimated and in having the English-speaking Squanto's diplomatic services. The Puritan communities expanded so rapidly, however, that they soon intruded on land populated by Indians who had no intention of giving them exclusive rights to it.

Within a few years of the founding of the Massachusetts Bay Colony, small groups of Puritans were spreading out in all directions (see Map 3–2). The Reverend John Wheelwright, Anne Hutchinson's brother-in-law and most ardent supporter, took a party into what is now New Hampshire. Others settled in Maine. In 1638, New Haven, Connecticut, was founded by the Reverend John Davenport and a London merchant, Theophilus Eaton, who purchased land from local Indians. Four years earlier, the first Puritan settlers had reached the Connecticut River in western Massachusetts. In 1636, the Reverend Thomas Hooker led his followers to the site of Hartford, Connecticut.

The Pequot War grew out of conflicts among Europeans about who would govern the fertile Connecticut River valley and among Native Americans about who would trade with the Europeans. Until the arrival of the English, the Dutch had controlled trade along the Connecticut River. They had granted trading privileges to the Pequots, which frustrated other tribes, who could trade only through these middlemen. When the English arrived, the Pequots' enemies attempted to attract them to the valley as trading rivals to the Dutch. The Pequots, afraid of losing their monopoly, made the

Map 3–2 New England in the 1640s This map shows the land settled by each of the New England colonies, the regions inhabited by Indian tribes, and the region of Dutch settlement. *Source:* John Murrin et al., *Liberty, Equality, Power* (Orlando, FL: Harcourt College Publishers, 1995), p. 73.

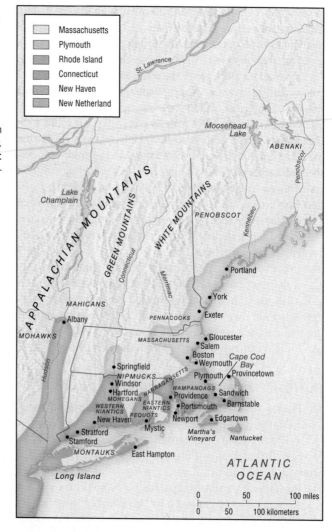

mistake of inviting Massachusetts Bay to establish a trading post in the region. They were counting on their ability to control not only their Indian enemies but also the Dutch and English. As hundreds of settlers poured in, the Pequots became alarmed. They appealed to their one-time enemies, the Narragansetts, to join with them to get rid of the English. The Narragansetts, however, had already been approached by the Puritans to join them in fighting the Pequots. That is where the Narragansetts calculated that their long-term advantage lay. They themselves were in desperate need of land, having been squeezed beyond endurance by the English settlements. Their leaders recognized the greater power of the English as allies than the Pequots.

The Pequots were caught in a rivalry for their lands between the parent colony in Massachusetts and the new offshoot in Connecticut. The Connecticut group struck first, avenging an attack by the Pequots, which in itself was in revenge for an attack on their allies. At dawn on May 26, 1637, 90 Connecticut men accompanied by 500 Narragansett allies attacked a Pequot village at Mystic filled with women, children, and old men. The raiders knew most of the warriors were away from home. As his men encircled the village, the commander, Captain John Mason, set a torch to the wigwams, shouting, "We must burn them." Those Pequots who escaped the fire ran into the ring of Mason's party, who killed between 300 and 700 Indians, while losing only two of their own men. The Narragansetts' Indian allies were horrified by the brutal attack.

Deeply demoralized, the remainder of the Pequot tribe was easily defeated. Prisoners were sold into slavery in the colony of Providence Island. By 1638, the Puritans declared the Pequot tribe dissolved, and in 1639 Connecticut established its dominance over the Pequots' land. In that year Connecticut established its own government, modeled after that of Massachusetts. In 1662, it became a royal colony. The Puritans had demonstrated that where ecological changes were insufficient to destroy the Indians, they were more than willing to use violence.

CONCLUSION

By the middle of the seventeenth century, the New England and Chesapeake colonies had already become quite different. Although the forces of capitalism shaped each region, other factors—disease, demographic patterns, relations with the Indians, and the objectives of the founders—left their distinctive imprints. The early history and relatively quick settlement of New England was shaped by the extraordinary cohesiveness and relatively high social standing and degree of wealth of the Puritan settlers, which made them uniquely successful. By contrast, New France and New Netherland were rough frontier societies for many decades, and the Chesapeake colonies were still raw outposts, populated largely by suffering indentured servants and enslaved Africans long after New England had achieved a secure order. All of the North American colonies, except those of New England, were outposts in the transatlantic political and economic order, created to enrich their mother countries and enhance those countries' power. New England was the exception, but so successful was New England in achieving a stable society that we sometimes forget that it was the exception and not the rule.

WHO, WHAT, WHERE

Anglo-Powhatan Wars   71

antinomianism   89

Arminianism   81

Calvinism   82

charter colony   74

commonwealth   85

headright   72

Hutchinson, Anne   88

indentured servants   83

Jamestown   79

Maryland   74

Massachusetts Bay   83

Pequot War   89

Plymouth   68

Pocahontas   66

Powhatan   66

proprietary colony   74

Puritans   78

CHAPTER 3:   The English Come to Stay, 1600–1660

Primary Sources

3.1   EDWARD WATERHOUSE'S REPORT ON THE UPRISING OF 1622

In March of 1622, the Powhatans launched a major attack, striking without warning at many sites up and down the James River. About a quarter of the colony's population was killed in one day. We do not know if the Powhatans hoped the surviving colonists would leave forever or would simply be content to stay in Jamestown and operate a trading post, leaving the Indians with their lands. Almost immediately, Edward Waterhouse sent this report back to London, in which he hatched the idea of exterminating the Indians.

These small and scattered Companies [of Indians] had warning given from one another in all their habitations to meete at the day and houre appointed for our destruction, at all our severall Townses and places seated upon the River; some were directed to goe to one place, some to another, all to be done at the same day and time, which they did accordingly: some entering their Houses under colour of trucking [trading], and so taking advantage, others drawing our men abroad upon faire pretencs, and the rest suddenly falling upon those that were at their labours.

. . . Thus have you seen the particulars of this massacre, out of Letters from thence written, wherein treachery and cruelty have done their worst to us, or rather to themselves; for whose understanding is so shallow, as not to perceive that this must needs bee for the good of the Plantation after, and the losse of this blood to make the body more healthfull, as by these reasons may be manifest.

First, Because betraying of innocency never rests unpunished: And therefore *Agesilaus*,[1] when his enemies (upon whose oath of being faithfull hee rested) had deceived him, he sent them thankes, for that by their perjury, they had made God his friend, and their enemy.

Secondly, Because our hands which before were tied with gentlenesse and faire usage, are now set at liberty by the treacherous violence of the Savages, not untying the Knot, but cutting it: So that we, who hitherto have had possession of no more ground then their waste, and our purchasse at a valuable consideration to their owne contentment, gained; may now by right of Warre, and law of Nations, invade the Country and destroy them who

---

[1]Agesilaus was a king of Sparta who lived from 444 BCE to 360 BCE. In making reference to him, Waterhouse is showing off his classical education, and thus proving his credentials as a "gentleman" to anyone who might read his work.

sought to destroy us: whereby wee shall enjoy their cultivated places, turning the laborious Mattocke into the Victorious Sword (wherein there is more both ease, benefit, and glory) and possessing the fruits of others labours. Now their cleared grounds in all their villages (which are situate in the fruitfullest places of the land) shall be inhabited by us, whereas heretofore the grubbing of woods was the greatest labour.

Thirdly, Because those commodities which the Indians enjoyed as much or rather more than we, shall now also be entirely possessed by us. The Deere and other beasts will be in safety, and finitely increase, which heretofore not onely in the generall huntings of the King (whereat foure or five hundred Deere were usually slaine) but by each particular Indian were destroied at all times of the yeare, without any difference of Male, Damme, or Young....

Fourthly, Because the way of conquering them is much more easie then of civiliz-ing them by faire meanes, for they are a rude, barbarous, and naked people, scattered in small companies, which are helps to Victories, but hinderances to Civilitie: Besides that, a conquest may be of many, and at once, but civility is in particular, and slow, the effect of long time, and great industry. Moreover, victorie of them may bee gained many waies; by force, by surprise, by famine in burning their Corne, by destroying and burning their Boats, Canoes and Houses, by breaking their fishing Weares, by assailing them in their huntings, whereby they get the greatest part of their sustenance in Winter, by pursuing and chasing them with our horses, and blood-Hounds to draw after them, and Mastives to teare them, which take this naked, tanned, deformed Savages, for no other then wilde beasts, and are so fierce and fell upon them, that they feare them worse than their old Devill which they worship, supposing them to be a new and worse kind of Devils then their owne. By these and sundry other wayes, as by driving them (when they flye) upon theire enemies, who are round about them, and by animating and abetting their enemies against them, may their ruine or subjection be soone effected ...

Fiftly [sic], Because the Indians, who before were used as friends, may now most justly be compelled to servitude and drudgery, and supply the roome of men that labour, whereby even the meanest [poorest] of the Plantation may imploy themselves more entirely in their Arts and Occupations, which are more generous, whilest Savages performe their inferiour workes of digging in mynes, and the like, of whom also some may be sent for the service of the Sommer Ilands [in the Caribbean].

Sixtly, This will forever hereafter make us more cautelous and circumspect, as never to bee deceived more by any other treacheries, but will serve for a great instruction to all pos-terities there, to teach them that *Trust is the mother of Deceipt*, and to learne them that of the *Italian, Chi no fida, non s'ingamuu*, Hee that trusts not is not deceived; and make them know that kindnesses are misspent upon rude natures, so long as they continue rude; as also, that Savages and Pagans are above all other for matter of Justice ever to be suspected. Thus upon this Anvile shall wee now beate out to our selves an armour of proofe, which shall for ever after defend us from barbarous Incursions, and from greater dangers that otherwise might happen. And so we may truly say according to the French Proverb, *Aquelq chose Malheur est bon*, Ill lucke is good for something.

Source: Edward Waterhouse, "A Declaration of the State of the Colony and Affaires in Virginia, with a Relation of the Barbarous Massacre in the Time of Peace and League, Treacherously Executed by the Native Infidels upon the English." Imprinted at London for Robert Mylbourne, 1622. Appearing in Susan Myra Kingsbury, ed., *The Records of the Virginia Company of London*, vol. III (Washington, DC: United States Government Printing Office, 1933), pp. 541–564.

3.2   LETTER FROM RICHARD FRETHORNE TO HIS PARENTS ABOUT LIFE IN VIRGINIA (1623)

Almost nothing is known about Richard Frethorne, other than what a letter he sent home to his parents tells us. Frethorne was a young indentured servant who arrived in Jamestown in December of 1622, a few months after the uprising described in the previous source. Life in Virginia was not what he had expected, and he wrote to beg his parents to try to buy him out of his indenture. Someone apparently turned the missive over to the Company, as it was found in their records. The spelling here has been modernized, as the original is too idiosyncratic to read with ease.

Loving and kind father and mother,

My most humble duty remembered to you, hoping in God of your good health, as I myself am at the making hereof. This is to let you understand that I your child am in a most heavy case by reason of the nature of the country is such that it causeth much sickness, as the scurvy and the bloody flux and divers other diseases, which maketh the body very poor and weak. And when we are sick, there is nothing to comfort us, for since I came out of the ship, I never ate anything but peas and loblolly (that is, water gruel). As for deer or venison, I never saw any since I came into this land. There is indeed some fowl, but we are not allowed to go and get it, but must work hard both early and late for a mess of water gruel and a mouthful of bread and beef. . . . People cry out day and night—Oh that they were in England without their limbs—and would not care to lose any limb to be in England again, yea, though they beg from door to door. For we live in fear of the enemy every hour, yet we have had a combat with them on the Sunday before Shrovetide, and we took two alive and make slaves of them. But it was by policy, for we are in great danger, for our plantation is very weak by reason of the dearth and sickness of our company. . . . We are but 32 to fight against 3000 if they should come. And the nighest help that we have is ten miles of us, and when the rogues overcame this place last they slew 80 persons. How then shall we do, for we live even in their teeth [that is, close by]? They may easily take us, but that God is merciful and can save with few as well as with many . . .

And I have nothing to comfort me, nor there is nothing to be gotten here but sickness and death, except that one had money to lay out in some things for profit. But I have nothing at all—no, not a shirt to my back but two rags, nor no clothes but one poor suit, nor but one pair of shoes, but one pair of stockings, but one cap, but two bands. My cloak is stolen by one of my own fellows. . . . I have not a penny, nor a penny worth, to help me to either spice or sugar or strong waters, without which one cannot live here. For as strong beer in England doth fatten and strengthen them, so water here doth wash and weaken these here, only keeps life and soul together. But I am not half a quarter so strong as I was in England, and all is for want of victuals: for I do protest unto you that I have eaten more in a day at home than I have allowed me here for a week. You have given more than my day's allowance to a beggar at the door . . .

If you love me, you will redeem me suddenly, for which I do entreat and beg. And if you cannot get the merchants to redeem me for some little money, then for God's sake get a gathering [that is, take up a collection] or entreat some good folks to lay out some little sum of money in meat and cheese and butter and beef. . . .

Good father, do not forget me, but have mercy and pity my miserable case. I know, if you did but see me, you would weep to see me.... Wherefore, for God's sake, pity me. I pray you to remember my love to all my friends and kindred. I hope all my brothers and sisters are in good health, and as for my part I have set down my resolution that certainly will be; that is, that the answer of this letter will be life or death to me. Therefore, good father, send as soon as you can ... I thought no head had been able to hold so much water as hath and doth daily flow from mine eyes. But this is certain: I never felt the want of father and mother till now; but now, dear friends, full well I know and rue it, although it were too late before I knew it. Your loving son,

Richard Frethorne
Virginia, 3rd April, 1623.

Source: Susan Kingsbury, ed., *The Records of the Virginia Company*, vol. 4 (Washington, DC: US Government Printing Office, 1935), pp. 58–62.

3.3   EXCERPTS FROM ANNE HUTCHINSON'S TRIAL TRANSCRIPT (1637)

When the Massachusetts Bay Colony was still very young, Anne Hutchinson, a merchant's wife, held meetings in her house for those who wished to discuss religion. She was accused of promoting a schism, or division within the spiritual community, and on November 7, 1637, was brought to trial in Boston. She stonewalled the prosecution by avoiding their questions, arguing that she had not actually been accused of any specific wrongdoing. Nevertheless, she was found guilty and banished from the colony.

Gov. John Winthrop:
Mrs. Hutchinson, you are called here as one of those that have troubled the peace of the commonwealth and the churches here: you are known to be a woman that hath had a great share in the promoting ... those opinions that are the cause of this trouble, and to be nearly joined not only in affinity and affection with some of those the court had taken notice of and passed censure upon, but you have spoken divers thing ... very prejudicial to the honour of the churches and ministers thereof, and you have maintained a meeting and an assembly in your house that hath been condemned by the general assembly as a thing not tolerable nor comely in the sight of God nor fitting for your sex, and notwithstanding that was cried down you have continued the same. Therefore we have thought good to send for you to understand how things are, that if you be in an erroneous way we may reduce you that so you may become a profitable member here among us. Otherwise if you be obstinate in your course that then the court may take such course that you may trouble us no further. Therefore I would entreat you to express whether you do assent and hold in practice to those opinions and factions that have been handled in court already, that is to say, whether you do not justify Mr. Wheelwright's sermon and the petition.

Mrs. Anne Hutchinson:
I am called here to answer before you but I hear no things laid to my charge.

Source: David Hall, ed., *The Antinomian Controversy*, 1636–1638: *A Documentary History* (Durham, NC: Duke University Press, 1990).

3.4 LETTER FROM ANNE BRADSTREET TO HER CHILDREN (UNDATED)

Anne Dudley Bradstreet, born to a prosperous London family, came to the Massachusetts Bay Colony in 1630 where first her father and then her husband later served as governor. She was well educated and, in 1650, a volume of her poems was published in London under the title *The Tenth Muse Lately Sprung Up in America*. It was met with a positive reception. This letter to her children is undated but was probably written later in her life.

To My Dear Children

This book by any yet unread,
I leave for you when I am dead,
That being gone, here you may find
What was your living mother's mind.
Make use of what I leave in love
And God shall bless you from above.

A.B.

My dear children,—

I, knowing by experience that the exhortations of parents take most effect when the speakers leave to speak, and being ignorant whether on my death bed I shall have opportunity to speak to any of you much less to all, thought it the best whilst I was able to compose some short matters (for what else to call them I know not) and bequeath to you, that when I am no more with you, yet I may be daily in your remembrance (although that is the least in my aim in what I now do) but that you may gain some spiritual advantage by my experience. I have not studied [that is, aimed] in this you read to show my skill, but to declare the Truth, not to set forth myself, but the Glory of God. If I had minded the former it had been perhaps better pleasing to you, but seeing the last is the best, let I be best pleasing to you. The method I will observe shall be this—I will begin with God's dealing with me from my childhood to this day.

In my young years, about 6 or 7 as I take it, I began to make conscience of my way, and what I knew was sinful as lying, disobedience to parents, etcetera, I avoided it. If at any time I was overtaken with the like evils, it was a great trouble. I could not be at rest 'till by prayer I had confessed it unto God. I was also troubled at the neglect of private duties, though too often tardy that way. I also found much comfort in reading the Scriptures, especially those places I thought most concerned my condition, and as I grew to have more understanding, so the more solace I took in them.

In a long fit of sickness which I had on my bed, I often communed with my heart, and made my supplication to the most high who set me free from that affliction.

But as I grew up to be about 14 or 15, I found my heart more carnal, and sitting loose from God, vanity and the follies of youth took hold of me.

About 16, the Lord laid his hand sore upon me and smote me with the small pox. When I was in my affliction, I besought the Lord, and confessed my pride and vanity and he was entreated of me, and again restored me. But I rendered not to him according to the benefit received.

After a short time I changed my condition and was married and came into this country, where I found a new world and new manners, at which my heart rose. But after I was convinced it was the way of God, I admitted to it and joined to the church at Boston.

After some time I fell into a lingering sickness like a consumption, together with a lameness, which correction I saw the Lord sent to humble and try me and to do me good: and it was not altogether ineffectual.

It pleased God to keep me a long time without a child which was a great grief to me, and cost me many prayers and tears before I obtained one, and after him gave me many more, of whom I now take the care, that as I have brought you into the world, and with great pains, weakness, cares and fears brought you to this, I now travail in birth again of you till Christ be formed in you.

Among all my experiences of God's gracious dealings with me I have constantly observed this, that he hath never suffered me long to sit loose from him, but by one affliction or another hath made me look home, and search what was amiss—so usually thus it hath been with me that I have no sooner felt my heart out of order, but I have expected correction for it, which most commonly hath been upon my own person, in sickness, weakness, pains, sometimes on my soul, in doubts and fears of God's displeasure, and my sincerity towards him. Sometimes he hath smote a child with sickness, sometimes chastened by losses in estate, and these times (through his great mercy) have been the times of my greatest getting and advantage, yet I have found them the times when the Lord hath manifested the most love to me. Then have I gone to searching, and have said with David, Lord search me and try me, see what ways of wickedness are in me, and lead me in the way everlasting: and seldom or never but I have found either some sin I lay under which God would have reformed, or some duty neglected which he would have performed. And by his help I have laid vows and bonds upon my soul to perform his righteous commands.

If at any time you are chastened of God, take it as thankfully and joyfully as in greatest mercies. For if ye be his, ye shall reap the greatest benefit by it. It has been no small support to me in times of darkness, which the Almighty hath hid his face from me, that yet I have had abundance of sweetness and refreshment after affliction and more circumspection in my wailing after I have been afflicted. I have been with God like an untoward child, that no longer than the rod has been on my back (or at least in sight) but have been apt to forget him and myself too. Before I was afflicted I went astray, but now I keep thy statutes.

I have had great experience of God's hearing my prayers, and returning comfortable answers to me, either in granting the thing I prayed for, or else in satisfying my mind without it; and I have ben confident it hath bene from him, because I have found my heart through his goodness enlarged in thankfulness to him.

I have often been perplexed that I have not found that constant joy in my pilgrimage and refreshing which I supposed the most of the servants of God have, although he hath not left me altogether without the witness of his Holy Spirit, who hath oft given me his word and set to his seal that it shall be well with me. I have sometimes tasted of that hidden manna that the world knows not, and have set up my Ebenezer, and have resolved with myself that against such a promise, such tastes of sweetness, the fates of Hell shall never prevail. Yet have I many sinkings and droopings, and not enjoyed that felicity that sometimes I have done. But when I have been in darkness and seen no light, yet have I desired to stay myself upon the Lord. And, when I have been in sickness and pain, I have thought if the Lord would but lift up the light of his countenance upon me, although he ground me to powder, it would be but light to me. Yea, often have I thought were it Hell itself and could there find the love of God toward me, it would be a Heaven. And, could I have been in Heaven without the love of God, it would have been a Hell to me. For, in Truth, it is the absence of presence of God that makes Heaven or Hell.

Many times hath Satan troubled me concerning the verity of the Scriptures, many times by atheism. How could I know whether there was a God if I never saw any miracles to confirm me, and those which I read of, how did I know, but they were feigned. That there is a God my reason would soon tell me by the wondrous works that I see, the vast frame of the Heaven and the earth, the order of all things, night and day, summer and winter, spring and autumn, the daily providing for this great household upon the earth, the preserving and directing of all to its proper end. The consideration of these things would with amazement certainly resolve me that there is an Eternal Being.

But how should I know he is such a God as I worship in Trinity, and such a Saviour as I rely upon? Though this hath thousands of times been suggested to me, yet God hath helped me over. I have argued thus with myself. That there is a God I see. If ever this God hath revealed himself, it must be in his word, and this must be it or none. Have I not found that operation by it that no humane invention can work upon the soul? Hath not judgments befallen diverse who have scorned and contend it? Hath it not been preserved through all ages maugre [that is, despite] all the heathen tyrants and all of the enemies who have opposed it? Is there any story but that which shows the beginning of times, and how the world came to be as we see? Do we not know the prophecies in it fulfilled which could not have been so long foretold by any but God himself?

When I have got over this block, then have I another put in my way. That admit this be the true God whom we worship, and that be his word, yet why may not the popish religion be the right? They have the same God, the same Christ, the same word. They only interpret it one way, we another.

This hath sometimes stuck with me, and more it would, but the vain fooleries that are in their religion, together with their lying miracles, and cruel persecutions of the saints, which admit were they as they term them, yet not so to be dealt withal.

The consideration of these things and many the like would soon turn me to my own religion again.

But some new troubles I have had since the world has been filled with blasphemy, and sectaries, and some who have been accounted sincere Christians have been carried away with them, that sometimes I have said, "Is there faith upon the earth?" And I have not known what to think; but then I have remembered the words of Christ that so it must be, and that, if it were possible, the very elect should be deceived. "Behold," saith our Saviour, "I have told you before," that hath stayed my heart, and I can now say, "Return, o my soul, to thy rest, upon this rock Christ Jesus will I build my faith, and if I perish, I perish." But I Know all the powers of Hell shall never prevail against it. I know whom I have trusted, and whom I have believed, and that he is able to keep that I have committed to his charge.

Now to the King, immortal, eternal, and invisible, the only wise God, be honor and glory forever and ever. Amen.

This was written in much sickness and weakness, and is very weakly and imperfectly done; but if you can pick any benefit out of it, it is the mark which I aimed at.

Source: Adelaide Amore, ed., *A Woman's Inner World: Selected Poetry and Prose of Anne Bradstreet* (Lanham, MD: University Press of America, 1982).

Turmoil in England

In the middle of the seventeenth century, the British government was thrown into turmoil as Parliament and the king struggled over the future direction of the nation. Two issues were at stake: religion and royal power. The uneasy balance that Elizabeth I had established between Puritans and the Church of England collapsed under her successors James I (r. 1603–1625) and Charles I (r. 1625–1649). Archbishop of Canterbury William Laud moved the Church of England away from the Calvinist belief in predestination, brought back worship that smacked of Catholicism, and persecuted Puritans, prompting Presbyterian Scotland to revolt.

Parliament refused to appropriate the funds that King Charles requested to quash the revolt. Instead, in 1628, Parliament passed the Petition of Right, which reasserted such basic freedoms as no taxation except by act of Parliament, no arbitrary arrest or imprisonment, and no quartering of soldiers in private homes. After years of stalemate, in 1642 Charles raised an army and moved against the Parliament, beginning the English Civil War. It concluded in 1647 with Parliament's victory. Two years later, Charles was beheaded. Oliver Cromwell, a Puritan, ruled as Lord Protector until his death in 1658. When Cromwell's son and successor proved an inept leader, Charles II was invited to reclaim the Crown in 1660.

Although the monarchy had been restored, its authority had been diminished. Britain had been transformed into a constitutional monarchy in which the power of the Crown was balanced by that of Parliament. Britain also found a middle way between Calvinist Protestantism and Catholicism. When the Catholic King James II (r. 1685–1688) tried to fill the government with Catholics and to rule without the consent of Parliament, he was removed in a bloodless revolution, known as the **Glorious Revolution** (1688). It brought Mary, James's Protestant daughter, and her Protestant husband, William of Orange (Holland), to the throne.

The Meaning of Mercantilism

After the reassertion of Parliament's authority in 1688, the British state became increasingly strong and centralized. Britain then embarked on a course that would make it the world's most powerful nation by the early nineteenth century.

Throughout the political turmoil of the seventeenth century, Britain's economic policies were guided by a theory called **mercantilism**, which held that the chief object of a nation's economic policies was to serve the state. Mercantilism was developed to facilitate the consolidation of the new European nation-states, which required vast amounts of money to support their growing military and bureaucracies. Mercantilists considered the economy and politics as zero-sum games; one side's gain was another's loss. Wealth was defined exclusively as hard money—that is, gold and silver. With only a finite amount of gold and silver in the world, a nation could best improve its position by capturing a share of other nations' money. Mercantilism thus led to rivalry between nations. Between 1651 and 1696, the mercantilist British government passed a series of trade regulations, the **Navigation Acts**, requiring that all goods shipped to England and its colonies be carried in ships owned and manned by the English (including colonists). All foreign goods going to the colonies had to be shipped via Britain, where they could be taxed, and some colonial products (tobacco, sugar, indigo, and cotton, to start) had to be sent first to England before being shipped elsewhere. In mercantilist doctrine, the mother country was to produce finished products, and the colonies, raw materials. Hence, when the colonies began to manufacture items such as woolen cloth and hats, Parliament restricted those industries.

NEW COLONIES, NEW PATTERNS

Lacking tight English control, each colony developed differently. In the second half of the seventeenth century, two important new English colonies, Pennsylvania and South Carolina, were established, and New Netherland was seized from the Dutch. As a rule, the most successful colonies were the ones that offered the most opportunity to free white people and the greatest amount of religious toleration.

New Netherland Becomes New York

By the middle of the seventeenth century, the British were ready to challenge their chief trade rival, the Dutch, whom they defeated in three wars between 1652 and 1674. The Navigation Acts cut the Dutch out of international trade, and Britain began to challenge Dutch dominance of the slave trade. In 1663, King Charles II chartered the Royal Africa Company to carry slaves out of Africa to the British West Indies. Britain also made a move for New Netherland.

James, the Duke of York and King Charles II's younger brother, persuaded Charles to grant him the territory between the Connecticut and Delaware Rivers (present-day Pennsylvania, New Jersey, New York, and part of Connecticut), which was occupied by the Netherlands. In 1664, James sent a governor, 400 troops, and several warships that easily conquered the small colony of New Amsterdam. In 1665, James gave away what is now New Jersey to two of his royal cronies, Lords John Berkeley and George Carteret; and in 1667, New York's governor gave the territory on the western side of the Connecticut River to Connecticut. New Netherland had become New York.

The new colony was part Dutch (in New York City and along the Hudson) and part English (on Long Island, where New England Puritans had migrated). The first governors attempted to satisfy both groups. The governors confirmed Dutch landholdings, including huge estates along the Hudson, and guaranteed the Dutch religious freedom. The governors also distributed 2 million more acres of land, most of it in enormous chunks called manors. The owners of these manors, like feudal lords, rented land to tenants and set up courts on their estates.

If religious toleration attracted diverse peoples to the region, feudal land policies and England's failure to restore self-government kept others away. Without an elective legislature to raise taxes, the governors, following English mercantilist policy, used customs duties to raise the revenue necessary to run the colony and send a profit to James. These attempts to regulate trade and direct the economy angered local merchants and harmed the economy. Eventually, James gave in to popular discontent and, in 1683, allowed New York to have an elective assembly.

At its first meeting, this group of English and Dutch men passed a "Charter of Libertyes and Priviledges," which, had the king approved it, would have guaranteed New Yorkers a number of civil liberties and the continuing right to self-government

American Landscape

New Amsterdam/New York

Today it is called Wall Street, and it represents the center of world finance, but in 1660, it was literally a wall that marked the northernmost edge of settlement on the island of Manhattan. Although some of the street grid remains—and today's Broad Street was once a huge canal—most of the other traces of the Dutch settlement of New Amsterdam have disappeared.

Lower Manhattan did not become a business and commercial center until the nineteenth century, however. Until then, it was a little urban village, first Dutch and then English. Even after the English takeover in 1664, the town retained its Dutch character and distinctive Dutch architectural styles. The original New Amsterdam was home to a variety of crafts- and tradespeople: not only the merchants, brokers, lawyers, and shipmasters one would expect in a commercial port but also druggists, painters, printers, tailors, and boardinghouse keepers. The homes and workshops were built in the Dutch style, out of red and yellow brick, with leaded-glass casement windows and terracotta tiles on the roofs. The comfortable feel of such homes was not unlike a middle-class home in Amsterdam.

Because buildings often functioned as both homes and workshops, they might contain not only the nuclear family but also the employees of the family business and enslaved people, both Indian and African. (In 1703, 40 percent of New York's households contained African slaves.) If New Amsterdam and its successor, New York, looked and felt like a European town, the presence of large numbers of Africans and Indians gave the little settlement a distinctive New World character.

From its earliest years, New Amsterdam was an urban village in a global economy, home to immigrants and natives, all buying and selling in a global market. The Kierstede family built its house at the corner of what today are Pearl and Whitehall Streets, looking out on the East River. Hans Kierstede, a German religious refugee, came to New Amsterdam and served as its first surgeon. His wife, Sara Roelofs, had been born in Amsterdam and lived as a child near present-day Albany, where she played with the local Indians and learned their languages. In New Amsterdam, she built a backyard shed where Indian women crafted goods to sell in the market across the street from the Kierstedes' home. In 1664, Sara Roelofs Kierstede served as a translator when Peter Stuyvesant negotiated a treaty with the local Indians.

by their elected assembly. The charter expressed the principles of liberalism starting to spread through both Britain and the Netherlands. Liberalism places an emphasis on individual liberty and holds that all human beings are equally entitled to enjoy the freedom and fulfillment to be found in their social lives—their work, families, and churches. The charter would have guaranteed all free men the right to vote and to be taxed only by their elective representatives. It also provided for trial by jury, due process, freedom of conscience for Christians, and certain property

The Lenape Indian Sachem Oratam was so pleased with her translating abilities that he gave her some 2,000 acres of land on the Hackensack River, in present-day Bergen County, New Jersey.

When archeologists excavated the family home late in the twentieth century, they found bits and pieces of the cultures that mixed on the island of Manhattan: pipes made in Holland and imported even after the English takeover; a German wineglass; a piece of a sword; hair curlers for curling wigs; whistles carved from clay pipes and traded to the Indians for furs; and ceramic gambling tokens, similar to ones found at plantations in the South and the West Indies.

New Amsterdam was a crossroads of empire. There people—and goods—from both sides of the Atlantic, Europeans, Indians, and Africans, met and traded with each other, creating a new world made out of bits and pieces from each of their cultures.

NIEUW AMSTERDAM OFTE NUE NIEUW IORX OPT TEYLANT MAN

New Amsterdam New Amsterdam was an urban village in a global economy.

rights for women, the latter two items reflecting Dutch practices. However, the king refused to approve the charter on two grounds: it would give New Yorkers more rights than any other colonists, and the New York Assembly might undermine the power of Parliament. Without secure self-government, New Yorkers fell to fighting among themselves, and political instability in combination with feudal land holdings slowed New York's population growth.

Diversity and Prosperity in Pennsylvania

Pennsylvania demonstrated the potential of a colony that offered both religious toleration and economic opportunity. Its founder, **William Penn**, was a Quaker and the son of one of King Charles II's leading supporters. After his restoration to the throne, Charles had a number of political debts to repay, and giving away vast chunks of North America was a cheap way of doing it. As a Quaker, Penn was eager to get out of England. In 1661 alone, 4,000 English **Quakers** were jailed, and Penn was imprisoned four times. The Quakers were a radical sect of Protestants who believed that God offered salvation to all and placed an "inner light" inside everyone. Hardworking, serious, and moral, Quakers rejected violence and refused to serve in the military or pay taxes for its support.

Penn received his charter in 1681. To raise money, he sold land to a group of wealthy Quaker merchants, who received government positions and economic concessions in return. To attract ordinary settlers, Penn promised self-government (although stacked in favor of the merchant elite), freedom of religion, and reasonably priced land.

In 1682, when Penn arrived at Philadelphia (Greek for "city of brotherly love"), the colony already had 4,000 inhabitants. Penn had clear ideas about how he wanted his colony to develop. He expected the orderly growth of farming villages, neatly laid out along rivers and creeks, and mapped the settlement of the city along a grid, with each house set far enough from its neighbors to prevent the spread of fires. He wanted harmonious relations with local Indians.

Penn's policies attracted a wide variety of Europeans. Soon Pennsylvania was populated by self-contained communities, each speaking a different language or practicing a different religion. Pennsylvania's early history was characterized by rapid growth and prosperity. However, this progress undermined Penn's plans for a cohesive, hierarchical society. People lived where and how they wanted, pursuing the economic activities they found most profitable.

While moving away from the inequalities of the Old World, Pennsylvania replicated those of the New World. Many of its European immigrants were indentured servants or **redemptioners**, people who worked for a brief period to pay back the ship's captain for the cost of transportation to the colony. And by 1700, the Pennsylvania Assembly had passed laws recognizing slavery, although not unanimously. That slavery could take root in a colony where some questioned its morality suggests both the force of its power in shaping early America and the weakness of the opposition.

Indians and Africans in the Political Economy of Carolina

Like Pennsylvania and Maryland, South Carolina was a proprietary colony. One of the proprietors, Anthony Ashley Cooper, the Earl of Shaftesbury, and his secretary, **John Locke**, drafted the Fundamental Constitutions for the new colony. Locke later became a leading political philosopher, and the Constitutions reflect the liberal, rights-guaranteeing principles that he later developed more fully.

The Constitutions provided for a representative government and widespread religious toleration. At the same time, they embodied the traditional assumption that liberty could be guaranteed only in a hierarchical society. Shaftesbury and Locke tried to set up a complex hierarchy of nobles at the top and hereditary serfs

Chickasaw Map This eighteenth-century French copy of a Chickasawmap represents an indigenous conception of the local political landscape.

at the bottom. The Constitutions also recognized African slavery, and Carolina was the first colony that introduced slavery at the outset. The Constitutions never went into full effect, for the first Carolina representative assembly rejected many of its provisions. Predictably, the attempt to transplant a British-style nobility failed. The only aristocracy that the Carolinas developed was one of wealth, supported by the labor of slaves.

The first settlers arrived at Charles Town (later moved and renamed **Charleston**) in 1670. The area had a semitropical climate, wonderfully fertile soil, and a growing season of up to 295 days a year. The region had once been explored by the Spanish, who still claimed it. It was inhabited by mission Indians, that is, Indians who had converted to Catholicism.

As happened so often when Europeans arrived, Indian tribes competed to trade with them, and rival groups of Europeans struggled to dominate the trade. In the colonial period, Indian wars usually pitted one group of Europeans and their Indian allies against another group of Europeans and their native allies, with the

Indians doing most of the fighting. Such wars were an extension of Europe's market economy: Indians fought for European goods, and Europeans fought for a monopoly over Indian products. The English were particularly successful in achieving dominance because of their sophisticated market economy. London's banks had perfected the mechanisms of credit, which financed a fur trade in the forests half a world away.

The Westos elbowed their way ahead of other tribes by offering the Carolina traders a commodity more valuable even than deerskins: Indian slaves. In fact, until about 1690, slaves were the most valuable commodity sold by the Carolina colony.

Carolina merchants quickly established control over the entire Southeast (see Map 4–1), pushing out the Spanish, the French, and even the Virginians. At the

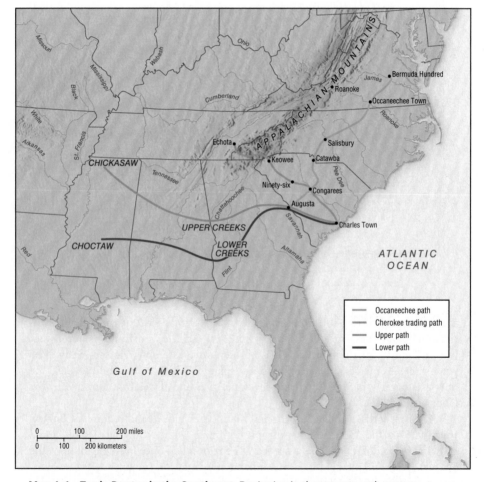

Map 4–1 Trade Routes in the Southeast Beginning in the seventeenth century, English traders from Virginia and later Carolina followed several paths to trade with Southeastern Indians as far west as the Mississippi.
Source: Adapted from W. Stitt Robinson, *The Southern Colonial Frontier* (Albuquerque: University of New Mexico Press, 1979), p. 103.

same time, Indian tribes fought to become the chief slave supplier. In 1680, in the Westo War, the Carolina traders sent their allies, the Savannah Indians, out to destroy the Westos, who were the Virginians' link to the Native American trade of the Southeast. The Carolinians vanquished the Spanish by sending in other Indian allies to destroy the mission towns. In this way, the Carolina traders eliminated their European rivals. At the same time, the Chickasaws emerged to replace the Westos and, like them, obliterated less powerful tribes in order to obtain a steady supply of slaves. Altogether, between 1670 and 1715, somewhere between 25,000 and 50,000 Indians were enslaved, with many more killed in the slaving raids. The slave trade increased dramatically the level of violence among Native Americans.

This violence was turned against the Carolinians in the Yamasee War (1715–1716). Although the Yamasees had been reliable trading partners for 40 years and had fought with the British in Queen Anne's War (see later in the chapter), South Carolina traders cheated them out of their land and enslaved their women and children. In retaliation, the Yamasees and their allies attacked, pushing the settlers almost back to Charleston before they were stopped. The war killed 400 white South Carolinians, crippled the Indian slave trade, forced the colony to abandon frontier settlements, and revealed the fragility of the entire South Carolina venture. When international war began again in 1739, the frontier regions were, as they had been a quarter of a century earlier, dangerous and unstable for settlers, traders, and Indians alike.

The Barbados Connection

Carolina was part of a far-flung Atlantic political economy based on trade, plantation agriculture, and slavery. Many of the early Carolina settlers had substantial experience with African slavery in **Barbados**, a small Caribbean island settled in 1627 that within a decade became a major source of the world's sugar. By then, it had an African majority and was Britain's first slave society. By the end of the seventeenth century, Barbados was the most productive of all Britain's colonies, its per-person income much higher than in England.

This income was not shared equally, however. Owners of the largest plantations became fabulously wealthy, and even lesser planters enjoyed a high standard of living. Conditions for enslaved Africans, however, were brutal. The British magnified differences between Europeans and Africans to enhance the distinction between landowners and slaves. Barbadians were the first to portray Africans as beasts, and the racism of Caribbean planters was intense. Slave codes were the harshest of any in the Atlantic world, prescribing that enslaved men convicted of crimes could be burned at the stake, beheaded, starved, or castrated. When Caribbean slavery was imported into Carolina, these attitudes came with it. The Carolina slave code was the harshest in North America. Laws and attitudes separated whites from Blacks, but differences among Europeans were minimized, as some restrictions against Irish Catholics and Jews were lifted after Barbados became a slave society. In 1650, Barbados allowed the immigration of Jews and other religious minorities six years before England did. As in the Chesapeake, increasing freedom for Europeans developed alongside the enslavement of Africans.

The sugar plantations of Barbados and Britain's other Caribbean islands made their extraordinary profits from the labor of enslaved Africans. British planters worked Africans harder than European indentured servants. Profits came from keeping labor costs down, as well as from the growing demand for sugar. It is important to remember that the New World slave system would not have grown as it did without European demand for plantation crops. Enslaved Africans were imported into Carolina from the outset, but only after 1690 did the colony develop a staple crop—rice—that increased the demand for slave labor. After rice became the region's major cash crop, enslaved Africans became more valuable. By 1720, Africans composed more than 70 percent of Carolina's population. With a Black majority, a lethal environment, and wealth concentrated in an elite, Carolina resembled the Caribbean islands more than it did the other English colonies on the mainland. In only a few decades, Carolina had become a slave society, not simply a society with slaves: slavery stood at the center of everything.

THE TRANSFORMATION OF VIRGINIA

At the same time that a newly vigorous England was planting new colonies, those established earlier were reshaped. In the final quarter of the seventeenth century, the older colonies experienced political and sometimes social instability, followed by the establishment of a lasting order. In Virginia, the transition was marked by a violent insurrection known as Bacon's Rebellion. Significantly, the rebels sought not to overthrow the social and political order but to secure a legitimate government that could protect economic opportunity. In its aftermath, Virginia became a slave society.

Social Change in Virginia

As Virginia entered its second half-century, the health of its population finally began to improve. Apple orchards had matured, so Virginians could drink cider instead of impure water. Ships bringing new servants arrived in the fall, a healthy time of year. Increasingly, they lived to serve out their periods of indenture and set out on their own to plant tobacco. However, most of the best land in eastern Virginia had already been claimed, and the land to the west was occupied by Indian tribes with peace treaties with the English. In addition, the government was controlled by a small clique of men using it as a means of getting rich. Taxes, assessed in tobacco, were extraordinarily high, and as taxes rose, the price of tobacco began to fall. Caught in a squeeze, many ordinary planters went to work for others as tenants or overseers.

Still, servants kept coming to the colony, most from the lower ranks of society. Restless and unhappy, they joined in a series of disturbances beginning in the middle of the century. The elite responded by lengthening the time of service and stiffening the penalties for running away.

Bacon's Rebellion and the Abandonment of the Middle Ground

When the revolt came, it was led not by one of the poor or landless but by a member of the elite. **Nathaniel Bacon** was young, well educated, wealthy, and a member of a prominent family. Bacon made an immediate impression on Virginia's ruling clique, and Governor William **Berkeley** invited him to join the colony's Council of State. For unknown reasons, Bacon cast his lot with Berkeley's enemies among the elite. The instability of elites created political factions in a number of colonies. When ruling elites, such as Berkeley's in Virginia, levied exorbitant taxes and ignored their constituents, they left themselves open to challenge.

The contest between Bacon and Berkeley might have remained minor had not Bacon capitalized on the discontent of the colony's freedmen (men who had served out their indentures). In 1676, Bacon's Rebellion was triggered by a routine episode of violence on the middle ground inhabited by Indians and Europeans. Seeking payment for goods they had delivered to a planter, a band of Doeg Indians killed the planter's overseer and tried to steal his hogs. Over the years, Europeans and Indians who shared the middle ground had adapted the Indian custom of providing restitution for crimes committed by one side or the other. Although this practice resulted in sporadic violence, it also helped maintain order. But this time, the conflict escalated, as Virginians sought revenge, prompting further Indian retaliation.

Soon an isolated incident escalated into a militia expedition of 1,000 men, an extraordinarily large force at the time. For six weeks the war party laid siege to the reservation of the Susquehannocks, a tribe drawn unwillingly into the conflict, who in turn avenged themselves on settlers on the frontier.

When Berkeley refused to fight the Susquehannocks, the frontier planters were infuriated. They complained that their taxes went to Berkeley's clique instead of being used to police the frontier. Planter women used their gossip networks to spread the idea that Berkeley was "a greater friend to the Indians than to the English."

With his wife's encouragement, Nathaniel Bacon agreed to lead a wholesale war on "all Indians whatsoever." After his rebels massacred some formerly friendly Occoneechees, Bacon marched on the government at Jamestown with 400 armed men, demanding to fight "all Indians in general, for that they were all Enemies." Berkeley agreed, and then changed his mind, but it was too late. By then Bacon was in control, and Berkeley fled to the Eastern Shore.

By the time a royal commission and 1,000 soldiers arrived in January 1677 to put down the disorder, Bacon had died, and Berkeley had regained control. Twenty-three rebel leaders were executed, then the king removed Berkeley from office. After Bacon's death, support for the rebellion quickly dissipated.

After Bacon's Rebellion, the government remained in the hands of the planter elite, but the rebels had achieved their primary objective. The frontier Indians had been dispersed, and their land was now free for settlement. Those in power became more responsive to white freedmen. Other factors also improved economic conditions: tobacco prices began to climb, and planters replaced servants with slaves.

Virginia Becomes a Slave Society

With new colonies such as New York and Pennsylvania offering greater opportunity to poor whites, the supply of European indentured servants to the Chesapeake dried up just when more Africans were becoming available. Britain entered the slave trade on a large scale at the end of the seventeenth century, authorizing private merchants to carry slaves from Africa to North America in 1698. It seemed planters could not get enough slaves to meet their needs. In 1680, only 7 percent of Virginia's population

Table 4-1 Population of British Colonies in America, 1660 and 1710

Colony	1660			1710		
	White	Black	Total	White	Black	Total
Virginia	26,070	950	27,020	55,163	23,118	78,281
Maryland	7,668	758	8,426	34,796	7,945	42,741
Chesapeake	33,738	1,708	35,446	89,959	31,063	121,022
Massachusetts	22,062	422	22,484	61,080	1,310	62,390
Connecticut	7,955	25	7,980	38,700	750	39,450
Rhode Island	1,474	65	1,539	7,198	375	7,573
New Hampshire	1,515	50	1,565	5,531	150	5,681
New England	33,006	562	33,568	112,509	2,585	115,094
Bermuda	3,500	200	3,700	4,268	2,845	7,113
Barbados	26,200	27,100	53,300	13,000	52,300	65,300
Antigua	1,539	1,448	2,987	2,892	12,960	15,852
Montserrat	1,788	661	2,449	1,545	3,570	5,115
Nevis	2,347	2,566	4,913	1,104	3,676	4,780
St. Kitts	1,265	957	2,222	1,670	3,294	4,964
Jamaica				7,250	58,000	65,250
Caribbean	36,639	32,932	69,571	31,729	136,645	168,374
New York	4,336	600	4,936	18,814	2,811	21,625
New Jersey				18,540	1,332	19,872
Pennsylvania				22,875	1,575	24,450
Delaware	510	30	540	3,145	500	3,645
Middle Colonies	4,846	630	5,476	63,374	6,218	69,592
North Carolina	980	20	1,000	14,220	900	15,120
South Carolina				6,783	4,100	10,883
Lower South	980	20	1,000	21,003	5,000	26,003
Totals	109,209	35,852	145,061	318,574	181,511	500,085

Source: Jack P. Greene, *Pursuits of Happiness* (Chapel Hill: University of North Carolina, 1988), pp. 178–179.

was African in origin, but by 1700 the proportion had increased to 28 percent, and half the labor force was enslaved (see Table 4–1). Within two decades, Virginia had become a society in which slavery was central to the political economy and the social structure. With the bottom tier of the social order enslaved and hence unable to compete for land or wealth, opportunity for all whites necessarily improved.

As the composition of Virginia's labor force changed, so did the laws to control it. Although all slave societies had certain features in common, each colony enacted its own slave code to maintain and define the institution. By 1705, Virginia had a thorough slave code in place.

All forms of slavery have certain elements in common: perpetuity, kinlessness, violence, and the master's access to the slave's sexuality. First, slavery is a lifelong condition. Second, an enslaved person has no legally recognized family relationships. Third, slavery rests on violence or its threat, including the master's sexual access to the slave.

American slavery added other elements. First, slavery in all the Americas was hereditary, passed on from a mother to her children and to their children, for all time. Second, compared with other slave systems, including that of Latin America, manumissions—the freeing of slaves—in the American South were quite rare. Finally, slavery in the South was racial. Slavery was reserved for Africans and some Indians. The line between slavery and freedom was defined as one of color.

Slave codes also defined gender roles. Two early pieces of legislation denied African women the privileges of European women. A 1643 statute made all adult men and African women taxable, assuming that they (and not white women) were performing productive labor in the fields. In 1662, another law said that children were to inherit the status of their mother, not their father.

The same laws that created and sustained racial slavery also increased the freedom of whites. New World plantation slavery was developed in a world in which the freedom of most Europeans also was limited in various ways. In fact, two-thirds of the Europeans who migrated to British America before the American Revolution were unfree—servants or redemptioners. (When Africans are added, virtually all of whom were enslaved, the total increases to 90 percent.) The increase in freedom for whites was the product of several sorts of policies. First, it depended on the widespread availability of cheap land, which whites could obtain only by dispossessing the Indians who inhabited it. Second, it depended on British government policies, such as permitting self-government in the colonies, which were designed to attract immigrants. Third, it depended on specific laws that improved the conditions of whites, often at the same time limiting the freedom of Blacks. For example, in 1705, Virginia made it illegal for white servants to be whipped without an order from a justice of the peace (see Table 4–2).

NEW ENGLAND UNDER ASSAULT

New England's prosperity led to problems, both internal and external. How would a religion born in adversity cope with good fortune? A combination of internal colonial conflicts and a growing population encroaching on Indian lands led to the region's deadliest Indian war in 1675.

Social Prosperity and the Fear of Religious Decline

In many ways, the Puritan founders of the New England colonies saw their dreams come true. Although immigration virtually halted as the English Revolution broke out, natural increase kept the population growing, from about 23,000 in 1650 to more than 93,000 in 1700. Life expectancy was higher than in England, and families were larger.

Most New Englanders enjoyed a comfortable, if modest, standard of living. By the end of the century, the simple shacks of the first settlers had been replaced by two-story frame homes. By our standards, these homes would still have been almost unbearably cold in the winter, when indoor temperatures routinely dropped into the 40s. Still, New Englanders were beginning to enjoy the prosperous village life their ancestors had once known in England.

Table 4–2 Codifying Race and Slavery in Virginia

1640—Masters are required to arm everyone in their households except Africans

1643—All adult men and African women are taxable, on the assumption that they were working in the fields

1662—Children follow the condition of their mother

1662—Double fine charged for any Christian who commits fornication with an African

1667—Baptism as a Christian does not make a slave free

1669—No punishment is given if punished enslaved person dies

1670—Free Blacks and Indians are not allowed to purchase Christian indentured servants

1670—Indians captured elsewhere and sold as slaves to Virginia are to serve for life; those captured in Virginia, until the age of 30, if children, or for 12 years, if grown

1680—In order to prevent "Negroes Insurrections": no slave may carry arms or weapons; no slave may leave his or her master without written permission; any slave who "lifts up his hand" against a Christian will receive 30 lashes; any slave who runs away and resists arrest may be killed lawfully

1682—Slaves may not gather for more than four hours at other than owner's plantation

1682—All servants who were "Negroes, Moors, Mollattoes or Indians" were to be considered slaves at the time of their purchase if neither their parents nor country were Christian

1691—Owners are to be compensated if "negroes, mulattoes or other slaves" are killed while resisting arrest

1691—Forbidden is all miscegenation as "that abominable mixture"; any English or "other white man or woman" who marries a "negroe, mulatto, or Indian" is to be banished; any free English woman who bears a "bastard child by any negro or mulatto" will be fined, and if she can't pay the fine, she will be indentured for five years and the child will be indentured until the age of 30

1691—All slaves who are freed by their masters must be transported out of the state

1692—Special courts of "over and terminer" are established for trying slaves accused of crimes, creating a separate system of justice

1705—Mulatto is defined as "the child of an Indian, the child, grandchild, or great grandchild of a negro"

1705—Africans, mulattoes, and Indians are prohibited from holding office or giving grand jury testimony

1705—Slaves are forbidden to own livestock

1705—"Christian white" servants cannot be whipped naked

1723—Free Blacks explicitly excluded from militia

1723—Free Blacks explicitly denied the right to vote

Note: Slavery is a creation of law, which defines what it means to be a slave and protects the master's rights in his slave property. Slave codes developed piecemeal in the Chesapeake, over the course of the seventeenth century. Legislators in the Chesapeake colonies defined slavery as a racial institution, appropriate only for Africans, and protected it with a series of laws, which, in the process, also created a privileged position for whites.

For Puritans, such good fortune presented a problem. Prosperity became a cause for worry, as people turned their minds away from God to more worldly things. In the 1660s and 1670s, New England's ministers preached a series of jeremiads, lamentations about spiritual decline. They criticized problems ranging from public drunkenness and sexual license to land speculation and excessively high prices and wages. If New Englanders did not change their ways, the ministers predicted, "Ruine upon Ruine, Destruction upon Destruction would come, until one stone were not left upon another."

Most of the churches were embroiled in controversy in the 1660s concerning who could be members. The founders had assumed that most people, sooner or later, would have the conversion experience that entitled them to full church membership. By the third generation, however, many children and grandchildren of full members had not had the experience of spiritual rebirth. In 1662, a group of ministers adopted the **Half-Way Covenant**, which set out terms for church membership and participation. Full church membership was reserved for those who could demonstrate a conversion experience. Their offspring could still be "half-way" members of the church, receiving its discipline and having their children baptized. Those who wished to maintain the purity and exclusivity of the church resisted. Rather than settle this question, the Half-Way Covenant aggravated tensions always present in the Puritan religion.

Turmoil broke out as well in the persecution of Quakers, despite Charles II's having issued a protection order. In 1660, Massachusetts had executed the Quaker Mary Dyer, who had returned to Boston after her banishment. The Quakers had been brazen in their defiance of authority, not only returning to the colony when they knew it meant certain death but also even running naked through the streets or in church.

King Philip's War

Although New England's colonies developed along a common path, conflicts among them were intense and led to the region's deadliest Indian war. As in Bacon's Rebellion, the underlying cause of the war was the steady encroachment of English settlers on Native American lands. In the 1660s, Rhode Island, Massachusetts, and Plymouth all claimed the land occupied by the Wampanoags, Massasoit's tribe, now ruled by his son Metacom, known by the colonists as King Philip. By 1671, the colonies had resolved their dispute and ordered King Philip and his people to submit to the rule of Plymouth. No longer able to play one colony against another,

King Philip (Metacom) signs a deed of sale, 1668 A sketch of the lands that Metacom (known by New Englanders as King Philip) sold in 1668. Note that Metacom's understanding of what it meant to "sell" land differed from English conceptions: He insisted that the Indians who sometimes hunted on the land could continue to do so.

the threats presented by political instability, imperial war, and conflict with the Indians. In 1692, Massachusetts executed 20 people who had been convicted of witchcraft in Salem. Even in a society that believed in witchcraft, the execution of so many people at once was an aberration that revealed deep tensions.

The Social and Cultural Contexts of Witchcraft

Although the majority of New England's colonists were Puritan, many seem to have believed in magic. They subscribed to such tenets of Puritanism as predestination, but they also believed that they could use supernatural powers to predict the future, protect themselves from harm, and hurt their enemies. Although the ministry identified the use of magic with the devil, many New Englanders were influenced by folk religion. Before the development of scientific modes of explanation for such catastrophes as epidemics, droughts, and sudden death, people looked for supernatural causes.

In 1692, the inhabitants of Massachusetts were unusually anxious. They were without an effective government because they had not yet received their new charter. King William's War had just begun, with the French Catholics of Canada and their Algonquian Indian allies raiding the northern and eastern frontiers. Enslaved people reported that the French were planning to recruit New England's Africans as soldiers. These sources of stress increased underlying tensions, many of which concerned gender. Although men and women both attempted to use magic, the vast majority of those accused of witchcraft were women. Almost 80 percent of the 355 persons officially accused of practicing witchcraft were women, as were an even higher proportion of the 103 persons actually put on trial. Because most of these women had neither sons nor other male heirs, they could control property, which made them an anomaly in Puritan society. By the end of the seventeenth century, local land was an increasingly scarce commodity, and any woman who controlled it could be seen as threatening to the men who wanted it.

In addition, declining opportunity also disrupted the tight Puritan social order. Because land was scarce, it became difficult for young couples to start out. Consequently, the age of marriage increased, and the number of women who were pregnant on their wedding days began to climb, as did the number of women who gave birth without marrying at all. Courts increasingly shifted the burden of child support from fathers to mothers. By the end of the seventeenth century, New Englanders were more inclined than ever to hold women responsible for sin.

Witchcraft at Salem

In this context of strain and anxiety, on February 29, 1692, magistrates John Hathorne and Jonathan Corwin went to Salem to investigate recent accusations of witchcraft. By the time the investigation and trials ended, 156 people had been jailed and 20 executed. As in previous more minor witchcraft scares, most of the accused were women past the age of 40, and most of the accusers were women in their late teens and 20s.

Most of the accused fell into categories that revealed the stresses in Puritan society. Many, like Sarah Good, were the sort of "disagreeable" women who had always attracted accusations of witchcraft. Others had ties to Quakers or Baptists.

Several were suspiciously friendly with the Indians. An enslaved woman named Tituba, who was probably an Arawak Indian, was particularly vulnerable and was the first to be accused. Notably, some of the accusers, like Mercy Lewis, had been orphaned or displaced by the recent Indian wars, and they described the devil they feared as "a Tawney, or an Indian color." In addition, most of the accusers lived in Salem Village, an economic backwater, whereas most of the accused lived in or had ties to the more prosperous merchant community of Salem Town. The pattern of accusations suggested resentment on a variety of levels.

By late September, accusations were falling on wealthy and well-connected men and women, such as the wife of the governor. Accusers were paraded from town to town to root out local witchcraft, and other people were drawn to Salem like medieval pilgrims. Finally, the leading ministers of Boston, most of whom believed in witchcraft but had been skeptical of the trials, stepped in, and the governor adjourned the court. No one was ever convicted of witchcraft in New England again.

The End of Witchcraft

The epidemic of panic and resentment was eventually brought under control. Although many colonists continued to believe in witchcraft, magic, and the occult, by the end of the seventeenth century they more often believed that the universe was orderly and that events were caused by natural, and knowable, forces. By the eighteenth century, educated people took pride in their rational understanding of nature and disdained a belief in the occult as mere superstition. This change in thinking reflected a new faith not only in human reason but also in the capacity of ordinary people to shape their lives. Increasing numbers of people, especially those who were well educated, prosperous, and lived in cities, believed that they could control their destinies and were not at the mercy of invisible evil forces. The seed of individualism had been planted in New England's rocky soil.

The witchcraft trials ended New England's belief in itself as a covenanted society with a collective future. Because Puritans had believed that God had chosen them for a mission, they read special meaning into every event, from a sudden snowstorm to an Indian attack. By the eighteenth century, however, they began to evaluate events separately, rather than always as part of God's master plan.

EMPIRES IN COLLISION

As late as the middle of the eighteenth century, Native Americans still outnumbered Europeans on the North American continent. At the end of the seventeenth century in the territory that became the United States, Britain was the only European power with a substantial presence (see Map 4–3). The French and Spanish both had mainland outposts north of the Rio Grande, but these nations concentrated their resources on more valuable colonies: for the Spanish, Mexico and Latin America, and for the French, the West Indies. Nonetheless, imperial ambitions brought European powers into conflict in North America, where they jostled against each other and the Native Americans.

The Pueblo at Acoma The Acoma Pueblo sits atop a mesa that rises 400 feet aboveg-round. In January 1699, Spanish soldiers destroyed the pueblo and killed 800 of its inhab-itants, in retaliation for the killing of a dozen soldiers. All the male survivors over the age of 12 and all female survivors were sentenced to 20 years of servitude to the Spanish, and the men over the age of 25 each had a foot cut off as well. The pueblo was rebuilt after its destruction.

by force what they could no longer get by trade. Under siege, Pueblos turned once again to their tribal gods and religious leaders.

When the Spanish punished the Indians who returned to their traditional reli-gion, they pushed the Pueblos into revolt. A medicine man named **Popé** united the leaders of most of the Pueblos, promising that if the Indians threw out the Spanish and prayed again to their ancient gods, food would be plentiful. Indians would never have to work for the Spanish again, he said, and Indian customs would be restored.

Popé's revolt began on August 10, 1680, when the Spanish were low on supplies. First, the Indians seized all horses and mules, immobilizing the Spanish. Next, they blocked the roads to Santa Fe. Then they destroyed all the Spanish settlements, one at a time. At day's end, more than 400 Spanish had been killed. The Pueblos laid siege to Santa Fe, forcing Spanish survivors to retreat to El Paso. In the most successful Indian revolt ever in North America, the Spanish had been driven from New Mexico.

The Pueblos held off the Spanish for 13 years, until the mid-1690s, but the struggles took a heavy toll. Contrary to Popé's promise, the drought continued. Warfare took more lives, and the population continued to drop.

The revolt taught the Spaniards several lessons. The new Franciscan mis-sionaries were far less zealous than their predecessors. The *encomienda* was not

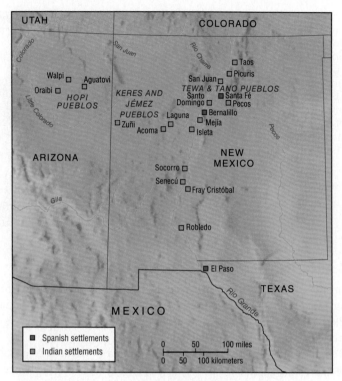

UTAH

COLORADO

Colorado

San Juan

Rio Chama

□ Taos
□ Picuris

Walpi □   Aguatovi
Oraibi □   □
HOPI
PUEBLOS

San Juan □

TEWA & TANO PUEBLOS

KERES AND
JÉMEZ

Santo   ■ Santa Fé
Domingo □   □ Pecos

Little Colorado

PUEBLOS Laguna
□ Zuñi   □□
Acoma □

■ Bernalillo
□ Mejía
□ Isleta

Pecos

ARIZONA

NEW
MEXICO

Socorro □

Senecú □
□ Fray Cristóbal

Gila

□ Robledo

□ El Paso

TEXAS

Rio Grande

MEXICO

■ Spanish settlements
□ Indian settlements

0   50   100 miles
0   50   100 kilometers

**Map 4–4   Region of Spanish Reconquest of New Mexico,
1692–1696** This map includes the pueblos reconquered by the
Spanish, as well as Spanish settlements.
Source: Adapted from Oakah L. Jones Jr., *Pueblo Warriors and Spanish
Conquest* (Norman: University of Oklahoma Press, 1966), p. 37.

reestablished, and brutal exploitation was less common. Slowly the Spanish colony began rebuilding (see Map 4–4).

The population was divided into four groupings, from a small elite at the top to enslaved Indians at the bottom. The elite, a hereditary aristocracy of 20 or so families, included government officials. They developed codes of honor to distinguish themselves from lower orders. This local nobility prided itself on its racial purity, considering white skin a clear sign of superiority. It scorned those of mixed blood, many of whom, of course, were the illegitimate children of elite Spanish men and the Indian women they coerced. Aristocratic men placed a high value on the personal qualities of courage, honesty, loyalty, and sexual virility. Female honor consisted of extreme modesty and sexual purity.

The second group was landed peasants, most of them *mestizos*, half-Spanish and half-Indian. In this highly color-conscious colonial society, the *mestizos* often prized the Spanish part of their heritage and scorned the Indian. Next came the Pueblo Indians, living in their own communities, influenced by Spanish values but still largely faithful to their own traditions. The *genízaros*, Indians who had left their own communities by choice or whose ancestors had been enslaved, lived in Spanish settlements. Sometimes these urban immigrants were outcasts, such as women who had been raped by Spanish men, but most of them eagerly participated in town life.

Eighteenth-Century Spanish Illustration of New World Racial Mixture In this case, the union of an Indian ("Yndio") and a "Mestiza" produces a "Coyote" child. The Spanish developed a large vocabulary so that they could make racial distinctions with great precision.

De Yndio y Mestiza
Coyote.

Native Americans and the Country Between

Spain paid little attention to its impoverished outposts in New Mexico, leaving them vulnerable to the Indians to the east. When the French in Louisiana started arming their Comanche, Wichita, and Pawnee trading partners, New Mexicans—Spanish and Pueblos alike—were challenged.

The Indians of the Great Plains, however, profited from the conflict, obtaining guns from the French and horses from the Spanish. After the Pueblo revolt, the

TIME LINE

▼**1598**
Juan de Oñate colonizes
New Mexico for Spain

▼**1610**
Santa Fe established

▼**1627**
Barbados settled

▼**1628**
Parliament passes Petition
of Right

▼**1642–1647**
English Revolution

▼**1649**
King Charles I beheaded

▼**1651–1696**
Navigation Acts passed to
regulate trade

▼**1652–1674**
Three Anglo-Dutch Wars

▼**1660**
British monarchy restored,
Charles II crowned king

▼**1662**
Half-Way Covenant

▼**1664**
British seize New Netherland,
renaming it New York

▼**1665**
New Jersey established

▼**1669**
Fundamental Constitutions
written for South
Carolina

▼**1670**
Carolina settled

▼**1673**
Marquette and Joliet
explore Mississippi for
France

▼**1675–1676**
King Philip's War

▼**1676–1677**
Bacon's Rebellion

▼**1680**
Pueblo Revolt in New
Mexico reestablishes
Indian rule
Westo War, Carolina
defeats the Westos

Spanish left behind hundreds of horses that Pueblo and Apache Indians passed on to the Plains Indians. By the middle of the eighteenth century, all the Plains Indians were on horseback, which transformed their lives dramatically. They became more effective buffalo hunters, thus making them better fed, clothed, and housed. Their new mobility gave them an increasing sense of freedom, too. But the horses attracted other Indians to the Great Plains. In fact, most of the Indians we now associate with the Great Plains—Sioux, Arapaho, Cheyenne, Blackfoot, Cree—did not arrive there until the eighteenth century.

The result was increased warfare among the Plains Indians, and those with the best access to horses fared the best. For example, the Comanches came to dominate the southern plains, from western Kansas to New Mexico, where they intruded on both the Apaches and the Spanish. The Comanches raided the Apaches, taking not only their horses but also their women and children as captives, some of whom they sold as slaves—*genízaros*—to the Spanish. The Comanches cut the Apaches off from French traders to the east. The Apaches in turn moved west and south, bringing them into conflict with the Pueblos and the Spanish. In defense, the Spanish built a string of armed settlements in current-day Texas, but they could not withstand the Comanches, and even the New Mexican settlements were endangered.

Eventually, the new horse-centered way of life took its toll. Although some tribes grew stronger at the expense of others, all suffered from the increasing violence. European diseases proved deadly as well. Under such pressures, gender roles changed. Men sought distinction as warriors, demonstrating success by the number of scalps or captives they seized. Yet so many fell in battle that they were

▼**1681**
William Penn granted charter for Pennsylvania

▼**1683**
New York's assembly meets for first time

▼**1685**
King Charles II dies and James, Duke of York, becomes King James II

▼**1686**
Massachusetts, Plymouth, Connecticut, Rhode Island, and New Hampshire combined in Dominion of New England; New York and New Jersey added two years later

▼**1688**
Glorious Revolution

▼**1689**
Leisler's Rebellion in New York, Coode's Rebellion in Maryland
William and Mary become King and Queen of Britain; Dominion of New England overthrown

▼**1689–1697**
King William's War

▼**1690**
Publication of John Locke's *Two Treatises of Government*

▼**1691**
Massachusetts made a royal colony

Maryland made a royal colony New Hampshire made a royal colony

▼**1692**
Salem witchcraft trials

▼**1696**
Reconquest of New Mexico

▼**1702–1713**
Queen Anne's War

▼**1715–1716**
Yamasee War

▼**1718**
French establish settlement at New Orleans

soon outnumbered by women, which led to an increased frequency of polygamy, as surviving warriors took multiple wives. As men's status as warriors and hunters rose, that of women—the agriculturalists—fell. The American West was already changing.

CONCLUSION

After a period of considerable instability, by the beginning of the eighteenth century, almost all of the British North American colonies had developed the societies that they would maintain until the American Revolution. For the most part, the colonies were prosperous, with a large white middle class. The efforts to replicate a European hierarchical order had largely failed. Each region had found a secure economic base: farming and shipping in New England, mixed farming in the middle colonies, and single-crop planting in the southern ones. The southern colonies had become slave societies, although slavery was practiced in every colony. The colonies had mostly figured out how to control their own populations, whether by affording them increased opportunity and political rights, in the case of Europeans, or by exercising tighter control, in the case of enslaved Africans. These strong economic foundations, when combined with political stability, were the preconditions for the rapid population growth of the eighteenth century, when the British population on the mainland would far surpass that of the French and Spanish colonies. The French and Spanish colonies on the mainland were still little more than frontier outposts, although both nations maintained imperial visions for North America. Native Americans remained a strong presence, but the competition among the European powers—and even the individual colonies—for the loyalty of the Indian tribes, their trade, and their land remained a source of conflict.

WHO, WHAT, WHERE

REVIEW QUESTIONS

1. What was Britain's plan of empire? What role were the American colonies supposed to play in it?

2. What effect did political turmoil and the change of leadership in Britain have on the American colonies in the second half of the seventeenth century?

3. Describe Indian–white relations in the American colonies in the second half of the seventeenth century. Why was competition between the colonies an important element?

CRITICAL-THINKING QUESTIONS

1. Many of the American colonies experienced a period of political instability in the last quarter of the seventeenth century. In many cases, ranging from the Salem witch trials to Popé's Rebellion of 1680, the sources of the instability appear specific and local, yet they may also reveal a pattern. To what extent were these instances of instability local, and to what extent may they reveal larger processes at work in the colonies of European imperial powers?

2. In this period, a number of colonies became slave societies. What forces propelled these changes? Were different outcomes possible?

3. What patterns, if any, do you see in Native Americans' accommodation and resistance to European expansion in North America in this period?

SUGGESTED READINGS

Bailyn, Bernard. *The New England Merchants in the Seventeenth Century.* Cambridge, MA: Harvard University Press, 1955.

Green, Jack P. *Pursuits of Happiness: The Social Development of Early Modern British Colonies and the Formation of American Culture.* Chapel Hill: University of North Carolina Press, 1988.

Isaac, Rhys. *The Transformation of Virginia.* Chapel Hill: University of North Carolina Press, 1982.

Norton, Mary Beth. *In the Devil's Snare: The Salem Witchcraft Crisis of 1692.* New York: Knopf, 2002.

Weber, David. *The Spanish Frontier in North America.* New Haven, CT: Yale University Press, 1992.

For further review materials and resource information, please visit www.oup.com/us/ofthepeople

CHAPTER 4:   CONTINENTAL EMPIRES, 1660–1720
Primary Sources

4.1   THE DUTCH LOSE POWER IN AMERICA: A MEETING WITH INDIANS ON THE DELAWARE (1670)

In 1664, the Dutch officially withdrew from New Netherland and left it to the English. On the surface, the event seems simple enough. In fact, however, thousands of Dutch people continued to reside in the colony. They still spoke Dutch but now answered to English authorities. The local Lenape people quickly learned that they no longer needed to fear them. This report from some settlers in Delaware shows how complicated interactions soon became.

Report of a Meeting with Indians on the Delaware about a Murder

The sachems[1] present: Rinnawiggen, Oebequeme, Menninckta, Oyagrakun, Quequirimen Megeras, Pemenacken, Colopapan, Magaecksie, [illegible] rensies, Mannanengen

On Friday being the 23rd of September, 1670, we, namely Marten Roseman, Edman Kantwel, Pieter Cock, Pieter Rambo, Israel Helm and Matheus de Ringh, clerk, came, at the request of the Honorable Lords of Justice to a Indian settlement called Annockenink, where a group of [Lenape] Indians had been and still were meeting, in order to cantico[2] with some sachems whose names appear above. After having waited there three or four days for the arrival of the rest of the sachems and other Indians, who did not all come, we placed our matter before them and asked them for what reason they killed and murdered our people and we named all of those whom they have murdered from the time when the English came here into the country [in 1664] until the present, being ten in number, with many other details too long to relate. [ ][3] replied that they did not know of [ ] namely from Kohansy to [ ]. Whereupon they at once showed and presented us with a small bundle of white sewant[4] about three or four fathoms, on the condition that we would be patient while they looked for the murderers and brought them in, if they could find them. They then gave us another bundle of white wampum adding these words: that they did not seek war and that they desired to go out hunting ad trade up and down among the Christians just as before. They then told the Minquaesen,[5] that is the sachem of the Minquaesen, whom we had among us, that they should kill no more Christians. Whereupon they also gave the Minquaesen a gift, namely, a belt of sewantwith a bundle of white sewant, after the Minquasen had first given them a gift and delivered a whole oration; saying, that we were brothers one to the other, and that they wanted to remain brothers and friends, and that they were sorry that they had done such things and that they must know that they lived scattered among the Christians and pointed out, "Christians are living here and Christians

---

[1]Chiefs.

[2]The Dutch scribe wrote "kintekayen," almost certainly from the Lenape word kantka meaning to dance, to have a social gathering.

[3]When the scribe did not catch a name, he left a blank space, intending to fill it in later. Sometimes, he never did.

[4]The word the Dutch used for wampum, beads used as currency made from whelk and clamshell. They were strung on cords measured in "fathoms" (vadem in Dutch, a length of about six feet).

[5]Probably from Maquas. Under the Anglos, the word came to mean Mohawk, but originally, the Dutch used it to refer to the Mahicans, who lived just to the noth of the Lenape.

are living there" and brought to their attention that since they lived scattered among the Christians, and if they made war, where would the get their gun powder and lead, along with many more similar things which they recited to them. We answered them, when we accepted this money or sewant, saying that when we accept this money or sewant, we accept it not as atonement for the murders which they committed but that we accepted it only provisionally as a pledge that they would look for and bring in the murderers; for our great sachem, we told them, was not satisfied with money but wants you to bring in murderers. We also said that we were surprised that not one of the sachems or Indians knew who had committed the murders and named those whom we thought had committed the murders, who were by name Allomgack, Kecksioes, and the brother of Wissapoes.

They answered that they had [ ] and that [ ] the night when the murders took place [ ] Allomgack was in Assiskonck, Kecksioes was at home with the sachems and the brother of Wissapoes was at the Maleboer's brother's house and further, that we should be content that they would look for those who had done it. We also asked them why they had stolen and plundered the goods belonging to Pieter Jiego and Pieter Alrichs.

They replied that they had not done that and had not even known about it, but that the Indians from Asissconck had done it and that they absolve themselves from it. These were our dealings with the savage Indians.

Signed: Matheus de Ring, Clerk

Source: "Report of a Meeting with Indians on the Delaware about a Murder," in Charles T. Gehring, ed., *New York Historical Manuscripts: Dutch*, Vol. 20: *Delaware Papers, English Period, 1664–1682* (New York: The Holland Society, 1977), 17–18. The New Netherland Project, seated in the New York State Library, has devoted itself to translating all surviving Dutch archival material into English.

4.2   LETTER FROM WILLIAM PENN TO HIS BACKERS (1683)

William Penn was the son of a wealthy English admiral. As a young man, he converted to the Quaker faith and suffered imprisonments. In 1682, the King paid a debt to Penn's father by giving him lands in the New World, and the younger Penn immediately set off to govern them, founding "Pennsylvania" that same year. In 1683, after touring the lands and meeting with the Lenni Lenape, or Delaware Indians, he wrote a letter describing his experiences with them to his backers in London. That same year, a printed version was published. In 1684, Penn returned to England but went back to Pennsylvania for an extended stay from 1699 to 1701.

August 6, 1683

… Every King hath his Council, and that consists of all the Old and Wise men of his Nation, which perhaps is two hundred People: nothing of Moment Is undertaken, be it War, Peace, Selling of Land or Traffick, without advising with them; and which is more, with the Young Men too. 'Tis admirable to consider, how Powerful the Kings are, and yet how they move by the Breath of their People.

I have had occasion to be in Council with them upon Treaties for Land, and to adjust the terms of Trade; their Order is thus: The King sits in the middle of an half Moon, and hath his Council, the Old and Wise on each hand; behind them, or at a little distance, sit the younger Fry, in the same figure. Having consulted and resolved their business, the King ordered one of them to speak to me; he stood up, came to me, and In the Name of his King saluted me, then took me by the hand, and told me, That he was ordered by his King to speak to me, and that now it was not he, but the King that spoke, because what he should say, was the King's mind. He first pray'd me, To excuse them that they had not yet complyed

4.5   ROBERT CALEF, EXCERPTS FROM *MORE WONDERS OF THE INVISIBLE WORLD* (1700)

As the witch hunts of 1692 unfolded in the colony of Massachusetts, many residents looked on in horror. Some colonists later wrote about the experience, while some collected other people's testimonies regarding the events that occurred in the ensuing months and years. Robert Calef, a Boston merchant, sent an extensive manuscript back to London in 1697. When it was published in 1700, Puritan minister Increase Mather had copies burned in Harvard Yard.

May 24, 1692. Mrs. Cary of Charlestown [Massachusetts], was examined and committed. Her husband Mr. Nathaniel Cary has given account thereof, as also of her escape, to this effect,

I having heard [for] some days, that my wife was accused of witchcraft, being much disturbed at it, by advice, we went to Salem Village, to see if the afflicted did know her; we arrived there, 24 May, it happened to be a day appointed for examination; accordingly soon after our arrival, Mr. Hathorne and Mr. Corwin, etc., went to the meeting house, which was the place appointed for that work, the minister began with prayer, and having taken care to get a convenient place, I observed, that the afflicted were two girls of about ten years old, and about two or three others, of about eighteen. One of the girls talked most, and could discern more than the rest. The prisoners were cavalled in one by one, and as they came in were cried out of,[13] etc. The prisoner was placed about 7 or 8 foot from the justices, and the accusers between the justices and them; the prisoner was ordered to stand right before the justices, with an officer appointed to hold each hand, lest they should therewith afflict them, and the prisoner's eyes must be constantly on the justices; for if they looked on the afflicted, they would either fall into their fits, or cry out of being hurt by them; after examination of the prisoners, who it was afflicted these girls, etc., they were put upon saying the Lord's prayer, as a trial of their guilt; after the afflicted seemed to be out of their fits, they would look steadfastly on some one person, and frequently not speak; and then the justices said they were struck dumb, and after a little time would speak again; then the justices said to the accusers, "which of you will go and touch the prisoner at the bar?" then the most courageous would adventure, but before they had made three steps would ordinarily fall down as in a fit; the justices ordered that they should be taken up and carried to the prisoner, that she might touch them; and as soon as they were touched by the accused, the justices would say, they are well, before I could discern any alteration; by which I observed that the justices understood the manner of it. Thus far I was only as a spectator, my wife also was there part of the time, but no notice taken of her by the afflicted, except once or twice they came to her and asked her name.

But I having an opportunity to discourse [with] Mr. Hale (with whom I had formerly an acquaintance) I took his advice, what I had best to do, and desired of him that I might have an opportunity to speak with her that accused my wife; which he promised should be, I acquainting him that I reposed my trust In him.

Accordingly he came to me after the examination was over, and told me I had now an opportunity to speak with the said accuser, viz. Abigail Williams, a girl of 11 or 12 years old; but that we could not be in private at Mr. Parris's house, as he had promised me; we went therefore into the alehouse, where an Indian man attended us, who it seems was one of the afflicted: to him we gave some cider, he showed several scars, that seemed as if they had been long there, and showed them as done by witchcraft, and acquainted us that his wife,

---

[13]Those accused of witchcraft were jeered at, yelled at.

who also was a slave, was imprisoned for witchcraft. And now Instead of one accuser, they all came in, who began to tumble down like swine, and then three women were called in to attend them. We in the room were all at a stand, to see who they would cry out of; but in a short time they cried out, Cary; and Immediately after a warrant was sent from the justices to bring my wife before them, who were sitting in a chamber nearby, waiting for this.

Being brought before the justices, her chief accusers were two girls; my wife declared to the justices, that she never had any knowledge of them before that day; she was forced to stand with her arms stretched out. I did request that I might hold one of her hands, but it was denied me; then she desired me to wipe the tears from her eyes, and the sweat from her face, which I did; then she desired she might lean herself on me, saying, she should faint.

Justice Hathorne replied, she had strength enough to torment those persons, and she should have strength enough to stand. I speaking something against their cruel proceedings, they commanded me to be silent, or else I should be turned out of the room. The Indian before mentioned, was also brought in, to be one of her accusers; being come In, he now (when before the justices) fell down and tumbled about like a hog, but said nothing. The justices asked the girls, who afflicted the Indian? They answered she (meaning my wife) and now lay upon him; the justices ordered her to touch him, In order to his cure, but her head must be turned another way, lest instead of curing, she should make him worse, by her looking on him, her hand being guided to take hold of his; but the Indian took hold on her hand, and pulled her down on the floor, In a barbarous manner; then his hand was taken off, and her hand put on his, and the cure was quickly wrought. I being extremely troubled at their inhumane dealings, uttered a hasty speech (that God would take vengeance on them, and desired that God would deliver us out of the hands of unmerciful men). Then her Mittimus was writ. I did with difficulty and charge obtain the liberty of a room, but no beds In It; if there had [been], [she] could have taken but little rest that night. She was committed to Boston prison; but I obtained a habeas corpus to remove her to Cambridge prison, which is in our County of Middlesex. Having been there one night, next morning the jailer put Irons on her legs (having received such command) the weight of them was about eight pounds; these irons and her other afflictions, soon brought her into convulsion fits, so that I thought she would have died that night. I sent to entreat that the irons might be taken off, but all entreaties were in vain, if it would have saved her life, so that in this condition she must continue. The trials at Salem coming on, I went thither, to see how things were there managed; and finding that the spectre evidence was there received, together with Idle if not malicious stories, against people's lives, I did easily perceive which way the rest would go; for the same evidence that served for one, would serve for all the rest. I acquainted her with her danger; and that if she were carried to Salem to be tried, I feared she would never return. I did my utmost that she might have her trial in our own county, I with several others petitioning the judge for it, and were put in hopes of it; but I soon saw so much, that I understood thereby it was not intended, which put me upon consulting the means of her escape; which through the goodness of God was effected, and she got to Rhode Island, but soon found herself not safe when there, by reason of the pursuit after her; from thence she went to New York, along with some others that had escaped their cruel hands; where we found his Excellency Benjamin Fletcher, Esqu., governor, who was very courteous to us. After this some of my goods were seized In a friend's hands, with whom I had left them, and myself Imprisoned by the sheriff, and kept in custody half a day, and then dismissed; but to speak of their usage of the prisoners, and their Inhumanity shown to them, at the time of their execution, no sober Christian could bear; they had also trials of cruel mockings; which is the more, considering what a people for religion, I mean the profession of it, we have been; those that suffered being many of them church members, and most of them unspotted In their conversation, till their adversary the devil took up this method for accusing them.

Source: Robert Calef, *More Wonders of the Invisible World* (London, 1700), as found in Frances Hill, ed., *The Salem Witch Trials Reader* (New York: Da Capo Press, 2000), pp. 68–71.

The Eighteenth-Century World

1700–1775

COMMON THREADS

What were some of the choices that individual men and women made in the eighteenth century—for example, about where to live, how to work, what to purchase, what to believe—and how did those choices affect their society?

How did such choices make everyday life more democratic? What were the forces that worked against such democratization?

How were free Americans able to become wealthier even without significant technological innovations?

Was it possible yet to talk about a common American experience or culture?

< Enslaved Africans bound for the New World

Young Alexander Hamilton: One Immigrant's Story

In 1755, a woman named Rachel in the English Caribbean colony of Nevis gave birth to a child by a man who was not her husband. Her own father had been a French Huguenot doctor who had fled persecution in France and arrived in the Caribbean, and probably worked for slave dealers determining whether an ailing slave coming off the ships was likely to die. The doctor bought a small plantation with about seven enslaved people and married a local English woman, but they ended up separating. At his death, Rachel, then 16 years old, took her inheritance and her aging, impoverished mother and went to the town of Christiansted, in the Danish colony of St. Croix. There the girl was dazzled by a European gentleman, a Dane named Johann Lavien. They married immediately but got along so poorly that Lavien had his recalcitrant wife jailed. He thought it would teach her obedience, but instead he lost her entirely.

Once Rachel was released, she fled back to the English colony of Nevis. At age 21, she met James Hamilton, the fourth son of a Scottish lord. He was a ne'er-do-well whose family had sent him to the New World in hopes of improvement. He did not have the resources to marry a girl from an established family, and Rachel could not marry, so they set up household together, unbothered by the illegitimacy of their union. Both had benefited from the freedom afforded by the New World, where separate worlds existed in close proximity; but both had also suffered from the vulnerability that New World rootlessness bred. Not surrounded by extensive kin, they had no safety net to catch them when they made mistakes or had bad luck, and both experienced rapid downward social mobility as a result.

The couple named their first son James and their second Alexander. They had no money to send the boys to an elite school, but the island was home to many Sephardic Jews, some of whom ran informal schools in their homes. Alexander learned the English alphabet as well as the Decalogue in Hebrew. Eventually, money became so tight that the family returned to Christiansted, to be near Rachel's sister. Not long after, James Hamilton abandoned his family and Rachel opened a small grocery store to support herself. She and her sons lived in a room above the shop. In 1767, when she was 38 and Alexander was 12, they both contracted a fever; Rachel died. The boys' father did not reappear, so they went to live with a relative, but soon after, he also died. Thus, the colonial government put the boys into that era's version of foster care: their indentures were offered for sale. James was taken by a carpenter. Alexander had become good friends with a merchant's son, and his friend asked his father to take the clever boy on as a merchant's apprentice. Alexander went to work for the New York–based mercantile firm of Beekman and Cruger. He and his brother's life trajectories would thus be forever divergent.

As a merchant's apprentice, Alexander learned many things—about currencies, interest payments, and the need for insurance and stability. He also learned to hate slavery, for he was surrounded by its abuses without being cosseted by the wealth it generated. Most of all, he learned about migration and motion, about the possibility of going somewhere where the potential was richer. In his spare time, he wrote for the local paper. Without intending to, he wrote his ticket out of Nevis. After writing a particularly powerful piece about a hurricane that the town had experienced, his supporters took up a subscription to finance his education. Alexander was sent to New York to attend King's College (now Columbia University). In 1775, Alexander Hamilton packed his trunk and set off, hoping that the vagaries of life in the New World would be, for him, a blessing and not a curse.

THE POPULATION EXPLOSION OF THE EIGHTEENTH CENTURY

As the colonies matured, they were tied in to the North Atlantic world and brought dramatic changes. One of the most important changes was the increase in population, from both immigration and natural increase. This population produced products for the world economy and provided a market for them as well, and its boom was both the product of American prosperity and the precondition for its further growth.

The Dimensions of Population Growth

The population in the American colonies grew at a rate unprecedented in human history, from just over 250,000 people in 1700 to more than 1 million by 1750. The rate of growth was highest in the free population in prosperous farming regions, but it was rapid everywhere, even among enslaved people.

Much of the colonies' population growth was caused by their unquenchable thirst for labor. They attracted an extraordinary number of immigrants, and when free labor did not meet the demand, unfree labor (enslaved people, indentured servants, and redemptioners) filled the gap. Increasingly, these immigrants reflected the broad reach of the North Atlantic political world. At the beginning of the eighteenth century, the population of the American colonies was primarily English in origin. By the beginning of the American Revolution, the population had changed significantly. There were small numbers of people with Finnish, Swedish, French, Swiss, and Jewish heritage, and large numbers of Welsh, Scotch-Irish, Germans, Dutch, and Africans. The foundation for American diversity had been laid.

Bound for America: European Immigrants

In the eighteenth century, about 425,000 Europeans migrated to the colonies, with large numbers from Scotland, Ireland, Wales, and Germany. The largest numbers of European immigrants were **Scotch-Irish**, that is, Scottish people who had moved to Northern Ireland to escape famine in their own country. As many as 250,000 came to seek a better life and to escape the religious persecution they experienced as Presbyterians in an Anglican society. At first, Massachusetts invited the Scotch-Irish to settle on its borders, as a buffer between the colony and the Indians. Once the impoverished Scotch-Irish began to arrive in large numbers, however, the English inhabitants worried that they would have to provide for them. In 1729, a Boston mob turned away a shipload of Scotch-Irish immigrants, and in 1738 the Puritans of Worcester burned down a Presbyterian church. Thereafter, the vast majority of Scotch-Irish immigrants headed for the more welcoming middle colonies and the South.

Going where land was the cheapest, the Scotch-Irish settled between the English seaboard settlements and the Indian communities to the west, from Pennsylvania to Georgia (see Map 5–1). As their numbers increased, the Scotch-Irish pressed against the Indians, seizing their lands. Like the Scotch-Irish, most German migrants settled in the backcountry from Pennsylvania to the Carolinas. Between 1700 and the start of the Revolution, more than 100,000 Germans arrived, and by 1775, a third of Pennsylvania's population was German. Including not only Lutherans and Catholics but also Quakers, Amish, and Mennonites, Germans established prosperous farming communities wherever they settled. Indeed, colonies such as Pennsylvania that welcomed the widest variety of immigrants became not only the most prosperous but also the ones in which prosperity was most widely shared. Unlike most seventeenth-century migrants, a large proportion of eighteenth-century migrants were artisans drawn to America by the demand for their labor. The majority of European migrants to the colonies were unfree—not only indentured servants and redemptioners but also the 50,000 British convicts whose sentences were commuted to a term of service in the colonies. Most English and Welsh migrants were single men between the ages of 19 and 23 who came as indentured servants. The Scotch-Irish migration included a larger number of families, and three-fourths of the Germans came in family groups. For all, the passage to America, which could take three months or more, was grueling and profoundly unhealthy. Once the migrants arrived, servants and convicts were sold for terms of service at auctions (see Figure 5–1).

Bound for America: Enslaved Africans

The increase in the African population was even more dramatic than that of Europeans. In 1660, there were only 2,920 African or African-descended inhabitants of the mainland colonies. A century later there were more than 300,000. The proportion of Africans grew most rapidly in the southern colonies, to almost 40 percent on the eve of the Revolution. By 1720, South Carolina had an African majority. Most of the increase in the African population came from the slave trade. By 1808, when Congress closed off the importation of enslaved people to the United States, about 523,000 enslaved Africans had been imported into the nation (see Figure 5–2).

The African slave trade was a profitable and well-organized segment of the world economy. Until the eighteenth century, when demand from the New World increased, the transatlantic slave trade was controlled by Africans, in the sense that enslaved people were brought to the coast by other Africans for sale to Europeans. African nations had to participate in this activity because it was the only way

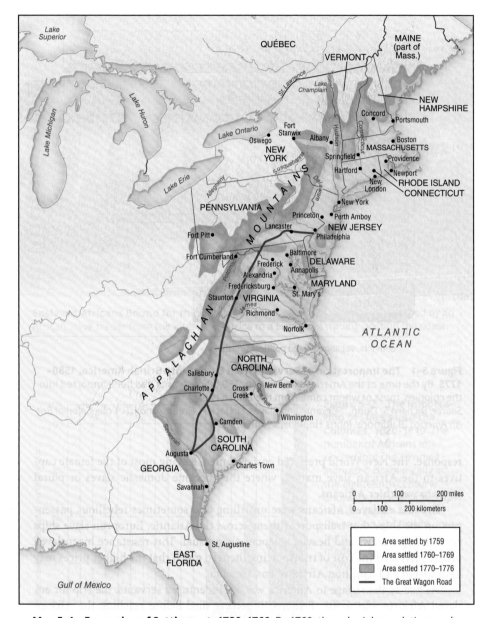

Map 5–1 Expansion of Settlement, 1720–1760 By 1760, the colonial population made up an almost continuous line of settlement from Maine to Florida and was pushing west over the Appalachian Mountains.

they could purchase guns, and without guns, they were vulnerable to neighbors who had already bought them. Some nations supplied a steady stream of slaves, whereas others offered them intermittently, stopping when they had enough arms to defend themselves for a while. Most enslaved people were captives of war, and as the demand for slaves increased, the tempo of warfare in Africa intensified in

THE TRANSATLANTIC ECONOMY: PRODUCING AND CONSUMING

In the eighteenth century, as the colonies matured, they became **capitalist** societies in an Atlantic trade network. More and more, people produced for the market, so that they could buy the goods the market had to offer. Throughout the Atlantic world, ordinary people reshaped their lives so they could buy more goods. Historians talk about two economic revolutions in this period: a **consumer revolution**—a steady increase in the demand for and purchase of consumer goods—and an **industrious revolution** (not *industrial* but *industrious* revolution), in which people worked harder and organized their households (their families, servants, and enslaved people) to produce goods for sale so that they would have money to pay for items they wanted. Income went up only slightly in the eighteenth century, yet people were buying more. In the process, they created a consumer society, in which most people eagerly purchased consumer goods.

The Nature of Colonial Economic Growth

Throughout human history, population growth has usually led to a decline in the standard of living as more people compete for a finite supply of resources. In the American colonies, however, population growth led to an expansion of the economy, as more of the continent's abundant natural resources were brought under human control. The standard of living for most free Americans probably improved, although not dramatically. As the economy matured, a small segment—urban merchants and owners of large plantations—became wealthy. At the same time, the urban poor and tenant farmers began to slip toward poverty.

All of these changes took place, however, without any significant changes in technology (such as the power looms that would be invented later in the century). Most wealth was made from shipping and agriculture. Eighty percent of the colonies' population worked on farms or plantations, areas with no major technological innovations. Virtually all gains in productivity came instead from labor: more people were working, and they were working more efficiently.

The economy of colonial America was shaped by three factors: abundance of land and shortages of labor and of capital. The plantation regions of the South and the West Indies were best situated to take advantage of these circumstances, and the small-farm areas of New England were the least suitable. Tobacco planters in the Chesapeake and rice and indigo planters in South Carolina sold their products on a huge world market. Their large profits enabled them to purchase more land and more slaves to work it.

Because northern farmers raised crops and animals that were also produced in Europe, profits from agriculture alone were too low to permit them to acquire large tracts of land or additional labor (see Table 5–1). Northerners had to look to other opportunities for wealth. They found them in trade, exchanging their raw goods for European manufactured ones and selling them to American consumers.

The Transformation of the Family Economy

In colonial America, the family was the basic economic unit, and all family members contributed to it. Work was organized by gender. On farms, women were responsible for the preparation of food and clothing, child care, and care of the home.

Table 5–1   How Wealthy Were Colonial Americans?

Property-Owning Class	New England	Mid-Atlantic Colonies	Southern Colonies	Thirteen Colonies
Men	169	194	410	260
Women	42	103	215	132
Adults 45 and older	252	274	595	361
Adults 44 and younger	129	185	399	237
Urban	191	287	641	233
Rural	151	173	392	255
Esquires, gentlemen	313	1,223	1,281	572
Merchants	563	858	314	497
Professions, sea captains	271	241	512	341
Farmers only, planters	155	180	396	263
Farmer-artisans, ship owners, fishermen	144	257	801	410
Shop and tavern keepers	219	222	195	204
Artisans, chandlers	114	144	138	122
Miners, laborers	52	67	383	62

Source: Alice Hanson Jones, Wealth of a Nation to Be: The American Colonies on the Eve of the Revolution (New York: Columbia University Press, 1980), p. 224.

Note: Numbers given are in pounds sterling.

Women grew vegetables and herbs, provided dairy products, and transformed flax and wool into clothing. Daughters worked under their mothers' supervision, perhaps spinning extra yarn to be sold for a profit.

Men worked the rest of the farm. They raised grain and maintained the pastures. They cleared the land, chopped wood for fuel, and built and maintained the house, barn, and other structures. They took crops to market. Men's and women's work were complementary and necessary for survival. For example, men planted apple trees, children picked apples, and women pressed the apples into cider. When a husband was disabled, ill, or away from home, his wife could perform virtually all of his tasks as a sort of "deputy husband." Men almost never performed women's work, however, and men whose wives died remarried quickly to have someone to care for the household and children.

The eighteenth century's industrious revolution transformed the family economy: when people decided to produce goods to sell, they changed their family economies. Historians believe that increased production in this period came primarily from the labor of women and children, who worked harder and longer than they had before.

Sources of Regional Prosperity

The South, the most productive region, accounted for more than 60 percent of colonial exports (see Map 5–2). Tobacco was its chief cash crop. Next came cereals such as rice, wheat, corn, and flour, and then indigo, a plant used to dye fabric.

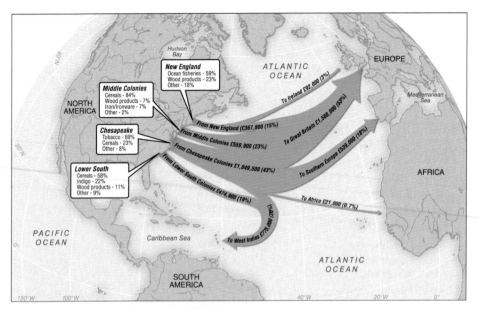

Map 5–2   Exports of the Thirteen Colonies, ca. 1770 Almost two-thirds of the exports from the colonies came from the South, and more than one-half went to Great Britain alone. Tobacco and grains were the most important exports of all.
Source: Jacob Cooke, ed., *Encyclopedia of North American Colonies* (New York: Scribner's, 1993), pp. 1, 514.

Slave labor accounted for most of the southern agricultural output and was organized to produce for the market. When tobacco profits began to slip because of falling prices and the depletion of the soil, planters worked their slaves harder and, in the Chesapeake, began to plant corn and wheat. By diversifying their crops, planters were able to make maximum use of their slave labor force by keeping enslaved people busy throughout the year.

The work routine of enslaved people depended on the crops they tended. On tobacco plantations, where careful attention to the plants was necessary to ensure high quality, planters or white overseers worked the slaves in small gangs carefully selected and arranged to maximize productivity.

In the rice-growing lower South, however, the enslaved were usually assigned specific tasks, which they would work at until the job was completed. Rice growing required far less supervision than did tobacco planting. Because many Africans had grown rice in Africa and had likely taught Europeans how to grow it in America, rice planters let the enslaved people set their own pace. In addition, the people were sometimes allowed to use the evenings as they chose. Many planted gardens to supplement their own diets or to earn a small income. Enslaved people trafficked in a wide range of products, from rice, corn, chickens, hogs, and catfish to canoes, baskets, and wax.

The inhabitants of the **middle colonies** grew prosperous by raising and selling wheat and other grains. The ports of Baltimore, Philadelphia, Wilmington, and

New York became thriving commercial centers that collected grain from regional farms, milled it into flour, and shipped it to the West Indies, southern Europe, and other American colonies. Farmers relied on indentured servants, cottagers, and enslaved people to supplement the labor of family members. **Cottagers** were families who rented out part of a farmer's land, which they worked for wages.

As long as land was cheap and accessible, the middle colonies enjoyed the most evenly shared prosperity on the continent. Most inhabitants fell into the comfortable middle class, with the gap between the richest and the poorest relatively small. Pennsylvania, which offered both religious toleration and relatively simple ways to purchase land, was particularly prosperous. The energy that elsewhere went into religious conflict here fueled work and material accumulation. Gottlieb Mittelberger, who endured a horrendous journey to Pennsylvania, described his new home as a sort of paradise: "Our Americans live more quietly and peacefully than the Europeans; and all this is the result of the liberty which they enjoy and which makes them all equal."

When land became expensive or difficult to obtain, however, conflict might ensue. In the 1740s and 1750s, both New Jersey and New York experienced land riots when conflicting claims made land titles uncertain. In the Chesapeake and southeastern Pennsylvania, increasing land prices drove the poor into tenancy or to the urban centers. Widespread prosperity led Americans to expect that everyone who wished to would be able to own a farm. When land ownership was not fully possible, tension and anger grew.

New England was also primarily a farming region. Here, however, male family members, rather than indentured servants, cottagers, or enslaved people, provided most farm labor. Although farms in some regions, such as the Connecticut River valley, produced surpluses for the market, most farm families had to look for other sources of income to pay for consumer goods.

Town governments in New England encouraged enterprise, sometimes providing gristmills, sawmills, and fields on which cattle could graze. The region prospered, and New Englanders came to expect their governments to enhance the economy. Agricultural exports were relatively slight, although both grain and livestock were sold to the slave plantations of the West Indies, which received more than 25 percent of the American colonies' exports (and more than 70 percent of New England's).

The other major colonial exports in the eighteenth century were fur and hides. By the eve of the Revolution, 95 percent of the furs imported into England came from North America—most of them provided by Indians, who traded them to European middlemen.

Merchants and Dependent Laborers in the Transatlantic Economy

Almost all colonies participated in a transatlantic economy. In each region, those most involved in the market were those with the most resources: large planters in the southern colonies, owners of the biggest farms in the middle colonies, and urban merchants in the northern colonies. The wealthiest never made their fortunes from farming or planting alone but always added income from activities such as speculating in land, practicing law, or lending money.

Interpreter. I was both a School master and Minister to the Indians, yea I was their Ear, Eye & Hand, as well as Mouth. I leave it with the World, as wicked as it is, to Judge, whether I ought not to have had half as much, they gave a young man Just mentioned which would have been but 50 pounds a year; and if they ought to have given me that, I am not under obligations to them, I owe them nothing at all; what can be the Reason that they used me after this manner? I can't think of anything, but this as a Poor Indian Boy said, Who was Bound out to an English Family, and he used to Drive Plow for a young man, and he whipt and beat him almost every Day, and the young man found fault with him, and Complained of him to his master and the poor Boy was Called to answer for himself before his master, and he was asked, what it was he did, that he was So Complained of and beat almost every Day. He Said, he did not know, but he Supposed it was because he could not drive any better; but says he, I Drive as well as I know how; and at other Times he Beats me, because he is of a mind to beat me; but says he believes he Beats me for the most of the Time "because I am an Indian."

Source: Colin Calloway, ed., *The World Turned Upside Down: Indian Voices from Early America* (New York: Bedford), p. 61.

5.3   OLAUDAH EQUIANO, EXCERPTS FROM *THE INTERESTING NARRATIVE AND OTHER WRITINGS* (1789)

The late eighteenth-century autobiography of Gustavus Vassa, or Olaudah Equiano, is probably the most famous slave narrative ever published. He claimed to have been born in Africa and brought to America, but scholars have recently demonstrated that it is far more likely that Equiano was American-born and made this claim about himself so as to be able to speak about—and criticize—the slave trade with "authenticity." In any case, having been at sea during the French and Indian War, acting first as a naval officer's personal servant and then as a fighter, he assumed he was to be freed by his master but was disappointed instead.

Our ship having arrived at Portsmouth, we went into the harbour and remained there till the latter end of November, when we heard great talk about peace, and to our very great joy in the beginning of December we had orders to go up to London with our ship to be paid off. We received this news with loud huzzas and every other demonstration of gladness, and nothing but mirth was to be seen throughout every part of the ship. I too was not without my share of the general joy on this occasion. I thought now of nothing but being freed and working for myself, and thereby getting money to enable me to get a good education: for I always had a great desire to be able at least to read and write, and while I was on ship-board I had endeavoured to improve myself in both. While I was in the *Ætna* particularly, the captain's clerk taught me to write, and gave me a smattering of arithmetic as far as the rule of three. There was also one Daniel Queen, about forty years of age, a man very well educated, who messed [that is, ate] with me on board this ship, and he likewise dressed and attended the captain. Fortunately this man soon became very much attached to me and took very great pains to instruct me in many things. He taught me to shave and dress hair a little and also to read in the Bible, explaining many passages to me which I did not comprehend. I was wonderfully surprised to see the laws and rules of my country written almost exactly here, a circumstance which I believe tended to impress our manners and customs more deeply on my memory. I used to tell him of this resemblance, and many a time we have sat up the whole night together at this employment. In short, he was like a father to me, and some even used to call me after his name; they also styled me the black Christian. Indeed I almost loved him with the affection of a son. Many things I have denied myself that he might have them, and when I used to play at marbles or any other game and won a few halfpence, or got any little money, which I sometimes did, for shaving anyone, I used to buy him a little sugar or tobacco, as far as my stock of money would go. He used to say that he and I never should part, and that when our ship was paid off, as I was as free as himself or any other man on board, he would instruct me in his business by which I might gain a good livelihood. This gave me new life and spirits, and my heart burned within me while I thought the time long till I obtained my freedom. For though my master had not promised it to me, yet besides the assurances I had received that he had no right to detain me, he always treated me with the greatest kindness and reposed in me an unbounded confidence; he even paid attention to my morals, and would never suffer me to deceive him or tell lies, of which he used to tell me the consequences; and that if I did so God would not love me; so that from all this tenderness, I had never once supposed, in all my dreams of freedom, that he would think of detaining me any longer than I wished.

In pursuance of our orders we sailed from Portsmouth for the Thames and arrived at Deptford 10 December, where we cast anchor just as it was high water. The ship was up about half an hour, when my master ordered the barge to be manned, and all in an instant, without having before given me the least reason to suspect anything of the matter, he forced me into the barge, saying I was going to leave him, but he would take care I should not. I was so struck with the unexpectedness of this proceeding that for some time I did not make a reply, only I made an offer to go for my books and chest of clothes, but he swore I should not move out of his sight, and if I did he would cut my throat, at the same time taking his hanger [a short sword]. I began, however, to collect myself, and plucking up courage, I told him I was free and he could not by law serve me so. But this only enraged him the more, and he continued to swear, and said he would soon let me know whether he would or not, and at that instant sprung himself into the barge from the ship to the astonishment and sorrow of all on board. The tide, rather unluckily for me, had just turned downward, so that we quickly fell down the river along with it till we came among some outward-bound West Indiamen, for he was resolved to put me on board the first vessel he could get to receive me. The boat's crew, who pulled against their will, became quite faint, different times, and would have gone ashore, but he would not let them. Some of them strove then to cheer me and told me he could not sell me, which revived me a little, and I still entertained hopes, for as they pulled along he asked some vessels to receive me, but they could not. But just as we had got a little below Gravesend, we came alongside of a ship which was going away the next tide for the West Indies; her name was the *Charming Sally*, Captain James Doran, and my master went on board and agreed with him for me, and in a little time I was sent for into the cabin. When I came there Captain Doran asked me if I knew him; I answered that I did not; "Then," said he, "you are now my slave." I told him my master could not sell me to him, nor to anyone else. "Why," said he, "did not your master buy you?" I confessed he did. "But I have served him," said I, "many years, and he has taken all my wages and prize-money, for I only got one sixpence during the war; besides this I have been baptized, and by the laws of the land no man has a right to sell me." And I added that I had heard a lawyer and others at different times tell my master so. They both then said that those people who told me so were not my friends, but I replied, "It was very extraordinary that other people did not know the law as well as they." Upon this Captain Doran said I talked too much English, and if I did not behave myself well and be quiet he had a method on board to make me. I was too well convinced of his power over me to doubt what he said, and my former sufferings in the slave-ship presenting themselves to my mind, the recollection of them made me shudder. However, before I retired I told them that as I could not get any right among men here I hoped I should hereafter in Heaven,

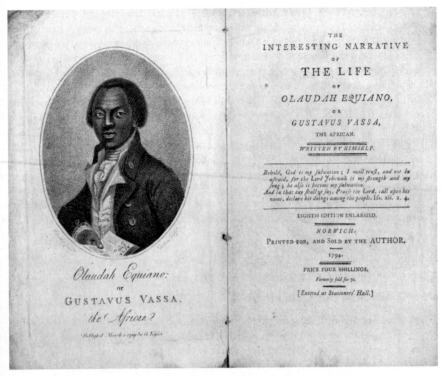

THE

INTERESTING NARRATIVE

OF

THE LIFE

OF

OLAUDAH EQUIANO,

OR

GUSTAVUS VASSA,

THE AFRICAN.

WRITTEN BY HIMSELF.

Behold, God is my falvation; I will truft, and not be afraid, for the Lord Jehovah is my ftrength and my fong; he alfo is become my falvation. And in that day fhall ye fay, Praife the Lord, call upon his name, declare his doings among the people. Ifa. xii. 2. 4.

EIGHTH EDITION ENLARGED.

NORWICH:

PRINTED FOR, AND SOLD BY THE AUTHOR.

1794.

PRICE FOUR SHILLINGS.

Formerly fold for 7s.

[*Entered at Stationers' Hall.*]

Olaudah Equiano;

or

GUSTAVUS VASSA.

the African?

Source: Library of Congress Rare Book and Special Collections Division, Washington, DC.

and I immediately left the cabin, filled with resentment and sorrow. The only coat I had with me my master took away with him, and said if my prize-money had been £10,000 he had a right to it all and would have taken it. I had about nine guineas which, during my long seafaring life, I had scraped together from trifling perquisites and little ventures, and I hid it that instant lest my master should take that from me likewise, still hoping that by some means or other I should make my escape to the shore; and indeed some of my old shipmates told me not to despair for they would get me back again, and that as soon as they could get their pay, they would immediately come to Portsmouth to me, where this ship was going: but, alas! all my hopes were baffled and the hour of my deliverance was yet far off. My master, having soon concluded his bargain with the captain, came out of the cabin, and he and his people got into the boat and put off; I followed them with aching eyes as long as I could, and when they were out of sight I threw myself on the deck, while my heart was ready to burst with sorrow and anguish.

Source: Olaudah Equiano, *The Interesting Narrative and Other Writings*, edited by Vincent Carretta (New York: Penguin Books, 1995), pp. 91–94.

5.4   GEORGE WHITEFIELD, ACCOUNT OF A VISIT TO CAROLINA (1740)

George Whitefield, the leading preacher of the Great Awakening, maintained a diary in which he recorded his travels to spread the word of the Lord. He edited and published these journals in regular installments so as to reach a wider audience.

Though an Englishman by birth, he visited America seven times. This selection comes from his second trip, which was in general very successful. Yet here we see evidence that not everyone was disposed to hear his message, and that he himself suffered from racial blinders.

Tuesday, January 1, 1740. Rode about ten miles, and where we waited, met with one who I had great reason to believe, was a child of God. It grieved me that I could stay no longer, but being in haste, we passed over a half-mile ferry. About sunset, we came to a tavern, five miles within the province of South Carolina. Here I immediately perceived the people were more polite than those we generally met with; but I believe the people of the house wished I had not come to be their guest that night; for, it being New Year's Day, several of the neighbours were met together to divert themselves by dancing country dances. By the advice of my companions, I went in amongst them whilst a woman was dancing a jig. At my first entrance I endeavoured to shew the folly of such entertainments, and to convince her how well pleased the devil was at every step she took. For some time she endeavoured to outbrave me; neither the fiddler nor she desisted; but at last she gave over, and the musician laid aside his instrument. It would have made any one smile to see how the rest of the company, one by one attacked me, and brought, as they thought, arguments to support their wantonness; but Christ triumphed over Satan. All were soon put to silence, and were, for some time, so overawed, that after I had discoursed with them on the nature of baptism, and the necessity of being born again, in order to enjoy the Kingdom of Heaven, I baptized, by their entreaty, one of their children, and prayed afterwards as I was enabled, and as the circumstances of the company required. I and my companions then took a little refreshment; but the people were so bent on their pleasure, that notwithstanding all that had been said, after I had gone to bed, I heard their music and dancing, which made me look back upon my own past follies with shame and confusion of face; for such an one, not long since, was I myself. Lord, for Thy mercies' sake, shew all unhappy formalists of the same favour, and suffer them not to go in such a carnal security till they lift up their eyes in torment! Draw them, O draw them from feeding upon such husks. Let them know what it is to feast upon the fatted calf, even the comforts of the Blessed Spirit. Amen.

Wednesday, Jan. 2. Rose very early, prayed, sung a hymn, and gave a sharp reproof to the dancers, who were very attentive, and took it in good part. At break of day, we mounted our horses, and I think, never had a more pleasant journey. For nearly twenty miles, we rode over a beautiful bay as plain as a terrace walk, and as we passed along were wonderfully delighted to see the porpoises taking their pastime, and heard, as it were, shore resounding to shore the praises of Him Who hath set bounds to the sea that it cannot pass, and hath said, "Here shall your proud waves be stayed." At night we intended to call at a gentleman's house, where we had been recommended, about forty miles distant from our last night's lodging; but the moon being totally eclipsed, we missed the path that turned out of the road, and then thought it most advisable, as we were in the main road, to go on our way, trusting to the Almighty to strengthen both our beasts and us. We had not gone far when we saw a light. Two of my friends went up to it, and found a hut full of negroes; they enquired after the gentleman's house whither we had been directed, but the negroes seemed surprised, and said they knew no such man, and that they were new comers. From these circumstances, one of my friends inferred, that these negroes might be some of those who lately had made an insurrection in the province, and had run away from their masters. When he returned, we were all of his mind, and, therefore, thought it best to mend our pace. Soon after, we saw another great fire near the roadside, and imaging there was another nest of such negroes, we made a circuit into the woods, and one of my friends at a distance observed them dancing round the fire. The moon shining brightly, we soon found our way into the great road again; and after we had gone about a dozen miles (Expecting to find negroes in every place) we came to a great plantation, the master of which gave us lodging, and our beasts provender. Upon our relating the circumstances of our travels, he satisfied us concerning the negroes, informed us whose they were, and upon what occasion they were in those places in which we found them. This afforded us much comfort, after we had ridden nearly threescore miles, and, as we thought, in great peril of our lives. Blessed be Thy Name, O Lord, for this, and all other Thy mercies, through Jesus Christ!

Thursday, Jan.3. Had a hospitable breakfast; set out late in the morning, passed over a three mile ferry near George Town; and for the ease of our beasts, rode not above nineteen miles the whole day. "A good man," says Solomon, "is merciful to his beast."

Source: William Wale, ed., *Whitefield's Journals* (London: Henry Drane, 1905), pp. 379–381.

5.5   PHILLIS WHEATLEY, "TO THE UNIVERSITY OF CAMBRIDGE, IN NEW ENGLAND" (1773)

Phillis Wheatley was brought as an enslaved person from Africa to America in 1761, when she was about eight years old. She was purchased by the wealthy Boston merchant John Wheatley to be a companion to his wife. Wheatley proved to be an excellent student, and they tutored her in English, Latin, history, and Christianity. During this time, the students at Harvard University were becoming increasingly known for their wild and destructive behavior. Here, Wheatley reminds them what people of African descent would do with the education they were being offered if it was given to them. Years later, she would receive her freedom from the Wheatley family.

To the University of Cambridge, in New England

While an intrinsic ardor prompts to write,
The muses promise to assist my pen;
'Twas not long since I left my native shore
The land of errors, and *Egyptian* gloom:
Father of mercy, 'twas thy gracious hand
Brought me in safety from those dark abodes.
Students, to you 'tis giv'n to scan the heights
Above, to traverse the ethereal space,
And mark the systems of revolving worlds.
Still more, ye sons of science ye receive
The blissful news by messengers from heav'n,
How *Jesus'* blood for your redemption flows.
See him with hands out-stretcht upon the cross;
Immense compassion in his bosom glows;
He hears revilers, nor resents their scorn:a
What matchless mercy in the Son of God!
When the whole human race by sin had fall'n,
He deign'd to die that they might rise again,
And share with him in the sublimest skies,
Life without death, and glory without end.

Improve your privileges while they stay,
Ye pupils, and each hour redeem, that bears
Or good or bad report of you to heav'n.
Let sin, that baneful evil to the soul,
By you be shunn'd, nor once remit your guard;
Suppress the deadly serpent in its egg.
Ye blooming plants of human race devine,
An *Ethiop* tells you 'tis your greatest foe;
Its transient sweetness turns to endless pain,
And in immense perdition sinks the soul.

Source: Julian D. Mason, ed., *The Poems of Phillis Wheatley* (Chapel Hill: University of North Carolina Press, 1989 [1966]), p. 52.

Another round of international warfare broke out in 1739 and lasted nine years. In the War of Jenkins's Ear (1739–1744), Britain attempted to expand into Spanish territories and markets in the Americas. Urged on by merchants, and with the approval of colonists who wanted to eliminate Spain as a rival, Britain found an excuse for declaring war: a ship's captain, Robert Jenkins, turned up in Parliament in 1738 holding in his hand what he claimed was his ear, severed by the Spanish seven years earlier in the Caribbean. Once again, colonists joined in what they hoped would be a glorious international endeavor, only to be disillusioned. In 1741, 3,600 colonists, mostly poor young men lured by the promise of Spanish plunder, joined 5,000 Britons in a failed attack on Cartagena, Colombia. More than half the colonial contingent died.

Another ambitious move against the Spanish empire failed in 1740. James Oglethorpe and settlers hired by South Carolina, accompanied by Cherokee and Creek allies, failed to seize the Spanish outpost at St. Augustine and left the southern border vulnerable. When Oglethorpe's troops repulsed a Spanish attack in 1742, however, Spain's plan to arm the enslaved people of Georgia and South Carolina and thus destroy the Anglo colonies was thwarted.

Just as the War of Jenkins's Ear ended in stalemate, so did King George's War (1744–1748), a conflict between Britain and Austria on one side and France and Prussia on the other over succession to the Austrian throne. A French raid on a fishing village in Nova Scotia met with a huge retaliation by the British. Troops from Massachusetts, supported by the British navy, captured the French fort at Louisbourg. Finally, a joint British-colonial venture had succeeded. But a planned attack on Québec was called off when the British fleet failed to arrive. At war's end, Britain returned Louisbourg to France and warned the colonists that they had to maintain the peace. The British blockade of French ports cut off trade to Canada, including the all-important presents to Indian allies and trade partners. Without these European goods, the French-Indian empire began to crumble.

The Local Impact of Global War

Successive rounds of warfare had a significant impact on politics and society in British North America. Although the colonists identified strongly with the British cause, decades of warfare were a constant drain on the colonial treasury and population.

Wars are expensive. Generally, rates of taxation in colonial America were low, except when wars had to be financed. In a rehearsal for the conflicts that would lead to the American Revolution, the British government complained that the colonists were unwilling to contribute their fair share to the imperial wars. As a rule, colonial legislatures were willing to go only so far in raising taxes to pay for imperial wars or expeditions against Indians. Then they simply issued paper money. Inevitably, the currency depreciated, making even worse the boom-and-bust cycles that war economies always produce.

No colony did more to support the imperial war efforts than Massachusetts, but the result was heightened political conflict at home. Royal governors, eager to please officials in London, pushed the colony to contribute to the imperial wars. As many as one-fifth of the colony's men may have served in the military in the middle of the eighteenth century. In 1747, Boston mobs rioted for three days to resist the

Royal Navy's attempt to "impress" (force) men into service, and the local militia refused to restore order. For the first time, Bostonians began to speak about a right to resist tyranny.

Much more than in Europe, civilians in America became victims of war. By the eighteenth century, conventions of "civilized" warfare that held that civilians should be spared broke down in America for two reasons. First, without a transportation system to supply the army, troops often relied on plunder. Second, frontier Indians, adapting their traditional practices of war, routinely attacked villages, seizing captives to replenish their populations and to ransom to the French. Between 1675 and 1763, when frontier settlers such as Susannah Johnson were at risk, Indians took more than 1,600 New England settlers as captives, more than 90 percent during times of war (see Figure 6–1).

Almost half the colonists seized eventually returned home, but as with Johnson's son Sylvanus, who had forgotten English entirely, the former captives remained culturally Indian to some extent. Other captives died during the arduous march to Canada. Many died of disease, and some, typically girls between 7 and 15, remained with their captors voluntarily. Historians debate why this was so. Perhaps it was because Puritan culture trained girls to respond without question to those in authority. Or perhaps it was because, after the rigors of a Puritan upbringing, the relative freedom of Indian culture was inviting.

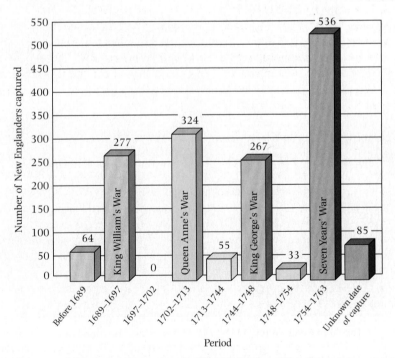

Figure 6–1 New England Captives, 1675–1763 During periods of war, the number of New Englanders taken captive by northern Indians and the French increased dramatically; more than 90 percent of captives were taken during wartime.
Source: Alden Vaughan, *Roots of American Racism* (New York: Oxford University Press, 1990), p. 31.

The French Empire Crumbles from Within

In the years after King George's War, a change in French policy offered a small band of Miami Indians the chance to gain an advantage over rivals. In the process, they started a chain of events that led to the **French and Indian War.**

Although King George's War had ended in a stalemate, it weakened the French position in North America. The costs of war had forced the French to cut back on their presents to allied Algonquian tribes, especially in the Ohio River Valley. To raise revenue, the French sharply increased their charges for the lease of trading posts; in turn, traders raised the prices that they charged the Indians for trade goods. These changes significantly weakened the French hold over their Indian allies, creating political instability that was the underlying North American cause of the French and Indian War.

The **Ohio River Valley** was home to small, refugee tribes (see Map 6–1). As long as the French provided liberal presents and cheap trade goods, they maintained a loose control. Once that control ended, however, each tribe sought to increase its advantage over the others, at a time when the British recognized the strategic and economic importance of the region.

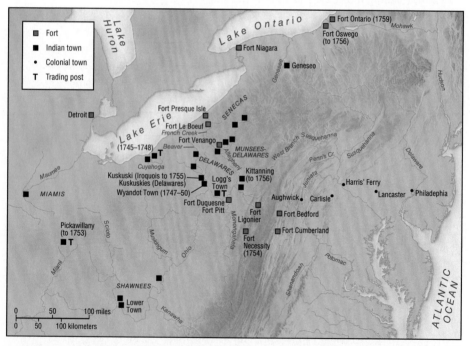

Map 6–1   The Ohio River Valley, 1747–1758 This territory, inhabited by a number of small bands of Indians, was coveted by both the French and the British, not to mention several competing groups of colonial land speculators. The rivalries between the imperial powers, among the Indian bands, and between rival groups of speculators made this region a powder keg.
Source: Adapted from Michael McConnell, *A Country Between* (Lincoln: University of Nebraska, 1992), pp. 116–117.

The temporary power vacuum afforded a small group of Miamis, led by a chieftain called **Memeskia**, an opportunity to play one group of colonists off another. The chain of events that led to the French and Indian War began in 1748 when Memeskia's group, originally allied to the French, established a new village, Pickawillany, near the head of the Miami River (in today's Ohio). Memeskia welcomed English traders from Pennsylvania, because their goods were better and cheaper than those of the French. He hoped to trade with the British free of political or military obligations.

Memeskia's move threatened not only the balance of power between Britain and France but also that between Pennsylvania and Virginia. The Pennsylvanians welcomed trade with the Miamis, for it gave them a claim to the western lands that Virginians sought. At the same time, Memeskia used his access to British traders to attract many small bands of followers to his village. Alarmed, the French shifted away from trade to force. In 1749, they sent a small expedition to cow their former Indian allies back into submission. When it failed, they began to raid dissident Indian encampments and planned to establish a fort in the Ohio River Valley. With this change in French policy, Indians faced two options: to gather Indian allies (Memeskia's tactic) or to make alliances with the British (the strategy of an Iroquois chieftain named Tanacharison). Neither route promised real security, but the chaos these bids for advantage created drew the French and British into war.

In 1752, Tanacharison agreed to give Virginia not only the 200,000 acres claimed by the Ohio Company, a group of Virginia speculators, but also all the land between the Susquehanna and Allegheny Rivers (today's Kentucky, West Virginia, and western Pennsylvania). In return, Virginia promised Tanacharison's people trade and protection from their enemies. Memeskia was isolated. With no European or Indian power dominant in the region, conflicts broke out, and the French pried off some of Memeskia's allies and conquered the rest. In a raid on Pickawillany, 250 pro-French Ottawas and Chippewas killed Memeskia. Their village destroyed, the demoralized Miamis returned to the French for protection. For the moment, the French regained power, but by shifting their policy from trade to force, they set a course that would lead to the loss of their North American empire.

The Virginians Ignite a War

Both France and Virginia now claimed the Ohio River Valley, and they raced to establish forts to secure their claims. Virginia entrusted the job to a well-connected 21-year-old with almost no qualifications for the post: **George Washington**. Washington was tied through his brother's marriage to the powerful Fairfax clan, a British family that owned 5 million acres in Virginia and held a share in the Ohio Company. In the Anglo-American world, advancement came through such linked ties of family and patronage.

In the spring of 1754, the French and Virginians scrambled to see who could build a fort first at the Forks of the Ohio (present-day Pittsburgh). The force that Virginia sent to the region, with Washington second in command, was pathetically small. Although the French army—numbering 1,000—was only 50 miles away, a combined Virginia-Indian band led by Washington attacked and defeated a small French reconnaissance party. The French and Indian War (known in Europe as the Seven Years' War) had begun.

The Virginians had bitten off more than they could chew. Washington's small fort was reinforced by British regulars but was quickly deserted by Indian allies, who recognized it as indefensible. The French overwhelmed the fort, driving Washington and his troops back to Virginia. Although war was not officially declared in Europe until May 1756, fighting soon spread throughout the frontier.

From Local to Imperial War

At the beginning of the war, the advantage was with the French. Although the population in the British colonies greatly outnumbered that of New France, France's population was three times larger than Britain's and its army 10 times the size. More important, the more centralized French state was better prepared to coordinate the massive effort an international war required. The British government, aware that lack of coordination among its colonies could cripple the war effort, in summer 1754 instructed all the colonies north of Virginia to plan for a collective defense and to shore up the alliance with the Six (Iroquois) Nations. Pennsylvania's Benjamin Franklin offered the delegates, who met in Albany, a plan, known as the **Albany Plan of Union**, which every colony rejected.

The localism of the American colonies made cooperation difficult if not impossible. A deeply ingrained value, localism was suspicious of the centralized European state and its army of professionals.

Britain was now in its fourth war with France in less than a century. It had authorized Virginia's foray into the Ohio River Valley and sent two regiments, under the command of General Edward Braddock, to Virginia in late 1754, hoping that the colonists could fight with only a little British assistance. But the disarray continued: colonial soldiers were reluctant to obey an officer from another colony, let alone one from the British army.

With four times as many troops as the British had in North America, superior leadership, and no intercolonial rivalries, the French dominated the first phase of the war, from 1754 through 1757. The British and colonial armies planned to besiege four French forts: Fort Duquesne (Pittsburgh), Fort Niagara (Niagara Falls), Fort St. Frédéric (Crown Point, at the southern end of Lake Champlain), and Fort Beauséjour (Nova Scotia).

Braddock was to attack Fort Duquesne with a combined force of British regulars and colonial troops, but without Indians. He had alienated the regional Indians, who rejoined the French alliance. After a grueling two-month march, on July 9, 1755, Braddock's forces were surprised close to their objective by a French and Indian force. Almost 1,000 British and colonial troops were killed or wounded; Braddock himself died from wounds suffered in the ambush. One of the survivors was George Washington, who had been serving as an unsalaried adjutant to Braddock to learn the art of war.

Two of the other three planned assaults ended in disappointment as well. William Shirley, who became the British commander in chief, led the attack on Fort Niagara himself and assigned Fort St. Frédéric to William Johnson, a Mohawk Valley Indian trader who was soon made superintendent of Indian affairs for the northern colonies. Well suited for leading Iroquois forays against the French, Johnson led a force of about 3,500, including 300 Iroquois. Their advance was stopped by the

French and their Native American allies, but with equal casualties on both sides and the capture of the French commander, the British declared victory and elevated Johnson to the nobility. In the winter of 1755–1756, the British built Fort William Henry, and the French, Fort Carillon (which the British renamed Ticonderoga).

Hampered by rough terrain and intercolonial wrangling, Shirley's force never made it to Fort Niagara. The only outright success was at Fort Beauséjour, near the British colony at Nova Scotia. A British-financed expedition of New England volunteers easily seized the fort, and the British evicted 10,000 Acadians (French residents of Nova Scotia) who would not take an oath of loyalty. About 300 ended up in French Louisiana, where their name was abbreviated to "Cajuns."

Both the British and the French expected their colonists to carry most of the load of the war. Their defeats and continued intercolonial rivalries left the British vulnerable and the frontier exposed. The French began a cautious but successful offensive. First, they encouraged Indian raids along the frontier from Maine to South Carolina. Indians swung back to the French because the French appeared less dangerous than the land-hungry British. The price for French friendship, however, was participation in the war against the British. By the fall of 1756, some 3,000 settlers had been killed, and the line of settlement had been pushed back 150 miles in some places.

The French and their Indian allies seized Fort Bull in March 1756 and Fort Oswego several months later. A little over a year later, a massive French force attacked Fort William Henry. This loosely organized army of 8,000 included 1,000 Indian warriors and another 800 converted Algonquians accompanied by their Catholic priests. After a seven-day siege and heavy bombardment,

DEFEAT and DEATH of GENERAL BRADDOCK in North America.

Braddock's Defeat This detail depicting Braddock's defeat is from a drawing by an engineer with the British army.

the British commander surrendered on August 9, 1757. Louis-Joseph de Montcalm, the French commander, offered European-style terms: the British were to return their French and Indian prisoners, keep their personal weapons, and march back to Fort Edward, on the lower Hudson River, promising not to fight the French for 18 months. Historians still debate whether Montcalm knew what was about to take place. The Indians had expected, as was their custom, to be allowed to take plunder and captives. Denied this opportunity, they fell on the British, including the sick, women, and children, as they were evacuating the fort the next morning.

The deaths at Fort William Henry had significant repercussions. Still angry at being denied the spoils of war, Montcalm's Indian allies returned home, taking smallpox with them. The French would never again have the assistance of such a significant number of Indian allies. The British were outraged. The new British commander, Lord Jeffrey Amherst, declared the surrender terms null and void. Later, under his order, Delaware Indians who had been invited to a peace talk were given, ostensibly as presents, blankets that had been infected with smallpox. Historians are not certain whether these blankets were responsible for the outbreak of the disease among local Indians, but that was certainly Amherst's intent.

Problems with British-Colonial Cooperation

The British and the colonists blamed each other for their defeats. There was some truth in their accusations: unwillingness to sacrifice and disastrous infighting among the colonists, and arrogance among the British. These recriminations, more than any side's failing, created problems. The colonists and the British had different expectations about their roles in the war. The colonists were not prepared for the high taxes or sacrifice of liberty that waging an international war required.

The British were dismayed by what they perceived as the colonists' selfishness, as they engaged in profiteering and trading with the enemy. Colonial governments were no more generous. Braddock's expedition to Fort Duquesne was delayed by the colonies' unwillingness to provision his army.

After Braddock's defeat, colonials deserted in droves. The British began recruiting servants and apprentices, angering their masters. Another serious problem was that of quartering soldiers over the winter. Under English law, which did not extend specifically to the colonies, troops in England could be lodged in public buildings rather than private homes. In the colonies, however, there weren't enough buildings in which to house soldiers without resorting to private homes. The residents of Albany took in soldiers only under threat of force. Philadelphians were rescued by the ever-resourceful Ben Franklin, who opened a newly built hospital to the troops. In Charleston, soldiers had to camp outdoors, where they fell victim to disease.

Other problems arose from joint operations. The British army was a disciplined professional fighting force, led by members of the upper classes; service in it was a career. In contrast, colonial soldiers were primarily civilian amateurs, led by members of the middle class from their hometowns. Colonial soldiers believed that they were fighting by contract for a set period of time, for a specific objective, for a set rate of pay, and under a particular officer. If any of the terms were violated, the soldier considered himself free to go home.

The British, however, expected the same discipline from the colonists as they did from their own army. All colonial soldiers operating with regular forces were subject to British martial law, which was cruel and uncompromising. One regular soldier, for example, was sentenced to 1,000 lashes for stealing a keg of beer, which a merciful officer reduced to a mere 900! The British officers were almost unanimous in their condemnation of colonial soldiers. According to Brigadier General James Wolfe, "The Americans are in general the dirtiest most contemptible cowardly dogs that you can conceive."

Yet the colonists certainly believed that they were doing their share. Tax rates were raised sharply, tripling in Virginia in three years, for example. The human contribution was even more impressive. At the height of the war, Massachusetts was raising 7,000 soldiers a year, from a colony of only 50,000 men. Perhaps as many as 3 out of 10 adult men served in the military during the war, and only the Civil War and the Revolution had higher casualty rates.

The British Gain the Advantage

Montcalm's victory at Fort William Henry marked the French high-water mark. After a change of government in 1757, Britain resolved to win the war, as **William Pitt** became head of the cabinet. His rise to power represented the triumph of the commercial classes and their vision of the empire. Pitt was the first British leader who was as committed to a victory in the Americas as in Europe, believing that the future of the British Empire lay in the extended empire and its trade. Britain's aim in North America now shifted from simply regaining territory to seizing New France itself. Pitt sent 2,000 additional troops, promised 6,000 more, and asked the colonies to raise 20,000 of their own. To support so large an army, Pitt raised taxes on the already heavily taxed British and borrowed heavily, doubling the size of the British debt. He won the cooperation of the colonies by promising that Britain would pay up to half of their costs for fighting the war. As all of this money poured into the colonies, it improved their economies dramatically.

Now the British could take the offensive (see Map 6–2). In a series of great victories, they won Louisbourg on Cape Breton Island in July 1758; then Fort Frontenac in August; and finally, in November, Fort Duquesne, which the British renamed Fort Pitt. The only defeat was at Fort Carillon (called Ticonderoga by the British). There, Susannah Johnson's husband, James, was one of the casualties. The British seized Fort Frontenac, disrupting the supply lines from the French to the Ohio Valley Indians, who shifted their allegiance. The British also moved from a policy of confrontation to one of accommodation. In the Treaty of Easton (1758), 13 Ohio Valley tribes agreed to remain neutral in return for a promise to keep the territory west of the Alleghenies free of settlers. Also, gifts to the Iroquois brought them back into the fold.

The British were now ready for the final offensive. Historians always argue about when and why a war is "lost": unless an army has been annihilated and the population entirely subjugated, which is rare, when to surrender is always a subjective decision. Political and military leaders must decide when the loss in lives and resources can no longer be justified, and the population must agree that further fighting is pointless. By 1759, some of the French believed that the war was essentially over. Casualties were extremely high, food was in short supply, and inflation was rampant. Most of the Indian allies had deserted the cause, and the French government was unable to match Pitt's spending on the war. It would take two

The colonies refused, however, to comply with the next piece of legislation, the Townshend Revenue Act of 1767, which levied import duties on lead, paint, glass, paper, and tea. Townshend believed that the colonists objected only to taxes within the colonies, "internal taxes," but that they would accept an "external tax," such as an import duty. The revenue would be used to support colonial officials, making them independent of the colonial assemblies that had paid their salaries.

Resistance to the Townshend Act built slowly, as it was hard for colonists to make a case against all duties. Merchants were now complying with the new Revenue Act of 1766, which reduced the duty on molasses. Those colonists most troubled by the first round of imperial legislation, however, were convinced that the Townshend Duties were part of a design for tyranny.

A body of thought known as **republicanism** helped the colonists make sense of British actions. Republicanism was a set of doctrines rooted in the Renaissance that held that power is always dangerous, because "it is natural for Power to be striving to enlarge itself, and to be encroaching upon those that have none." Republicanism supplied constitutionalism with a motive. It explained how a balanced constitution could be transformed into tyranny. Would-be tyrants had access to a variety of tools, including a standing army, whose ultimate purpose was not the protection of the people but their subjection. Tyrants also engaged in corruption, in particular by dispensing patronage positions. So inexorable was the course of power that it took extraordinary virtue for an individual to resist its corruption. Consequently, republican citizens, it was thought, had to be economically independent; the poor were dangerous because they could easily be bought off by would-be tyrants. A secular theory with connections to Puritanism, republicanism asserted that people were naturally weak and that exceptional human effort was required to protect liberty and virtue.

Not only did people have to keep a close eye on power-hungry tyrants, but they also had to look inside themselves. According to republican thought, history demonstrated that republics fell from within when their citizens lost their virtue. The greatest threat to virtue was luxury, an excessive attachment to the fruits of the consumer revolution. When colonists worried that they saw luxury and corruption everywhere, they were criticizing the world that the consumer revolution had created. Although it is understandable why poor people embraced republicanism, it might seem perplexing that wealthy merchants and planters would also strongly denounce "malice, covetousness, and other lusts of man." Yet the legacy of Puritanism was powerful, and even those profiting most from the new order felt ambivalent about its effects on their society. Joining with poorer people in criticizing British officials and accusing them of attempting to undermine colonial liberties helped forge a cross-class alliance.

The colonial legislatures slowly began to protest the duties. Massachusetts's House of Representatives, led by Sam Adams, asked each of the other lower houses in the colonies to join in resisting "infringements of their natural & constitutional Rights because they are not represented in the British Parliament." When Lord Hillsborough, a hardline secretary of state for the colonies, saw the request, he instructed the colonial governors to dissolve any colonial assembly that received the petition from Massachusetts. Massachusetts refused to rescind it, so Governor Francis Bernard dissolved the legislature. With representative government threatened,

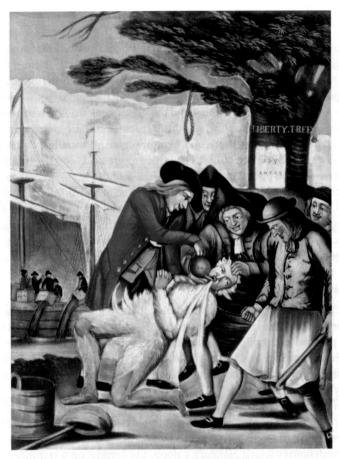

Tarring and Feathering the Customs Officer, 1774 Two Bostonians dress British customs officer John Malcolm in tar and feathers and force him to drink tea, turning him into a "macarony," an effete man who affected the latest fashion.

those colonial legislatures that had not already approved the Massachusetts petition did so now—and were then dissolved. In response, many legislatures met on their own, as extralegal bodies.

Not only did legislators assert their own authority, but ordinary people did so as well. In each colony, the radicals who called themselves **Sons of Liberty** organized a nonimportation movement using both coercion and patriotic appeal. Women were actively recruited into the movement, both to encourage household manufacture (an economic activity redefined as a political one) and to refuse British imports. In 1769, women in little Middletown, Massachusetts, wove 20,522 yards of cloth, and throughout the colonies women signed the nonimportation agreements. This politicization of ordinary people horrified conservative British observers. Although there were pockets of defiance, the movement succeeded in cutting imports dramatically. By the time that the Townshend Duties were repealed in 1770, Britain had collected only £21,000 and lost £786,000 in trade.

Table 6–1   Major Events Leading to the Revolutionary War, 1763–1774

1763	Proclamation of 1763	Confines colonists to the east of an imaginary line running down the spine of the Allegheny Mountains.
1764	Sugar Act	Drops duty on molasses to 3 cents/gallon, but institutes procedures to make sure it is collected, such as trial at Admiralty Court (closest is in Nova Scotia), where burden of proof is on defendant and verdict is rendered by judge rather than jury.
1764	Currency Act	Forbids issuing of any colonial currency.
1765	Stamp Act	Places a tax on 15 classes of documents, including newspapers and legal documents; clear objective is to raise revenue.
1765	Quartering Act	Requires colonies to provide housing in public buildings and certain provisions for troops.
1766	Declaratory Act	Repeals Stamp Act, but insists that Parliament retains the right to legislate for the colonies "in all cases whatsoever."
1767	Townshend Revenue Act	Places import duty on lead, paint, glass, paper, and tea; objective is to raise money from the colonies.
1770	Boston Massacre	Several citizens killed by British soldiers whom they had pelted with snowballs; grew out of tensions caused by quartering of four army regiments in Boston to enforce customs regulations.
1773	Tea Act	After Townshend Duties on all items other than tea are removed, British East India Company is given a monopoly on the sale of tea, enabling it to drop price—and cut out middlemen.
1773	Boston Tea Party	To protest Tea Act, Bostonians dump 90,000 pounds of tea into Boston Harbor.

TIME LINE

▼**1718**
French build New Orleans

▼**1720**
French build Louisbourg and Fort Niagara

▼**1731**
French build Fort St. Frédéric

▼**1733**
Molasses Act

▼**1739–1744**
War of Jenkins's Ear

▼**1741**
Attack upon Cartagena fails

▼**1744–1748**
King George's War

▼**1748**
Village of Pickawillany established by Memeskia and his band of Miamis

▼**1749**
French military expedition fails to win back dissident Indians in Ohio Valley

▼**1752**
Tanacharison cedes huge chunk of Ohio Valley to Virginia

▼**1753**
French build small forts near forks of Ohio River

▼**1754**
Albany Plan of Union

▼**1754–1763**
French and Indian War

▼**1755**
Braddock's forces defeated

▼**1757**
British defeated at Fort William Henry, survivors massacred
William Pitt accedes to power in Britain

1774	Intolerable Acts	To punish Massachusetts in general and Boston in particular for the "Tea Party":
		1. Port of Boston closed until East India Company repaid for dumped tea.
		2. King to appoint Massachusetts's Council; town meetings to require written permission of governor; governor will appoint judges and sheriffs, and sheriffs will now select juries.
		3. Governor can send officials and soldiers accused of capital crimes out of Massachusetts for their trials.
		4. Troops may be quartered in private homes.
1774	Quebec Act	Gives Ohio River Valley to Québec; Britain allows Québec to be governed by French tradition and tolerates Catholic religion there.
1774	First Continental Congress	Representatives of 12 colonies meet in Philadelphia and call for a boycott of trade with Britain, adopt a Declaration of Rights, and agree to meet again in a year.

At the same time, General Thomas Gage was appointed governor of Massachusetts and authorized to bring as many troops to Boston as he needed. Boston soon became an armed camp. The Port Act was easily enforced as Gage deployed troops to close the ports of Boston and Charlestown. The Government Act was another matter. Citizens summoned by the sheriff simply refused to serve on juries, and some judges even refused to preside. When Gage called for an election to the legislature, only some towns elected delegates, and a shadow "Massachusetts Provincial Congress" met in Concord in October 1774. The citizens of Massachusetts had taken government into their own hands.

▼**1758**
Treaty of Easton secures neutrality of Ohio Valley tribes in return for territory west of Alleghenies

▼**1759**
British seize Québec

▼**1763**
Treaty of Paris, ending French and Indian War, signed
Pontiac's Rebellion
Proclamation of 1763
Parliament increases size of peacetime army to 20 regiments

▼**1764**
Sugar Act
Currency Act

▼**1765**
Stamp Act
Quartering Act
Stamp Act Congress

▼**1766**
Declaratory Act

▼**1767**
Townshend Revenue Act

▼**1768**
John Hancock's sloop *Liberty* seized

▼**1770**
Boston Massacre

▼**1773**
Tea Act
Boston Tea Party

▼**1774**
Intolerable Acts (known as Coercive Acts in Britain)
Lord Dunmore's War

▼**1775**
First Continental Congress

The British had thought that Massachusetts could be isolated, but they underestimated the colonists' attachment to their liberties. The threat to representative government presented by the Intolerable Acts was so clear that the other colonies soon rallied around Massachusetts. In June 1774, the Virginia Burgesses sent out a letter suggesting a meeting of all the colonies. At about the same time, Massachusetts had issued a similar call for a meeting in Philadelphia. These two most radical colonies spurred the others to meet in early September.

The First Continental Congress

Every colony except Georgia sent delegates to the **First Continental Congress**, which convened on September 5, 1774. Only a few of the delegates had ever met any of their counterparts from the other colonies, so provincial were the colonies. For seven weeks these strangers met in formal sessions and social occasions. Together they laid the foundation for the first national government.

With Massachusetts and Virginia almost ready to take up arms, and the middle colonies favoring conciliation, the greatest challenge was how to achieve unity. Since Massachusetts needed the support of the other colonies, it was ready to abandon any discussion of offensive measures against the British. In return, the Congress ratified the Suffolk Resolves, a set of Massachusetts resolutions that recommended passive resistance to the Intolerable Acts.

The delegates could now consider national action. Hoping to exert economic pressure on Britain, Congress issued a call for a boycott of all imports and exports between the colonies, Britain, and the West Indies. Then the delegates adopted a Declaration of Rights that for the first time expressed as the collective determination of every colony (except Georgia) what had become standard constitutional arguments. The colonists were entitled to all the "rights, liberties, and immunities of free and natural-born subjects" of England. Parliament could regulate trade for the colonies only by the "consent" of the colonies. Parliament could neither tax nor legislate for the colonies. Again and again, the Declaration reiterated the twin principles on which resistance to imperial legislation had been based: consent and the rule of law.

Finally, Congress agreed to reconvene in half a year, on March 10, 1775, unless the Intolerable Acts were repealed. The delegates had achieved consensus on the principles that would shortly form the basis for a new and independent national government.

CONCLUSION

Within a decade, the British Empire had come apart on its westernmost edge. The stage had been set decades earlier when Britain unintentionally allowed the colonies to develop more self-government and personal freedom than in Britain itself, without requiring them to pay a proportionate share of the costs of empire. As a result, the colonies created their own vision, one that linked democratic government and prosperity. Once Britain decided to knit the colonies more tightly into the empire and impose on them the controls of the centralized state, conflict was inevitable. At the same time, both Britons and Americans revered the same constitution, whose values and protections Americans invoked in their protests. That those protests would end in revolution was by no means a foregone conclusion. Revolution would require two key elements: Britain's unwillingness to compromise on issues of governance, and the ability of colonial radicals to convince moderates that there was no other way. By the end of 1774 that point had almost been reached.

WHO, WHAT, WHERE

REVIEW QUESTIONS

1. What were the reasons for the conflicts among the British, French, Spanish, and the various Indian tribes on the North American continent?

2. How and why did Britain attempt to reorganize its North American colonial empire?

3. Why did the colonies resist Britain's attempts to reorganize its North American colonial empire?

CRITICAL-THINKING QUESTIONS

1. For much of the eighteenth century, Britain and France were at war, involving the American colonies. How did this warfare affect the colonies and their people?

2. What was the series of events that brought Britain and the colonies to the brink of war by 1774? To what extent were they the product of poor leadership? Differing theories of government? Different social experiences?

3. At what point did the American Revolution become unavoidable? Until that point, how might it have been avoided?

SUGGESTED READINGS

Demos, John. *The Unredeemed Captive: A Family Story from Early America*. New York: Knopf, 1994.

Morgan, Edmund S., and Helen M. Morgan. *The Stamp Act Crisis: Prologue to Revolution*. Chapel Hill: Published for the Institute of Early American History and Culture at Williamsburg, Virginia, by the University of North Carolina Press, 1953.

White, Richard. *The Middle Ground: Indians, Empires, and Republics in the Great Lakes Region, 1650–1815 (Studies in North American Indian History)*. New York: Cambridge University Press, 1992.

For further review materials and resource information, please visit www.oup.com/us/ofthepeople

6.2 BENJAMIN FRANKLIN, EXCERPTS FROM "A NARRATIVE OF THE LATE MASSACRES" (1764)

The fullest account we have of the Paxton Boys' attacks on the Conestoga Indians comes from Benjamin Franklin, who joined with other civic leaders to persuade a force of 250 men to turn back when they began marching on Philadelphia. Franklin's sympathy for the Natives, who were Christian converts, is evident, as is his contempt for the men who attacked them. Shehaes, mentioned in the excerpt that follows, was an elderly Conestoga who had been present in 1701 when William Penn entered into a treaty with the Indians "and ever since continued a faithful and affectionate Friend to the English."

These Indians were the Remains of a Tribe of the Six Nations, settled at Conestogoe [Conestoga], and thence called Conestogoe Indians. On the first Arrival of the English in Pennsylvania, Messengers from this Tribe came to welcome them, with Presents of Venison, Corn and Skins; and the whole Tribe entered into a Treaty of Friendship with the first Proprietor, William Penn, which was to last "as long as the Sun should shine, or the Waters run in the Rivers." This Treaty has been since frequently renewed, and the Chain brightened, as they express it, from time to time. It has never been violated, on their Part or ours, till now. It has always been observed, that Indians, settled in the Neighbourhood of White People, do not increase, but diminish continually. This Tribe accordingly went on diminishing, till there remained in their Town on the Manor, but 20 Persons, viz. 7 Men, 5 Women, and 8 Children, Boys and Girls . . .

On Wednesday, the 14th of December, 1763, Fifty-seven Men, from some of our Frontier Townships, who had projected the Destruction of this little Common-wealth, came, all well-mounted, and armed with Firelocks, Hangers and Hatchets, having travelled through the Country in the Night, to Conestogoe Manor. There they surrounded the small Village of Indian Huts, and just at Break of Day broke into them all at once. Only three Men, two Women, and a young Boy, were found at home, the rest being out among the neighbouring White People, some to sell the Baskets, Brooms and Bowls they manufactured, and others on other Occasions. These poor defenceless Creatures were immediately fired upon, stabbed and hatcheted to Death! The good Shehaes, among the rest, cut to Pieces in his Bed. All of them were scalped, and otherwise horribly mangled. Then their Huts were set on Fire, and most of them burnt down. When the Troop, pleased with their own Conduct and Bravery, but enraged that any of the poor Indians had escaped the Massacre, rode off, and in small Parties, by different Roads, went home. . . .

The Magistrates of Lancaster sent out to collect the remaining Indians, brought them into the Town for their better Security against any further Attempt, and it is said condoled with them on the Misfortune that had happened, took them by the Hand, comforted and promised them Protection. They were all put into the Workhouse, a strong Building, as the Place of greatest Safety.

When the shocking News arrived in Town, a Proclamation was issued by the Governor, in the following Terms:

"Whereas I have received Information, That on Wednesday, the Fourteenth Day of this Month, a Number of People, armed, and mounted on Horseback, unlawfully assembled together, and went to the Indian Town in the Conestogoe Manor, in Lancaster County, and without the least Reason or Provocation, in cool Blood, barbarously killed six of the Indians settled there, and burnt and destroyed all their Houses and Effects: And whereas so cruel and inhuman an Act, committed in the Heart of this Province on the said Indians, who have lived peaceably and inoffensively among us, during all our late Troubles, and for many Years before, and were justly considered as under the Protection of this Government and its Laws, calls loudly for the vigorous Exertion of the civil Authority, to detect the Offenders, and bring them to condign Punishment."

. . . Notwithstanding this Proclamation, those cruel Men again assembled themselves, and hearing that the remaining fourteen Indians were in the Work-house at Lancaster, they suddenly appeared in that Town, on the 27th of December. Fifty of them, armed as before, dismounting, went directly to the Work-house, and by Violence broke open the Door, and entered with the utmost Fury in their Countenances. When the poor Wretches saw they had no Protection nigh, nor could possibly escape, and being without the least Weapon for Defence, they divided into their little Families, the Children clinging to the Parents; they fell on their Knees, protested their Innocence, declared their Love to the English, and that, in their whole Lives, they had never done them Injury; and in this Posture they all received the Hatchet! Men, Women and little Children—were every one inhumanly murdered!—in cold Blood!

The barbarous Men who committed the atrocious Fact, in Defiance of Government, of all Laws human and divine, and to the eternal Disgrace of their Country and Colour, then mounted their Horses, huzza'd in Triumph, as if they had gained a Victory, and rode off—unmolested!

The Bodies of the Murdered were then brought out and exposed in the Street, till a Hole could be made in the Earth, to receive and cover them.

But the Wickedness cannot be covered, the Guilt will lie on the whole Land, till Justice is done on the Murderers. The Blood of the Innocent will cry to Heaven for Vengeance. . . .

There are some (I am ashamed to hear it) who would extenuate the enormous Wickedness of these Actions, by saying, "The Inhabitants of the Frontiers are exasperated with the Murder of their Relations, by the Enemy Indians, in the present War." It is possible; but though this might justify their going out into the Woods, to seek for those Enemies, and avenge upon them those Murders; it can never justify their turning in to the Heart of the Country, to murder their Friends.

If an Indian injures me, does it follow that I may revenge that Injury on all Indians? It is well known that Indians are of different Tribes, Nations and Languages, as well as the White People. In Europe, if the French, who are White People, should injure the Dutch, are they to revenge it on the English, because they too are White People? The only Crime of these poor Wretches seems to have been, that they had a reddish brown Skin, and black Hair; and some People of that Sort, it seems, had murdered some of our Relations.

Source: "A Narrative of the Late Massacres [January 30, 1764]," Founders Online, National Archives (http://founders.archives.gov/documents/Franklin/01-11-02-0012, ver. 2014-05-09). *Source: The Papers of Benjamin Franklin*, vol. 11, *January 1, through December 31, 1764*, ed. Leonard W. Labaree (New Haven, CT: Yale University Press, 1967), p. 42ff.

6.3   A VISITING FRENCHMAN'S ACCOUNT OF PATRICK HENRY'S CAESAR–BRUTUS SPEECH (1765)

Patrick Henry may be best known as the man who said, "Give me liberty or give me death!" His radicalism, however, appeared much earlier than that 1775 speech. As the Virginia House of Burgesses was about to conclude its business in May 1765, Henry introduced a series of resolutions protesting the Stamp Act. He came close to committing treason when he named historic dictators who had been assassinated and suggested King George III might deserve the same fate, but he quickly backed away, pleading "the heat of passion." This description of his speech comes from the travel diary of a Frenchman who was visiting Virginia at the time.

May the 30th. Set out early from half-way house in the chair and broke fast at York[town], arived at Williamsburg at 12, where I saw three negroes hanging at the galous for having robbed Mr. Waltho[w] of 300 pounds. I went immediately to the Assembly which was seting, where I was entertained with very strong debates concerning dutys that the Parlement wants to lay on the America colonys, which they call or stile stamp dutys. Shortly after I came in, one of the members stood up and said he had read that in former time Tarquin and Julius had their Brutus, Charles had his Cromwell, and he did not doubt but some good American would stand up in favour of his Country; but (says he) in a more moderate manner, and was going to continue, when the Speaker of the House rose and, said he, the last that stood up had spoke traison, and [he] was sorey to see that not one of the members of the House was loyal enough to stop him before he had gone so far. Upon which the same member stood up again (his name is Henery) and said that if he had afronted the Speaker or the House, he was ready to ask pardon, and he would shew his loyalty to His Majesty King George the third at the expence of the last drop of his blood; but what he had said must be attributed to the interest of his country's dying liberty which he had at heart, and the heat of passion might have lead him to have said something more than he intended; but, again, if he said anything wrong, he begged the Speaker and the House's pardon. Some other members stood up and backed him, on which that afaire was droped.

May the 31st. I returned to the Assembly today, and heard very hot debates stil about the stamp dutys. The whole House was for entering resolves on the records but they differed much with regard [to] the contents or purport thereof. Some were for shewing their resentment to the highest. One of the resolves that these proposed, was that any person that would offer to sustain that the Parlement of England had a right to impose or lay any tax or dutys whatsoever on the American colonys, without the consent of the inhabitants therof, should be looked upon as a traitor, and deemed an enemy to his country: there were some others to the same purpose, and the majority was for entring these resolves; upon which the Governor disolved the Assembly, which hinderd their proceeding.

Source: A visiting Frenchman's account of Patrick Henry's Caesar-Brutus Speech. http://www.redhill.org/life/1765_2.html.

6.4   THE STAMP ACT RIOTS: THE DESTRUCTION OF THOMAS HUTCHINSON'S HOUSE (1765)

As Lieutenant Governor of Massachusetts, a royal appointment, Thomas Hutchinson was required to enforce the Stamp Act and widely (if incorrectly) believed to support it. On the evening of August 26, 1765, a well-organized mob protesting the Act drove Hutchinson and his family from their home, looted it, and left the house in shambles. Four days later, Hutchinson described the events to a British official.

Boston Aug. 30 1765
    My Dear Sir, I came from my house at Milton the 26 in the morning. After dinner it was whispered in town there would be a mob at night ans that Paxton, Hallowell, and the custom-house, and admiralty officers' houses would be attacked; but my friends assured me the rabble were satisfied with the insult I had received and that I was become rather popular. In the evening whilst I was at supper and my children round me, somebody ran in & said the mob were coming. I directed my children to fly to a secure place and shut up my house as I had done before, intending not to quit it; but my eldest daughter repented her leaving me and hastened back and protested she would not quit the house unless I

did. I could n't stand against this, and withdrew with her to a neighbouring house where I had been but a few minutes before the hellish crew fell upon my house with the rage of devils, and in a moment with axes split down the door & entered. My son being in the great entry heard them cry: "Damn him, he is upstairs we'll have him." Some ran immediately as high as the top of the house, others filled the rooms below and cellars, and others remained without the house to be employed there. Messages soon came one after another to the house where I was, to inform me the mob were coming in pursuit of me, and I was obliged to retire through yards and gardens to a house more remote, where I remained until 4 o'clock, by which time one of the best finished houses in the Province had nothing remaining but the bare walls and floors. Not contented with tearing off all the wainscot and hangings, and splitting the doors to pieces, they beat down the partition walls; and altho that alone cost them near two hours they cut down the cupola or lanthorn, and they began to take the slate and boards from the roof and were prevented only by the approaching daylight from a total demolition of the building. The garden-house was laid flat, and all my trees, etc., broke down to the ground. Such ruins were never seen in America. Besides my plate and family pictures, household furniture of every kind, my own, my children's, and servants' apparel they carried off about £900 sterling in money and emptied the house of everything whatsoever except a part of the kitchen furniture, not leaving a single book or paper in it, and have scattered or destroyed all the manuscripts and other papers I had been collecting for 30 years together, besides a great number of publick papers in my custody.

The evening being warm I had undressed me and put on a thin camlet surtout over my waistcoat. The next morning the weather being changed, I had not cloathes enough in my possession to defend me from the cold and was obliged to borrow from my friends. Many articles of clothing and a good part of my plate have since been picked up in different quarters of the town, but the furniture in general was cut to pieces before it was thrown out of the house, and most of the beds cut open and the feathers thrown out of the windows. The next evening, I intended with my children to Milton, but meeting two or three small parties of the ruffians, who I suppose had concealed themselves in the country, and my coachman hearing one of them say, "There he is!" my daughters were terrified and said they should never be safe, and I was forced to shelter them that night at the Castle.

The encouragers of the first mob never intended matters should go this length, and the people in general express the utmost detestation of this unparalleled outrage, and I wish they could be convinced what infinite hazard there is of the most terrible consequences from such demons when they are let loose in a government where there is not constant authority at hand sufficient to suppress them. I am told the government here will make me a compensation for my own and my family's loss, which I think cannot be much less than £3000 sterling. I am not sure that they will. If they should not, it will be too heavy for me and I must humbly apply to his Majesty in whose service I am a sufferer; but this and a much greater sum would be an insufficient compensation for the constant distress and anxiety of mind I have felt for some time past, and must feel for months to come. You cannot conceive the wretched state we are in. Such is the resentment of the people against the Stamp-Duty, that there can be no dependence upon the General Court to take any steps to enforce, or rather advise, to the payment of it. On the other hand, such will be the effects of not submitting to it, that all trade must cease, all courts fall, and all authority be at an end. Must not the ministry be extremely embarrassed? On the one hand, it will be said, if concessions be made, the Parliament endanger the loss of their authority over the Colony: on the other hand, if external force should be used there seems to be danger of a total lasting alienation of affection. Is there no alternative? May the infinitely wise God direct you.

Source: James K. Hosmer, *The Life of Thomas Hutchinson, Royal Governor of the Province of Massachusetts Bay* (1896), 91–94.

6.5 THE INTOLERABLE ACTS (1774)

In response to the 1774 Boston Tea Party, Parliament passed a series of acts to try to bring Massachusetts back under the authority of the British Crown. The acts, which American patriots called the "Intolerable Acts," closed the Boston Harbor, allowed for trials to take place in Great Britain rather than Massachusetts, suspended local elections, and allowed for the quartering of troops on private property. Although the Quebec Act did not directly affect Boston, many patriots were angry that the British government seemed to grant more freedom to the French Catholics living in recently conquered Quebec while simultaneously curtailing political liberty in Massachusetts.

BOSTON PORT ACT:

AN ACT to discontinue . . . shipping, of goods, wares, and merchandise, at the town, and within the harbour, of Boston, in the province of Massachuset's Bay, in North America

Whereas dangerous commotions and insurrections have been fomented and raised in the town of Boston, in the province of Massachuset's Bay, in New England, by divers ill affected persons, to the subversion of his Majesty's government, and to the utter destruction of the publick peace, and good order of the said town; in which commotions and insurrections certain valuable cargoes of teas, being the property of the East India Company, and on board certain' vessels lying within the bay or harbour of Boston, were seized and destroyed: And whereas, in the present condition of the said town and harbour, the commerce of his Majesty's subjects cannot be safely carried on there, nor the customs payable to his Majesty duly collected; and it is therefore expedient that the officers of his Majesty's customs should be forthwith removed from the said town: . . . be it enacted . . ., That from and after June 1, 1774, it shall not be lawful for any person or persons whatsoever to lade, put, or cause to procure to be laden or put, off or from any quay, wharf, or other place, within the said town of Boston, or in or upon any part of the shore of the bay, commonly called The Harbour of Boston.

ADMINISTRATION OF JUSTICE ACT:

AN ACT for or the impartial administration of justice in . . . Massachuset's Bay, in New England

Whereas in his Majesty's province of Massachuset's Bay, in New England, an attempt hath lately been made to throw off the authority of the parliament of Great Britain over the said province, and an actual and avowed resistance, by open force, to the execution of certain acts of parliament, hath been suffered to take place, uncontrouled and unpunished, . . .: and whereas, in the present disordered state of the said province, it is of the utmost importance . . . to the reestablishment of lawful authority throughout the same; be it enacted . . . , That if any inquisition or indictment shall be found, or if any appeal shall be sued or preferred against any person, for murther, or other capital offense, in the province of the Massachuset's Bay, and it shall appear, by information given upon oath to the governor . . . that an indifferent trial cannot be had within the said province, in that case, it shall and may be lawful for the governor . . . , to direct, with the advice and consent of the council, that the inquisition, indictment, or appeal, shall be tried in some other of his Majesty's colonies, or in Great Britain.

MASSACHUSETTS GOVERNMENT ACT:

AN ACT for the better regulating the government of the province of the Massachuset's Bay, in New England

Whereas the method of electing such counsellors or assistants, to be vested with the several powers, authorities, and privileges, therein mentioned, . . . hath been found to be extremely ill adapted to the plan of government established in the province of the Massachuset's Bay . . . , and hath . . . for or some time past, been such as had the most manifest tendency to obstruct, and, in great measure, defeat, the execution of the laws; to weaken the attachment of his Majesty's well disposed subjects in the said province to his Majesty's government, and to encourage the ill disposed among them to proceed even to acts of direct resistance to, and defiance of, his Majesty's authority: And it hath accordingly happened, that an open resistance to the execution of the laws hath actually taken place in the town of Boston, and the neighbourhood thereof, within the said Province: And whereas it is, under these circumstances, become absolutely necessary, . . . that the said method of annually electing the counsellors or assistants of the said Province should no longer be suffered to continue, . . . Be it therefore enacted . . . that the council, or court of assistants of the said province for the time being, shall be composed of such of the inhabitants or proprietors of lands within the same as shall be thereunto nominated and appointed by his Majesty.

QUARTERING ACT OF 1765:

Whereas doubts have been entertained whether troops can be quartered otherwise than in barracks . . . in such cases, it shall and may be lawful for . . . the officer . . . in command of His Majesty's forces in North America, to cause any officers or soldiers in His Majesty's service to be quartered and billeted in such manner as is now directed by law where no barracks are provided by the colonies.

And be it further enacted by the authority aforesaid that, if it shall happen at any time that any officers or soldiers in His Majesty's service shall remain within any of the said colonies without quarters for the space of twenty four hours after such quarters shall have been demanded, it shall and may be lawful for the governor of the province to order and direct such and so many uninhabited houses, outhouses, barns, or other buildings as he shall think necessary to be taken (making a reasonable allowance for the same) and make fit for the reception of such officers and soldiers, and to put and quarter such officers and soldiers therein for such time as he shall think proper.

QUEBEC ACT:

AN ACT for making effectual Provision for the Government of the Province of Quebec, in North America

It is hereby declared, That His Majesty's Subjects professing the Religion of the Church of Rome, of, and in the said Province of Quebec, may have, hold, and enjoy, the free Exercise of the Religion of the Church of Rome . . . and that the Clergy of the said Church may hold, receive, and enjoy their accustomed Dues and Rights, with respect to such Persons only as shall profess the said Religion.

Source: US History.org, http://www.ushistory.org/declaration/related/intolerable.html.

Creating a New Nation
1775–1788

< John Trumbull, *The Capture of the Hessians at Trenton*

Abigail Adams and the Wartime Economy

For almost ten years, between 1774 and 1784, John Adams was away from home. He left his beloved wife Abigail in Braintree, Massachusetts, with four small children and a farm to manage. Two years after his departure, Abigail Adams still felt "unequal to the cares which fall upon me." Over the course of the decade, however, she became a shrewd manager, even better at business than her husband. While John dealt with pressing matters of state, playing a leading role in establishing both the principles and structures of the new government, Abigail handled the day-to-day challenges of a wartime economy.

Unable to hire men to work the farm, with labor scarce and wages consequently high, Abigail turned to tenant farmers who shared a portion of the produce with her in return for use of the land. Equally challenging was John's situation as a creditor: those who owed him money for his services as a lawyer or for farm produce paid him in currency that, with wartime inflation, was worth less and less. As a solution, Abigail purchased the bonds the US government sold to finance the war; at 6 percent interest, they were an excellent investment. However, it wasn't enough money to pay the mounting state taxes necessary to finance the war effort. So Abigail went into business, asking John to send her trunks of merchandise—handkerchiefs, fabric, gloves, ribbons—from Paris, where he was negotiating the alliance with France. A male relative resold the items for her locally, at a profit.

Abigail embarked upon other ventures as well—lending money at interest, investing in land, and speculating in bonds, specifically, depreciated government war bonds, selling at less than face value because of doubts that the federal and state governments would ever redeem them. This was a risky venture with no guarantees. But, as Abigail reassured her anxious husband, "Nothing venture, nothing have." Here was one of the great economic debates of the era: whether to invest in land or capital, whether to take risks or to stick with the sure thing. Remarkably, a married woman—prevented by the laws of the time from holding property in her own name or entering into any sort of business transaction on her own—was risking the family's finances on capital. Even though such a thing was not legally possible, Abigail thought of her profits as "this money which I call mine." The responsibility of managing her family's farm in her husband's absence during the war had convinced Abigail that bonds "were less troublesome to take charge of than Land," and her investments brought a handsome return once the new nation was on a sound economic footing.

The challenges presented by the creation of a new nation also offered opportunities, which men and women faced in different ways, sometimes stretching far beyond their expected roles.

THE WAR BEGINS

By the end of 1774, conflict between the colonists and Britain seemed unavoidable. The British government, under the leadership of Lord North and King George III, seemed unwilling to make significant concessions. In the colonies, the radical opponents of British rule dominated politics. Despite these signs, no one anticipated eight years of warfare that would make the colonies a single nation under a centralized government.

The First Battles

Before he became governor of Massachusetts in 1774, General Thomas Gage had a long record of advocating force. He had called for the stationing of troops in Boston in 1768, leading to the Boston Massacre. Even before the Boston Tea Party, he recommended limiting democratic government in Massachusetts. Because he believed that Boston merchants and lawyers were instigating dissent among the poor, he wanted to isolate the colonial Revolutionary elite, by force if necessary.

In the spring of 1775, Gage received orders from England to act decisively against the colonists. He planned to seize the colonists' military supplies, stored at Concord, but alert Bostonians tipped off the patriot leaders. On the night of April 18, the silversmith Paul Revere and the tanner William Dawes slipped out of Boston on horseback to carry the message that British troops were on the move. Militiamen from several towns began to gather.

The British soldiers arrived at Lexington at daybreak and ordered the militia to surrender, which they refused to do. Exactly what happened next remains unclear. The colonists swore that British soldiers opened fire, saying, "Ye villans [sic], ye Rebels, disperse; Damn you, disperse." The British major insisted that the first shot came from behind a tree. British soldiers lost control and fired, and the colonists returned fire. Eight Americans were killed, most while attempting to flee.

At the same time, the Concord militia had assembled and then pulled back about a mile, allowing the British to enter an almost-deserted town. Fighting broke out when a fire the British troops had set to the Concord liberty pole spread to the courthouse. To protect their town, the militia began marching on the British, who fired when the Americans drew near. In the exchange, three British soldiers were killed and several more injured. The British were forced back across the bridge. The actual battle took two or three minutes (see Map 7–1), though the settlers continued to harass the troops all the way back to the city.

Once news of the fighting at **Lexington and Concord** spread, militias converged on Boston to evict Gage and his troops. More than 20,000 men soon were encamped in Boston. Gage declared that all the inhabitants of Massachusetts who bore arms were rebels and traitors, although he was willing to pardon everyone but John Hancock and Sam Adams, two leaders of the defiant Provincial Congress. Rather than backing down, the colonists fortified Breed's Hill (next to the more famous Bunker Hill) in Charlestown, overlooking Boston. On June 17, Gage sent 2,400 soldiers to take the hill. The cost was enormous: 1,000 soldiers and 92 officers killed or wounded (compared with 370 casualties among the colonists). The British learned not to make frontal assaults against fortified positions.

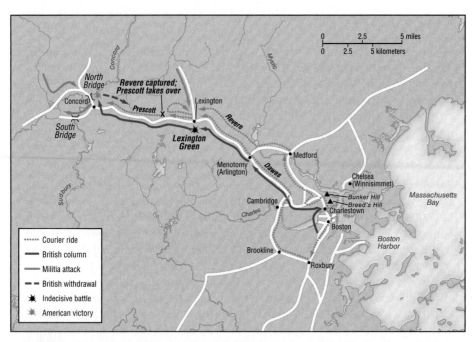

Map 7–1   Battles of Lexington, Concord, and Breed's Hill This map shows the sites of the first battles of the Revolution in and around Boston, along with the routes taken by Paul Revere and William Dawes to warn the colonists of the approach of British troops.

Other New Englanders were also taking matters into their own hands. A group under Benedict Arnold, an ambitious New Haven merchant, and Ethan Allen, the leader of the Vermont Green Mountain Boys, seized the crumbling fort at Ticonderoga on Lake Champlain and other small posts. In these heady days early in the Revolution, many colonists thought that this would be a quick and painless war.

Congress Takes the Lead

When the Second Continental Congress convened in Philadelphia on May 10, its greatest challenge was to maintain consensus. The most radical leaders, such as Sam and John Adams from Massachusetts and Richard Henry Lee from Virginia, were ready for war. However, many leaders, especially in the middle colonies, still hoped that war could be avoided.

Because Congress was an extralegal body, the elected colonial assemblies might easily have rejected its authority. But one after another, they transferred their allegiance from the British government to Congress. Although some moderates hoped for a negotiated settlement with Britain, they were caught between two sides that both anticipated war. The British refused even to acknowledge the petition sent by the First Continental Congress. That refusal, combined with Gage's attack on Breed's Hill, convinced the moderates that military preparations were necessary. Congress voted to create a Continental army and put it under the leadership of Virginia's George Washington. Not only was Washington experienced in military matters and widely respected, but his selection also helped solidify the alliance between New England and the South. Congress decided to attack Canada in the hope that a significant defeat would force the British to accede to American demands. To justify all of these actions, Congress also adopted the Declaration of the Causes and Necessity of Taking Up Arms, a rousing indictment of British "despotism," "perfidy," and "cruel aggression" drafted by Virginia's **Thomas Jefferson.**

At the same time, to preserve unity with the moderates, the radicals agreed to petition the king one more time. Without making any concessions, the Olive Branch Petition appealed to George's "magnanimity and benevolence." Nevertheless, on August 23, 1775, the king declared the colonists to be in "an open and avowed Rebellion." Although Congress had neither declared war nor asserted independence, the American Revolution had begun.

Military Ardor

Military ardor in the colonies reached its high point between the fall of 1775 and the spring of 1776. Colonists expected war, and they thought it would be quick and glorious. As a consequence, the first enlistments were for a term of only a year. Even if the war was not over by then, Revolutionaries were fearful of creating a permanent standing army.

In the summer of 1775, the Continental army marched on Canada. Victory would have either forced the British to the bargaining table or at least protected New York and New England from assault from the north. The contingent under General Benedict Arnold's command sailed from Newburyport, Massachusetts, to Maine and then marched 350 miles to Québec. In November, after a grueling march, Arnold's forces prepared to assault Québec, joined by troops under General Richard Montgomery, who had just seized Montréal. The battle was a disaster. Half of the 900 Continental soldiers were killed, captured, or wounded, including Montgomery. By the time the expedition retreated to New York in the spring, 5,000 men had been lost. The suffering was extraordinary, but it only increased American resolve.

Declaring Independence

By the beginning of 1776, moderates in Congress who still hoped for a peaceful settlement found themselves squeezed from both directions. The king and Parliament were unyielding, and popular opinion increasingly favored independence. Word arrived from Britain that all American commerce was to be cut off and that the British navy would seize American ships and their cargoes. Britain also began hiring German mercenaries known as Hessians, and Virginia's Governor Dunmore shelled Norfolk from warships. He had already offered freedom to any enslaved person who would fight for the British. Every prediction the radicals had made seemed to be coming true.

Public opinion pushed Congress toward a declaration of independence. In January 1776, Thomas Paine, an expatriate English radical in Philadelphia, electrified the public with his pamphlet *Common Sense*, which sold 75,000 copies in a short time. In it, Paine liberated Americans from their past ties to the British so that they could start their government fresh. The idea of a balanced constitution that combined king, nobles, and common people in one government was "farcical," and monarchy was "exceedingly ridiculous." Paine had a message for Congress, too: "The period of debate is closed."

Most members of Congress either desired a declaration of independence or thought it inevitable. Most delegates also agreed that unanimity was more important than speed, so they waited through the spring of 1776 as, one by one, the state delegations received instructions in favor of independence. Then, under instructions from his colony, on June 7, 1776, Virginia's Richard Henry Lee asked Congress to vote on the resolution that "these United Colonies are, and of right ought to be, free and independent States." A committee of five, including Thomas Jefferson, Benjamin Franklin, and John Adams, was appointed to draft a declaration of independence. Adams asked Jefferson, a 33-year-old Virginian who could write stirring prose, to create the first draft. For four days, the delegates debated the draft and took preliminary votes. Congress was not ready to reject slavery: a clause that accused King George of forcing African slavery on the colonies was deleted. On July 2, the delegates voted unanimously to declare independence.

Many years later Jefferson insisted that there was nothing original about the Declaration of Independence, and he was not entirely wrong. The long list of accusations against King George, which formed the bulk of the Declaration, contained

Cover of Common Sense Thomas Paine's *Common Sense* sold more than 75,000 copies in just a few weeks.

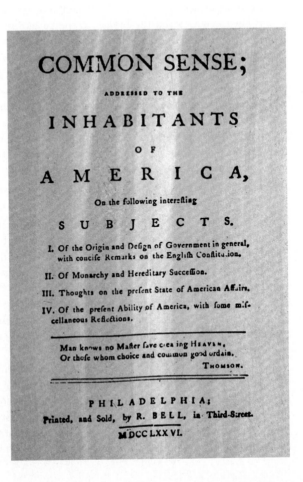

Destruction of Statue of King George Here, a small crowd in New York City pulls down the statue of King George on July 9, 1776, a few days after independence was declared.

little that was new, and even some of the stirring words in the preamble had been used by the radicals time and again. Moreover, the Revolutionaries borrowed ideas from a number of British and European sources, including constitutionalism, republicanism, Enlightenment thought (see Chapter 6), and even a strain of millennial Christian thought.

However, in a different sense the Declaration of Independence was truly original. Jefferson's achievement was to reformulate familiar principles in a way that made them simple, clear, and applicable to the American situation.

The most important of these principles was **human equality**, that all people were born with certain fundamental rights. Second, and closely related, was the belief in a universal, common human nature. If all people were the same and had the same rights, then the purpose of government was to protect those rights. Just as people created government to protect their rights, they could abolish any government that became despotic. Third, government should represent the people.

It was many years, however, before the radical implications of the Declaration became fully evident to the American people and slavery and other forms of oppression were rejected. At the moment, more attention was focused on immediate political struggles. The Revolution succeeded because moderates and radicals were able to create effective alliances, reversing the pre-Revolutionary trend toward class and regional conflict. To remain leaders of the opposition to Britain, elite Revolutionaries such as John Hancock continually appealed to poorer, more radical people and looked out for these people's interests, as well as their own. The result was a more moderate revolution than it might otherwise have been and a revolution that succeeded. Just as military fervor reached its high point in the spring of 1776, so did political unity, even if there were ongoing struggles over the meaning of the Revolution.

Creating a National Government

Although treated as if it were a legitimate national government, Congress actually had no more authority over the states than the states were willing to give it, and it had none whatsoever over the people. At the same time that Richard Henry Lee presented Congress with his proposal for independence, he also suggested that Congress create a permanent national government, a confederation of the states with a written constitution. John Dickinson, a moderate, was assigned to draft the **Articles of Confederation**. He sketched out a weak central government with the authority to make treaties, carry out military and foreign affairs, request the states to pay its expenses, and very little else. There was no chief executive, only a Congress in which each state would have one vote. Term limits were imposed on representatives. Any act of Congress would require 9 votes (of 13), and the Articles would not go into effect until all 13 states had approved them.

With state jealousies strong, it took Congress more than a year to revise and accept a watered-down version of the Articles of Confederation. Not until March 1781, near the end of the war, did the final state ratify the Articles of Confederation, putting them into effect. By then, the weaknesses in a national government with no means of enforcing its regulations were becoming evident.

Creating State Governments

In 1776, all attention was focused on state governments, where the new ideas about liberty, equality, and government were put into practice. Americans were exhilarated by the prospect of creating their own governments. Between 1775 and 1780, each of the 13 states adopted a new written constitution.

Because the Revolutionaries feared concentrations of power, the powers of governors in the new states were sharply limited. In Pennsylvania and Georgia, the position of governor was abolished and replaced with a council. Governors were given term limits or required to run for reelection every year. Because royal governors had appointed cronies to powerful positions, the new governors also were stripped of their power of appointment.

The new state constitutions made the legislatures more democratic. The number of representatives was doubled in South Carolina and New Hampshire and more than tripled in Massachusetts. Many constitutions also imposed either term limits or frequent elections for representatives. As the property qualifications for holding office were lowered, poorer men sat in legislatures alongside richer ones. The admission of more ordinary men into government was one of the greatest changes brought about by the Revolution. Now the elite had to learn to share power and to win the votes of men they had once scorned.

WINNING THE REVOLUTION

The British entered the war with clear advantages in population, wealth, and power, but with a flawed premise about how to win the war. Britain, arguably the world's most powerful nation, had the mistaken idea that the colonists could be defeated by a swift and effective use of force. It also assumed that Americans loyal to the Crown would support British troops, but they alienated Americans with their actions.

Probably no more than one-fifth of the population remained loyal to Britain, but many more shifted loyalties depending on local circumstances. The war ultimately became a struggle for the support of this unpoliticized population.

Competing Strategies

British political objectives shifted during the war. The first goal, based on the belief that resistance was being led by a handful of radical New Englanders, was to punish and isolate Boston. This was the strategy of 1774 and 1775, with the Intolerable Acts and the battles of Lexington, Concord, and Breed's Hill. It failed miserably, due to the faulty assumption that well-trained British regulars were necessarily superior to untrained colonial rustics. However, if the British had a misplaced faith in their invincibility, the Americans had a misplaced faith in their moral superiority; but neither faith could guarantee victory. The result was a long war, as both sides tried to avoid decisive engagements that might prove fatal.

For seven years, the two armies chased each other across the Eastern Seaboard. Neither side had huge armies. Moreover, with no consensus in Britain about the strategic or economic value of the colonies, there was always opposition to the war and a limit to the investment that the British were prepared to make in it. Consequently, every battle presented a significant risk that troops who were lost could not be replaced.

Manpower was also a serious problem for the Americans. It was difficult to recruit enough soldiers into the Continental army. After a defeat in battle or near the end of the year when terms of enlistment were up, men left the army to return home. Any defeat demoralized the public, depressing enlistments. Hence, there was limited incentive for the army to risk all in battle.

Early in the war, however, both sides hoped for a decisive victory. After the Americans failed in Québec, the British pursued them back to Ticonderoga on Lake Champlain, where Benedict Arnold's leadership stopped the rout. The war then shifted to southern New York and the middle colonies. Having given up hopes of crushing New England directly, the British planned to isolate the region and defeat the Continental army under George Washington's leadership.

The British also sought to seize all the major American cities, and they did capture Boston, Newport, New York, Philadelphia, Charleston, and Savannah. The capture of these cities, however, did not bring about an American surrender. With 90 percent of Americans living in the countryside, the seizure of a major city did not strike the hoped-for psychological or economic blow.

The British on the Offensive: 1776

Preparing for an offensive in 1776, the new British commander, General William Howe, assembled a huge force on Staten Island: 32,000 soldiers and 13,000 seamen. Some of these soldiers were actually Hessians, German mercenaries. Anticipating battle and hoping to protect New York, Washington moved his army south to New York (see Map 7–2). He had about 19,000 soldiers, too few for a pitched battle. Half his troops were in Manhattan while the other half, in Brooklyn Heights, dug in to protect Long Island. The British sneaked up behind the Americans in Brooklyn, inflicting heavy casualties, and on August 27, 1776, Washington pulled his remaining forces back into Manhattan. Had the British pursued rapidly, they probably could have crushed Washington's army, but Howe may have been more concerned with winning a peace than a war. After Washington retreated, Howe invited members of the Continental Congress to meet with him privately on Staten Island. He was unable to recognize American independence, which was what the representatives insisted on, so his peace strategy failed.

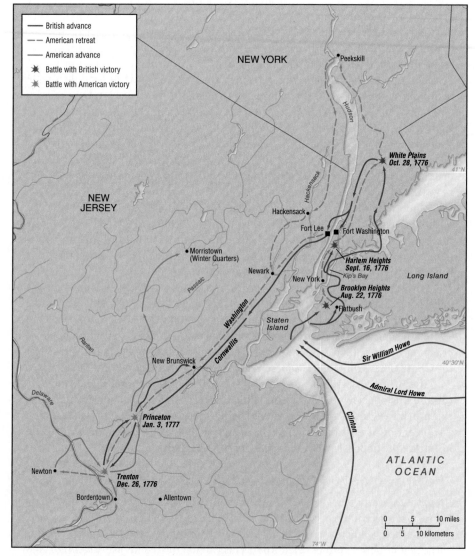

Map 7-2   New York and New Jersey Campaigns, 1776-1777 In the second half of 1776, British troops chased Washington out of New York and across New Jersey. As he would for the remainder of the war, Washington took care never to let the British capture him and his troops, leaving him free to attack at Trenton and Princeton.

Still hoping for peace, Howe began pushing Washington back out of Manhattan. Simultaneously, he offered peace to any colonists in the region who would declare their loyalty, and thousands accepted. On November 16, the British forced the Americans out of Manhattan and pursued them to White Plains and then through New Jersey to New Brunswick. The British almost caught Washington twice in New Jersey, but on December 8 the Americans crossed the Delaware at Trenton, taking every boat with them to prevent pursuit. By Christmas Eve, Washington had only 3,000 soldiers, and General Charles Lee, the commander of the other half of the Continental army, had been captured. As Thomas Paine wrote, "These are the times that try men's souls."

Howe had captured New York and New Jersey and was poised to seize Philadelphia (which fell in September 1777). At the end of 1776, the British were close to achieving their objective. Then, on Christmas night, with morale in his army dangerously low, Washington took it across the ice-clogged Delaware and surprised the British garrison at Trenton at dawn, capturing almost 900 Hessian soldiers. About a week later, Washington evaded a British trap and sneaked behind the lines to capture an outpost at Princeton.

These American successes brought another 1,000 troops into the army. More significant, the British decided to concentrate their troops near New Brunswick, fearing the loss of any more garrisons, which were needed to defend the **Loyalists**. This strategic decision revealed the weakness in the British position and demonstrated why, when victory seemed closest, it was very far away. Without enough troops to overcome the Americans' home advantage, the British needed to ensure that civilians did not aid the Revolutionary War effort. To assure the allegiance of Loyalists, the British had to offer them protection from American reprisals. However, the British were seizing the Americans' goods and property for the war effort. Then, once the garrisons were withdrawn, Loyalists were left alone and vulnerable to the reprisals of the patriots.

A Slow War: 1777–1781

Washington settled in and enlisted soldiers for a long war. Lacking enough soldiers to confront the British head-on, he mostly led the British on chases across the countryside. Maintaining such an army year after year was expensive, but the Americans were unwilling to be taxed at high rates. Continental soldiers who were from the bottom tier of society suffered grievously; at Jockey Hollow, New Jersey, in the winter of 1779–1780, men roasted their own shoes to eat and even devoured their pet dogs.

In 1777, the British political objective was still the same: to isolate New England by seizing the middle colonies. General John Burgoyne, coming down from Canada, was authorized to arm Native American allies. This caused settlers to join up in droves. American troops soon outnumbered Burgoyne's forces three to one, and they defeated the British decisively at Saratoga, stopping the British advance.

The crucial victory at Saratoga convinced the French to enter into a formal alliance, negotiated by Benjamin Franklin, the American envoy. Winning French support was perhaps the major accomplishment of the middle phase of the war: the

and using them as soldiers, they might possibly have won the war. But the British were fighting to preserve social and political order, not to overturn it. The British nonetheless disrupted the slave system significantly, and this disruption was another aspect to the civil war that beset the region for most of the Revolutionary period.

The British southern strategy had failed, but the Americans were not yet ready to win the war. Cornwallis moved on to Virginia in 1781, capturing Richmond, the new capital, and Charlottesville, coming within a few minutes of capturing Thomas Jefferson. Yet the British had been seriously weakened by the war of attrition. George Washington, working closely with the French—who sent a huge fleet into the Chesapeake near Cornwallis's quarters at **Yorktown**—led most of his forces, accompanied by French troops, to Virginia and laid siege. Trapped, Cornwallis surrendered on October 19, 1781. Although the Treaty of Paris officially ending the war would not be signed for two more years, the war was effectively over.

Securing a Place in the World

The United States revolted to escape from the British Empire and to turn its back on European power politics. However, to win the war, the new nation had to strike bargains with those same European powers. These alliances and treaties set the stage for America's struggle for a place in the world order.

Early in the war the United States called on Britain's enemies—France, Spain, and Holland—for support, and it played these new allies off against Britain with the cunning of an Old World diplomat. Benjamin Franklin, Congress's envoy to France, now 70, arrived at court in 1776 dressed like a country rustic instead of wearing the expected silks and powdered wig. His appearance was a ruse, intended to make the French think that he was innocent and uncalculating. France entered the war in the hope of breaking up the British Empire and reestablishing itself as the world's most powerful nation, and the Spaniards hoped to regain Florida and secure other Gulf Coast territory. France and Spain both wanted the United States to be independent but small and weak.

The United States wanted to secure its independence, first and foremost, but it had no intention of remaining small or feeble. Americans sought a large chunk of Canada, the territory between the Appalachians and the Mississippi River, and the right to navigate the Mississippi. In return for French and Spanish assistance, the United States at first offered only the right to trade, vastly overrating the value in Europe of American trade.

Because America wanted France and Spain to fight for expanded American territory, whereas those countries wanted instead to keep the new nation small, it took three years, until 1778, to negotiate formal treaties. Franklin prodded the French by holding secret truce discussions with a British agent late in 1777 and then leaking reports to well-placed French friends. Although the alliance was an impressive accomplishment, it involved concessions. The Americans promised not to negotiate separately with Britain and to remain France's ally "forever."

Surrender of British Army Here, Cornwallis surrenders to Washington.

The United States broke both promises, the first within a few years and the second in the 1790s. In April 1782, after Cornwallis's surrender at Yorktown but before France and Spain had gained their military objectives, Franklin began peace negotiations with the British. By November, a draft of the treaty had been completed, although Franklin assured the French that nothing would be signed without their consent. The agreement primarily served British and American interests, however. In the Treaty of Paris, signed in 1783, Britain recognized American independence, and the United States acquired the territory between the Appalachians and the Mississippi River and south of the Great Lakes (see Map 7–3).

Neither France nor Spain gained much from the war. Although Spain won Florida, neither country achieved its other territorial objectives, and France was left with a large debt.

If America's allies were relative losers, so also were Britain's allies, the American Loyalists and Indian tribes that fought with them. The best the British could do for the Loyalists was to secure a commitment of no further reprisals against them and Congress's promise to consider making restitution. The British sold their Indian allies out by transferring their land (the territory between the Appalachians and the Mississippi) to the United States. They were left desperate. Although a stunning achievement, the Treaty of Paris also set the stage for future conflicts.

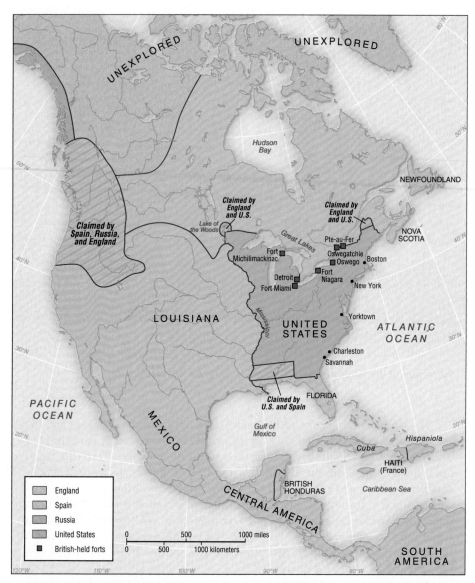

Map 7–3   The Treaty of Paris The Treaty of Paris confirmed the boundaries of the new United States, north to the Great Lakes, south to Spanish Florida, and west to the Mississippi. But it left the British in several forts west of the Appalachians, forts that they did not abandon until 1797.
Source: Walter LaFeber, *The American Age, 2nd ed.* (New York: Norton, 1994), p. 29.

THE CHALLENGE OF THE REVOLUTION

During and after the Revolution, Americans experienced all the upheavals of war: death, profiteering, and inflation, followed by economic depression. Other challenges were also presented by the new Revolutionary ideas about liberty and equality.

Radicals and moderates had compromised for victory, yet significant disagreements resurfaced once the fighting ended. One of the greatest challenges that Americans faced was designing political structures to contain these conflicts. The other great challenge came from the philosophy of revolution itself. Equality implied a transformed society. Followed to its natural conclusion, not only would the transformation lead to prosperity, but it would also necessarily challenge slavery and the subordination of women.

The Departure of the Loyalists

About 15 to 20 percent of the white population had remained loyal to the Crown during the Revolution, along with a majority of the Indians and a minority of enslaved people. Although sizable in number (almost half a million whites), the Loyalists were never well organized enough to threaten the success of the Revolution.

During the war, partisan fighting was fierce in contested regions such as the Carolinas and New Jersey, but there was relatively little retribution after the war. There were no trials for treason, mass executions, or significant mob actions directed against whites. Nor was there any significant resistance from the Loyalists. Perhaps as many as 80,000 left for Canada, Great Britain, or the West Indies. Among them were thousands of formerly enslaved people who had accepted the British offer of freedom.

The white exiles came disproportionately from the top tier of society, and their departure left a void. Confiscated Loyalist property represented a great deal of wealth to be redistributed, and people just below the top rung of society scrambled to take the Loyalists' places. The departure of the Loyalists enhanced the democratizing tendencies of the Revolution by removing the most conservative element in American society and creating an opportunity for many white Americans to rise to power.

The Challenge of the Economy

Wars disrupt the economy in two ways. First, they interfere with production and exchange, hurting some people and creating opportunity for others. Second, because wars are expensive, they require some combination of increased taxation and deficit spending.

Those who suffered the greatest economic hardships and enjoyed the greatest opportunities from the Revolution were those most deeply involved in the market. During the war, trade with Britain and the British West Indies was cut off, and the British navy seized American ships and destroyed the New England fishing industry. After the war, Britain still excluded American ships from the West Indies. Congress, under the Articles of Confederation, was too weak to negotiate a better trade relationship, and merchants trading with Britain and the West Indies were ruined.

At the same time, other opportunities opened up. Merchants willing to risk seizure of their ships continued the trade with Europe and sold the goods they imported at astronomical prices. Privateering made other merchants rich, as did provisioning the Continental army. In 1779 alone, the army spent $109 million on provisions, fueling a wartime economic boom. The army's demand for supplies drove prices up. Prices for grain increased 200 to 600 percent and, in Maryland, 5,000 percent.

Enterprising Americans with a little capital to invest could rise quickly. Not everyone could take advantage of the Revolutionary economy, however. In fact, although the Revolution eliminated some of the ruling elite, it did not level social classes. Those who could not profit from the war had to work harder and struggle with rising prices. To meet the army's demand for cloth, women increased the pace of home production. Because there were set prices for cloth, women were unable to reap exorbitant profits.

Skyrocketing prices were hardest on those with limited incomes. While Congress debated price controls and some cities set them, aggrieved citizens sometimes took matters into their own hands. In Boston, a mob of at least a hundred women seized a hogshead of coffee from the merchant Thomas Boylston, who was hoarding it. Such conflicts pitted the community against the entrepreneur and raised serious questions about the purpose of the Revolution: Was it to create opportunities for the individual or to protect the well-being of the community?

After the war, opportunities for profit and prosperity for some increased, whereas a postwar deflation pushed others to misery. Speculation in land and currency offered the fastest ways to become rich. Entrepreneurs bought up paper currency and land titles at a fraction of their worth, counting on the day when they would be redeemed at their face value.

Even before the war ended, there was a clamor for land. Between 1776 and 1790, America's population grew by almost 70 percent, from 2.3 million to 3.9 million, almost all from natural increase. Colonists had long been pushing against the Indians to the west, and by 1783, the Wilderness Road had taken thousands into Kentucky; seven years later, 100,000 settlers were living in Kentucky and Tennessee.

With the demand for land so great, speculators who could corner huge tracts stood to reap extraordinary profits. Before the Revolution, seven men had secured a **patent** to 29,350 acres in upstate New York as a grant from the Crown. By the end of the Revolution, three of them were dead; one—a Loyalist—had left the country; and the others were broke or close to it, all victims of the dislocations of war. William Cooper, a small-scale merchant and speculator, bought the patent in a possibly rigged auction for the bargain-basement price of £2,700. Yet his investment was worthless unless Cooper could get others to buy portions of the huge patent from him. After a few months, Cooper sold off thousands of acres not to poor farmers but to speculators, who in turn sold farm-sized plots to their own townsmen, turning a profit by increasing the price.

All along the western frontier, farmers rushed to take the new lands, reversing the pre-Revolutionary trend toward the cities. With the opening of new regions to the west, America would remain a farming nation for decades more, rather than industrializing rapidly along the rigid class lines of European industrial economies. At the same time, slavery expanded into new territories in the South, ensuring the persistence of inequalities based on race.

Even more than the dislocations of the Revolutionary economy, the financing of the Revolution challenged the American economy. Taxing the population was out of the question, not only because Americans had begun the Revolution precisely to avoid high taxes but also because Congress had no authority to tax. Instead, it simply printed more money. There was no increase in underlying wealth to back up this currency, and the more Congress printed, the less it was worth. By 1780, Congress had printed more than $241 million. In addition, Congress paid for supplies and soldiers' wages with certificates that circulated like money. These certificates put another $95 million into circulation.

The plan was for each state to raise taxes to buy up the Continental currency and remove it from circulation. However, the states were either unable or unwilling to buy up enough currency to maintain its value. Moreover, the states issued their own paper money. Eventually, the states had to tax their inhabitants at rates far higher than had ever been seen before. Collecting taxes was difficult: people could not pay in hard money, and the Continental currency depreciated so rapidly that it was almost worthless (see Figure 7–1).

By April 1777, Continental currency was worth only half its face value, and by April 1781, only half a percent. By the end of the war, some creditors were refusing to accept paper money for debts owed to them, insisting on hard money instead. When trade with Britain resumed, imports increased sharply (because of pent-up demand for consumer goods), while exports fell (because restrictions kept American goods out of British markets). The result was severe deflation and a flood of cheap imports.

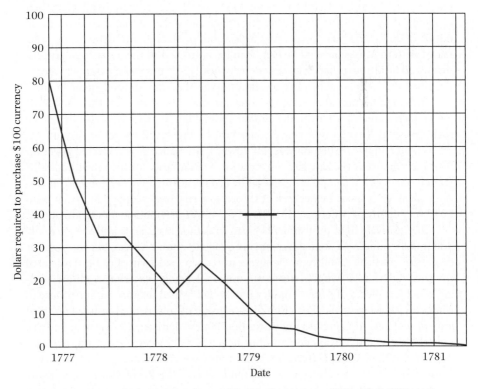

Figure 7–1 Depreciation of Continental Currency, January 1770–April 1781 At the same time that prices were rising, the value of Continental currency was falling dramatically. Between 1777 and 1781, it lost almost all of its value, becoming close to worthless.

The weak central government was almost powerless to address these economic upheavals. In 1780, it stopped paying the army, which almost led to a mutiny at Newburgh, New York. Congress looked to each state to decide what to do about its debt and which element of its population to serve. Many states showed mercy to debtors. To help pay off debts, some states sold confiscated Loyalist property, whereas others tried to seize Indian lands in the west. Wherever states increased taxes to pay off state debts (as the postwar depression hit), hard-pressed debtors clamored for tax relief. In western Massachusetts, farmers led by Revolutionary War captain Daniel Shays shut down the courts to prevent them from collecting debts. This episode is known as **Shays's Rebellion.**

Contesting the New Economy

Economic upheaval and popular uprisings against state governments led many Americans to question whether democratic government could survive. The process of rebellion that started in 1765 seemed to be starting again, this time directed against the new republican state governments. Americans now faced the same issue that had led to conflict with Britain: Were they willing to pay for a huge war? Could they avoid the perils of tyranny, on the one hand, and anarchy, on the other? Could they, in short, maintain democratic forms of government?

Shays's Rebellion was simply an extreme form of the protest that occurred in many states. It was an attempt by debtors to force the government to alleviate their economic distress, primarily by shutting down the courts so that their debts could not be collected, but also by passing legislation for the relief of debtors. By 1786, many western Massachusetts farmers had become used to the absence of government, and local courts had been shut down since 1774. Those who put down Shays's Rebellion did so in republican terms, faulting the Shaysites for inadequate virtue.

Such popular uprisings raised serious questions about whether the democratic governments created after the Revolution could contain anarchy. States that faced such uprisings learned that peace could best be preserved by going easy on the rebels. After Shays's Rebellion was put down, John Hancock was elected governor with the support of the Shaysites on a platform of amnesty for the rebels and relief for debtors. As a rule, popular uprisings by economically independent men (as distinguished from those by dependent laborers or enslaved people) have been punished very lightly in America, which may be a source of American political stability.

The relatively light punishments given to debtor insurgents and the generally inflationary policies of state governments quelled popular unrest, but the postwar depression and the inability of Congress to reopen trade with Britain devastated commerce. The huge national debt went unpaid, leaving numerous creditors holding worthless pieces of paper. Popular unrest had helped debtors but hurt those to whom they owed money. The nationalists, a group of commercial-minded political leaders centered in Congress and including James Madison, Gouverneur Morris, Robert Morris, and Alexander Hamilton, began to make a case for a strong national government that would actively advance commerce and protect private property. These nationalists were, in general, the moderates of the Revolutionary era. Radicals envisioned a weaker central government, a more localized democracy, and a hands-off approach to the economy. Whether these two visions of America could be reconciled was one of the greatest challenges of the Revolution.

Can Women Be Citizens?

The American Revolution raised questions that threatened and in some cases changed the social order. A revolution based on beliefs in human equality and a common human nature brought into question all social relations, including the role of women.

Many women were drawn into the Revolution as consumers. They had eagerly participated in the boycotts of the 1760s and 1770s and had increased home production. Many women identified with the goals of the Revolution and often led riots against merchants suspected of unfair dealings. Women could challenge the Revolutionary governments, as well, when they perceived interference with their rights as consumers and duties as homemakers.

If women were able to extend their traditional economic roles as producers and consumers to support the war effort, there was no consensus on expanding their political roles. Some women pointed out that the right to be taxed only by one's own representatives should apply to them, too. Under the principle of **coverture**, married women were generally denied the right to own property, but what was the basis for denying the vote to unmarried women who owned property? In 1776, New Jersey extended the vote to unmarried women who met the property qualification (although this right was rescinded in 1807). Although American Revolutionaries were not prepared to let women vote, except in New Jersey, they began to broaden their views of women's intellectual and political capabilities. The state laws that confiscated Loyalists' property, for example, often presumed that married women were capable of making their own political choices. This notion broke with the past, when married women were thought to have no political will separate from that of their husbands.

The Revolution challenged the idea that women lacked independent minds and could not think for themselves. The Enlightenment belief that all human beings had the capacity to reason led to significant improvements in women's education after the war. Reformers, many of them women, argued that if women appeared ignorant or incapable, it was only because of their inferior education.

Enlightenment ideas about women's intellectual abilities meshed neatly with republican ideas about the need for virtue and liberal ideas about the necessity of consent. If the nation's fate depended on the character of its citizens, both men and women should be able to choose intelligent, upright, patriotic partners. The Revolution also accelerated a trend for people to choose their own marriage partners and marry for love rather than for material interest. If women were to make such choices wisely, they must be educated well.

Yet once again the Revolutionary impulse had its limits. Discussions about women's citizenship and capacities implicitly applied only to prosperous white women. Moreover, almost no one advocated professional education or even knowledge for its own sake for women. Overly intellectual women were ridiculed as "women of masculine minds." Women's education was supposed to make them better wives and mothers and enable them to perform their domestic roles better. Because the family was still the bedrock of the nation, no one was willing to answer a question posed by Abigail Smith Adams in a letter to her husband, John Adams: What recourse was open to women who found that they were treated with "cruelty and indignity" at home?

North Carolina, and Virginia all attempted to seize land within their borders. Speculators moved in, knowing they could sell land at an immense profit. At the end of the Revolution, one-third of the men in western Pennsylvania were landless, and they believed that the Revolution's promise of equality entitled them to cheap land. Some of the poorest crossed the Appalachians into Kentucky and Ohio, even during the war, squatting on Indian-owned lands.

Those already on the frontier who both suffered from and inflicted violence maintained a visceral hatred of Indians, sometimes advocating their extermination. These settlers expected government to secure frontier land for them and to protect them from the Indians. Congress and the states moved quickly to force Indians, some with no authority to speak for their tribes, to sign treaties ceding their land.

Such treaties (15 were signed between 1784 and 1796) were almost meaningless. Native Americans refused to honor agreements made under duress and that did not include the customary exchange of gifts, and the states would not recognize another state's claims or those of the national government. Indian leaders were encouraged by the British and the Spanish. The Mohawk leader Joseph Brant took his followers to Ontario. Alexander McGillivray united the Creeks and secured military support from the Spanish in Florida. Not until well into the nineteenth century were American claims to Indian land east of the Mississippi secured and Indian resistance put down.

Settling the West

Establishing effective government in the West was one of the biggest problems the new nation faced. Many frontier regions (in particular Kentucky and the area north of the Ohio River, as well as portions of Vermont and Maine) were claimed by competing groups of speculators. The Articles of Confederation gave Congress limited powers of government in the West, but a national policy was necessary. Just after the Revolution, dissident settlers in New York, Pennsylvania, Kentucky (then part of Virginia), and Tennessee (then part of North Carolina) all hatched plans to create their own states.

Both state governments and nationalists in Congress believed that the Union was in peril. Yet it was difficult to reach a compromise among the competing interests. States wanted Congress to recognize their western claims, whereas states without any claims wanted all of the western lands to be turned over to Congress. Also at issue was which speculators' claims would be upheld, as speculators with dubious claims to the land were selling them to settlers at bargain prices.

The Northwest Ordinance, ratified by Congress on July 13, 1787, was a compromise among these competing interests. Finally realizing that they could not manage vast areas of territory, the large states yielded their claims to Congress (see Map 7–4). Because Congress validated the claims only of respectable speculators, it made losers not only out of unscrupulous ones but also out of anyone who had bought land from them at cheap prices.

The Northwest Ordinance set out a model of government for the western territories that reflected the liberal political philosophy of nationalists in Congress and established a process for the admission of new states into the nation. Rejecting Britain's colonial model of expansion, it declared that territories would be eligible

Map 7–4 Western Land Cessions Between 1782 and 1802, eastern states ceded to the national government the territory they claimed in the West. Under the principle established by the Northwest Ordinance, new states were carved out of this territory. Never before had a nation developed such a procedure for bringing in new regions not as colonies but as fully equal states.

to apply for statehood once they had 60,000 free inhabitants. There were other important breaks with the past. Slavery was forbidden north of the Ohio River, the first time that a line was drawn barring enslavement in a particular region. Trial by jury and habeas corpus were guaranteed, as well as the right to bail and freedom of religion. Cruel and unusual punishments were barred. These were important principles that, except for the provision excluding slavery, would all appear again in the Constitution and Bill of Rights.

The Northwest Ordinance was designed to create an orderly world of middle-class farmers who obeyed the law, paid their debts, worshiped as they pleased, and were protected from despotic government and the unruly poor. The ordinance represented the triumph of the moderate Revolutionaries' vision of government.

A GOVERNMENT OF THE PEOPLE

At the beginning of the Revolution, radicals and moderates had worked together to accomplish common goals. The years of war, however, slowly pulled radicals and moderates apart. Many moderates, particularly those who served in Congress or as officers in the Continental army, became nationalists. They worked with men from other states on national projects and came to think of the states as a threat to the success of the Revolution. Many of the radicals, meanwhile, retained a local, republican perspective. They dreaded a centralized government and feared that the Continental army would become a standing army that might take away their liberties.

This split between moderate nationalists and radical localists culminated in the battle over the Constitution, written by the nationalists to create a stronger central government and resisted by the localists, afraid it would subvert liberty. Almost all the problems that led the nationalists to wish for a stronger national government concerned the economy: paying the war debt, paying the soldiers, and improving commerce. The nationalists were deeply involved in the market economy as merchants, financiers, farmers, and planters. The localists, as a rule, were much less involved in the market and suspicious of those who were. As long as taxes were low and their creditors did not harass them, they were satisfied. The Articles of Confederation provided them all the national government and economy they needed.

A Crippled Congress

Nationalists in Congress soon realized that the national government was powerless to address the most pressing economic questions. By 1779, after printing $200 million in paper money that was dropping in value by the day, Congress had shut down its printing presses. It then gave the states the responsibility to provision the army. As legislatures dithered, the unclothed, unfed, and unpaid army threatened mutiny. Congress gave up trying to pay its war debt and passed that back to the states as well. Some states refused. States such as Massachusetts that raised taxes to pay off their portion courted armed upheavals such as Shays's Rebellion.

Congress was powerless to alleviate the economic distress. At the end of the war, British goods flooded in again to meet a consumer demand that seemed insatiable. However, there was no comparable British demand for American exports; in fact, Britain closed its ports to American trade. America could not close its ports to British ships, because the Articles of Confederation denied Congress the authority to regulate commerce. Additional foreign loans were out of the question. Congress could not pay back those it had already taken out. Even western policy, Congress's greatest triumph, presented problems. Once the states had ceded western territory to Congress (leading to the Northwest Ordinance), Congress discovered that it takes an army and a great deal of money to police a territory inhabited by Indians and coveted by land-hungry settlers. Congress lacked that money and could not pay the army it had.

Nationalist attempts to strengthen Congress failed, however, lacking the approval of the states. By the middle of the 1780s, several nationalists abandoned that reform in favor of a new and stronger form of government. James Madison and other nationalists began talking about calling a constitutional convention. But the challenge they faced was how to effect changes that the states did not seem to want.

The road to the Constitutional Convention in Philadelphia in 1787 ran through two earlier meetings. First, in 1785, at Madison's suggestion, commissioners from Virginia and Maryland met at George Washington's home, Mount Vernon, to resolve disputes about navigating the Potomac River. Madison suggested a further meeting of representatives from all the states in Annapolis, Maryland, to build on the accomplishments from Mount Vernon. When only 12 men from five states arrived, they called for another meeting, in Philadelphia, nine months later. In those nine months, Shays's Rebellion and the stalemate in Congress persuaded nationalists to consider strengthening the government. Over the summer of 1787, 55 men from 12 states met in Philadelphia to write one of the most influential documents in the history of the world.

Writing a New Constitution

The men assembled in Philadelphia were primarily moderate nationalists. Committed to the goals of the Revolution, they sought, in Madison's words, "republican remedies" for the problems of republican government. The 55 delegates met for almost four months during the summer of 1787, finally ratifying the Constitution on September 17. They deliberated in secret, in order to talk freely and achieve compromises.

Although there were sharp differences of opinion, there were also wide areas of agreement. Most of the delegates had considerable experience in state and national government. George Washington, a member of Virginia's delegation, was the most widely respected man in the nation. He was elected the presiding officer of the convention.

The delegates were young, with most in their 30s and 40s. No one was more important to the convention than James Madison, just 36. He came with a design for the new government already worked out. Known as the Virginia Plan, it became the outline for the Constitution.

The Virginia Plan was a blueprint for substantial change: a strong central government divided into three branches, executive, legislative (itself with two branches), and judicial, that would check and balance one another; a system of federalism that guaranteed every state a republican government; and proposals for admitting new states and amending the Constitution. The only alternative, the New Jersey Plan, was offered on June 15 and quickly rejected. It proposed a single-house legislature, with all states having an equal vote, and a plural executive, chosen by the legislature (see Table 7–1).

The delegates agreed that the new national government would have to be much stronger: Congress would now have the power to collect taxes and duties, to pay the country's debts, to regulate foreign commerce, and to raise armies and pay for them. Once the delegates compromised on a method for choosing the president (by

Table 7–1 Key Provisions of the Articles of Confederation, the Virginia Plan, the New Jersey Plan, and the Constitution

	Articles of Confederation	Virginia Plan	New Jersey Plan	Constitution
Executive	None	Chosen by Congress	Plural; chosen by Congress	President chosen by Electoral College
Congress	One house; one vote per state	Two houses	One house	Two houses
Judiciary	None	Yes	Yes	Yes
Federalism	Limited; each state retains full sovereignty	Yes; Congress can veto state laws	Yes; acts of Congress the "supreme law of the states"	Yes; Constitution the "supreme law of the land"; states guaranteed a republican form of government; Supreme Court to adjudicate disputes between states
Powers of Congress	Conduct diplomacy and wage war; cannot levy taxes or raise army	All powers of Articles of Confederation, plus power to make laws for nation	All powers of Articles of Confederation, plus power to regulate commerce and make states pay taxes	Numerous powers, such as levy taxes, declare war, raise army, regulate commerce, and "make all laws which shall be necessary and proper" for carrying out those powers

representatives to the **Electoral College** chosen in each state) and the length of his term (four years, eligible for reelection), they readily agreed to grant him considerable power to propose legislation, veto bills of Congress (subject to congressional override), conduct diplomacy, and command the armed forces.

The delegates vested judicial authority in the Supreme Court and inferior federal courts and granted them authority over the state constitutions as well. Although the delegates could agree rather easily on the structure and powers of the new government, they argued bitterly anytime the interests of their states seemed in jeopardy. The most difficult issues related to representation: Would the numbers of senators and representatives be based on population or wealth, or would each state have equal numbers? If based on population or wealth, would enslaved people be counted? Large states generally wanted representation to be based on either population or wealth (they had more of both), whereas northern states did not want the enslaved to be counted, either as population or as wealth. The conflict between the large and small states was resolved by Roger Sherman's Connecticut (or Great) Compromise: Each state would have an equal number of senators, satisfying the small states. The number of representatives would be based on either population or wealth, satisfying the large states.

The Connecticut Compromise solved the conflict between small and large states, but only by creating another between slave and free states. The South

Carolinians were adamant: whether slavery was called population or wealth, the institution must be protected. The argument was fierce, with several delegates threatening to walk out. Finally, the convention compromised. Representation in the House would be based on the entire free population (including women and children, but not Indians) plus three-fifths of the enslaved people, thus increasing the South's representation. The delegates recognized that the Three-Fifths Compromise was fundamentally illogical, but its acceptance was needed to make the Connecticut Compromise possible.

The Three-Fifths Compromise, or Clause, became the most notorious provision in the Constitution. Although the delegates were careful not to use the word "slave" (instead using bland phrases such as "other persons"), clearly they were establishing a racial line. The convention made two other concessions to slavery. First, it agreed, over Madison's vehement protest, that Congress could not ban the slave trade until 1808 at the earliest. In addition, the Constitution included a fugitive slave clause, which required states to return runaway slaves. The reopening of the slave trade did more to strengthen slavery than the other compromises on slavery. Madison predicted accurately that "twenty years will produce all the mischief that can be apprehended from the liberty to import slaves." Between 1788 and 1808, thousands and thousands of Africans were sold into slavery in the United States.

The nationalists were determined not to leave Philadelphia without a constitution, and they were willing to make whatever compromises seemed necessary. Those compromises were eventually achieved, and the convention adjourned on September 17. The delegates' work was not over, however. Now the Constitution had to be ratified.

Ratifying the Constitution: Politics

There was nothing inevitable about the nation, the Constitution, or the particular form either took. The Constitution was the creation of a small group of men who thought nationally, the **Federalists**. They then had the difficult task of getting the Constitution ratified by a nation that still thought about government in almost wholly local terms. That the Constitution would be ratified was by no means a given.

The Philadelphia Convention decided that the Constitution would go into effect once nine states had ratified it. They could not bind any states that had not ratified, but the nine signatories could go ahead. Small states were the first to ratify, because they most needed the union. For example, Georgia, the fourth state to ratify, was still in many ways a frontier region, vulnerable to Indian assault, its capital at Augusta an armed camp. The most serious opposition came from the large, powerful states of Massachusetts, New York, and Virginia.

The convention had concluded on September 17, and by December 7, Delaware had already ratified the Constitution. By January 9, 1788, New Jersey, Georgia, and Connecticut followed, with barely any dispute. The Federalists in Pennsylvania forced ratification by using strong-arm tactics. The Federalists in other states learned from this mistake and more willingly made concessions to the **Antifederalists** (as the opponents of the Constitution were called).

Struggles For Democracy

The Ratification of the Constitution

In writing the Constitution, the Founding Fathers drew from their knowledge of world history and political theory, but once it was time to turn their new document into an actual government, they were in uncharted territory. Not only was a written Constitution an innovation but so was the process for putting it into effect. The creators of the new United States government were making up the processes of democratic government as they went along.

Approval of the Constitution was by no means assured. Its supporters, the Federalists, made a series of strategic decisions, however, that not only enabled them to prevail but also strengthened the Constitution and enhanced its legitimacy in the process. The first of these decisions was to send the Constitution back to Congress, asking *it* to send the document along to the state legislatures, requesting them to convene ratifying conventions of the people. This tactic was at once democratic and a bit devious. It reflected the Lockean basis of the Constitution: Government is created by the people—the "We the People" of the Constitution's Preamble who "establish this Constitution for the United States of America." But this process broke so sharply from the past that some delegates could not reconcile themselves to it. Maryland's Luther Martin, an Antifederalist, had consistently argued against any representation based upon population. He argued that "the Genl Govt ought to be formed for the States, not for individuals." Nationalists such as James Wilson carried the day with their Lockean understanding: "The Genl Govt is not an assemblage of States, but for the individuals composing them; the *individuals* therefore not the *States*, ought to be represented." It also brought Congress back into the process, giving the Constitution added legitimacy. At the same time, sending it out to "the people" for ratification was a bit sly, for had the Convention asked for ratification from the state legislatures, that process would have been slow and difficult, with legislators who were jealous of their states' powers stalling the process; moreover, two-thirds majorities would have been necessary in many states. Had the Constitution

In Massachusetts, as in Pennsylvania, considerable opposition came from the western part of the state among those sympathetic to Shays's Rebellion. In an inspired move that would be used also in Virginia, the Federalists made certain that the Constitution was debated section by section, enabling them to win point by point. And in another key strategic decision, the Federalists agreed that the convention in Massachusetts should propose amendments, not as a condition for ratification but as part of a package that recommended ratification. This concession, which made the Constitution both stronger and more democratic, was critical in winning ratification.

been sent to the state legislatures, it is unlikely it would have been adopted.

Consider how close the Pennsylvania assembly came to refusing to call a ratifying convention. The day the assembly was scheduled to vote on whether to issue the call, two Antifederalists intentionally did not show up; without them, the minimum number of necessary members was not present, and no convention could be called. The Federalist Speaker of the House ordered the sergeant-at-arms to bring the two absent legislators to the assembly, which he did, with the assistance of a mob. The Federalists won, but their tactic was considered distasteful.

At each of the state ratifying conventions, the Federalists used different tactics, as the situation seemed to warrant. Especially important to enhancing the legitimacy of the Constitution was the decision to accept amendments to the document. The Convention had defeated with almost no debate a proposal to add a Bill of Rights, but the Antifederalists pushed the idea in the state conventions. In Pennsylvania, Wilson explained the Federalist position: enumerating the rights of the people was downright "dangerous" because it might limit rights to those listed. The Pennsylvania Federalists voted down a proposal for amendments, but their counterparts in Massachusetts, where John Hancock offered amendments as a compromise to "remove the fears and quiet the apprehensions of many of the good people of the commonwealth," were much wiser. They accepted the amendments. At least as important was the form that these amendments would take, not as a condition for ratification, but as a recommendation to the new government. Only Maryland would not attach a list of amendments.

Other decisions were purely tactical. The Federalists were able to get a postponement in New Hampshire, which at that point was unlikely to ratify. They knew that momentum was important and that even one rejection might prove fatal. Then, Maryland and South Carolina ratified, requiring only one more state's approval for the Constitution to go into effect. As it turned out, both New Hampshire and Virginia ratified at almost the same time, unbeknownst to each other.

Democratic government is a combination of procedure and principle. The Federalist proponents of the Constitution were skilled political tacticians who used the processes of government to their own advantage, but they also compromised with their Antifederalist opponents. Their contestation—their arguments, struggles, and compromises—gave meaning to the Constitution and form to the new government of the United States.

Only three more states were necessary for the Constitution to go into effect. The Federalists postponed or stalled the debate until the states most favorable to the Constitution had ratified it, as it would go into effect once nine states had ratified it. The Virginia ratifying convention was one of the most dramatic and divided. Patrick Henry, who had refused to attend the Philadelphia Convention, saying that he "smelt a rat," spoke in opposition. His impassioned speeches were rebutted by James Madison's careful and knowledgeable remarks. Having worn down the Antifederalists with logic, the Federalists carried the day, and the Constitution was ratified. The Antifederalists agreed to abide by the result, even though there had been threats of armed rebellion. The decision of Antifederalists to accept the Constitution and to participate in the government it created was one of the most important choices made in this era.

In New York, the Federalists stalled debate until news of Virginia's ratification arrived. Then they posed the inevitable question: Ten states had now voted in favor and the Constitution had been ratified; would New York join in or not? New York did, and eventually the Constitution was ratified by all the states. As a condition for ratification, several states had insisted that the first Congress consider a number of amendments. These amendments became the Bill of Rights.

Ratifying the Constitution: Ideas

The Constitution was the product of many compromises, and it did not precisely fit anyone's previous ideas. As the Federalists explained the benefits of the Constitution to skeptical Americans, and as the Antifederalists tried to explain what they thought was wrong with it, a new understanding of what American government should be evolved. Despite significant disagreements, this new understanding, which incorporated the Bill of Rights, was sufficiently broad that Antifederalists could join the new government.

Nonetheless, the differences between the Federalists and Antifederalists were profound. As a rule, the Antifederalists were more rural and less involved in the market, came from the western or backwoods regions, and were more likely to be veterans of the militia than of the Continental army. The Antifederalists were, above all, old-line republicans who warned of the dangers to liberty of corruption, tyranny, and enslavement, although now they spoke against the Federalists, not the British.

TIME LINE

▼**1774**
Intolerable Acts

▼**1775**
Battles of Lexington and Concord
Fort Ticonderoga seized
Battle of Breed's Hill
Second Continental Congress convenes
Continental army created, with George Washington in charge
Congress adopts "Declaration of the Causes and Necessity of Taking Up Arms"

George III declares colonists in rebellion
Governor Dunmore offers freedom to Virginia's enslaved people who fight for the British
Continental army attacks Canada

▼**1776**
Thomas Paine writes *Common Sense*
Declaration of Independence
Articles of Confederation drafted

British capture Manhattan
Washington captures Trenton and Princeton
New Jersey Constitution allows unmarried, property-owning women to vote

▼**1777**
British capture Philadelphia
American victory at Saratoga

▼**1778**
French enter into treaty with United States
British conquer Georgia

The Antifederalists believed passionately in the local community. They asserted that republics could survive only in homogeneous communities, where all people had the same interests and values. They believed that too much diversity, whether economic, cultural, ethnic, or religious, destroyed a republic. One Massachusetts Antifederalist criticized the Constitution because it would not allow states to stop immigration so as "to keep their blood pure." Although Antifederalists, like Federalists, generally supported freedom of religion, they also favored the spread of Protestantism as a means of ensuring morality.

At the same time, the Antifederalists were committed to individual rights, and it is to them that the nation is indebted for the Bill of Rights. They retained the republican fear of power, and they did not trust the person they could not see. If government were remote, then it would become oppressive, it would deprive the people of their liberties, and it would tax them. One of the most consistent complaints of the Antifederalists was not so much that taxation would be enacted without representation as that it would be enacted at all. If the national government needed money, let it ask the states for it (a system that failed under the Articles of Confederation). The Antifederalists displayed the same fear of centralized government and hatred of taxation that had led to their revolt against Britain. The Antifederalist contribution to American political thought was a continuing critique of government itself.

Federalists shared many of the beliefs of the Antifederalists, such as individual rights. Hence, they readily accepted the Antifederalist proposal to list and protect those rights as amendments to the Constitution. They were also suspicious of government, most agreeing with Thomas Paine that "government even in its best state is but a necessary evil." The separation of powers and elaborate series of checks and balances

Sullivan expedition
into New York and
Pennsylvania

▼**1779**
Continental troops winter
at Jockey Hollow

▼**1780**
British conquer South
Carolina

▼**1781**
Articles of Confederation
ratified

Battle of Guilford Court
House
Cornwallis surrenders

▼**1782**
Franklin begins peace
discussions with British

▼**1783**
Treaty of Paris

▼**1785**
Virginia and Maryland
commissioners meet at
Mount Vernon

▼**1786–1787**
Shays's Rebellion
Meeting at Annapolis

▼**1787**
Northwest Ordinance
Constitutional Convention

▼**1787–1788**
Federalist Papers published
Constitution ratified

that the Constitution created, as well as the system of federalism itself, reflects this fear. The Federalists divided power; unlike the Antifederalists, they did not deny it.

Their experience in the market economy, as officers in the Continental army and as members of the national government, provided the Federalists with a different perspective on political economy. They had come to believe that all people were motivated by self-interest. Unlike the Antifederalists, the Federalists were willing to accept self-interest and build a government around it.

The Federalists were convinced that no government could rest entirely on the virtue of its people. The challenge was to build a government out of imperfect human materials that would preserve liberty instead of destroying it. In *The Federalist* No. 10 (one of a series of 85 essays known as the *Federalist Papers*, written by Madison, Hamilton, and John Jay and published anonymously to influence the ratification debate), Madison explained that the causes of conflict "are sown into the nature of man." The only way of eliminating them would be either by "giving to every citizen the same opinions, the same passions, and the same interests" (the Antifederalist solution) or by destroying liberty itself. But "as long as the reason of man continues fallible, and he is at liberty to exercise it, different opinions will be formed." Toleration was the price of liberty and the necessary result of human imperfection.

In the Philadelphia Convention, the Federalists had been so intent on working out compromises and reconciling competing interests that they did not develop a philosophy to explain the profound changes they were proposing. That philosophy emerged from the ratification debates, in which it was met by the alternative philosophy of the Antifederalists. Both these bodies of thought, sometimes in harmony, sometimes in disagreement, constitute the legacy of the Revolution. This dialogue has continued to frame American government from their day until ours.

CONCLUSION

In rejecting the increasingly centralized British state, the Revolutionaries were clear about what they did not want. Over the course of the Revolution, they began to envision the kind of society and nation that they hoped to create. It would ensure individual liberty and economic opportunity. But this was a vague vision for the future. As the first modern nation created by revolution, the United States was entering uncharted territory. Winning independence from the world's most powerful nation, ratifying the federal Constitution, and planning for the admission of new territories into the federal union were all extraordinary accomplishments, unique in world history.

Yet there were many problems left unresolved. Not only was Britain still occupying forts in the Northwest Territory, but also the European nations were skeptical that the new nation would survive. Although the United States had more than doubled its size, much of the new territory could not be settled because it was inhabited by Indians who refused to recognize America's sovereignty. There were also disagreements among Americans themselves, particularly about the meaning of democracy. How could a nation founded on the principle of liberty practice slavery? How would individual rights be reconciled with the general welfare? Whose economic interests would be served? The American people had begun a great experiment whose outcome was far from assured.

WHO, WHAT, WHERE

REVIEW QUESTIONS

1. What was Revolutionary ardor, and why was it highest at the beginning of the war?

2. What were American and British strategies for winning the war? What were the chief challenges the Americans faced in mounting the war, and how did they affect military strategy? What were the constraints on the British in waging a war on American soil?

3. Which Americans believed a stronger central government was needed, and why? What were the compromises they made in writing the Constitution?

4. Describe the political philosophies of the Federalists and Antifederalists.

CRITICAL-THINKING QUESTIONS

1. Which group was more democratic, the Federalists or Antifederalists? Or were they democratic (or undemocratic) in different ways?

2. How did Americans respond to the challenges to the social order presented by their doctrine of equality?

3. Assess the relative importance of ideals and economic interests in shaping the history of the period 1775–1787.

SUGGESTED READINGS

DuVal, Kathleen. *Independence Lost: Lives on the Edge of the American Revolution*. New York: Random House, 2015.

Holton, Woody. *Abigail Adams: A Life*. New York: Free Press, 2009.

Parkinson, Robert. *The Common Cause: Creating Race and Nation in the American Revolution*. Chapel Hill: Omohundro Institute and University of North Carolina Pres, 2016.

For further review materials and resource information, please visit www.oup.com/us/ofthepeople

CHAPTER 7: CREATING A NEW NATION, 1775–1788
Primary Sources

7.1 THOMAS PAINE, *COMMON SENSE* (1776)

In 1775, the political strife between the colonies and Great Britain turned into outright warfare. Nevertheless, many Americans questioned whether the goal of the conflict should be the creation of an independent nation or simply a renegotiation of the colonies' relationship with Great Britain. Thomas Paine's pamphlet *Common Sense*, published in January 1776, helped convince the colonists that monarchy was a corrupt and tyrannical system and that they would be better off independent. The document was widely read and helped shift American public opinion toward revolution.

OF THE ORIGIN AND DESIGN OF GOVERNMENT IN GENERAL

Some writers have so confounded society with government, as to leave little or no distinction between them; whereas they are not only different, but have different origins. Society is produced by our wants, and government by our wickedness; the former promotes our happiness POSITIVELY by uniting our affections, the latter NEGATIVELY by restraining our vices. The one encourages intercourse, the other creates distinctions. The first a patron, the last a punisher.

Society in every state is a blessing, but government even in its best state is but a necessary evil; in its worst state an intolerable one; for when we suffer, or are exposed to the same miseries BY A GOVERNMENT, which we might expect in a country WITHOUT GOVERNMENT, our calamity is heightened by reflecting that we furnish the means by which we suffer. Government, like dress, is the badge of lost innocence; the palaces of kings are built on the ruins of the bowers of paradise. For were the impulses of conscience clear, uniform, and irresistibly obeyed, man would need no other lawgiver; but that not being the case, he finds it necessary to surrender up a part of his property to furnish means for the protection of the rest; and this he is induced to do by the same prudence which in every other case advises him out of two evils to choose the least. WHEREFORE, security being the true design and end of government, it un-answerably follows, that whatever FORM thereof appears most likely to ensure it to us, with the least expense and greatest benefit, is preferable to all others.

In order to gain a clear and just idea of the design and end of government, let us suppose a small number of persons settled in some sequestered part of the earth, unconnected with the rest, they will then represent the first peopling of any country, or of the world. In this state of natural liberty, society will be their first thought. A thousand motives will excite them thereto, the strength of one man is so unequal to his wants, and his mind so unfitted for perpetual solitude, that he is soon obliged to seek assistance and relief of another, who in his turn requires the same. . . . Thus necessity, like a gravitating power, would soon form our newly arrived emigrants into society, the reciprocal blessings of which, would supersede, and render the obligations of law and government unnecessary while they remained perfectly just to each other; but as nothing but heaven is impregnable to vice, it will unavoidably happen, that in proportion as they surmount the first difficulties of emigration, which bound them together in a common cause, they will begin to relax in their duty and attachment to each other; and this remissness will point out the necessity of establishing some form of government to supply the defect of moral virtue.

Some convenient tree will afford them a State-House, under the branches of which, the whole colony may assemble to deliberate on public matters. It is more than probable that their first laws will have the title only of REGULATIONS, and be enforced by no other penalty than public disesteem. In this first parliament every man, by natural right, will have a seat.

But as the colony increases, the public concerns will increase likewise, and the distance at which the members may be separated, will render it too inconvenient for all of them to meet on every occasion as at first, when their number was small, their habitations near, and the public concerns few and trifling. This will point out the convenience of their consenting to leave the legislative part to be managed by a select number chosen from the whole body, who are supposed to have the same concerns at stake which those who appointed them, and who will act in the same manner as the whole body would act, were they present. If the colony continues increasing, it will become necessary to augment the number of the representatives, and that the interest of every part of the colony may be attended to, it will be found best to divide the whole into convenient parts, each part sending its proper number; and that the ELECTED might never form to themselves an interest separate from the ELECTORS, prudence will point out the propriety of having elections often; because as the ELECTED might by that means return and mix again with the general body of the ELECTORS in a few months, their fidelity to the public will be secured by the prudent reflection of not making a rod for themselves. And as this frequent interchange will establish a common interest with every part of the community, they will mutually and naturally support each other, and on this (not on the unmeaning name of king) depends the STRENGTH OF GOVERNMENT, AND THE HAPPINESS OF THE GOVERNED.

Here then is the origin and rise of government; namely, a mode rendered necessary by the inability of moral virtue to govern the world; here too is the design and end of government, viz. freedom and security. And however our eyes may be dazzled with show, or our ears deceived by sound; however prejudice may warp our wills, or interest darken our understanding, the simple voice of nature and of reason will say, it is right.

Source: Thomas Paine, *Common Sense*, New York: Penguin Editions, 2005 [1776].

7.2   ALEXANDER HAMILTON RECOMMENDS ARMING SLAVES AND GEORGE WASHINGTON REJECTS THE IDEA (1779)

As the site of warfare moved south, American leaders struggled to raise troops. Colonel John Laurens, a member of a prominent South Carolina slave-owning family, and one of Washington's aides, proposed arming enslaved people and granting them freedom at the end of the Revolution. His friend and fellow Washington aide, Alexander Hamilton, passed this proposal on to John Jay, the president of the Continental Congress, in March 1779. Although as much of a quarter of Washington's army was made up of Black men, in a letter to John Laurens's father, Henry, then a delegate to Congress, Washington himself rejected the idea of formally recruiting enslaved people to fight.

HAMILTON TO JAY, MARCH 14, 1779

Col Laurens, who will have the honor of delivering you this letter, is on his way to South Carolina, on a project, which I think, in the present situation of affairs there, is a very good one and deserves every kind of support and encouragement. This is to raise two three or four batalions of negroes; with the assistance of the government of that state, by contributions from the owners in proportion to the number they possess. If you should think proper to enter upon the subject with him, he will give you a detail of his plan. He wishes to have it recommended by Congress to the state; and, as an inducement, that they would engage to take those batalions into Continental pay.

It appears to me, that an expedient of this kind, in the present state of Southern affairs, is the most rational, that can be adopted, and promises very important advantages. Indeed, I hardly see how a sufficient force can be collected in that quarter without it; and the enemy's operations there are growing infinitely serious and formidable. I have not the least doubt, that the negroes will make very excellent soldiers, with proper management; and I will venture to pronounce, that they cannot be put in better hands than those of Mr. Laurens. He has all the zeal, intelligence, enterprise, and every other qualification requisite to succeed in such an undertaking. It is a maxim with some great military judges, that with sensible officers soldiers can hardly be too stupid; and on this principle it is thought that the Russians would make the best troops in the world, if they were under other officers than their own. The King of Prussia is among the number who maintain this doctrine and has a very emphatical saying on the occasion, which I do not exactly recollect. I mention this, because I frequently hear it objected to the scheme of embodying negroes that they are too stupid to make soldiers. This is so far from appearing to me a valid objection that I think their want of cultivation (for their natural faculties are probably as good as ours) joined to that habit of subordination which they acquire from a life of servitude, will make them sooner bec[o]me soldiers than our White inhabitants. Let officers be men of sense and sentiment, and the nearer the soldiers approach to machines perhaps the better.

I foresee that this project will have to combat much opposition from prejudice and self-interest. The contempt we have been taught to entertain for the blacks, makes us fancy many things that are founded neither in reason nor experience; and an unwillingness to part with property of so valuable a kind will furnish a thousand arguments to show the impracticability or pernicious tendency of a scheme which requires such a sacrifice. But it should be considered, that if we do not make use of them in this way, the enemy probably will; and that the best way to counteract the temptations they will hold out will be to offer them ourselves. An essential part of the plan is to give them their freedom with their muskets. This will secure their fidelity, animate their courage, and I believe will have a good influence upon those who remain, by opening a door to their emancipation. This circumstance, I confess, has no small weight in inducing me to wish the success of the project; for the dictates of humanity and true policy equally interest me in favour of this unfortunate class of men.

WASHINGTON TO HENRY LAURENS, MARCH 20, 1779

Dear Sir:

. . . . The policy of our arming Slaves is, in my opinion, a moot point, unless the enemy set the example; for should we begin to form Battalions of them, I have not the smallest doubt (if the War is to be prosecuted) of their following us in it, and justifying the measure upon our own ground; the upshot then must be, who can arm fastest, and where are our Arms? besides, I am not clear that a discrimination will not render Slavery more irksome to those who remain in it; most of the good and evil things of this life are judged of by comparison; and I fear a comparison in this case will be productive of much discontent in those who are held in servitude; but as this is a subject that has never employed much of my thoughts, these are no more than the first crude Ideas that have struck me upon the occasion. . . .

Mrs. Washington joins me in respectful compliments to you, and with every sentiment of regard and attachment. I am etc.

Sources: Philip Kurland and Ralph Lerner, eds., *The Founders' Constitution* (Indianapolis: Liberty Fund, 1987), vol. 1, chapter 15, document 24. And George Washington Papers, series 3, Varick Transcripts, subseries 3H, Letterbook 1 (1775-1779). Library of Congress, Washington, D.C., https://www.loc.gov/resource/mgw3h.001/?sp=237&st=text

7.3 LETTER FROM ABIGAIL ADAMS TO JOHN ADAMS (1776)

The American Revolution had a profound impact on the lives of women. Whether they were directly affected by fighting, or struggling to hold down the home front in the absence of their sons, fathers, husbands, and brothers, women played a vital role in the war years. Abigail Adams's letters to her husband, John, when he was away in Philadelphia at the Continental Congress and, later, serving as a diplomat in France and the Netherlands, captured both the ties of affection and the practical concerns felt by many American women. In addition, Abigail Adams was deeply engaged politically. Note the way that she framed her appeal for women's rights.

I wish you would ever write me a Letter half as long as I write you; and tell me if you may where your Fleet are gone? What sort of Defence Virginia can make against our common Enemy? Whether it is so situated as to make an able Defence? Are not the Gentery Lords and the common people vassals, are they not like the uncivilized Natives Brittain represents us to be? I hope their Riffel Men who have shewen themselves very savage and even Blood thirsty; are not a specimen of the Generality of the people.

I am willing to allow the Colony great merrit for having produced a Washington but they have been shamefully duped by a Dunmore.

I have sometimes been ready to think that the passion for Liberty cannot be Eaqually Strong in the Breasts of those who have been accustomed to deprive their fellow Creatures of theirs. Of this I am certain that it is not founded upon that generous and christian principal of doing to others as we would that others should do unto us.

Do not you want to see Boston; I am fearfull of the small pox, or I should have been in before this time. I got Mr. Crane to go to our House and see what state it was in. I find it has been occupied by one of the Doctors of a Regiment, very dirty, but no other damage has been done to it. The few things which were left in it are all gone. Cranch has the key which he never deliverd up. I have wrote to him for it and am determined to get it cleand as soon as possible and shut it up. I look upon it a new acquisition of property, a property which one month ago I did not value at a single Shilling, and could with pleasure have seen it in flames.

The Town in General is left in a better state than we expected, more oweing to a percipitate flight than any Regard to the inhabitants, tho some individuals discoverd a sense of honour and justice and have left the rent of the Houses in which they were, for the owners and the furniture unhurt, or if damaged sufficent to make it good.

Others have committed abominable Ravages. The Mansion House of your President is safe and the furniture unhurt whilst both the House and Furniture of the Solisiter General have fallen a prey to their own merciless party. Surely the very Fiends feel a Reverential awe for Virtue and patriotism, whilst they Detest the paricide and traitor.

I feel very differently at the approach of spring to what I did a month ago. We knew not then whether we could plant or sow with safety, whether when we had toild we could reap the fruits of our own industery, whether we could rest in our own Cottages, or whether we should not be driven from the sea coasts to seek shelter in the wilderness, but now we feel as if we might sit under our own vine and eat the good of the land.

I feel a gaieti de Coar [French: *gaieté de Coeur*, lightness of heart] to which before I was a stranger. I think the Sun looks brighter, the Birds sing more melodiously, and Nature puts on a more chearfull countance. We feel a temporary peace, and the poor fugitives are returning to their deserted habitations.

Tho we felicitate ourselves, we sympathize with those who are trembling least the Lot of Boston should be theirs. But they cannot be in similar circumstances unless pusilanimity and cowardise should take possession of them. They have time and warning given them to see the Evil and shun it.—I long to hear that you have declared an independency—and by the way in the new Code of Laws which I suppose it will be necessary for you to make I desire you would Remember the Ladies, and be more generous and favourable to them than your ancestors. Do not put such unlimited power into the hands of the Husbands. Remember all Men would be tyrants if they could. If perticuliar care and attention is not paid to the Laidies we are determined to foment a Rebelion, and will not hold ourselves bound by any Laws in which we have no voice, or Representation.

That your Sex are Naturally Tyrannical is a Truth so thoroughly established as to admit of no dispute, but such of you as wish to be happy willingly give up the harsh title of Master for the more tender and endearing one of Friend. Why then, not put it out of the power of the vicious and the Lawless to use us with cruelty and indignity with impunity. Men of Sense in all Ages abhor those customs which treat us only as the vassals of your Sex. Regard us then as Beings placed by providence under your protection and in immitation of the Supreem Being make use of that power only for our happiness.

Source: Letter from Abigail Adams to John Adams, 31 March–5 April 1776 [electronic edition]. *Adams Family Papers: An Electronic Archive.* Massachusetts Historical Society. https://www.masshist. org/digitaladams/archive/doc?id=L17760331aa.

7.4   SLAVE PETITION FOR FREEDOM TO THE MASSACHUSETTS LEGISLATURE (1777)

Although many slave owners supported the patriot cause without questioning the morality of slavery, the rhetoric of liberty profoundly challenged slavery. This petition for freedom, submitted by a group of eight people enslaved in Massachusetts, failed. They and others continued to petition the courts, arguing that slavery was inconsistent with Article I of the Massachusetts Constitution, which declared "all men are born free and equal." In 1781, a local court ruled in favor of Elizabeth Freeman (also known as Mum Bett), and in response to the enslaved Quock Walker's suit in 1783, the Massachusetts Supreme Judicial Court ruled that the Massachusetts Constitution prohibited slavery.

The petition of A Great Number of Blackes detained in a State of slavery in the Bowels of a free & Christian Country Humbly shuwith that your Petitioners apprehend that thay have in Common with all other men a Natural and Unaliable Right to that freedom which the Grat Parent of the Unavers hath Bestowed equalley on all menkind and which they have Never forfuted by any Compact or agreement whatever—but thay wher Unjustly Dragged by the hand of cruel Power from their Derest friends and sum of them Even torn from the Embraces of their tender Parents—from A popoulous Pleasant and plentiful contry and in violation of Laws of Nature and off Nations and in defiance of all the tender feelings of humanity Brough hear Either to Be sold Like Beast of Burthen & Like them Condemnd to Slavery for Life—Among A People Profesing the mild Religion of Jesus A people Not Insensible of the Secrets of Rational Being Nor without spirit to Resent the unjust endeavours of others to Reduce them to a state of Bondage and Subjection your honouer Need not to be informed that A Life of Slavery Like that of your petioners Deprived of Every social privilege of Every thing Requisit to Render Life Tolable is far worse then Nonexistence.

[In Imitat]ion of the Lawdable Example of the Good People of these States your petitononers have Long and Patiently waited the Evnt of petition after petition By them presented to the Legislative Body of this state and cannot but with Grief Reflect that their Success hath ben but too similar they Cannot but express their Astonishment that It has Never Bin Consirdered that Every Principle form which Amarica has Acted in the Cours of their unhappy Dificultes with Great Briton Pleads Stronger than A thousand arguments in favowrs of your petioners they therfor humble Beseech your honours to give this petion [petition] its due weight & consideration & cause an act of the Legislatur to be past Wherby they may be Restored to the Enjoyments of that which is the Naturel Right of all men—and their Children who wher Born in this Land of Liberty may not be heald as Slaves after they arrive at the age of twenty one years so may the Inhabitance of this Stats No longer chargeable with the inconsistancey of acting themselves the part which they condem and oppose in others Be prospered in their present Glorious struggle for Liberty and have those Blessing to them, &c.

Prince Hall

Lancaster Hill

Peter Bess

Brister Slenser

Jack Pierpont

Nero Funelo

Newport Sumner

Job Look

Source: Slave Petition for Freedom to the Massachusetts Legislature, 1777. Printed in *Collections of the Massachusetts Historical Society*, 5th Series, III (Boston, 1877), pp. 436–37.

7.5   THE FEDERALISTS AND THE ANTI-FEDERALISTS (1787–1788)

The Federalist Papers appeared anonymously under the classical name "Publius" in various New York State newspapers in 1787 and early 1788. The Tenth, by James Madison, is perhaps the most philosophically central. The essays were reprinted widely and contributed to local legislative debates. For more than three weeks, delegates to the Virginia Ratifying Convention argued the merits of the proposed Constitution. James Madison, George Wythe, and John Marshall argued passionately for it, while Patrick Henry, George Mason, and James Monroe argued just as passionately against it. Marshall later said, "If I were called upon to say who of all men I have known had the greatest power to convince, I should perhaps say Mr. Madison; while Mr. Henry had without doubt the greatest power to persuade." Here is an excerpt from The Federalist #10 and then one from one of Henry's speeches given on June 7, 1788.

Among the numerous advantages promised by a well-constructed Union, none deserves to be more accurately developed than its tendency to break and control the violence of faction. The friend of popular governments never finds himself so much alarmed for their character and fate, as when he contemplates their propensity to this dangerous vice. He will not fail, therefore, to set a due value on any plan which, without violating the principles to which he is attached, provides a proper cure for it. The instability, injustice, and confusion introduced into the public councils, have, in truth, been the mortal diseases under which popular governments have everywhere perished. . . . By a faction, I understand a number of citizens, whether amounting to a majority or a minority of the whole, who are united and actuated by some common impulse of passion, or of interest, adversed to the rights of other citizens, or to the permanent and aggregate interests of the community.

There are two methods of curing the mischiefs of faction: the one, by removing its causes; the other, by controlling its effects.

There are again two methods of removing the causes of faction: the one, by destroying the liberty which is essential to its existence; the other, by giving to every citizen the same opinions, the same passions, and the same interests.

It could never be more truly said than of the first remedy, that it was worse than the disease. Liberty is to faction what air is to fire, an aliment without which it instantly expires. But it could not be less folly to abolish liberty, which is essential to political life, because it nourishes faction, than it would be to wish the annihilation of air, which is essential to animal life, because it imparts to fire its destructive agency.

The second expedient is as impracticable as the first would be unwise. As long as the reason of man continues fallible, and he is at liberty to exercise it, different opinions will be formed. As long as the connection subsists between his reason and his self-love, his opinions and his passions will have a reciprocal influence on each other; and the former will be objects to which the latter will attach themselves. The diversity in the faculties of men, from which the rights of property originate, is not less an insuperable obstacle to a uniformity of interests. The protection of these faculties is the first object of government. From the protection of different and unequal faculties of acquiring property, the possession of different degrees and kinds of property immediately results; and from the influence of these on the sentiments and views of the respective proprietors, ensues a division of the society into different interests and parties.

The latent causes of faction are thus sown in the nature of man; and we see them everywhere brought into different degrees of activity, according to the different circumstances of civil society. A zeal for different opinions concerning religion, concerning government, and many other points, as well of speculation as of practice; an attachment to different leaders ambitiously contending for pre-eminence and power; or to persons of other descriptions whose fortunes have been interesting to the human passions, have, in turn, divided mankind into parties, inflamed them with mutual animosity, and rendered them much more disposed to vex and oppress each other than to cooperate for their common good. So strong is this propensity of mankind to fall into mutual animosities, that where no substantial occasion presents itself, the most frivolous and fanciful distinctions have been sufficient to kindle their unfriendly passions and excite their most violent conflicts. . . . The inference to which we are brought is, that the *causes* of factions cannot be removed, and that relief is only to be sought in the means of controlling its *effects*.

Mr. Henry [in arguing against Congress's power to tax] continued: I will exchange that *abominable* word for *requisitions*. Requisitions, which gentlemen affect to despise, have nothing degrading in them. On this depends our political prosperity. I never will give up that *darling* word *requisitions*: my country may give it up; a majority may wrest it from me, but I will never give it up till my grave. Requisitions are attended with one singular advantage. They are attended by deliberation. They secure to the states the benefit of correcting oppressive errors. If our Assembly thought requisitions erroneous, if they thought the demand was too great, they might at least supplicate Congress to reconsider—that it was a little too much. The power of direct taxation was called by the honorable gentleman the *soul* of the government: another gentleman called it the *lungs* of the government. We all agree that it is the most important part of the body politic. If the power of raising money be necessary for the general government, it is no less so for the states. If money be the vitals of Congress, is it not precious for those individuals from whom it is to be taken? Must I give my soul, my lungs, to Congress? Congress must have our souls; the state must have our souls. This is dishonorable and disgraceful. These two coordinate, interfering, unlimited powers of harassing the community are unexampled: it is unprecedented in history. They are the visionary projects of modern politicians. Tell me not of imaginary means, but of reality; this political solecism will never tend to the benefit of the community. It will be as oppressive in practice as it is absurd in theory. If you part from this, which the honorable gentleman tells you is the soul of Congress, you will be inevitably ruined. I tell you, they shall not have the soul of Virginia. They tell us that one collector may collect the federal and state taxes. The general government being paramount to the state legislatures, if the sheriff is to collect for both,—his right hand for Congress, his left for the state,—his right hand being paramount over the left, his collections will go to Congress. We shall have the rest. Deficiencies in collections will always operate against the states. Congress, being the paramount, supreme power, must not be disappointed. Thus Congress will have an unlimited, unbounded command over the soul of this commonwealth. After satisfying their uncontrolled demands, what can be left for the states? Not a sufficiency even to defray the expense of their internal administration. They must therefore glide imperceptibly and gradually out of existence. This, sir, must naturally terminate in a consolidation. If this will do for other people, it never will do for me.

Source: James Madison, excerpt from Federalist Paper #10, *The New York Packet*, November 23, 1787. Guides.loc.gov/federalist-papers/text-1-10. Patrick Henry, excerpt from speech to the Virginia Ratifying Convention, June 7, 1788. http://www.constitution.org/rc/rat_va_06.htm#henry-02.

8

Contested Republic
1789–1800

< "Congressional pugilists," 1798

Among Congress's first tasks was deciding what the president should be called. Believing that the president needed an impressive title to demonstrate that the new nation was "civilized," a Senate committee recommended "His Highness the President of the United States of America, and Protector of the Liberties." But the House argued that the suggestion smacked of aristocratic pretension and in the end insisted simply on "the President of the United States."

Meanwhile, Congress approved official advisers to the president (the cabinet). Washington's first administration reflected both his own close circle of friends and the political clout of the large states. The president was from Virginia, the most populous state, as were his secretary of state, **Thomas Jefferson**, and his attorney general, Edmund Randolph. For his secretary of the treasury, he chose former aide-de-camp **Alexander Hamilton** of New York. Washington's vice president (**John Adams**), his secretary of war (Henry Knox), and his postmaster general (Samuel Osgood) were from Massachusetts. The Constitution had specified the existence of a third branch of government, a federal judiciary, but had not offered much of a blueprint for its structure. Congress might have created a federal system that dominated state courts. Recalling the high-handedness of British courts, however, with the Judiciary Act of 1789 Congress created a federal court system with limited power. Under its first chief justice, John Jay, the Supreme Court remained a minor branch of government.

The States and the Bill of Rights

The Federalists had agreed to let the state ratifying conventions propose amendments to the Constitution, possibly to be added as a **bill of rights**. Two hundred of these had been suggested. Some Federalists originally opposed the idea of a bill of rights: if the Constitution did not protect liberty and property, no appended list of rights would help. But they agreed to allow Congress to make amendments to the Constitution when several states made it a condition for ratification (see Chapter 7).

Within a month of Washington's inauguration, **James Madison**, recently elected to the House, set about making good on the promise. Madison never expected to incorporate all 200 of the state proposals in a bill of rights, and he never imagined that he could placate all of the groups critical of the Constitution. But he did believe that adding a bill of rights could secure the Antifederalists' support for the Constitution without harming "the structure and stamina of the Government." This belief guided Madison's selection of proposed amendments. He ignored those that would alter the structure of the central government or strengthen the powers of the states at the expense of the federal government, and he dismissed outright one that would have limited the power of Congress to levy taxes. Instead, he focused on amendments that affirmed human rights within the structure already ratified (although the reference to a "well-regulated Militia" in the Second Amendment and the Third Amendment's restrictions on the quartering of soldiers reflected Americans' profound mistrust of standing national armies). The First Amendment protected citizens against congressional interference with freedom of religion, speech, the press, the right of assembly, and the right of petition. The Fourth Amendment protected the rights of citizens "against unreasonable [government] searches and seizures." The Fifth, Sixth, Seventh, and Eighth Amendments laid down the rights of citizens accused of crimes and established protection from "cruel and unusual punishments." The Ninth affirmed that the Constitution's silence on a specific right of the people "shall not be construed" as a denial of that right, and the Tenth ambiguously reserved all rights not delegated to the new government "to the States respectively, or to the people."

Congress eventually sent twelve amendments to the states for ratification. Two were rejected: one on congressional compensation (adopted in 1992 as the Twenty-seventh Amendment) and one covering representation. The remaining ten amendments were declared in force on December 15, 1791.

Debating the Economy

As Congress deliberated the structure of government, Secretary of the Treasury Alexander Hamilton turned to the problem of financial solvency, the problem that had plagued the Confederation (see Chapter 7). His proposals to strengthen the nation by strengthening the economy soon brought to the fore underlying disagreements about the future of the nation.

The first challenge was to raise money for current expenses. Hamilton proposed that Congress place a tariff on imported goods and the foreign ships carrying them. The Tariff Act of 1789 passed easily. In the coming years the federal government would depend on tariffs for the vast majority of its funds (see Table 8–1).

The next challenge was how to pay off the debt left over from the Revolution, a total of $79 million that included not only the amounts the government had borrowed from foreign countries and promised to soldiers and suppliers but also the debts owed by state governments. In a plan known as "funding and assumption," Hamilton proposed that the government assume all of the debt and pay it off at full value, even the parts that were in badly depreciated paper money. But rather than paying off the national debt immediately, the government would give creditors new federal bonds that paid interest (which in turn would be paid for by a new federal excise tax on whiskey and other luxuries). In this way, Hamilton thought he could turn the national debt into a "blessing" by making sure that people with money had a literal investment in the success of the nation.

Table 8–1 Sources of Federal Revenue, 1790–1799

Year(s)	Tariffs	Internal Taxes	Other (incl. sale of public lands)
1790–1791	$4,399,000	—	$10,000
1792	$3,443,000	$209,000	$17,000
1793	$4,255,000	$338,000	$59,000
1794	$4,801,000	$274,000	$356,000
1795	$5,588,000	$338,000	$188,000
1796	$6,568,000	$475,000	$1,334,000
1797	$7,550,000	$575,000	$563,000
1798	$7,106,000	$644,000	$150,000
1799	$6,610,000	$779,000	$157,000

Source: Curtis P. Nettels, *The Emergence of a National Economy, 1775–1815* (New York: Holt, Rinehart and Winston, 1962), p. 221.

Madison and Jefferson were alarmed, however. Not only had most southern states paid their debts by 1790, but many soldiers and ordinary people had sold off their paper money to speculators at far less than its face value—sometimes as little as 10 percent. The speculators would now reap huge profits. Why should they benefit? At the same time, southerners were also unhappy about the possibility that the nation's capital (temporarily located in New York) might be moved permanently to Philadelphia. They preferred a site in Virginia, closer to the center of the country. At last, representatives struck a compromise: Hamilton got his debt plan, and southerners got the nation's capital.

Hamilton next recommended the creation of a national bank that would ensure a stable currency and enable the government to mobilize capital for development, two activities he considered essential to an expanding commercial economy. The bank would be chartered by Congress to collect, hold, and pay out government receipts; hold the new federal bonds and oversee their payment; and issue currency; and it would be backed up by government bonds.

The bank proposal passed Congress against the opposition of Madison, Jefferson, and other Virginians, who viewed the bank as an extralegal structure to support the interests of merchants and financiers against "the republican interest." Jefferson advised the president to veto the bill on the grounds that the Constitution gave the federal government no expressed authority to create such an institution, a position known as *strict constructionism*. Hamilton countered that every specified power in the Constitution implied "a right to employ all the means requisite . . . to the attainment" of that power. In granting the federal government the responsibility to coin and regulate money, pass and collect taxes, pay debts, and "make all laws which shall be necessary and proper" to these ends, the Constitution implied the power to create a bank. Washington accepted Hamilton's position and signed the bank bill.

Hamilton's final major recommendation to Congress was that the federal government subsidize domestic manufacturing. Jefferson and Madison were now convinced that the republic was being sold out to speculators and financiers. Hamilton had been using a Philadelphia newspaper, John Fenno's *Gazette of the United States*, to promote his views. In October 1791, Jefferson and Madison prevailed on their friend Philip Freneau to come to Philadelphia to establish a newspaper favorable to their position, and Madison began to use Freneau's *National Gazette* to publish essays in which he framed the rationale for the permanent necessity of political parties in a republic. There would always be schemers who placed self-interest above the good of the whole. Parties, according to Madison, arose in a struggle of the true "republican interest" against such dangerous conspirators, a struggle of "good" against "evil." He identified the two groups as "Republicans" and "Anti-Republicans."

Hamilton's efforts to create a strong government based on a commercial economy alienated those such as Madison and Jefferson who believed Hamilton's policies were "subverting step by step the principles of the Constitution." This theme was taken up by the Democratic Republican Societies, groups that had come together in late 1792 and early 1793 to support the French Revolution. They became the nucleus of the first political party, the Democratic Republicans. They believed that the new government was becoming too strong and thus a threat to "liberty and equality." The societies included some common people, but most members were from middling and even prosperous families. Washington blamed the societies for spreading "suspicions, jealousies, and accusations of the whole government."

At the same time, the supporters of Hamilton's policies became known as the Federalists, to suggest their commitment to the new government. At first, most candidates resisted formal party alignment, however, and congressional voting patterns showed little sense of "party" discipline. There were several reasons for this, including the tendency of most citizens (including many partisans themselves) to associate political parties with corruption and a loss of independence. By 1796, the opposing groups coalesced into Democratic Republicans and Federalists, and congressional voting patterns revealed a distinct tendency to vote on one side or the other.

A SOCIETY IN TRANSITION

The new political parties reflected growing divisions in society itself. The end of the Revolution ushered in a period of explosive growth—in the economy, in population, and in territory. As one American observed, "Population is encreasing, new houses building, new lands clearing, new settlements forming, and new manufacture establishing with a rapidity beyond conception." So much change offered both opportunity and danger. Americans responded with both optimism and fear.

A People on the Move

A quarter-century of political unrest, compounded by the depression of the 1780s, had stalled the development of the American economy, but once peace was restored, the patterns of growth and development of the mid-eighteenth century resumed. Even with the disruptions of the Revolution, the American population grew at the greatest rate in its entire history in the 1780s, and it continued to double every 20 years, primarily from natural increase. In the 1790s, the United States added 1.4 million people, only 100,000 of whom were immigrants. Many of those immigrants were political refugees, fleeing revolutions in France and Saint-Domingue and political repression in Britain and Ireland. For most of the growing population, native born or refugees, democracy meant opportunity and political freedom. Thirty thousand, however, were enslaved Africans, purchased to enhance their owners' opportunity at the denial of their own.

The United States was overwhelmingly a rural nation and would remain so until well into the nineteenth century. (Ninety-seven percent of its almost 4 million people enumerated in the first census lived in the countryside, most of them on family farms of 50–100 acres.) As the population grew, thousands of families looked for fertile, inexpensive land so that they could continue as farmers. They found it in the hinterlands of established states and in the territories that would become states over the next several decades. Seeking quick revenue, the government sold large tracts of land to speculators and large proprietors, some of whom were federal officials. Alexander Hamilton and Secretary of War Henry Knox were both silent partners in the huge Macomb Purchase in New York. Speculators also bought up land abandoned by Loyalists. William Cooper, for example, purchased— for a suspiciously low price—the huge Otsego, New York, tract that had been owned by William Franklin.

In regions such as frontier Maine, squatters simply occupied the land that such "great proprietors" hoped to sell for a huge profit. Squatters built small cabins, cleared the land, and planted crops, resisting when the legal owners tried to oust them. Such disputes were typically resolved when the squatters purchased the land—but for far less than the speculators had wanted. The population of Kentucky and Tennessee tripled in the 1790s. By 1800, 220,000 people lived in Kentucky, and not a single adult (excluding Native Americans) had been born in the state. At the same time, settlers were trickling into what would become Indiana, Alabama, and Mississippi, and almost 50,000 moved into Ohio. Because land in these territories was still held by Native Americans, conflict was almost inevitable as settlers pressed the new government to secure the land for them (see Map 8–1).

American cities grew rapidly, too. Philadelphia and New York grew by almost 50 percent between 1789 and 1800. St. Louis, Detroit, Pittsburgh, Cincinnati, Lexington, Cleveland, Nashville, and Louisville all became important regional centers, serving the surrounding populations. As in the farming regions, the rapid influx of population and its youthfulness—two-thirds of the white population was 25 or younger—made it hard to control. Philadelphia had a particularly large number of young people who were on their own. The result was a boisterous culture, particularly among the

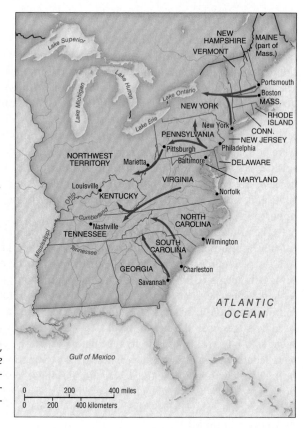

Map 8–1 Western Expansion, 1785–1805 Between the Treaty of Paris (1783) and the Louisiana Purchase (1803), Americans flooded into the territories that lay between the Appalachians and the Mississippi River. Then (as later) migration often followed rivers and valleys into the interior of the continent.
Source: Gregory Evans Dowd, *A Spirited Resistance: The North American Indian Struggle for Unity, 1745–1815* (Baltimore: Johns Hopkins University Press, 1991), p. 92.

lower classes. Men and women of all classes took advantage of a more liberal sexual environment. Rates of adultery and divorce increased, and the proportion of children born outside of marriage doubled. Houses of prostitution flourished, as did taverns such as the one owned by the free African American John York, where "all the loose and idle characters of the city, whether whites, blacks, or mulattoes . . . indulge in riotous mirth and dancing til dawn."

In later decades this growing population would provide the workforce for the Industrial Revolution, but in the first decades of the new nation, most people worked as farmers.

In spite of their hostility to the growing merchant "monied interest," most farmers sought international as well as local markets for their crops. The principal exports were all farm or plantation products—grains, tobacco, and rice. But without the protection of Britain (which banned Americans from trading with British colonies), Americans struggled to secure old markets and establish new ones, at the same time that the British were dumping manufactured goods into the American market at low prices that undercut American manufacturers. As farm families struggled, much of the burden fell on women, who were required to increase production

The Quilting Frolic What appears to be a cozy domestic scene actually reveals the complexity of urban life in Philadelphia at the time: we see women putting away their work as fashionably dressed guests arrive. The many consumer objects, from the well-stocked cupboard to the plates on the table and the tea set on the tray held by the African American girl, show that the family is prosperous. So too does the presence of African American servants, both with the exaggerated features that were beginning to become racist stereotypes.

(where "we shall find nobody to reproach us for being black, or for being slaves") and advocated gradual emancipation. As Phillis Wheatley (1753–1784), an African American poet, wrote in "On Being Brought from Africa to America," the subject of salvation spoke to the subject of slavery: "Some view our sable race with scornful eye, / 'Their colour is a diabolic die.' / Remember, Christians, Negros, black as Cain, / May be refin'd, and join th' angelic train."

Although the process of **emancipation** in the North was sometimes slow and often contested, the first steps toward the elimination of slavery had been taken. By 1804, every state north of Delaware had placed slavery on the road to extinction. In the North, free Blacks collected in the port cities, where they found employment, the men most often in the maritime trades and the women as domestic servants. The free Black population of New York almost doubled in the 1790s, while that of Philadelphia tripled. Once they were able to choose freely where to live, African Americans began establishing their own neighborhoods (such as the one where Ona Judge sought refuge), their own schools, churches, burial grounds, and organizations. Free property-owning African American males enjoyed the right to vote in many northern and even some southern states in the first years of the **republic**, although few Black men had sufficient property to exercise that right, and it was revoked shortly after.

Even in the South there were signs of a growing opposition to slavery. Virginia, Delaware, and Maryland all passed laws permitting the private manumission of enslaved people. As a result, the number of free Blacks in the upper South tripled between 1790 and 1810. Although the emancipation movement never took hold in the lower South, even there, slave owners were put on the defensive. In the 1790s, many Americans hoped, and even believed, that slavery would gradually be eliminated.

Conflicting Visions of Republican Society

Agreeing on a structure for the new republic had not been easy. It had taken free Americans thirteen years to frame their government: a year to propose the Articles of Confederation, four years to pass them, seven more to fight over them and devise an alternative (the federal Constitution), and two years to ratify it. Even then, many Americans still opposed ratification, and two states (North Carolina and Rhode Island) had not yet ratified the Constitution when George Washington was sworn into office. Moreover, supporters of the Constitution did not necessarily agree on its meanings or on the principles of a republican society.

Still, there was a common ground of beliefs for many white inhabitants of the new republic. Most free Americans thought the success of the republic depended on the character of its citizens, by which they meant the traits that would enable citizens to protect themselves against either would-be tyrants or lawless mobs. For many, these traits included industriousness, independence, and an ability to put self-interest aside for the larger good. Very often, these qualities were associated with certain types of economic life. When people grew too wealthy and used to luxury, many believed, they grew lazy and were willing to support corrupt governments for their own selfish purposes. Poverty, on the other hand, led to desperation, riots, and anarchy.

This consensus obscured real disagreements about the nature of a republic and about who really embodied its key virtues. In 1790, 97 percent of free Americans lived in nuclear households (parents and children) on farms or in rural villages, where they produced much of their own food, clothes, tools, and furnishings. For this great mass of the people, republican virtue was rooted in the land, and particularly in the working freehold farm. In *Letters from an American Farmer* (1782), **J. Hector St. John de Crevecoeur** had identified the new nation as "a people of cultivators scattered over an immense territory . . . animated with the spirit of an industry that is unfettered and unrestrained, because each person works for himself." Thomas Jefferson echoed this view in his *Notes on the State of Virginia* (1785). He thought that only the independent farmer could achieve true self-reliance, warning that "dependence begets subservience and venality, [and] suffocates the germ of virtue."

This emphasis on labor and the private ownership of land did not mean that rural Americans opposed manufacturing and trade. Farms were tied to villages that were tied to larger markets in the port cities and overseas. Even Jefferson considered overseas trade essential to rural virtue, because it gave Americans access to manufactured goods without the blight of industrialization. As trade with Britain improved and the demand for American agricultural products grew both in Europe and in the plantation slave colonies of the West Indies, rural Americans agreed that a successful new nation required a booming free international trade.

The profits made by large merchants and landowners were another matter. Farmers, small shopkeepers, landless settlers, and craft workers saw the wealth of large merchant families and families with great landed estates as the moral equivalent of theft. "No person can possess property without laboring," farmer and tavern keeper William Manning emphasized, "unless he get it by force or craft, fraud or fortune, out of the earnings of others." Manning viewed this distinction as "the great dividing line" of society.

Unsurprisingly, merchants and landed proprietors saw matters differently. They agreed that republican virtue resided in labor, but they included commercial labor, which opened markets and expanded trade, nurtured invention, taught discipline, and contributed new wealth to society. Alexander Hamilton, the first secretary of the Treasury, was a chief proponent of this view. Hamilton, who was born in the West Indies, was left on his own at the age of 13 when his mother, a shopkeeper, died. His father, who had never married his mother, had abandoned the family earlier. Hamilton then entered the merchant firm of Beekman and Cruger as a clerk, becoming so valuable that Cruger paid for his college education. These experiences taught Hamilton that the merchant class (traders, investors, and financiers who took risks to generate new wealth, new markets, and new ideas) best embodied the qualities needed in republican citizens.

Just as farmers viewed merchants and financiers with distrust, so wealthy merchants and proprietors often regarded Americans of the middling and laboring ranks as their inferiors. Most people were undisciplined and gullible, Hamilton believed. Easily deceived by fanatics and demagogues, they required proper leadership. City elites dismissed their backcountry compatriots as "yahoos" and "clodpoles." To the rich, the rude huts of homesteaders, their barefoot children, and their diets of beans, potatoes, and coarse bread all signaled not the hardships of settlement but rather the laziness of the settlers. The merchants and proprietors especially disliked the casualness with which country people treated debt. Rural people conducted trade in a combination of barter, cash, and promissory notes, with records kept casually and payments constantly renegotiated. Large-scale merchants and proprietors needed timely payment, preferably in hard currency, to pay off their own debts or to make new deals and investments.

Most white Americans denied that hard work produced republican character in the enslaved. They argued that because enslaved people could not own the property they produced, their labor could never lead to self-reliance or the stake in the public order essential to citizenship. This view was rife with contradictions. As Thomas Jefferson, himself a slave owner, pointed out in *Notes on the State of Virginia*, slavery undermined the ambition of slave owners. "In a warm climate, no man will labor for himself who can make another labor for him," Jefferson wrote. If enslaved people were of bad character, simply because of their status as slaves, then surely the institution of slavery was itself unrepublican.

Nevertheless, the unrepublicanism seemed to attach itself to the enslaved themselves, rather than to the institution. Even as northern states moved to abolish slavery, many expressed concerns about the ability of the formerly enslaved to adjust to freedom and democracy and suggested that freed people should be resettled in the territories or Africa. In the northern states, although some working-class whites socialized freely with African Americans, other Americans refused to work with them. White passengers refused to ride in stagecoaches alongside them, and landlords refused to rent them any but the worst housing. Meanwhile, the Naturalization Act of 1790 restricted naturalized citizenship to "free white persons" (who had resided in the country for two years).

Although free white women were citizens of the nation, women labored under severe legal disabilities and restrictive social prejudices. Under the English common-law principle of coverture, a married woman subsumed her separate legal identity under that of her husband. While some individual women (usually wealthy women with access to special legal measures) did own property in their own names, as a category married women could not own property or wages, could not enter into contracts, and were not the legal guardians of their own children. Most women lost control of their property when they married and took little property other than their own clothing in divorce.

Social prejudice also made it difficult for most women to earn an independent living. Wives and unmarried women continued to ply their skills as midwives, seamstresses, hucksters, grocers, and milliners and in a variety of other trades. But the more lucrative male crafts and professions were closed to them, and most working women struggled to make ends meet.

A growing bias against the idea of female autonomy marked the final years of the eighteenth century. The earlier years of the century were by no means a golden age of female independence, yet age, wealth, and family appear to have mattered as much as gender in delineating individual status. And for a time it seemed that women (especially wealthy white women) might be among the beneficiaries of the Revolutionary spirit. Indeed, New Jersey granted single, property-owning women the right to vote in 1776 (but rescinded it in 1807), and women participated actively in the discussions both of their own new republic and of the French Revolution. In France and in England, women spoke out publicly against restraints on the natural rights of women.

In the wake of the creation of the new republic, however, attitudes toward women grew more conservative. As the *Apollo Magazine* put it in 1795, the exemplary woman married and asked no more than that "Her good man [was] happy and her Infants clean." Ironically, these hardening attitudes may in some ways have resulted from the experiment in democracy itself. In the face of social and political disorder, controlling the conduct of females may have seemed reassuring to some Americans.

The Culture of the Republic

Americans discussed these views, both the agreements and the disagreements, through a variety of practices—written and simply enacted.

Perhaps most important was the circulation of information through newspapers. Although fewer than 20 newspapers were being published in all the British North American colonies in 1760, by 1790 the new republic claimed 106 newspapers, and by 1800 more than 200. Most stories were strictly local, but editors also published official government documents and reprinted articles from other cities, states, and even countries.

The 1790s also saw the beginnings of an American fictional literature. In 1789, William Hill Brown published *The Power of Sympathy*, often considered the first genuinely American novel because some of its content was based on events in Boston. Other novelists also tried to develop distinctly American stories and themes. Actress and author Susanna Rowson wrote the historical novel *Rachel and Reuben* (1798), which imagined the lives of the fictional heirs of Columbus, and Charles Brockden Brown chose the countryside near Philadelphia as the setting for *Wieland* (1798), a tale of religious zealotry and the fallibility of human reason. In Connecticut, a group of poets known as the Hartford Wits produced a series of political satires celebrating New England as the model for national order and self-discipline.

News was easiest to come by in the cities, but a variety of information sources linked city to backcountry and region to region. Copies of periodicals and books found their way into the countryside, and comparatively high literacy rates produced a reading audience that went beyond urban elites. In shops, taverns, and homes, those who could not read listened as stories were read aloud. Where papers did not reach, travelers, peddlers, and preachers brought information and opinion.

In cities, prosperous Americans established salons (where local luminaries, male and female, gathered to discuss politics and culture), museums, libraries, and specialized societies of learning. Many of these reflected Americans' keen sense of themselves as involved in an important historical undertaking. The Philadelphia subscription library, founded in 1731 by Benjamin Franklin and others, became the de facto library of the government until 1800, when the capital moved to Washington, and the Library of Congress was founded.

For every occasion that drew American citizens together, however, there seemed to be another that divided them. Strong attachments to place and great disparities of condition often transformed seemingly shared values and ideas into fodder for sharp conflicts. Many, if not most, Americans felt stronger attachments to the neighborhoods or states where they lived, rather than to the nation as a whole. If anything, the process of ratification had underscored just how many differences remained among Americans. Advocates had won approval only by putting together a different coalition of interests in each state, not by drawing on a uniform set of interests across all the states. Even so, a bare nine states had ratified the document, and virtually all of these had made qualifications.

The localism of American society in 1789 was evident in daily life, as well as in formal politics. Never traveling far from home, ordinary Americans knew little about other parts of the country and tended to view them as quite different, becoming more exotic—and frightening—the greater the distance. Writing from Massachusetts to Philadelphia in 1776, **Abigail Adams** had asked John whether it was true that in Virginia the "gentery" were "Lords" and "the common people vassals." Travelers often described other parts of the nation as if they were foreign countries. The hard economic times of the era also nursed a suspicion of strangers. Describing these differences as an East-West contrast was also common in the early years of the nation. Rural revolts in the Carolinas in the 1760s and Shays's Rebellion in western Massachusetts in 1786–1787 had underscored the differences between backcountry farmers and eastern commercial elites, differences that settlers experienced as conflicts between "the people" and eastern governments. This sense of division and distrust persisted in the 1790s.

These disagreements ran deep and were not confined to formal politics or to polite discussion and debate. Newspapers often revealed sharp local bias in

Congressional Pugilists Before the US Congress had time to formulate respected institutions and traditional protocols, chaos sometimes reigned. In 1798, a fight broke out on the floor of the House of Representatives between Matthew Lyon, a Democratic Republican, and Roger Griswold, a Federalist.

vituperative debates over the proper direction of republican politics. They were accompanied into the public arena by vitriolic political tracts and single-page "broadsides" that attacked individual politicians. Among these was William Manning's 1798 "Key of Liberty," condemning the predations of the "Few" upon the "Many."

Not all of the arguments took place in print. Wealthy city people met in parlors and salons to discuss the concerns of the day, and common Americans held their arguments outside courthouses and churches, on post office porches, at liveries and craft shops, and in taverns like the one run by William Manning. Travelers, peddlers, and preachers were sources of information and opinion.

The early republic was also an era of school building—primarily academies to prepare sons for professions or university training and daughters to participate in the discussions (if not the formal electoral politics) of republican society. More than 350 academies for females opened between 1790 and 1830. The first incorporated publicly was the Young Ladies' Academy of Philadelphia (1787). Intended for daughters of prosperous families, to educate them in "Reading, Writing, Arithmetic, English, Grammar, Composition, and Geography," its curriculum implicitly argued that women could flourish in a challenging academic environment.

Citizens also formed societies intended to provide relief to the needy. A group of prosperous Philadelphians established an almshouse to care for and house the poor (and to teach them the values of industry) and a penitentiary to reform criminals by isolating them from one another. Jewish organizations founded in New York in the late eighteenth century provided aid for the city's small Jewish community.

In a variety of occupational and manufacturing societies, masters and journeymen furthered their common interests, sometimes against what they perceived as the haughtiness of the merchants. Many of the trades of Philadelphia participated in the Federal Procession of 1789, for example—a sign to the elites that craft workers had their own expectations of the new republic. Promoting a different vision, Alexander Hamilton and his assistant secretary, Tench Coxe, formed the Society for Establishing Useful Manufactures in 1791, a joint-stock corporation meant to demonstrate the economic virtues of cooperation between the private sector and the government.

SECURING THE NATION

The internal turbulence the United States faced in these years was matched by conflict on the western borders of the nation and in the larger Atlantic community of which the new nation was inextricably a part. Moreover, those conflicts and disagreements about how to resolve them became the major sources of political conflict in the new nation.

Borders and Boundaries

The United States of America had come into formal existence as a republic with the Articles of Confederation in 1781, and its existence had been recognized in the Paris Peace Treaty with Britain in 1783 and again in the ratification of the federal Constitution. Still, much remained unclear, unfinished, and highly contested when George Washington took office in 1789.

On the simplest level, the new republic lacked even clear external borders. Although the Treaty of Paris seemed to describe a very specific territory being ceded from Britain to the United States, things were much less clear on the ground. For example, the treaty set a boundary beginning "from the northwest angle of Nova Scotia, viz., that angle which is formed by a line drawn due north from the source of the St. Croix River to the highlands; along the said highlands which divide those rivers that empty themselves into the river St. Lawrence, from those which fall into the Atlantic Ocean, to the northwesternmost head of Connecticut River; thence down along the middle of that river to the forty-fifth degree of north latitude" across the Great Lakes, down the Mississippi River, and across the border of New Spain to the Atlantic. But what exact spot marked "the source of the St. Croix River"? Where was the "middle" of the Connecticut River? These were not abstract problems: Britain and the United States would argue for years over present-day Maine, and Spain claimed a sizable chunk of present-day Mississippi and Alabama.

A related problem was that much of the territory America claimed was literally unmapped. When his nation sent him to England to resolve trade and boundary disputes (resulting in Jay's Treaty; see "To the Brink of War"), John Jay was handicapped by a lack of basic geographical knowledge about North America. How could he argue for favorable terms when it was unknown how far north "the Mississippi River extends"?

European empires were not the only ones challenging the territorial integrity of the new nation. There were also a hundred thousand or so Native Americans who lived within the boundaries of the republic, many of them crisscrossing large expanses of hunting and growing grounds in seasonal migrations. The United States had acknowledged the sovereignty of Indian nations in eight treaties before the ratification of the Constitution and again in Article I of the Constitution, granting Congress the power "to regulate commerce with . . . the Indian tribes." But the Native Americans rejected both European American ideas of fixed borders and the specific borders delineated in the Treaty of Paris. Most of the "United States of America" was still Indian land to them—the land of the Shawnee, for example, or of the people of the longhouses, or of the turtle people. Settlers kept moving into these lands, however.

Even the states of the new nation disagreed on the division of lands within its borders. Many of the original boundary conflicts had been settled in the 1780s, but Virginia, Georgia, and North Carolina still claimed lands running to the Mississippi River (although North Carolina wanted to cede the land to the United States). Massachusetts, New Hampshire, and New York still fought over present-day Maine. Finally, the attachment of many western settlers to the new nation was so weak that, well into the nineteenth century, some flirted with detaching portions of the West and turning them over to the Spanish or creating another independent nation.

Controlling the Borderlands

For all of its symbolic importance as a source of republican order, the backcountry had so far been marked by constant conflict among owners and settlers and between Indians and Americans. Americans fought with each other over land prices and rights of ownership. In spite of these conflicts, squatters, proprietors, and governments shared the assumption that the land was theirs to fight over. The Treaty of Paris did not acknowledge Indian claims, and treaties promising Indians peace in exchange for land proved illusory (see Chapter 7). By the time Washington took office in 1789, the backcountry was in an uproar. Undisciplined federal troops and state militias roamed western lands in search of a fight, often attacking neutral or sympathetic Indian villages. Betrayed and angry, Indians banded together in loose confederations, retaliating against settlers and striking alliances with the British and Spanish.

By 1789, the Eastern Woodland and Great Lakes nations had been deeply altered by the westward pressure of white settlement. In the North, a group of battered Iroquoian villages traded large tracts of land for promises of security and called on tribes of the **Northwest Territory** to do the same. However, these peoples refused and effectively shut down settlement north of the Ohio River Valley. In the South, the Creeks, trapped between white settlements and the Native American nations of the Mississippi River valley, allied with militant Cherokees to keep the Georgia, Tennessee, and Kentucky frontiers ablaze with war parties.

Washington had more reasons to worry about the western territories. By 1789, Spain was actively luring US settlers into New Spain at the foot of the Mississippi River in order to weaken the loyalty of the West to the new US government. In the Great Lakes region, Britain hung on to the string of forts it had promised to give up in the Treaty of Paris. Many Americans believed that Britain was biding its time to regain control of the lands south of the Great Lakes.

This turmoil took its toll in the East. The inability of the national government to control Native Americans angered states, would-be settlers, and small-business owners. Landowners complained that their property rights were not being protected, and small settlers complained of favoritism in land distribution. Understanding that both external relations and the domestic authority of the federal government were at stake, Washington turned immediately to the problem of the backcountry. Working with Secretary of War Henry Knox, Washington sought to reduce bloodshed by encouraging Indians to become farmers, thus "civilizing" them. He assumed their settlements would gradually disappear if they did not choose this option. Less than a month after assuming office, Washington submitted to Congress a report by Knox on Indian affairs. Knox argued that the United States should acknowledge a residual Indian "right in the soil" not affected by a treaty between Britain and the United States. That right could be extinguished, he insisted, only by dealing directly with the Indians; he recommended that the United States purchase Indian claims to disputed lands.

In part, Knox and Washington shifted policy in the name of justice, but they also sought to avoid the costs of having to take the western territories by war. A change in tactics did not mean a change in ultimate goals, however. Although Knox tried to keep white settlers outside treaty boundaries, his policy did not recognize Native Americans' right to refuse to negotiate. Seeking to bolster the authority of the national government, Knox argued that Indian bands were not communities within state borders but rather foreign entities, on the level of nations. Indian relations were therefore properly the business of the federal government. Knox in effect declared Indians aliens on their own lands, using federal policy to define Indians as the ultimate outsiders.

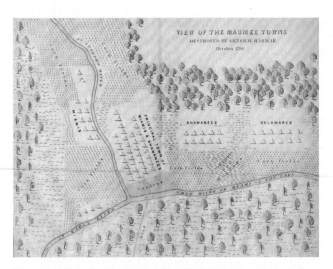

Maumee River Indian Towns This 1790 drawing suggests the complex economic arrangement of the Maumee River Indian towns and the diverse groups that occupied the towns.

By 1790, continuing troubles in the Northwest Territory convinced Washington to send troops there (see Maps 8–1 and 8–3). His first two efforts were dismal failures. In 1790, a combined Native American force led by the Miami war leader Little Turtle routed the US Army, led by General Josiah Harmar. The next year a much smaller party crushed the troops of territorial governor general Arthur St. Clair. In 1792, Congress authorized a "strong coercive force" (bigger, better paid, and better trained) and Washington turned to a seasoned infantry officer, Pennsylvanian major general Anthony Wayne. By the time Wayne found the Indians in 1794 at Fallen Timbers, near Lake Erie, his army was more than 3,000 strong. Facing a force of only 400 warriors, Wayne claimed a decisive victory.

According to the Treaty of Greenville, signed August 3, 1795, Indians ceded two-thirds of the later state of Ohio and a piece of present-day Indiana. In return, they received annual federal payments ranging from $500 to $1,000 per band. The annuities bought the United States influence within Indian communities and rendered the Indians more economically dependent. The treaty also tried to impose white ideas of work and economy by offering Indians annuities in the form of farm equipment, cows, and pigs.

Indian efforts at confederacy proved somewhat less successful in the South, where deep fractures existed within the Cherokee and Creek nations. Older leaders, wearied by constant warfare, and mixed-heritage populations familiar with white economic and social ways sometimes favored accommodation and entered into agreements they lacked the authority to make. At the Treaty of New York in 1790, Alexander McGillivray and other Creek leaders agreed to exchange lands belonging to the entire Creek nation for annual payments from the federal government and promises of US protection for their remaining lands. A faction of the Cherokee nation signed a similar pact in 1791.

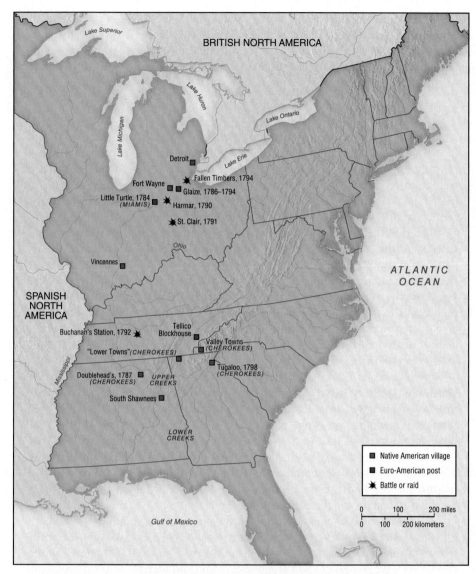

Map 8-3   Major Indian Villages and Indian–US Battle Sites, 1789–1800 During its first decade of existence, the new federal government struggled to assert control over the trans-Appalachian territories, claimed by Native Americans as their homelands and coveted by US settlers and land speculators.

These internal disputes weakened Indian military efforts. When the government proved unable to stop settlers flowing into the future state of Tennessee, younger Creeks, Chickamaugas, Cherokees, and Shawnees repudiated the treaties and attacked the Americans at Buchanan's Station, near Nashville, Tennessee, planning to move on Nashville itself. Fearing reprisals, older Cherokee leaders betrayed the plan, and the assault was thrown back. US Indian commissioners used military victories to coerce new land cessions and to insinuate white customs more deeply into Indian cultures, especially that of the Cherokees.

Resistance continued, in the North and the South, but dreams of a pan-Indian confederation were temporarily stymied. They would be resurrected at the turn of the century by two Shawnees. One, Tenskwatawa, would become an important prophet. The other, his half-brother, was named Tecumseh and would prove to be important (see Chapter 9).

The Whiskey Rebellion

Another threat to the federal government came from western settlers themselves. By 1791, western settlers were disenchanted with the seeming inability of the government to protect their interests and had begun disregarding federal policy. They trespassed on Indian lands, sent unorganized militias to enforce their claims, and traded illegally with Indians. In 1791, western Pennsylvanians rejected federal authority explicitly, setting the stage for a direct confrontation.

The trouble began with the passage of Hamilton's excise tax. Living in a gateway to the Northwest Territory, residents of western Pennsylvania anticipated an economic bonanza from westward migration but were frustrated with the failure of the government to secure safe passage into the Ohio River Valley. Hamilton's tax on spirits fueled their simmering anger over the question of republican fairness. Many Americans regarded excise taxes (internal taxes on specific goods) as unfair in principle. This particular tax seemed targeted specifically at western farmers, who found it cheaper to transport their grain in liquid than in bushel form.

Popular protests intensified at each new report of the army's failure in the Northwest Territory (efforts the tax was supposed to fund). Western Pennsylvanians vowed that they would not pay the tax and urged citizens to treat tax collectors with "contempt." Washington took the challenge seriously, and in August 1794 he sent 13,000 troops into western Pennsylvania. Against this show of force, the Whiskey Rebellion fizzled, but the government drove its point (and power) home. Remaining protestors were rounded up; twenty were sent to Philadelphia to face treason charges, and two were sentenced to death. Washington pardoned them both, but he had proven the authority of federal law.

Western Pennsylvanians were not without sympathizers, however. The congressional elections of 1792 were contests between the policies of Alexander Hamilton, on the one hand, and the beliefs of the self-named "republican interest," on the other, over what it meant to be a republican nation and society.

Democratic Revolutions

Just as the United States was launching its federal republic, France entered the throes of revolution. After years of fiscal mismanagement by the Crown, high unemployment, and widespread malnutrition and starvation, the French bourgeoisie began a reform of the monarchy that soon led to wholesale grassroots revolution. In July 1789, just eight weeks after Washington took the oath of office, the people of Paris stormed the Bastille prison in symbolic rejection of the power of the monarchy. The next month the new National Constituent Assembly abolished feudalism and promulgated the Declaration of the Rights of Man and of the Citizen, modeled on the American Declaration of Independence.

Initially, most Americans, including many Federalists, supported the French Revolution. As a part of its long eighteenth-century conflict with Great Britain, France had aided the Americans in their own revolution and had recognized the nation and its diplomats after the war. Americans now saw the efforts of the French people to overthrow monarchy as a reflection of their own struggle against Britain, and they read events in France as a confirmation that the United States would lead the world into a new era of democracy.

By 1793, however, as the Parisian mob grew more violent and moderate politicians lost power, many Americans lost their enthusiasm for the French republic. Although many, Jefferson and Madison among them, remained avid French partisans, others grew convinced that France was spiraling into chaos—which would spread to the United States.

Part of their alarm may have derived from events on the French island colony of Saint-Domingue (present-day **Haiti**) in the West Indies. In 1791, its free people of color led an insurgency against the white planter class but soon lost control in the face of a full-scale revolution by the island's tens of thousands of enslaved people. Eventually, under the leadership of the formerly enslaved François-Dominique Toussaint-Louverture, Saint-Domingue would become the first Black republic in the Americas.

Washington's response to the revolution in Saint-Domingue was complicated. He did not support the revolutionaries, especially after the movement for equality for free Blacks turned into a slave rebellion. Like other slave owners, Washington feared that supporting the Saint-Dominguans would encourage slave rebellion in the southern United States. Still, he did not want to enter into an alliance with France (which sent soldiers to put down the rebellion), as that might seem hostile to the British. His compromise was to order supplies and ammunition sent directly to the island's white-planter ruling class.

Between France and England

Washington would later summarize his foreign policy goals: "The great rule of conduct for us, in regard to foreign nations, is, in extending our commercial relations, to have with them as little political connexion as possible." The United States wanted to trade freely with every nation, but other nations used trade barriers to protect not only their economic but their political interests as well. Washington and his successors thus found that it was one thing to announce a policy and another to achieve it.

Washington's efforts to avoid the appearance of pro-French partiality were soon tested. On February 1, 1793, France and Spain declared war on Great Britain and Holland. American sentiments were divided. Many Democratic Republicans (among them Jefferson and Madison) viewed with horror the possibility that America might join with its former colonial master against a fellow republic. Hamiltonians, meanwhile, believed that friendly relations with Britain best served American interests. Searching for a middle ground, President Washington endorsed neutrality.

Then, on May 16, Edmond-Charles Genêt, citizen of France, arrived in Philadelphia, the temporary capital. France had several hopes for the Genêt mission. Genêt was supposed to incite the European colonies in the Americas to revolution. He was also to press the United States for a new treaty allowing French naval forces and privateers to resupply in American ports. France's hopes were not entirely fanciful. The impoverished Washington administration had lent money to the new French government and recognized the Republic as the legitimate government of France.

But the French overestimated American support. Giving preferential treatment to French ships could only strain relations between America and England. Barely able to muster a force to the Northwest, Washington was not about to risk a foreign war or to inflame tensions on western borders. Washington considered Genêt's proposals reckless.

Genêt, however, did not believe that Washington's views represented the sentiments of Americans generally. In Philadelphia, he authorized the refitting of a captured English ship as a French privateer, and he encouraged American settlers in Kentucky to attack the Spaniards who lived along the Mississippi.

Washington was furious. "Is the Minister of the French Republic to set the Acts of this Government at defiance, with impunity?" he fumed. Issuing a formal Proclamation of Neutrality, Washington disavowed Genêt and demanded that he be recalled. Disappointed by Washington's growing support of Federalist policies, Jefferson resigned as secretary of state.

To the Brink of War

Even without Genêt's provocations, by 1794 tensions with Britain were high. There were already issues left over from the Revolution—debts owed to British creditors, compensation due to southerners whose enslaved people had been seized, and forts the British still occupied in the Northwest. To these were added new irritants: the British navy was confiscating US merchant ships trading with (and for) the French in the Caribbean and impressing their sailors into the British navy. The Americans wanted compensation. Still, Washington sought to avoid confrontation. Even though the British kept the Americans out of West Indian and Canadian ports, US shipping had been steadily expanding, making it hard to argue that British policies were injurious enough to risk a war. Washington dispatched Chief Justice of the Supreme Court John Jay to England to resolve outstanding issues.

Already at war with France, Britain was ready to reduce tensions with the United States. Although Britain was unwilling to let the United States trade with France, Britain agreed to open West Indies ports to smaller US ships. Both countries agreed that (with some exceptions) their ships would receive equal treatment. They agreed as well to establish arbitration boards to determine compensation for prewar debts and the seized ships, as well as to set the boundary between Canada and the United States. Britain also promised to evacuate its forts in the Northwest by June 1, 1796. Jay, an opponent of slavery, did not try very hard to get compensation for the enslaved.

Most Americans knew nothing about Jay's Treaty until after it was approved, for the Senate debated it in secret. When Democratic Republicans learned of its contents and its ratification, they were outraged. They protested the closed deliberations and the failure to gain "neutral rights," the right to trade with Britain's enemies. They feared being drawn closer to Britain, their old enemy, and being

Map 8–4   Extension of US National Territories, 1783 and 1795 The Treaty of Paris with Great Britain (1783) left the United States' borders with Spain (much of the western and southern boundaries) ambiguous. Those borders were clarified in the Pinckney Treaty with Spain (1795).

pulled from France, the nation's first ally. But positive developments in the West helped the fury to subside. First came news of Anthony Wayne's victory against the Great Lakes tribes at Fallen Timbers. Word followed that Thomas Pinckney had also concluded a treaty with Spain, opening the Mississippi River to US navigation and permitting Americans to use the port at New Orleans. (Pinckney's Treaty also set the boundary between the United States and Florida.) Once the United States made peace with Britain, a weak Spain feared a formal alliance would come next and accepted an American presence in the West as a price for peace.

Wayne's victory and Jay's and Pinckney's negotiations seemed at last to open the territories to settlement (see Map 8–4). Western land prices soared, and the US export trade boomed. By the time opponents in the House of Representatives tried to scuttle Jay's Treaty by denying necessary funds, popular sentiment had shifted to strong support for the treaty as a key to prosperity.

The Administration of John Adams

George Washington, reluctant to serve a second term, had been convinced to do so when Jefferson and Hamilton argued that no one else could bring the republic's fractious politics together. But Washington refused to run for a third term, and in 1796 the nation faced its first contested presidential election.

In his farewell address, published on September 19, 1796, Washington made clear his Federalist concern with social order and personal discipline. Having acknowledged the right of the people to alter their Constitution, he stressed the "duty of every individual to obey the established Government" until it was changed "by an explicit and authentic act of the whole people." Sounding themes that would echo through the first half-century of the republic, he warned against unlawful "combinations and associations" with designs on the rightful "power of the people"—an image that, 30 years later, would drive the emergence of Jacksonian democracy.

With Hamilton too controversial to be an effective candidate, Federalists selected Vice President John Adams as their choice. Adams had served in the Continental Congress, been a part of the committee to draft the Declaration of Independence, served as representative to France, helped negotiate the peace treaty, and served two terms as vice president. Thomas Pinckney of South Carolina was their vice-presidential choice. For president, Democratic Republicans supported former secretary of state Thomas Jefferson, along with Madison, the most visible opponent of Hamilton. New Yorker Aaron Burr was intended as vice president.

Although contested, the election of 1796 was not decided by popular majority. State legislatures chose two-fifths of the members of the **Electoral College**. Moreover, procedures in the Electoral College did not distinguish between votes for the offices of president and vice president. The person who received the most electoral votes became president. The person who received the second-highest number of electoral votes became vice president.

This procedure proved dangerously unpredictable in a new age of political parties. Although the Federalist Adams received a majority of electoral votes (71) and became president, the Democratic Republican Jefferson received the second-highest count (68 to Pinckney's 59) and became vice president.

Benjamin Franklin once said that John Adams was "always an honest man, often a wise one, but sometimes, and in some things, absolutely out of his senses." Also cranky, defensive, and self-doubting, he was not the man to negotiate growing party rifts successfully. Against a background of partisan resentment, Adams confronted an increasingly hostile relationship with France. Unsurprisingly, Franco–American relations had been harmed by Jay's Treaty—which seemed to France to ally America with England—and by the French practice of plundering American ships. There was also the issue of Saint-Domingue. By the time John Adams took office, the revolutionaries (now led by Toussaint-Louverture) were seeking to resume trade with the United States as a step toward full independence. The abolitionist Adams had no qualms about supporting the revolutionaries and saw a number of advantages in allying with them. A trade deal with Haiti would further isolate the island from French control, it would help the US economy, and it might prompt Louverture to close his ports to the French privateers attacking US merchant ships. In June 1799, the Adams administration signed a three-way British–US–Saint-Dominguan trade agreement. Although that agreement was unratified when Adams left office, in the last months of his presidency Adams stationed US warships outside Saint-Dominguan ports to help quash an internal rebellion of conservative free people of color wishing to reimpose slavery, while members of his administration discussed with Louverture the form that an independent Saint-Dominguan republican government might assume. None of this pleased France, particularly not after the rise of Napoleon and the resurgence of French imperial ambitions in the late 1790s.

Even before his inauguration on March 4, 1797, Adams thought about sending a special envoy to France to resolve these issues. When Adams's cabinet objected, the president temporarily abandoned the plan. At the end of March, he learned that new American ambassador Charles Pinckney had been kicked out of France because the French government would "no longer recognize or receive" an ambassador from the United States. Adams decided to send a mission to France, appointing Elbridge Gerry, John Marshall, and Pinckney.

When the American mission arrived, French foreign minister Talleyrand made clear that he expected a bribe for his willingness to talk. Such arrangements were not uncommon in European politics, but to the starched and wary Adams, the idea was abhorrent. He turned over all documentation of the affair to Congress, identifying Talleyrand's agents by the letters X, Y, and Z.

The so-called XYZ Affair prompted a largely Federalist Congress to suspend commercial ties to France, empower American ships to seize armed French vessels, and expand the nation's military. In what became known as the "Quasi-War" (neither nation formally declared war), between 1798 and 1800 the United States and France skirmished on the seas, with the United States capturing more than 80 French ships. In the Convention of 1800, France and the United States agreed to end these hostilities. France agreed to return captured American ships; the United States assumed Americans' claims against the French for damages in shipping; and the earlier Franco-American Alliance was replaced by mutual most-favored-nation status.

Tensions at Home

The military expansion necessary for this conflict soon created tensions at home. Adams and Congress needed $2 million for it, which they found by imposing a tax on houses, land, and slaves. Each state had a specified portion of the cost to pay. The levy on houses, assessed according to the size of the house, fell especially hard on residents of states with few or no huge plantation estates and was particularly odious to German immigrants, whom it reminded of harsh taxes exacted by the kings of Germany. When the assessors reached eastern Pennsylvania, settled predominantly by German immigrants, unrest became civil disobedience. Led by John Fries, men of the area raised a small army to chase collectors away, while women poured hot water on the assessors. When the governor tried to have the resisters arrested, Fries's supporters freed them. Adams sent a militia of 1,000 men to capture the leaders. Fries and most of the other leaders were arrested, tried for treason, and sentenced to hang. In the face of strong public sentiment, Adams pardoned the rebels. (This was the second uprising in less than a decade, and in both cases, the rebels were pardoned.)

The Federalists had also used the XYZ Affair and hostilities with France for domestic political purposes. Insisting that pro-French influence endangered the nation, in 1798 Congress passed the Alien and Sedition Acts, aimed at gagging the Democratic Republican opposition and preventing it from using the war issue to win the 1800 election. The acts required a 14-year naturalization period, the highest at any period in American history, and targeted immigrants, whom the Federalists presumed to be Democratic Republicans. The acts also empowered the president to deport any "suspicious" aliens and established a broad definition of sedition, intended to stop all Democratic Republican criticism of the administration's policies.

The Alien and Sedition Acts backfired against the Federalists. Twenty-five prosecutions were eventually brought under the Sedition Act (all against Democratic

Struggles For Democracy

Sedition and the Limits of Dissent

What are the limits of dissent in a democracy? The new American government struggled with this question at the end of the 1790s. By that time, two political parties had developed in a nation that still considered such organized opposition as illegitimate. When the French Revolution became more violent, the parties were driven even further apart. The Federalists feared the spread of French radicalism to the United States, while the Democratic Republicans remained sympathetic to the aims of the Revolution, if not always its tactics.

The debates over the Alien and Sedition Acts reflected the Federalists' fears that the American republic was vulnerable to both external and internal foes. No amount of reasoning by their Democratic Republican opponents could convince them otherwise because they were not even convinced of the other party's loyalty to the United States. Federalist Jonathan Dayton believed that "the time was arrived when we ought to take measures for our own security," and his colleague David Brooks warned that "we have those within our bosom who would give up our country too." When Nathaniel Macon, a Revolutionary War veteran, asked if the Federalists truly thought that "men who had fought and won the Revolution" would now "relinquish the prize to any nation," a Federalist Congressman replied that he had no doubts. Some Federalists imagined tens of thousands of French radicals coming to invade the United States. The Democratic Republicans asked for proof, and Robert Livingston insisted that "we must legislate upon facts, not on surmises; [we] must have evidence,

TIME LINE

▼**1781**
Articles of Confederation
  ratified

▼**1787–1788**
Constitution ratified

▼**1789**
George Washington
  inaugurated
Judiciary Act of 1789

Tariff Act of 1789
John Fenno founds *Gazette
  of the United States*
William Hill Brown
  publishes *The Power of
  Sympathy*

▼**1790**
Alexander Hamilton's
  Report on the Public
  Credit

Assumption Act
Naturalization Act

▼**1791**
Excise tax (including tax on
  whiskey) passes
First Bank of the United
  States
Philip Freneau establishes
  National Gazette
Bill of Rights ratified

not vague suspicions." A Federalist Congressman responded, "Because proof is not produced in a fortnight, it does not follow that it will not be produced" at some later time. Then again, "legal proof was one thing, and he did not know that he should ever be able to produce it."

It was in this heated environment that the Sedition Act was passed, making it illegal to "write, print, utter or publish . . . any false, scandalous and malicious writing against the government of the United States, or either house of the Congress of the United States, or the President . . . with intent to defame [them], or to bring them . . . into contempt or disrepute; or to excite against them . . . the hatred of the good people of the United States." The Democratic Republicans believed it was a political bill, aimed at undermining their party. Indeed, the pattern of prosecutions—against Republican newspaper editors and critics of President John Adams—suggests that they were right. Republican newspapers were either suppressed or put out of business altogether. Pennsylvania

editor Thomas Cooper was jailed for listing what he believed to be Adams's chief failures as president, while a mob that included soldiers beat another editor, William Duane, unconscious. Vermont Congressman Matthew Lyon, in the middle of his campaign for re-election in a swing district, was jailed for publishing a letter in a local newspaper that accused Adams of "unbounded thirst for ridiculous pomp, foolish adulation or selfish avarice."

If the goal of the Sedition Act was to ensure Adams' reelection, it was a failure. Indeed, some of the prosecutions—for example, of the inebriated New Jersey man who said he hoped the ceremonial cannon welcoming the president to Newark would shoot President Adams "thro' his arse"—now seem ridiculous. But the effect was to shut down a number of newspapers and to make radicalism itself suspect. Although Jefferson won the election, he subsequently distanced himself from former radical allies. And this pattern of questioning the loyalty of opponents would be repeated in years to come.

▼**1792–1794**
Whiskey Rebellion

▼**1793**
Fugitive Slave Act
Edmond-Charles Genêt
   arrives in the United
   States

▼**1794**
Battle of Fallen Timbers

▼**1795**
Jay's Treaty
Treaty of Greenville
Pinckney's Treaty

▼**1796**
John Adams elected
   president

▼**1798**
Alien and Sedition Acts

▼**1798–1799**
Virginia and Kentucky
   resolutions

▼**1798–1800**
XYZ Affair and Quasi-War

▼**1801**
Judiciary Act of 1801

Republicans), and 10 men were convicted. The acts were so transparently partisan that individuals convicted under them became martyrs to the Democratic Republican cause. A Vermont congressman who published criticisms of administration policies was reelected even as he served out his four-month jail term. But by targeting those believed to be "radical," especially newspaper editors, and warning immigrants away, the acts silenced the most outspoken opponents of the government.

Although Democratic Republicans insisted that the acts were unconstitutional, they hesitated to challenge them in the Supreme Court, both because the Court was dominated by Federalists and because Democratic Republicans did not want to set a precedent for giving the Supreme Court the power to rule on constitutionality. Instead, Madison and Jefferson encouraged the states to pass resolutions denouncing the Alien and Sedition Acts. Madison, now retired from Congress, authored a set of resolutions in Virginia affirming the rights of states to judge the constitutionality of federal laws. Jefferson, vice president of the United States, framed a more militant set of resolutions for the Kentucky legislature, saying that states might declare federal laws they deemed unconstitutional to be without force within their state boundaries.

Jefferson and Madison expected that other states would support the Virginia and Kentucky resolutions, but they did not. Rather, voters simply returned the Democratic Republicans to power in the election of 1800, and the acts expired in 1801.

Before retiring, the Federalist Congress got off one more shot at the Democratic Republicans. Just as the session expired, Congress passed the Judiciary Act of 1801, which gave John Adams the power to expand the federal judiciary by appointing new judges, justices of the peace, attorneys, clerks, and marshals. He promptly filled these positions with good Federalists and then left office.

CONCLUSION

After a tumultuous first decade, it was not clear that the United States' experiment in government of, by, and for the people could survive. As the nation grew in size and population, the government struggled to maintain not simply order but, even more, the allegiance of its peoples. Americans had fallen into two rival political parties, with rival visions for the future and rival international attachments. Yet in the midst of all this turmoil, Americans such as Ona Judge maintained a deep commitment to the principle and, even more, realization of freedom. Out of these conflicts and aspirations, a new nation was being born.

WHO, WHAT, WHERE

REVIEW QUESTIONS

1. What were the key elements of Hamilton's fiscal and economic policies?

2. Why did political parties emerge during Washington's administration? How did the two parties differ, and why was the conflict between them so intense?

3. What was the Whiskey Rebellion? How did it reflect larger tensions in the early republic?

CRITICAL-THINKING QUESTIONS

1. Why were foreign and domestic affairs so intertwined in the 1790s?

2. How fragile do you think the new nation was? What were the reasons for that fragility?

3. Could slavery have been eliminated in the 1790s?

SUGGESTED READINGS

Cotlar, Seth. *Tom Paine's America: The Rise and Fall of Transatlantic Radicalism in the Early Republic.* Charlottesville: University of Virginia Press, 2011.

Dunbar, Erica Armstrong. *Never Caught: The Washingtons' Relentless Pursuit of Their Runaway Slave, Ona Judge.* New York: Atria, 2017.

Sachs, Honor. *Home Rule: Households, Manhood, and National Expansion on the Eighteenth-Century Kentucky Frontier.* New Haven, CT: Yale University Press, 2015.

For further review materials and resource information, please visit www.oup.com/us/ofthepeople

CHAPTER 8: CONTESTED REPUBLIC, 1789–1800
Primary Sources

8.1 HENRY KNOX, REPORT ON THE INDIANS (1789)

Washington's Secretary of War, Henry Knox, submitted a report to Congress on the question of the Indians almost as soon as Washington took office. What he said aligned closely with what Washington himself believed, as he revealed in his letters.

In examining the question how the disturbances on the frontiers are to be quieted, two modes present themselves, by which the object might perhaps be effected; the first of which is by raising an army and extirpating the refractory tribes entirely, or 2dly, by forming treaties of peace with them, in which their rights and limits should be explicitly defined, and the treaties observed on the part of the United States with the most rigid justice, by punishing the whites, who should violate the same.

In considering the first mode, an inquiry would arise, whether, under the existing circumstances of affairs, the United States have a clear right, consistently with the principles of justice and the laws of nature, to proceed to the destruction or expulsion of the savages ... supposing the force for that object easily attainable.

It is presumable, that a nation solicitous of establishing its character on the broad basis of justice, would not only hesitate at, but reject every proposition to benefit itself, by the injury of any neighboring community, however contemptible and weak it might be, either with respect to its manners or power ... The Indians being the prior occupants, possess the right of the soil. It cannot be taken from them unless by their free consent, or by the right of conquest in case of a just war. To dispossess them on any other principle, would be a gross violaton of the fundamental laws of nature, and of that distributive justice which is the glory of a nation.

But if it should be decided, on an abstract view of the question, to be just, to remove [them] by force from the territory they occupy, the finances of the United States would not at present admit of the operation. ... As the settlements of the whites shall approach near to the Indian boundaries established by treaties, the game will be diminished, and the lands being valuable to the Indians only as hunting grounds, they will be willing to sell further tracts for small considerations. ... It is most probable that the Indians will, by the invariable operation of the causes which have hitherto existed in their intercourse with the whites, be reduced to a very small number.

Source: Report of Henry Knox on the Northwestern Indians, June 15, 1789. *American State Papers, Indian Affairs,* 1:13–14.

8.2 ALEXANDER HAMILTON, REPORT ON MANUFACTURES (1791)

Washington's Secretary of the Treasury, Alexander Hamilton, proposed a number of initiatives to strengthen the American economy and make it more like that of the European nations, with a national bank, a funded debt, and increased commerce and manufacturing. In his Report on Manufactures, he described the benefits that would come from national support of manufacturing, including increasing the productivity of women and children. He also advocated increased immigration, to provide workers for the growing industries. Jefferson, Madison, and others who organized to oppose Hamilton feared that a shift from agriculture to manufacturing would create a permanent dependent class that would undermine the new republic.

III. As to the additional employment of classes of the community, not ordinarily engaged in the particular business.

This is not among the least valuable of the means, by which manufacturing institutions contribute to augment the general stock of industry and production. In places where those institutions prevail, besides the persons regularly engaged in them, they afford occasional and extra employment to industrious individuals and families, who are willing to devote the leisure resulting from the intermissions of their ordinary pursuits to collateral labours, as a resource of multiplying their acquisitions or [their] enjoyments. The husbandman himself experiences a new source of profit and support from the increased industry of his wife and daughters; invited and stimulated by the demands of the neighboring manufactories.

Besides this advantage of occasional employment to classes having different occupations, there is another of a nature allied to it [and] of a similar tendency. This is—the employment of persons who would otherwise be idle (and in many cases a burthen on the community), either from the byass of temper, habit, infirmity of body, or some other cause, indisposing, or disqualifying them for the toils of the Country. It is worthy of particular remark, that, in general, women and Children are rendered more useful and the latter more early useful by manufacturing establishments, than they would otherwise be. Of the number of persons employed in the Cotton Manufactories of Great Britain, it is computed that 4/7 nearly are women and children; of whom the greatest proportion are children and many of them of a very tender age.

And thus it appears to be one of the attributes to manufactures, and one of no small consequence, to give occasion to the exertion of a greater quantity of Industry, even by the same number of persons, where they happen to prevail, than would exist, if there were no such establishments.

IV. As to the promoting of emigration from foreign Countries.

Men reluctantly quit one course of occupation and livelihood for another, unless invited to it by very apparent and proximate advantages. Many, who would go from one country to another, if they had a prospect of continuing with more benefit the callings, to which they have been educated, will often not be tempted to change their situation, by the hope of doing better, in some other way. Manufacturers, who listening to the powerful invitations of a better price for their fabrics, or their labour, of greater cheapness of provisions and raw materials, of an exemption from the chief part of the taxes burthens and restraints, which they endure in the old world, of greater personal independence and consequence, under the operation of a more equal government, and of what is far more precious than mere religious toleration—a perfect equality of religious privileges; would probably flock from Europe to the United States to pursue their own trades or professions, if they were once made sensible of the advantages they would enjoy, and were inspired with an assurance of encouragement and employment, will, with difficulty, be induced to transplant themselves, with a view to becoming Cultivators of Land.

If it be true then, that it is the interest of the United States to open every possible [avenue to] emigration from abroad, it affords a weighty argument for the encouragement of manufactures; which for the reasons just assigned, will have the strongest tendency to multiply the inducements to it. . . .

V. As to the furnishing greater scope for the diversity of talents and dispositions, which discriminate men from each other.

. . . The results of human exertion may be immensely increased by diversifying its objects. When all the different kinds of industry obtain in a community, each individual can find his proper element, and can call into activity the whole vigour of his nature. And the community is benefitted by the services of its respective members, in the manner, in which each can serve it with most effect.

If there be anything in a remark often to be met with—namely that there is, in the genius of the people of this country, a peculiar aptitude for mechanic improvements, it would operate as a forcible reason for giving opportunities to the exercise of that species of talent by the propagation of manufactures. . . .

Source: Alexander Hamilton, "Report on Manufactures," 1791, http://press-pubs.uchicago.edu/founders/documents/v1ch4s31.html.

8.3   THOMAS JEFFERSON'S LETTER TO PHILIP MAZZEI (1796)

Out of government and deeply discouraged about the state of American politics, Thomas Jefferson vented privately to his old friend Philip Mazzei, complaining that much of the government was now in the hands of those who preferred "the calm of despotism to the boisterous sea of liberty." When the letter became public the next year, Federalists suggested that Jefferson was a traitor who preferred France to his own country.

. . . . The aspect of our politics has wonderfully changed since you left us. In place of that noble love of liberty and republican government which carried us triumphantly thro' the war, an Anglican, monarchical and aristocratical party has sprung up, whose avowed object is to draw over us the substance as they have already done the forms of the British government. The main body of our citizens however remain true to their republican principles, the whole landed interest is with them and so is a great mass of talents. Against us are the Executive, the Judiciary, two out of three branches of the legislature, all of the officers of the government, all who want to be officers, all timid men who prefer the calm of despotism to the boisterous sea of liberty, British merchants and Americans trading on British capitals, speculators and holders in the banks and public funds a contrivance invented for the purposes of corruption and for assimilating us in all things, to the rotten as well as the sound parts of the British model. It would give you a fever were I to name to you the apostates who have gone over to these heresies, men who were Samsons in the field and Solomons in the council, but who have had their heads shorn by the harlot England. In short we are likely to preserve the liberty we have obtained only by unremitting labors and perils. But we shall preserve them, and our mass of weight and wealth on the good side is so great as to leave no danger that force will ever be attempted against us. We have only to awake and snap the Lilliputian cords with which they have been entangling us during the first sleep which succeeded our labors.

Source: Thomas Jefferson's letter to Philip Mazzei, April 24, 1796, https://jeffersonpapers.princeton.edu/selected-documents/thomas-jefferson-philip-mazzei-0.

8.4   CHARLES BROCKDEN BROWN'S DEFENSE OF EDUCATION FOR WOMEN (1798)

Many in the young United States were eager to make a better world. Charles Brockden Brown (1771–1810), from a Quaker family in Philadelphia, became known as a significant novelist writing about American themes. One of his work's, *Alcuin: A Dialogue* (1798), presented a lengthy fictionalized dialogue between a young man and a lady who was hosting an evening party.

If I understand you rightly (said the lady), you are of opinion that the sexes are essentially equal?

It appears to me (answered I) that human beings are molded by the circumstances in which they are placed. In this they are all alike. The differences that flow from the sexual distinction, are as nothing in the balance.

And yet women are often reminded that none of their sex are to be found among the formers of States, and the instructors of mankind—that Pythagoras, Lycurgus, and Socrates, Newton, and Locke, were not women.

True; nor were they mountain savages, nor helots, nor shoemakers. You might as well expect a Laplander to write Greek spontaneously, and without instruction, as that any one should be wise or skillful, without suitable opportunities. I humbly presume one has a better chance of becoming an astronomer by gazing at the stars through a telescope, than in eternally plying the needle, or snapping the scissors. To settle a bill of fare, to lard a pig, to compose a pudding, to carve a goose, are tasks that do not, in any remarkable degree, tend to instill the love of or facilitate the acquisition of literature and science. . . . Men are the slaves of habit. . . . Hence it is that certain employments have been exclusively assigned to women and that their sex is supposed to disqualify them for any other. Women are defective. They are seldom or never metaphysicians, chemist, or law-givers. Why? Because they are sempstresses [seamstresses] and cooks. This is unavoidable. Such is the unalterable constitution of human nature. They cannot read who never saw an alphabet. They who know no tool but the needle, cannot be skillful at the pen.

Yes (said the lady); of all forms of injustice, that is the most egregious which makes the circumstance of sex a reason for excluding one half of mankind from all those paths which lead to usefulness and honour.

Source: Charles Brockden Brown, *Alcuin: A Dialogue* (New Haven: Carl & Margaret Rollins, 1935 [1798]), 21–24.

8.5   UNITED STATES CONGRESS, "AN ACT TO ESTABLISH AN UNIFORM RULE OF NATURALIZATION" (1790) AND AN ACT RESPECTING ALIEN ENEMIES (1798)

The first naturalization policy, established by Congress in 1790, set liberal terms for residency, only two years, but restricted citizenship to persons who were free and white. In 1795, as fear of foreigners increased, the residency period was extended to 5 years, and then, in 1798, to 14 years. At the same time the Alien Enemies Act empowered the president, if there were a declared war, to apprehend, confine, or deport any adult male aliens who were natives of the enemy country, while the Alien

Friends Act enabled him to deport any alien he considered "dangerous to the peace and safety of the United States." Following are two of these pieces of legislation.

UNITED STATES CONGRESS, "AN ACT TO ESTABLISH AN UNIFORM RULE OF NATURALIZATION" (MARCH 26, 1790)

Be it enacted by the Senate and House of Representatives of the United States of America, in Congress assembled, That any Alien being a free white person, who shall have resided within the limits and under the jurisdiction of the United States for the term of two years, may be admitted to become a citizen thereof on application to any common law Court of record in any one of the States wherein he shall have resided for the term of one year at least, and making proof to the satisfaction of such Court that he is a person of good character, and taking the oath or affirmation prescribed by law to support the Constitution of the United States, which Oath or Affirmation such Court shall administer, and the Clerk of such Court shall record such Application, and the proceedings thereon; and thereupon such person shall be considered as a Citizen of the United States. And the children of such person so naturalized, dwelling within the United States, being under the age of twenty one years at the time of such naturalization, shall also be considered as citizens of the United States. And the children of citizens of the United States that may be born beyond Sea, or out of the limits of the United States, shall be considered as natural born Citizens: Provided, that the right of citizenship shall not descend to persons whose fathers have never been resident in the United States: Provided also, that no person heretofore proscribed by any States, shall be admitted a citizen as aforesaid, except by an Act of the Legislature of the State in which such person was proscribed.

AN ACT RESPECTING ALIEN ENEMIES (JULY 6, 1798)

SECTION 1. *Be it enacted by the Senate and House of Representatives of the United States of America in Congress assembled,* That whenever there shall be a declared war between the United States and any foreign nation or government, or any invasion or predatory incursion shall be perpetrated, attempted, or threatened against the territory of the United States, by any foreign nation or government, and the President of the United States shall make public proclamation of the event, all natives, citizens, denizens, or subjects of the hostile nation or government, being males of the age of fourteen years and upwards, who shall be within the United States, and not actually naturalized, shall be liable to be apprehended, restrained, secured and removed, as alien enemies. . . . Provided, that aliens resident within the United States, who shall become liable as enemies, in the manner aforesaid, and who shall not be chargeable with actual hostility, or other crime against the public safety, shall be allowed, for the recovery, disposal, and removal of their goods and effects, and for their departure, the full time which is, or shall be stipulated by any treaty, where any shall have been between the United States, and the hostile nation or government, of which they shall be natives, citizens, denizens or subjects: and where no such treaty shall have existed, the President of the United States may ascertain and declare such reasonable time as may be consistent with the public safety, and according to the dictates of humanity and national hospitality.

SEC. 2. *And be it further enacted,* That after any proclamation shall be made as aforesaid, it shall be the duty of the several courts of the United States, and of each state, having criminal jurisdiction, and of the several judges and justices of the courts of the United States, and they shall be, and are hereby respectively, authorized upon complaint, against any alien or alien enemies, as aforesaid, who shall be resident and at large within such jurisdiction or district, to the danger of the public peace or safety, and contrary to the tenor or intent of such proclamation, or other regulations which the President of the United States shall and may establish in the premises, to cause such alien or aliens to be duly apprehended and convened before such court, judge or justice; and after a full examination and hearing on such complaint. and sufficient cause therefor appearing, shall and may order such alien or aliens to be removed out of the territory of the United States, or to give sureties of their good behaviour, or to be otherwise restrained, conformably to the proclamation or regulations which shall and may be established as aforesaid, and may imprison, or otherwise secure such alien or aliens, until the order which shall and may be made, as aforesaid, shall be performed.

SEC. 3. *And be it further enacted*, That it shall be the duty of the marshal of the district in which any alien enemy shall be apprehended, who by the President of the United States, or by order of any court, judge or justice, as aforesaid, shall be required to depart, and to be removed, as aforesaid, to provide therefor, and to execute such order, by himself or his deputy, or other discreet person or persons to be employed by him, by causing a removal of such alien out of the territory of the United States; and for such removal the marshal shall have the warrant of the President of the United States, or of the court, judge or justice ordering the same, as the case may be.

Source: United States Congress, "An Act to Establish an Uniform Rule of Naturalization" (March 26, 1790); "An Act Respecting Alien Enemies" (July 6, 1798).

8.6   THE VIRGINIA AND KENTUCKY RESOLUTIONS (1798–1799)

As the Democratic Republicans debated how best to respond to the Alien and Sedition Acts, rumors spread that Thomas Jefferson's home state of Virginia was going to rise in revolution—which Alexander Hamilton seemed ready to put down by force. Jefferson and Madison, however, chose a more moderate path, one with lasting implications for states' rights: They encouraged the states to pass resolutions opposing the Acts, which Virginia and Kentucky did. The 1798 Virginia resolution affirmed the right of states to determine the constitutionality of federal laws, while in 1799 the Kentucky Act went even further, suggesting a state might nullify any federal law it deemed unconstitutional.

VIRGINIA ACT

RESOLVED, That the General Assembly of Virginia, doth unequivocably express a firm resolution to maintain and defend the Constitution of the United States, and the Constitution of this State, against every aggression either foreign or domestic, and that they will support the government of the United States in all measures warranted by the former.

... That the General Assembly doth also express its deep regret, that a spirit has in sundry instances, been manifested by the federal government, to enlarge its powers by forced constructions of the constitutional charter which defines them; and that implications have appeared of a design to expound certain general phrases (which having been copied from the very limited grant of power, in the former articles of confederation were the less liable to be misconstrued) so as to destroy the meaning and effect, of the particular enumeration which necessarily explains and limits the general phrases; and so as to consolidate the states by degrees, into one sovereignty, the obvious tendency and inevitable consequence of which would be, to transform the present republican system of the United States, into an absolute, or at best a mixed monarchy.

That the General Assembly doth particularly protest against the palpable and alarming infractions of the Constitution, in the two late cases of the "Alien and Sedition Acts" passed at the last session of Congress.

... That this state having by its Convention, which ratified the federal Constitution, expressly declared, that among other essential rights, "the Liberty of Conscience and of the Press cannot be cancelled, abridged, restrained, or modified by any authority of the United States," and from its extreme anxiety to guard these rights from every possible attack of sophistry or ambition, having with other states, recommended an amendment for that purpose, which amendment was, in due time, annexed to the Constitution; it would mark a reproachable inconsistency, and criminal degeneracy, if an indifference were now shewn, to the most palpable violation of one of the Rights, thus declared and secured; and to the establishment of a precedent which may be fatal to the other.

That the good people of this commonwealth, having ever felt, and continuing to feel, the most sincere affection for their brethren of the other states; the truest anxiety for establishing and perpetuating the union of all; and the most scrupulous fidelity to that constitution, which is the pledge of mutual friendship, and the instrument of mutual happiness; the General Assembly doth solemnly appeal to the like dispositions of the other states, in confidence that they will concur with this commonwealth in declaring, as it does hereby declare, that the acts aforesaid, are unconstitutional. ...

That the Governor be desired, to transmit a copy of the foregoing Resolutions to the executive authority of each of the other states, with a request that the same may be communicated to the Legislature thereof; and that a copy be furnished to each of the Senators and Representatives representing this state in the Congress of the United States.

KENTUCKY ACT

... RESOLVED, That this commonwealth considers the federal union, upon the terms and for the purposes specified in the late compact, as conducive to the liberty and happiness of the several states: That it does now unequivocally declare its attachment to the Union, and to that compact, agreeable to its obvious and real intention, and will be among the last to seek its dissolution: That if those who administer the general government be permitted to transgress the limits fixed by that compact, by a total disregard to the special delegations of power therein contained, annihilation of the state governments, and the erection upon their ruins, of a general consolidated government, will be the inevitable consequence: That the principle and construction contended for by sundry of the state legislatures, that the general government is the exclusive judge of the extent of the powers delegated to it, stop nothing short of despotism; since the discretion of those who adminster the government, and not the constitution, would be the measure of their powers: That the several states who formed that instrument, being sovereign and independent, have the unquestionable right to judge of its infraction; and that a nullification, by those sovereignties, of all unauthorized acts done under colour of that instrument, is the rightful remedy: That this commonwealth does upon the most deliberate reconsideration declare, that the said alien and sedition laws, are in their opinion, palpable violations of the said constitution; and however cheerfully it may be disposed to surrender its opinion to a majority of its sister states in matters of ordinary or doubtful policy; yet, in momentous regulations like the present, which so vitally wound the best rights of the citizen, it would consider a silent acquiesecence as highly criminal: That although this commonwealth as a party to the federal compact; will bow to the laws of the Union, yet it does at the same time declare, that it will not now, nor ever hereafter, cease to oppose in a constitutional manner, every attempt from what quarter soever offered, to violate that compact:

AND FINALLY, in order that no pretexts or arguments may be drawn from a supposed acquiescence on the part of this commonwealth in the constitutionality of those laws, and be thereby used as precedents for similar future violations of federal compact; this commonwealth does now enter against them, its SOLEMN PROTEST.

Source: Virginia and Kentucky resolutions, 1798–1799, https://billofrightsinstitute.org/primary-sources/virginia-and-kentucky-resolutions

8.7   EXCERPTS FROM "AN ACT FOR THE GRADUAL ABOLITION OF SLAVERY," IN *LAWS OF THE STATE OF NEW YORK*, 22ND SESSION (1799)

After the Revolution, a number of northern states began to abolish slavery within their borders. State legislatures found themselves balancing carefully the rights of slave owners to their property with the Revolutionary promise of equality. While Massachusetts enacted general emancipation in 1783, most other northern states, including Pennsylvania, New Hampshire, Connecticut, Rhode Island, Vermont, New York, and New Jersey, decided upon a "gradual" method that emancipated the enslaved on a certain future date, or only emancipated those born after a given day. Here is New York's 1799 Act.

Be it enacted . . . That any child born of a slave within this state after the fourth day of July next shall be deemed and adjudged to be born free: Provided nevertheless. That such child shall be the servant of the legal proprietor of his or her mother until such servant, if a male, shall arrive at the age of twenty-eight years, and if a female, at the age of twenty-five years.

And be it further enacted. That such proprietor, his, her or their heirs or assigns, shall be entitled to the service of such child until he or she shall arrive to the age aforesaid, in the same manner as if such child had been bound to service by the overseers of the poor.

And be it further enacted. That every person being an inhabitant of this state who shall be entitled to the service of a child born after the fourth day of July as aforesaid, shall, within nine months after the birth of such child, cause to be delivered to the clerk of the city or town whereof such person shall be an inhabitant, a certificate in writing containing the name and addition of such master or mistress, and the name, age and sex of every child so born, which certificate shall be by the said clerk recorded in a book to be by him for that purpose provided, which record shall be good and sufficient evidence of the age of such child; and the clerk of such city or town shall receive from said person twelve cents for every child so registered . . .

And be it further enacted. That the person entitled to such service may, nevertheless, within one year after the birth of such child, elect to abandon his or her right to such service, by a notification of the same from under his or her hand, and lodged with the clerk of the town or city where the owner of the mother of any such child may reside; in which case every child abandoned as aforesaid shall be considered as paupers of the respective town or city where the proprietor or owner of the mother of such child may reside at the time of its birth; and liable to be bound out by the overseers of the poor on the same terms and conditions that the children of paupers were subject to before the passing of this act.

And be it further enacted. That every child abandoned as aforesaid shall be supported and maintained till bound out by the overseers of the poor as aforesaid, at the expence of this state: Provided however. That the said support does not exceed three dollars and fifty cents per month for each child; and the comptroller is hereby authorized and directed to draw his warrant on the treasurer of this state for the amount of such account, not exceeding the allowance above prescribed. . . . And provided also, That the person so abandoning as aforesaid, shall, at his own expence, support and maintain every such child till it arrives at the age of one year, and every owner omitting to give notice in due form as aforesaid shall be answerable for the maintenance of every such child until the arrival of the respective periods of servitude specified in the first section of this act.

And be it further enacted. That it shall be lawful for the owner of any slave, immediately after the passing of this act, to manumit such slave by a certificate for that purpose under his hand and seal.

Source: "An Act for the Gradual Abolition of Slavery," passed March 29, 1799, in *Laws of the State of New York*, 22nd Session, 1799. http://www.archives.nysed.gov/education/ act-gradual-abolition-slavery-1799

A Republic in Transition

1800–1819

< 1812 Cartoon accusing the British of offering bounties to their Indian allies for American scalps

Andrew Jackson: A Man of the People

Andrew Jackson came of age with the new nation. Already fatherless by the age of one, he later lost "everything that was dear" to him—his mother, his two brothers, and his South Carolina home, too—while he "embarked in the struggle for our liberties" during the Revolution. Jackson's hatred of the British, as well as any form of aristocracy, was deep and enduring. By the age of 21, Jackson had tried out a few trades, settling on that of lawyer; bought his first enslaved person; fought his first duel; and made his way to Tennessee, which had been opened up to settlement by the Americans' victory in the Revolution. In this region, a smart and aggressive young white man like Jackson could succeed, but he would need land and enslaved people. Political connections helped individuals secure land, some of which they would then sell to settlers at a higher price, using the profits to buy enslaved people to grow cotton. Profits from cotton, in turn, would go toward more land and slaves. Jackson quickly began moving up the social and economic ladder in this frontier region, as a lawyer, politician, land speculator, and slave-owning planter. He was aided by his marriage to a well-connected young woman, Rachel Donelson Robards—who actually married him before her divorce from another man was finalized.

Jackson rose quickly in Tennessee, in short order occupying the offices of representative, senator, and judge. He built, lost, and rebuilt a fortune as a land speculator and planter. (The frontier economy was unstable, and after his first reversal, Jackson developed a strong hatred of banks.) More than anything, though, he longed for a military career, both for the glory and for the opportunity to fight those who blocked his countrymen's occupation of fertile lands: the British (who had not yet vacated the West), the Spanish (who held Florida), and the Indian tribes who claimed the land. Jackson offered to round up a "thousand brave Tennesseeans" to help William Henry Harrison defeat the Shawnee chief, **Tecumseh**: "That banditti ought to be swept from the face of the earth."

At the outbreak of the War of 1812, Jackson received a US commission to lead Tennessee volunteers to Louisiana. Then, in 1813, came orders to avenge a serious attack by the Red Stick faction of the Creek Indians on a group of white settlers and their Creek allies at Fort Mims, near Mobile, Alabama. The influx of settlers onto Indian lands and the political contests among the Spanish, British, and Americans had destabilized the Indian tribes, encouraging the most violent tribal members to fight more moderate members for supremacy. Even before receiving orders, Jackson rallied his volunteers. "Your frontier is threatened with invasion by the savage foe! Already do they advance towards your frontier with their scalping knifes unsheathed, to butcher your wives, your children, and your helpless babes."

Jackson's forces defeated the Red Sticks in a series of battles known as the Creek War. More Indians died in the final battle at Horseshoe Bend than in any other American-Indian battle in US history. A whole village was killed. To assure an accurate body count, the Tennessee soldiers cut off the tips of the dead Indians' noses—557 of them. With the victory in the Creek War, Jackson secured his reputation, an appointment in the regular US army, and a treaty that ceded 23 million acres to the United States. It covered not only land that had been occupied by the rebellious Red Sticks but also land occupied by the more moderate Creeks, including those who had actually fought *with* Jackson.

Further triumphs—and controversy—lay ahead. General Jackson and his troops defeated the British in New Orleans in 1815, at the end of the War of 1812. He then assumed command of the US army in the southern territory to defend against Indians and the Spanish. Jackson secured tens of millions more acres by treaties. He also moved against the Spanish and the Seminoles in Florida, even exceeding his orders; he secured Florida for the United States; and executed two British agents in the process. Jackson's aggressive measures gained him powerful critics in Washington but made him a hero to other Americans. What cannot be denied is his role in the expansion of the United States and the southern slave-based economy.

Jackson's advance helped people like him: poor whites looking for opportunity. And the most important factors for advancement in the South remained land and enslaved people. In this way, opportunity for whites came directly at the expense of Native Americans and enslaved African Americans.

A POLITICS OF TRANSITION

In his inaugural address in 1801, Jefferson strove to put the partisan bitterness of the previous decade behind American politics. He asked Americans to come together "in common efforts for the common good" and assured Federalists that he was committed to the rights of the minority. "Let us, then, fellow-citizens, unite with one heart and one mind," he encouraged. In some ways, Jefferson got his wish: over time many of the policies of the Democratic Republicans would so come to resemble the policies of the Federalists that it would seem as if the two parties had grown closer. In the daily battle of national politics, however, the Democratic Republicans and the Federalists seemed not to share any common ground at all.

A Contested Election, an Anxious Nation

As a fractured country approached its second contested presidential election, in 1800, it was not clear that the nation could survive. Virginia had just thwarted a revolt led by a 24-year-old enslaved man named **Gabriel**. Recruited from taverns and religious meetings around Richmond, as many as 500 or 600 enslaved people

Struggles For Democracy

The Gabriel Revolt

On the evening of August 30, 1800, a torrential rain fell on the city of Richmond, Virginia. Despite the weather, an enslaved man named Gabriel and a number of his companions met to launch a long-planned rebellion, but they agreed the cause was presently hopeless. They postponed the uprising and promised each other to try to get the word out to their fellow enslaved. They had to reconstitute the movement quickly, as it was only a matter of time before the plot was discovered. On an agreed-upon date they would set fire to the dockyards and warehouses, and while the white population was distracted, they would rouse the Black population to fight for freedom. It was, however, already too late. Someone had given them away. In the ensuing days, some enslaved people were taken in for questioning and were probably tortured. The authorities had a list of people they wanted to arrest, including Gabriel, who had escaped. Eventually, on September 24, he was captured. By then, the trials of his colleagues were already under way. He and over two dozen others were sentenced to death.

Gabriel was born in 1776, as the Declaration of Independence was being read aloud throughout the thirteen colonies. He was the youngest of three sons born to an enslaved couple living on a tobacco plantation in Henrico County. All three children were given biblical names; Gabriel was named for the angel who visited Mary to tell her she would bear the baby Jesus. Gabriel was exactly the same age as the master's son and almost certainly played with him when they were children. Both boys grew up hearing about the course of the fight for freedom from Britain.

were prepared to assemble outside of Richmond, take the city, and then spread through the countryside, freeing the enslaved. Inspired by the American, French, and Haitian Revolutions, the conspirators hoped to rally "the poor white people" to their cause of liberty. Gabriel planned to spare those who were "friendly to liberty" and the "poor white women who had no slaves." The conspiracy was discovered, however, and 27 African Americans, including Gabriel, were executed. According to white witnesses, all went to their deaths with "a sense of their rights and a contempt of danger." It was a determination, Congressman John Randolph later cautioned, "which, if it becomes general, must deluge the Southern country in blood."

Would bloodshed among whites follow? Deeply unpopular, John Adams nonetheless ran for a second term. Thomas Jefferson came out of retirement to oppose him. Each side predicted disaster if the opposition won. The election's uncertain outcome only compounded the sense of danger. The Constitution required the presidency to go to the man with the highest number of electoral votes, but both Jefferson and another candidate from his party, Aaron Burr, received

By the 1790s, Gabriel, who was tall and strong, had become a blacksmith and lived at least part of each month in the city of Richmond, where he was hired out to others. He kept some of the money he earned. When he wasn't working, he socialized with both free and enslaved folk. The biggest news of the day was the drama of the Revolution of Saint-Domingue (today's Haiti). A formerly enslaved man named Toussaint L'Ouverture was leading a successful revolution against the master class. Some of the whites who fled and the Black servants and enslaved people they brought with them landed in Richmond, carrying their tales. Gabriel was intelligent and able to read. He would have been aware that the situation in Saint-Domingue was different from the one in Virginia, for on the island, the Black population outnumbered the white, and the French government could not come to the colonists' aid, for they were engulfed in their own revolution. But in Richmond, Gabriel lived in a world in which the Black population outmatched the white, albeit by a slim margin, and on the countryside plantations, Blacks more dramatically outnumbered whites. He also knew that the election of 1800 was bitterly contested. There was so much rancor between the Federalists and the Republicans that many people spoke of the danger of civil war. Gabriel reasoned that this was the enslaved people' moment to demand their freedom.

Given that the memory of the American Revolution was still so recent, and the French and Haitian Revolutions still ongoing, many people, even whites, could not help but recognize Gabriel's motivation. Two years later, **Thomas Jefferson** wrote in a private letter to a friend, "[Slave rebels] are not felons, or common malefactors, but persons guilty of what the safety of society, under actual circumstances, obliges us to treat as a crime, but which their feelings may represent in a far different shape." Still, few whites were ready to remedy the gaping hole in American logic. Gabriel stood in the tumbril with his hands bound behind his back and was taken to the gallows. The time of freedom for the enslaved had not yet come after all.

73 votes. The choice was thrown into the House of Representatives, where Federalists threatened to block Jefferson by supporting Burr. Only after 34 ballots was Jefferson elected, once the Federalists had secured Jefferson's promise to keep Hamilton's financial system.

Democratic Republicans in Office

The peaceful transition of power in 1800 proved that the government could contain intense political conflict. Immediately on gaining office, Democratic Republicans closed the loophole in the Constitution that had led to the electoral stalemate. They quickly passed the legislation that became the Twelfth Amendment (1804), providing for party tickets in national elections. The Democratic Republicans also attempted to reduce the Federalist presence on the Supreme Court by impeaching Associate Supreme Court Justice Samuel Chase. Chase was notorious for his open partisanship during the Sedition Act prosecutions, but it was unclear whether his behavior met the constitutional standard of "Treason, Bribery, and high Crimes and Misdemeanors." In the final vote, Chase was acquitted, and the Supreme Court remained Federalist, five to one. Jefferson's desire for a Democratic Republican Court had to wait.

Before leaving office, the Federalists had tried to pack the courts with Federalists. The Judiciary Act of 1801, passed by the lame-duck Federalist Congress, increased the number of federal judgeships. Adams promptly appointed—and Congress confirmed—loyal Federalists. He also issued commissions for 41 justices of the peace, but they had not yet been acted on when he left office, and Jefferson ordered their appointments withheld. One of those "midnight" appointees, William Marbury, went directly to the Supreme Court, asking it for a "writ of mandamus," a court order compelling the executive to issue the commission. In a landmark decision, Chief Justice **John Marshall**, speaking for the Federalist-dominated Court, refused—but in a ruling that actually enhanced the Court's power. The provision in the Judiciary Act of 1789 that gave the Supreme Court the power to issue writs of mandamus was unconstitutional. The Constitution had set out the powers of the Supreme Court, and no act of legislation could change them. Marbury was out of luck, but the principle of judicial review (itself nowhere mentioned in the Constitution) had been established. Henceforth, the Supreme Court would decide whether acts of legislation were constitutional or not. Jefferson had won the battle but lost a very big constitutional war.

Jefferson also set out to reduce the size of the federal government. Working with Secretary of the Treasury Albert Gallatin, he slashed the army budget by half and the navy budget by more than two-thirds. He also supported congressional efforts to reduce the $80 million national debt and to repeal internal taxes, including the hated one on whiskey. By 1807, the national debt had been cut in half.

These efforts at thrift were soon derailed by the politics of overseas commerce. The monarchs of the North African nations of Tunis, Algeria, Morocco, and Tripoli had long sought to dominate shipping on the Mediterranean, seizing the ships and enslaving the crews of those nations that refused to pay tribute. In 1794, Congress appropriated a million dollars to ransom captives and another million to build a navy to protect American shipping. By the end of the decade, tribute and ransoms absorbed 20 percent of the US budget. The conflict was about trade and money, not religion. The 1796 Treaty of Tripoli reassured the Arab nations that "the Government of the United States of America is not, in any sense, founded on the Christian religion" and "has in itself no character of enmity against the laws, religion, or tranquility, of Mussulmen [Muslims]."

Jefferson had long opposed paying tribute. When he became president, he was still convinced that it would be "more economical and more honorable" to go to war than continue paying tribute. He asked Congress for an appropriation for warships and gunboats "to protect our commerce and chastise their insolence—by sinking, burning, or destroying their ships and vessels wherever you shall find them."

Results were mixed. Democratic Republicans managed to avoid new internal taxes, and they cut the national debt substantially. They were not, however, able to dismantle Hamilton's economic system, which provided the revenue to finance the country's defense. America's military intervention in the Mediterranean was not particularly successful. The United States signed a second treaty with Tripoli in 1805—and paid $60,000 to ransom prisoners. Payments to the other North African states continued until 1815.

The Louisiana Purchase

Many citizens, including Jefferson himself, had long presumed that white Americans would eventually settle west of the Mississippi River, but Pinckney's Treaty of 1795 (which improved American access to the Mississippi) had removed any need for immediate action.

Napoleon Bonaparte changed all that. By the turn of the century, American–French relations had chilled. Ambitious to establish his own empire in the Americas and determined to prevent further United States expansion, in 1800 Napoleon acquired Louisiana from Spain. Jefferson worried that France would eventually send troops to occupy New Orleans. Hoping to thwart Napoleon, Jefferson secretly sent help to the rebels in Saint-Domingue, pushed Native Americans across the Mississippi, and raised an army. He then dispatched Robert Livingston and James Monroe to France to purchase New Orleans and West Florida, too.

By then, Napoleon had lost 30,000 troops in a failed effort to put down the rebellion in Saint-Domingue. Defeated by the island's formerly enslaved people and by infectious disease, Napoleon was ready to unload his American territory. He stunned the American agents by offering to sell not only New Orleans but also the entire Louisiana Territory—883,000 square miles. (The Americans claimed that the purchase included West Florida, but Spain denied selling the territory to France. This issue was not resolved until 1819; see Chapter 10.) On April 12, 1803, the deal was struck. The United States purchased the entire Louisiana Territory for $15 million, or roughly 3.5 cents an acre.

Selling the deal to Congress was another matter. Many Democratic Republicans, including Jefferson himself, questioned whether the territory could be acquired and made part of the United States without a constitutional amendment. Federalists worried about whether the United States could govern so vast a territory or make citizens out of its multiracial, largely foreign populace. Reversing the position they had held when the Federalists were in power, Jeffersonians decided that the "necessary and proper" and "general welfare" clauses of the Constitution provided adequate authority. Using the precedent of the Northwest Ordinance (see Chapter 7), Congress set out a path to statehood, granted citizenship to French and Spanish inhabitants of the territory, and ignored the status of Indians living there. Congress also established a government for Louisiana, which soon passed laws to make Louisiana's practices more American: a Black Code defined enslaved people as property and instructed free people of color never "to conceive of themselves as equal to whites."

Congress also banned the foreign slave trade in Louisiana, fearing that enslaved people imported from Saint-Domingue would spread revolution. Louisiana had long been a cauldron of slave unrest. This was probably buttressed by events in revolutionary France and Saint-Domingue and by the arrival in New Orleans in 1810 and 1811 of perhaps 10,000 refugees from the revolution in Saint-Domingue—whites, free people of color, and enslaved people. Some of them joined the 1811 uprising on the German Coast of the Mississippi led by a Louisiana-born enslaved man of mixed racial background, Charles Deslondes. As many as 300 well-organized enslaved people marched on New Orleans, burning plantations, destroying crops, and gathering weapons on the way. West of the city, they were met by a planter militia and US troops. Deslondes and 15 other enslaved people were captured, tried, and executed, their decapitated heads raised on pikes along the road as a warning to any other enslaved people thinking of rebellion.

Even before Louisiana belonged to the United States, Jefferson began to plan its exploration. Jefferson appointed his trusted secretary, Captain Meriwether Lewis, and another officer, William Clark, to lead the expedition. Lewis was an ambitious soldier with some experience in the **Old Northwest**. Clark, who had commanded troops on the Mississippi, was a skilled surveyor and mapmaker. Their mission was to follow the Missouri River, chart the territory as far as the Pacific, and scout opportunities for commerce with the Indians of the northern Missouri River, who traded chiefly with the British.

The expedition left St. Louis on May 14, 1804, on three boats containing 45 men and a dog, firearms, medicines, scientific instruments, tools, flour, and salt. The party traveled first up the Missouri River, closely observed by the Mandans, the Minnetarees, and the Hidatsas, who visited their camps and sent ahead stories of these curious people. In early November, the white men made their winter camp. When the expedition broke camp the following spring, a Shoshone woman, **Sacagawea**, her French-Canadian trapper husband, and their newly born child left with them. She became an invaluable guide and interpreter. Native women such as Sacagawea and Malinche often served as cultural mediators.

Some encounters with Native Americans were less friendly. Far more dangerous than the Indians, however, were waterfalls and rapids, freezing temperatures and paralyzing snows, accidents, diseases (especially dysentery), and dead-end trails. After a difficult portage across the Rocky Mountains in the fall of 1805, the expedition finally reached the Pacific Ocean on November 7, 1805.

Throughout their journey, Lewis and Clark had represented themselves as the envoys of a great nation with whom the Native Americans should now trade. But they also kept an eye out for future settlements. After their return, in 1806, parts of their journals and letters, including detailed maps and drawings, slowly found their way into print, advertising what Jefferson called America's new "empire for liberty."

Other Americans had other plans for the territory west of the Mississippi. In 1805, former vice president Aaron Burr, who had recently killed Alexander Hamilton in a duel, went to New Orleans, looking for a fresh start. He immediately fell in love with it, and saw, too—or so he later claimed—that the United States might extend its sovereignty to include some of Spanish Mexico, where settlers were unhappy with high taxes and little government attention. By 1806, Burr had raised a force of several thousand men. Convinced that Burr intended treason, and wanting to avoid trouble with Spain, Jefferson ordered his arrest. Burr was brought back to Richmond to stand trial before John Marshall, who happened to be presiding over the federal circuit. Marshall interpreted treason in the narrowest sense possible. "Conspiracy is not treason," he instructed the jury. Burr was acquitted, but he was also disgraced. The incident indicated the government's weakness, when a former vice president could raise his own army for his own purposes, whether treasonous or not.

Embargo

In the fall of 1804, Jefferson's popularity was soaring. Internal taxes had been abolished; the national debt was falling; the United States had (seemingly) stood up to international coercion; and, most amazingly, it had acquired a huge western empire. Jefferson won reelection handily, and the Democratic Republicans took control of both houses of Congress. Faced with the prospect of federal surpluses, Jefferson began to contemplate a future role for the federal government encouraging "the great objects of public education, roads, rivers, canals, and such other objects of public improvement as may be thought proper." But Jefferson's second term had barely begun when his attention was riveted to developments in Europe.

In his first inaugural address, Jefferson had counseled "peace, commerce, and honest friendship with all nations, entangling alliances with none." He remained committed to American neutrality, but by 1805 Napoleon's growing power in France and his expansionistic designs on Europe had complicated this policy. On the one hand, Jefferson knew he might need Napoleon's help to settle the unresolved question of West Florida, still claimed by Spain. On the other hand, France's increasing indifference toward American shipping rights raised the possibility that the United States might need Britain as an ally. Napoleon's victory over Austria in 1805 made France the undisputed master of western Europe. At the same time, English victories over the fleets of France and Spain had made England the undisputed master of the seas. The stalemate had dire consequences for American shipping.

Jefferson's hopes that Britain might respect the neutrality of American ships were dashed in 1805 when Britain again began seizing ships traveling between enemy ports, taking more than 200 American ships in that year alone. Then Napoleon declared a blockade of England and also began confiscating American ships. In June 1807, the British ship *Leopard* stopped the American frigate *Chesapeake* as it left Norfolk, Virginia. The captain of the *Leopard* demanded the right to search the American ship, insisting that it had recruited British deserters for its crew. When he was denied, he fired on the ship, boarded it, and took four men prisoner, leaving the *Chesapeake* to limp home.

Jefferson immediately ordered all British ships out of American waters and demanded reparation for the *Chesapeake*. In secret sessions, Congress passed an act that permitted only those American ships with the president's express approval to sail into foreign ports and prohibiting foreign ships from the American export trade. In effect, the United States had embargoed itself.

It was the most disastrous policy of Jefferson's career. Because enforcement was impossible, wealthy merchants enjoyed the large profits of smuggling. At the same time, small merchants, sailors, and shopkeepers who depended on steady maritime trade were thrown into crisis, and farmers in the South and West had trouble finding overseas trading outlets. As the economy settled into depression in 1808, the remaining Federalists charged that the embargo was helping Napoleon. Adding to American frustration, Napoleon then slyly claimed the right to attack

A Philosophic Cock This 1804 cartoon caricatured Jefferson as a "philosophic cock" courting his enslaved woman Sally Hemings. Jefferson's Federalist opponents tried to tarnish his reputation by publicizing his relationship with an enslaved woman, but the voters reelected Jefferson by a decisive margin.

US ships in any continental port because, by Jefferson's own order, they could not be legal carriers.

The ironies of the embargo did not end there. As violations mounted, ever more repressive versions of the embargo were enacted. The final, fifth Embargo Act (signed January 9, 1809) swept away protections against self-incrimination and the right to due process and trampled on the right to trial by jury. By comparison, even the Alien and Sedition Acts looked tame.

As he himself acknowledged, the Embargo Acts represented the failure of Jefferson's agrarian political economy. His dream of a republic of farmers was dead, the victim of the principles of territorial expansion and free trade on which he had based it. Meeting America's need for manufactured goods solely by "this exuberant commerce," as Jefferson admitted in 1809, "brings us into collision with other powers in every sea, and will force us into every war of the European powers. The converting of this great agricultural country into a . . . mere headquarters for carrying on the commerce of all nations, is too absurd."

The anguish caused by the Embargo Acts exposed long-simmering dissension within Democratic Republican ranks. The most serious rupture came after the **Louisiana Purchase.** Although Jefferson insisted that West Florida was a part of the Louisiana Purchase, Spain denied ever ceding it to France. Napoleon hedged, but his ministers let it be known that the right price might convince them to lobby the American cause with Spain. Jefferson asked Congress for the money. To Jefferson's most radical critics, this was the Louisiana Purchase all over again—the government exercising powers unauthorized by the Constitution. These critics, led by the Virginian John Randolph, took the name Tertium Quids (the "third something"), neither Federalists nor Democratic Republicans. By 1808, the Quids were threatening open rebellion. To avoid the risk of public brawling, in 1808 party loyalists met in a closed caucus to select Jefferson's successor. They chose **James Madison**. In the election, Madison captured 122 electoral votes to Federalist Charles C. Pinckney's 47. The Democratic Republicans again won both houses of Congress.

From 1801 until 1829, the federal government would remain under the control of a single party. By itself, that did not challenge Democratic Republican principles, as neither Madison nor Jefferson considered a two-party system necessary to American political life. Both, however, warned against the day when a small cadre of like-minded men would meet in secret to choose the nation's ruler. Democratic Republican ascendancy itself had now come to rest on just such a closed institution. Meanwhile, with American hopes for international prestige now a joke, and with commerce and agriculture in trouble, on March 1, 1809, Jefferson signed a bill repealing the Embargo Act. Three days later, Jefferson left the office he now described as a "splendid misery."

THE WAR OF 1812

Facing ruptures in his party serious enough to compel him to accept nomination by the kind of closed and antirepublican institution he himself had once condemned, James Madison took office on March 4, 1809. Madison had stood side by side with Thomas Jefferson on virtually every important political and ideological issue since the founding of the nation. Now he inherited his friend's presidential woes.

Madison and the War

In 1809, with Madison's approval, Congress replaced the embargo with the Non-Intercourse Act, reopening trade with all of Europe except England and France but authorizing the president to resume commerce with whichever of these countries dropped its restrictions and attacks on American shipping. The act set off a series of diplomatic feints by England and France, both pretending to change policies without making actual concessions.

France eventually won the game. In the summer of 1810, Napoleon's ministers officially told Madison that, as of November of that year, France would stop seizing American ships if Britain would do likewise. Probably correctly, Britain did not believe France would follow through on this policy. But Madison accepted the French declarations, and he altered American Non-Intercourse Act policy to apply to Britain alone.

Still, war might have been averted. A quarter of a century of European wars and Napoleon's continental policy—which closed continental markets to English goods—had taken its toll on Britain's economy. Although far more powerful militarily than the United States, Britain would have been happy to avoid the cost of an additional war. On June 1, 1812, in light of continuing British attacks on American shipping, Madison requested that Congress declare war on Great Britain. He listed several other reasons, including that the British were "impressing" American seamen into service and, perhaps most importantly, instigating Indian attacks in the west. On June 4, the House voted to pass a war bill. On June 18, the Senate concurred. Ironically, unaware of these events, England announced that it was revoking its maritime policy against US ships.

The war vote in Congress went largely along party and regional lines. Proponents, led by Henry Clay of Kentucky and John C. Calhoun of South Carolina, mostly hailed from the West and South. Known as the War Hawks, they were fiercely nationalistic and expansionist young men who had come of age since the Revolution. They predicted an easy conquest of Canada— "a mere matter of marching," in Jefferson's words—where they fantasized the people would rise up against British rule. Farmers and planters in the South wanted to open up the seas, while western migrants were convinced that Creek and Shawnee resistance was the work of the British, with their forts still along the Great Lakes. Tensions with Indians fueled their desire to fight.

New Englanders, however, were adamantly opposed to more war. Shipping was just beginning to recover and their region's prosperity depended on trade with Britain. Even moderate Democratic Republicans were hesitant. They dreaded the cost of the war and doubted that the nation could gear up to take on such a formidable foe.

All of these tensions were reflected in the election of 1812. Maverick Democratic Republican De Witt Clinton rallied Federalist support and ran against

A Scene on the Frontiers as Practiced by the "Humane" British and Their "Worthy" Allies This 1812 cartoon accuses the British of offering their Indian allies bounties for American scalps. A Native American is depicted scalping an American soldier, while a British officer says to another Native American, "Bring me the Scalps and the King our master will reward you."

Madison. He lost, with 89 electoral votes (to Madison's 128), but with a higher proportion than the Federalists had enjoyed since the election of 1800.

Doubts about America's war readiness were soon justified. An ill-planned attempt to invade Canada in the summer of 1812 failed. Two thousand American troops surrendered at Detroit, and two advances failed when state militiamen insisted they were not required to leave the country to fight. Commodore Oliver Hazard Perry's dramatic victory on Lake Erie, however, led to another attempt on Canada and a victory at the Battle of the Thames, where the famed Shawnee leader Tecumseh (see "Ways of Life In Flux," this chapter) was killed. Demoralized by his death, the Britons' Indian allies withdrew from the war.

A comparable victory eluded Americans in the Atlantic. After initial successes, the tiny American navy was easily overwhelmed by superior British sea power. Americans turned to private schooners and sloops and by the war's end managed to capture more than 1,300 British vessels. Nevertheless, by 1813 the British navy had succeeded in blockading the American coast from the Chesapeake Bay to New Orleans; in the following year, the blockade extended to New England. The British fleet pummeled coastal cities and villages. On August 24, 1814, British troops invaded Washington, DC, burned the Capitol, the White House, the Treasury Building, and the Naval Yard, and terrorized civilians. The entire cabinet, including President James Madison, had already evacuated.

While Washington smoldered, the British turned to Baltimore. Through the night of September 13, its ships fired on **Fort McHenry**, the island citadel guarding Baltimore's harbor. Among the anguished observers was a Washington lawyer by the name of Francis Scott Key. Elated that the United States flag still flew over the fort at dawn, Key quickly scribbled the words that would, many years later in 1931, become the lyrics of the national anthem, "The Star-Spangled Banner."

In the Old Southwest, Andrew Jackson used the war to suppress Indian resistance to US settlement. In March 1814, he defeated the Red Stick faction of the Creeks at Horseshoe Bend, forcing them to sign a treaty ceding two-thirds of remaining Creek lands to the United States.

Federalist Response

For a time the war worked in favor of the Federalists. In 1812, they doubled their numbers in Congress. New Englanders actively impeded the war effort. Governors refused to call out their militias, and trade with the enemy was rampant. Then, in October 1814, emboldened Massachusetts Federalists called for a convention of the New England states "to lay the foundation for a radical reform in the National compact." They would meet on December 15 in Hartford, Connecticut.

The Federalists meeting in Hartford were divided. Extreme Federalists, arguing that the Union could not be saved, lobbied for a separate New England confederacy that could immediately seek an end to the war. More moderate voices prevailed, and in the end, the convention sought amendments to the Constitution that they hoped would give more power to the North. The Federalists demanded restrictions on the power of Congress to declare war, an end to the Three-Fifths Compromise allowing enslaved people to be counted for purposes of representation, exclusion of naturalized citizens from elective federal office, and restrictions on the admission of new states. They also sought to limit the number of terms a president could serve and the frequency with which the presidential candidate could be chosen from a given state.

Federalists mistimed their efforts. The unpopular war was already finishing. By 1814, a weary Britain was ready to end the war. Emerging as the dominant power in Europe, Britain had little incentive to offer Americans more than simple peace. Signed in Ghent, Belgium, on December 24, 1814, the treaty that ended the War of 1812 was silent on the issues of free trade and impressment that had triggered the war. The Treaty of Ghent also sidestepped boundary disputes between Canada and the United States. British negotiators did agree to remove British troops from the Old Northwest, in effect acknowledging the failure of Indian resistance to white settlement.

Only Andrew Jackson's victory at New Orleans saved Americans from outright humiliation in the war. After the victory at Horseshoe Bend, his troops moved on to New Orleans (see Map 9–1), where a British fleet prepared to take control of the mouth of the Mississippi River. Unaware that two weeks earlier, on January 8, 1815, a peace treaty had been signed in Ghent, 7,500 British regulars stormed Jackson's position. In 30 minutes the battle was over, and, miraculously, the Americans had won and Jackson had become a national hero.

In 1815, the chief political importance of Jackson's victory was the lift it gave to American nationalism and the light it cast on the Federalist Hartford Convention, still meeting in Connecticut. Threatening secession was one thing in a failing war, but quite another in a moment of national triumph. Suddenly, the proceedings at Hartford seemed downright traitorous.

AN ECONOMY IN TRANSITION

The end of the war ushered in a half century of fundamental economic change and growth. These changes, sometimes called the **market revolution**, were reflected in every aspect of society, from religion and politics to family life and everyday values. Paternalistic employment arrangements (apprenticeship, indenturing) gave way to labor contracts and wage labor, and informal transactions to formal contracts. Self-sufficiency declined, while longer distance market exchange increased. All of these changes were enhanced by improvements in technology and transportation as well as laws to encourage commerce.

International Markets

The economic transformation of the late eighteenth and early nineteenth centuries had many sources. One of the most significant was the gradual revival of overseas commerce at the end of the eighteenth century, much of which was supported by conflicts in Europe. As Napoleon tried to spread the French Revolution (and his own power) throughout Europe, Europe remained at war—disrupting agriculture on the Continent and impeding European overseas trade. American shippers happily filled the gap.

This American shipping was of three kinds: export/import (exporting American wheat, rice, indigo, tobacco, and especially cotton to Europe and importing European manufactured goods to growing United States markets); reexport (carrying goods between two foreign ports with an intermediate stop in the

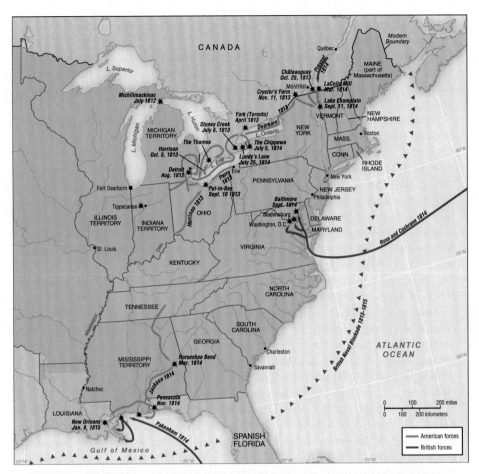

Map 9-1   Battles and Campaigns of the War of 1812   The War of 1812 was largely a naval war, fought along the Atlantic coast, in the Gulf of Mexico, and on the Great Lakes. Several land campaigns proved important, however: the British ground attack that ended in the looting and burning of the capital and Andrew Jackson's trek overland to New Orleans.

United States, often to avoid French and English embargoes on each other's Caribbean colonies); and the simple carrying trade between two foreign ports (as US ships became the main carriers between warring England and France). In addition to farm products and manufactured goods, American ships also carried people: political refugees from France and from Ireland's ill-fated rebellion seeking safety in the new republic and—before 1808, when the slave trade was officially ended—captives from Africa sold into slavery in the Caribbean and the United States.

American shipping tonnage tripled between 1780 and 1810, reaching almost 11 million tons annually. The American share of the traffic between England and the United States grew from 50 percent in 1790 to 95 percent by 1800. The value of the reexport carrying trade also increased from about $500,000 a year in the 1790s to about $60 million a year in 1807. By the first decade of the nineteenth century, American ships were in the harbors of India, the East Indies, China, the

Philippines, Japan, and Hawaii and on the Pacific coast of North America and the eastern coast of South America.

The return of overseas trade fed an already rampant inflation (the result of a shortage of gold and silver and a surfeit of local- and state-issued currencies of doubtful values). But it also created many jobs and helped alter the way Americans understood the terms of labor.

Merchants contracted for vessels (built at an astonishing rate), captains hired crews, and teamsters hurried goods to port. Some merchants also invested in port-city manufacturing. They gathered tailors, for example, into large central shops to turn out cheap clothing for sailors or to sell to planters for their enslaved people—even though the new merchant-manufacturers seldom recognized the traditional obligations of shop master to worker: food, housing, and training. Rather, they tended to hire unattached workers, apprentices, or jobless young men and put them to work at some single, specialized aspect of the craft. Some traditional shop masters became merchants, taking investments in ships to carry their goods to southern and Caribbean markets.

The growth of overseas shipping also spurred the development of business services in the early republic, particularly in port cities. The National Bank of the United States would be reauthorized in 1816. In the meantime, citizens formed insurance companies against the risks of loss in trading and local institutions for pooling capital for investment. By 1810, there were more than 100 banks in the nation. Many of these banks, corporations, and insurance companies operated under special state charters that allowed them to function as legal entities. As the businesses mushroomed, so did new jobs for clerks and lawyers.

In the countryside, farming families shifted from a relatively self-sufficient model of agriculture to more commercially oriented enterprises. Farmers were willing to travel longer distances to sell their goods. Whenever possible, they expanded the size of their holdings. In Delaware, for example, families used the profit from women's dairying activities to finance new land to grow wheat for sale in the cities or in Europe. Farmers, like merchants and shop masters, tried to hedge their bets by reducing their costs and liabilities. They ceased using indentured servants, to whom they would have owed year-round room and board and a freedom bonus at the end of their term, in favor of hiring seasonal wage workers, to whom they had no responsibilities in the off-season.

The most significant boost to American commercial agriculture arose from the late eighteenth-century mechanization of the English textile mills and the resulting increased demand for cotton. The colonies had not been an important source of raw cotton, because the only variety that grew well in most of North America was extremely laborious and time-consuming to clean. Spurred by the new English markets, in 1793 Eli Whitney invented a mechanism that increased the amount of this short-staple cotton that could be cleaned in a day from 1 pound to 50 pounds. Almost at a stroke, Whitney's gin made cotton a viable cash crop for much of the South.

The invention occurred at a critical moment. American indigo was losing market share to indigo from the East Indies. The tobacco trade was in decline. The market for rice was still strong, but rice cultivation required such large investments of land and labor as to exclude most farmers from production. Cotton gave the South a new commodity crop, and one that, unlike rice, could be grown on small farms without significant investment. Between 1790 and 1810, American cotton production increased from 3,000 bales to 178,000 bales a year. Increasingly after 1800, cotton was the largest single US export commodity, making the development of the nation, not merely that of the South, dependent on cotton and its labor system, slavery.

At the same time, the United States banned another kind of international trade: that of enslaved Africans. The Constitution forbade a national ban until 1808, but by 1806 every state except South Carolina, which imported almost 40,000 enslaved people between 1803 and 1807, had ended the trade. In early 1807, Congress banned the international slave trade as of January 1, 1808, but only after debating one troubling issue: What was to be done with the enslaved people confiscated from ships that defied the ban? Slavery's opponents thought the enslaved people should be freed, while the institution's defenders feared the introduction of more free Blacks. A compromise left it up to the individual states to decide, which meant that Africans confiscated in the South could be sold into slavery there. Americans could agree that no more Africans should be brought into the United States, but not what to do with those who were already there. The ending of the international slave trade was a significant achievement, but the debate gave signs of trouble to come.

Crossing the Appalachian Mountains

After the Treaty of Greenville with the Indians (see Chapter 8) opened the Ohio River Valley to white settlers, the expansion of overseas markets fed a pent-up desire for new lands in Tennessee, Kentucky, and the soon-to-be state of Ohio (1803). The Land Ordinance of 1785 had provided for sales to private individuals who could afford sections of 640 acres or more at $1 an acre, but that was far beyond the reach of ordinary citizens. Sales were effectively restricted to speculators. Hoping to find a source of revenue, in 1796 Congress made matters worse by raising the price to $2 an acre.

Finally, in 1800, poorer settlers got some relief. The Land Act of 1800 reduced the size of the minimum parcel from 640 acres to 320 acres. For the first time, buyers were permitted to spread their payments over time. In 1804, the minimum size was decreased to 160 acres and the price reduced from $2.00 to $1.64 an acre. Even though the cost of the land and the journey were still prohibitive for many Americans and easy credit sometimes led to unmanageable debt, lower prices per acre, lower minimums, and the promise of credit opened the West to tens of thousands of settlers.

The unprecedented migration set off by the peace brought by the Treaty of Ghent swelled the population of the trans-Appalachian region. Kentucky grew from 220,955 in 1800 to 564,317 in 1820; Tennessee from 105,602 to 422,823; and Ohio from 42,159 to 581,434. Equally important, settlement led to the organization of new states. After Ohio in 1803, nine years passed before Louisiana entered in 1812. But then the admissions came rapid-fire. Indiana became a state in 1816, Mississippi in 1817, Illinois in 1818, and Alabama in 1819. By then both Missouri and Maine were also eager to join the Union.

The westward migration was a remarkably diverse parade. The earliest arrivals were usually hunters, fur traders, explorers, and surveyors. Wealthy speculators (European and American) sometimes traveled to the backcountry just long enough

entrepreneur. In 1819, the monopoly was withdrawn, but many small operators remained convinced of the state's favoritism toward the wealthy. In fact, few got rich running steamboats on the Mississippi. The twists and hidden snags of the shallow river saw to that. Only in the East, where rivers were deeper and where steamboats became fashionable transportation for wealthy travelers, did investors realize large profits early on.

Even steamboats were limited by the existing waterways. Since the turn of the century, investors and inventors had sought to enlarge those water routes by linking them artificially with canals, but the early history of canals did not portend great success. By the end of the War of 1812, only about 100 miles of canals existed in the United States (the longest ran 27 miles between the Merrimack River and Boston Harbor). None earned much money. Yet some investors could see their potential.

When at the end of the war New York City mayor De Witt Clinton proposed building a canal to connect Albany and Buffalo (see Map 9–2), he was thought to have taken leave of his senses. The canal would run 364 miles, making it the longest canal in the world. It would require an elaborate system of aqueducts and locks to negotiate a 571-foot rise in elevation and would cost $7 million, the largest investment of the sort in the nation's history. Clinton argued that the canal would "create the greatest inland trade ever witnessed" and would tie the "most fertile and extensive regions of America" to the city of New York, making that city "the granary of the world, the emporium of commerce, the seat of manufactures, the focus of great moneyed operation." In 1817, he convinced the state legislature not only to authorize the project but also to pay for it entirely in state funds, a gamble that amounted to a $5-per-capita levy for the entire population of New York.

Begun on July 4, 1817, the **Erie Canal** was completed in 1823 and officially opened two years later. At 10:30 on the morning of Wednesday, November 2, 1825, the first boats cleared the final locks and made their way into the Albany basin. Bells pealed, bands played, a huge crowd cheered, and 24 cannons fired successively in a national salute.

Clinton's gamble paid off spectacularly. Passenger boats and transport barges produced revenues high enough for the state to pay for later stages of construction with the profits of early ones. Transportation costs from Buffalo to New York City fell from $100 a ton to about $10 a ton when the canal opened and dropped even lower later on. The Erie Canal set off an explosion of canal building that lasted up to the Civil War, but few later canals duplicated its success.

Early Industrial Society in New England

New Englanders had been experimenting with the idea of water-powered textile mills since the 1780s, when prominent Massachusetts merchants tried to convince the state legislature to support the creation of textile machinery in the United States. In 1790, émigré mechanic Samuel Slater had replicated the English water-powered carding and spinning machines in his mill in Pawtucket, Rhode Island. But Slater lacked the power loom necessary to turn yarn into finished cloth. It took Eli Whitney's invention of the cotton gin in 1793, some industrial sabotage, and the devastating trade losses during the embargo and the War of 1812 to finally propel Americans to devise a power loom and invest seriously in a domestic textile industry. Boston merchant Francis Cabot Lowell pioneered the shift.

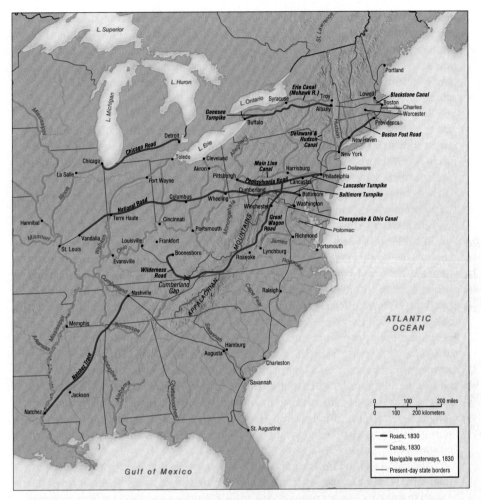

Map 9–2   The Development of Regions and of Roads and Canals By 1830, internal development had fostered a growing transportation infrastructure throughout the United States. That development was regional in character, however. In the southern states, where natural waterways ran from deep in the interior to the coast, citizens saw little need to build additional linkages. In the North, where natural waterways seldom ran directly to coastal outlets, investors were far more willing to spend money on internal development, especially canals.

A graduate of Harvard with a knack for machine design, Lowell traveled to England to see the loom for himself and surreptitiously to memorize its plan. Back home, working with mechanic Paul Moody, he duplicated the English model in 1814. With a special charter from the Massachusetts legislature, Lowell and his Boston associates (organized as the Boston Manufacturing Company) opened the United States' first fully mechanized textile mill in Waltham, Massachusetts. Within three years the mill had expanded and was paying a whopping 20 percent dividend.

Lowell died in 1817, but under Nathan Appleton's leadership the company (now the Merrimack Manufacturing Corporation) raised more than $8 million to finance a second group of mills in East Chelmsford, Massachusetts. The new mills turned out their first finished cloth in 1823. A sleepy rural village of 200 in 1820, by 1826 East Chelmsford had grown to 2,600 and had incorporated as the city of Lowell, America's first industrial town. The mills relied entirely on the South for their raw cotton. Northern domestic purchase of raw southern cotton grew from 8 million pounds in 1800 to 31.5 million by the end of the war in 1815.

The **Waltham system**, as Lowell's approach was called, differed from earlier American manufacturing enterprises in several ways. The Waltham mill was the largest industrial undertaking attempted in America up to that time. It housed the full production process, from fiber to finished cloth. It relied on a new organization plan in which a professional managerial rank (separate from the owners) oversaw daily operations. Finally, to cultivate an appearance of benevolence (in contrast to the plight of workers in the English mills), the Waltham system required that employees live on-site in subsidized and supervised housing.

For their workforce, the owners turned to the young rural women from Vermont, New Hampshire, and western Massachusetts. Textiles were traditionally women's work, and power-driven textile machinery was not necessarily identified with either sex. Moreover, female workers were cheaper than men, the result of their long exclusion from customary craft protections and their loss of the right to make contracts if they were married.

In the early years, parents and daughters both saw benefits in mill work for unmarried young women. Presumably, a daughter would leave her family anyway when she married. Having her work in the mills before marriage reduced the number of mouths to be fed at home. The residential system allayed fears that a young woman was compromising her respectability. Matrons supervised company-owned boardinghouses, where operatives lived together in single-sex settings. Strict rules of behavior guided leisure time, and factory bells regulated the workday.

The success of the mills underscored the paradoxes of American slavery and American freedom in the early nineteenth century. In the early years, at least, the women operatives enjoyed a financial and social independence virtually unknown under the parental roof. They lived together under the guidance of a female head of household. They returned home for vacation largely at their own discretion. Many of the young women kept all or most of their pay, enjoying (perhaps for the only time in their lives) a separate disposable income. They developed pride in their work and in their community and began to see themselves as part of a long Yankee history of hard work and independence. All of this was made possible by the fact of slavery in the American South.

The final irony of this contradiction would play out only in the later years of the mills, after employers had cut pay and intensified production. In 1834 and again in 1836, the operatives turned out in defiant strikes—condemning the mill owners for reducing them, "the daughters of freemen," to the condition of slaves the Rule of Law and Lawyers

Americans had long emphasized the importance of the written law to the preservation of the republic, but the law became important in new ways in the growing commercial economy. Overseas trade, internal expansion, the buying and selling of land, new inventions—all required complex legal documents and lawyers to draw them up and execute them. The revival of commerce and the work of government converged to make the legal profession attractive. By 1815, lawyers made up about half the members of Congress.

The growing importance of lawyers reflected the growing importance of courts and of the judiciary. Again and again, judicial interpretation reinforced and set the course for market development. When tradition clashed with economic development, judges tended to side with the entrepreneurs. For example, as businesses experimented with the use of water power in manufacturing, they sought to erect dams and millraces that altered the flow of streams. English common law protected the use of waterways undisturbed by alterations upstream. But in 1805, in *Palmer v. Mulligan*, a New York court ruled in favor of the right of development, against customary common-law rights.

On the federal level, the power of the Democratic Republicans (and, later, the Jacksonian Democrats) in the executive and legislative branches was countered by the power of Federalist John Marshall, who was chief justice of the Supreme Court from 1801 until 1835. Between 1805 and 1824, the Marshall Court issued three decisions that brought the Constitution to bear in support of the new market-based economy.

The first, *Dartmouth v. Woodward* (1819), explicitly reinforced the rights of contract. The case concerned an attempt by the New Hampshire legislature to alter the original charter of Dartmouth College, given to the college by King George III in 1769 when the nation was still a set of British colonies. New Hampshire argued that the original charter was not binding on the current state government, but Dartmouth insisted that the charter was in fact a contract, protected under Article VI of the US Constitution, which protected debts and engagements entered into before the Revolution. Acting to ensure the stability of contract in the broadest sense, the Court ruled in Dartmouth's favor.

The case of *McCulloch v. Maryland*, also decided in 1819, upheld the constitutionality of the Second Bank of the United States. The creation of the bank had been one of the successes of the new Democratic Republicans, who had managed to overpower their party's objections to national banks by attracting Federalist votes. The Second Bank had created a number of branches, one of which was in Baltimore. Viewing the presence of the bank within its borders as a threat to its sovereignty, Maryland attempted to assert its authority over the Baltimore branch by taxing it. James W. McCulloch, chief clerk of the branch, refused. Maryland appealed to the Supreme Court, arguing that because the federal government was a creation of the states, its branch institutions could be taxed in the states in which they existed. Marshall's Court unanimously rejected this position. The federal government was superior to the states, the Supreme Court concluded. Because "the power to tax involves the power to destroy," the states could not tax the creations of the federal government, whatever their location. The ruling was a victory for federal power and the Bank both.

Gibbons v. Ogden (1824), the last in Marshall's long line of landmark decisions, concerned a disputed ferryboat monopoly in New York. Having exclusive rights to operate steamboats in the state's waters, Robert Fulton and Robert Livingston had, in turn, "contracted" a part of this right out to Aaron Ogden, giving him a ferry monopoly across the Hudson River from New York to New Jersey. At the same time, however, Thomas Gibbons had obtained a federal license to operate a boat line along a coastal route that came into conflict with Ogden's line. Who controlled these waters and therefore had the right to grant licenses, New York or the federal government? Consistent with its national view of power and development, the Marshall Court found in favor of the federal power. The decision noted that the Constitution had given to Congress (Article I, Section 8) the right "to regulate Commerce with foreign nations, and among the several States." Because the waterways under dispute did not fall clearly within the boundaries of a single state, state power was in this case in conflict with federal power. In such cases, the Marshall Court found, federal power took precedence.

WAYS OF LIFE IN FLUX

Americans at the turn of the century played active roles in the political, social, and economic changes affecting their communities. Those changes grew out of choices some Americans made—to invest in an overseas venture, for example, or to buy new lands in the West to grow wheat or cotton. Their choices affected their own lives and the lives of others and slowly added up to a far more market-driven way of life.

Indian Resistance to American Expansion

Although he expressed benevolence toward Indians, President Jefferson believed that they must give way to American settlement. Not only did the territories represent the supply of land necessary to nurture republican virtues and stabilize republican institutions, but they also provided a western buffer against Britain, France, and Spain. Preferring peaceful American expansion westward, Jefferson fostered a growing Indian dependency on American agents that would, he hoped, lead them to sell off their lands.

By the turn of the century, that westward migration was devastating native life and culture. As settlers occupied new lands, Indians lost their villages and fields. Thrown back on the fur trade, they overhunted dwindling grounds. By 1800, many of the pelts and skins brought to traders in the Northwest Territory had actually been hunted west of the Mississippi River, and the deer were all but gone in the Southeast. Protestant missionaries urged the Indians to adopt European American religious and social practices, including male-headed households and private ownership of property. Unscrupulous agents bullied Indian nations into signing away their land. When the Indians resisted, the agents made deals with leaders they knew the people did not recognize as chiefs, promising bounties and annuities for territory.

Native Americans resisted these assaults on their autonomy. Seneca communities accepted some missionary aid but refused to abandon their holdings, gendered division of labor, and matrilineal households. The southern nations declined Jefferson's promise of new lands in the West and focused on constructing internal institutions Americans might recognize as "civilized." For example, the Cherokees adopted a series of laws that functioned as a constitution, established a congress, and executed individual land titles. Meanwhile, resistance to European American culture also took the form of a broad movement for spiritual revitalization. Ganioda'yo (Handsome Lake), who rose to influence among the Senecas after 1799, preached revival through a synthesis of traditional beliefs and Christianity, but for other groups revitalization meant cleansing themselves of European American practices. Cherokees revived the Green Corn Ceremony, celebrating personal bonds and repudiating material wealth.

This crisis of survival virtually ensured armed confrontation. As early as 1807, William Henry Harrison, governor of the Indiana Territory, heard rumors of "a general combination of the Indians for a war against the United States." Two Shawnee leaders, the chief Tecumseh and his half-brother, Tenskwatawa (known as the Prophet), coalesced the diffuse anger into organized resistance. Indians' struggles against whites in the Old Northwest and in the South helped Tecumseh build a pan-Indian alliance. After 1805, Tenskwatawa became the leader of a movement that rejected white culture. About 1808, Tecumseh and Tenskwatawa founded a village in present-day Indiana on the banks of the Tippecanoe River. Thousands of Indians from different tribes came to live there. The Prophet remained in the town while Tecumseh traveled widely, encouraging organized resistance to white settlement.

By 1811, Tecumseh's success alarmed Harrison. That fall, Harrison marched an army toward Tecumseh's village. Although cautioned by Tecumseh not to be drawn into battle in his absence, on November 7, 1811, the Prophet engaged Harrison's troops and was defeated. The Prophet was discredited, but when war broke out between Britain and the United States the following year, Tecumseh was still able to amass a huge force for the British. He played a decisive role in the British victory at Detroit but then was killed soon after in the Battle of the Thames in 1813. Tecumseh's death marked the end of organized Indian resistance east of the Mississippi.

Tenskwatawa (known as the Prophet) The Shawnee Prophet was about 60 in 1830 when George Catlin painted him holding his "medicine fire" in one hand and sacred beads in the other. Catlin said he "has been a very shrewd and influential man, but circumstances have destroyed him . . . and he now lives respected, but silent and melancholy in his tribe."

Winners and Losers in the New Economy

For many Americans, the more cash- and contract-based society at the turn of the century offered both new freedom and new wealth. Large merchants who were able to absorb the risks of war might realize enormous profits in transatlantic shipping. Owners of shipbuilding and related enterprises benefited from the prolonged boom in American shipping. Farmers able to expand their holdings and take advantage of trade networks thrived in the increasingly commercial environment.

The blessings of these new liberties were mixed. New, unskilled workers took jobs away from journeymen, but they were as quickly fired as hired. Wages fell. Near poverty, journeymen in Philadelphia, New York, and Baltimore began to form mutual aid societies, helping each other and laying the foundations for trade associations. But when they tried to organize for higher wages, they discovered that in the eyes of the law, these assertions of liberty amounted to a conspiracy against the rights of trade. When Philadelphia journeyman shoemakers demanded a bill of higher wages in 1805–1806 (in the first strike in US history), they were arrested and required to pay stiff fines.

But craft masters paid, too. New opportunities in manufacturing lured entrepreneurs and merchants who organized bigger shops, hired cheap workers, and offered cut-throat competition. Initially, the traditional craft masters refused to associate with these new entrepreneurs. By the early 1800s, however, their solidarity eroded. Wanting to take advantage of economic opportunities or to cut costs, shop masters began to hire runaway servants with no questions asked or unskilled workers to whom they had fewer lasting obligations.

Americans described these changing relations of labor and society in the language of the Revolution. Elites fretted that the masses were unfit for republican self-government, whereas workers condemned the older structures of authority as repugnant to a free people. However, local conditions were also sources of new social instability. Apprentices ran away not to express allegiance to Jeffersonianism but to escape cruel masters or to seek higher wages. Masters did not hire untrained workers to affirm republican freedom but to protect profits by cutting costs.

Religion

These were years of ongoing religious upheaval, some of it evidence of a new freedom of belief and some of it expressing a sense of profound personal dislocation.

The new demands for personal liberty focused on religion, as well as work and family, as Americans increasingly objected to paying taxes to support state churches. Anglicanism had been disestablished in the South in the 1780s, replaced by the Protestant Episcopal Church. The Congregational Church was disestablished in New England in 1834, and new denominations began thriving in all regions.

Southerners were drawn especially to new evangelical Christian faiths, principally Methodism and various forms of Baptist practice. In contrast to the more staid and ritual-based Episcopal Church, these sects stressed the personal, emotional nature of religion and the ability of individuals to struggle actively for their own redemption. Methodists rejected what they deemed artificial differences among Christians, pronouncing "one condition, and only one" required for salvation: "a real desire." Their system of itinerant preaching (preachers traveled among congregations, rather than associating with a single church) enabled the clergy to reach out to the dispersed and the displaced. Emphasizing inner truth, a plain style, and congregational independence, evangelical denominations offered a relatively egalitarian vision of the community of believers that was especially attractive to the poor, to enslaved and free African Americans, and to white women. Some congregations questioned the morality of slaveholding itself.

Even before Congregationalism was fully disestablished, it was plagued by breakaway movements from within and by competition from the evangelical sects. The most important splinter groups were the Unitarian and Universalist movements, which held generally positive views of human nature, embraced universal salvation, and offered an alternative to strict Calvinism. Everywhere, the far greater threat to established religion came from the Methodists and Baptists, who found converts among country folks and city workers.

This widespread religious turmoil was expressed in a series of highly emotional **revivals** at the turn of the century, sometimes called the Second Great Awakening. These began in Virginia and western New England and spread quickly into newly settled areas of Kentucky and Tennessee. The most famous of these revivals occurred in August 1801, in the tiny rural community of Cane Ridge, Kentucky, where thousands of men, women, and children, Black and white, free and enslaved, came to watch and experience mass conversions. Eventually, the awakening spread to all parts of the country and to virtually all faiths. Yet many members of older denominations were displeased that revivals were led by unschooled preachers and encouraged unconventional beliefs and extravagant emotionalism. From 1803 to 1805, these misgivings led to schism, as the "Old Light" members of the Kentucky Synod purged "New Light" revivalists. Where Congregationalists and Presbyterians saw confusion in the revivals, Methodists and Baptists saw converts. In the first years of the nineteenth century, the number of Baptist congregations grew from about 400 to about 2,700, and membership in Methodist churches more than doubled, from 87,000 to 196,000. Eager for new members, Methodists founded the national Sunday School Union and the first denominational publishing house in the United States.

Federalists often viewed this religious upheaval as a sign of the deterioration of both politics and morality, but the linkages were seldom so simple. Neither Jefferson nor Madison, the founding lights of the Democratic Republican Party, embraced evangelical faiths. Moreover, far from signaling a drift toward irreligion, this contentious fragmentation of belief at the turn of the century had the effect of securing the language of religion, especially Protestant Christianity, as an idiom of both identity and exclusion in the new nation. Even as they fought over the correct form of Christian practice, many Americans formulated their visions of the ideal political community in the language of Protestant Christianity and suspected those who disagreed with them not only of bad politics but also of bad faith.

The Problem of Trust in a Changing Society

As old friends headed west for new lands, as young people slipped away from parents or masters, as newcomers swelled the port cities, many Americans began to wonder whom or what they could trust.

American Landscape
American Indians Watch Home Slip Away

On a warm day in 1802, twelve wagons lumbered toward the docks at the small port of New Brunswick, New Jersey. They carried all the worldly possessions of about eighty-five Lenape Indians. Perched on top of the barrels and bundles were the elders and the youngest children. The able-bodied walked alongside. Now they ferried their goods to the boats on which they had booked passage to New York City. The muddy waters of the Raritan River lapped at them, wetting their feet and sometimes their packages, but this aspect of things didn't bother them. The Lenape had long been people of the waters, living alongside New Jersey's creeks, rivers, and seashores. It was leaving yet another home that distressed them.

During the French and Indian War, a Lenape chief named Stephen Calvin had translated at a major conference between the New Jersey settlers and the Delaware Indians of eastern Pennsylvania, who were threatening war. The "Delaware" were actually the Lenape people, renamed by the whites, who had left New Jersey over the past two generations, and so the translator knew them personally—was even related to some of them—and he successfully maintained peace. As a reward, his people were given a small reservation in the southern part of New Jersey, in today's Burlington County in the area called the Pine Barrens. It was marshy land, almost useless for farming, but the whites said it would be theirs forever, and there was a useful sawmill on the property. Thus the people left central Jersey, where they had felt

The Pine Barrens When the Lenape departed from New Jersey, they were forced to leave behind the environment that had been home to them for generations.

Particularly distressing to middling and wealthy Americans were signs that workers and children were forgetting their proper place. The customary discipline of the craft shop seemed to be crumbling. Apprentices demanded better treatment, refused drudgery work, or just ran away. In the larger port cities, unemployed young men gathered on the streets shouting obscenities, frightening children, hassling hounded, and joyfully named their new community Brotherton, short for "Brother Town." The swamplands had long been hunting grounds for them, and they loved them.

Sadly, the sawmill later burned down, and during the Revolution, the British pillaged the territory. After the war, American settlers felt no scruples about hunting and foraging on the Indians' land—which the law said they could not be prosecuted for. The young people were forced to leave home to seek work as servants or sailors. By the end of the century, the remaining residents were so poor that they simply had to go elsewhere. They sold their land, packed up, and rented twelve carts to take them to New Brunswick.

That was how they found themselves sailing to New York on a day in 1802; from there, they would go up the Hudson River to Albany, and then travel along the Mohawk River as far as they could, eventually walking overland to Oneida country. The Oneida Indians (of the Haudenosaunee Confederacy, or, Iroquoian League of Six Nations) had once sold some land to another group of Lenape who had left years ago to found a mission as far from white people as possible. Now the New Jersey Lenape joined them at the Stockbridge-Munsee community.

The land in the rolling hills of central New York was good farmland, and the people made new lives for themselves. They missed hunting squirrels and gathering cranberries in the bogs of south Jersey, but they had known the use of a plow for many years now, and the women were able to earn extra money weaving blankets. They were adaptable people and could learn to love these hills. It was a good life, they decided.

Perhaps it was too good. By 1820, white settlers were hungry for their land once again, and again, the community considered moving, this time far to the west, to Wisconsin, hoping to isolate themselves from the white world. It took years of negotiations, but eventually, the Lenape boarded boats once more and traveled over the Great Lakes, various groups docking at Green Bay, Wisconsin, over the course of the 1820s and 1830s.

Stephen Calvin's son Bartholomew Calvin—who had once attended Princeton for a year—eventually traveled back east to speak to the New Jersey State Assembly. It was 1832, and many northerners regretted the pressures Andrew Jackson's government was putting on Indians. He pointed out that when his people were given the Brotherton Reservation, they were also given hunting rights to all the Pine Barrens, and those rights had never been legally extinguished. The Assembly granted the Indians $2000, to be used in their new home in Wisconsin. Calvin thanked them. "There may be some who would despise an Indian benediction," he said to them. But he insisted that "the ear of the great Sovereign of the Universe . . . is still open to our cry." He returned to the woodlands of Wisconsin, where once again his people operated a sawmill. Some of their descendants were pressured to move further west later in the century—but others are there still.

shopkeepers, and sometimes attacking strangers. Journeymen in Philadelphia and New York demanded better pay and threatened to take their skills elsewhere.

Household society seemed to be falling apart, too. Domestic workers told masters and mistresses that they should now be called "help" instead of "servants." Indentured workers balked at having their lives closely scrutinized. Even children seemed to have found a new "republican" determination to make their own decisions about whom to marry, where to live, and what work to pursue.

To their parents and masters and mistresses, it seemed that the youth and laboring classes were out of control. Indeed, in 1820, half the nation's population was under the age of 16 (compared with 24 percent under 18 in 2010). Parents threatened and cajoled. Masters offered rewards for runaway apprentices. Ministers warned against libertinism (especially young women's fashions, cut too daringly, they thought). Meanwhile, local authorities responded with laws intended to control apprentices and regulate public behavior.

For several reasons, these efforts were largely doomed. The Revolution and its aftermath had changed society. Young people coming of age at the turn of the century had been nurtured on the rhetoric of independence. The market revolution offered them numerous alternatives to older structures of authority. Why should a young person remain on the family farm when there were jobs in nearby towns? Why not just leave the controls of indentures or an apprenticeship? Why languish in Temple, Maine, when New York beckoned?

Rumor and deception thrived everywhere in this landscape. On the brink of war in 1812, one Charles Redheffer told the Philadelphia city government that he had invented a perpetual motion machine. When the city commissioners discovered that Redheffer was actually powering his machine through a hidden cranking device, rather than simply crying foul, they responded with a hoax of their own. They had a local engineer build a similar but even more cleverly deceptive machine. Redheffer fled Philadelphia for New York City, where he was exposed by Robert Fulton (who had his own interest in debunking the machine).

Meanwhile, the New England countryside was filled with treasure hunters who had heard countless rumors of long-buried riches. Some of these seekers were amateur scientists and historians. Some were charlatans, trying to make a quick buck off gullible visitors. Some were just the down-and-outers of New England's

TIME LINE

▼**1800**
Thomas Jefferson elected president

▼**1801**
Judiciary Act of 1801

▼**1803**
Louisiana Purchase
Marbury v. Madison

▼**1804**
Jefferson reelected
Lewis and Clark begin exploration of Louisiana

▼**1805**
Palmer v. Mulligan (New York)

▼**1806**
Conspiracy trial of Philadelphia journeyman shoemakers

▼**1807**
First Embargo Act
Hudson River trial of Fulton's *North River Steamboat of Clermont*

▼**1808**
External slave trade becomes illegal
Madison elected president

▼**1809**
Non-Intercourse Act

▼**1810**
American cotton production reaches 178,000 bales

changing economy who still believed in miracles that might turn their fortunes around.

One of these was the treasure-seeker **Joseph Smith**. Smith was born in 1805 to a family of poor farmers in Vermont and grew up in western New York surrounded by economic and religious uncertainty. Although the family moved constantly in a region bursting with development, economic security eluded the Smiths. Perhaps in search of some sense of constancy, Smith was drawn to the religious revivalism that scorched upstate New York, and he believed in direct spiritual revelation. Occasionally Smith and his father used what they claimed were supernatural powers to hire out as guides in what an observer described as "the money digging business." In 1819, however, Joseph Smith's powers of divination took a different turn: he experienced the first of a series of revelations in which he claimed that God had instructed him to found a new church that would teach the true lessons of Jesus Christ. In a second vision a few years later, an angel gave him the location of golden tablets, buried near his home, which described God's intentions for the "latter days" of creation, now approaching. In 1830, Smith published his translation of the ancient writings on the tablets as the Book of Mormon. He formally founded the church now known as the Church of Jesus Christ of Latter-day Saints (or the Mormon Church).

The Panic of 1819

In 1819, Americans learned that the market revolution could produce dream-shattering plunges, as well as exhilarating rises. After he signed the bill chartering the Second Bank of the United States in 1816, James Madison appointed an old political ally, Captain William Jones, as its director. Jones was a poor choice, speculating in bank stock and willing to accept bribes to overlook reckless local practices. By the time he was replaced, bank stock was at an all-time low, and the state banks had glutted the economy with unsecured paper money.

▼**1811**
Tecumseh at peak of
    influence
Battle of Tippecanoe River

▼**1812**
War of 1812 begins
James Madison reelected

▼**1814**
Federalist Hartford
    Convention

Treaty of Ghent ends War
    of 1812
Fully steam-powered tex-
    tile mills established in
    Waltham, Massachusetts

▼**1815**
Battle of New Orleans

▼**1817**
Work on Erie Canal begins
Steamboats common on
    Mississippi River

▼**1819**
Panic of 1819
Dartmouth v. Woodward
McCulloch v. Maryland

▼**1824**
Gibbons v. Ogden

▼**1825**
Erie Canal opens

Jones's successor, Langdon Cheves, moved quickly to cut the supply of paper money (too quickly, given that Great Britain was taking the same measures). Cheves began to call in loans and to redeem the bank's holdings of currency issued by the various state banks. Dangerously overextended, the state banks were forced to respond with their own programs of retrenchment. As credit dried up and the value of paper money plummeted, the nation was thrown into depression. Without credit or sufficient circulating money, commodity prices crashed throughout the Atlantic community. The market in cotton, basic to the growing American economy, fell by almost two-thirds. Their mortgages unpaid, farms and businesses failed. And tens of thousands of workers lost their jobs. For three long years, the economy stalled. Visitors to America warned potential immigrants not to come.

Because the branches of the Second Bank of the United States reached far beyond the East Coast, so did the distress of the panic. When the branch in Cincinnati, Ohio, suddenly cashed in the paper money it held from local banks, for example, Cincinnati's booming economy felt the blow, as local banks scurried to collect enough debts to make good on the face value of their paper. Similar shock waves rolled through Kentucky and Tennessee and into the lower South.

Cheves had saved the monetary system of the United States but did not make many friends for the Second Bank. State legislators, who saw the national bank (not runaway local speculation or wildcat state banks) as the villain, scrambled to reduce its power. Fourteen states passed laws preventing the bank from collecting its debts, Kentucky abolished imprisonment for debt, and six states levied heavy taxes on bank branches (a practice soon banned by the Supreme Court in *McCulloch v. Maryland*, discussed earlier). After opening 18 branches in 1817, the Second Bank opened no additional new branches until 1826.

CONCLUSION

In 1819, Andrew Jackson returned home physically exhausted. He had gone to Washington, DC, where Congress was debating censuring him for his actions in the Seminole War. Henry Clay charged that Jackson's "inhumanity, and cruelty, and ambition" made him no better than the despots of Europe. Jackson's supporters replied, however, that "when at war with a nation which observes no rules . . . the attempt may be made of bringing them to the laws of humanity." Congress could not agree. Nor could the American people. Although some crowds cheered Jackson, an important question lingered: After more than a half-century of conflict, the United States was finally at peace with both Britain and France, and it had acquired a vast new territory, rapidly filling with an ever-expanding population. As Jackson regained his strength, he and his fellow Americans asked themselves once again what kind of nation they were to be.

WHO, WHAT, WHERE

REVIEW QUESTIONS

1. What were the primary challenges facing the Jefferson and Madison administrations? How well did the administrations handle those challenges?

2. What was the market revolution?

3. In what ways were Native Americans affected by changes in the new nation? Did others suffer some negative consequences as well?

CRITICAL-THINKING QUESTIONS

1. The War of 1812 was hardly an American victory, yet at its conclusion, the United States was stronger than it had ever been. Why was this so?

2. What challenges did the addition of vast new territories create for the United States, and how did it address them? Why didn't it make colonies out of the new territories?

3. This period saw the development of both cotton plantations in the South and factories in the North. Though seemingly quite different, both were expressions of the market revolution. How so?

SUGGESTED READINGS

Freeman, Joanne B. *The Field of Blood: Violence in Congress and the Road to Civil War*. New York: Farrar, Straus & Giroux, 2018.

Gordon-Reed, Annette, and Peter S. Onuf. *"Most Blessed of the Patriarchs": Thomas Jefferson and the Empire of the Imagination*. New York: Norton, 2016.

Taylor, Alan S. *The Civil War of 1812: American Citizens, British Subjects, Irish Rebels, & Indian Allies*. New York: Knopf, 2010.

For further review materials and resource information, please visit www.oup.com/us/ofthepeople

CHAPTER 9: A REPUBLIC IN TRANSITION, 1800–1819
Primary Sources

9.1 THOMAS JEFFERSON, FIRST INAUGURAL ADDRESS (1801)

The election of 1800 aroused great anxiety for both the Federalists, the party of the incumbent, John Adams, and the Republicans, the party of the challenger, Thomas Jefferson. Each party had feared the takeover of the government by force. The goal of Jefferson's inaugural address was reconciliation and a vigorous statement of his liberal principles, which he presented as if they were the simple truth, with which every American would naturally agree. In this memorable speech, he achieved his goal.

Friends & Fellow Citizens,

Called upon to undertake the duties of the first Executive office of our country, I avail myself of the presence of that portion of my fellow citizens which is here assembled to express my grateful thanks for the favor with which they have been pleased to look towards me, to declare a sincere consciousness that the task is above my talents, and that I approach it with those anxious and awful presentiments which the greatness of the charge, and the weakness of my powers so justly inspire. A rising nation, spread over a wide and fruitful land, traversing all the seas with the rich productions of their industry, engaged in commerce with nations who feel power and forget right, advancing rapidly to destinies beyond the reach of mortal eye; when I contemplate these transcendent objects, and see the honour, the happiness, and the hopes of this beloved country committed to the issue and the auspices of this day, I shrink from the contemplation & humble myself before the magnitude of the undertaking....

During the contest of opinion through which we have past, the animation of discussions and of exertions has sometimes worn an aspect which might impose on strangers unused to think freely, and to speak and to write what they think; but this being now decided by the voice of the nation, announced according to the rules of the constitution all will of course arrange themselves under the will of the law, and unite in common efforts for the common good. All too will bear in mind this sacred principle, that though the will of the majority is in all cases to prevail, that will, to be rightful, must be reasonable; that the minority possess their equal rights, which equal laws must protect, and to violate would be oppression. Let us then, fellow citizens, unite with one heart and one mind, let us restore to social intercourse that harmony and affection without which liberty, and even life itself, are but dreary things. And let us reflect that having banished from our land that religious intolerance under which mankind so long bled and suffered, we have yet gained little if we countenance a political intolerance, as despotic, as wicked, and capable of as bitter and bloody persecutions. During the throes and convulsions of the ancient world, during the agonising spasms of infuriated man, seeking through blood and slaughter his long lost liberty, it was not wonderful that the agitation of the billows should reach even this distant and peaceful shore; that this should be more felt and feared by some and less by others; and should divide opinions as to measures of safety; but every difference of opinion is not a difference of principle. We have called by different names brethren of the same principle. We are all republicans: we are all federalists. If there be any among us who would wish to dissolve this Union, or to change its republican form, let them stand undisturbed as monuments of the safety with which error of opinion may be tolerated, where reason is left free to combat it. I know indeed that some honest men fear that a republican government cannot be strong; that this government is not strong enough. But would the honest patriot, in the full tide of successful experiment, abandon a government which has so far kept us free and firm, on the theoretic and visionary fear, that this government, the world's best hope, may, by possibility, want energy to preserve itself? I trust not. I believe this, on the contrary, the strongest government on earth. I believe it the only one, where every man, at the call of the law, would fly to the standard of the law, and would meet invasions of the public order as his own personal concern.—Sometimes it is said that man cannot be trusted with the government of himself. Can he then be trusted with the government of others? Or have we found angels, in the form of kings, to govern him? Let history answer this question.

Let us then, with courage and confidence, pursue our own federal and republican principles; our attachment to union and representative government. Kindly separated by nature and a wide ocean from the exterminating havoc of one quarter of the globe; too high minded to endure the degradations of the others, possessing a chosen country, with room enough for our descendants to the thousandth and thousandth generation, entertaining a due sense of our equal right to the use of our own faculties, to the acquisitions of our own industry, to honor and confidence from our fellow citizens, resulting not from birth, but from our actions and their sense of them, enlightened by a benign religion, professed indeed and practised in various forms, yet all of them inculcating honesty, truth, temperance, gratitude and the love of man, acknowledging and adoring an overruling providence, which by all its dispensations proves that it delights in the happiness of man here, and his greater happiness hereafter; with all these blessings, what more is necessary to make us a happy and a prosperous people? Still one thing more, fellow citizens, a wise and frugal government, which shall restrain men from injuring one another, shall leave them otherwise free to regulate their own pursuits of industry and improvement, and shall not take from the mouth of labor the bread it has earned. This is the sum of good government; and this is necessary to close the circle of our felicities. . . .

Source: Thomas Jefferson, Inaugural Address, March 4, 1801, in *The Papers of Thomas Jefferson*, vol. 33 (Princeton: Princeton University Press, 2006), pp.134-52.

9.2   TECUMSEH'S SPEECH TO GOVERNOR HARRISON, AUGUST 20, 1810

The Shawnee chief Tecumseh was known in his lifetime as a great orator, but most of the existing speeches come to us through the notes of newspaper reporters, and they changed his words as they saw fit. However, in August of 1810, William Henry Harrison, then the governor of the Indiana Territory, met with Tecumseh in the presence of an interpreter and a scribe, so we have a full record. Tecumseh spoke frankly of his desire to unite the tribes.

Brother When we were first discover'd it was by the French who told us that they would adopt us as their children and gave us presents without asking anything in return but our considering them our fathers. Since we have changed our fathers, we find it different.

Brother, This is the manner that the treaty was made by us with the French. They gave us many presents and treated us well. They asked us for a small piece of country to live on which they were not to leave and continued to treat us as their children. After some time the British and French came to quarrel, the British were victorious yet the French promised to think of us as their child and if they ever could serve us to do it. "Now my red children,

. . . It is a fact much to be lamented, that there exists in this country an organized opposition to the constituted authorities, whose influence is seen and felt on this floor, and whenever an appeal is made to the patriots of the people, its effects are transfused from one extremity of the United States to the other, for the purpose of defeating the measures which are adopted to maintain the honor of the nation. Ye, sire, every exertion has been made to weaken the arm of the Government, by means the most disgraceful. The people have been admonished to withhold their resources from us, in an hour of great public difficulty and danger. Sir, on the eve of a war with a foreign Power, it is surely no subject of contragulation to see a set of men combining together to weaken their own country, and thereby indirectly give an advantage to the enemy. Sir, I venture to predict, that if war is once begun, the difficulties which now present themselves [for paying for the war] will vanish. The distinction of Federalists and Republicans will cease; the united energies of the people will be brought into action; the inquiry will be, are you for your country or against it?

. . . The gentleman from New York admonishes us that if we go to war, we ought to take the hearts of the people with us. Sir, we all know that without this nothing effectual can be done. But is this object to be attained by a variable policy, which is to-day one thing and tomorrow another? No; convince them by a firm and determined conduct of your intentions, and they will go with you in every extremity, against any foreign foe with whom you come in collision. . . .

Source: War Hawk Tennessee Congressman Felix Grundy's Predictions About the War of 1812, Annals of Congress, House of Representatives, 12th Congress, 1st Session, pp. 1406–1411.

9.4   CONSTITUTION OF THE LOWELL FACTORY GIRLS ASSOCIATION (1834)

While women had always contributed to the family economy, the establishment of factories in the early nineteenth century offered a new type of employment, outside the home, for wages. The Lowell textile factories hired women to work in the mills while also providing room and board for their workers, most of whom were young, unmarried women. The "Factory Girls" united to protest some of the conditions in the factory and fight for higher wages, creating the first union for working women in the United States.

PREAMBLE.

Whereas we, the undersigned, residents of Lowell, moved by a love of honest industry and the expectation of a fair and liberal recompence, have left our homes, our relatives and youthful associates, and come hither, and subjected ourselves to all the danger and inconvenience, which necessarily attend young and unprotected females, when among strangers, and in a strange land; and however humble the condition of Factory Girls, (as we are termed,) may seem, we firmly and fearlessly (though we trust with a modesty becoming our sex,) claim for ourselves, that love of moral and intellectual culture, that admiration of, and desire to attain and preserve pure, elevated and refined characters, a true reverence for the divine principle which bids us render to every one his due; a due appreciation of those great and cardinal principles of our government, of justice and humanity, which enjoins on us "to live and let live"—that chivalrous and honorable feeling, which with equal force, forbids us to invade others rights, or suffer others, upon any consideration, to invade ours; and at the same time, that utter abhorence and detestation of whatever is mean, sordid, dishonorable or unjust—all of which, can alone, in our estimation, entitle us to be called the daughters of freemen, or of Republican America.

And, whereas, we believe that those who have preceded us have been, we know that ourselves are, and that our successors are liable to be, assailed in various ways by the wicked and unprincipled, and cheated out of just, legal and constitutional dues, by ungenerous, illiberal and avaricious capitalists,—and convinced that "union is power," and that as the unprincipled consult and advise, that they may the more easily decoy and seduce—and the capitalists that they may the more effectually defraud—we (being the weaker,) claim it to be our undeniable right, to associate and concentrate our power, that we may the more successfully repel their equally base and iniquitous aggressions.

And, whereas, impressed with this belief, and conscious that our cause is a common one, and our conditions similar, we feel it our imperative duty to stand by each other through weal and woe: to administer to each others wants, to prevent each others backsliding—to comfort each other in sickness, and advise each other in health, to incite each other to the love and attainment of those excellences, which can alone constitute the perfection of female character—unsullied virtue, refined tastes and cultivated intellects—and in a word, do all that in us lies, to make each other worthy ourselves, our country and Creator.

Therefore, for the better attainment of those objects, we associate ourselves together, and mutually pledge to each other, a females irrefragable vow, to stand by, abide by, and be governed by the following

PROVISIONS.

It shall be denominated the LOWELL FACTORY GIRLS' ASSOCIATION.

Any female of good moral character, and who works in any one of the Mills in this city, may become a member of this Association, by subscribing to this Constitution.

The officers of the Association shall be, a President, Vice President, a Recording Secretary, a Corresponding Secretary, a Treasurer, a Collector, and a Prudential Committee, two of whom shall be selected from each Corporation in this city.

The officers shall be chosen by the vote of the Association; that is, by the vote of a majority of the members present.

The duties of the President, Vice President, Secretaries, Treasurer, and Collector, shall be the same as usually appertain to such offices. The duties of the Prudential Committee shall be to watch over the interests of the Association generally; to recommend to the Association, for their consideration and adoption, such By-Laws and measures as in their opinion the well-being of the Association may require: and also to ascertain the necessities of any of its members, and report the same, as soon as may be, to the Association. And whenever, in the opinion of the Committee, there are necessities so urgent as to require immediate relief, they shall forthwith report the same to the President, who shall immediately draw upon the Treasurer for the sum recommended, and which sum the Committee shall forthwith apply to the relief of the necessitous.

The Treasurer and Collector shall be subject to the supervision of the Prudential Committee, to whom they shall be accountable, and to whom they shall give such security for the faithful discharge of their duties, as the Committee shall require.

All moneys shall be raised by vote of a majority of the Association, or of the members present, and shall be assessed equally on all the members.

All the officers shall hold their office for the term of one year, with the privilege of resigning, and subject to be removed by vote of the Association, for good cause.

The Association shall meet once in three months, and may be convened oftener, if occasion require, by the President, upon a petition of twenty of the members first.

It shall forever be the policy of the members of this Association, to bestow their patronage, so far as is practicable, upon such persons as befriend, but never upon such as oppose our cause.

The Association shall have power to make all necessary By-Laws, which shall be consistent with these Provisions, and such By-Laws, when made, shall be binding upon all the members.

Any member may dissolve her connection with the Association, by giving two weeks notice to the Recording Secretary; and any member shall be expelled from the Association by a vote of a majority of the members present, for any immoral conduct or behavior unbecoming respectable and virtuous females . . .

Source: Constitution of the Lowell Factory Girls Association, 1834. This is a pamphlet of which only a few copies survive. There is one in the possession of the American Antiquarian Society: https://americanantiquarian.org/millgirls/items/show/54.

9.5   ELDER DAVID PURVIANCE'S DESCRIPTION OF THE CANE RIDGE REVIVAL (1801)

When David Purviance, a Kentucky farmer, was forced out of politics because of his opposition to slavery, he turned instead to religion, studying for the ministry. He attended the huge religious revival at Cane Ridge and left this first-person account, which was published in 1848 by his son.

The Great Meeting at Caneridge commenced on Friday before the third Lord's day of August, 1801. From the commencement the roads were literally crowded with wagons, carriages, horsemen, and people on foot; all pressing to the appointed place; till by the Sabbath day, the grove that was then open near Caneridge meeting-house, was filled with wagons, tents, and people. It was supposed that there were between twenty and thirty thousand people there. Elder Stone in his journal remarks "A particular description of this meeting would fill a large volume, and then the half would not be told."

From the very commencement, an uncommon solemnity appeared to rest on the countenances of the people. Not unfrequently several preachers would be speaking within the bounds of the encampment without any interruption to each other. Wagons, stumps, and logs were used for stands. The preaching and exhortations, were interesting and impressive. Salvation free to all mankind, was proclaimed, and the willingness of Jesus, to save all that would come, was urged universally by the speakers. . . . many sinners were cut to the heart, and fell prostrate under an awful guilt and condemnation for sin. This was not confined to any one class. The moral, genteel and well raised: the giddy and profane, the wicked, the drunkard, and the infidel, the poor and also the rich, as well as the proud and vain, with all their gaudy attire, were brought down by the spirit of the ALMIGHTY, and they appeared to have forgotten every thing in this world in view of their souls eternal salvation.

I recollect having seen a small girl, not more than ten or eleven years of age, held up by a friend that stood in a wagon, while she invited sinners to the Savior. All who heard her, seemed to be astonished at her eloquence and judgment manifested in inviting sinners to God. . . . I have gone from the camp-ground into the woods, and it was difficult to get away from prayer; for more than a half mile, I could see people on their knees before God in humble prayer.

Perfect friendship, unanimity, and brotherly kindness prevailed. . . . The meeting lasted six days—the last sermon that was delivered on the occasion, was by a Methodist preacher, by the name of Samuel Hitt. It is known only to God, how many were converted at this meeting. There were no means, by which, even to ascertain how many professed religion.

The object of the meeting was not to build up any sect or party; but to bring sinners to the Savior. When the meeting was over, the people returned to their homes and friends.— There were many there from Ohio, and some from Tennessee, and the excitement spread with the people, and the young converts joined the churches of their choice; and the good work of reformation went on with irresistible force, and appeared like carrying every thing before it. Many were fully persuaded that the glorious millennial day had commenced, and that the world would soon become the Kingdom of our Lord Jesus Christ. But alas! That enemy of God and man, sectarianism, raised its hydra head, and "made war upon the saints of the most High God and overcame them," and the fair prospects of Zion were in some degree blasted.

Source: *The Biography of Elder David Purviance, with His Memoirs* (1848), Documenting the American South, University of North Carolina. http://docsouth.unc.edu/nc/purviance/purviance.html.

Henry Clay Henry Clay was 44 when Charles Bird King painted this portrait in 1821, but he looks much younger. He charmed both women and men. Margaret Bayard Smith said that he had a "power of captivation, which no one who was its object could resist."

and vice president. Although both Calhoun and South Carolina later became symbols of states' rights sentiment, in the postwar years South Carolinians believed that their international export economy was best served by a strong federal government.

Adams and Webster, both New Englanders, illustrated the compatibility of **National Republicanism** with the old Federalist views. Webster promoted the interests of New England's banking classes. He was a strong supporter of protective tariffs after the War of 1812, as Massachusetts merchants shifted from importing to manufacturing. Born in 1767, John Quincy Adams was influenced by his father's Federalist views and was first elected to the Senate in 1800 by the Federalist Massachusetts legislature. Adams broke rank with his party when it opposed the Louisiana Purchase.

Led by Clay, the new nationalists fashioned a vision of a Republican political economy based on individual entrepreneurial and market development (including domestic manufacturing), guided by an active federal government. Not surprisingly, their platform, loosely called the **American System**, was devised to appeal to local interests and identities. In the West and South, that meant promoting a national subsidy to improve transportation, whereas in the Northeast, it meant a protective tariff for domestic industries. To protect federal credit and stabilize currency and internal credit, they supported a national bank.

The various elements of the American System came before Congress as separate bills after the War of 1812, each with its own supporters. The bills to create the

Second Bank of the United States and to increase the national tariffs passed easily and were signed by President Madison. Authorized in 1816, the Second Bank of the United States was chartered for 20 years and located in Philadelphia, with the federal government providing one-fifth of its capital and appointing one-fifth of its directors. The tariff bill was less protective than some nationalists wished.

Transportation subsidies fared less well. Madison was skeptical about the constitutionality of this form of federal intervention. In his annual messages of 1815 and 1816, he urged Congress to initiate a constitutional amendment to clarify federal power in this area. A torn Congress eventually passed a bill creating a federal fund for internal improvements. On his last day in office, Madison vetoed it. In 1818, the federal government opened a section of the National Road, a highway that connected Baltimore to Wheeling, Virginia (later West Virginia). Otherwise, federal transportation initiatives fell victim to questions of constitutionality and regional jealousies; such projects were left to individual states.

James Monroe and National Republicanism

In 1816, Republican James Monroe ran for the presidency against Rufus King, the last Federalist to vie for that office. In the flush of postwar victory and prosperity and in the aftermath of the New Englanders' Hartford Convention, the returns were lopsided in Monroe's favor: 183 electoral votes to King's 34. He was the third Virginian in a row to hold the office.

Monroe's inaugural address sounded many familiar Republican themes: he praised the virtue of the American people and warned against corruption, greed, and the usurpation of power by foes of the republic. But in explaining the principles that would guide him in office, Monroe seemed almost to sound Federalist themes. He suggested the need for a more vigorous national defense and a more aggressive foreign policy toward Europe generally. He also recommended federally subsidized internal improvements as necessary for a prosperous, cohesive nation.

In office, Monroe governed with the nationalist bent suggested in his inaugural address. He asked former Federalist John Quincy Adams to be secretary of state (the presumed stepping-stone to the presidency). Together Monroe and Adams moved toward a more assertive foreign policy.

First, the administration arrived at agreements with Britain limiting British and American forces on the Great Lakes and along the 49th parallel to the Rocky Mountains. Then, in 1819, the United States forced Spain to fix definite borders to the Louisiana Purchase. After the purchase, Jefferson had attempted unsuccessfully to buy Florida from Spain. His successor, Madison, had simply declared that West Florida had been a part of the Louisiana Purchase all along. Taking the Florida peninsula had been left for James Monroe, who sent Andrew Jackson to lead a raid into Florida, ostensibly to frighten the Seminoles. When Jackson appeared to exceed his intentionally vague orders, he faced investigation by Congress (see Chapter 9), but he demonstrated that Spain was too weak, both politically and militarily, to hold onto Florida.

Capitulating to American forcefulness, in the Transcontinental Treaty of 1819, Spain ceded all of Florida to the United States in return for the US government's agreement to assume private American claims against Spain of about $5 million. The Transcontinental Treaty also clarified the border between the United States and

Spanish Mexico. The United States gave up claims not only to California (which few considered part of the original purchase) but also to Texas (which many Americans had hoped for). The boundary gained in return ran in a series of ascending steps from Louisiana to the Pacific, defining the United States as a nation that spanned the continent.

In the 1820s, under Monroe, the United States began to view itself as American, not quasi-European, and as protector of the Americas against Europe. By 1815, a number of former Spanish colonies, including Argentina, Chile, and Venezuela, had revolted, and an independence movement was under way in Mexico. As these new republics won their independence, they turned to the United States for recognition and support, while the absolute monarchies in Europe sought to preserve and extend their territorial empires. France offered to help Spain regain its colonies in South America. Russia reasserted and strengthened its long-standing claims in the Pacific Northwest.

Disavowing any future new territorial ambitions for itself in the Americas, Great Britain offered to make a joint declaration with the United States warning other nations against intruding in the internal affairs of Western Hemisphere countries. An alliance with Britain would have enhanced US diplomatic credibility, but many Americans suspected that Britain would use its position to squeeze the United States out of South American markets.

Secretary of State John Quincy Adams convinced Monroe to refuse the British offer, and instead to act independently and issue a unilateral statement of support for the new republics. Adams hoped that being identified with this policy would help him shed the pro-British tag that was associated with many New Englanders.

In his annual message to Congress in 1823, Monroe enunciated the policy that has since become known as the **Monroe Doctrine**. Monroe asserted a special relationship between the United States and all parts of North and South America, with which, he insisted, "we are of necessity more immediately connected." "We . . . declare," he added, "that we should consider any attempt on their part to extend their system to any portion of this hemisphere as dangerous to our peace and safety." The Monroe Doctrine marked an important milestone in the development of American nationalism and internationalism. The United States asserted not only a new relation (as peer) to the European nations but also a new relation to the Americas. Surveillance over the nations of North and South America would be claimed as the domestic right of the United States.

The Missouri Compromise

Yet just as a more assertive nation flexed its muscles, internal divisions threatened to pull it apart. Since the first compromises on slavery at the Constitutional Convention in 1787 (see Chapter 7), it was clear that slavery had the potential to create fierce conflict. For decades, no one was willing to call the institution a positive good, and northerners and southerners both seemed to agree publicly that slavery was unfortunate and in due course it would just fade away. Nonetheless, each time slavery entered national politics—the debate over Louisiana, setting the terms for ending the slave trade (see Chapter 9)—southerners did all they could to protect the institution. Then, as slavery spread to newly acquired territories, northern opponents of the institution saw clearly that, rather than disappearing, as it seemed to be doing in the North, the institution was becoming stronger elsewhere. In the decade after 1810, the number of enslaved people in the United States increased 30 percent.

In 1819, when Missouri applied for permission to organize as a state, antislavery politicians made their move. In the House debate, New York representative James Tallmadge proposed that Missouri be admitted under two conditions. First, no more enslaved people were to be brought into the state, and second, slavery was to be gradually abolished after the state was admitted to the Union. Southerners unanimously opposed the amendment, whereas northerners voted unanimously for it. The more populous North carried the vote. Slavery's defenders warned that such an attack on private property was unconstitutional and would incite "servile war." But slavery's opponents insisted that the institution was both immoral and antirepublican. "You boast of the freedom of your Constitution," Tallmadge told them, "and yet you have slaves in your country."

But when the House bill reached the Senate committee charged with its consideration, the vote was reversed. The Tallmadge amendment died in committee, to be reintroduced in the next session.

By the time Congress reconvened, positions on both sides had hardened. All notions of an antislavery South were now dead. A northern congressman said, "I awoke as from a trance." The struggle over Missouri foreshadowed later congressional debates over slavery and made southerners wary of a strong federal government. As North Carolina senator Nathaniel Macon explained, "If Congress can make canals, they can with more propriety emancipate."

The firestorm over Missouri was finally resolved when Maine applied for statehood as a free state. At that time there were 22 states in the Union, 11 free and 11 slave. Under Speaker of the House Henry Clay's guidance, the bills admitting both states were linked, preserving the balance in the Senate. The compromise also provided that slavery would be permitted in the Arkansas Territory but excluded from the rest of the Louisiana Purchase. The compromise passed narrowly in March 1820.

Almost immediately, another problem arose when Missouri submitted a state constitution that barred free Black people and free persons of mixed heritage from the state. This was a clear violation of Article IV of the Constitution, which provided that citizens of one state should enjoy the rights of citizens in all states. Here was another sign of an emerging sectional division over the issue of Black citizenship. In 1821, during the second round of the Missouri crisis, that division was just beginning to show itself, as Henry Clay struggled to engineer a second compromise. Congress allowed Missouri to enter under the proposed constitution, but it demanded that the new state legislature promise never to interpret the clause to mean what it so obviously meant, that Missouri reserved the right to deny free African Americans their constitutional rights. The Missouri territorial legislature made the promise but withheld any power to bind the people of the state to what it said. Finally, in August 1821, President James Monroe greeted Missouri as the 24th state of the Union.

The Election of 1824 and the "Corrupt Bargain"

In the usual order of custom in the young republic, Secretary of State John Quincy Adams would have been Monroe's presumed successor. But by 1824 the Republican Party housed experienced men who considered themselves next in line. In addition to Adams, there were John C. Calhoun (secretary of war), Henry Clay (Speaker of the House), and William H. Crawford of Georgia (secretary of the Treasury). This group, which called itself the National Republicans, contained some of the nation's most experienced and respected leaders.

And then there was the outlier, Andrew Jackson. In spite of his fame as a war hero, when the Tennessee legislature nominated Jackson for the presidency in 1822, few politicians took the candidacy seriously, given his competition. But by 1824 voting Americans were beginning to pull back from the new expansive Republican vision. As a political unknown, without a legislative record, Jackson was free to run on his image, as a forceful leader and an outsider. An early indication of the storminess of the election came with the Republican nomination. Because James Monroe had not designated a successor, the selection was thrown to the Republican congressional caucus and was expected to benefit Crawford. But this time, the other candidates disowned the caucus as a corrupt and irregular institution so effectively that only 66 of a possible 216 Republican members of Congress even attended. Crawford did get the nod, but its value had been diminished.

In the election, no candidate claimed a majority either of the popular vote or of the Electoral College. The underdog Andrew Jackson came closest, with 43 percent of the popular vote and 99 electoral votes. Next was Adams, with 31 percent of the popular vote and 84 electoral votes. Crawford managed only 41 electoral votes, and Clay came in last with 37. (Calhoun had withdrawn.) See Map 10–1.

The election was thus thrown to the House of Representatives, where members had to select from among the three candidates with the highest electoral count. As the highest vote getter, Jackson was confident at first, but by late December he began to hear rumors "that deep intrigue is on foot." Those rumors were correct. Although Adams did not receive a single popular vote in Kentucky, and although

Map 10–1
The Election of 1824 Almost all of Adams's electoral votes came from the Northeast, while Jackson's were spread through the South, the Midwest, and the Mid-Atlantic.

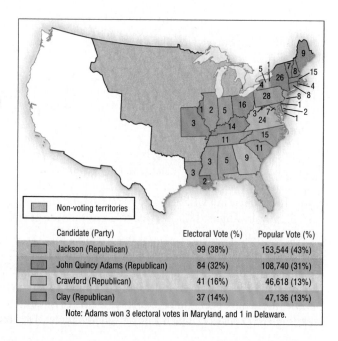

Candidate (Party)	Electoral Vote (%)	Popular Vote (%)
Non-voting territories		
Jackson (Republican)	99 (38%)	153,544 (43%)
John Quincy Adams (Republican)	84 (32%)	108,740 (31%)
Crawford (Republican)	41 (16%)	46,618 (13%)
Clay (Republican)	37 (14%)	47,136 (13%)

Note: Adams won 3 electoral votes in Maryland, and 1 in Delaware.

the Kentucky legislature had directed its delegation to vote for Jackson, Clay overrode those instructions and also marshaled support for Adams in other states. Adams received the votes of 13 of the 24 state delegations. Jackson received 7, and Crawford received 4.

Jackson later charged that Adams had bought Clay's support with the promise of the post of secretary of state. Adams did give Clay that job, but Clay had had good reasons for allying himself with Adams. They shared similar political philosophies. In addition, Jackson and Clay vied for the same regional vote. Clay's support for him in 1824 would have helped Jackson build a stronger western base for 1828.

Jackson was furious. His supporters charged that the election had been stolen in a "**corrupt bargain**" brokered by insiders who debased the virtue of the republic and disregarded the clear will of the electorate.

The Adams Presidency and the Gathering Forces of Jacksonianism

In many respects, Adams's choice of Clay made perfect sense. Since the postwar period both men had shared a commitment to the so-called American System: the preservation of a national bank, the levying of a national tariff, and the improvement of infrastructure.

Adams continued to support these policies in office, even using his first annual message to Congress in 1825 to lay out a grand vision for federal involvement in the political economy. He called not only for economic projects, such as transportation improvements, but also for the creation of a national university, a national observatory, a naval academy, and an elaborate system of roads and canals supported by federal expenditures. He urged Congress not to be "palsied by the will of our constituents." His opponents railed that this was clear evidence of his intention to benefit the wealthy at the expense of the common people and that this branch of the Republican Party (increasingly identifying itself as the National Republicans) seemed more Federalist than Jeffersonian.

John Quincy Adams was a wise and principled statesman, but he was never able to set an independent agenda for his presidency. He was shadowed by the political battle that began with his election and by his unpopular identification with banking and mercantile interests. Defensive and prickly in public, he did not build strong political alliances, and he misread the gulf developing within the American electorate.

And Jackson's supporters worked hard to discredit Adams, especially on the issue of the tariff. Early on, the federal government had depended on the tariff and on land sales for most of its revenue. By the end of the War of 1812, the importance of the tariff for generating funding had declined, but its role in addressing the growing regional economic differences had increased. The 1816 tariff was protectionist, but only very mildly so, working to give some recognition to the importance of domestic manufactures. But the Panic of 1819, brought on in part by the United States' reliance on world markets, reenergized protectionists: a bill to raise tariffs on the entire list of imported products by 5 percent (even higher for cotton, wool, iron, and glass) failed passage by only one vote. It was broadly supported in the western and middle states and opposed in the South (where it was seen as favoring high-priced New England products), whereas New England split on the issue. But by 1824 New

England was committed enough to industrial growth to become solidly pro-tariff. That year, when Congress proposed a tariff that included levies of 35 percent on imported cotton, wool, hemp, and iron, passage was a forgone conclusion.

Passage of the 1824 tariff was ominous for several reasons. First, of course, it was vehemently opposed by the South. Second, neither the North nor the federal government really needed it. In 1824, the federal government reported a surplus of funds, a year when New England manufactures were doing well enough not to need the help. The tariff had become the language of sectionalism, but the underlying conflict was over the power of the federal government. This was not a simple question of nationalism versus localism. Jackson, a nationalist willing to support some level of protective tariff, had even conceded, "It is time we became a little more Americanized." The difference between Adams and Jackson was the question of federal legitimacy. In what actions could the federal government claim the authority of the American people? And in what actions did it overstep that authority? That conflict was now infused with a new energy.

THE SOCIAL AND POLITICAL BASES OF JACKSONIAN DEMOCRACY

Jacksonian democracy captured the hopes and fears of a rapidly changing country. As settlers looked for opportunity in the West, city dwellers struggled to make a living in the new urban landscape. Anyone who wanted to enter the market—to purchase land or establish a business—needed credit, but in a volatile economy, risk accompanied opportunity. When things went wrong, Americans looked for someone to blame—and for bold politicians to advocate their causes.

Settlers

The migration into the backcountry continued throughout the 1820s. After Maine in 1820 and Missouri in 1821, no new states entered the Union until Arkansas in 1835. But in the meantime the populations of the new states grew steadily, in some cases doubling and tripling in a single decade: Mississippi grew from 75,448 in 1820 to 136,621 in 1830, Illinois from 55,211 to 157,445, and Indiana from 147,178 to 343,031.

North or South, migrants wanted land. They also wanted easy credit and low prices—but they weren't always convinced that government was their friend in getting these. To be sure, the price of land per acre and the size of the minimum-permitted individual purchase had fallen steadily during the early nineteenth century. The Land Act of 1820 reduced the price to $1.25 per acre for a minimum purchase of 80 acres. In lowering the minimal outlay to $100, however, Congress also eliminated the 1800 provision that had permitted settlers to buy on credit from the government and added the requirement that land that wasn't promptly paid for would go back up for sale. This made small buyers even more dependent on easy credit from local or state banks. There were plenty of these institutions, but state and local bankers were often more interested in putting together big deals with land speculators than in making smaller loans to risky individual settlers. In 1819, when local banks had tried to foreclose on mortgages in arrears, other settlers had formed vigilante committees to intimidate potential buyers and convince the banks that foreclosure was not in their financial interest.

The obstacles to land purchase for ordinary citizens had kept alive the practice of squatting, of claiming land simply by occupying it, demanding that a person's labor on it over time be recognized as a legal claim. As they had in the late eighteenth century, squatters harassed surveyors and ran off sheriff's deputies. Even when a small settler had a legal claim, if the land was good, or the area promising, the settler was likely to have to fight off high-powered lawyers and their clients. Backwoodsmen, squatters, and settlers did not always share the same interests, but probably all would have agreed with William Manning that "no person can possess property without laboring, unless he get it by force or craft," and that "those that labor for a living and those who get one without laboring—or, as they are generally termed, the Few and the Many"—was "the great dividing line" of society.

Free Labor

Settlers were not alone in feeling abandoned to the wiles of the wealthy. Although farm labor would dominate the workforce for decades to come, by the second decade of the nineteenth century nonfarming wage labor was becoming more common. Especially in the cities of the coasts, growing numbers of people worked for wages in increasingly precarious circumstances. They had been hard hit by the war, and even improved prosperity afterward left many wage workers with barely enough money to meet their own and their families' needs. Like the frustrated settlers, wage workers worried that the new economy was keeping common working people

Emigrants Crossing the Appalachians This early nineteenth-century engraving depicts emigrants crossing the Appalachians on their way to Pittsburgh, Pennsylvania.

dependent on the rich. Workers had stuck with Jefferson and Madison through the embargo and the War of 1812, but their patience grew thin.

The Panic of 1819 strengthened that skepticism and gave rise to the beginnings of organized protest in the 1820s. Workers turned out in huge numbers to hear critics denounce the growing inequities of American life. Scotswoman Frances Wright, one of the most popular of these speakers, charged that the clergy conspired to keep workers shackled to superstition, inveighed against slavery, and advocated for women's rights.

In addition, workers began to form unions and go out on strike. Printers, weavers, carpenters, tailors, cabinetmakers, masons, stevedores, and workers in other crafts turned out on strike throughout major cities, protesting poor pay and long hours. Strikers argued that the shorter day was essential if they were to have time to refresh themselves, to be with their families, and to obtain the education necessary for newly enfranchised voters. Over time, these separate strikes merged into citywide and regional labor organizations. The first, the Mechanics' Union, was established in Philadelphia in 1827. Pledged to the 10-hour day, the union protested the exhaustion associated with industrialization and the "evils which . . . arise from a depreciation of the intrinsic value of human labor."

Suffrage Reform

At the founding of the nation, **suffrage** was restricted not just by gender and race but even more on the basis of property ownership and tax payment. Urban craft workers, who often owned little more than their tools and clothing, demanded the vote as the emblem of liberty. "Suffrage," as one editor insisted, "is the first right of a free people."

Territorial expansion also raised the question of suffrage. Settlers who owned little more than the mortgages on their land saw themselves as the chief embodiment of the democratic spirit.

The new, less settled states led in expanding white male suffrage. Vermont entered the Union in 1791 (the first new state after the original thirteen) with virtually universal white manhood suffrage. The next year, New Hampshire dropped its last qualification, and Kentucky entered the Union without restrictions on adult white males. Tennessee, which became a state in 1796, required that voters own property but did not set a minimum value. Ohio became a state in 1803 without property requirements for voting, and all the six states admitted between 1812 and 1821 entered with universal white male suffrage (see Map 10–2).

In 1817, Connecticut became the first of the older states to abolish all property qualifications for white men. In 1824, when Jackson made his first run for the presidency, only Virginia, Louisiana, and Rhode Island retained any significant restrictions on white male suffrage, and only 6 of the 24 states retained indirect selection of the delegates to the Electoral College.

The struggle for an expanded male suffrage was fought openly on the landscape of race. As suffrage was extended to all white males, it was withdrawn from African American men in New York, Maryland, Pennsylvania, Connecticut, and New Jersey (where single, propertied women also lost the right to vote). In addition, every new state admitted after 1819 specifically excluded African Americans from the vote. Through suffrage reform, white Americans refashioned the vote as the

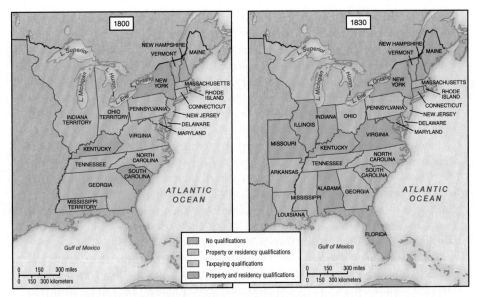

Map 10-2 Toward Universal White Male Suffrage As the western territories organized and entered the Union, they formed a band of states in which there were no property qualifications on white male suffrage, and often minimal taxpaying qualifications.
By 1830, Virginia and Connecticut were unusual in the nation for restricting white male
suffrage based on both property and tax payment. At the same time, free Black males
and women lost the vote where they had enjoyed it.

domain of white citizenship. "The people of this state are for . . . a political community of white persons," one Pennsylvanian asserted bluntly.

The partial exception to this pattern was Rhode Island, where elites blocked
universal white male suffrage throughout the 1830s. When, in 1841, white working
men called a People's Convention to demand universal white male suffrage, they rejected pleas to include African American men in their demands. Spurned by white
working men, African Americans supported the conservative opposition. When
state conservatives later broadened the franchise, they repaid African American
men for their earlier support by including them.

Opposition to Special Privilege and Secret Societies

Since the nation's founding, one strain of American political rhetoric had focused
on corrupt insiders who enjoyed opportunities not available to other citizens. In the
early nineteenth century, politics became a symbolic battle of the virtuous "many"
against the corrupt "few."

Early in the century, specially chartered corporations became visible symbols
of affluence and the target of these suspicions. Created by special acts of state legislatures, these corporations were, theoretically, open to all Americans. However, the
charters were granted on a personal basis to people of wealth, power, and reputation
who were known to individual legislators. The movement to use charters to promote
development accelerated after the War of 1812. States chartered companies to build
roads, provide transportation, and establish banks. Local reactions to chartered

projects were mixed. Many shared journalist William Leggett's bitterness that "not a road can be opened, not a bridge can be built, not a canal can be dug, but a charter of exclusive privileges must be granted for the purpose." Some of the specially chartered initiatives, especially banks, provided easy credit to local farmers and workers. When the Panic of 1819 ended that bubble of easy credit, shopkeepers, farmers, and urban workers were devastated. They focused their anger on eastern bankers, especially the Second Bank of the United States, and grew suspicious that the new Republican leadership would increase preferential rules. By 1820, John C. Calhoun noticed the appearance, in "every part of the Union," of "a general mass of disaffection to the Government . . . looking out anywhere for a leader."

Corporations were not the only focus of hard feelings. The old Republican fears of special privilege extended to secret societies that might give their members special access to money and success. In western New York, where the opening of the Erie Canal had ushered in an economic boom and widespread social instability, tensions exploded in a virulent fear of **Masons** in the late 1820s.

The Masonic movement had originated to counter aristocratic power and protect craft masons, but in the eighteenth century a new Order of Freemasons emerged, made up of urban businessmen, professionals, and politicians who pledged to support one another. By the 1820s, the Masons seemed to many working people to embody a dangerous antidemocratic spirit. This distrust was galvanized into popular opposition in 1826 by the mysterious disappearance (and presumed murder) of New Yorker William Morgan, who had written an exposé of the order's purported secret designs on public power. The story spread that Morgan had been abducted to Niagara Falls and then drowned. The outcry against this subversion of justice was magnified by the fact that public officials, including Andrew Jackson and Henry Clay, were also Masons. By 1827, New Yorkers had organized a separate political party to oppose the Masons. The **Antimason Party** spread from New York into other states, winning local elections in Massachusetts, Pennsylvania, and Vermont. In 1831, Antimasons held the first open presidential nominating convention, choosing William Wirt of Maryland as their candidate. Wirt carried only one state, and the party remained a minor player in national politics. Nevertheless, the battle against cabals illustrated the belief that American party politics was a struggle of common people against the monied aristocracy. This would become a staple of Jacksonian rhetoric.

SOUTHERN SLAVERY

Yet there was a darker side to the promise of a more popular democracy. Southern slavery was in fact another base of Jacksonian democracy: opportunity for southern whites meant the opportunity to own enslaved people. Between the Revolutionary and the Civil Wars, slave plantations spread across the southern frontier, creating one of the largest slave societies in history, stretching from Delaware to Texas. The freedom of some people was to come at the expense of the liberty of others.

Although only a minority of whites owned enslaved people at any one time, almost all hoped that they might. Moreover, the southern economy rested on slave property. By mid-century, the 4 million enslaved Americans were worth $3 billion—representing 19 percent of the wealth of the entire nation.

"Property in Man"

In this era, southern enslaved people worked in a variety of different circumstances—in cities, in factories, as skilled artisans, cooks, housekeepers, nurses, and most often as field hands. But what made all of them "slaves," no matter what they did or where they lived, was the fact that they were defined as property, treated as property, and defended as property.

By defining enslaved people as personal property, the slaveholders gave themselves the freedom to buy and sell their slaves almost without restraint. To be sure, Congress banned the foreign slave trade in the United States as of 1808 (the earliest date permitted by the Constitution). In anticipation of this action, between 1800 and 1808 slave traffickers delivered and southern planters purchased at least 40,000 Africans into American slavery. But by then a domestic trade in enslaved people was beginning to flourish, becoming a mainstay of southern slavery until the Civil War.

Slavery had already begun to expand westward when Eli Whitney built the first **cotton gin** in 1793. Nevertheless, his invention stimulated a boom in cotton production and with it the aggressive expansion of the South into the new cotton lands in the West. In response, eastern slave owners began to enhance their profits by trading in enslaved people—selling their own excess labor farther south and west to newer farms in Mississippi, Alabama, and western Tennessee and Kentucky. There is evidence that slaveholders were aware of the additional profits to be garnered from enslaved women who bore many children, and many went out of their way to encourage slave reproduction.

The Domestic Slave Trade

Wherever there was slavery, there were slave markets. Between 1790 and 1860, more than 850,000 enslaved people were forced to migrate south, perhaps as many as one-third by 1820, transported by slave traders. The internal slave trade was often a highly organized business, with firms of 10 or 20 employees (bosses, clerks, guards, agents) in fine offices in Charleston, Richmond, and Baltimore. Professional traders enabled slave owners in the upper South to turn their enslaved people, particularly valuable young people, into a lucrative commodity. Any enslaved person had a 50 percent chance of being sold. More than the plantation, the slave market reflected the defining feature of slavery as "property in man."

The slave market was a ghastly collision of worlds: for potential buyers, sellers, and onlookers, it was a lively gathering place (like a club or tavern) for white men, whose easy camaraderie stood in stark contrast to the terror of the Black people about to be offered for sale. Indeed, the amiability of the market helped potential buyers more easily to see themselves as rational, well-motivated businessmen, rather than purveyors of misery. And yet the truth of the transaction permeated the place—in the audible sobs of mothers and children, in the rough, physical inspections of the naked enslaved people, and in the absence of white females, a powerful silent admission that what was occurring at the slave market was so nakedly brutal as to taint the purity of white women.

The formerly enslaved **Frederick Douglass**, born in Maryland, later described the terror that the threat of being "sold South" struck in the hearts of enslaved

African Americans. After his owner died when Douglass was eight or nine years old, the enslaved workers were hustled together to be appraised and allotted—some to be retained by family members, some to be "sold at once to the Georgia traders." "I have no language to express the high excitement and deep anxiety which were felt among us poor slaves during this time," Douglass wrote. "Our fate for life was now to be decided. We had no more voice in that decision than the brutes among whom we were ranked. A single word from the white men was enough—against all our wishes, prayers, and entreaties—to sunder forever the dearest friends, dearest kindred, and strongest ties known to human beings." One in three enslaved children under 14 was separated from at least one parent as a result of westward migration. One in three slave marriages in the upper South was destroyed.

Plantation Slavery

The symbol of the nineteenth-century South was the cotton plantation, a large commercial farm owned and operated by a single white family and worked by a large number of enslaved laborers, toiling up and down plowed rows planting the seed in the spring, hoeing the young plants in the hot summer sun, and picking the sticky cotton balls in the autumn. For good reason, this image seemed to capture life in the slave South. Although slavery existed in America long before the cotton boom of the late 1790s, that boom vastly increased the demand for enslaved people. Cotton was a crop highly suitable to slave economies. It could be grown on large plantations tended by gangs of coerced workers who (thanks to the relatively short height of the cotton plant) could be kept under supervision at all times.

The number of enslaved on a plantation varied widely. Of the nearly 4 million enslaved inhabitants of the South in 1860, probably three-quarters lived on plantations with 10 or more enslaved people. Sugar plantations averaged 30 or more workers. Rice plantations were smaller, but still larger on average than cotton and tobacco farms. The wealthiest families of the South owned hundreds of people on several different plantations, often hundreds of miles apart. Owning large tracts of land and large numbers of enslaved workers was the highest symbol of status in the South. Cotton plantations proliferated in the new western lands. Meanwhile, tobacco plantations in Virginia and North Carolina, rice plantations in South Carolina and Georgia, and sugar plantations in Louisiana continued to flourish.

The conditions of enslaved life varied with the crop. For an enslaved person, there was nothing worse than the harsh life on the sugar plantation. Masters there drove workers hardest, producing the highest rates of sickness and death in the South. The crop cycle for sugar was 13 months or more, which meant that the planting of a new crop overlapped with the harvesting of the old one—producing weeks of almost unbearably intense labor. Because sugar, unlike cotton or tobacco, had to be processed immediately on harvesting, sugar plantations had to have the boiling and pressing machinery to rush the cane immediately into production. For these reasons sugar planters preferred to buy strong adult men. Fewer women meant fewer slave families on sugar plantations. To top it off, this intense exploitation took place in the hottest, swampiest parts of the South.

Higher rates of sickness and death combined with lower rates of reproduction meant that sugar planters had to restock their slave labor force frequently with newly purchased enslaved people. The cost of the sugar presses, plus the cost of buying large numbers of the most expensive slaves—strong young men—meant that only the wealthiest owners could afford to set up sugar plantations. The needs of the sugar parishes of southern Louisiana sustained the Old South's largest slave market, in New Orleans.

Rice cultivation was not quite as lethal, but it was also centered in the sickliest low-country regions of the South—the coastal tidewater regions of South Carolina and Georgia, where rice workers stood ankle deep in mud under the blazing sun in snake-infested, swampland fields. Skilled rice cultivators sometimes operated under a task system, in which workers were assigned a specific task for the day and were able to exercise some autonomy over their labor. Over time, however, rice planters shifted to a gang-labor system more familiar to cotton plantations.

Sugar and rice were restricted by geography to relatively contained coastal regions of the South. The vast majority of enslaved people worked cultivating cotton and, to a lesser extent, tobacco on farms and plantations in the drier inland regions. Growing seasons for these crops were shorter, and the plantations were more self-sufficient in foodstuffs. As a result, cotton and tobacco slaves were relatively healthy. On large cotton plantations, enslaved people were more likely to be organized in gangs, set at repetitive tasks under close supervision. Cotton workers dragged their harvest to the gins that pulled the sticky cotton fibers from their bolls, continuing by the light of torches long after sunset. Tobacco workers were busier in the spring, carefully transplanting young plants and pruning off extra shoots.

Not all plantation slaves were field workers. On tobacco farms, enslaved people tended the drying leaf. On sugarcane plantations, workshops were needed to wash, chop, and squash the stalks and reduce their juices to sugar. On big cotton and tobacco plantations, as much as one-quarter of the workforce was assigned to domestic service or to crafts intended to make the plantation more self-sufficient. Although white observers tended to view household servants as fortunate, their lot was not necessarily better than that of field workers. Constantly on call, their workday could last even longer than that of field workers. They were also more vulnerable to the whims and moody outbursts of owners.

More independent than the house slaves were the 5 to 8 percent of the workforce trained for craft work. Men became carpenters, ironworkers, and boatmen. A smaller number of women became spinners, weavers, seamstresses, and dairymaids. Because they worked in separate shops, craft workers often enjoyed a degree of autonomy rare for most enslaved people.

Other Varieties of Slavery

Although most enslaved African Americans were held on fairly sizable plantations, some of the enslaved worked in other settings. On large plantations that did not always require the work of everyone, and on older plantations where the soil was exhausted, planters made part of their income by renting out

A smaller number of the enslaved worked in extractive industries or mills in the South. In Kentucky, Virginia, and West Virginia, for example, enslaved people toiled in saltworks. White people held virtually all of the supervisory positions, but the enslaved tended and stirred the boiling kettles of brine and prepared the salt for drying and packing. As the industry grew, it supported an expanding economy in lumber, coal mining, boatbuilding, and shipping (down the Ohio and Mississippi Rivers). Some of these related jobs (cutting lumber, operating boats and ferries, coal—and even gold-mining) were also done by enslaved people, and some by free workers whose employment depended on a slave-based industry.

Neither slave owning nor plantation farming typified the experiences of southern whites, most of whom lived on small holdings of several hundred acres or less. In 1860, three out of four southern households had no enslaved people. Some of these "yeoman" farmers hired enslaved people from nearby planters, a stepping-stone into the slaveholding class for the most successful. They often relied on nearby planters to gin their cotton, sell their crops, or rent them an enslaved person for a brief period of time.

Although most white people did not own enslaved people, the institution of slavery influenced their material lives and personal values. Slaveholders could afford to buy the best lands near rivers that provided them with ready access to markets. A workforce of millions of unpaid laborers meant that there were fewer stores and businesses in the slave states than in the North. A large number of rivers flowing from inland regions to coastal ports reduced the need for expensive railroads and canals. All of this meant that the southern economy remained less developed than the North's, and this had important consequences for the southern whites who owned no enslaved people. For subsistence farmers, the relatively underdeveloped slave economy offered some measure of protection. For more ambitious farmers, slavery restricted economic opportunity to the accumulation of land and enslaved people. Small farmers could hire field slaves from larger planters more cheaply than they could hire free labor, and planters could put a person to craft work for less than it would cost to hire a free artisan.

Because southern slavery was overwhelmingly agricultural, the South had fewer and smaller cities than the North. Even in the older seacoast states, less than 3 percent of southerners lived in cities. This number included planters taking refuge during the malaria season, enslaved people in domestic service for the urban professional class, and the free African American population. Traditionally, southern planters looked to Philadelphia and New York for services and luxury goods. When planters sought alternatives to this pattern of external dependence, they looked not to local villages or towns but to their own plantations, reassigning field workers to produce the butter, cheese, and tools they might otherwise have purchased locally. With a few exceptions, the economies of southern cities were based narrowly on the commerce of enslaved people and cotton.

As ideas about the family became more sentimental in the nineteenth century, prosperous slaveowners adapted these new ideas to the plantation. They tried to convince slavery's critics—and perhaps themselves—that the plantation was like a family presided over by affectionate parents who had only the best interests of their "children" at heart, and, as preposterous as it might seem, that their enslaved people loved them. The South Carolina planter Henry Hammond explained to a British abolitionist, "We . . . content ourselves with our dear labor under the consoling reflection that what is lost to us is gained to humanity." The more slavery came under attack, the more slave owners insisted, even in the face of powerful evidence to the contrary, that the plantation and its owners were both modern and moral.

But make no mistake: enslaved people were another part of the master's property and were fiercely defended as such. Because the accumulation of enslaved people was a source of wealth in its own right, southern reformers argued that the economic interests of the master could dovetail with the benign treatment of his human property. That was the ideal, of course, but planters determined to secure a quick profit provided the enslaved with as little as possible and used the whip freely. One Mississippi slave owner hired an overseer to "whip up" the enslaved, calculating that the harsh treatment would double their productivity. Slavery was a system designed to turn a profit.

Resistance and Creativity Among Southern Enslaved People

For enslaved people, slavery was not merely a system of enforced and often harsh labor. It was also a system of daily survival, practically and emotionally. It was a struggle against arbitrary authority, a monotonous diet, the constant threat of brutal treatment, and the breakup of families and communities. Slavery gave masters so much power over their enslaved people that the treatment they meted out necessarily varied widely from one owner to another. The enslaved people themselves spoke of "good masters" and "mean" ones. On any given plantation the impulses of a brutal or a paternalistic master could be offset by an overseer who might be competent or cruel, or by a mistress who might be kindly or mean-spirited. Particular enslaved people might be singled out as favorites, others for especially harsh treatment.

Yet most masters and enslaved people came to an accommodation that allowed the system to function on a day-to-day basis. Plantation routine created norms and expectations. The enslaved worked "from sunup to sundown" and ate their predictable meals at predictable hours. Diligent masters set clear expectations for the amount of labor their enslaved people were to perform and equally clear guidelines for the food, clothing, and shelter provided them, as well as the punishments meted out for infractions of the rules. Enslaved people in turn came to expect certain "privileges" such as free time—generally Saturday afternoon and Sunday, as well as a yearly holiday at Christmas—and passes to leave the plantation to visit spouses and children on neighboring farms. Arbitrary punishments, cruel overseers, or the withdrawal of privileges could disrupt the smooth operation of the plantation and undermine its profitability.

At the same time, slavery vested so much arbitrary power in the master that the system could be defined less by what was routine than by what it allowed. Wanton murder of an enslaved person was illegal, but killing an enslaved person who resisted the master's authority was not. People were maimed and branded often enough that inventors devised special instruments for them, and owners included descriptions of scars and other signs of torture in their advertisements for those who had escaped.

Enslaved Person with Scars Slave owners used a variety of methods to maintain worker disciplne. Some masters tried to entice their enslaved people with small privileges in exchange for hard work and cooperation. Many others relied instead on the cruelty of the lash.

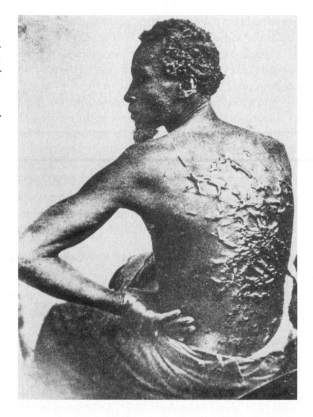

Few enslaved people escaped the familiar casual humiliations of the system. It was not unusual for enslaved women to bear children whose fathers were free and white. Undoubtedly, some intimate relations between enslaved women and free men were consensual, but most were not. In her memoir *Incidents in the Life of a Slave Girl*, Harriet Jacobs described the limited choices available to enslaved women. Jacobs's master began making sexual advances when she was only 15: "Shudder[ing] to think of being the mother of children who should be owned by my old tyrant," and hoping to make him so angry that he would sell her, Jacobs entered a sexual relationship with another white man, with whom she eventually bore two children.

Among southern whites, nothing was so fearful as the prospect of outright slave rebellion. Historically, slave rebellions were quite rare and almost never successful. But slave revolts and their rumor periodically shook the white population—the Gabriel rebellion in 1800 and the German Coast uprising a decade later (see Chapter 9), then the Denmark Vesey conspiracy in South Carolina in the 1820s and finally the **Nat Turner** rebellion in 1831(see "Nullification Crisis," this chapter)—and southern masters never fully let down their guard. While southern whites feared the prospect of slave rebellion, slave resistance usually took forms other than outright or attempted rebellion. Although masters and mistresses were ready enough to punish enslaved people without cause, individual enslaved people also set boundaries on that punishment. In his *Narrative of the Life of Frederick Douglass, An American Slave*, Douglass recalled how he had been rented out to

Edward Covey, who whipped Douglass regularly for six months. And then one day Douglass fought back, brawling with Covey for two hours until, exhausted and bleeding, the white man gave up. He never tried to whip Douglass again.

Most forms of resistance were less dramatic than Douglass's act of defiance. Feigned illness or ignorance, carelessness, a slow pace of work—all of these diminished the power of the master or mistress or driver, forcing him or her to adjust to the distinctive tempo or personality of the laborer. Field workers carved out implicit understandings with their masters about at least some of the terms of their labor. For example, task groups finishing early expected to be rewarded with free time and individuals with particular expertise expected deference from drivers, overseers, and even owners. Enslaved people were also able to accumulate a certain status, based on age or expertise or their place in the slave community, which owners could not completely ignore altogether.

To focus solely on their acts of resistance, however, is to see unfree African Americans only in relation to the institution of slavery. Albeit with one eye always on survival, enslaved African Americans also established familial and community bonds and cultural traditions. Parenthood often came to the enslaved unchosen or, if chosen, still under circumstances choreographed by owners (who often tried to arrange partners). Certainly, some enslaved people—like some free people—were unable to navigate the responsibilities of parenthood successfully. Separated from spouses and children, many enslaved people never had the chance to try. All these conditions make the record of slave parenting all the more impressive. Parents taught their children to fish and hunt and cook. They praised their children. They told them stories about their grandparents and great-grandparents. White owners felt they were the masters of all their chattel, but African American parents made certain their children understood that, as Jacobs remembered her father's words, "You are my child, and when I call you, you should come immediately, if you have to pass through fire and water."

Enslaved Americans also created communities of custom, both formally and informally. Market women carried produce and handicrafts to county seats and gossiped while they traded with local whites. Men fished and trapped small game. Men and women perfected skills at cooking and storytelling, quilt making and wrestling, and gained reputation and status among their friends. Whites denied legal recognition to slave marriages, but enslaved people sanctioned their own relationships, combining African ceremonies with European wedding rituals.

As enslaved people built the economy of the South, they also left a lasting imprint on the culture of southern whites and Blacks. Enslaved African Americans began converting to Christianity in the late eighteenth century, and many embraced the religious revivals of the early nineteenth century. Yet as they accepted Christianity, they made it their own. Slave preachers made selective use of Christian themes, emphasizing the story of Moses and the escape from bondage over homilies on the importance of absolute obedience. Newly arrived Africans provided a constant infusion of African religious forms, such as dancing, spiritual singing, chanting, and clapping, as well as distinctly African and Afro-Caribbean religions, such as voodoo. Slave religious practice became both the embodiment and the instrument of self-assertion. The call to "cross over Jordan" in the refrain of many slave songs symbolized the harshness of slave life but perhaps also the singer's intention to escape.

SLAVERY AND NATIONAL DEVELOPMENT

By 1827, when New York finally concluded its long abolition process, few enslaved people resided in the North and Northwest. But in the North, as in the South, dependency on slavery was not a simple matter of owning or not owning enslaved people. A free American worker might never see an enslaved person and yet be dependent on the shipping business that carried slave-produced goods or the manufacturing or farming enterprises that supplied planters' needs. An American proud of the country's growth might cherish elaborate shirts and petticoats without ever wondering where the cotton came from. A white American might never have seen an enslaved person and yet believe that there was some natural association of African Americans with servility.

Slavery and Industrialization in the Northeast

As capitalism developed in northwestern Europe and the northern United States, it generated an explosion of commerce that reached across the globe. But instead of spreading freedom, the profits of commerce intensified the various forms of social organization it touched. Commerce made plantation slavery more profitable in the Americas; and it made factory labor more profitable in England and the northern United States. Here was the paradox that would one day bring civil war to the United States: commerce tied two incompatible societies together, one in the South based on slave labor, the other in the North based on free labor.

The seagoing economy of the central and northern coast had long benefited from commercial ties to southern slavery. Yankee ships and crews carried food to the slave islands of the Caribbean and slave-produced commodities to European markets. In the early nineteenth century, the northern economy began to develop robustly on its own, whereas the slave economy continued to depend on the northern and European markets for the sale of its cash crops.

In the North, cities such as Philadelphia, New York, and later Chicago began to stretch their economic tentacles deep into the surrounding countryside, and northern farms fed a growing army of city factory workers and other wage laborers. Meanwhile, southern cities such as Charleston and New Orleans remained chiefly commercial ports with few signs of the economic development beginning to emancipate northern cities from their long-standing commercial dependence on the southern slave economy.

Boosters of the southern slave economy missed the signs of the North's slowly emerging economic independence because their own cotton economy was thriving. The slaveholders were shipping ever-larger volumes of cash crops to the North—evidence, they thought, of increasing northern commercial dependence on southern slave society. In many ways the slaveholders were right. In the first half of the nineteenth century, merchants in New York and Philadelphia began to specialize in consolidating shiploads of consigned cotton and sending it to England, where agents arranged for sales to English textile manufacturers. Those agents then put together shipments of consumer goods for sale in the United States, often to southern planters. The importance of this commerce to the economy of the North cannot be measured in voyages alone. Every voyage required a ship and a crew. The ships were made in Boston, Salem, Essex, and other New England towns, where local residents were employed in logging or as carpenters, caulkers, or sailmakers and on the rope walks. The crews were mostly New England bred but also came from around the world and included African Americans and Native Americans. Overseas trade also developed the business services of seaport cities. Insurance companies and banks in mid-Atlantic and New England ports catered to southern planters, providing agents for their sales, protecting their goods against the risks of oceanic trade, and holding their debts.

Northerners also benefited from southern consumers. Planters' annual shopping trips to Philadelphia or New York prompted merchants to import expensive English furniture and Chinese porcelain and encouraged tailors, seamstresses, milliners, and glove makers to keep up with the latest European fashions. Peddlers carried household goods into the southern countryside, and northern bookbinders sold religious tracts and prescriptive manuals to southern households. The symbiotic relationship of northern industry and the slave South is nowhere clearer than in the textile mills of early nineteenth-century New England that powered the Industrial Revolution in the North. The desire for such mills was an old story in the republic, but it took slave-produced southern cotton to make that aspiration viable.

The cotton boom proved that commerce can intensify the differences between buyers and sellers. During and after the War of 1812, as the cotton economy was exploding, Francis Cabot Lowell and his associates made large investments in northern textile mills that employed free wage laborers. The profits of the cotton trade also paid for large tracts of land with rivers and falls and eventually supported industrial towns, with all their ancillary commerce, across Rhode Island and Massachusetts. As the textile factories flourished, their commercial ties to the South flourished. In a sense, this was mutual dependency. Northern factory workers needed the cotton enslaved people produced, and the slaveholders needed northern factories as customers for their cotton. But the cotton trade forged a potentially explosive connection, for it enhanced rather than diminished the differences between northern capitalism and southern slavery.

The many linkages between northern and southern economies led some slaveholders to predict defiantly that the Yankees would never wage war on slavery because they were too dependent on the South. But this was an illusion. What the northerners wanted was cotton, whether it came from Egypt or Alabama, whether it was produced by wage laborers or by enslaved people. The statistics showing the importance of cotton to America's overseas trade impressed slaveholders. But what those statistics did not show was the far greater volume of trade and commerce within the northern states themselves that was dependent on the development of cities and industry at home rather than oceanic commerce. The textile mills needed the cotton produced by southern enslaved people, but the mill owners and shoe manufacturers of New England needed even more the northern workers and western farmers who were steadily becoming each other's best customers. Due to industrialization, the South was more dependent on the North than ever, but the North was not nearly as dependent on the South as it had once been.

Slavery and the Laws of the Nation

The men who wrote the Constitution had compromised on the issue of slavery, and it is the nature of compromises to produce ambiguities. After the Constitution was ratified, for example, both New York and New Jersey abolished slavery in their states—completing the process of emancipation in the North. Congress reenacted the Ordinance of 1787, prohibiting the importation of enslaved people into the Old Northwest and into the federal territories of the Old Southwest. And in 1807, the earliest possible date allowed by the Constitution, Congress prohibited the importation of any more enslaved people from the Atlantic slave trade. Under the Constitution, the states were now free to abolish slavery on their own, and the federal government assumed the power to regulate and even prohibit slavery in the territories. The Founders' sensibilities were reflected in their deliberate decision to refer to the enslaved as "persons" rather than property throughout the Constitution.

At the same time, however, the Constitution recognized and even protected slavery from federal interference in the states where it already existed. The Three-Fifths Clause, for example, gave white southerners disproportionate power in the House of Representatives and the Electoral College (in which the number of electors for each state was based on the number of senators and representatives). Article IV gave masters the right to capture and return enslaved people who ran away: "No person held to service or labour in one state, under the laws thereof, escaping into another, shall, in consequence of any law or regulation therein, be discharged from such service or labour, but shall be delivered up on claim of the party to whom such service or labour may be due." The article avoided the word "slave," but everybody referred to it as the "fugitive slave clause" of the Constitution.

Legal experts and lawmakers agreed that the Constitution prohibited the federal government from interfering with slavery in the states where it existed. But this left several questions unanswered. Did Congress have the power to interfere with slavery in the territories? Could Congress regulate the interstate slave trade? Was the federal government constitutionally obliged to protect the interests of slaveholders on the high seas? And who was responsible for enforcing the fugitive slave clause, the federal government or individual states? In 1793, for example, Congress enacted a fugitive slave law that made it a federal crime to aid an escaping enslaved person. But it left enforcement of the law to the states, and in the North accused runaways were often guaranteed the due process rights of free citizens, much to the dismay of the slaveholders. The slaveholders objected because enslaved people were, by definition, not citizens. But northerners resented the Three-Fifths Clause for precisely the same reason. In principle, only citizens were supposed to be counted for purposes of representation. By counting as citizens three-fifths of the enslaved population, the Constitution rewarded southern states with enough extra representatives and Electoral College votes to help ensure the election of a string of presidents from the South. Their support for a limited federal government helped protect slavery from federal interference.

Local and state laws concerning slavery affected the lives of people in all the states. Northern states, for example, passed personal-liberty laws designed to protect free Blacks from being kidnapped into slavery by bounty hunters in search of fugitives from slavery.. These personal-liberty laws made it much harder for masters to enforce the fugitive slave clause of the Constitution. Southern masters deeply resented what they saw as northern-state interference with their rights of property. Conversely, when Charlestonians, fearful of the influence of free Black sailors over South Carolina enslaved people, empowered sheriffs in southern ports to lock up free Black sailors, they affected the lives and the employment of men from Boston and Nantucket and New York. The South Carolina Negro Seamen Act of 1822 not only specified the imprisonment of Black sailors but also required a bond from their captains to cover the costs of incarceration. Under pressure from a planters' organization, the sheriff of Charleston imprisoned free Jamaican sailor Harry Elkinson. In court, lawyers argued that any treaty that interfered with the power of the state to guard against internal revolution must be unconstitutional. The court rejected this position, but South Carolina continued to enforce the act. By this time, Black sailors made up roughly a fifth of northern seamen—a proportion far higher than their presence in the free population. Sailing was an important occupation for them and their families. The act in effect made hiring them a handicap to any captain using South Carolina's ports and jeopardized the sailors' employment. The South Carolina act was later copied by Louisiana, North Carolina, Alabama, Georgia, Florida, and Texas.

Free Black People in a Republic of Slavery

By 1815, some 200,000 African Americans lived as free inhabitants of the United States, most of them in urban areas. Whether they were more than inhabitants—whether they were citizens—varied from state to state and from North to South.

Free Blacks faced formidable discrimination in all parts of the country. In the slave South, their very existence was a threat to the system, both in the possibilities of freedom they represented and in the avenues of communication they offered enslaved people. Southern and border states responded by tightening laws permitting individual emancipation, by increasing surveillance of enslaved people, and by regulating the movement and occupations of free Black people. Southern courts increasingly argued that the "taint" of color followed African Americans out of slavery, assuming that free Blacks lacked the privileges and immunities of citizens. Free Blacks in the South were barred from militias, from the ownership of weapons, and from occupations that might bring them into contact with enslaved people, such as operating groceries or taverns. What's more, they lived in daily danger of being enslaved, especially as the demand for slaves in the new southern territories increased. It was worth a free Black person's life to cultivate ties with the white community, should he or she need authority to ward off the greed of traders. Some border states—including Maryland, New Jersey, and Ohio—barred free Blacks from settling within their borders.

Free Blacks in the North suffered from similar discriminations, but their conditions varied from state to state. In New England, Blacks could vote and send their children to public schools alongside white children. In other states, such as New York, free Black men could vote only if they met a property qualification not required of white men. Elsewhere, Blacks were barred from voting altogether. Most northern courts assumed that Blacks were citizens entitled to own property, to make contracts, to move about freely, and, if accused of crimes, to have a jury trial. But some northern states, particularly along the borders of the South, prohibited free Blacks from moving into the state, thus denying them one of the traditional "privileges and immunities" of citizenship. And as in the South, Blacks were often segregated from whites in schools, churches, theaters, cemeteries, hotels, streetcars, ferries, and railways.

In the North and the South, however, the laws were not always a reliable measure of social practice. Often, free Blacks and whites interacted every day in ways that defied state statutes. They did business with one another, attended the same churches, and helped one another in times of need. In some southern states, the laws restricted free Blacks from owning land and houses, but free Blacks did so anyway. Periodically, states and localities would require free Blacks to be licensed for certain jobs or to carry freedom papers with them at all times, but the laws were only erratically enforced. The threat of enforcement, however, was a constant source of pressure on free Black communities across the South.

Within this complicated mosaic of formal and informal discriminations, free African Americans found ways to survive, to earn a living, and, once in a while, to flourish. By the 1820s, the self-help movement founded at the beginning of the republic had yielded many African American mutual-aid and benevolent associations. Organizing was most lively in Philadelphia, where free Blacks established more than 40 new societies between 1820 and 1835, but the self-help impulse extended south to Baltimore and Charleston and north to New York and Boston. Although some societies were clearly limited in membership to relatively prosperous free Blacks, self-help organizing crossed economic lines: coachmen, porters, barbers, brick makers, sailors, cooks, and washer-women all formed associations.

The growth of white racial prejudice in the nineteenth century was reflected not simply in the spread of laws discriminating against Blacks but also in the form that renewed calls for the abolition of slavery sometimes took. In 1816, a group including prominent national politicians, northerners, and slave owners formed the **American Colonization Society** (ACS). Styling itself as a benevolent organization, the Society (whose founders included Andrew Jackson, Francis Scott Key, Daniel Webster, and Henry Clay) determined that because of "unconquerable prejudice resulting from their color," African Americans could succeed only in Africa, which was declared their home (although by 1816 almost all enslaved Americans had been born in the republic). Made up of wealthy, influential white men, the ACS lobbied Congress for funds. It received $100,000 in 1819 and sent out its first emigrant ship in 1820. Dedicated to removing free African Americans from their native land to Liberia, in Africa, the ACS signaled waning white support for a racially integrated republic.

JACKSONIAN DEMOCRACY IN ACTION

The Democratic campaign of 1828 ushered in a new era of national politics, one that mobilized the public in support of a popular president. To make the point that they were a new breed, Jacksonians began to refer to themselves as "Jacksonian Democrats" (or just "the Democrats").

The Election of 1828

The campaign was personal and vicious. Adams's supporters tarred Jackson as an undisciplined liar and blasphemer. They accused him of having married Rachel Robards before her own divorce was final. Jackson supporters retorted that Adams was an aloof aristocrat, corrupted by his years of living abroad, his victory in 1824 illegitimate.

Earlier campaigns had been fought primarily on the local level and among a far smaller group of potential voters, but in 1828 New York senator Martin Van Buren coordinated a Democratic national campaign designed to appeal to a mass electorate. Van Buren oversaw the creation of a highly controlled party hierarchy of local and state societies linked to the national organization. He pioneered the use of carefully choreographed demonstrations and converted nonpartisan occasions (such as Fourth of July celebrations) into Democratic rallies. Van Buren also used political imagery to evoke campaign themes. Trading on Jackson's nickname, "Old Hickory" (for the hardest wood in the United States), campaign workers handed out hickory canes at political events. Supporters also used editorials and campaign tracts to describe Jackson as the embodiment of the common man.

When the votes were counted in 1828, almost three times as many men had voted than in 1824, and Jackson had won a clear majority (see Map 10–3): 56 percent of the popular vote and 178 electoral votes to Adams's 83 electoral votes. Although Adams had retained New England, New Jersey, Delaware, and northern Maryland, Jackson had solidly taken the South and the West, as well as Pennsylvania, much of New York, and even northern Maine.

Jackson was elected by a cross section of voters who identified with his stance as an outsider to, and victim of, eastern elites. Van Buren had put together a coalition of "planters of the South and plain Republicans of the North," actively suppressing the divisive issue of slavery and instead appealing to those who believed that special privilege was denying them their chance of prosperity. He was the candidate of westerners, migrants, settlers, and landowners who opposed eastern banks and congressional land policies, but he also drew support from urban professionals, shopkeepers, laborers, and craftsmen. Jackson claimed the mantle of Jefferson, who also had favored the individual common American and warned against concentrations of economic and political power.

At the same time, the Jacksonians were vague about exactly where the heart of their new democratic movement resided. Structurally, they believed that it evolved from the states, which restrained federal power. At the same time, however, Jackson's strong conviction that he was the people and that his will was indistinguishable from theirs confused matters. The ironic result was a shift of power from the states to the executive during the presidency of the man elected to protect the common man.

The tendency to personalize political struggle characterized Jackson's presidency. He never forgave the National Republicans for publicly questioning the legitimacy of his marriage. Later, he viewed his battle against the Second Bank of the United States in the same highly personal terms: "The Bank," he informed Van Buren, "is trying to kill me, but I will kill it."

If Jackson understood himself as the embodiment of the people's will, he understood the new Democratic Party as its direct instrument. After personal loyalty to Jackson, party loyalty became the avenue to appointment and the justification for an unprecedented turnover in appointees. The overall results were mixed. Jackson expanded the powers of the presidency, but his conviction that he alone embodied the true virtue of the republic also led to personal pettiness, widespread patronage, and turmoil within his cabinet. His efforts to abolish the Second Bank of the United

Map 10-3 The Election of 1828 In 1828, Jackson solidified his hold on the South and Midwest and even made inroads in the Northeast. Almost three times as many men voted as in 1824, and while Adams received almost 400,000 more votes, Jackson got almost half a million more.

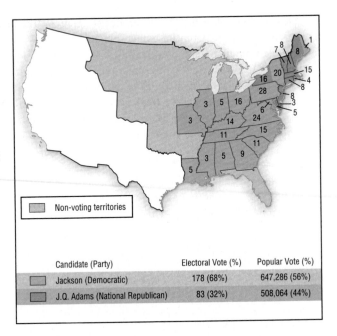

Candidate (Party)		Electoral Vote (%)	Popular Vote (%)
	Jackson (Democratic)	178 (68%)	647,286 (56%)
	J.Q. Adams (National Republican)	83 (32%)	508,064 (44%)

States created serious hardship for average Americans, and his hostility to Native Americans resulted in widespread death and impoverishment.

The Bank War

The message of the new presidency was clear: reform. Jackson turned his eye on the special privileges and unfair advantages of the rich and well connected. Jackson had long associated this obstacle with Henry Clay, John Quincy Adams, John Calhoun, and the Republican caucus. By 1828, Jackson focused his anger on the Second Bank of the United States.

Jackson hated the bank for all the reasons southerners and westerners did: it was powerful and privileged, and wealthy easterners and foreign investors controlled its private stock. Also, as much as they liked easy credit, most Americans were suspicious of banknotes of all kinds. They had been stung too often by counterfeiters and deadbeats.

But Jackson also had very personal reasons for his opposition. Soon after his first election, Jackson heard rumors that the bank had used its power to buy votes for Adams in 1828. Declaring that the bank threatened "the purity of the right of suffrage," Jackson vowed to oppose it.

Nicholas Biddle, the bank's president, rebuffed Jackson's criticisms. Confident the bank enjoyed broad support, Biddle decided to force the issue before the next presidential election. Although the bank's authorization ran until 1836, on January 6, 1832, Biddle asked Congress to take up renewal early. Jackson may have felt Biddle's behavior to be a personal challenge, because he vetoed it in 1832. "The rich and powerful," he thundered, "too often bend the acts of government to their selfish purposes. . . . When the laws undertake . . . to make the rich richer, . . . the humble members of society ... have a right to complain of the injustice of their Government."

The Democrats carried the bank veto proudly into the 1832 election as a contest of "the Democracy and the people, against a corrupt and abandoned aristocracy." The Republicans responded that Jackson's veto showed his tendency toward despotism. The Supreme Court had ruled the national bank constitutional, and Congress had voted to recharter it. Jackson had trammeled the authority of the other branches of government, assuming the sole right to determine the future of the bank.

Dismembering the Bank

Jackson won reelection in 1832, although by a smaller majority than in 1828. By 1833, he was ready to disassemble the Second Bank of the United States. He asked Secretary of the Treasury Louis McLane to select other banks into which the federal government could move its deposits. McLane balked, worried that the selection would be compromised by politics and that the state banks would lose all fiscal restraint. Impatient, Jackson replaced McLane with William J. Duane, and then replaced Duane with Attorney General Roger Taney. On October 1, 1833, the federal government began to distribute its deposits to 22 state banks. By the close of the year, the government deposits had been largely removed.

The deposits had been used to make loans to individuals and corporations around the country. To make the funds available, the Second Bank began furiously calling in loans and foreclosing on debts. In effect, Biddle was repeating the process that triggered the Panic of 1819. In six months he took more than $15 million worth of credit out of the economy.

As recession gripped the nation, the Senate passed an unprecedented resolution censuring Jackson for assuming "authority and power not conferred by the constitution and laws." Jackson's response underscored the new "democratic" politics of the times: "The President," he maintained (and no other branch of government), "is the direct representative of the American people." The expansion of white male suffrage (and the spreading practice of electing members of the Electoral College directly) made Jackson the first president who could claim to be elected directly by the voters. Congress, on the other hand, would soon become the power base of elites.

The first recession passed quickly as state banks tapped their federal deposits to churn out loans, and new wildcat banks took advantage of the glut of paper money. Much of the borrowing went for land sales.

The Specie Circular

Although he did not understand many aspects of banking, Jackson correctly believed that the excess of paper money in circulation had caused the recession. As soon as conditions improved, he implemented a hard-money policy. In 1833, he had announced that the federal government would no longer accept drafts on the Second Bank in payment of taxes, a move that reduced the value of the bank's notes. In 1834, Jackson declared that the "deposit" banks receiving federal monies could not issue paper drafts for amounts under $5 (later raised to $20), an action that reduced the small-denomination paper in circulation. In July 1836, he had the Treasury Department issue the Specie Circular, which directed land offices to accept only coins or precious metals in payment for western lands. This shut out actual settlers, who could not get together enough gold or silver for their purchases. Meanwhile, the Deposit Act, passed in 1836, expanded the number of "pet banks" to nearly 100 and distributed a federal surplus of more than $5 million to the states, on top of the more than $22 million already deposited in the state banks from the Second Bank of the United States. Underregulated and under local pressure, the state banks could not absorb these funds. They issued loans and printed money that vastly exceeded their assets. When the bubble burst in 1837, the nation faced the worst financial disaster of its young history.

A POLICY OF REMOVING INDIGENOUS PEOPLE

When Jackson looked west, he saw a different sort of problem. For Andrew Jackson, the quintessential "common man" was the western settler, struggling to bring new lands under cultivation and new institutions to life. Pioneers confronted many obstacles in their trek west, but none loomed larger than the resistance of Indian peoples.

Jackson and Native Peoples

The War of 1812 had ended intertribal resistance east of the Mississippi River. By 1828, most of the Great Lakes nations had been pushed out of Ohio, southern Indiana, and Illinois, but the Ojibwa, Winnebago, Sauk, Mesquakie, Kickapoo, and Menominee tribes retained sizable homelands in the region. In the South, in spite of repeated forced cessions, the Chickasaws, Choctaws, Creeks, Cherokees, and Seminoles—the Five "Civilized" Tribes that had adopted American ways—retained ancestral territories.

Jackson's views concerning Native Americans had been settled in the crucible of the Indian wars of the 1790s. "Does not experience teach us that treaties answer no other Purpose than opening an Easy door for the Indians to pass [through to] Butcher our citizens?" he wrote in 1794. Congress should "Punish the Barbarians."

In these views, Jackson was no different from many American settlers—some of whom had directly experienced the violence of white incursions into Indian Country, but many of whom formed their ideas long before they ever saw an Indian, basing their preconceptions on inflamed newspaper accounts in the new mass-produced "penny press." Most American settlers saw Indians only in passing. Some of these encounters were surely unnerving, but they were usually of no harm to the settlers. The harm that Indians represented was more basic: they occupied lands recognized as belonging to them in treaties with the federal government. Despite recurrent wars and land cessions, western settlers were no happier with federal initiatives in the 1820s than they had been in the 1790s.

Tension ran especially high in Georgia. There officials complained that the federal government had not kept its promise to remove all Indians from the state, a condition of Georgia's 1802 agreement to cede its western land claims to the federal government. A few Creeks and most of the Cherokee nation remained. In 1826, the federal government pressured the Creeks to give up all but a small strip of their remaining lands in Georgia, but white Georgians were not satisfied. Georgia governor George Michael Troup sent surveyors onto that last piece of Creek land. When President Adams objected to this encroachment on federal treaty powers, Troup threatened to call up the state militia.

The election of Andrew Jackson emboldened Georgians to go after Cherokee land. They invalidated the constitution of the Cherokee nation within Georgia and proclaimed that the Cherokees were subject to the authority of the state of Georgia. When discoveries of gold sent white prospectors surging onto Cherokee land, Georgia refused to stop the trespassers or to protect the Indians. To the contrary, the state passed laws that stripped Cherokees of their rights and their land. Jackson quickly notified the Cherokees that it was his duty, as president, to "sustain the States in the exercise of their rights."

In fact, those rights were arguable. In 1830, the Cherokee nation took the state of Georgia to the Supreme Court, arguing that the Cherokee nation was a "foreign nation in the sense of our constitution and law" and that, as a state, Georgia had no right to pass laws over the inhabitants of a foreign nation. In *Cherokee Nation v. Georgia*, Chief Justice John Marshall agreed that the Cherokees were a distinct political society, but he also said that as a foreign entity, they "cannot maintain an action in the courts of the United States." But the following year, *Worcester v. Georgia*, which was not brought by the Cherokee nation, but rather by a young New Englander living in Georgia, gave Marshall the opportunity to say more. He identified the Cherokee nation as "a distinct community, occupying its own territory, with boundaries accurately described in which the laws of Georgia can have no force, and which the citizens of Georgia have no right to enter but with the assent of the Cherokees themselves or in conformity with treaties and with the acts of Congress." Marshall concluded, "The whole intercourse between the United States and this nation is, by our Constitution and laws, vested in the government of the United States." Georgia had acted unconstitutionally.

Jackson very publicly refused to enforce this decision. He had long believed that the best policy would be to remove the Indians entirely from lands sought by settlers. The place he had in mind was across the Mississippi River. Because full-scale removal of the Indians involved shifting populations across state lines and into federal territories, however, it required congressional consent.

The proposed policy was not unopposed. "If, in pursuance of a narrow and selfish policy, we should . . . drive away these remnants of tribes, in such a manner, and under such auspices, as to insure their destruction," Jeremiah Evarts, secretary of the American Board of Commissioners for Foreign Missions, warned, "then the sentence of an indignant world would be uttered in thunders." In Congress, the Native Americans found unexpected allies. To the old Adams men, now led by Henry Clay, "removal" was the policy of states, forced on the federal government. For Congress to pass an act authorizing the policy would mean encouraging states to trample on federal powers.

Van Buren responded by forming a counterlobby, the Board for the Emigration, Preservation, and Improvement of the Aborigines of America, which argued rather disingenuously that Indians were ill equipped for contact with white civilization and that removing them was actually humane. In the end, the bill passed by only five votes and only after four months of debate.

The Removal Act

In 1830, Congress passed and President Jackson signed an act "to provide for an exchange of lands with the Indians residing in any of the states or territories, and for their removal west of the river Mississippi." In one sense, the act only made official and accelerated a policy that Americans had pursued since the founding of the nation. In his State of the Union address that year, Jackson praised the Removal Act as an act of "Philanthropy." He reminded Congress that for generations European Americans had been "leav[ing] the land of their birth to seek new homes in distant regions" and that new lands meant opportunity and liberty. "Doubtless it will be painful to leave the graves of their fathers," he acknowledged of the eastern Indians, "but what do they more than our ancestors did or than our children are now doing?" In fact, leaving "the land of their birth" was for Native Americans not an act of opportunity but rather an eviction from their very identity as a people.

In 1830, the Choctaws were forced from their lands in Mississippi to present-day Oklahoma. The Chickasaws and the Creeks followed in 1832. Then, in 1836, a small splinter group of the Cherokees at last agreed to removal. Since they had won their case before the Supreme Court, but the president refused to uphold it, they felt that they had exhausted all other options. The Treaty of New Echota provided that within two years the Cherokees would leave the mountains for Indian Territory, in return for safe passage, $5 million, and food, shelter, equipment, and medicine for a year after their arrival. The Senate ratified the treaty in the spring of 1836. The protreaty Cherokees began to leave almost immediately. The overwhelming majority of Cherokees, who considered the treaty fraudulent, remained in the East, with their chief, John Ross, continuing to fight for them.

In 1838, the Cherokees were removed from their eastern lands. In a forced march that became known as the Trail of Tears, they were driven off their homelands to Indian Territory in what is now eastern Oklahoma. Most people had delayed leaving until the last moment and had made few preparations for the journey. Thousands died of disease, malnutrition, dehydration, and exhaustion along the way.

Indians did not accept removal willingly. In 1831, the Sauk and Fox people (descended from Native Americans who had earlier been pushed across the Great Lakes region) were forced to relocate once again. In their new lands, however, they began to hear rumors of whites desecrating their former burying grounds. When Indians recrossed the Mississippi to rebury their dead and harvest produce from their old fields, white farmers and the Illinois militia attacked them. The Sauk and Fox Indians turned to a revered old fighter, **Black Hawk**, who raised a band of 500 warriors. Attacked by state militiamen, they spent the summer fighting a series of skirmishes called Black Hawk's War. Finally, on August 2, 1832, the exhausted remnants of Black Hawk's band were cornered and massacred by the army.

More successful were the Florida Seminoles, also a diverse community including militant Creek warriors, known as Red Sticks, and fugitives from slavery. When

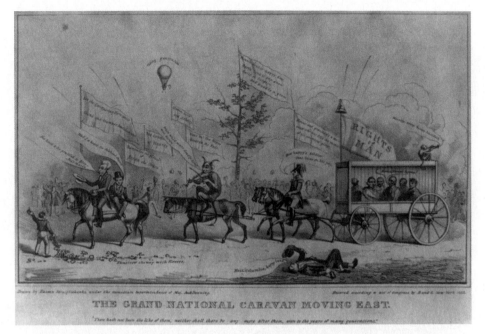

THE GRAND NATIONAL CARAVAN MOVING EAST.

The Grand National Caravan Moving East About half of all Americans were against Removal. In this satirical cartoon, Jackson and Van Buren are on the left, followed by the devil, an army officer, and a group of caged Indians, who represent Indian removal. On the ground, a drunken Jacksonian proclaims, "Hail! Columbia, happy land."

federal troops arrived to remove the Seminoles in 1832, the Indians resisted with skill and determination. Unfamiliar with the terrain and vulnerable to malaria, the American troops were picked off by both disease and snipers. The war dragged on for seven years. Not until 1842 could President John Tyler proclaim victory.

History, Destiny, and the Remaking of Indian Societies

Beginning with Washington, federal policy had encouraged Indians to adopt American ways of life—a private-property-based agrarian economy in which men worked in the fields and women in the home. At the same time, another strand in American thought held that Native Americans were incapable of change and Native American dispossession was inevitable, not only because white Americans were perfectly matched to the land but also because Indians were not. Americans who wanted to seize Indian lands claimed to have tried again and again to help Native Americans survive but considered them incapable of taking full advantage of the land. Ignoring the example of the **Five Civilized Tribes**, Jackson reflected this view in his 1833 address to Congress. Native Americans, he declared, had "neither the intelligence, the industry, the moral habits, nor the desire of improvement which are essential" to realizing the potential of the land.

This understanding of manifest destiny as entailing the inevitable disappearance of Native Americans made its way into American literature in the 1820s, just as white Americans were considering Indian removal as an official government policy. Its venue was the historical novel. The depiction of Native Americans in antebellum historical novels represented a departure from earlier Indian captivity narratives, which often described Indians as almost incapable of human feeling and bent on the violent destruction of European American civilization. Although the historical novels of the 1820s did not romanticize all Native Americans, they did identify among the Indians individuals of high character—of integrity, intelligence, and great sensitivity—but who, significantly, were always doomed to extinction. The most famous of such stories was *The Last of the Mohicans* (1826), by James Fenimore Cooper.

Although dispossession was a devastating experience for Native Americans, native societies adapted. The Comanches agreed to make room for removed Indians who would trade with them. Soon the displaced tribes, which had reestablished their agricultural way of life, were trading their crops and government-issued guns and ammunition to the Comanches for their new neighbors' chief commodities, horses and enslaved prisoners of war. When they were forced to migrate, the southeastern Indians had brought 5,000 enslaved Blacks with them, a workforce they replenished with the enslaved Indians, Mexicans, and Anglo-Americans sold by the Comanches. Ironically, the Indians who were displaced because they supposedly could not adapt took American values and practices with them: representative government, Christianity, and racial slavery. Drawing from their experience, they became middlemen, facilitating the trade between the Comanches to the west and Americans to the east.

As American weapons made their way to the western edge of the

Western Comanche in War Dress Comanche culture rewarded risk taking and prowess in war. Warriors made headdresses out of the hair of their captives and the hair of their own wives.

Comanche empire, the Spanish became alarmed. They now found that thousands of dollars' worth of gifts no longer purchased the loyalty of the Comanches, who increasingly wanted trade with the wealthier Americans. As Spanish influence in the West waned after Mexico achieved independence in 1821, American traders began moving into the region, at first destabilizing it. By 1840, however, the Comanche Empire had established commercial dominance in the southern plains. Josiah Gregg, an American trader, observed that the Comanches "acknowledge no boundaries, but call themselves the lords of the entire prairies."

THE GROWTH OF SECTIONAL TENSION

The growing fiscal strains in Jacksonian America were matched by brewing sectional conflict. Americans had not always viewed the differences between the political economies of the North and South as bad. Those regional differences had powered northern industrialization during the War of 1812 and had laid the foundation for the National Republican vision of robust nationalism after the war. But economic expansion brought old differences into open conflict. The immediate catalyst was the tariff, but by 1832 the tariff question had ignited a broader debate over the institution of slavery.

The Sources of Southern Discontent

Despite an apparent victory in the Missouri controversy, many white southerners had felt betrayed by northern criticisms of slavery. Economic and political frustrations in the 1820s nurtured that sense of mistreatment, leading the planter class, which had so far dominated the presidency, to see itself as the victim of the federal government.

White southerners read signs of shifting public attitudes toward slavery. Proslavery advocates in Illinois (where many African Americans were already held in indentures comparable to slavery) were unable to elect a proslavery congressman in 1820. In 1824, Ohio asked Congress to consider a plan for the gradual abolition of slavery throughout the United States. On July 4, 1827, New York completed its long process of gradual emancipation, an occasion celebrated by free African Americans as far south as Virginia. And news from England had it that abolitionist William Wilberforce was likely to get slavery outlawed in the British West Indies.

Most important, though, was the economy. By 1828, cotton prices were only about one-third of their 1815 levels. Many planters and farmers tried to compensate for falling profits by planting more acres, but worn-out fields kept production low. Large eastern planters often sold off enslaved people, lands, and city houses. Many smaller farmers, dependent on cotton as their cash crop to pay off debts, were forced to sell out. Although the Panic of 1819 hurt northern farms and businesses, most of the Northeast bounced back faster than the South, which focused planter attention on the 1816 protective tariff as a sign of government favoritism. They complained that the tariff was unnaturally driving up the prices of European imports, forcing strapped southerners to purchase expensive northern-made products and driving down southern export sales. "We have no objection to the North being enriched by our riches," one Charleston *Mercury* reporter wrote sarcastically in 1827, "but not from our poverty."

the Virginia legislature debated, but ultimately rejected, a proposal for the gradual abolition of slavery in the state.

In an 1832 convention, South Carolina radicals voted to nullify the tariffs of 1828 and 1832, passing the Ordinance of Nullification by 136 votes to 26 votes. The act forbade the collection of the tariffs within South Carolina. For Jackson, the act of nullification transformed the crisis from a question of regional interests to one of national union. "The laws of the United States must be executed," he declared. "I have no discretionary power on the subject; my duty is emphatically pronounced in the Constitution." He asked Congress for a law specifically affirming his responsibility to compel the collection of the tax in South Carolina, by force of arms if necessary.

Congress rushed to find a compromise. In early 1833, it passed a tariff that gradually reduced duties over the next decade but also passed the law Jackson had requested, known as the Force Bill. Jackson signed both the new tariff law and the Force Bill, a signal to South Carolina that nullification and secession would not be tolerated.

In 1832, with South Carolina virtually alone even among southern states, supporters of nullification had no choice but to withdraw their ordinance. At the same time, they voted to nullify the Force Bill within the boundaries of South Carolina. Jackson let the gesture pass, and at least for the time being, the constitutional crisis was over.

CONCLUSION

The Jacksonian consensus was forged from belief in the efficacy of the individual, a distrust of unfair privilege, a commitment to geographic expansionism, and, ironically, an insistence that slavery be kept out of national politics. Few of these elements were new to Americans, but their meanings had shifted since 1776. The republic was becoming a democracy in some regards. But the harmony that seemed to be expressed in the Jacksonian celebration of democracy was misleading. Consensus was always partial, and conflict always present and growing. African Americans and Native Americans were excluded altogether; workers and women were included only contingently. Within 25 years of Jackson's election, workers were in the streets, hundreds of thousands of Americans were petitioning to end slavery, political parties were in chaos, and the nation stood on the brink of civil war.

WHO, WHAT, WHERE

REVIEW QUESTIONS

1. How did the United States show its self-confidence at the end of the War of 1812?

2. What was the Missouri Compromise?

3. How was slavery generally practiced in the United States?

4. Describe the relationship between southern slavery and northern capitalism.

5. Why did Jackson oppose the South Carolina Exposition and Protest? Why didn't other southern states support South Carolina in the nullification crisis?

CRITICAL-THINKING QUESTIONS

1. How could the Jacksonians create a coalition between two such different interests as southern planters and northern workers?

2. The Cherokees and the other "civilized" tribes were removed from the Southeast, even though they had adopted American customs and forms of government. Why?

3. The Second Bank of the United States and Indian removal were simultaneously symbolic and substantial issues. How was this the case?

4. Compare and contrast how slavery brought the North and South closer together and how it drove the two regions apart. How did the cotton trade enhance rather than diminish the differences between northern capitalism and southern slavery?

SUGGESTED READINGS

Dusinberre, William. *Them Dark Days: Slavery in the American Rice Swamps*. New York: Oxford University Press, 1996.

Opal, J. M. *Avenging the People: Andrew Jackson, the Rule of Law, and the American Nation*. New York: Oxford University Press, 2017.

Perdue, Theda, and Michael Green. *The Cherokee Nation and the Trail of Tears*. New York: Viking, 2006.

For further review materials and resource information, please visit www.oup.com/us/ofthepeople

CHAPTER 10: Jacksonian Democracy, 1820–1840
Primary Sources

10.1 RUFUS KING, EXCERPTS FROM *THE SUBSTANCE OF TWO SPEECHES DELIVERED IN THE SENATE OF THE UNITED STATES, ON THE SUBJECT OF THE MISSOURI BILL* (1820) AND WILLIAM PINKNEY, EXCERPTS FROM HIS RESPONSE ON THE MISSOURI QUESTION (1820)

Politicians and leaders had known since the early days of the nation that slavery would be a divisive and contested issue. Congress had banned the importation of enslaved people in 1807, while still allowing the slave trade to continue via the internal slave market. Many hoped that the institution would slowly decline into oblivion. The acquisition of new territory, however, along with rising cotton prices, caused new debates over slavery to erupt. In 1820, Congress debated whether or not Missouri could be required to abolish slavery before becoming a state.

RUFUS KING, NEW YORK, FEBRUARY 11 AND 14, 1820

The constitution declares, "that Congress shall have power to dispose of, and make all needful rules and regulations respecting the territory and other property of the United States."

... The question respecting slavery in the old thirteen states, had been decided and settled before the adoption of the constitution, which grants no power to Congress to interfere with, or to change, what had been so previously settled: the slave states therefore are free to continue or to abolish slavery....

The constitution contains no express provisions respecting slavery in a new state that may be admitted into the union: every regulation upon this subject, belongs to the power whose consent is necessary to the formation and admission of such state. Congress may therefore make it a condition of the admission of a new state, that slavery shall be forever prohibited within the same. We may with the more confidence pronounce this to be the true construction of the constitution, as it has been so amply confirmed by the past decisions of Congress....

The existence of slavery impairs the industry and the power of a nation; and it does so in proportion to the multiplication of its slaves: where the manual labour of a country is performed by slaves, labour dishonours the bands of freemen.

If her labourers be slaves, Missouri may be able to pay money taxes, but will be unable to raise soldiers, or to recruit seamen; and experience seems to have proved that manufactures do not prosper where the artificers are slaves. In case of foreign war or domestic insurrection, misfortunes from which no states are exempt, and against which all should be seasonably prepared, slaves not only do not add to, but diminish the faculty of self defence; instead of increasing the public strength, they lessen it, by the whole number of free persons whose place they occupy, increased by the number of freemen that may be employed as guards over them.

... If Missouri, and the other states that may be formed to the west of the river Mississippi, are permitted to introduce and establish slavery, the repose, if not the security, of the union may be endangered; all the states south of the river Ohio and west of Pennsylvania and Delaware, will be peopled with slaves, and the establishment of new states west of the river Mississippi, will serve to extend slavery instead of freedom over that boundless region.

Such increase of the states, whatever other interests it may promote, will be sure to add nothing to the security of the public liberties, and can hardly fail hereafter to require and produce a change in our government....

WILLIAM PINKNEY, MARYLAND, RESPONDS, FEBRUARY 15, 1820

... The whole amount of the argument on the other side is, that you may refuse to admit a new State, and that therefore if you admit, you may prescribe the terms.

The answer to that argument is—that even if you can refuse, you can prescribe no terms which are inconsistent with the act you are to do. You can prescribe no conditions which, if carried into effect, would make the new State less a sovereign State than, under the Union as it stands, it would be. You can prescribe no terms which will make the compact of Union between it and the original States essentially different from that compact among the original States. You may admit, or refuse to admit: but if you admit, you must admit a State in the sense of the Constitution—a State with all such sovereignty as belongs to the original parties: and it must be into this Union that you are to admit it, not into a Union of your own dictating, formed out of the existing Union by qualifications and new compacts, altering its character and effect...

The truth is, that the restriction has no relation, real or pretended, to the right of making slaves of those who are free, or of introducing slavery where it does not already exist. It applies to those who are admitted to be already slaves, and who (with their posterity) would continue to be slaves if they should remain where they are at present; and to a place where slavery already exists by the local law.

... I trust, then, that I shall be forgiven if I suggest that no eccentricity in argument can be more trying to human patience than a formal assertion that ... a clause commanding Congress to guarantee a republican form of government to [slaveholding] States, as well as to others, authorizes you to determine that slavery and a republican form of government cannot coexist.

But if a republican government is that in which all the men have a share in the public power, the slaveholding States will not alone retire from the Union. The constitutions of some of the other States do not sanction universal suffrage, or universal eligibility. They require citizenship, and age, and a certain amount of property, to give a title to vote or to be voted for; and they who have not those qualifications are just as much disfranchises ... as if they were slaves.... If it be true that all men in a republican Government must help to wield its power, and be equal in rights, I beg leave to ask ... and why not all the *women*? ... If the ultra republican doctrines which have now been broached should ever gain ground among us, I should not be surprised if some romantic reformer, treading in the footsteps of Mrs. Wolstonecraft, should propose to repeal our republican law ... and claim for our wives and daughters a full participation in political power, and to add to it that domestic power which, in some families, as I have heard, is as absolute and unrepublican as any power can be.

Sources: Rufus, King. *The Substance of Two Speeches Delivered in the Senate of the United States, on the Subject of the Missouri Bill.* Philadelphia: Clark and Raser. Rufus King, February 11 and 14, 1820, http://archive.org/stream/substanceoftwosp00king/substanceoftwo sp00king_djvu.txt.

William Pinkney's response from: Johnston, Alexander. *American Eloquence: Studies in American Political History.* New York: G. P. Putnam's Sons, 1896. Additionally: *Annals of Congress,* Senate, 16th Congress, 1st session, pp. 414–415.

10.2   ANDREW JACKSON, EXCERPTS FROM BANK VETO MESSAGE (1832) AND VISUAL DOCUMENT: H. R. ROBINSON, "GENERAL JACKSON SLAYING THE MANY HEADED MONSTER" (1836)

In 1832, shortly before the end of President Andrew Jackson's first term, Congress proposed rechartering the Bank of the United States. Jackson vetoed the bill, and he and the Democrats used the veto as an issue in the reelection campaign. As much as any other address to the American people, Jackson's veto message, a brief excerpt of which follows, sets out his vision for the role of government in advancing economic equality and preventing undemocratic concentrations of political and economic power.

To the Senate.

... A bank of the United States is in many respects convenient for the Government and useful to the people. Entertaining this opinion, and deeply impressed with the belief that some of the powers and privileges possessed by the existing bank are unauthorized by the Constitution, subversive of the rights of the States, and dangerous to the liberties of the people, I felt it my duty at an early period of my Administration to call the attention of Congress to the practicability of organizing an institution combining all its advantages and obviating these objections. I sincerely regret that in the act before me I can perceive none of those modifications of the bank charter which are necessary, in my opinion, to make it compatible with justice, with sound policy, or with the Constitution of our country.

The present corporate body ... will have existed at the time this act is intended to take effect twenty years. It enjoys an exclusive privilege of banking under the authority of the General Government, a monopoly of its favor and support, and, as a necessary consequence, almost a monopoly of the foreign and domestic exchange. The powers, privileges, and favors bestowed upon it in the original charter, by increasing the value of the stock far above its par value, operated as a gratuity of many millions to the stockholders....

Every monopoly and all exclusive privileges are granted at the expense of the public, which ought to receive a fair equivalent. The many millions which this act proposes to bestow on the stockholders of the existing bank must come directly or indirectly out of the earnings of the American people. It is due to them, therefore, if their Government sell monopolies and exclusive privileges, that they should at least exact for them as much as they are worth in open market.

. . .

It is to be regretted that the rich and powerful too often bend the acts of government to their selfish purposes. Distinctions in society will always exist under every just government. Equality of talents, of education, or of wealth can not be produced by human institutions. In the full enjoyment of the gifts of Heaven and the fruits of superior industry, economy, and virtue, every man is equally entitled to protection by law; but when the laws undertake to add to these natural and just advantages artificial distinctions, to grant titles, gratuities, and exclusive privileges, to make the rich richer and the potent more powerful, the humble members of society—the farmers, mechanics, and laborers—who have neither the time nor the means of securing like favors to themselves, have a right to complain of the injustice of their Government. There are no necessary evils in government. Its evils exist only in its abuses. If it would confine itself to equal protection, and, as Heaven does its rains, shower its favors alike on the high and the low, the rich and the poor, it would be an unqualified blessing. In the act before me there seems to be a wide and unnecessary departure from these just principles.

Nor is our Government to be maintained or our Union preserved by invasions of the rights and powers of the several States. In thus attempting to make our General Government strong we make it weak. Its true strength consists in leaving individuals and States as much as possible to themselves—in making itself felt, not in its power, but in its beneficence; not in its control, but in its protection; not in binding the States more closely to the center, but leaving each to move unobstructed in its proper orbit.

Experience should teach us wisdom. Most of the difficulties our Government now encounters and most of the dangers which impend over our Union have sprung from an abandonment of the legitimate objects of Government by our national legislation, and the adoption of such principles as are embodied in this act. Many of our rich men have not been content with equal protection and equal benefits, but have besought us to make them richer by act of Congress. By attempting to gratify their desires we have in the results of our legislation arrayed section against section, interest against interest, and man against man, in a fearful commotion which threatens to shake the foundations of our Union. It is time to pause in our career to review our principles, and if possible revive that devoted patriotism and spirit of compromise which distinguished the sages of the Revolution and the fathers of our Union. If we can not at once, in justice to interests vested under improvident legislation, make our Government what it ought to be, we can at least take a stand against all new grants of monopolies and exclusive privileges, against any prostitution of our Government to the advancement of the few at the expense of the many, and in favor of compromise and gradual reform in our code of laws and system of political economy.

Source: Andrew Jackson, "Bank Veto, July 10, 1832," in *The Addresses and Messages of the Presidents of the United States, from 1789 to 1839: Together with the Declaration of Independence and Constitution of the United States* (New York: MacLean and Taylor, 1839), pp. 398–399, 409–410.

GENERAL JACKSON SLAYING THE MANY HEADED MONSTER.

Here, the Second Bank of the United States is depicted as a monster, the mythological many-headed Hydra. The largest of the heads, in the top hat, is that of Nicholas Biddle, the president of the Bank.

Source: Library of Congress LC-USZ62-1575

10.3   THEODORE FRELINGHUYSEN'S ARGUMENT AGAINST THE REMOVAL ACT (1830)

About half of all Americans were against the passage of the Removal Act, and many followed the debates in Congress, parts of which were printed in the newspapers and read aloud. Senator Theodore Frelinghuysen of New Jersey became a hero for like-minded people. On April 9, 1830, he spoke for over four hours on the subject.

God, in his profidence, planted these tribes on this Western continent, so far as we know, before Great Britain herself had a political existence. I believe, sir, it is not now seriously denied that the Indians are men, endowed with kindred faculties and powers with ourselves; that they have a place in human sympathy, and are justly entitled to a share in the common bounties of a benignant Providence. And, with this conceded, I ask in what code of the law of nations, or by what process of abstract deduction, their rights have been extinguished?

Where is the decree or ordinance that has stripped these early and first lords of the soil? Sir, no record of such measure can be found. And I might triumphantly rest the hopes of these feeble fragments of once great nations upon this impregnable foundation. However mere human policy, or the law of power, or the tyrant's pleas of expediencey, may have found it convenient at any or in all times to recede from the unchangeable principles of eternal justice, no argument can shake the political maxim, that, where the Indian always has been, he enjoys an absolute right still to be, in the free exercise of his own modes of thought, government and conduct.

In the light of natural law, can a reason for a distinction exist in the mode of enjoying that which is my own? If I use it for hunting, may another take it because he needs it for agriculture? I am aware that some writers have, by a system of artificial reasoning, endeavored to justify, or rather excuse the encroachments made upon Indian territory; and they denominate these abstractions the law of nations, and, in this ready way, the question is dispatched. Sir, as we trace the course of this law, we find its authority to depend either upon the conventions or common consent of nations. And when, permit me to inquire, were the Indian tribes ever consulted on the establishment of such a law? Whoever presented them or their interests in any congress of nations, to confer upon the public rules of intercourse, and the proper foundations of dominion and property? The plain matter of fact is, that all these partial doctrines have resulted from the selfish plans and pursuits of more enlightened nations; and it is not matter of any great wonder, that they should so largely partake of a mercenary and exclusive spirit toward the claims of the Indians.

It is, however, admitted, sir, that when the increase of population and the wants of mankind demand the cultivation of the earth, a duty is thereby devolved upon the proprietors of large and uncultivated regions, of devoting them to such useful purposes. But such appropriations are to be obtained by fair contract, and for reasonable compensation. It is, in such a case, the duty of the proprietor to sell: we may properly address his reason to induce him; but we cannot rightfully compel the cession of his lands, or take them by violence, if his consent is withheld. It is with great satisfaction that I am enabled, upon the best authority, to affirm, that this duty has been largely and generously met and fulfilled on the part of the aboriginal peoples of this continent. Several years ago, official reports to Congress stated the amount of Indian grants to the United States to exceed 21 millions of acres. Yes, sir, we have acquired and now own more land as the fruits of their bounty than we shall dispose of at the present rate to actual settlers in two hundred years. For, very recently, it has been ascertained, on this floor, that our public sales average not more than about one million of acres annually. It greatly aggravates the wrong that is now meditated against these tribes, to survey the rich and ample districts of their territories, that either by force or persuasion have been incorporated into our public domains. As the tide of our population rolled on, we have added purchase to purchase. The confiding Indian listened to our professions of friendship: we called him brother, and he believed us. Millions after millions he has yielded to our importunity, until we have acquired more than can be cultivated in centuries—and yet we crave more. We have crowded the tribes upon a few miserable acres on our southern border; it is all that is left to them of their once boundless forest, and still, like the horse-leech, our insatiated cupidity cries, give! give!

Source: Register of Debates in Congress, 6: 311–16, in Francis Paul Prucha, ed., *Documents of United States Indian Policy* (University of Nebraska Press, 2000 [1975]), 48–52.

10.4   FRANCES KEMBLE'S JOURNAL (1838–1839)

Frances Kemble was a young English actress, touring the United States, where she met the Georgia planter Pierce Butler. She married him in 1832, when she was 23 years old. From 1838 to 1839, she kept a journal, written in the form of letters to a friend, of her life on the plantation, one much like Gowrie, on an island off the coast of Georgia. Horrified by what she found among the enslaved, Kemble fought with her husband, soon leaving him and the plantation. She was particularly sensitive to the sufferings of women, some of which she described in the following excerpts.

This morning I had a visit from ... Louisa [who told me the story of her escape]. She told it very simply, and it was most pathetic. She had not finished her task one day, when she said she felt ill, and unable to do so, and had been severely flogged by Driver Bran, in whose "gang" she then was. The next day, in spite of this encouragement to labour, she had again been unable to complete her appointed work; and Bran having told her that he'd tie her up and flog her if she did not get it done, she had left the field and run into the swamp. "Tie you up, Louisa" said I, "what is that?" She then described to me that they were fastened up by their wrists to a beam or a branch of a tree, their feet barely touching the ground, so as to allow them no purchase for resistance or evasion of the lash, their clothes turned over their heads, and their backs scored with a leather thong, either by the driver himself, or if he pleases to inflict their punishment by deputy, any of the men he may choose to summon to the office; it might be father, brother, husband, or lover, if the overseer so ordered it. I turned sick, and my blood curdled listening to these details from the slender young slip of a lassie, with her poor piteous face and murmuring pleading voice. "Oh," said I, "Louisa; but the rattlesnakes, the dreadful rattlesnakes in the swamps; were you not afraid of those horrible creatures?" "Oh, missis," said the poor child, "me no tink of dem, me forget all 'bout dem for de fretting." "Why did you come home at last?" "Oh, missis, me starve with hunger, me most dead with hunger before me come back." "And were you flogged, Louisa?" said I, with a shudder at what the answer might be. "No, missis, me go to hospital; me almost dead and sick so long, 'spec Driver Bran him forgot 'bout de flogging." I am getting perfectly savage over all these doings, E[lizabeth]—, and really think I should consider my own throat and those of my children well cut, if some night the people were to take it into their heads to clear off scores in that fashion.

Yesterday evening I had a visit that made me very sorrowful—if anything connected with these poor people can be called more especially sorrowful than their whole condition; but Mr. [Butler]s declaration that he will receive no more statements of grievances or petitions for redress through me, makes me as desirous now of shunning the vain appeals of these unfortunates as I used to be of receiving and listening to them . . . to the entreaty, "Oh missis, you speak to massa for us! Oh missis, you beg massa for us! Oh missis, you tell massa for we, he sure do as you say!"—I cannot now answer as formerly, and I turn away choking and with eyes full of tears from the poor creatures. . . .

Before closing this letter, I have a mind to transcribe to you the entries for to-day recorded in a sort of daybook, where I put down very succinctly the number of people who visit me, their petitions and ailments, and also such special particulars concerning them as seem to me worth recording.

Fanny has had six children, all dead but one. She came to beg to have her work in the field lightened.

Nanny has had three children, two of them are dead; she came to implore that the rule of sending them into the field three weeks after their confinement might be altered.

Leah, Caesar's wife, has had six children, three are dead.

Sophy, Lewis' wife, came to beg for some old linen; she is suffering fearfully, has had ten children, five of them are dead. The principal favour she asked was a piece of meat, which I gave her.

Sally, Scipio's wife, has had two miscarriages and three children born, one of whom is dead. She came complaining of incessant pain and weakness in her back. This woman was a mulatto daughter of a slave called Sophy, by a white man of the name of Walker, who visited the plantation.

Charlotte, Renty's wife, had had two miscarriages, and was with child again. She was almost crippled with rheumatism, and showed me a pair of poor swollen knees that made my heart ache. I have promised her a pair of flannel trowsers, which I must forthwith set about making.

Sarah, Stephen's wife,—this woman's case and history were, alike, deplorable, she had had four miscarriages, had brought seven children into the world, five of whom were dead, and was again with child. She complained of dreadful pains in the back, and an internal tumour which swells with the exertion of working in the fields; probably, I think, she is ruptured. She told me she had once been mad and ran into the woods, where she contrived to elude discovery for some time, but was at last tracked and brought back, when she was tied up by the arms and heavy logs fastened to her feet, and was severely flogged. After this she contrived to escape again, and lived for some time skulking in the woods, and she supposes mad, for when she was taken again she was entirely naked. She subsequently recovered from this derangement, and seems now just like all the other poor creatures who come to me for help and pity. I suppose her constant child-bearing and hard labour in the fields at the same time may have produced the temporary insanity.

Source: Frances Anne Kemble, *Journal of a Residence on a Georgian Plantation, 1838–1839* (1863).

Reform and Conflict
1820–1848

< The burning of Pennsylvania Hall in 1838

347

Millennialism and Communitarians

Separatist communities were not new to the American spiritual landscape in these years, and they never accounted for more than a minority of the American people. Nevertheless, they enjoyed renewed success in the 1820s. As a group, these religious communitarians sought to create more perfect societies on earth by withdrawing from daily contact with their neighbors and instituting tightly controlled spiritual, social, and economic regimens. Collectively, they revealed the fault lines in a rapidly changing society.

One of the earliest of these religious communities was the United Society of Believers in Christ's Second Appearing, a radical branch of Quakerism dubbed **Shakers** by its critics, for the "dancing, singing, leaping, clapping ... groans and sighs" that characterized its services. Shakerism was rooted in the experiences of Ann Lee, a late-eighteenth-century English factory worker and lay preacher who believed that she was the second, female embodiment of the Messiah. Lee preached that believers should return to the simplicity and purity of the early Christian church, pooling their worldly resources, withdrawing from the vanities of society, and observing celibacy. The Shakers migrated to North America in 1774 and established their first community near Watervliet, New York (see Map 11–1). By the turn of the century, the Shakers had established a dozen communities in New England and four settlements in Ohio and Kentucky. By the 1830s, membership approached 4,000.

Shaker beliefs required a community based on a "union of faith, of motives, and of interest" of all members. To ensure this perfect unity, Shakers organized themselves into "families" of 30 to 100 members, each of which was supervised by a panel of eight people (two women and two men to oversee spiritual matters, and two men and two women to oversee temporal concerns), guided by a ministry also composed equally of men and women.

Their search for perfection led the Shakers to repudiate the values of contemporary society. They embraced celibacy while rejecting materialism and competitive individualism, allocating individual labor according to the needs of the community. This alternative political and economic arrangement resulted in prosperity and innovation, as Shakers sold their goods to outsiders.

Women appear to have been especially drawn to Shakerism, probably because of the Shaker belief in the spiritual equality of women and men, which was reflected in the organization of the communities, with "sisters" and "female elders" supervising the women's lives and "brothers" and "male elders" supervising the men's. The practice of celibacy afforded women freedom from the dangers of childbirth.

The largest and most long-lived of the **millennial** communities of the early nineteenth century was the Church of Jesus Christ of Latter-day Saints, also known as the Mormons, founded by Joseph Smith Jr. in 1830 (see Chapter 9). In addition to traditional Christian doctrine, the Mormon Articles of Faith included a belief "in the literal gathering of Israel and in the restoration of the Ten Tribes; that Zion (the New Jerusalem) will be built upon the American continent; that Christ will reign personally upon the earth; and, that the earth will be renewed and receive its paradisiacal glory."

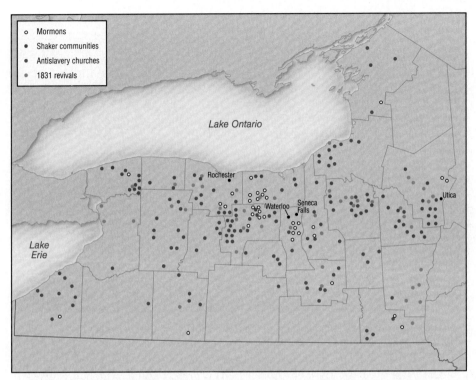

Map 11-1   Revival and Reform Social and economic transformation, religious revival, and social reform movements went hand in hand in the antebellum North. The so-called burned-over district of New York (the region directly served by the Erie Canal) nurtured numerous millennial sects (including Mormons and Shakers), Antimasonry, Finneyite revivals, and antislavery activism, as well as the Seneca Falls Woman's Rights Convention.

Smith's preaching attracted rural followers, most of them displaced by the changing antebellum North. To them, Smith preached that it was God's will that they go forth into the wilderness to found the city of Zion, where they would reign over the coming millennium.

The opposition of their neighbors, who considered Mormon beliefs blasphemous, forced the Mormons to leave New York. Smith first moved his followers to Ohio, and then to Missouri. In 1839, a large group moved on to Illinois, founding the city of Nauvoo. By the early 1840s, Smith had begun to preach the doctrine of plural marriage. The Mormon community split, and anti-Mormon outrage flared anew. Smith was arrested and thrown in jail in Carthage, Illinois, where, on June 27, 1844, he was murdered by a mob (allegedly helped by a jail guard supported by leading citizens). In 1847, following Brigham Young, the Mormons left again, reaching the Great Salt Lake in the West. By 1850, hard work, irrigation, and careful cultivation had turned the desert into a garden paradise inhabited by more than 11,000 people.

The success of such communities reflected the dissatisfaction with the gender and economic norms of the wider society. Others, however, focused outward, attempting to change the wider society.

Shakers Outsiders labeled members of the United Society of Believers in Christ's Second Appearing "Shakers" after the active twirling and shaking movements that accompanied their services.

The Benevolent Empire

Separatist millennialists were a relatively minor stream in the floods of religious organizing during the 1820s and 1830s. Far more numerous were the Americans who sought to perfect society by carrying the spirit of reform into their own communities. This massive evangelizing of America took many forms. Itinerant Methodists and Baptists continued to minister to newly settled churches in the backcountry. By the 1820s, however, even such great metropolises as Boston, Philadelphia, and New York became hothouses of evangelism.

The career of Presbyterian minister Ezra Stiles Ely reflects this shift in mainstream religious life. From 1811 to 1813, Ely was a chaplain for the Society for Supporting the Gospel, working with people who lived in public shelters. He led religious services, distributed Bibles, and prayed at the bedsides of the sick and dying, observing firsthand the growing poverty of American cities. After the War of 1812, he worked the shanties and tenements of New York's poor neighborhoods. He increasingly understood his mission to be not merely providing solace but also converting souls.

"Every truly converted man turns from selfishness to benevolence," Charles Finney, the most famous revivalist preacher of the era, said, "and benevolence surely leads him to do all he can to save the souls of his fellow man." The new evangelical emphasis on personal agency soon fostered a broad impulse for social reform, expressed in religious terms and organized through a network of charities and associations, often referred to as the **Benevolent Empire.**

The Benevolent Empire reflected Americans' love of organizing, a tendency observed by Frenchman Alexis de Tocqueville when he visited the United States in 1831–1832. Americans, Tocqueville wrote, "combine to … found seminaries, build churches, distribute books, and send missionaries to the antipodes. … If they want to proclaim a truth or propagate some feeling by the encouragement of a great example, they form an association."

Local societies linked up into national umbrella groups. Among the largest of these were the American Bible Society (which distributed Bibles in cities and new settlements), the Female Moral Reform Society (devoted to reclaiming women from prostitution), and the American Board of Commissioners for Foreign Missions (which promoted missions in the West). Every major city fostered Bible groups, asylums to help the poor, houses of industry, orphanages, and humane societies, among other charitable organizations. By 1830, evangelicals had also created a Sunday school movement and a movement to prohibit the delivery of mail on the Christian Sabbath.

Benevolent societies combined emotional and rational approaches to reform. The method of the Benevolent Empire was moral suasion. Reformers believed that social change came about not from external rules but rather through the gradual internal awakening of individual moral purpose through personal contact, testimony, and (where needed) exhortation. Yet the Benevolent Empire soon resembled a bureaucratic corporation.

Founded in 1816 in New York by wealthy Christian men, the American Bible Society illustrates this paradox. The society consisted initially of a volunteer board of managers who hired out the printing of Bibles. By 1832, the society was run by a professional staff in its own building in Manhattan. However, the society still depended on idealistic young ministers as its traveling agents and local volunteer organizations as its community contacts.

As they pursued their good deeds—distributing Bibles or religious tracts, praying with the sick—evangelicals came into intimate contact with the poor and ministered to their material needs. They arranged fuel deliveries and medical care, helped homeless families find lodging, and organized soup kitchens. Both men and women were engaged in the charitable associations of the early nineteenth century, but voluntary reform offered special opportunities for women. Women had already been active in organizing maternal societies to improve their parenting habits and Bible societies to discuss their moral failings. By the second decade of the nineteenth century, women were becoming active in the Sunday school movement and founding orphan asylums, homes for wayward girls, and asylums for "respectable" homeless adults. By the 1830s, women were the acknowledged volunteer backbone of the Benevolent Empire.

ORGANIZING AGAINST SLAVERY

Although to some it seemed as if opposition to slavery suddenly became a national issue when Missouri applied to enter the Union in 1819 (see Chapter 10), the issue had long simmered under the surface as northern states moved to abolish slavery and the institution became entrenched in the South with the spread of slavery and cotton culture into the Southwest.

Free Blacks and a significant number of whites continued to attack slavery as immoral and proposed to abolish it. In the 1820s, new religious perspectives joined with older egalitarian ones and gave rise to a new abolitionist movement that challenged both the institution of slavery and the national political parties. At the same time, a larger group of white people, though far from committed abolitionists, felt increasingly uncomfortable supporting the institution, and many northern churchgoers were uneasy with their denominations' acquiescence to slavery. Still, northern mill owners and merchants, tied to the institution, nevertheless shied away from acknowledging that linkage publicly. Religious perspectives did not all lead to antislavery sentiments.

The Antislavery Movement

The **Missouri Compromise** was a devastating defeat for the opponents of slavery. For decades they had struggled to hold back the expansion of slavery and the growing power of the slaveholders in national politics. Disgusted by the increasing belligerence of proslavery politicians, antislavery northerners had campaigned to stop slavery once and for all, they hoped, by keeping it out of Missouri. But they had failed, and the consequences of their failure were soon apparent. Slavery's defenders had always used racial politics to try to stop antislavery politics, but their successes were limited and local until the 1820s. Impressed by the strength of antislavery sentiment during the Missouri crisis, southerners joined an emerging political coalition that came to be known as the Democratic Party. This coalition started from the premise that slavery would henceforth be excluded from national politics. It worked by demonizing the emerging **abolitionist movement.** By the late 1820s, a broad national antislavery politics was effectively dead, not to reemerge again until the late 1840s.

Black Abolitionists

With the collapse of antislavery politics, leadership of the movement passed to a small group of articulate abolitionists. Free Black leaders in the North led the way. They began to wonder whether the **American Colonization Society** (ACS) had become a cover for slaveholders who wanted to forestall abolition by insisting that Blacks were unfit for self-government. Colonization, which began as a conservative means of supporting abolition, looked more and more like an effort by slaveholders to rid themselves of the troubling presence of free Blacks.

There was another, bigger, problem with colonization. By the 1820s, almost all African Americans in the United States were American born. Although some later thought about migrating to Haiti or to Canada, most claimed the United States as their own. They strongly rebuffed the ACS's attempt to recruit them for relocation efforts. Many earlier Black efforts had focused understandably on self-help and community building. The emphasis on self-help grew in the wake of the Missouri debates, the organization of the ACS, and the racism of the early nineteenth century. It was a constant refrain from Black abolitionists: "Too long have others spoken for us," John Russwurm and Samuel E. Cornish declared in the first issue of the first independent Black newspaper, *Freedom's Journal.*

In the 1820s, free Blacks began to form their own all-Black antislavery groups, beginning in 1826 with the General Colored Association of Massachusetts.

Their protest, which drew from the older Revolutionary tradition, was not timid. In 1829, David Walker, an early member of the association, published a pamphlet titled *An Appeal to the Colored Citizens of the World*, calling on Blacks to take resistance to slavery into their own hands by armed insurrection, if necessary. Walker's protest, like those of other Black antislavery writers in this period, targeted the hypocrisies of white people, but at the same time drew from the Declaration of Independence. Many whites were furious, and southerners put a $3,000 bounty on Walker's head. Walker was undeterred: "Somebody must die in this cause," he added. "I may be doomed to the stake and the fire, or to the scaffold tree, but it is not in me to falter if I can promote the work of emancipation."

Black organizing continued to grow more assertive over the 1830s. Most Black abolitionists did not counsel armed insurrection, but a growing number wrote and lectured on slavery and the condition of African Americans in the republic. In 1832, Maria Stewart, a free Black woman in Boston, urged African Americans to take their destinies into their own hands. "If they kill us," she said of white opponents, "we shall but die."

These entreaties found responsive audiences. From 1830 until 1835 (and less regularly thereafter), free African Americans met in annual conventions to coordinate antislavery efforts and to secure free African American men "a voice in the disposition of those public resources which we ourselves have helped to earn." This National Negro Convention movement consistently framed its goals in the idiom of "manhood," calling for "the speedy elevation of ourselves and brethren to the scale and standing of men." At the same time, African American women worked to raise funds for the antislavery press and to raise awareness by inviting antislavery speakers to address their societies.

By the 1840s, militant abolitionism had grown common in African American communities. In 1841, former slave Frederick Douglass delivered his first public abolitionist speech in Nantucket, Massachusetts; four years later he published his moving autobiography about the brutalities of slavery, *Narrative of the Life of Frederick Douglass, An American Slave, Written by Himself*. In 1843, the formerly enslaved itinerant preacher Isabella Baumfree changed her name to Sojourner Truth and became a powerful and popular antislavery speaker throughout New England. Also in 1843, Henry Highland Garnet delivered "An Address to the Slaves of the United States of America," in which he called 4 million American slaves to open rebellion: "Arise, arise!" he cried. "Strike for your lives and liberties. Now is the day and the hour. … Rather die freemen than live to be slaves."

Immediatism

Although always a minority, a growing number of whites in the North began to confront the issue of slavery directly. The most significant was William Lloyd Garrison, who founded his own abolitionist newspaper, *The Liberator*, in Boston in 1831. In the first issue, he announced his absolute rejection of any compromise with slavery: "I will not equivocate—I will not excuse—I will not retreat a single inch—and I will be heard." Garrison's approach was known as immediatism—by which abolitionists meant not the immediate abolition of slavery but the immediate beginning of the process that would lead to slavery's ultimate extinction. In 1831, under Garrison's leadership, the immediatists formed the New England Anti-Slavery Society.

Increasingly inspired by the philosophy of **perfectionism**, Garrison and his followers eventually rejected all forms of compromise with slavery, public or personal. They became fierce critics of American religion and even ended up repudiating the Constitution. Few abolitionists went that far. Most were willing to risk contact with the imperfect world. One of these was Theodore Dwight Weld, an early supporter of the Colonization Society. After his conversion in the Finneyite revivals of 1825 and 1826, however, he began to doubt that the Society would ever risk alienating its southern constituency. By the 1830s, Weld was a committed abolitionist, and in 1834 he became a full-time antislavery organizer.

There were quick converts to the new, energized antislavery movement, especially in urban areas of the Northeast, upstate New York, Pennsylvania, and in western states heavily settled by New Englanders, especially Ohio. Quakers and liberal Congregationalists were particularly active. Local antislavery societies formed throughout New England in 1832. By the end of 1833, local and state organizations had grown strong enough to support a national society, the American Anti-Slavery Society, which included six African Americans on its original board. This integration was unparalleled in the United States at that time.

The American Anti-Slavery Society dedicated itself to abolishing slavery without compensation for owners and to the admission of African Americans to full citizenship. Society members pledged to pursue their goals through nonviolent moral suasion, exhorting individuals to undertake voluntary self-reform and the reform of society.

Antiabolition Violence

Although it was nonviolent, moral suasion did not exclude confrontation. In 1835, in the wake of Virginia's unwillingness to take any action against slavery, the Society ratcheted up its challenge to American society, especially the South. The Society dramatically increased its publication of antislavery pamphlets from 100,000 to 1 million pieces.

The response, in the North as well as the South, was immediate and fierce, in part orchestrated by the Jackson administration as a tactic to pave the way for Martin Van Buren's election by unifying the Democratic Party around opposition to the abolitionists, whom it depicted as dangerous radicals (see Chapter 10). In the South, anger and panic turned violent. With the memory of Nat Turner still fresh, slave owners denounced the campaign. Southern communities offered rewards for prominent abolition leaders, dead or alive. Vigilante committees were appointed to police free African American neighborhoods, to patrol waters looking for fugitives, and to search post offices for offending materials. The abolitionists were now outcasts.

Even before the 1835 campaign, northerners who opposed slavery still had reservations about racial equality. In 1833, some whites boycotted a Connecticut school for young women when its principal, Prudence Crandall, admitted two African American scholars. When Crandall admitted an entirely African American student body, white citizens lobbied for laws to bar Black students from the state, threatened Crandall, and burned the school to the ground.

The antiabolitionist campaign led to a new fury in the North. Anti–African American and antiabolitionist riots tore through St. Louis, Pittsburgh, Cincinnati, and Philadelphia, and abolitionist meetings were regularly broken up by mobs. In Boston in 1835, a crowd captured William Lloyd Garrison and dragged him through the streets on a rope. Antiabolitionist mobs also targeted newspapers. Rioters in Alton, Illinois, destroyed abolitionist newspaper editor Elijah Lovejoy's press four times in 1837. In the last attack, they murdered Lovejoy himself.

Abolitionists were undeterred and even began to find more converts. Anti-abolition violence suggested to some moderates that proslavery forces would stop at nothing—the flagrant violation of civil rights, the destruction of property, or murder.

Jackson and the Democrats, however, were not prepared to let opponents of slavery rupture their party. In 1835, Jackson asked Congress for measures curtailing antislavery organizing. Congress refused but Jackson prevailed with the use of the "gag rule," passed in 1836 and under which the House of Representatives automatically tabled antislavery petitions, thus assuring that Congress would not discuss the issue of slavery (see Chapter 10). The gag rule was renewed by succeeding Congresses until 1844.

The American Anti-Slavery Society, however, was quick to capitalize on the passage of the gag rule. In July1836, the society published *An Appeal to the People of the United States*, charging that it violated the right of petition. That summer, female antislavery leaders organized a systematic drive to obtain signatures on antislavery petitions. They traveled across the North, speaking in private parlors and in public halls, and within two years collected some 2 million signatures, more than two-thirds of which were women's.

The petition campaign called attention to the gag rule, to congressional support of slavery, and to the ability of proslavery forces to abridge the rights of all Americans. It also provided moderate northerners with a nonconfrontational avenue of protest. Thanks to a growing awareness of slavery, the American Anti-Slavery Society grew from 225 local auxiliaries in 1835 to more than 1,500 by the end of the decade. Thus, at the same time that national political parties succeeded in keeping slavery out of national politics, the abolitionist movement slowly picked up support in northern cities and towns.

The Emergence of Political Abolitionism

Fearful that the slavery issue would destroy the Union, politicians north and south determined to maintain a political coalition that would prevent a reoccurrence of the kind of crisis that had erupted over the admission of Missouri. The result was a new party system that began with the emergence of the Democrats, led by Andrew Jackson, and later an anti-Jackson coalition eventually known as the Whigs. Democrats and Whigs were both national parties: each had strong northern and southern wings, meaning that both parties were committed to keeping the slavery issue out of national politics.

Hence, the focus of antislavery politics shifted to the states. By the mid-1820s, popular clamor had prompted a few northern states to pass laws divorcing them from the national Fugitive Slave Act of 1793 and making it more difficult for masters to recapture fugitives. An 1820 state law made it illegal for Ohio officials to enforce the Fugitive Slave Act and made kidnapping free people of color in Ohio punishable by fines of up to $2,000 and "seven to twenty-one years' imprisonment at hard labor." When proslavery forces tried to scuttle the act in 1826, antislavery workers—Black and white—combined to pass another bill that essentially restated the first.

But the emergence of radical abolitionism, and the backlash it provoked, demonstrated that slavery was a threat not simply to the freedom of southern Blacks but to the civil rights of northern whites. In defense of slavery, northern speakers were hounded from their lecterns; northern editors were dragged through the streets and murdered. The government even proposed to interrupt the flow of the US mail. The threat slavery posed to northern freedom was the wedge issue that began to push slavery back into national politics.

The lack of support for the petition campaign in Congress led abolitionists to the conclusion that they would have to elect more antislavery men. At first, they tried interviewing candidates to sound them out and endorsing only those who expressed satisfactory antislavery views. But it quickly became clear that campaign promises were an unreliable predictor of support for antislavery issues by elected officials. By late 1839 and early 1840, a small group of abolitionists, most of them in New York, decided to launch a political party of their own.

The new interest in electoral politics divided abolitionism. Garrison's growing commitment to perfectionism led him and his followers to object to all forms of government coercion; therefore, they reacted with increasing vehemence against the move into politics. And even among "political abolitionists" there was no clear agreement on the desirability of establishing a third party, what the party should stand for, and whether it should focus on the single issue of slavery or try to broaden its appeal by adopting positions on additional issues. Most abolitionists also flinched at the increasingly aggressive tactics of Garrison's movement and at the visible participation of women and African Americans.

These tensions were palpable in 1840 at the American Anti-Slavery Society's national convention. Participants quickly divided over whether women should participate in deliberations and whether the organization should work to elect abolitionist candidates to office. The Garrisonian branch stacked the convention. When Abby Kelley was elected to a previously all-male committee, anti-Garrisonians walked out. The exodus freed the majority of abolitionists to launch an abolitionist political party. The Liberty Party fielded its first presidential candidate, James Gillespie Birney, in 1840 and again in 1844. Birney had no chance of being elected president, and Liberty Party organizers understood that. Their hope was to gain enough strength in different localities to give antislavery men leverage in swing districts. Though Liberty Party candidates themselves won few elections, they were more successful in many northern localities than Birney's meager presidential votes might otherwise indicate. But the most enduring achievement of the Liberty Party was in its formulation of an antislavery constitutional doctrine and a political platform that went on to become the basis of later electoral success.

Freedom National, Slavery Local

The first premise of the Liberty Party was that freedom was national and slavery merely local. This meant that slavery had no reach beyond the borders of the states where it existed. Everywhere outside those borders—in the western territories, on the high seas, in Washington, DC, and in the free states of the North—the

Constitution obliged the federal government to promote freedom and oppose slavery. The Constitution did not allow the federal government to abolish slavery in the states where it already existed, but that did not mean that there could be no national antislavery politics. On the contrary, the federal government could exclude slavery from the western territories, refuse to admit any new slave states, regulate the interstate slave trade, abolish slavery in the nation's capital, and join Great Britain in the suppression of the Atlantic slave trade.

Because political abolitionists had alerted northerners to the disproportionate influence of a "Slave Power" on national politics, they paved the way for a much more successful foray into politics in 1848. By then the War with Mexico (see Chapter 12) had dramatically increased the size of the western territories and many northerners had come to suspect that this was a way of creating more new slave states, increasing the influence of the Slave Power on federal policy. Armed with the same basic principle of "Freedom National, Slavery Local," most of the Liberty Party men joined in a much more successful Free-Soil Party in 1848. This time their candidate, former president Martin Van Buren, garnered a respectable 225,000 votes. The ideological continuity of antislavery politics was provided by Salmon P. Chase, who drafted both the Liberty Party platform of 1844 and the Free-Soil platform of 1848.

Chase did not expect the Free-Soil Party to displace either of the two major parties. Instead, he placed his hopes on a "fusion" with either the Whigs or the Democrats. Over the next four years, successful fusion movements got Chase elected to the Senate from Ohio and Charles Sumner from Massachusetts. But after 1850, both major parties committed themselves more firmly than ever to suppressing all discussion of slavery in national politics. However successful it was in some localities, "fusion" could not be the basis of a successful antislavery political movement.

But neither could the two major parties withstand the pressure of the slavery issue. Over the next several years, the Whig Party collapsed and the Democratic Party split into hostile northern and southern wings. Once that happened, the path was clear for the establishment of a new antislavery party, the Republicans, committed to the same basic principle of "Freedom National, Slavery Local" that had animated political abolitionists for nearly 20 years. With the emergence of abolition as a force in national politics, the era of antebellum reform, drawing from both the Revolutionary and religious traditions, came to fruition and made its mark on American democracy.

REFORM AND THE URBAN CLASSES

Drawing from both the Revolutionary egalitarian tradition and evangelical Christianity, Americans in this era also created organizations to address concerns about secular life, particularly in the cities. There, the market revolution and immigration opened a new rift between the haves and the have-nots.

Wage Dependency and Labor Protest

By 1830, in response to growing markets, master craftsmen had subdivided the production process into smaller, discrete tasks, sending part production (of shoes, hats, or shirts) to outworkers who worked from home and were paid by the number of pieces they completed rather than the hours they worked. In house, employers relied more and more on apprentices or poorly trained helpers, who worked more cheaply than journeymen. As work was subdivided, workers became more interchangeable, and their wages dropped, threatening not only their livelihoods but their belief in democratic equality.

The Panic of 1819 had thrown thousands of people out of work, driving wages down and prices up. The reviving economy of the 1820s did not reverse those trends, which were deepened by depressions in 1829 and 1837. The lives of outwork seamstresses, of whom there were tens of thousands in the eastern cities, were particularly harrowing. Philadelphia philanthropist Mathew Carey estimated the wages of Philadelphia seamstresses at $1.25 a week, but a committee of seamstresses revealed that they were lucky to earn $1.12 a week. After rent, they were left with a little more than a nickel a day for food, clothing, heat, and anything else they needed.

By 1830, the urban Northeast was witnessing the damages of wage dependency and the subdivision of labor. In the largest cities, neighborhoods had become stratified by class. The New York neighborhood of **Five Points**, once a thriving community of master craftsmen and trade shops, by 1829 was home to prostitutes, beggars, public drunks, thieves, and confidence men. High rents crowded whole working families into single unventilated rooms. Many went homeless or threw up shanties.

The organizing begun in the 1820s exploded in the 1830s, both among craft workers and in occupations long excluded from craft recognition. When the

Five Points, New York City Once the site of a thriving community of craft shops and smaller retailers, Five Points had become one of New York City's poorest neighborhoods and, as this drawing suggests, a symbol of urban poverty, immorality, and crime.

Philadelphia Mechanics' Union dissolved, leadership passed to the New England Association of Farmers, Mechanics, and Other Workingmen, founded in 1831 by, among others, Seth Luther. The association used its newspaper, the *New England Artisan*, for worker self-education and organizing.

In February 1831, protest erupted in an unexpected quarter. With wages in sharp decline, over 1,800 tailoresses (women who worked in specific aspects of the tailoring craft) struck the New York garment industry. The tailoresses had been advised not to strike to avoid harsh public censure and to wait for times to improve. Sarah Monroe, the secretary of the union, resisted the advice: "Long have the poor tailoresses of this city borne their oppression in silence, until patience is no longer a virtue—and in my opinion to be silent longer would be a crime." The women drew up a constitution, elected officers, and stayed out on strike for five months.

Deteriorating labor conditions led to protest even in that industrial paradise, Lowell (see Chapter 9). After a decade of rapid expansion, the market stalled in 1834. When prices fell and owners cut wages by 12.5 percent, 800 female operatives walked off their jobs. The protest failed, but two years later, when owners tried to increase the price of company housing, 2,000 operatives went out on strike, forcing owners to rescind the increases. The 1836 victory was fleeting, however. Business was booming, and the owners had a vested interest in keeping the mills open. When business was slow or inventories high, workers would have far less power.

Workers tried to strengthen their position by forming regional and national associations. The most successful national association was the National Trades' Union (NTU), formed in 1834. The NTU survived for a number of years but was unable to effect statewide coordinated actions. In the end, much of its energy went into lobbying for currency reform, worker access to education and free land, and the 10-hour day.

A New Urban Middle Class

If the new working classes turned to Revolutionary principles and collective action to address their status, the new middles classes looked increasingly to revitalized religion and individual responsibility.

Seth Luther framed his criticisms of American industrial society as a struggle between the "producing classes" and the "rich." However, this was not an accurate description. The concept of the "producing classes" was ambiguous, encompassing Americans of many different standards of living and levels of wealth. For Luther, the term meant primarily urban households dependent on wage labor. Luther sometimes distinguished among the "poor," the "rich," and the "middling classes." Americans were proud of their great "middling" ranks of solid farmers and artisans, the bedrock of democracy. But the composition of the category had changed by the 1830s, as had its relation to the group Luther now called the "working classes."

These new middling classes were difficult to define exactly. Like the new working classes, the middling classes were primarily urban based. Middle-class households tended to receive their income as fees and salaries, rather than wages, and their paid workers held jobs that required mental, rather than physical, labor. These included doctors, lawyers, ministers, middle managers, agents, supervisors, tellers, clerks, shopkeepers, editors, writers, and schoolteachers.

The relationship of these urban households of moderate means to the new industrial economy was complicated. On the one hand, they were highly susceptible to catastrophic economic reversal, whether sudden unemployment, business failure, or bad speculation. At the same time, the new middle class was created by and benefited from the industrial transformation. The paid occupations on which middle-class families depended had expanded enormously. These jobs brought annual salaries ranging roughly from $1,000 to $1,500, compared with the $300 to $400 an average working man might earn. Middle-class families also tended to have access to other resources through family, friends, and business connections.

The middle class celebrated the new economy, the expansion of democracy, and the growth of individual opportunity even as it deplored the special privilege of the wealthy. Deeply religious and committed to the doctrines of personal agency, middle-class citizens were churchgoers who both donated to and participated in the causes of the Benevolent Empire.

Individuals who aspired to urban middle-class status began to distinguish themselves from the urban poor rather than the rich. This was especially evident in their understanding of personal responsibility and material success. In sermons and tracts, children's books, and novels, members of the new middle class described the commercial economy as a test of personal character. Success demonstrated superior individual industriousness and self-discipline; failure signified the opposite. These beliefs took their toll on middle-class families that failed, bringing on social and psychological censure. Nevertheless, middle-class writers continued to hone the idiom of the "common man" into the more class-based language of the "self-made man" of business. From this point of view, the middle class was the repository of moderation in a changing world, the heir of Jefferson's idealized "husbandmen."

Meanwhile, middle-class families struggled to distinguish themselves from the working class. Middle-class parents recoiled from manual labor and urged their sons to become "a rich merchant, or a popular lawyer, or a broker." They expressed a new value for education, even for their daughters. Whereas workers crowded into smaller and smaller homes, the emerging middle class expressed itself in increasingly elaborate residential spaces. The ideal middle-class home, the "cottage," offered a private sitting room for the family and a separate "public" parlor for guests. The parlor was a stage on which the family could proclaim its success through a display of costly furnishings and decorations.

To emphasize their distance from the industrial world, members of the new urban middle class insisted on a "natural" division of temperament and capability between men and women. Although men were required to confront the degradations of labor, women were intended by nature to remain at home to restore the sensibilities of husbands and raise children protected from the ravages of industrialization.

This view of women as the primary influence on children represented a dramatic change in attitude. It was, however, largely inaccurate, as many middle-class women pursued paid labor. They took in boarders, did fancy sewing, opened schools, and worked in family-owned businesses. They all worked unpaid at the daily labor of cooking, cleaning, washing, ironing, preserving food, sewing, and caring for children. Domestic womanhood became the primary symbol of middle-class respectability and a bulwark against the contradictions of the new industrial society.

Immigration and Nativism

Facing enormous changes, even economically secure Americans were alert for sources of potential danger. While labor leaders and utopians felt that industrialists were posing that danger, others focused their anxieties on the poor, deemed incapable of self-improvement. Immigrants became natural targets, and especially the Catholic Irish.

In spite of the difficulties facing wage workers, the robust economy drew increasing numbers of immigrants from Europe, 90 percent of whom came from England, Germany, or Ireland. The largest group by far was Irish. Plagued by chronic poverty and harsh British rule, almost 60,000 Irish immigrants arrived in the 1820s, 235,000 in the 1830s, and 845,000 during the potato famines of the 1840s. Through most of the period, the Irish accounted for more than one-third of all immigrants.

Their customs and their poverty made Irish immigrants conspicuous. Unable to afford land, they remained crowded in the seaports where they arrived. Desperate, they often had to accept jobs and conditions that native-born workers scorned. With no other place to go, one boss observed, the Irish could "be relied on at the mill all year round."

Not all of the Irish went into mills. Many built roadways, dredged river bottoms, and built canals. Irish women cooked and did laundry for the camps or hired out as domestic workers in middle-class households.

Most of all, the Irish were distinguished by their Catholic religion. By 1830, immigration had virtually doubled the number of Catholics in the country. Not all Catholics were Irish, but many were, making the Irish visible targets of long-standing anti-Catholic prejudices. Anti-Irish stereotypes represented Catholics as given to superstition and unthinking obedience. Funded by the new middle class and supported by Protestant ministers, anti-Catholic newspapers charged the Catholic hierarchy with "tyrannical and unchristian" acts "repugnant to our republican institutions."

By the early 1830s, anti-Catholicism spilled over into street violence. Organizations such as the New York Protestant Association sponsored "public discussions" on the immorality of monks, the greed of priests, and the pope's alleged designs on the American West. The debates deteriorated into small riots. Anti-Catholicism was especially strong in Massachusetts. In 1834, the associated Congregational Clergy of Massachusetts issued a frantic challenge to Protestants to rescue the republic from "the degrading influence of Popery." Sermons and editorials whipped up a frenzy of anti-Catholic fear. The hysteria was aimed at an Ursuline convent in Charlestown, Massachusetts, in which, purportedly, nuns were brainwashing innocent Protestant students. On the night of August 11, 1834, a cheering mob burned the convent to the ground. Anti-Catholicism was beginning to serve as a bond among Americans who otherwise had little in common with one another.

Internal Migration

The constant stream of internal migrants also heightened the sense of turmoil in antebellum American society. Strong internal migration signaled growth and opportunity, but it also produced a steady flow of individuals who seemed to have no settled stake in American society.

Many of these were westward settlers, but many were marginalized rural folks seeking employment in the cities. There was both a push and a pull to this movement. Children were pushed out from farming families whose land could no longer support them.

In the cities, these young people often lived in rented rooms without adult guidance. Young men joined neighborhood fire companies that served as gathering places for fun and sport. Young women navigated the city unescorted. Young people used their earnings to buy the things unavailable in the countryside: new shoes, clothing of the latest cut, hats, and canes. Migrants usually traveled fairly short distances to the nearest large towns and cities and swelled the populations of the midsized cities in which most American manufacturing took place.

At the same time, the constant migration of Americans westward provoked alarm among the eastern, urban middle class. Moralistic observers worried that this migration was draining ambitious, upright citizens from the East Coast, leaving the dregs of society behind. Observers also worried about the influence of the West on future American citizens. The West lacked the institutions that easterners associated with civilization and civic responsibility. There were few schools and churches and too many unattached young men, saloons, and brothels. Moreover, westward migration stood for the materialism and greed that easterners were beginning to worry about. The desire for money drove some families on an almost endless migration. One family, the Shelbys, had made four moves west by 1850, when they ended up in Oregon.

Into this changing land were being born more and more of the nation's young. Once families had begun to pour in, fertility rates in the newly settled areas became far higher than they were in the older, coastal regions. Easterners were alarmed by the specter of a generation of children growing up in the wilderness without proper social constraints. The values of self-reliance, industry, and civic virtue, which only a decade before had seemed to capture the essence of American nationalism, appeared in danger of disappearing.

SELF-REFORM AND SOCIAL REGULATION

Americans during this era felt both hope and fear that the foundations of American character and democracy were disappearing, but that they could be reclaimed, if only Americans exercised sufficient control of themselves and others. Faced with deep divisions and seemingly impossible obstacles to an ideal industrial society, reformers began to turn away from broad programs of social perfection to endeavors that centered on self-control and external restraint.

A Culture of Self-Improvement

Answering criticisms from fellow senators that only the rich and well-connected enjoyed the benefits of the new American industrial order, in 1832 Henry Clay rose to defend the entrepreneurial class. "In Kentucky," he asserted, "almost every manufactory known to me is in the hands of enterprising and self-made men, who have acquired whatever wealth they possess by patient and diligent labor." Clay's emphasis on personal enterprise captured a perspective increasingly shared by ambitious Americans by the 1830s. Success or failure was less a matter of external injustice and constraint than of individual striving. Those who truly worked hard—who were industrious and clever and frugal—would succeed. Thus was born the concept of American "individualism," a term coined by the French traveler Alexis de Tocqueville, who visited the United States in 1831–1832, and observed that Americans "are apt to imagine that their whole destiny is in their own hands."

Individualism led directly to a culture of **self-improvement** among members of the new middle class. The emphasis on self-creation helped to resolve their ambivalence about industrial society: middle-class families had escaped the worst ravages of wage labor not because they were lucky or had some special advantage but because they worked harder.

The culture of self-improvement embraced the body as well. From the 1820s to the 1840s, health reform became a national obsession, as Americans experimented with new diets, clothing, exercise programs, abstinence, and hydropathy, the cleansing of the body through frequent bathing and drinking of water.

Middle-class men and women crowded lectures and devoured writings that espoused the philosophy of self-culture. By 1831, the **lyceum movement** claimed several thousand local organizations under a national association and sponsored such speakers as the writer Ralph Waldo Emerson, Daniel Webster, and later Abraham Lincoln. Meanwhile, middle-class readers supported a publishing bonanza in novels, periodicals, and tracts devoted to self-improvement.

These publications promoted a variety of images of the self-made American. In his *Leatherstocking Tales*, James Fenimore Cooper celebrated the pioneer. Novels like Catharine Sedgwick's *The Poor Rich Man, and the Rich Poor Man* romanticized urban poverty and suggested that hard work put "true wealth" (virtue) within the reach of even the most humble family.

Although in most cases the myth of the self-made American was decidedly male, it also had important implications for women. On the one hand, it highlighted the importance of childrearing. Periodicals such as the *Ladies Magazine* and *Godey's Lady's Book* and advice books such as Lydia Maria Child's *The Mother at Home* and William Alcott's *The Young Mother* instructed women on the

Lyceum Movement Americans' enormous interest in self-improvement in the antebellum years was reflected in their enthusiasm for public lectures, known as the lyceum movement. This cartoon gently spoofed a lecture by James Pollard Espy, a meteorologist. As the drawing suggests, women were prominent in lyceum audiences.

development of the proper mental and moral habits in the young. On the other hand, a generation of female novelists appropriated the themes of self-culture to emphasize female self-reliance. In her 1827 novel *A New-England Tale*, Sedgwick told the story of a young orphan left penniless by an improvident wealthy father and a pampered mother. Jane, the protagonist, learns that hard work builds both economic independence and strength of character and is appropriately rewarded with a prosperous husband, children, and a safe middle-class home.

Some writers mounted a determined assault on the new American political and economic order. Transcendentalists such as Ralph Waldo Emerson, Margaret Fuller, and Henry David Thoreau believed in the power of the independent mind not only to understand the material environment but also to achieve a spiritual wholeness with the world. They saw that, in contemporary America, self-improvement was often cultivated only for immediate material gain. In his essay "Self-Reliance" (1841), Emerson tried to distinguish true independence of mind from slavish rushing after privilege and celebrity.

Temperance

Of the many movements for regulating the body, the largest by far—and the longest lived—was the **temperance movement**. By the 1840s, hundreds of thousands of Americans had taken the pledge to swear off demon rum.

Prior to the nineteenth century, liquor played a central role in the lives of Americans. The Puritans (even ministers) had insisted on having their supply of wine, beer, and hard cider, and in craft shops, workers took rum breaks from their labor.

Some religious groups, especially the Quakers and the Methodists, had opposed the drinking of hard liquor in the eighteenth century, but it was only in 1808, in Saratoga, New York, that the first temperance society was formed. Within the next five years, at least four more temperance societies were established in New England.

In the 1820s, the temperance movement was taken over by evangelicals who saw demon rum as the enemy not just of piety but of the self-control essential to the perfection of society. Evangelists began to depict drinking as a sign of social disorder. In a series of six sermons preached in 1825, Lyman Beecher effectively changed the debate over alcohol. He did not call for absolute abstinence, and he urged his followers to form voluntary associations to drive the demon rum from American society. The following February saw the formation of the American Society for the Promotion of Temperance (ASPT). The ASPT quickly set about organizing local chapters across the country. By 1834, there were at least 5,000 state and local temperance societies.

The Common School Movement and Democracy

By the 1830s, workers, members of the new middle class, and elite philanthropists all identified education as a critical arena for reform. The drive to expand public education, like so many movements of this era, grew out of both hope and fear. As in other reform movements, however, the motives of different groups varied widely.

Since the founding of the nation, educational opportunities for the sons and daughters of prosperous parents had steadily increased. Children from wealthy urban families had private tutors, followed (for boys) by training in private seminaries and academies. By the 1820s, young women from prosperous northern families could choose from a growing number of seminaries. Meanwhile, subscription schools offered basic education to rural children.

These schools were out of reach for working-class children and even much of the growing middle class. Labor reformers linked this lack of schooling directly to the larger process of industrial oppression. In their 1831 constitution, the Working Men's Association of New York placed the demand for "a system of equal, republican education" above every other goal, because education "secures and perpetuates every political right we possess." Only free public education, workers argued, could defy "the siege of aristocracy." At the same time, middle-class fathers in Utica, New York, called for a public school system that would permit children to "keep pace with the age in its improvements" and "calculate their own profits in the world."

Middle-class parents knew that their daughters might not marry or might marry into families that would face financial ruin; they worried that traditional housewifery skills would be of little use to daughters who faced an increasingly complex market culture and new domestic technologies. At the same time, reformers who were concerned that expanded suffrage would introduce volatility into the American electoral process often supported expanded public education as "the great bulwark of republican government," in the words of New York governor De Witt Clinton. If white working men and their sons were to vote, it was important that they first be educated.

This convergence of interests led to a growing demand for more **common schools**. Nevertheless, broad segments of the public resisted the idea. In Cincinnati, wealthy property owners opposed paying taxes to send poor children to school. Other skeptics considered the whole idea an invasion of their rights as free citizens. States were often left to passing simple enabling legislation such as Pennsylvania's 1834 act that made public schools a local option.

In 1837, the Massachusetts legislature went further, creating a state board of education and appointing educational reformer Horace Mann as its first secretary. Mann addressed the anxieties of more prosperous Americans. On the one hand, he reassured middle-class parents that relying on an extrafamilial institution was both right and natural, given the changing society. On the other hand, he assured them that nothing else needed to change about the industrial society on which they depended. Only the lack of education barred the poor from prosperity, and benevolence and education would "disarm the poor of their hostility toward the rich."

The commitment to public education did not extend to the education of the small free African American community. Until the 1850s, free African American children were excluded from public common schools, and tax monies were not used to establish schools for them. Education for free Black children came almost entirely from the work of the free African American community. In the North, the efforts bore fruit, but in the South, opposition to the education of enslaved people hardened. In fact, many enslaved and free African American southerners did learn to read and write, but usually surreptitiously.

Penal Reform

In the first years of the republic, with memories of British injustice still fresh, Americans tended to think of crime as a problem of bad laws, not flawed people. Fair laws would nurture good republican character, and good republican citizens would respect laws they had had a hand in passing.

Yet by the 1820s, eastern cities were incarcerating thousands of citizens—some for debt but many for robbery, larceny, fraud, vagrancy, and disorderly conduct. Where individuals failed to obey the law, the community must devise some mechanism for its own protection.

The most popular solution from the 1820s on was the establishment of state prison systems, where deviant individuals could be kept apart from the community but could also be rehabilitated. State and city prisons soon began to replace older charity institutions. The two primary models, devised by New York and Pennsylvania, were variants on a single principle: the first step in making prisons places of real reform was to prevent inmates from influencing one another.

The New York version became most widely associated with the penitentiary at Ossining, New York, known as Sing Sing. There, prisoners worked side by side all day but were prevented from talking or even looking at one another. They slept in separate cells. The Pennsylvania model called for absolute isolation of the prisoners.

Visitors often toured these prisons and frequently applauded them, but they also noted the exaggerated hopes that Americans seemed to invest in them. Alexis de Tocqueville observed of American reformers: "They have caught the monomanie of the penitentiary system, which to them seems to remedy for all the evils of society."

Electoral Politics and Moral Reform

Frustrated with the seeming resistance of social problems to moral suasion, reformers turned increasingly to electoral politics for solutions, just as the abolitionists did, but without facing the same national backlash. The effect was to fragment and weaken party organization rather than to consolidate it. The political landscape became littered with specialized and often largely local parties, demonstrating the inability of the major parties to absorb basic social conflicts into their agendas.

Nowhere was possession of the vote more important than among newly enfranchised white male workers. During the struggles of the 1820s and 1830s, laboring people, drawing on the democratic heritage of the Revolution, believed that many of their problems would be remedied only through electoral action. As long as the economic power of employers was backed by laws that oppressed workers (debt laws that imprisoned them, bankruptcy laws that took their property, conspiracy laws that made union organizing illegal), strikes and petitions would never be enough.

By the late 1820s, workers had begun to mobilize politically. In 1827, a group of workers in Philadelphia formed the Mechanics' Union of Trade Associations. Within a year that group became the Philadelphia Working Men's Party, a new political party dedicated to "the interests and enlightenment of the working classes." Over the next five years, under various names, the movement spread through most of the nation, becoming strongest in northern cities.

Workers were at a political crossroads. On the one hand, the formation of the Working Men's Party implied that workers were still optimistic that change was possible and that working men thought of themselves as citizens with the right and power to affect the makeup of the republic in such issues as public education, broadened incorporation laws, an end to imprisonment for debt, and banking reform. On the other hand, the organization of a separate political party indicated that workers remained deeply skeptical of the responsiveness of existing parties. Workers were moving toward a distinct identity within the new political economy.

In the winter of 1835–1836, anger at the legal system came to a head. With inflation and unemployment running high, New York City journeymen tailors went out on strike. The leaders of the union were arrested, tried, convicted on conspiracy charges, and fined. The labor press denounced the courts as "the tool of the aristocracy, against the people!" Nearly 30,000 people (the largest crowd in American history to that date) protested the convictions. The protestors resolved to meet the following fall in Utica, New York, to organize a "separate and distinct" political party to represent workers' interests. The 93 "workers, farmers, and mechanics" who met in Utica six months later voted to form the Equal Rights Party.

Labor movements in other states also began to focus on legislative reform. The 10-hour day, a long-standing demand, reemerged in the late 1840s as a central point of labor organizing. Workers in New England supported candidates friendly to the 10-hour day, petitioned legislatures for laws setting work hours, and testified before legislative committees. Female workers testified as well, using their life stories to create sympathy for the cause. It was male workers, however, who had the power to vote representatives out of office.

Other reform movements, ones with roots in the Benevolent Empire, began to focus on electoral strategies. The Female Moral Reform Society, which had long worked to redeem prostitutes from their sins, shifted strategies and began working for the passage of rent laws and property protections for women. This growing emphasis on legal reform grew out of an enhanced sense of connection between the reformer and the recipient of her aid.

Throughout the 1840s, temperance workers turned increasingly toward the passing of state laws. Among some temperance advocates (especially women), the shift was motivated by concern for legal protections for the wives and families of alcoholic men. But the use of legal strategies also expressed a growing belief on the part of middle-class, native-born reformers that alcoholism was a problem of the unruly immigrant working classes. As they identified drinkers as fundamentally different from themselves, temperance workers grew less interested in aiding drinkers directly and more willing to take recourse to legal controls.

WOMEN'S RIGHTS

Many of the antebellum reform movements generated widespread controversy and passionate disagreement. But no others touched the central nerve of society like the organized abolition movement after 1830 and the women's rights movement. Race and gender, it seemed to many Americans, were defining their nation and society.

Elizabeth Cady Stanton Stanton, one of the founders of the women's rights movement, is pictured here holding her daughter Harriot in 1856.

Women and Reform Movements

Women from all classes and ranks in antebellum society were beginning to chafe under cultural and legal restrictions on their full autonomy as Americans. The young women workers who marched at Lowell called themselves "daughters of freemen" and edged closer to claiming an independent status as citizens, as did the tailoresses, who were tired of waiting for chivalry to improve their lot. Educated women and women who worked as authors, editors, and educators participated actively in the public discourse and profoundly influenced public opinion. Were they to be regarded as mere subordinates to fathers and husbands?

For many women, the growing importance of suffrage and electoral tactics to reform movements created a new consciousness of their precarious status. Reform work permitted women to participate in shaping the new democratic order and to perfect skills useful in civic culture. They ran meetings, kept track of money and records, and honed their skills at public speaking. Elite women involved in charities also learned to make use of the new institutions of the market revolution. Because married women could not hold property or make contracts in their own names, most women would have had trouble accumulating the money to fund asylums and schools. But these married women, wives and daughters of wealthy and influential men, could use their social position to obtain donations, endorsements, and even special charters (comparable to those granted to male entrepreneurs) that permitted a group of married women to function legally as males.

Reform women soon learned that there were limits to their authority. Even women who were involved in the mildest of reform activities (e.g., as members of the American Bible Society) were rebuked for "acting out of their appropriate sphere." Women engaged in more controversial activities such as labor reform or abolition work were heckled and hounded by mobs.

In 1837, in her *Essay on Slavery and Abolitionism*, Catharine Beecher attacked female abolitionists for violating the bounds of "rectitude and propriety" and for being motivated by unwomanly "ambition." The same year, the Massachusetts clergy criticized Sarah and Angelina Grimké for daring to take "the place and tone of man as public reformer."

By the late 1830s, women involved in abolition work were subjected to growing criticism from within. Although William Lloyd Garrison remained a staunch ally, other leaders, such as Arthur and Lewis Tappan, believed that outspoken, assertive women were embarrassing the movement. For women who had given years of their labor and had endangered their lives in the cause of abolition, these attacks were

Struggles For Democracy

The Seneca Falls Convention

"We hold these truths to be self-evident: that all men and women are created equal; that they are endowed by their Creator with certain inalienable rights; that among these are life, liberty, and the pursuit of happiness; that to secure these rights governments are instituted, deriving their just powers from the consent of the governed." The speaker who first read these words aloud was not a twentieth-century feminist presenting a more "politically correct" version of the Declaration of Independence. The person who wrote and then read these words was Elizabeth Cady Stanton, speaking on a summer day in 1848. She was passionately convinced that the words of the Declaration of Independence were flawed because they did not explicitly apply to everyone.

Weeks before she read those words, Elizabeth Cady Stanton had been chafing under the endless round of household responsibilities that belonged to a wife and mother. Her husband, Henry Stanton, was frequently away from home campaigning against the spread of slavery, and Elizabeth was left at home in **Seneca Falls**, New York, to care for their family. She kept up with the newspapers and learned that in Europe, revolutionary movements were brewing. One day in July, a Quaker neighbor named Jane Hunt invited her to tea with several other Quaker friends, among them Lucretia Mott, a well-known abolitionist whom Elizabeth had met years before on a trip to England, where she and her husband attended an antislavery conference. Elizabeth poured out her heart to sympathetic ears, and the conversation turned to the need to organize on behalf of women, who were barred from higher education, the right

to enter lucrative professions, and in most states, if they were married, the right to own property or keep their children after a divorce. The group decided to hold a convention at the local Wesleyan chapel and see what came of it.

They advertised in local papers and wrote to a number of well-known activists and reformers, including Frederick Douglass. The women were pleased and surprised when about 300 people turned up, including over 40 men on the first day. Walking from her home to the chapel that first morning, the nervous Elizabeth confessed to her sister that she felt like "abandoning all her principles and running away." She had never spoken in public before. During the convention, which took place on July 19 and 20, the women read aloud and debated each section of the document they called their "Declaration of Rights and Sentiments." Only one segment aroused resistance from the otherwise largely sympathetic audience, and that was the demand that women be given the right to vote. Not even all the organizers were in favor of it. Lucretia Mott had warned, "Lizzie, thee will make us ridiculous." But Elizabeth was determined to defend the measure. Frederick Douglass helped immensely. The former slave, nationally known as a speaker and writer, declared that he could not possibly demand the right to vote for himself and his brethren if he did not also ask for it on behalf of all women. All the measures, even the demand for the franchise, were approved by the audience in a vote.

Several New York State newspapers covered the convention and the coverage was picked up by many papers around the nation. That was the good news, as far as the organizers were

continued

Struggles For Democracy continued

concerned. The bad news was that much of the commentary was negative, even derisive. The women had not been prepared for that. The cause seemed so right and just to them; reform and change were in the air. However, several of the attendees later held conferences of their own in their home communities, and far more people than before began to write about women's issues in various periodicals. The need to end slavery soon became the preeminent cause, and then the Civil War absorbed reformers' energies.

A generation later, however, in the late nineteenth century, women's rights and especially women's suffrage became major national concerns. In some ways, the Seneca Falls convention became mythologized, envisioned as far larger and grander than it really was. Its actual spontaneity was masked when people looked back upon it as a founding moment. But the meeting had certainly constituted an important step in the forging of American democracy. When Elizabeth Cady Stanton died in 1902, she still could not vote, but she was rightly convinced that her daughters would be able to; they had already obtained the college education she herself had hungered for.

galling. Disappointing, too, was the willingness of such men to abandon the old moral-reform strategies, which embraced gender equality. The turn toward electoral reform reduced women to second-class status in the movement. They could still raise money, lobby, and speak, but they could not perform the new essential act of reform, voting.

TIME LINE

▼**1824**
Charles Grandison Finney begins preaching in up-state New York

▼**1826**
American Society for the Promotion of Temperance formed
General Colored Association of Massachusetts formed

▼**1827**
John Russwurm and Samuel E. Cornish found *Freedom's Journal*

▼**1829**
David Walker publishes *An Appeal to the Colored Citizens of the World*

▼**1830**
Joseph Smith founds the Church of Jesus Christ of Latter-day Saints (Mormons)
National Negro Convention movement begins

▼**1831**
New England Association of Farmers, Mechanics, and Other Workingmen founded

New York Protestant Association founded
Lyceum movement begins
William Lloyd Garrison founds *The Liberator*
New England Anti-Slavery Society founded

▼**1831–1832**
Alexis de Tocqueville visits United States

▼**1832**
Maria Stewart lectures in Boston

The Seneca Falls Convention

After the 1840 division of the American Anti-Slavery Society over women's participation, abolitionist women spearheaded a drive for an organized women's rights movement. In Seneca Falls, New York, on July 14, 1848, five women (including the seasoned Quaker abolitionist Lucretia Mott and the much younger Elizabeth Cady Stanton) placed an advertisement in the *Seneca County Courier* stating, "A convention to discuss the social, civil and religious condition and rights of woman will be held in the Wesleyan Chapel, Seneca Falls, New York, on Wednesday and Thursday, the 19th and 20th of July current, commencing at 10 a.m."

The response was overwhelming. The packed house debated, voted on, and passed a Declaration of Sentiments (modeled after the Declaration of Independence, and adapting the Revolutionary legacy for a new purpose) and a list of resolutions. They demanded specific social and legal changes for women, including a role in lawmaking, improved property rights, equity in divorce, and access to education and the professions. All of the resolutions passed unanimously but one: a demand for the vote. Even as reform became ever more tied to electoral strategies, some reformers considered suffrage too radical for women.

CONCLUSION

When Andrew Jackson took office in 1829, he declared his mission to be "reform." Jackson, of course, meant reform of America's political society, and specifically, personal revenge on the politicians who had earlier denied him the presidency. By the time Jackson left office in 1837, Americans had begun to take the cause of

▼**1833**
American Anti-Slavery Society founded

▼**1834**
Anti-Catholic mob burns Ursuline Convent in Charleston, Massachusetts
Lowell operatives go on strike
National Trades' Union formed
Female Moral Reform Society formed
Anti–African American riots in major cities

▼**1835**
Lyman Beecher publishes *A Plea for the West*
American Anti-Slavery Society begins postal campaign

▼**1836**
Congress passes "gag rule"

▼**1837**
Bread riots in New York City
Massachusetts creates first state board of education; Horace Mann appointed secretary
Abolitionist editor Elijah Lovejoy murdered

▼**1838**
Angelina Grimké presents abolitionist petitions to the Massachusetts legislature

▼**1840**
James Gillespie Birney runs for president as first Liberty Party candidate

▼**1848**
Women's rights movement begins at Seneca Falls, New York
Martin Van Buren runs for president on Free Soil Party ticket

reform into their own hands. For some, it was a purifying mission, returning the nation to its founding promises of justice and equality. For others, it was an impossible task, tearing apart the fabric of the democracy. In the nation's short history, the West had always functioned as the republic's social and cultural release. Soon that symbol of reconciliation and prosperity would become the site of America's insoluble conflicts.

WHO, WHAT, WHERE

abolitionist movement   354

American Colonization
   Society   354

Benevolent Empire   352

common schools   369

Five Points   362

Garrison, William Lloyd   348

lyceum movement   367

millennial   350

Missouri Compromise   354

perfectionism   358

Purvis, Harriet Forten   357

self-improvement   367

Seneca Falls   373

Shakers   350

temperance movement   368

REVIEW QUESTIONS

1. What conditions gave rise to labor protest in the 1820s and 1830s? What forms did that protest take?

2. What conditions gave rise to the development of religious communities such as the Shakers?

3. Why did some reformers abandon the tactic of moral suasion over time?

4. What does the phrase "Freedom National, Slavery Local" refer to?

CRITICAL-THINKING QUESTIONS

1. Antebellum reformers created large organizations to pursue their various goals but also placed a strong emphasis on personal agency and helped shape the image of the self-made man. How were these two seemingly contradictory ideas able to exist side by side?

2. Did the rise of perfectionism and the Benevolent Empire reflect a new democratic impulse or a desire for social control?

3. Which of the reform movements of this period do you think was most successful? Explain your answer.

4. Compare and contrast the tactics that different abolitionists used to further their cause (for example, speeches, mailings, working within the political system). What are the strengths and weaknesses of each? Which seems to have been most effective?

5. The reforms of this period had many sources: both hope and fear, and both the Revolutionary commitment to equality and an evangelical Christian commitment to individual and social moral reform. Describe how these trends worked in shaping the era's reform movements.

SUGGESTED READINGS

Ginzberg, Lori D. *Elizabeth Cady Stanton: An American Life.* New York: Hill and Wang, 2009.

Sinha, Manisha. *The Slave's Cause: A History of Abolition.* New Haven, CT: Yale University Press, 2016.

Thatcher Ulrich, Laurel. *A House Full of Females: Plural Marriage and Women's Rights in Early Mormonism, 1835–1870.* New York: Knopf, 2017.

For further review materials and resource information, please visit www.oup.com/us/ofthepeople

CHAPTER 11:   Reform and Conflict, 1820–1848
Primary Sources

11.1   DAVID WALKER, EXCERPTS FROM "WALKER'S APPEAL" (1829)

The son of a free Black woman and an enslaved man, David Walker was born free in South Carolina. As an adult, he moved to Boston, where he became a successful businessman, an outspoken abolitionist, and a vociferous critic of racial slavery. The following selection comes from "Walker's Appeal," a pamphlet he published in 1829 that encouraged fellow Blacks, both enslaved and free, to fight racism and slavery. Walker's passionate critique of slavery encouraged people of all races to become more radical in their opposition to slavery.

... I therefore ask the whole American people, had I not rather die, or be put to death, than to be a slave to any tyrant, who takes not only my own, but my wife and children's lives by the inches? Yea, would I meet death with avidity far! far! in preference to such *servile submission* to the murderous hands of tyrants. For let no one of us suppose that the refutations which have been written by our white friends are enough—they are *whites*—we are *blacks*. We, and the world wish to see the charges of Mr. Jefferson [in *Notes on Virginia*, 1785] refuted by the blacks *themselves,* according to their chance; for we must remember that what the whites have written respecting this subject, is other men's labours, and did not emanate from the blacks. I know well, that there are some talents and learning among the coloured people of this country, which we have not a chance to develope, in consequence of oppression; but our oppression ought not to hinder us from acquiring all we can. For we will have a chance to develope them by and by. God will not suffer us, always to be oppressed. Our sufferings will come to an *end,* in spite of all the Americans this side of *eternity.* Then we will want all the learning and talents among ourselves, and perhaps more, to govern ourselves.—"Every dog must have its day," the American's is coming to an end.

But let us review Mr. Jefferson's remarks respecting us some further. Comparing our miserable fathers, with the learned philosophers of Greece, he says: "Yet notwithstanding these and other discouraging circumstances among the Romans, their slaves were often their rarest artists. They excelled too, in science, insomuch as to be usually employed as tutors to their master's children; Epictetus, Terence and Phædrus, were slaves,—but they were of the race of whites. It is not their *condition* then, but *nature,* which has produced the distinction."

See this, my brethren!! Do you believe that this assertion is swallowed by millions of the whites? Do you know that Mr. Jefferson was one of as great characters as ever lived among the whites? See his writings for the world, and public labours for the United States of America. Do you believe that the assertions of such a man, will pass away into oblivion unobserved by this people and the world? If you do you are much mistaken—See how the American people treat us—have we souls in our bodies? Are we men who have any spirits at all? I know that there are many *swellbellied* fellows among us, whose greatest object is to fill their stomachs. Such I do not mean—I am after those who know and feel, that we are MEN, as well as other people; to them, I say, that unless we try to refute Mr. Jefferson's arguments respecting us, we will only establish them. ...

Are we MEN!!—I ask you, O my brethren! are we MEN? Did our Creator make us to be slaves to dust and ashes like ourselves? Are they not dying worms as well as we? Have they not to make their appearance before the tribunal of Heaven, to answer for the deeds done in the body, as well as we? Have we any other Master but Jesus Christ alone? Is he not their Master as well as ours?—What right then, have we to obey and call any other Master, but Himself? How we could be so *submissive* to a gang of men, whom we cannot tell whether they are *as good* as ourselves or not, I never could conceive. However, this is shut up with the Lord, and we cannot precisely tell—but I declare, we judge men by their works.

The whites have always been an unjust, jealous, unmerciful, avaricious and bloodthirsty set of beings, always seeking after power and authority. We view them all over the confederacy of Greece, where they were first known to be any thing, (in consequence of education) we see them there, cutting each other's throats—trying to subject each other to wretchedness and misery—to effect which, they used all kinds of deceitful, unfair, and unmerciful means. We view them next in Rome, where the spirit of tyranny and deceit raged still higher. We view them in Gaul, Spain, and in Britain.—In fine, we view them all over Europe, together with what were scattered about in Asia and Africa, as heathens, and we see them acting more like devils than accountable men. But some may ask, did not the blacks of Africa, and the mulattoes of Asia, go on in the same way as did the whites of Europe. I answer, no—they never were half so avaricious, deceitful and unmerciful as the whites, according to their knowledge.

Source: David Walker, *An Appeal to the Coloured Citizens of the World*. Boston: published for the author, 1829, pp. 17–20, http://docsouth.unc.edu/nc/walker/walker.html.

11.2 WILLIAM LLOYD GARRISON, EXCERPT FROM THE FIRST ISSUE OF *THE LIBERATOR* (1831)

William Lloyd Garrison was one of the most dedicated and radical abolitionists of the antebellum period. At a time when most opponents of slavery supported gradual abolition, colonization, and political negotiation, Garrison advocated for immediate and uncompensated emancipation. He considered the Constitution a proslavery document and resisted any suggestions for compromise on the issue of slavery. Following is an excerpt from the first edition of Garrison's abolitionist newspaper, *The Liberator*, which he published every week from 1831 to 1865.

During my recent tour for the purpose of exciting the minds of the people by a series of discourses on the subject of slavery, every place that I visited gave fresh evidence of the fact, that a greater revolution in public sentiment was to be effected in the free States—and particularly in New-England—than at the South. I found contempt more bitter, opposition more active, detraction more relentless, prejudice more stubborn, and apathy more frozen, than among slave-owners themselves. Of course, there were individual exceptions to the contrary. This state of things afflicted, but did not dishearten me. I determined, at every hazard, to lift up the standard of emancipation in the eyes of the nation, within sight of Bunker Hill and in the birthplace of liberty. That standard is now unfurled; and long may it float, unhurt by the spoliations of time or the missiles of a desperate foe—yea, till every chain be broken, and every bondman set free! Let Southern oppressors tremble—let their secret abettors tremble—let their Northern apologists tremble—let all the enemies of the persecuted blacks tremble.

I deem the publication of my original Prospectus unnecessary, as it has obtained a wide circulation. The principles therein inculcated will be steadily pursued in this paper, excepting that I shall not array myself as the political partisan of any man. In defending the great cause of human rights, I wish to derive the assistance of all religions and of all parties.

Assenting to the "self-evident truth" maintained in the American Declaration of Independence, "that all men are created equal, and endowed by their Creator with certain inalienable rights—among which are life, liberty and the pursuit of happiness," I shall strenuously contend for the immediate enfranchisement of our slave population. In Park-Street Church, on the Fourth of July, 1829, I unreflectingly assented to the popular but pernicious doctrine of gradual abolition. I seize this moment to make a full and unequivocal recantation, and thus publicly to ask pardon of my God, of my country, and of my brethren the poor slaves, for having uttered a sentiment so full of timidity, injustice, and absurdity. A similar recantation, from my pen, was published in the *Genius of Universal Emancipation* at Baltimore, in September, 1829. My conscience is now satisfied.

I am aware that many object to the severity of my language; but is there not cause for severity? I will be as harsh as truth, and as uncompromising as justice. On this subject, I do not wish to think, or to speak, or write, with moderation. No! no! Tell a man whose house is on fire to give a moderate alarm; tell him to moderately rescue his wife from the hands of the ravisher; tell the mother to gradually extricate her babe from the fire into which it has fallen;—but urge me not to use moderation in a cause like the present. I am in earnest—I will not equivocate—I will not excuse—I will not retreat a single inch—AND I WILL BE HEARD. The apathy of the people is enough to make every statue leap from its pedestal, and to hasten the resurrection of the dead.

It is pretended, that I am retarding the cause of emancipation by the coarseness of my invective and the precipitancy of my measures. The charge is not true. On this question of my influence,—humble as it is,—is felt at this moment to a considerable extent, and shall be felt in coming years—not perniciously, but beneficially—not as a curse, but as a blessing; and posterity will bear testimony that I was right. I desire to thank God, that he enables me to disregard "the fear of man which bringeth a snare," and to speak his truth in its simplicity and power …

Source: Wendell Phillips Garrison, *William Lloyd Garrison, 1805–1879: The Story of His Life, Told by His Children*, vol. I (New York: The Century Company, 1885), pp. 224–226.

11.3   WILLIAM APESS, "AN INDIAN'S LOOKING GLASS FOR THE WHITE MAN" (1833)

William Apess was the first Native American to publish a book. Born in 1798, he was of Connecticut Pequot descent. As a child, he was "bound out" as an indentured servant to a white family. When he was an adolescent, he ran away and joined the army, fighting in the War of 1812. After having a religious conversion experience, he became a minister to Indians, and made his living speaking and writing. This is an excerpt from an essay printed in his book *The Experiences of Five Christian Indians* (1833). When the book was reprinted in 1837, he was pressured to remove it.

Reader, I acknowledge that this is a confused world, and I am not seeking for office, but merely placing before you the black inconsistency that you place before me—which is ten times blacker than any skin that you will find in the universe. And now let me exhort you to do away that principle, as it appears ten times worse in the sight of God and candid men than skins of color—more disgraceful than all the skins that Jehovah ever made. If black or red skins or any other skin of color is disgraceful to god, it appears that he has disgraced himself a great deal—for he has made fifteen colored people to one white and placed them here upon this earth.

Now let me ask you, white man, if it is a disgrace to eat, drink, and sleep with the image of God, or sit, or walk, and talk with them. Or have you the folly to think that the white man, being one in fifteen or sixteen, are the only beloved mages of god? Assemble all nations together in your imagination, and then let the whites be seated among them, and then let us look for the whites, and I doubt not it would be hard to finding them; for to the rest of the nations, they are but a handful. Now suppose these skins were put together, and each skin had its national crimes written upon it—which skin do you think would have the greatest? I will ask one question more. Can you charge the Indians with robbing a nation almost of their whole continent, and murdering their women and children, and then depriving the remainder of their lawful rights, that nature and God require them to have? And to cap the climax, rob another nation to till their grounds and welter out their days under the lash with hunger and fatigue under the scorching rays of a burning sun? I should look at all the skins, and I know that when I cast my eye upon the white skin, and if I saw those crimes written upon it, I should enter my protest against it immediately and cleave to that which is more honorable. And I can tell you that I am satisfied with the manner of my creation, fully—whether others are or not. ...

Source: William Apess, "An Indian's Looking Glass for the White Man," in Barry O'Connell, ed., *A Son of the Forest and Other Writings by William Apess, A Pequot* (Amherst: University of Massachusetts Press, 1997), 97–100.

11.4 ANGELINA GRIMKÉ, EXCERPT FROM *AN APPEAL TO THE WOMEN OF THE NOMINALLY FREE STATES* (1838)

After publishing a letter criticizing slavery in William Lloyd Garrison's abolitionist publication *The Liberator* in 1835, Angelina Grimké found her voice as a writer. Her next major publication was *An Appeal to the Christian Women of the South* (1836), followed by an appeal to the women in the North, where she had moved to avoid the evils of slavery. In this excerpt, she describes the way the easy access to enslaved women corrupted the morals of not only southern but also northern men, making this an issue that directly concerned women.

And, dear sisters, in a country where women are degraded and brutalized, and where their exposed persons bleed under the lash—where they are sold in the shambles of "negro brokers"—robbed of their hard earnings—torn from their husbands, and forcibly plundered of their virtue and their offspring; surely in *such* a country, it is very natural that women should wish to know "the reason *why*"—especially when these outrages of blood and nameless horror are practiced in violation of the principles of our national Bill of Rights and the Pre-amble of our Constitution. We do not, then, and cannot concede the position, that because this is a *political subject* women ought to fold their hands in idleness, and close their eyes and ears to the "horrible things" that are practiced in our land. The denial of our duty to act, is a bold denial of our right to act; and if we have no right to act, then may we well be termed "the white slaves of the North"—for, like our brethren in bonds, we must seal our lips in silence and despair.

This, however, is not merely a political subject; it is highly moral, and as such claims the attention of every moral being. Slavery exerts a most deadly influence over the morals of our country, not only over that portion of it where it actually exists as "a domestic institution" but like the miasma of some pestilential pool, it spreads its desolating influence far beyond its own boundaries. Who does not know that licentiousness is a crying sin at the North as well as at the South? and who does not admit that the manners of the South in this respect have had a wide and destructive influence on Northern character? Can crime be fashionable and common in one part of the Union and unrebuked by the other without corrupting the very heart's blood of the nation, and lowering the standard of morality everywhere? Can Northern men go down to the well-watered plains of the South to make their fortunes, without bowing themselves in the house of Rimmon and drinking of the waters of that river of pollution which rolls over the plain of Sodom and Gomorrah? Do they return uncontaminated to their homes, or does not many and many a Northerner dig the grave of his virtue in the Admahs and Zeboims of our Southern States. And can our theological and academic institutions be opened to the sons of the planter without endangering the purity of the morals of our own sons, by associations with men who regard the robbery of the poor as no crime, and oppression as no wrong? Impossible!

… our people have erected a false standard by which to judge of men's character. Because in the slaveholding States colored men are plundered and kept in abject ignorance, are treated with disdain and scorn, so here, too, in profound deference to the South, we refuse to eat, or ride, or walk, or associate, or open our institutions of learning, or even our zoological institutions to people of color, unless they visit them in the capacity of *servants*, of menials in humble attendance upon the Anglo-American. Who ever heard of a more wicked absurdity in a Republican country?

Have Northern women, then, nothing to do with slavery, when its demoralizing influence is polluting their domestic circles and blasting the fair character of *their* sons and brothers? Nothing to do with slavery when their domestics are often dragged by the merciless kidnapper from the hearth of their nurseries and the arms of their little ones? Nothing to do with slavery when Northern women are chained and driven like criminals, and incarcerated in the great prison-house of the South? Nothing to do with slavery?

Source: Angelina Grimké, *An Appeal to the Women of the Nominally Free States* (Boston: Isaac Knapp, 1838).

11.5 LOUISA MAY ALCOTT, EXCERPTS FROM "TRANSCENDENTAL WILD OATS" (1873)

Louisa May Alcott, best known as the author of *Little Women* (1868), was also an abolitionist and feminist. Her father was involved in the transcendentalist movement, along with Ralph Waldo Emerson and Henry David Thoreau, and believed that humans could achieve perfection by living in harmony with nature. As a child, Louisa lived for seven months at a transcendentalist commune founded by her father. Although the experiment was short-lived, the community's beliefs influenced her writing career. Years later, she wrote a short story based on her experience at the commune, satirically describing how the idealism of the male leaders created more work for the women.

… Thus these modern pilgrims journeyed hopefully out of the old world, to found a new one in the wilderness.

This prospective Eden at present consisted of an old red farm-house, a dilapidated barn, many acres of meadow-land, and a grove. Ten ancient apple-trees were all the "chaste supply" which the place offered as yet; but, in the firm belief that plenteous orchards were soon to be evoked from their inner consciousness, these sanguine founders had christened their domain Fruitlands.

Here Timon Lion intended to found a colony of Latter Day Saints, who, under his patriarchal sway, should regenerate the world and glorify his name for ever. Here Abel Lamb, with the devoutest faith in the high ideal which was to him a living truth, desired to plant a Paradise, where Beauty, Virtue, Justice, and Love might live happily together, without the possibility of a serpent entering in. And here his wife, unconverted but faithful to the end, hoped, after many wanderings over the face of the earth, to find rest for herself and a home for her children.

"There is our new abode," announced the enthusiast, smiling with a satisfaction quite undamped by the drops dripping from his hat brim, as they turned at length into a cart-path that wound along a steep hillside into a barren looking valley.

"A little difficult of access," observed his practical wife, as she endeavored to keep her various household goods from going overboard with every lurch of the laden ark.

"Like all good things. But those who earnestly desire and patiently seek will soon find us," placidly responded the philosopher from the mud, through which he was now endeavoring to pilot the much-enduring horse.

"Truth lies at the bottom of a well, Sister Hope," said Brother Timon, pausing to detach his small comrade from a gate, whereon she was perched for a clearer gaze into futurity.

"That's the reason we so seldom get at it, I suppose," replied Mrs. Hope, making a vain clutch at the mirror, which a sudden jolt sent flying out of her hands.

The new-comers were welcomed by one of the elect precious,—a regenerate farmer, whose idea of reform consisted chiefly in wearing white cotton raiment and shoes of untanned leather. This costume, with a snowy beard, gave him a venerable, and at the same time a somewhat bridal appearance.

The goods and chattels of the Society not having arrived, the weary family reposed before the fire on blocks of wood, while Brother Moses White regaled them with roasted potatoes, brown bread and water, in two plates, a tin pan, and one mug; his table service being limited. But, having cast the forms and vanities of a depraved world behind them, the elders welcomed hardship with the enthusiasm of new pioneers, and the children heartily enjoyed this foretaste of what they believed was to be a sort of perpetual picnic. ...

"Every meal should be a sacrament, and the vessels used should be beautiful and symbolical," observed Brother Lamb, mildly, righting the tin pan slipping about on his knees. "I priced a silver service when in town, but it was too costly; so I got some graceful cups and vases of Britannia ware."

"Hardest things in the world to keep bright. Will whiting be allowed in the community?" inquired Sister Hope, with a housewife's interest in labor-saving institutions.

"Such trivial questions will be discussed at a more fitting time," answered Brother Timon, sharply, as he burnt his fingers with a very hot potato. "Neither sugar, molasses, milk, butter, cheese, nor flesh are to be used among us, for nothing is to be admitted which has caused wrong or death to man or beast."

"Our garments are to be linen till we learn to raise our own cotton or some substitute for woollen fabrics," added Brother Abel, blissfully basking in an imaginary future as warm and brilliant as the generous fire before him ...

"Haou do you cattle 'ate to treat the ten-acre lot? Ef things ain't 'tended to right smart, we shan't hev no crops," observed the practical patriarch in cotton.

"We shall spade it," replied Abel, in such perfect good faith that Moses said no more, though he indulged in a shake of the head as he glanced at hands that had held nothing heavier than a pen for years. He was a paternal old soul and regarded the younger men as promising boys on a new sort of lark.

... "Each member is to perform the work for which experience, strength, and taste best fit him," continued Dictator Lion. "Thus drudgery and disorder will be avoided and harmony prevail. We shall rise at dawn, begin the day by bathing, followed by music, and then a chaste repast of fruit and bread. Each one finds congenial occupation till the meridian meal; when some deep-searching conversation gives rest to the body and development to the mind. Healthful labor again engages us till the last meal, when we assemble in social communion, prolonged till sunset, when we retire to sweet repose, ready for the next day's activity."

"What part of the work do you incline to yourself?" asked Sister Hope, with a humorous glimmer in her keen eyes.

"I shall wait till it is made clear to me. Being in preference to doing is the great aim, and this comes to us rather by a resigned willingness than a wilful activity, which is a check to all divine growth," responded Brother Timon.

"I thought so." And Mrs. Lamb sighed audibly, for during the year he had spent in her family Brother Timon had so faithfully carried out his idea of "being, not doing," that she had found his "divine growth" both an expensive and unsatisfactory process …

Source: Louisa May Alcott, "Transcendental Wild Oats: A Chapter from an Unwritten Romance," *The Independent* (New York), vol. 25, no. 1307, December 18, 1873, pp. 1569–1571.

11.6   ALEXIS DE TOCQUEVILLE, EXCERPTS FROM *DEMOCRACY IN AMERICA: VOLUME II* (1840)

Alexis de Tocqueville, a French political scientist and historian who traveled the United States in 1831–1832, published his observations in a two-volume book, *Democracy in America* (Volume 1 was published in 1835 and Volume 2 in 1840). Having been involved in political struggle in his own country, Tocqueville paid keen attention to the workings of democracy in American society. In the following selection, he notes the proclivity of Americans to form groups, perhaps based on his observations of the Anti-Slavery Society, the American Temperance Society, and numerous other reform societies founded in the 1820s and 1830s.

… The political associations that exist in the United States are only a single feature in the midst of the immense assemblage of associations in that country. Americans of all ages, all conditions, and all dispositions constantly form associations. They have not only commercial and manufacturing companies, in which all take part, but associations of a thousand other kinds, religious, moral, serious, futile, general or restricted, enormous or diminutive. The Americans make associations to give entertainments, to found seminaries, to build inns, to construct churches, to diffuse books, to send missionaries to the antipodes; in this manner they found hospitals, prisons, and schools. If it is proposed to inculcate some truth or to foster some feeling by the encouragement of a great example, they form a society. Wherever at the head of some new undertaking you see the government in France, or a man of rank in England, in the United States you will be sure to find an association.

… Thus the most democratic country on the face of the earth is that in which men have, in our time, carried to the highest perfection the art of pursuing in common the object of their common desires and have applied this new science to the greatest number of purposes. Is this the result of accident, or is there in reality any necessary connection between the principle of association and that of equality?

Aristocratic communities always contain, among a multitude of persons who by themselves are powerless, a small number of powerful and wealthy citizens, each of whom can achieve great undertakings single-handed. In aristocratic societies men do not need to combine in order to act, because they are strongly held together. Every wealthy and powerful citizen constitutes the head of a permanent and compulsory association, composed of all those who are dependent upon him or whom he makes subservient to the execution of his designs.

Among democratic nations, on the contrary, all the citizens are independent and feeble; they can do hardly anything by themselves, and none of them can oblige his fellow men to lend him their assistance. They all, therefore, become powerless if they do not learn voluntarily to help one another. If men living in democratic countries had no right and no inclination to associate for political purposes, their independence would be in great jeopardy, but they might long preserve their wealth and their cultivation: whereas if they never acquired the habit of forming associations in ordinary life, civilization itself would be endangered. A people among whom individuals lost the power of achieving great things single-handed, without acquiring the means of producing them by united exertions, would soon relapse into barbarism.

… When the members of an aristocratic community adopt a new opinion or conceive a new sentiment, they give it a station, as it were, beside themselves, upon the lofty platform where they stand; and opinions or sentiments so conspicuous to the eyes of the multitude are easily introduced into the minds or hearts of all around. In democratic countries the governing power alone is naturally in a condition to act in this manner, but it is easy to see that its action is always inadequate, and often dangerous. A government can no more be competent to keep alive and to renew the circulation of opinions and feelings among a great people than to manage all the speculations of productive industry. No sooner does a government attempt to go beyond its political sphere and to enter upon this new track than it exercises, even unintentionally, an insupportable tyranny; for a government can only dictate strict rules, the opinions which it favors are rigidly enforced, and it is never easy to discriminate between its advice and its commands. Worse still will be the case if the government really believes itself interested in preventing all circulation of ideas; it will then stand motionless and oppressed by the heaviness of voluntary torpor. Governments, therefore, should not be the only active powers; associations ought, in democratic nations, to stand in lieu of those powerful private individuals whom the equality of conditions has swept away.

As soon as several of the inhabitants of the United States have taken up an opinion or a feeling which they wish to promote in the world, they look out for mutual assistance; and as soon as they have found one another out, they combine. From that moment they are no longer isolated men, but a power seen from afar, whose actions serve for an example and whose language is listened to. The first time I heard in the United States that a hundred thousand men had bound themselves publicly to abstain from spirituous liquors, it appeared to me more like a joke than a serious engagement, and I did not at once perceive why these temperate citizens could not content themselves with drinking water by their own firesides. I at last understood that these hundred thousand Americans, alarmed by the progress of drunkenness around them, had made up their minds to patronize temperance.

… Nothing, in my opinion, is more deserving of our attention than the intellectual and moral associations of America. The political and industrial associations of that country strike us forcibly; but the others elude our observation, or if we discover them, we understand them imperfectly because we have hardly ever seen anything of the kind. It must be acknowledged, however, that they are as necessary to the American people as the former, and perhaps more so. In democratic countries the science of association is the mother of science; the progress of all the rest depends upon the progress it has made.

Among the laws that rule human societies there is one which seems to be more precise and clear than all others. If men are to remain civilized or to become so, the art of associating together must grow and improve in the same ratio in which the equality of conditions is increased.

Source: Alexis de Tocqueville, *Democracy in America: Volume II*, New York: Harper & Row, 1966 [1840].

Political Parties in Crisis

In some ways, the expansion of white male suffrage and the translation of moral-reform agendas into electoral politics energized American politics in the 1830s and 1840s: voting day became a bonding experience for white working men. In 1840, 66 percent of the electorate voted in Massachusetts, 75 percent in Connecticut, and 77 percent in Pennsylvania, higher than today. Yet the capacity of major political parties to accommodate a wide range of conflicting interests and beliefs was limited. Increasingly fractured since the election of 1824, the Republican Party had struggled to reorganize in opposition to Andrew Jackson. Jackson's war on the national bank had offered the immediate occasion. Although unable to save the bank, **Henry Clay** and the anti-Jacksonians narrowly passed a Senate resolution in 1834 censuring Jackson for assuming "authority and power not conferred by the Constitution and the laws." In the debate before the censure, Clay identified his own anti-Jackson position as "Whiggish," meant to evoke memories of the English "Whigs" who opposed royal tyranny in the eighteenth century. That label stuck as the name of the new political party.

Former National Republicans in the urban Northeast and upper West made up the bulk of the new **Whig Party**. Some of these were beginning to doubt the wisdom of uncontrolled territorial expansion, which seemed to promote political corruption, economic disorder, sectional conflict, and the extension of slavery. They feared the disruptive power of wildcat settlers, wage workers, the urban poor, and immigrants. Whigs supported market expansion guided closely by a strong, interventionist central government. They continued to embrace the elements of the earlier "American System": a new national bank, a strong protective tariff, and government-sponsored internal improvements.

By 1834, some former Democrats were also disenchanted with the party of Jackson. Prosperous shopkeepers and middling merchants began to see their own interests as distinct from those of the urban laboring classes and were attracted by the Whig emphasis on discipline and order. Some southerners were still angry over the tariff and the nullification crisis. Later, some small farmers and shopkeepers wiped out by the depression of 1837 blamed Jackson for their hard times. Workers, however, who had little trust for the merchant classes at the core of the new Whig Party, tended to form splinter parties or to stay with the Democrats.

Through the 1830s the Whigs were a loose and disorganized opposition. Unable to decide on a single candidate, in 1836 they ran four regional challengers, hoping to deny Van Buren a majority in the Electoral College. The Whig field included William Henry Harrison (governor of Indiana Territory and victor at the Battle of Tippecanoe, nominated by Pennsylvania Antimasons), Senator Hugh Lawson White (Jackson's disenchanted replacement in the Senate, nominated by unhappy Democrats in Tennessee), Senator Daniel Webster (former National Republican and famous orator, nominated by the Massachusetts legislature), and Willie P. Mangum (a protest candidate of the South Carolina Nullifiers).

Jackson's vice president, Martin Van Buren, seemed well positioned for the race. Van Buren was instrumental in creating a successful Democratic coalition, so he was surely the one to hold it together. Van Buren had been constantly at Jackson's side, as secretary of state and as vice president. Few politicians seemed better situated to inherit Jackson's popularity. What was more, Van Buren seemed

Martin Van Buren One of the most powerful politicians of his time, Martin Van Buren extolled the virtues of party competition. He was also among the first presidents ever to be photographed.

perhaps uniquely positioned to bridge the growing gulf between northern antislavery and southern proslavery Democrats: his popularity in New York appeared strong enough for him to risk alienating some of the antislavery vote in the effort to gain southern support, a risk he took by publicly declaring himself "the inflexible and uncompromising opponent of any attempt on the part of Congress to abolish slavery in the District of Columbia" or to interfere with slavery "in the states where it exists."

The election was close. Van Buren won part of New England (but not Massachusetts or Vermont). He took his home state of New York, Pennsylvania, Virginia, and North Carolina. And he took Far West states, most of them slave states: Michigan, Illinois (technically free but popularly proslavery, especially in the south), Missouri, Arkansas, Louisiana, Mississippi, and Alabama. He won 58 percent of the electoral vote (after the weighting of the Three-Fifths Compromise in the South) and a bare majority (51 percent) of the popular vote. A shift of fewer than 2,000 votes in Pennsylvania would have denied Van Buren an Electoral College majority and thrown the election to the House of Representatives.

Van Buren and the Legacy of Jackson

In his 1837 inaugural address, Van Buren announced that the nation had arrived at a "singularly happy" condition. Less optimistic, Missourian Thomas Hart Benton observed that in Van Buren's victory "the rising was eclipsed by the setting sun." Benton was closer to the truth. Van Buren's struggle to unite Jackson's party enough to get elected was only the first of the challenges he inherited.

The signs of the **Panic of 1837** were already visible when Van Buren was inaugurated that March. Jackson's pet banks had ensured that western land speculation would be built on easy credit. His hard-money measures that had effectively drained the nation of specie did not end the bubble of credit. It simply diverted its source to European financiers, who got higher interest in the United States than in their home countries. When European banks responded to specie shortages in their own countries by increasing interest on deposits and tightening credit, the Europeans called in their American loans. The sudden collapse of credit was exacerbated by crop failures in 1835 and 1837, which put farmers at greater risk for defaulting on their loans and reduced American exports.

As credit evaporated, interest rates rose, paper money depreciated, and debt mounted. The credit-dependent cotton market began to collapse, taking with it several large import-export firms in New York and New Orleans. After years of high inflation, the failures ignited a run on the overextended banks, as depositors tried to withdraw their savings before the hard currency was paid out for mercantile debts. "Even during the Embargo, & war that followed," merchant John Perkins Cushing reported in May of 1837, "there was nothing like the complete prostration of commercial credit & confidence that has taken place within the last two months."

A strong federal hand might have stemmed the damage, but Van Buren shared Jackson's view that the federal government should not manage currency. Van Buren's announcement on May 4 that he intended to maintain the Specie Circular in force ensured continued pressure on banks. On May 10, 1837, frightened depositors drained $650,000 from their reserves, and New York City banks closed. Only a show of military force prevented a riot.

Coinciding with large waves of German and Irish immigration, the depression hit the East Coast hard. Wages declined faster than prices. Unemployment was widespread, and losses touched even the prosperous middle classes. Troubled times remained until 1843. While Democrats scrambled to avoid political responsibility, the new Whig Party began to look ahead optimistically to 1840.

In an effort to return stability to the nation's monetary system, Van Buren proposed that the Treasury Department establish its own financial institutions to receive, hold, and pay out government funds. The institutions would exist solely to manage government accounts and would not issue paper currency or make loans to business.

The proposal for an independent treasury met with substantial opposition. Predictably, Whigs objected that removing government holdings from circulation would reduce capital investment. But many Democrats also thought the new system would retard growth. The independent treasury did not pass until 1840, enacted as an entirely separate, specie-based system, able neither to receive nor to pay out paper currency.

Van Buren's challenges spilled over from domestic to international crises. Twice, the fears and frustrations of Americans along the Canadian border almost brought the United States and Canada/Great Britain to blows. Americans and Canadians had long argued over who owned the rich timber reserves in the Aroostook Valley on the border of Maine and New Brunswick. When Americans heard rumors in 1838 that Canadian lumberjacks were infiltrating the region and taking trees at will, the Democratic governor of Maine declared that Maine was under invasion and demanded federal protection. Van Buren sent in the army under General Winfield Scott. Aware that the economy could not support a war, he also instructed Scott to offer terms for a truce. If Canada would acknowledge Maine's predominant interest in the valley, the United States would respect existing Canadian settlements pending final disposition of the area.

Meanwhile, Americans along the northern New York border were picking sides in an internal Canadian rebellion against Great Britain (1837–1838). Although the United States was technically neutral, disgruntled unemployed American workers saw the rebels embodying the spirit of the American Revolution and were drawn to support them against wealthy Canadians and the British government. Recruited by the rebels, sympathetic New Yorkers raised funds and offered ships to transport men and arms to Canada. On December 29, 1837, Canadian pro-British troops crossed the river into Schlosser, New York, captured the *Caroline* (owned by American William Wells), towed it out into the middle of the river, and set it afire. A few months later, Americans retaliated by sinking a British ship. The United States and Britain exchanged diplomatic demands until 1840, when Alexander McLeod, a Canadian deputy sheriff, got drunk in a New York tavern and began bragging that he had killed an American during the *Caroline* incident. New York authorities immediately arrested him and local mobs clamored for blood, while Britain protested that McLeod's status was an international matter, beyond New York's jurisdiction, and threatened to break diplomatic relations. Van Buren, fighting for reelection as the anti–big-government Democratic candidate, was not ready to intervene. Only with the election of a Whig president and Congress in 1840 was McLeod released.

ACQUIRING THE TRANS-MISSISSIPPI WEST

Jackson had embodied the restless energy and assumed right of white Americans to settle ever deeper in the North American continent. The belief that white Americans had a providential right to as much of North America as they wanted had been a core belief and policy since the founding of the republic: It was implicit in the Northwest Ordinance, in scores of Indian treaties, in the Louisiana Purchase, in the Transcontinental Treaty, in the 1824 Monroe Doctrine, and in the Removal Act of 1830. But only in 1845 did the now famous phrase "manifest destiny" enter the American vocabulary, when journalist John O'Sullivan proclaimed that it is "our manifest destiny . . . to overspread the continent allotted by Providence for the free development of our yearly multiplying millions." As the United States' treatment of Native Americans had long made clear, the manifest destiny of the nation was for many Americans racial, as well as territorial and political.

Manifest Destiny in Antebellum Culture

On the simplest level, **manifest destiny** was a political slogan and a crass claim for property, a way of asserting that Americans wanted and would have the continent all the way to the Pacific. But most Americans resisted such a naked statement of their ambitions and framed—and deeply understood—their aspirations in the language of democracy and freedom. This land was intended by Providence as the physical home of a unique national greatness. In antebellum culture, this understanding of the singularity of North America was often articulated through a linked pair of evocative images: first, the image of the awesome power and natural majesty of the American wilderness, and second, the image of the wilderness giving way to an even nobler state of cultivation on the arrival of American settlers.

Both images were evident in antebellum landscape painting, particularly in the work of a group of artists known as the **Hudson River school**. Like most Americans of the era, the Hudson River painters were influenced by the Romantic movement sweeping Europe, which emphasized the power and beauty of untamed nature. Thomas Cole was the leader of the Hudson River school. In his work, ancient trees spiked toward the heavens and wild waterfalls cascaded over crags. There was also sometimes a bittersweet sadness at the passing of the wilderness, even as he also celebrated the taming of the land for farming.

Antebellum poets and novelists took up the theme of the land as well, also often envisioning it as a shifting scenery in which the majesty of the wilderness seemed merely to await transformation at the hands of American pioneers. **James Fenimore Cooper**'s *Leatherstocking Tales* narrated European American settlement of the New York back-country as a grand myth of manifest destiny, in which settlement tamed the land even as the land itself became the agent through which the newcomers were forged into a new, ennobled society. In *The Last of the Mohicans*, Cooper described the New York back-country of 1757 as "an impervious boundary of forests" torn by dangerous rapids and rugged passes. By 1793, the fictional time of *The Pioneers,* that same landscape had become "a succession of hills" and "narrow, rich cultivated dales" dotted by "beautiful and thriving villages" and "neat and comfortable farms." In the same spirit, poet William Cullen Bryant visited

Thomas Cole, Study for *Home in the Woods*, 1847 Cole, founder of the Hudson River School, was known for portraying not only the beauty of the American landscape, but also the drama of its gradual possession by settlers.

the Illinois plains in the 1830s and saw not an austere landscape but a vision of "gardens" and "fields, boundless and beautiful." The uniting of the national culture and the land was the manifest destiny not only of American citizens but also of the land itself.

Jefferson had imagined this relationship of the people to the land chiefly in terms of the yeoman farmer, with the craftsman a secondary "handmaid." In the wake of innovations in travel and machinery design in the early nineteenth century, however, images of trade and manufacturing began to make their way into ideas about the abundance of the land. Americans would unleash the richness of the continent not only through farming but also through commerce. De Witt Clinton's prediction that the Erie Canal would help make New York City the emporium of the world captured this new vision in the politics of trade. Commerce, Clinton insisted in 1819, would not only collapse regional differences but also "increas[e] the stock of human happiness—by establishing the perpetuity of free government—and by extending the empire of improvement, of knowledge, of refinement and of religion. . . . " The American wilderness, first cultivated into a homestead, would become a huge highway for the transportation of goods and culture.

To this image of North America as a transportation network, Americans added the image of North American power harnessed into manufacturing output. The proof of America's greatness lay not only in the riches coaxed from the land but also in the seemingly endless array of manufactured goods. Reviewing an exhibit of goods manufactured in Massachusetts in 1839, one magazine correspondent argued that manufacturing "blended harmoniously together" the interests of all Americans. The enjoyments of abundant market goods did not extend to all people, however.

Texas

By the terms of the 1819 Transcontinental Treaty (see Chapter 10), the United States had given up claims to Spanish lands south of the 42nd parallel. Nevertheless, within a few years Americans began to enter the region.

Many of these immigrants were specifically invited; some were not. The Spanish saw their northern region as a buffer zone against the Lipan Apaches and Comanche Indians and between New Spain and the United States. After independence, the new Mexican government expanded those policies by offering land grants to Americans in return for the promise to bring settlers to bolster the sparse population. The first American to accept the invitation was Stephen F. Austin, who began settling a colony on the banks of the Brazos and Colorado Rivers in 1821. By 1830 there were more than 20,000 Americans (including 1,000 enslaved people) living in the northeastern province of Mexico, bordering Louisiana.

Conflict between immigrant Americans and prior residents of Texas—known as **Tejanos**—was inevitable. Tejanos resented the influx of Americans, who were often awarded lands that already belonged to Tejanos or that included Tejano communities. Tejanos complained that the *empresarios* (American landholders) were "nothing more than money-changing speculators" who had no respect for existing claims and did not control their settlers or squatters who used the American colonies to hide stolen livestock.

Although they were happy to take advantage of the cheap prices Mexico offered, many Americans had never fully acknowledged the right of Mexico to these
lands. Viewing the region as the natural next frontier for American plantation
agriculture, southerners had denounced the 1819 treaty and lobbied John Quincy
Adams and Andrew Jackson to purchase the tract free and clear. By 1839 some
Americans were convinced that Texas was destined to become the "land of refuge
for the American slaveholders."

The immigrants themselves criticized the Mexican government in the language
of republicanism, calling it autocratic. They objected to high taxes, but then so did everybody. They objected to being required to convert to Catholicism in order to intermarry with Mexicans and control their Mexican wives' property, but those laws were
not really enforced. They objected to having to adopt the Spanish language to carry
on official business. But beneath these objections were more fundamental issues, including a deep discontent with being ruled by people who were culturally alien.

Southerners who moved to Texas had a particular complaint: the Mexican government's inconsistent policies on slavery. Like the young United States, the new
and unstable Mexican government took an erratic course, at one point banning
slavery altogether, at another point allowing enslaved people to enter the nation but
mandating gradual abolition.

By the mid-1820s, however, the immigrants had developed a cotton economy
dependent on slave labor that they were determined to preserve. They regarded
Mexican inconsistency and resistance as evidence of betrayal. In 1824, Stephen
Austin, never a devoted supporter of slavery, devised regulations for his colony with
harsh provisions for enslaved people who tried to escape or free people who abetted
runaways. By 1830, Austin had concluded that "Texas must be a slave country. Circumstances and unavoidable necessity compels it. It is the wish of the people there."
In Austin's view, "the people" included only white US immigrants and others who
agreed with their goals.

But slavery was not the major reason for the increasing tension between Texas
and the Mexican government. After 1830, the government took steps to stem immigration and put troops on the United States–Mexican border. Immigrants saw
these measures as obstructions to their rightful claims. The rise of General Antonio
López de Santa Anna as president of Mexico provided the occasion for registering
their complaints. But when Santa Anna dissolved the Mexican Congress and made
himself dictator in 1834, Texans—both Anglo and Tejano—sharpened their criticisms. Casting themselves as the quintessential republicans, they and residents of
several other Mexican states joined in the rebellion. Hoping to secure US statehood,
Texas declared itself a sovereign republic on March 2, 1836.

Four days later the huge Mexican army, led by Santa Anna, attacked and wiped
out 187 Texas patriots barricaded in a former mission called the Alamo. It was a
costly and fleeting victory. Santa Anna's army suffered 1,544 casualties and created
martyrs for the rebels' cause. Led by Sam Houston, the rebels retreated east, gathering recruits as they went. On April 21, they surprised Mexican troops on the San
Jacinto River and scored a huge victory, capturing Santa Anna himself. Bargaining
for his life and freedom, Santa Anna declared Texas a free nation (see Map 12–1).
Ecstatic Texans drew up a constitution for the "**Republic of Texas**," made Sam
Houston their first president, and then called for annexation to the United States.

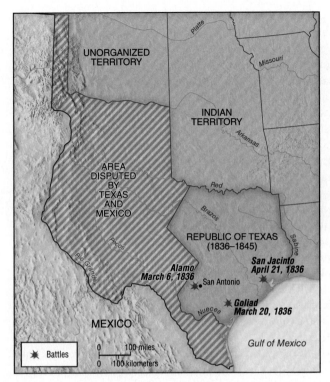

Map 12-1 Republic of Texas After the decisive American victory at San Jacinto that resulted in the independence of Texas, the border dispute between Texas and Mexico continued until it was resolved by the Mexican War a decade later.

With the nation in economic crisis and his own party bickering over who was responsible, the last thing Van Buren wanted as president was a bitter battle over Texas and slavery. He doubted that the Constitution permitted annexation, which he feared would be construed as meddling in Mexico's internal affairs. Anticipating Texas's application for admission, abolitionists had made opposition to annexation a central issue in their massive petition campaign of 1837–1838, expanding the controversy widely in the North. John Quincy Adams had delivered a stirring speech against annexation in the House, and some senators were publicly denouncing slavery in general and especially in Texas. Southerners had responded with their own states' rights petitions. In the end, Van Buren did not submit Texas's request for statehood to Congress.

On to Oregon

For most white Americans, however, Texas was not the fulfillment of America's manifest destiny. That goal lay in the rich lands beyond the plains. By the time Van Buren left office, the Mississippi River had become the staging ground for a massive migration west.

The migration began as a trickle of missionaries in the 1830s. In 1831, rumors reached the East of four young Indians who had appeared in St. Louis, exhausted and sick, imploring that religious teachers be sent to their people. Two years later, the Methodist *Christian Advocate and Herald* published a letter from a Wyandot Indian who claimed that western tribes hungered for instruction in Christianity. True or not, such stories enabled missionaries to claim they had been invited into Indian communities. In 1834, the Methodist Missionary Society sent the Reverend Jason Lee west to found a mission in the Willamette Valley of Oregon Territory. Two years later, the American Board of Commissioners for Foreign Missions sent six people (including two women) to settle permanent missions in Oregon.

For their first mission, the board selected Marcus and Narcissa Prentiss Whitman, a doctor and a Sunday school teacher. In 1836, the Whitmans established their mission among the Cayuse Indians near Fort Walla Walla on the Columbia River. Their fellow missionaries Henry and Eliza Hart Spalding founded a mission 125 miles away among the Nez Percés.

At first, all seemed well. Though a difficult man, Marcus Whitman preached and doctored among the Cayuses and taught the men agriculture, and Narcissa taught school and oversaw the operation of the large mission. Over the following decade, however, as white immigration swelled, the Cayuses came to view the missionaries as the cause of the influx of white people and new diseases. In 1847, after a deadly measles epidemic killed many children, a Cayuse band attacked the mission, killing Marcus and Narcissa Whitman and a number of other white people. But they couldn't stem the rising tide of settlers. Indeed, the famous incident seemed to work to bring more settlers.

By then, migrants to the West Coast were so numerous that the roads of Iowa "were literally lined with long blue wagons . . . slowly wending their way over the broad prairies," leaving deep, rutted tracks. In the years of heaviest migration, watering holes were so overused and sanitary conditions so poor that the road west became a breeding ground for typhoid, malaria, dysentery, and cholera.

Most of the migrants were farming families of moderate means. Men might decide to leave with little warning to their families. Sarah Cummins remembered returning home from school one day in Illinois to discover that her father had sold the farm and that "as soon as school closes we are to move." Yet even spur-of-the-moment decisions rarely meant immediate departure. Preparations for the trip took up to half a year, and families could expect to spend another half a year on the trail.

Travelers funneled through St. Louis, crossed Missouri to rendezvous with wagon trains near St. Joseph or Independence, Missouri, and then followed one of two main routes west (see Map 12–2). The northern route, known as the **Oregon Trail**, zigzagged northwest roughly parallel to the Rocky Mountains. The **Santa Fe Trail** headed southwest out of Independence along the Arkansas River through the future state of Kansas before reaching Mexican lands. At Santa Fe, the trail divided, feeding immigrants west along the Old Spanish Trail or south to Chihuahua, Mexico.

Most overland migrants traveled in families, in groups of families, and occasionally in entire communities. If they lacked team animals, families pulled their possessions in two-wheeled handcarts. For the most part, wagons carried supplies, not people. Most migrants walked west. Moreover, wagons broke down, were washed away in river crossings, or had to be emptied to ease the burden on the animals.

Map 12-2   Major Overland Trails The overland trails to the west started at the Missouri River. The Santa Fe Trail was a conduit for traders and goods to Mexico. The Oregon Trail passed through Wyoming and branched off to California and Oregon.

Past the plains, wagon trains sometimes went days without finding water or game. Women and men drove the wagons and herded the cattle, collected firewood, and caught small animals for food. When broken equipment or sickness slowed families, the trains were often forced to leave them behind, lest the others not clear the Rocky Mountains before winter. The harrowing dangers of that possibility were immortalized in the story of the ill-fated Donner Party, who took the wrong path and were caught in the Sierra Nevadas by an early winter. For four months the group was trapped by snow, slowly starving. When relief finally arrived in mid-February 1847, "the dead were lying about on the snow, some even unburied, since

Family Traveling West
This rare 1850s photograph shows a family traveling west in a covered wagon.

the living had not strength to bury their dead," according to one survivor. Of the 87 persons snowed in, 42 died.

For migrants who reached the West, the rewards were not always immediately apparent. "My most vivid recollection of that first winter in Oregon," one woman recalled, "is of the weeping skies and of Mother and me also weeping." As soon as they were settled, though, many newcomers proclaimed Oregon "this best country in the world." The climate was hospitable to crops of wheat, flax, and corn and to apple and pear orchards. Lumber was plentiful, and the streams were full of fish. Farther south was California, where, after 1848, rumors of "inexhaustible" gold strikes began to filter north and east.

Indian Nations of the Trans-Mississippi West

American settlers felt they were journeying through national territories. Indigenous communities, on the other hand, viewed the settlers as trespassers in Indian Country.

Most wagon trains departed from Missouri, which meant that settlers first crossed Oklahoma, where Native Americans like John Ross and the Cherokees (see Chapter 10) had been guaranteed refuge from white intrusion (see Map 12–3). Between Independence, Missouri, and the Rocky Mountains lay the Indian nations of the prairies and Great Plains: the Blackfoot and Crow to the northwest; the Sioux, Pawnee, Arapaho, Shoshone, and Cheyenne, through the northern and central plains; and the Kiowa, Apache, Comanche, and Navajo in the Southwest. Along the Pacific were the Yakima, Chinook, Cayuse, and Nez Percé Indians, and to the south, in California, Pomo, Chumash, Yuma, and many other tribes.

Because most of this vast territory was part of Mexico, and because Great Britain laid claim to Oregon, crossing to utopia meant transgressing the boundaries of those nations as well.

Penny novelists would depict this contact as a violent confrontation in which warlike Indians massacred well-meaning migrants, and years later, early Hollywood movies would pick up on this theme. In fact, however, of the more than 250,000 settlers who crossed the plains between 1840 and 1860, only about 350 were killed by Native Americans. Far more deaths were inflicted by white migrants on the Indians.

From the time of the Removal Act, official US policy toward eastern Indians was one of removal, by force or by pressured sale of lands and physical relocation to

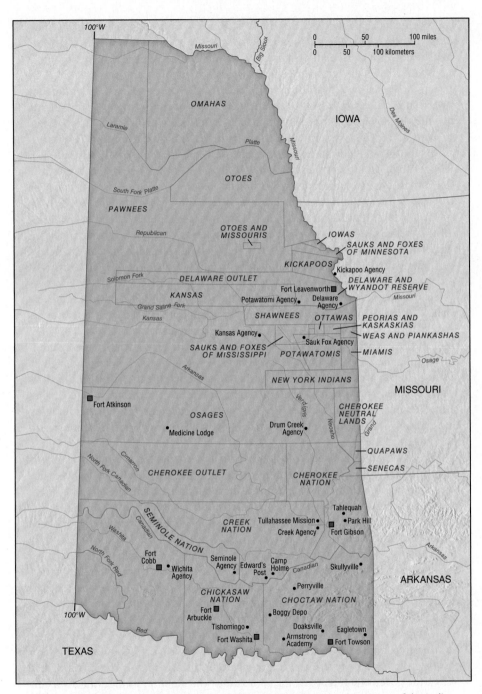

Map 12-3   Major Trans-Mississippi Indian Communities, ca. 1850 Most of the Indians living in the Indian Territories in the 1830s and 1840s had been "removed" from areas east of the Mississippi River. The territories were located west of Arkansas, Missouri, and Iowa. The section to the south (now Oklahoma) was home to Cherokees, Choctaws, Creeks, and Seminoles from the Old Southwest. The northern part (now Kansas and Nebraska) was inhabited by Indians from the Old Northwest.

a purportedly permanent home in the West. Observers saw no evidence that Americans really recognized any boundary short of the Pacific Ocean. Alexis de Tocqueville noted that "when it promises these unlucky people a permanent asylum in the West," the US government "is well aware of its inability to guarantee this." By the late 1830s, as the last of the eastern "removals" were completed, federal policy toward Indians began to shift to an unstated policy of subjecting western tribes to violence. Removal and resettlement continued to be the primary stated goal, and many western tribes were confined to reservations or moved to **Indian Territory.**

By the mid-1830s, when white Americans started crossing the Mississippi River in huge numbers, most of these nations had already felt the effects of expansionism. The Comanches (the largest of the southwestern nations) and the Apaches had been at war with European Americans for several centuries, having fought the Spanish, the Mexicans, and, since the 1820s, both the Mexicans and the US settlers in Texas. All of the Plains Indians, especially the Sioux, Kiowas, and Comanches, had felt the impact of eastern Indians arriving in their territory, displaced or officially relocated west. The Sioux had been at war for decades with the Indians of the Old Northwest Territory, who were being pushed across the Mississippi River.

For the western Indians, the effects of the settlers' migration of the 1840s were social, cultural, and economic. Although the number of deaths from warfare was low, deaths from disease and malnutrition were far higher and took especially high tolls on the children and the old, wiping out both the elders who carried a community's history and collective wisdom and the young people who represented its future. Contact gradually altered the Indians' social organization and gendered division of labor. As it became harder to claim and protect planting grounds, tribes shifted to more nomadic ways of life. The relative importance of women's foraging and planting diminished, and the relative importance of men's skills as hunters and warriors increased.

The northern grasslands and southern plains supported a complex economy of hunting and foraging. Indians consumed corn, melons, berries, wild sweet potatoes, turnips, and fowl and small game, harvested in a seminomadic way of life and traded through networks. At the center of this economy stood the bison: the glamorous, galloping hunts of this great beast supplied food and material for clothing, shelter, and trade.

This way of life was threatened as the number of bison declined. Settlers' need for food had only a minor impact on the buffalo. More deadly was their fascination with hunting and killing such a huge creature, regardless of whether they needed its meat and hides. Recreational hunting parties, as well as hunters intent on wiping out the Indians' means of support, took their toll. As early as 1842, the Teton Sioux had complained to federal agents that the heavy migrations were harming their hunting grounds. By 1846, the Sioux were demanding that the US government stem the migrations and prevent the migrants from killing animals indiscriminately. When the government ignored the complaints, the Sioux prevented wagon trains from passing until migrants had paid a toll in money, tobacco, or supplies.

In the mid-1840s, the energies of the federal government were primarily engaged in Texas, where American nationalists were demanding action against Mexico. In the northern plains, the government constructed a chain of forts intended as quarters for armed rifle units called dragoons, who would, theoretically,

Buffalo Hunt The Plains Indians were extremely adept at hunting buffalo, which served as an integral part of their economic systems. Over the course of the nineteenth century, white encroachments rapidly decimated the buffalo herds and brought the species to the brink of extinction.

protect overland migrants from the Indians. The strategy was not very effective, as Indians continued to exert control over white migration through northern Indian Country—though they were not able to stem the tide.

SLAVERY'S CONNECTION TO GEOGRAPHIC EXPANSION

As Americans poured west, expansion became a source of national political controversy. The problem was not the principle of manifest destiny, which few questioned. By the late 1830s, expansion was linked in the public debate with the extension of slavery and raised other problems. Southerners viewed northerners as unfaithful to a 50-year-old compromise ratified in the Constitution. Northerners looked at the spread of slavery into the new Southwest (Louisiana, Mississippi, Alabama, and Arkansas) and worried about the political leverage of a new slave state the size of Texas.

Log Cabins and Hard Cider: The Election of 1840

Approaching the election of 1840, the major parties were in a balancing act. Both hoped to exploit regional differences but without raising the divisive issues associated with slavery. Whigs considered Van Buren vulnerable, both because of the continuing effects of the depression of 1837 and because he was a northerner who seemed to be blocking the annexation of Texas. Henry Clay, leader of the Whigs, also opposed the annexation, but he calculated that southern Democrats would choose a Kentuckian over a New Yorker. Aware of Van Buren's liabilities in the South, Democrats sought to keep slavery out of the debates, although Van Buren was willing to have northerners see him as the alternative to a southern president. A number of northern Whigs were suspicious of Clay's ties to the South.

Van Buren received the Democratic nomination, but in an effort to skirt the explosive sectional issues, the Whigs turned to William Henry Harrison, the hero of the battle of Tippecanoe against Tecumseh's people (see Chapter 10) and an outspoken advocate of cheap western land. Harrison had run strongest against Van Buren in 1836. To bolster the appeal of their slate, for their vice-presidential candidate the Whigs chose a former Democrat, John Tyler of Virginia, a strong advocate of states' rights.

Harrison was a "sentimental" candidate who the Whigs hoped would evoke feelings of military glory and westward expansion. Avoiding tough issues, they crafted a Jackson-like campaign for "Tippecanoe and Tyler, too." When Harrison was derided as a country bumpkin content with sitting on his porch drinking cider, the Whigs took up the image with gusto. In the "Log Cabin and Hard Cider Campaign," the Whigs celebrated Harrison as a simple man of the people (like Jackson). In fact, Harrison was from a wealthy old Virginia family, but he could be linked to the West, and, as Daniel Webster observed, Harrison's main appeal was the vague "hope of a better time."

The turnout was large, and the popular results were close, but the Electoral College was a different story. Harrison triumphed with 234 electoral votes to Van Buren's 60. The Democrats held only New Hampshire, Illinois, Missouri, Arkansas, Alabama, Virginia, and South Carolina.

And Tyler, Too

Whig jubilation at their presidential victory was short-lived. Harrison fell ill shortly after his inauguration and died on April 4, 1841, the first president to die in office. Harrison was followed in office by his vice president, John Tyler, whom most observers assumed would serve as a caretaker president until the next general election. He soon proved them wrong, succeeding to the full stature and authority of the presidency.

Tyler's ascendancy threw the Whig Party into chaos, for once in office he reverted to his Democratic roots. Much about Tyler was reminiscent of Jackson. He opposed the American System and favored slavery and the annexation of Texas, and he was willing to use the full power of the executive to enforce those views. Unlike Jackson, Tyler strongly advocated extreme southern states' rights positions.

Tyler's attention was first drawn to diplomatic troubles with Britain. In 1841, the enslaved crew of the US ship *Creole*, en route from Virginia to New Orleans, had seized control of the vessel and forced it into the port of Nassau, in the Bahamas, where, by British law, the crew was freed. To no avail, white southerners demanded the return of the crew. Meanwhile, northern anti-British feeling flared over the question of the Oregon Territory, a vaguely defined expanse between California and Alaska that Britain and the United States had agreed in 1818 to occupy jointly. By 1842, reports of the North American Pacific Coast as a "storehouse of wealth in all its forests, furs, and fisheries" had stirred the American desire to claim the Oregon Territory.

In 1842, US secretary of state Webster and British emissary Ashburton concluded the Webster-Ashburton Treaty, which drew a boundary between the United States and Canada from Maine to the Rocky Mountains (Oregon was left undivided), established terms of extradition between the two nations, and created a joint effort to restrict the international slave trade. Great Britain also agreed not to interfere with foreign vessels.

Tyler's success in foreign relations was overshadowed by his 1841 break with his own party. Led by Henry Clay, Whigs in Congress passed legislation that embodied their platform, including tariff bills, a national bank bill, and a bill to distribute federal surpluses to states. Tyler vetoed almost every initiative. He denounced federal distribution as inappropriate when the federal government was in deficit. At last, in 1842, congressional Whigs offered lower tariff increases and detached the tariff from the question of distribution. Needing federal funds, Tyler signed the bill. Tyler supported the repeal of the independent treasury, a Whig goal, but this, too, proved a bitter victory for the Whigs, because Tyler vetoed the national bank with which the Whigs wanted to replace the independent treasury.

Tyler was soon a president without a party. As early as January 1843, there were calls in the House of Representatives for his impeachment. That year, when Tyler vetoed the bill rechartering the national bank, his entire cabinet resigned, except Webster.

"His Accidency," as opponents dubbed Tyler, proved resilient. Tyler interpreted Democratic gains in the 1842 elections as support for his positions, particularly on the national bank. Urged on by extreme states' rights advocates in Virginia and South Carolina, Tyler took up the cause of the annexation of Texas. After Daniel Webster resigned from the cabinet, Tyler fell almost entirely under the influence of southerners committed to Texas.

Texas did all it could to press for annexation. It allowed Great Britain to serve as an intermediary in Texas's efforts to win official recognition from Mexico and hinted that, as an independent republic, Texas might abolish slavery. The idea of an alliance between Texas and Great Britain reawakened old anti-British sentiments, and the prospect of a non–slave republic so nearby filled southerners with dread.

Seeking to capitalize on these anxieties, in 1843 President Tyler secretly opened negotiations with Texas for admission to the Union, expecting to justify the treaty as necessary protection against British influence. In 1844, Tyler submitted a treaty of annexation to Congress. He hoped that potential opposition would be countered by expansionist interests. He was wrong. Even before the treaty was submitted, John Quincy Adams and 12 other Whigs denounced it as constitutionally unauthorized and warned that it would bring the nation to "dissolution." Abolitionists labeled the move a naked power grab by slave owners. Even moderate northerners worried that annexing Texas would cause war with Mexico, without yielding the North any tangible gains. Some southerners worried that Texas would compete with the depleted cotton and sugar lands of the South.

By then, other election-year dramas were afoot. John Calhoun still longed for the presidency and felt he had a good chance against Tyler, another southerner, if he could deny Van Buren the Democratic nomination. To that end, Calhoun wrote a note to the British minister that the US goal in Texas was to protect slavery against British abolitionists. As Calhoun hoped, the note became public. The explicit association of Texas and slavery drove Van Buren away from endorsing the treaty of annexation, weakening his position in the South. An overwhelmingly sectional vote defeated the treaty in Congress, but Calhoun believed a Democratic victory in 1844 would revive it.

Occupy Oregon, Annex Texas

By the fall of 1844, the American political party system was in disarray. Harrison's impressive victory in 1840 had not really signaled a broad endorsement of the American System, any more than Van Buren's victory in 1836 had signaled a strong hard-money, antibank sentiment. To the contrary, between 1836 and 1844 the party system seemed most successful at polarizing American interests, which were already diverging economically (see Table 12–1).

Nowhere was that state of affairs more evident than in the 1844 Democratic convention in Baltimore. Van Buren's supporters believed the party owed him the nomination, yet his liabilities were legion. In the South, proslavery, proannexation Democrats led by Calhoun were vowing to have "a slaveholder for President next time regardless of the man." Andrew Jackson was disappointed with Van Buren's refusal to endorse annexation and encouraged former Tennessee governor James K. Polk to run. In the North, workers and entrepreneurs hard hit by years of deflation were disenchanted with Van Buren. His supporters were unable to block a convention rule requiring a candidate to receive a two-thirds vote to secure the nomination. Van Buren could not marshal that level of support, but neither could Tyler, Calhoun, or Lewis Cass, a compromise candidate. Finally, on the eighth ballot the convention fell back on Jackson's choice, James Polk. Tyler accepted renomination by a renegade group of supporters who styled themselves Democratic Republicans.

The 1844 Democratic Party ran on the platform of manifest destiny, calling for "the reoccupation of Oregon and the reannexation of Texas." It was an odd formulation, given that the United States had several times officially denied possession of Texas and had yet to occupy Oregon fully. The platform went even further on Oregon. Although the US claim to Oregon had never extended beyond the 49th parallel, the Democrats now declared their willingness to go to war to gain the entire region ("Fifty-four forty or fight!"). Their strategy incorporated war fears over Texas into a broader assertion of national destiny.

Meanwhile, in 1844 Henry Clay secured the Whig nomination. Clay was certain that opposition to the extension of slavery was strong enough to block a Texas-Oregon compromise and that Americans would not support a war with Mexico. Clay ran primarily as a supporter of the American System as the necessary means for stabilizing economic growth. His running mate, Theodore Frelinghuysen of New Jersey, was a staunch abolitionist who had once been known for his opposition to the Indian Removal Act.

The election results suggested a nation teetering on the edge of political division. Polk, annexation, and manifest destiny won, but by only 38,000 of more than 2.5 million votes cast. More striking, James G. Birney of Ohio, the candidate of the new, explicitly antislavery Liberty Party, drew 62,000 votes, most of them taken from Clay. Had Birney not run, the election might have been a dead heat (see Table 12–2).

Table 12-1 Personal Income per Capita by Region: Percentages of United States Average

	1840	**1860**	**1880**
United States	100	100	100
Northeast	135	139	141
North Central	68	68	98
South	76	72	51

Source: Richard A. Easterlin, "Regional Income Trends, 1840–1950," in *American Economic History*, ed. Seymour E. Harris (New York: McGraw-Hill, 1961), p. 528.

Table 12-2 The Liberty Party Swings an Election

Candidate	Party	Actual Vote in New York	National Electoral Vote	If Liberty Voters Had Voted Whig	Projected Electoral Vote
Polk	Democratic	237,588	170	237,588	134
Clay	Whig	232,482	105	248,294	141
Birney	Liberty	15,812	0	—	—

The idealists who had voted for a party demanding immediate abolition had, ironically, rendered possible the election of those they most decried.

Both Tyler and Congress read the election as a referendum on the Democratic platform, and specifically on Texas. Early in 1845, with Tyler still in office, a bill approving annexation passed the House. To move it through the Whig-dominated Senate, Senator Robert Walker of Mississippi suggested that the Senate version include the option of negotiating a whole new treaty. Only days away from the presidency, Polk was said to favor this approach, and Whigs thought a revised treaty might get them out of a politically costly position. The Senate approved the amended treaty annexing Texas. Mexico immediately severed relations with the United States.

War with Mexico

The annexation of Texas was the ostensible cause of the outbreak of war with Mexico in April 1846, but not the only cause. In Polk's eyes, the annexation of Texas was a piece of a larger acquisition: not only Oregon but also present-day New Mexico, Arizona, and California. Polk would have been happy to make these acquisitions peacefully, but he was willing to go to war.

Polk took a two-track approach to foreign relations. In December 1845, he announced his decision to withdraw from negotiations over Oregon, and he called on Congress to terminate the United States–Great Britain Convention of Joint Occupancy. Compromise would be an abandonment of American "territorial rights . . . and the national honour," he insisted, and would be unthinkable. Beyond the combative rhetoric, Polk informed his advisers that he was prepared

Meanwhile, Polk prepared for war. In the spring of 1845, he had sent 1,500 soldiers, under the command of General Zachary Taylor, allegedly to protect Texas against a possible invasion by Mexico. When Texas approved union with the United States, Polk reinforced Taylor's troops and ordered them to cross the Nueces and approach the Rio Grande, while also sending an army under Stephen Kearny into the northern part of the disputed territory. In August 1846, Kearny occupied Santa Fe. At the same time, Polk ordered the US squadron in the Pacific closer to the California coast and directed the US consul in California, Thomas Larkin, to encourage local disaffection with the Mexican government. When American settlers in the Sonoma Valley staged a rebellion in June and July, the representatives of the United States claimed California. Kearny later crossed into California to solidify the claim.

By then, Polk's brinkmanship on the Rio Grande had produced results. Mexican troops had crossed the river to drive out Taylor's force, and American soldiers had been killed and wounded. In May 1846, Congress declared that "a state of war exists" between the two nations.

The United States entered the war unprepared in that the United States Army had only 7,500 troops. However, 100,000 enthusiastic volunteers signed up at the outbreak of hostilities. With California guarded by John C. Frémont and the naval squadron, the United States could bring its military power to bear on Mexico City.

It was difficult for Mexico to mount a strong defense. Mexico (and New Spain before it) had always been less interested in its northern provinces than in other parts of the nation and did not have a strong presence or infrastructure there. Moreover, after a recent coup, the still young Mexican government was unstable. The defense force it mounted was composed almost entirely of deeply impoverished, conscripted men. For Polk, finding the right leader for the incursion into Mexico proved tricky. Taylor, the obvious choice, was a popular Whig. Polk finally settled on Winfield Scott, who also quietly harbored Whig ambitions. In the late winter of 1847, a squadron of 200 ships conveyed Scott's army of 10,000 soldiers to Veracruz, which surrendered in April. Scott's troops fought their way to the outskirts of Mexico City, which fell on September 14 (see Map 12–4).

TIME LINE

▼**1834**
First missionaries arrive in Oregon Territory

▼**1836**
Martin Van Buren elected president
Whig Party runs candidates for president
Texas declares independence

▼**1838**
"Aroostook" War
Anti-Slavery Petition campaign at height

▼**1839**
Assassination of Elias Boudinot and John Ridge

▼**1840**
Independent Treasury Bill

Large-scale overland migration to West Coast begins
Whig candidate William Henry Harrison elected president

▼**1841**
John Tyler succeeds Harrison in office
Creole Mutiny

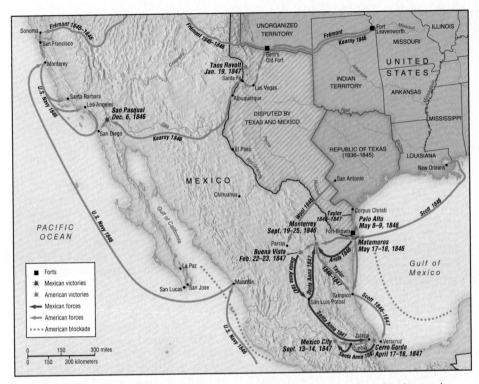

Map 12-4   Mexican War General Zachary Taylor's victories in northern Mexico established the Rio Grande as the boundary between Texas and Mexico. Stephen Kearny's expedition secured control of New Mexico. General Winfield Scott's invasion by sea at Veracruz and his occupation of Mexico ended the war.

For all the success of the American campaign, support for the war steadily eroded. From the beginning, the war raised the question of slavery. Northern Democrats saw the war as a transparent ploy to extend slavery. Antislavery activists spoke out against the war, and opposition grew as stories of US military atrocities

▼1842
Webster-Ashburton Treaty

▼1844
James Polk is elected president

▼1845
The United States annexes Texas

▼1846
The United States declares war on Mexico

▼1848
Treaty of Guadalupe Hidalgo

Teton Sioux attempt to tax white settlers passing through their lands

Struggles For Democracy

Mexicans in California Lose Their Rights

Many liberal-minded, educated people in the United States were against the Mexican-American war. They feared the spread of slavery and found the war to be an unjust effort to strip others of their property. Some of this thinking made its way into the 1848 Treaty of Guadalupe Hidalgo, which ended the war, and promised to deliver justice to Mexicans living in the territory that would henceforth be part of the United States. Article 8 of the treaty stipulated that Mexicans living in the territories ceded to the United States had one year to declare that they preferred Mexican citizenship; otherwise they would become US citizens. Article 9 of the treaty stated that Mexicans would be "maintained and protected in the free enjoyment of their liberty and property." Unfortunately, in the decades that followed, different states and courts interpreted the treaty in a wide range of ways.

In California, the discovery of gold in 1848 created a situation in which white North American settlers became eager to see the treaty overturned, and Mexicans were hard pressed to defend their lands. Many were driven away by mobs, and when the Mexican ambassador complained, he was told that the affected Mexicans must be new arrivals, not people who had been living there for generations. Of course, in this time of warfare against the indigenous people of the West, "Californios," who were primarily of Native American rather than Spanish descent, received no protection at all: the California state constitutional convention explicitly denied them US citizenship.

In 1851, in an effort to ameliorate the chaotic situation in California, Congress passed the Land Act. The legislation created a Board of Land Commissioners whose job was to adjudicate the validity of Mexican land claims in California. Those who had been granted land by Spain or Mexico were required to present documentation upholding their claims within two years. If they did not, their present holdings would pass into the public domain. The Commissioners were instructed to respect the Treaty of Guadalupe Hidalgo, Spanish and Mexican law, and any relevant previous US Supreme Court cases. The Committee received 813 claims and approved 604 of them. Among the successful claimants, however, it was not uncommon to find families who then had to turn around and sell the land they had just been awarded in order to pay the court costs. This was especially true where squatter settlers had brought multiple suits against them from which they had to defend themselves.

filtered back east. Senator **Thomas Corwin** of Ohio made scathing speeches on the floor of Congress, likening the war to thievery without moral justification. He reminded his hearers that though he was an experienced criminal lawyer, he had "never yet heard a thief, arraigned for stealing a horse, plead that it was the best horse he could find."

Adobe House on a California Hacienda, ca. 1880 Settlers from Mexico had lived in California for generations when their homeland suddenly became part of the United States.

The unsuccessful claimants tended to be poorer Californios whose titles had never been formalized but who simply had an understanding for generations either with a local plantation owner or the Church. However, some of those who lost their lands were not poor people with informal claims. One famous example eventually resulted in the 1889 Supreme Court case *Botiller v. Dominguez*. Dominga Dominguez, a wealthy woman from the San Fernando Valley, had perfect title to her lands, given to her family in a grant from the Mexican government dated 1835. Unfortunately, she ignored the political events happening around her and failed to turn in her claim before the two-year deadline. A Frenchman named Brigido Botiller led a group of squatters in a suit to claim her lands. The California State Supreme Court supported the dignified widow, ruling that by the terms of the Treaty of Guadalupe Hidalgo, doña Dominga should not have felt pressured to turn in papers according to a bureaucratic deadline imposed later.

Botiller and the squatters, who were still ranching there as unwelcome neighbors, were not prepared to give up. They brought their suit to the Supreme Court. As the years wore on, many Americans became less interested in promoting justice in connection with the Treaty of Guadalupe Hidalgo and more interested in furthering the connection between government and business. In 1889, the Supreme Court reversed the state court's decision and awarded the Dominguez lands to Botiller and his cohort. The Court reasoned that it would be dangerous to open the door to any other Mexican Americans who had perfect title but had lost their land years ago either because they had failed to present on time or due to some other technicality. *Botiller v. Dominguez* became a landmark case; henceforth, Mexican Americans tended to lose the cases that had been dragging on in the court system ever since the war. Many became deeply embittered and lost their faith in the American democratic system.

In spite of the unpopularity of the war, a defeated Mexico was so weak that Polk thought of extracting greater territorial concessions, including at least part of lower Mexico. His minister in Mexico, Nicholas P. Trist, opposed this proposal, however. In 1848, Trist negotiated the **Treaty of Guadalupe Hidalgo**, recognizing the Rio Grande as the border of Texas and granting the United States the territory encompassed in the present states of New Mexico, Arizona, Colorado, Utah, and Wyoming, as well as California. In return, the United States paid Mexico $15 million and assumed war claims of American citizens against Mexico. The Senate approved the treaty on March 10, 1848. The following May 25, Mexico, having no other option, concurred.

Polk shared with Andrew Jackson a broad understanding of politics and the use of political machinery. Like Jackson, Polk framed policy battles as battles between good and evil, between individual opportunity and elite finance and capital. At the same time, also like Jackson, Polk exercised executive power claiming it to be the tool of the people's will. He was convinced that the president, not the legislature (Whig controlled, by his final years in office), represented the people's will. Before he left office, virtually every important item on his political agenda had been accomplished. Lost in that flush of victory was the steady erosion of popular support for the Democratic Party.

CONCLUSION

The removal of the Indians was intended to create space for white settlers, but in reality, it created new problems for the country. What exactly was to be done with the lands in the West? The war with Mexico revealed just how far apart the North and South had grown. By 1848, the northern states were deeply committed to a society based on free labor. The southern states, meanwhile, had grown ever more committed to slavery. The Mexican War signaled the beginning of an era in which differences between the North and South would seem undeniable and intractable—and symbolized in the West.

In 1848, Henry David Thoreau spoke to an audience in Concord, Massachusetts, about his refusal to pay poll taxes, which he said supported the institution of slavery and its expansion in the war with Mexico. Thoreau declared himself ready to separate from his government—indeed, to see the Union itself destroyed—rather than support the United States in the West. "How does it become a man to behave toward this American government today?" he asked. "I answer, that he cannot without disgrace be associated with it. I cannot for an instant recognize that political organization as my government which is the slave's government also." A crisis was brewing.

WHO, WHAT, WHERE

REVIEW QUESTIONS

1. What caused the decline of Jacksonianism?

2. How did most Americans express their enthusiasm for westward migration?

3. Why were the annexation of Texas and later the invasion of Mexico so controversial?

CRITICAL-THINKING QUESTIONS

1. Support for American expansion was often expressed in the language of freedom and civilization. But was there also a racial component to manifest destiny?

2. Did the territorial additions of the 1840s represent a departure (in method or intent) from earlier acquisitions?

3. How and why did the Democratic Party change between 1828 and 1848?

SUGGESTED READINGS

Blackhawk, Ned. *Violence over the Land: Indians and Empires in the Early American West.* Cambridge, MA: Harvard University Press, 2006.

Guardino, Peter. *The Dead March: A History of the Mexican-American War* (Cambridge, MA: Harvard University Press, 2017).

Limerick, Patricia. *Legacy of Conquest: The Unbroken Past of the American West.* New York: Norton, 1988.

Schlissel, Lillian, ed. *Women's Diaries of the Westward Journey.* New York: Schocken Books, 1992.

For further review materials and resource information, please visit www.oup.com/us/ofthepeople

CHAPTER 12:   Manifest Destiny, 1836–1848
Primary Sources

12.1   CHIEF JOHN ROSS, THE PETITION AND MEMORIAL OF THE DELEGATES AND REPRESENTATIVES OF THE CHEROKEE NATION (1840)

In 1838, Cherokee Chief John and his people moved from Georgia to Oklahoma in the forced march known as the Trail of Tears. Once they arrived in the West, they starved. Their lives in Indian Territory threatened to devolve into chaos. In 1840, Chief Ross went to Washington in a desperate attempt to gain some financial and legal concessions after the fact.

To the Senate and House of Representatives
Washington City, Febry. 28th, 1840

The Petition and Memorial of the undersigned Delegates and representatives of the Cherokee Nation, respectfully shows and represents: That the present position of the Cherokee Nation, and the events which have taken place since its cause was humbly submitted two years ago to Congress, are of a character to call for deep and immediate attention.

Your memorialists [that is, petitioners] have no desire, at this juncture, to dwell on the harrowing causes of the removal of the great mass of their people from their native and cultivated country east of the Mississippi, to the wilderness of the west; the history of that capture is notorious, and that its agonies were mitigated is owing to the considerateness of the stronger, in not demanding of an entire people to say they had acknowledged what it was known they had disavowed; and to the permission humanely accorded to their leading men of personally supervising the compelled removal.

Your memorialists would here respectfully observe, that when it was found indispensable, under all the circumstances, to change the mode at first contemplated for effecting the transit in question, those of your memorialists who were intrusted with the charge of reconciling their countrymen to it, and of conducting them to their destination, encountered difficulties in the task, of which it may be almost impossible for your honorable bodies to form any imagination. Many were the stern minds they had to alter, who even when convinced of the hopelessness of retaining their inheritance they held so sacred, could only be persuaded not to die defending it, by a very slowly inspired reliance on promises that their consenting to remove would ensure peace and freedom to their children in a new and permanent home.

For the success of those of your Memorialists, and others of their fellow citizens, who performed this difficult office, it was fortunate that they were encouraged to assure their indignant, reluctant, and incredulous countrymen, that they would at length live unmolested in a region where their inspiriting national principle of self-government by the power of the majority was no more to be rendered inoperative; where they were to enjoy their own laws, and to be fore ever secured in the glorious privilege of feeling that they were men.

The Cherokee Nation was removed, though, on their first capture by the troops of the American republic, estates, large and small, were, upon the instant, seized and sold to any sordid adventurer, at large commissions to the auctioneers, and next to nothing for the owners; though, in the sudden and forced gathering of the people into separate masses by those troops, children were abruptly severed from doting parents who never met them more; though even the young husband was doomed to know that his wife, whom he was not permitted to protect, nor even to behold, had to pause before the rough soldiers, on the road to a military camp, and under these maddening circumstances, hear the first cry of her infant; though vast multitudes of both sexes and of all ages, were until then habituated to domestic comforts, were sickened by the wretchedness and unwholesomeness of being congregated in open fields, and crowded in Tents during the most scorching heat of summer, and thousands of those nearest and dearest to many of us at length sunk into miserable graves. Yes, though all these aggravations clustered around us on every side, still the drooping Cherokees were cheered on finding their armed captors eventually withdrawn and their conduct into exile transferred to persons among themselves in whom they could confide. The welcome change was hailed by them as the harbinger of a realization of the promise that the United States would secure to them elsewhere, that national independence, that exemption from intrusive meddlers, from prying and lying tale-bearers, and from military protection of the few, to overawe the many, from which the ill-starred peculiarities of their previous position had forever debarred them in the home whence they had departed. A few of their compatriots found themselves circumscribed by the chase by the advancing change in the modes of life, not only all around but within their native country, and that these few sought hunting grounds in the far west. The place they chose was at that time the property of Spain.[1] It passed into the hands of the United States, from whom, when the policy was arising to remove the Indians, our Mother Country east of the Mississippi purchased it, that her absent children might not be disturbed. Thus began the nucleus around which successive emigrants gathered, until at length its boundaries were outstretched by treaty for all Cherokees who might thenceforward follow. At the time the entire nation bent its course toward the region in question, about (as nearly as can be ascertained) one sixth of this whole population was already established there and this one sixth was generally designated as the western Cherokees. These facts will be well remembered by your honorable bodies; and your memorialists only state them to render their story more distinct.

The Cherokee Nation was removed . . . [Here follows a summary of all the efforts the relocated Cherokees had made between the 1838 removal and the present both to obtain aid from their western brethren, and to obtain that which was promised them by the US government, all to no avail.]

Your memorialists mostly humbly represent, that, if some mode of settling the concerns of the Cherokees with the United states is not presently adopted, their people will be reduced to ruin and despair; and it is their ardent hope that your honorable bodies will assist them to prevent such a result as all must deprecate, and not permit any pretence, however plausibly urged, to exclude us [chiefs] from being heard in the name of our people. The greater portion of them will presently be without goods; as the period of supplying the new Emigrants with rations is just expiring. They have no means. They have not so much as the implements of husbandry [that is, agricultural tools], and their arms which were taken from them some years ago, having never been restored, as promised, they cannot supply themselves with game. The existing relations between us and the United States are so ambiguous and capable of such opposite constructions, that even an obligation which is assumed, to preserve peace and to prevent intestine commotion, is, at this very moment, so exercised as to create the very evils it professes to remedy, and to defeat the very principle of recognizing the power of the majority which the Cherokees are instructed to consider as the principle of the Unites States in their dealings regarding them. We ask that these ambiguities may be cleared away. When our eastern country was lately taken from us without

---

[1]They are referring to today's Arkansas and eastern Oklahoma. These people are still known as the Western Band of Cherokee.

the consent of the majority, and the great mass of our people captured, they said that it was hard, but they were the weaker, and would not resist. They were doubted, but not a hand was raised, and now, those who have survived are in the West. We have done our part. We have given up all. What has been done by the United States? Nothing. Notwithstanding these things, have we yet acted towards the Unites States otherwise than with the meekest spirit of endurance. No one can say we ever did. We implore the great Republic to remember this in our favour and will then echo in its praise the benison [blessing] of the Saviour God himself, "Blessed are the peacemakers."

Your memorialists therefor humbly state that having full powers from the Cherokee people, to bring all questions between them and the United States to a close, they have been waiting for some time in Washington for the purpose;

1st Of obtaining indemnification for the country which has been taken away from them east of the Mississippi, and for the loss of private property and of injuries sustained in their forced removal:

2nd Of establishing a satisfactory definition of the tenure under which they are to hold their lands in the west:

3rd Of procuring some specific stipulations of the relations, which are to exist between them and the United States:

And 4th Of bringing the balance yet due for the expenses of their recent Emigration under General [Winfield] Scott to an immediate settlement:

And your memorialists throw themselves on the humanity and justice of your honorable bodies, as the only resource now left for the arrangement of these momentous affairs, to open the door for their relief, by such action as the wisdom of your honorable bodies may devise and the circumstances of our case urgently demand, and your memorialists will ever pray.

John Ross

John Looney (X)

E. Hicks

Archibald Campbell (X)

Joseph M. Lynch

Edward Gunter

Looney Price

George Hicks

Source: Gary Moulton, ed., *The Papers of John Ross, Volume II, 1840–1866* (Norman: University of Oklahoma Press, 1985), pp. 6–17.

12.2   VISUAL DOCUMENTS: THOMAS COLE, *LANDSCAPE* (1825); FREDERIC EDWIN CHURCH, *NIAGARA FALLS* (1857); LOUIS RÉMY MIGNOT, *LANDSCAPE IN ECUADOR* (1859)

In 1825, a New York City magazine reviewed the work of a young painter named Thomas Cole, who had hiked the Adirondacks and created works celebrating the beauty of the world he encountered. Soon a number of artists were producing sublime landscape paintings of the region. At first they were called "the Hudson River school" in gentle mockery, but soon the term's use changed. A second generation of Hudson River school painters worked in the same style but traveled all over North and South America for inspiration. They shared a belief that America's natural world revealed the hemisphere's greatness.

Source: Thomas Cole, *Landscape* (1825). Bequest of Mrs. Kate L. Dunwoody.

Source: Frederic Edwin Church, *Niagara Falls* (1857). Granger, NYC—

Source: Louis Rémy Mignot, *Landscape in Ecuador* (1859). Purchased with funds from gifts by the American Credit Corporation in memory of Guy T. Carswell, and various donors, by exchange.

12.3   LYDIA ALLEN RUDD, *ACCOUNT OF WESTWARD JOURNEY* (1852)

Lydia and Harry Rudd, Oregon Trail emigrants, had lost a baby girl named Margaret before they decided to go west and file for land in Oregon under the Donation Act. What especially interested Lydia was the fact that the Act allowed both husbands and wives to file for land claims. They went in 1852, together with two friends, whom Lydia identifies in her diary only as Henry and Mary. They were part of a larger wagon train that frequently purchased goods and services from local Indians.

May 6 1852 Left the Missouri river for our long journey across the wild uncultivated plains and unhabitated except by the red man. As we left the river bottom and ascended the bluffs the view from them was handsome! In front of us as far as vision could reach extended the green hills covered with fine grass.... Behind us lay the Missouri with its muddy water hurrying past as if in great haste to reach some destined point ahead all unheeding the impatient emigrants on the opposite shore at the ferrying which arrived faster than they could be conveyed over. About half a miles down the river lay a steamboat stuck fast on a sandbar. Still farther down lay the busy village of St. Joseph looking us a good bye and reminding us that we were leaving all signs of civilised life for the present. But with good courage and not one sigh of regret I mounted my pony (whose name by the way is Samy) and rode slowly on. In going some two miles, the scene changed from bright sunshine to drenching showers of rain this was not quite agreeable for in spite of our good blankets and intentions otherwise we got some wet. The rain detained us so that we have not made but ten miles today....

May 7 I found myself this morning with a severe headache from the effects of yesterday's rain....

There is a toll bridge across this stream kept by the Indians. The toll for our team in total was six bits. We have had some calls this evening from the Indians. We gave them something to eat and they left. Some of them [had] on no shirt only a blanket, whiles others were ornamented in Indian style with their faces painted in spots and stripes feathers and fur on their heads beeds on their neck brass rings on their wrists and arms and in their ears armed with rifles and spears.

May 8 ... We have come about 12 miles and were obliged to camp in the open prairie without any wood. Mary and myself collected some dry weeds and grass and made a little fire and cooked some meat and the last of our supply of eggs with these and some hard bread with water we made our supper.

May 9 ... We passed a new made grave today ... a man from Ohio. We also met a man that was going back: he had buried his Wife this morning She died from the effects of measels we have come ten miles today encamped on a small stream called Vermillion creek Wood and water plenty. Their [*sic*] are as many as fifty waggons on this stream and some thousand head of stock It looks like a village the tents and waggons extend as much as a mile....

Some are singing some talking and some laughing and the cattle are adding their mite by shaking their bells and grunt[ing]. Mosquitoes are intruding their unwelcome presence. Harry says that I must not sit here any longer writing but go to bed for I will not want to get up early in the morning to get breakfast.

May 10 I got up this morning and got breakfast and before sunrise we had eat in spite of Harry's prophecies to the contrary....

May 11 We had a very heavy fog this morning which cleared up about noon. Our men are not any of them very well this morning. We passed another grave to day which was made this morning. The board stated that he died of cholera. He was from Indiana. We met several that had taken the back track for the states homesick I presume let them go. We have passed through a handsome country and have encamped on the Nimehaw river, the most beautiful spot that ever I saw in my life. I would like to live here. As far as the eye can reach either way lay handsome rolling prairies, not a stone a tree nor a bush even nothing but grass and flowers meets the eye until you reach the valley of the river which is as level as the house floor and about half a mile wide, where on the bank of the stream for two or three rods wide is one of the heaviest belts of timber I ever saw covered with thick foliage so thick that you could not get a glimpse of the stream through it. You can see this belt of timber for three or four miles from the hills on both sides winding through the prairie like some huge snake. We have traveled twelve miles. . . .

May 12 . . . Our men not much better.

May 13 . . . Henry has been no better today. Soon after we stopped to night a man came along with a wheel barrow going to California: he is a dutchmann. He wheels his provisions and clothing all day and then stops where night overtakes him sleeps on the ground in the open air. He eats raw meat and bread for his supper. I think that he will get tired wheeling his way through the world by the time he gets to California.

May 14 Just after we started this morning we passed four men dig[g]ing a grave. They were packers. The man that had died was taken sick yesterday noon and died last night. They called it cholera morbus. The corpse lay on the ground a few feet from where they were dig[g]ing. The grave it was a sad sight. . . .

On the bank of the stream waiting to cross, stood a dray with five men harnessed to it bound for California. They must be some of the persevering kind I think. Wanting to go to California more than I do. . . . We passed three more graves this afternoon. . . .

Sept. 5 Traveled eighteen miles today encamped on a slough of powder river poor camp not much grass water nor wood. I am almost dead tonight. I have been sick two or three days with the bowel complaint and am much worse tonight.

Sept. 6 We have not been able to leave this miserable place today. I am not as well as yesterday and no physician to be had. We got a little medicine from a train tonight that has checked the disease some, the first thing that has done me any good.

Sept. 7 . . . I am some better today so much so that they ventured to move me this for the sake of a better camp. Mrs. Girtman is also sick with the same disease. Our cattle are most all of them ailing—there are two more that we expect will die every day. . . .

Oct. 8 started early this morning without any breakfast for the very good reason that we had nothing to eat still three miles from the falls safely landed about eight o'clock tired hungry and with a severe cold from last nights exposure something like civilization here in the shape of three or four houses there is an excuse here for a railroad of a mile and half on which to convey bag[g]age below the falls where they can again take water for the steamboat landing. Harry packed our bag[g]age down the railroad and the rest of us walked the car is drawn across the railroad by a mule and they will car[r]y no persons but sick. We again hired an Indian with his canoe to take us from the falls to the steamboat landing ar[r]ived about sundown a great many emigrants waiting for a chance to leave the steamboat and several flat boats lying ready to start out in the morning encamped on the shore for the night.

October 9–October 13 . . .

October 14 . . . I am so anxious to get some place to stop and settle that my patience is not worth much.

October 15–18 . . .

October 19 . . . We have had a very bad day today for traveling it has rained nearly all the time and it has rained very hard some of the time and we have had a miserable road the rain has made the hills very slippery and had to get up and down we have made but eleven miles of travel encamped on the prairie no water for our stock and not much for ourselves.

October 21 . . .

October 22 . . . Traveled three miles this morning and reached the village of Salem it is quite a pretty town a much handsomer place than Oregon City and larger. . . .

I am afraid that we shall be obliged to pack from here the rest of our journey and it will be a wet job another wet rainy day I am afraid that the rain will make us all sick. I am already begin to feel the affects of it by a bad cold.

October 23 . . . We cannot get any wagon to take us on our journey and are obliged to pack the rest of the way Mr. Clark and wife have found a house to live in and employment for the winter and they will stop here in Salem It took us until nearly noon to get our packs fixed for packing went about two miles and it rained so fast that we were obliged to stop got our dinner and supper in one meal cooked in a small cabin ignorant people but kind started again just.

October 24–25 . . .

October 26 . . . we reached Burlington about two o'clock. There is one store one blacksmith shop and three or four dwelling houses. We encamped close by found Mr. Donals in his store an old acquaintance of my husband's. I do not know what we shall yet conclude on doing for the winter. There is no house in town that we can get to winter in. We shall probably stay here tomorrow and by the time know what we are to do for a while at least.

October 27 . . . Our men have been looking around for a house and employment and have been successful for which I feel very thankful. Harry has gone into copartnership with Mr. Donals in the mercantile business and we are to live in the back part of the store for this winter. Henry and Mary are going into Mr. D—house on his farm for the winter one mile from here. Mr. D—will also find him employment if he wants. I expect that we shall not make a claim after all our trouble in getting here on purpose for one. I shall have to be poor and dependent on a man my life time.

Source: Lillian Schlissel, ed., *Women's Diaries of the Westward Journey* (New York: Schocken Books, 1982), pp. 188–197.

12.4 JOHN O'SULLIVAN, "ANNEXATION" (1845)

John O'Sullivan was a newspaper columnist and editor writing in the 1840s. In the summer of 1845, in the pages of *The United States Magazine and Democratic Review*, he was the first to use the phrase "manifest destiny" in connection with America's westward expansion. No one responded, but a piece he wrote a few months later in December for the *New York Morning News* was more widely read, and the term caught on. O'Sullivan was an influential Democrat, and at first, the term was only used derisively by Republicans. In fact, it did not become popular until late in the nineteenth century when the United States launched its career of imperialism.

It is now time for the opposition to the Annexation of Texas to cease, all further agitation of the waters of bitterness and strife, at least in connexion with this question,—even though it may perhaps be required of us as a necessary condition of the freedom of our institutions, that we must live on for ever in a state of unpausing struggle and excitement upon some subject of party division or other. But, in regard to Texas, enough has now been given to party. It is time for the common duty of Patriotism to the Country to succeed;—or if this claim will not be recognized, it is at least time for common sense to acquiesce with decent grace in the inevitable and the irrevocable.

Texas is now ours. Already, before these words are written, her Convention has undoubtedly ratified the acceptance, by her Congress, of our proffered invitation into the Union; and made the requisite changes in her already republican form of constitution to adapt it to its future federal relations. Her star and her stripe may already be said to have taken their place in the glorious blazon of our common nationality; and the sweep of our eagle's wing already includes within its circuit the wide extent of her fair and fertile land. She is no longer to us a mere geographical space—a certain combination of coast, plain, mountain, valley, forest and stream.... She comes within the dear and sacred designation of Our Country; no longer a *"pays,"* she is a part of *"la patrie"*; and that which is at once a sentiment and a virtue, Patriotism, already begins to thrill for her too within the national heart. It is time then that all should cease to treat her as alien, and even adverse—cease to denounce and vilify all and everything connected with her accession—cease to thwart and oppose the remaining steps for its consummation; or where such efforts are felt to be unavailing, at least to embitter the hour of reception by all the most ungracious frowns of aversion and words of unwelcome. There has been enough of all this. It has had its fitting day during the period when, in common with every other possible question of practical policy that can arise, it unfortunately became one of the leading topics of party division, of presidential electioneering. But that period has passed.... The next session of Congress will see the representatives of the new young State in their places in both our halls of national legislation, side by side with those of the old Thirteen. Let their reception into "the family" be frank, kindly, and cheerful, as befits such an occasion, as comports not less with our own self-respect than patriotic duty towards them. Ill betide those foul birds that delight to file their own nest, and disgust the ear with perpetual discord of ill-omened croak.

Why, were other reasoning wanting, in favor of now elevating this question of the reception of Texas into the Union, out of the lower region of our past party dissensions, up to its proper level of a high and broad nationality, it surely is to be found in the manner in which other nations have undertaken to intrude themselves into it, between us and the proper parties to the case, in a spirit of hostile interference against us, for the avowed object of thwarting our policy and hampering our power, limiting our greatness and checking the fulfillment of our manifest destiny to overspread the continent allotted by Providence for the free development of our yearly multiplying millions. This we have seen done by England, our old rival and enemy; and by France, strangely coupled with her against us, under the influence of the Anglicism strongly tinging the policy of her present prime minister, Guizot. The zealous activity with which this effort to defeat us was pushed by the representatives of those governments, together with the character of intrigue accompanying it, fully constituted that case of foreign interference, which Mr. Clay himself declared should, and would unite us all in maintaining the common cause of our country against foreigner and the foe. We are only astonished that this effect has not been more fully and strongly produced, and that the burst of indignation against this unauthorized, insolent and hostile interference against us, has not been more general even among the party before opposed to Annexation, and has not rallied the national spirit and national pride unanimously upon that policy. We are very sure that if Mr. Clay himself were now to add another letter to his former Texas correspondence, he would express this sentiment, and carry out the idea already strongly stated in one of them, in a manner which would tax all the powers of blushing belonging to some of his party adherents....

Away, then, with all idle French talk of *balances of power* on the American Continent. There is no growth in Spanish America! Whatever progress of population there may be in the British Canadas, is only for their own early severance of their present colonial relation to the little island three thousand miles across the Atlantic; soon to be followed by Annexation, and destined to swell the still accumulating momentum of our progress. And whosoever may hold the balance, though they should cast into the opposite scale all the bayonets and cannon, not only of France and England, but of Europe entire, how would it kick the beam against the simple, solid weight of the two hundred and fifty, or three hundred millions—and American millions—destined to gather beneath the flutter of the stripes and stars, in the fast hastening year of the Lord 1845!

Source: John O'Sullivan, "Annexation," *United States Magazine and Democratic Review* 17, no. 1 (July–August 1845): 5–10.

12.5 MARÍA AMPARO RUIZ DE BURTON, *THE SQUATTER AND THE DON* (1885)

Born in Lareto, Mexico, María Amparo Ruiz was the granddaughter of the governor of Baja California. When she was 15, she met Captain Henry S. Burton of the US Army, who arrived to take possession of Baja California at the same time as General Winfield Scott was marching on Mexico City. She married Burton in 1849, and she later moved with him to San Diego and then to the East Coast. After her husband's death, she supported herself and her children as a writer. She began work on what would become *The Squatter and the Don* in the late 1870s, based on experiences her friends and family had had in the preceding decades.

Don Mariano Alamar was silently walking up and down the front piazza of his house at the rancho; his hands listlessly clasped behind and his head slightly bent forward in deep thought. He had pushed away to one side the many armchairs and wicker rockers with which the piazza was furnished. He wanted a long space to walk. That his meditations were far from agreeable could easily be seen by the compressed lips, slight frown, and sad gaze of his mild and beautiful blue eyes. Sounds of laughter, music and dancing came from the parlor, the young people were entertaining friends from town with their usual gay hospitality, and enjoying themselves heartily. Don Mariano, though already in his fiftieth year, was as fond of dancing as his sons and daughters, and not to see him come in and join the quadrille was so singular that his wife thought she must come out and inquire what could detain him. He was so absorbed in his thoughts that he did not hear her voice calling him—"What keeps you away? Lizzie has been looking for you; she wants you for a partner in the lancers," said Doña Josefa, putting her arm under that of her husband, bending her head forward and turning it up to look into his eyes.

"What is the matter?" she asked, stopping short, thus making her husband come to a sudden halt. "I am sure something has happened. Tell me."

"Nothing, dear wife. Nothing has happened. That is to say, nothing new."

"More squatters?" she asked. Señor Alamar bent his head slightly in affirmative reply.

"More coming, you mean?"

"Yes, wife; more. Those two friends of squatters Mathews and Hagar, who were here last year to locate claims and went away, did not abandon their claims, but only went away to bring proselytes and their families, and a large invoice of them will arrive on tomorrow's steamer. The worst of it all is, that among the new comers is that terrible and most dangerous squatter William Darrell, who some years ago gave so much trouble to the Spanish people in Napa and Sonoma Counties by locating claims there. John Gasbang wrote to Hogsden that besides Darrell, there will be six or seven other men bringing their families, so that there will be more rifles for my cattle."

. . . Doña Josefa was silent and, holding on to her husband's arm, took a turn with him up and down the piazza.

"Is it possible that there is no law to protect us; to protect our property; what does your lawyer say about obtaining redress or protection; is there no hope?" she asked, with a sigh.

"Protection for our land, or for our cattle, you mean?"

"For both, as we get it for neither," she said.

"In the matter of our land, we have to await for the attorney general, at Washington, to decide."

"Lizzie was telling Elvira, yesterday, that her uncle Lawrence is a friend of several influential people in Washington, and that George can get him to interest himself in having your title decided."

"But, as George is to marry my daughter, he would be the last man from whom I would ask a favor."

"What is that I hear about not asking a favor from me?" said George Mechlin, coming out on the piazza with Elvira on his arm, having just finished a waltz—"I am interested to know why you would not ask it."

"You know why, my dear boy. It isn't exactly the thing to bother you with my disagreeable business."

"And why not? And who has a better right? And why should it be a bother to me to help you in any way I can? My father spoke to me about a dismissal of an appeal, and I made a note of it. Let me see, I think I have it in my pocket now"—said George, feeling in his breast pocket for his memorandum book—"yes, here it is—'For uncle to write to the attorney general about dismissing the appeal taken by the squatters in the Alamar grant, against Don Mariano's title, which was approved.' Is that the correct idea? I only made this note to ask you for further particulars."

"You have it exactly. When I give you the number of the case, it is all that you need say to your uncle. What I want is to have the appeal dismissed, of course, but if the attorney general does not see fit to do so, he can, at least, remand back the case for a new trial. Anything rather than this killing suspense. Killing literally, for while we are waiting to have my title settled, the *settlers* (I don't mean to make puns) are killing my cattle by the hundred head, and I cannot stop them."

"But are there no laws to protect property in California?" George asked.

"Yes, some sort of laws, which in my case seem more intended to help the law-breakers than to protect the law-abiding," Don Mariano replied.

"How so? Is there no law to punish the thieves who kill your cattle?"

"There are some enactments so obviously intended to favor one class of citizens against another class that to call them laws is an insult to law, but such as they are, we must submit to them. By those laws any man can come to my land, for instance, plant ten acres of grain, without any fence, and then catch my cattle which, seeing the green grass without a fence, will go to eat it. Then he puts them in a 'corral' and makes me pay damages and so much per head for keeping them, and costs of legal proceedings and many other trumped up expenses, until for such little fields of grain I may be obliged to pay thousands of dollars. Or, if the grain fields are large enough to bring more money by keeping the cattle away, then the settler shoots the cattle at any time without the least hesitation, only taking care that no one sees him in the act of firing upon the cattle. He might stand behind a bush or tree and fire, but then he is not seen. No one can swear that they saw him actually kill the cattle, and no jury can convict him, for although the dead animals may be there, lying on the ground shot, still no one saw the settler kill them. And so it is all the time. I must pay damages and expenses of litigation, or my cattle get killed almost every day."

"But this is infamous. Haven't you—the cattle owners—tried to have some law enacted that will protect your property?" George asked. "It seems to me that could be done."

"It could be done, perhaps, if our positions were reversed, and the Spanish people—'*the natives*'—were the planters of the grain fields, and the Americans were the owners of the cattle. But as we, the Spaniards, are the owners of the Spanish—or Mexican—land grants and also the owners of the cattle ranchos, our State legislators will not make any law to protect cattle. They make laws '*to protect agriculture*' (they say proudly), which means to drive to the wall all owners of cattle ranchos. I am told that at this session of the legislature a law more strict yet will be passed, which will be ostensibly '*to protect agriculture*' but in reality to destroy cattle and ruin the native Californians. The agriculture of this State does not require legislative protection. Such pretext is absurd."

"I thought that the rights of the Spanish people were protected by our treaty with Mexico," George said.

"Mexico did not pay much attention to the future welfare of the children she left to their fate in the hands of a nation which had no sympathies for us," said Doña Josefa, feelingly.

"I remember," calmly said Don Mariano, "that . . . Mexico did as much as could have been reasonably expected at the time. In the very preamble of the treaty the spirit of peace and friendship, which animated both nations, was carefully made manifest. That spirit was to be the foundation of the relations between the conqueror and conquered. How could Mexico have foreseen then that when scarcely half a dozen years should have elapsed the trusted conquerors would, In *Congress Assembled*, pass laws which were to be retroactive upon the defenseless, helpless, conquered people, in order to despoil them? The treaty said that our rights would be the same as those enjoyed by all other American citizens. But, you see, Congress takes very good care not to enact retroactive laws for Americans, laws to take away from American citizens the property which they hold now, already, with a recognized legal title. No, indeed. But they do so quickly enough with us—with us, the Spano-Americans, who were to enjoy equal rights, mind you, according to the treaty of peace. This is what seems to me a breach of faith, which Mexico could neither presuppose nor prevent."

"It is nothing else, I am sorry and ashamed to say," George said. "I never knew much about the treaty with Mexico, but I never imagined we had acted so badly."

"I think but few Americans know or believe to what extent we have been wronged by Congressional action. And truly, I believe that Congress itself did not anticipate the effect of its laws upon us and how we would be despoiled, we, the conquered people," said Don Mariano, sadly.

Source: María Amparo Ruiz de Burton, *The Squatter and the Don* (San Francisco: S. Carson & Co., 1885), chapter 2.

The Politics of Slavery

1848–1860

< John Brown

Frederick Douglass

Frederick Douglass denounced the war with Mexico as "disgraceful, cruel, and iniquitous." Northern support for what he saw as a slaveholders' war reinforced Douglass's conviction that the US Constitution had created an unholy union of liberty and slavery. The only solution was for New England to secede. "The Union must be dissolved," Douglass wrote, "or New England is lost and swallowed up by the slave-power of the country."

Douglass had been urging disunion for several years, ever since he became the most compelling antislavery voice in America. His authority derived from his extraordinary intelligence, his exceptional skill as a public speaker, and above all from his personal experience. Frederick Douglass was not simply an abolitionist; he was also the most famous runaway enslaved person in America.

He was born Frederick Augustus Washington Bailey in Talbot County, Maryland, in 1818. At the age of seven he was sent to Baltimore, where he became a skilled caulker in the shipyards. There he hired out his labor, paying his master three dollars each week and keeping the rest himself. He grew to resent the arrangement. For the rest of his life he would associate freedom with the right to earn a living. When his master demanded everything he had saved, Frederick planned his escape.

On May 3, 1838, he dressed as a sailor and boarded a northbound train using borrowed papers. By September he was calling himself Frederick Douglass and working in New Bedford, Massachusetts. He began attending antislavery meetings. He subscribed to William Lloyd Garrison's fiery abolitionist newspaper, The Liberator. In 1841, invited to speak during an abolitionist convention, Douglass stunned his listeners with an eloquent recital of his experience as an enslaved person. Garrison was in the audience, and he invited Douglass to speak for the American Anti-Slavery Society. For the next several years, Douglass was a leading voice for the Garrisonian wing of the abolitionist movement.

The Garrisonians saw the Constitution as hopelessly corrupted by its compromises with slavery. They saw no point in pursuing political reforms. Rather, North must separate from South. Nor could they endorse violent efforts to overthrow slavery, including slave rebellion; their one weapon was moral persuasion. So Frederick Douglass believed, too—at first.

The Mexican War was a turning point for him. Since the 1820s, the major parties had tried to stay clear of slavery-connected issues. Manifest destiny in the 1840s made that impossible: admitting Texas as a slave state and conquering Mexican territory spread slavery where the law forbade it. Many northern Whigs and Democrats called for keeping the newly acquired lands as "free soil." In 1848, a Free-Soil Party drew 300,000 votes. Its leaders made a compelling case for reading the Constitution as an antislavery document and for the government to act on that basis.

As antislavery thought entered the mainstream, Douglass reconsidered his views both on the Constitution and the possibilities of political action. Already his home had become a way station on the Underground Railroad. Douglass may have spirited as many as 200 fugitives from there into Canada. He also came to support slave resistance, even rebellion. However, a gulf remained between his own views and those of the Free-Soil Party's much bigger successor, the Republican Party. Douglass remained an abolitionist and struggled against all forms of racial discrimination; all too many Republicans treated the real issue as the politically powerful conspirators who ran the so-called Slave Power trying to lord it over white northern free labor. But at least, in Douglass's words, some northern voters no longer thought the abolitionists were crying wolf: they saw the wolf themselves.

THE POLITICAL ECONOMY OF FREEDOM AND SLAVERY

The politics of slavery reemerged at a moment of tremendous economic growth. As the depression of the 1840s lifted, the American zeal for internal improvements revived. The canals built between 1800 and 1830 were widened. Steamboats raced upriver as flatboats carried cheap freight down. Trains were redesigned to have more power to climb hills and looser joints to go around sharp curves. Double tracks were laid to permit train traffic in both directions at the same time. New passenger cars carried more customers by putting them in rows of seats rather than separate compartments. States and towns lent money to help railroads build and own long-distance through lines. Starting in 1850, the national government endowed companies like the Mobile and Ohio and the Illinois Central Railroads with millions of acres in land grants in order to expand business. As a result, railroad construction boomed. In the 20 years leading up to the Civil War, mileage rose from 3,000 to 31,000—more than the rest of the world combined. No less spectacular was the rapid adoption of the telegraph. Invented by Samuel F. B. Morse in 1844, the telegraph made virtually instantaneous communication possible across oceans and continents. By 1860, there were 50,000 miles of telegraph wire in America. The first transcontinental line was completed in 1861.

These developments might have inhibited the growth of sectionalism. An efficient transportation and communication network helped integrate the United States into a single national market. But the economic growth of the North created especially strong ties between the East and the West. Turnpikes, canals, and especially railroads tended to run east and west, linking northeastern cities to the western frontier; few, however, crossed the Mason-Dixon Line to link the northern and southern economies (see Map 13–1). By the 1850s, the differences between the North and the South overwhelmed the connections that bound them together.

A Changing Economy in the North

The 1850s were booming years for northern farmers, now connected firmly to the national market. Whereas it used to take two months to ship meat and grains from the Midwest to the East Coast in 1810, it now took less than a week. Railroads could carry a ton of wheat for a nickel a mile and a ton of coal for half that much. They could bring a half million bushels of wheat to Chicago in 12 hours. Because of the dramatic reduction in transportation costs, northern farmers could devote more time and effort to raising crops for sale rather than for subsistence at home. Thanks

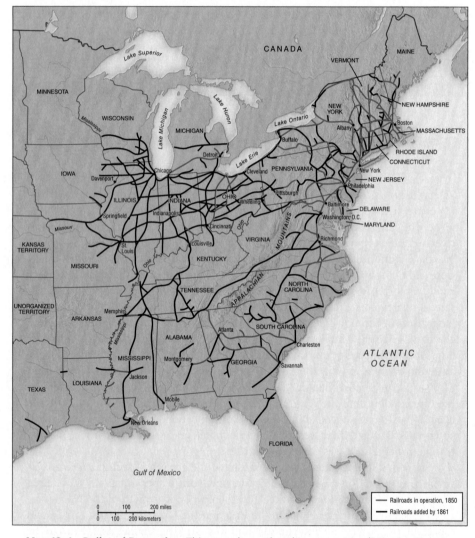

Map 13–1   Railroad Expansion This map shows that there were two distinct patterns of railroad development in the United States. In the North, rail lines connected the western states to the Eastern Seaboard. In the South, railroads tied the inland plantation districts to the coastal ports. Few lines connected the North to the South.

also to inventions like the steel plow, seed drills, and the McCormick reaper, northern farmers increased their production four times over between 1820 and 1860.

Farmers found expanding markets because more Americans were living in cities and working for wages, producing little of their own food, clothing, or shelter. Yet so productive was American agriculture that it took fewer farmers to supply a growing population. Between 1820 and 1860, the workforce engaged in agriculture dropped from 75 to 57 percent. Wage labor in the North grew too fast for native-born workers to fill the demand. In the mid-1840s, the number of Europeans coming to the United States jumped sharply, and 3 million arrived in the decade between 1845 and 1854.

As industrial production increased, businesses opened large downtown stores to sell their goods. Between 1859 and 1862, for example, A. T. Stewart built a huge dry goods store covering a full square block in lower Manhattan. The financial needs of these enterprises were met by an expanding number of banks, insurance companies, and accounting firms that employed armies of white-collar workers.

Economic growth in the North during the 1850s rested on important social changes. A rural society became more urban. Industry was complementing agriculture as a driving economic force. Wage laborers were supplementing small farmers and craftsmen. A Protestant nation saw its first great wave of Catholic immigrants. Machines made it possible for one person to cultivate more acres than ever before. A political economy based on new sources of wealth and new forms of work was being born.

The Slave Economy

It made sense for the wealthy South Carolina planter James Henry Hammond to declare in 1858, "Cotton is king." Recovering from the doldrums of the 1840s, cotton prices held steady while the price of enslaved people soared. Southern states threw themselves into railroad construction, building a substantial network. Steamboats plied the South's rivers. Telegraph wires sped news of cotton prices from New York to New Orleans and deep into the plantation belt. Slavery was thriving. So why shouldn't Hammond boast?

The South had changed in many ways during the previous century. It had expanded across half the continent (see Map 13–2). Cotton had become its most profitable crop. The Atlantic slave trade was over, and a native-born, largely Christian enslaved population had grown up. There were important signs of social change, especially in the upper South. The immigrant workers Frederick Douglass met on the Baltimore docks coped with the same process of economic development as New England dockworkers. The steady sale of enslaved people from the upper to the lower South reduced the influence of slaveholders in Maryland, Kentucky, and Delaware. Indeed, among whites across the South the proportion of slaveholding families had been declining for decades, from one in three in 1830 to one in four by 1860.

The expansion of slavery fostered commerce, but the benefits were spread unevenly. Slaveholders prospered the most. By 1860, they ranked among America's wealthiest classes. Wealth enabled slaveholders to monopolize the best lands, eliminating opportunity for small landowners. As a result, farmers without enslaved people were much poorer than their northern counterparts.

American Landscape

City of Broad Shoulders and Broader Implications: Chicago

Any town planner in 1811 would have rated Chicago the one location least likely to succeed. A trading post set in Potawatomie Indian country in a swamp on the edge of an unnavigable river that never reached the shallow edge of Lake Michigan, it had nothing to recommend it, even after easterners turned it into a village. Unpaved roads turned into rivers of mud in wet weather. "No Bottom Here. Shortest Road to China," one hotel sign warned. Yet by the start of the Civil War, it had become formidable.

Eastern money, public and private, made Chicago into a brawny western metropolis. A New York real estate promoter, William Ogden, came west to sell marshland and stayed to make it worth selling. Laying streets and parceling out property into lots was only the beginning. Residents needed access to eastern markets both for what they made and what they bought. With Ogden's backing, a canal opened a waterway from the Chicago River to Lake Michigan. The US government forced the Potawatomie to swap their lands for soil on the high plains west of Missouri and drove them forth at gunpoint. A harbor was dredged out. Later, the state financed a canal linking the city west to the Mississippi River. To entice immigrants, Ogden helped found a medical college and a city horticultural society. He ran a steamship line and built a brewery. By 1837, the community had grown large enough for a city charter. Ogden became its first mayor.

Most of all, Ogden grasped railroads' potential for developing the prairie west and enriching Chicago. Nearly 3,000 miles of track fed into the

Status in the South rested on owning land and enslaved people, not investing in industry. So while the South as a whole boasted of industrial growth, it fell further behind the North every year, especially below the border states. Most industry was extractive (coal mining or lumbering) or processed agricultural goods for market. The South had just 6 percent of the nation's cotton-manufacturing capacity. Lowell, Massachusetts, had more cotton spindles than fifteen slave states put together. New York City had as much banking capital as the whole South. Together, those limits explained why the surge of immigrants built the North and West rather than the South, and why by 1860 the states north of the Ohio River had 9 million people—more than the white population in the slave states. They also explained why the inventions transforming America—the sewing machine, the telegraph, reapers, harvesters, and circular saws—all came out of the North. Cyrus McCormick's "Virginia reaper" found few takers in Virginia; he found his buyers in the Midwest. Year by year those changes meant a North growing faster than the South, not just in wealth but in numbers and political power.

city by the mid-1850s. Within a generation, they had absorbed most of the trade from the Dakotas to Kansas City. Salesmen fanned out from the high plains to the upper south, taking orders from storekeepers and local merchants, enough to keep 500 Chicago factories at work full-time. Wisconsin's forests ended up in Chicago lumberyards before spreading across the treeless plains as boards for frame houses. Cincinnati, famed as "Porkopolis" for its hog butchering, could not match Chicago's sway in the Corn Belt. By the 1860s, tens of thousands of hogs were shipped to "Packingtown's" slaughterhouses to be killed, cured, and sold.

After struggling for years to sell his reapers in the east, Cyrus McCormick headed to Chicago with $300 in his pocket. He never regretted it. His factory sold 1,000 machines in 1851 and 23,000 six years later. Farmers once able to harvest only two acres a day now could do twelve. Instead of raising corn, they could put in wheat, which sold for twice as much per bushel.

Prairie land where stock had grazed turned into prime real estate, and nowhere more so than around Chicago, where railroads could haul the reapers in and haul the grain out. By 1853, Chicago shipped out 6 million bushels of grain every year; by 1856, 21 million.

Not surprisingly, the West's most famous figure, Stephen A. Douglas, made Chicago his home. No place better suited the go-ahead spirit that he represented. But Chicago did not just epitomize the West's vitality. It showed how steep the odds were against the South sharing the territories, whatever the fate of Kansas. The city's growth helped fill Illinois with northerners, Douglas among them. It bound white settlers' fortunes to northeastern markets, rather than to those of the Mississippi River cities and southern outlets. Ogden became the first president of the Union Pacific Railroad, tying Chicago to the west coast. When Republicans nominated a presidential candidate in 1860, fittingly, they held their convention in Chicago.

The Importance of the West

Both the North and the South coveted western lands. By 1850, many northerners believed that slavery, if allowed to expand into the West, would deprive free laborers of an important source of prosperity and independence. But slaveholders had come to believe that their prosperity depended on the spread of the slave economy into the West.

To white southerners, territorial expansion constituted progress. The westward movement of the southern frontier demonstrated the continued strength of the slave economy. Halting that movement would undermine southern prosperity. It was an affront to the moral decency of white southerners, an obstacle to their economic vitality. But above all else it was an infringement on the slaveholders' inalienable rights of property, which included the constitutional right to carry it with them wherever they saw fit and where state law did not forbid it. So argued slavery's defenders with increasing vehemence in the 1850s. For northerners, the West was essential to prosperity. The public lands of the West "are the great regulator of the

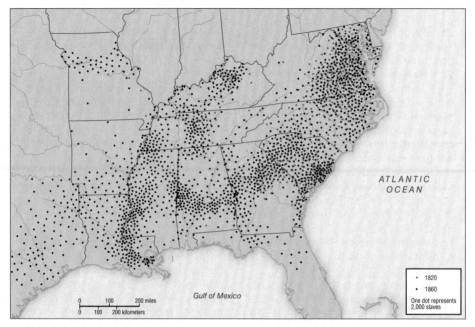

ATLANTIC
OCEAN

- 1820
- 1860

One dot represents
2,000 slaves

Gulf of Mexico

0   100   200 miles
0 100   200 kilometers

Map 13-2 Slavery's Expansion The westward expansion of the slave economy created political turmoil from 1820 until the Civil War. Sustained by an extensive internal slave trade that sold thousands of humans each year, slavery's expansion represented one of the greatest forced migrations in history.

relations of Labor and Capital," Horace Greeley explained, "the safety valve of our industrial and social engine." In fact, moving west to buy land and begin farming required resources most wage laborers lacked. For small farmers, however, the West remained a rich promise, and every landowner was one less potential competitor for a wage-earner's job. Not surprisingly, slavery's westward expansion stirred up deep anxiety in the North.

As free farmers saw it, slavery jeopardized their own prospects out west. Slaveholders were "settlers with means," bringing their wealth and their slave laborers with them. They easily bought up the best lands, usually river bottoms with the most productive soil and the readiest access to markets. Enslaved people provided a cheap means of clearing land, building homes, and raising profitable crops. Farmers without enslaved people could not compete because hired labor was scarce on the frontier. Farm families depended on their own efforts, plus whatever help neighbors could spare. Because the size of free farms was limited by how much labor a family could perform, excluding slavery resulted in more settlers sharing prime acreage.

SLAVERY BECOMES A POLITICAL ISSUE

Westward expansion forced the issue of slavery back into the political mainstream in the late 1840s. On the national level, Whigs and Democrats had avoided stirring up debates over slavery, but the Mexican War made it hard to maintain that silence.

For nearly 15 years, national politics would focus on one crucial question: Should Congress restrict the movement of slavery into the West? Behind that question lay a larger moral issue, the wrong and the right of "property in man."

Wilmot Introduces His Proviso

On August 8, 1846, Democratic congressman David Wilmot of Pennsylvania attached to an appropriations bill an amendment banning slavery from all the territories acquired in the war with Mexico. Slavery was illegal there already under Mexican law. The **Wilmot Proviso** wanted it to stay that way, to preserve the land for free white settlement. "The negro race already occupy enough of this fair continent," Wilmot argued; "let us keep what remains for ourselves and our children."

Reintroduced regularly, the proviso never passed Congress. Nevertheless, it roused furious debate and paralyzed action concerning the conquered territories. Antislavery northerners favored a congressional ban. South Carolina Senator John C. Calhoun's southern followers denied that Congress could bar slavery from the territories and unsuccessfully tried to open Oregon to slaveholding. Calhoun himself favored giving the North and the South veto power over any legislation affecting the other, with two presidents, one northern and one southern, as a last bulwark. In between, moderates talked of extending the Missouri Compromise's dividing line to the Pacific or "noninterference" coupled with "popular sovereignty": letting western settlers work out for themselves whether they would permit slavery.

With tempers rising, both parties finessed the issue during the 1848 presidential contest. Democrats nominated Senator Lewis Cass of Michigan, a "noninterference" man and a hearty supporter of expansion southward into Central America. Whigs ran General Zachary Taylor, known for his victories in Mexico, a professional soldier who may never have voted in his life. Antislavery men, Whig and Democrat alike, formed the Free-Soil Party and nominated former President Martin Van Buren. Favoring the institution's limitation, not its abolition, the movement made little headway outside of New England and got only 14 percent of the northern vote. But thousands in the mainstream organizations shared a distaste for slavery, and Taylor's presidential victory settled nothing.

Even as Congress deadlocked, westward settlement increased the pressure for a decision. In California, the discovery of gold in the Sierra foothills brought a rush of settlers. "Argonauts," as the gold-seekers were called, crammed whaling ships and sailed around South America or through Panama's fever-infested swamps to the west coast. Traveling associations like the Buckeye Rovers chartered wagon trains. Most prospectors endured a hard, monotonous life and had unrealistic hopes. Few struck it rich. One success story, however, was German-born Levi Strauss, who made a fortune making pants for miners from tent-cloth called "levis," or blue jeans. Philip Armour made $4,000 digging ditches, used his savings to open a butcher shop and ended up in Chicago, one of the biggest meatpackers in America. California's Anglo population soared. San Francisco swelled from 3,000 to 20,000 people by the end of 1849, and in gold country, mining towns sprang from nothing, with names like Whiskey Bar, Gouge Eye, and Mad Mule Gulch. Many newcomers discovered the real wealth in the frost-free climate and rich soil of the central valley. They came to stay—so many in fact that within a year California was ready to bypass territorial status entirely and apply for statehood. If admitted under its proposed free-state constitution, California would close off the richest, most promising part of the Mexican cession to slavery.

By early 1850, California's admission and continuing debate over the Wilmot Proviso had created an even more divided Congress. In the House, northerners called for ending slavery in Washington, DC, and free soil in the new territories. Texas claimed broad boundaries, taking in much of New Mexico and legalizing slavery there. It was ready to fight local authorities or even US troops to get its way. Fistfights and threats of disunion became commonplace. As a political amateur, President Taylor offered no leadership.

A Compromise Without Compromises

Called out of retirement, Senator Henry Clay of Kentucky proposed a solution: let all the flashpoints in the slavery debate be settled together. In a series of eight resolutions, he tried to balance northern and southern interests. California would be admitted as a free state, but the rest of the Mexican cession would be organized into territories with no mandate for freedom. Whether they could forbid slavery while still territories or needed to wait until applying for statehood was left unclear. Texas was denied its full geographical scope and, in return, the national government would assume its $10 million debt. The District of Columbia's slave trade was abolished, but not slavery itself. Finally, a new fugitive slave law would strengthen national power to retrieve runaway slaves. Clay's "Omnibus," as critics called it, met with immediate opposition at both ends of the political spectrum. Even though dying of tuberculosis, Calhoun was carried into the Senate to oppose any deal admitting California as a free state or giving less than an explicit guarantee to allow slaveholding throughout the Mexican cession. Senator William H. Seward of New York protested the North being forced to give concessions to get what was rightfully theirs, a free California. God and nature, he insisted, demanded that Congress keep the cession slave-free. As a firm nationalist, President Taylor opposed the "Omnibus" and insisted on admitting California unconditionally and promised, if Texas defied national authority, to lead forces against the Texans himself.

Northern and Southern centrists rallied to Clay's side. Appealing for harmony, Daniel Webster of Massachusetts spoke in favor of compromise. "Cotton Whigs," textile manufacturers, merchants relying on the southern trade, and conservatives fearful of agitation warned that the Union itself stood in peril from the controversies of slavery. On the Democratic side, Senator Stephen A. Douglas of Illinois rounded up support for the "Omnibus." At the same time, the forces against compromise weakened. Calhoun died in March of 1850, and no southern rights figure matched his influence. In July, President Taylor's sudden death put Millard Fillmore, a supporter of compromise, in the White House. Even so, the Omnibus failed to win approval because free-soil supporters would not vote for certain provisions, and southern rights supporters balked at others. Exhausted and ill, Clay quit Washington, leaving Douglas to carry the package through, piece by piece, as five separate bills designed to win different majorities. Referred to as the **Compromise of 1850**, the whole package was touted as banishing the slavery issue for good. A southern-rights convention at Nashville that had seemed to threaten secession fizzled. Free-Soil leaders and southern "fire-eaters," or extremists, however, swore that the day of reckoning had only been put off.

The Fugitive Slave Act Provokes a Crisis

The sorest point in the Compromise was the new **Fugitive Slave Act**. It took jurisdiction over fugitive slave cases away from northern courts. Any northerner could be forced into helping catch alleged runaways; to refuse was a federal crime. Accused Blacks had no right to a jury trial or a lawyer, and a federally appointed commissioner would be responsible for determining their status.

Enslaved people who had run away years earlier now risked arrest and reenslavement. Freeborn Blacks had no legal protection if an unscrupulous slave catcher identified them as a runaway, which happened. Vulnerable African Americans fled further north, out West, or into Canada, but they were not guaranteed safety. Like some abolitionists, Frederick Douglass advocated violent resistance. "A half dozen or more dead kidnappers carried down South," he contended, "would cool the ardor of Southern

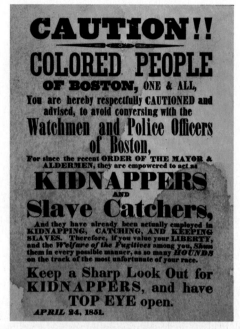

Poster Warning of Fugitive Slave Act The Fugitive Slave Act met strong resistance in many parts of the North. This Boston poster captures the atmosphere of fear and civil disobedience that gripped the city following the Compromise of 1850. It warns all Blacks, free or fugitive, to be on the lookout for slave catchers.

gentlemen." For many northern communities, slavery's evils were no longer something remote, easy to ignore. In Christiana, Pennsylvania, antislavery resisters killed a slave owner who tried to take back a fugitive. Crowds saved one accused man in Syracuse, New York; authorities had to call out the militia to enforce another's return from Boston.

Appalled by the new law, Harriet Beecher Stowe published *Uncle Tom's Cabin* in 1852. In time, the book was issued in dozens of languages. Theatergoers watched Eliza flee slave-catching bloodhounds over ice floes and Simon Legree lay a murderous whip to Uncle Tom, his Christian enslaved man. The sensational success of Stowe's antislavery novel showed how deep northern misgivings had become about the institution's spread. So did the "personal liberty laws" passed in many northern states to protect the rights of the accused. Although these statutes did not prevent one single enslaved person from being remanded south, white southerners were incensed and insulted at what they saw as disrespect for their property rights.

The Election of 1852 and the Decline of the Whig Party

In 1852, both the Democratic and Whig parties pronounced the Compromise of 1850 as a finality, and both went out of their way to find a candidate who was not

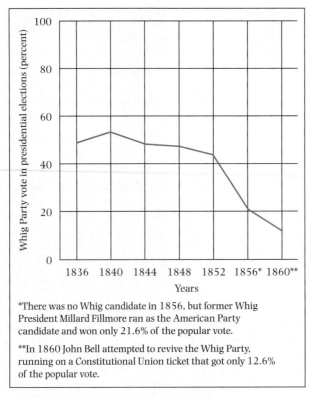

*There was no Whig candidate in 1856, but former Whig
President Millard Fillmore ran as the American Party
candidate and won only 21.6% of the popular vote.

**In 1860 John Bell attempted to revive the Whig Party,
running on a Constitutional Union ticket that got only 12.6%
of the popular vote.

Figure 13-1   The Decline of the Whig Party

directly connected to it. The Whigs rejected Fillmore and Webster, both of whom
had endorsed and enforced the law. Instead, they chose another war hero, this time
General Winfield Scott. Democrats chose then-governor of New Hampshire, Franklin Pierce. Southerners deserted Scott in droves, not because of his own views—like
Pierce, he favored the Compromise—but because of his friends, free-soil Whigs like
Seward. Every new western state meant a likely new Democratic stronghold, and,
it seemed, every new Catholic immigrant a new Democratic voter. The party's old
issues—a national bank and a protective tariff—no longer inspired anyone, but no
practical new issues replaced them. Pompous and aristocratic, Scott had none of
Taylor's appeal, and his attempts to reach foreign-born voters offended Protestant
Whigs. The outcome was a landslide for Pierce (see Figure 13–1). He carried 254 electoral votes to Scott's 42 and won every state but four. Severely weakened, the Whigs
were unable to meet the two political challenges that soon altered national politics:
the issue of slavery and hostility toward immigrants, also known as nativism.

THE ORIGINS OF THE REPUBLICAN PARTY

The calm of the early 1850s did not last. By the middle of the decade, two forces,
nativism—the fear of foreigners and Catholics—and a revived slavery issue had
undone the Jacksonian party system. These challenges also brought on a fresh

sectional crisis. But this time, there would be no rescue. With the deaths of states-men Henry Clay and Daniel Webster in 1852, the spirit of accommodation and the foundation of trust between the North and South also seemed to have perished.

Nativism's Political Moment

With the foreign born helping tilt politics Democrats' way, it was only natural that some Whigs would lash out against newcomers and make common cause with the overwhelmingly Protestant groups already treating the Pope as the republic's number one threat. By 1854, nativists and anti-Catholics had organized. Secret so-cieties spread, often called **Know-Nothings** because when asked about it, members claimed to "know nothing." Taking over local party organizations and endorsing candidates, the Know-Nothings carried the mayor's offices in San Francisco and Philadelphia, swept Massachusetts, from the governor's office to the state legisla-ture, and across the country, it elected congressmen. Temperance reformers voted Know-Nothing to close the saloons, conservative Whigs to affirm their support for the Union and compromise, and antislavery activists to punish the Democrats for bowing to the South's will. Voters joined the new "American Party" to toss the old politicians out; old politicians joined to ride the movement into office. With so many cross-purposes, the movement rose overnight and perished almost as fast. Among the forces unleashing the Know-Nothing movement was the one that ended up destroying it: the fight over the expansion of slavery into the western territories.

Slavery as a Foreign Policy

If not for the revival of the slavery issue, Franklin Pierce's administration might have revived manifest destiny and pushed into the Caribbean. If all of Pierce's ex-pansionist efforts were southward into land fit for plantations and enslaved people, this was no accident. Southerners and their northern sympathizers dominated Pierce's cabinet, and he appointed slaveholders to crucial diplomatic posts.

Pierce sent a South Carolinian, James Gadsden, to Mexico with instructions to spend up to $50 million to acquire a large portion of northern Mexico. In spite of his country's straitened circumstances, Mexico's leader, Antonio López de Santa Anna, resisted the offer. Gadsden returned with a treaty giving the United States quite a bit less, a swath of desert territory suited for a transcontinental railroad across the southern tier of the nation. Most northern senators balked even at that and forced Congress to cut the size of the Gadsden Purchase by a fourth and the price by a third, to $10 million.

The expansionist Pierce fared worse in Cuba. He appointed Pierre Soulé, a Louisianan, as minister to Spain. Soulé was instructed to negotiate the purchase of Cuba, with the threat that if Spain refused to sell he should encourage the Cubans to rebel. The Spanish government would not be bullied. It proposed to free and arm millions of Cuban enslaved people, if that was what it took to defend the island against an American invasion. The United States responded in 1854 with the **Ostend Manifesto**, which declared that Cuba was "naturally" a part of the United States and urged Spain to accept an offer of $120 million for the island. If Spain re-fused, the United States would "wrest" the island by force. (Spain did refuse, but the Manifesto was more than bluster; through the early 1850s, adventurers launched invasions of Cuba and northern Mexico in hopes of founding republics that, like

Frederick Douglass, arrived for unspeakable purposes. In the end, though, it was not John Brown's raid that brought on disunion. It was the election of Abraham Lincoln.

Northerners Elect a President

In February 1860, as the nation's focus shifted from John Brown to the coming presidential election, Abraham Lincoln traveled to New York to address influential eastern Republicans, doubtful of a backwoods figure's fitness for national office. Speaking in the newly opened Cooper Institute, Lincoln grounded Republican doctrine in the Founders' own opposition to slavery and to its spread. Under the Constitution, the enslaved were seen as persons, not property; Congress had never doubted its power to regulate the institution where state and local law did not prevail. Denying any wish to harm slavery in the states, the candidate treated its ban from the territories as a restoration, not a revolution.

Both conservative and radical, Lincoln's Cooper Union address vaulted him to the front of eligible Republican presidential nominees. Any one of them would need a united North in November in order to win the presidency. There was no chance of carrying a single slave state. But then, by 1860, even supporters of popular sovereignty like Douglas faced bitter opposition there. Candidates from the South stood almost as poor a chance up north. As a result, the party system was torn four ways, rather than two. In the slave states two southerners strove against each other, and in the free states, two northerners—both from Illinois. All had to cope with the same issues: What, if anything, should be done about slavery? And how best could the Union itself be saved?

When the Democrats met in Charleston, South Carolina, in April 1860, southern delegations insisted that the platform endorse a federal slave code, using national authority to protect slavery in every territory. Any such program would be political suicide up north, dooming the ticket, and northern delegates supporting Stephen A. Douglas knew it. When they insisted on reaffirming popular sovereignty, 49 southern delegates walked out. With too few members left to nominate a presidential candidate successfully, the party adjourned and reconvened in Baltimore in June. There, southerners staged another walkout. This time they picked a presidential candidate of their own, Vice President John C. Breckinridge, on a slave-code platform. The remaining delegates had had enough. They nominated Douglas, the only Democrat with any chance of carrying a single northern state.

To add to the complications, former Whigs and conservatives created a Constitutional Union ticket headed by Senator John Bell of Tennessee. Most onlookers assumed that Republicans would pick the affable and long-experienced Senator William H. Seward of New York. But Seward's "irrepressible conflict" remarks gave him too radical a reputation to carry Pennsylvania, Indiana, or Illinois. The party needed all three. Nativists thought him too cozy with immigrants, especially Catholic ones. New Yorkers recoiled at the hard-eyed political racketeers around him, like Thurlow Weed, "King of the Lobby." Compared to Seward, Lincoln seemed moderate, clean, and refreshingly unpolitical: he had served just one two-year term in Congress. If anybody could carry Illinois against Douglas, he could. So Lincoln was nominated, not because he was the party's best option, but because he could win.

Lincoln-Hamlin Presidential Campaign, 1860 Abraham Lincoln and Hannibal Hamlin as the Republican Party candidates for president and vice president on a lithograph campaign poster.

Lincoln's appeal went far beyond his Cooper Institute address. Born in Kentucky, raised in a log cabin, he had all the homespun qualities that Americans liked to associate with the frontier. Posters celebrated him as the self-made man, splitting rails or running a flatboat down the Mississippi. Sloganeers hailed "Honest Abe," a refreshing contrast to the crooked politicians infesting Washington, in Buchanan's administration particularly. Republicanism meant free homesteads for western farmers, a government-funded railroad across the prairies, and a higher tariff desired by Pennsylvania. There never was any question about Lincoln's conviction that slavery was immoral, that the entire slave system should be placed "in the course of ultimate extinction." Shutting slavery out of all the western territories was the one issue on which neither he nor his party would compromise, and doing so, leading southerners warned, would put the institution in mortal danger.

Threats came from fire-eaters that if Lincoln won, their states would depart from the Union. Republicans refused to believe them because they had heard those threats too often before. Breckinridge and Bell protested that their supporters, mostly southern, all cherished the Union. Only Douglas warned that the country faced a mortal peril. So alarmed was he that he broke the political rules of the day and campaigned, "not to ask for your votes for the Presidency," he told his audiences, "but to make an appeal to you on behalf of the Union."

Even without Democrats split between Douglas and Breckinridge, Lincoln would have won. He took barely 39 percent of the vote, with Douglas in second place. Only in the border South could Republicans mount a campaign or cast a ballot and live, and even there, they took only a few thousand votes. Breckinridge carried 11 slave states, with the richer plantation counties favoring John Bell, the Constitutional Union candidate. But Lincoln's often narrow majorities across the North gave him an electoral landslide, winning every state but one. Missouri alone favored Douglas (see Map 13–5).

Republicans had not carried the Senate. They had lost seats in the House. The Supreme Court remained in proslavery hands; and Democrats were sure to gain two years hence, when united against a common enemy. All the same, antislavery forces felt doubly vindicated: not only did the Republican victory demonstrate the Free-Soil platform's wide appeal, but it also suggested that political power was shifting as a dynamic economy based on free labor outpaced slave society. The future, they told themselves, belonged to them. In their own way, some white southerners agreed. They concluded that no matter what assurances Lincoln gave them, slavery had no future in the Union.

CONCLUSION

Frederick Douglass had doubts about Lincoln but sincerely hoped that the Republicans would win the 1860 elections. "Slavery is the issue—the single bone of contention between all parties and sections," he insisted. Slavery and freedom had guided the nation along two diverging pathways. The North was developing an urban, industrial economy based on the productive energy of wage labor. In the South, a

TIME LINE

▼**1838**
Frederick Douglass escapes from slavery

▼**1844**
Samuel F. B. Morse invents the telegraph

▼**1846**
David Wilmot introduces his proviso

▼**1848**
Gold discovered in California; start of the Gold Rush
Zachary Taylor elected president

▼**1850**
Zachary Taylor dies; Millard Fillmore becomes president
Compromise of 1850

▼**1852**
Uncle Tom's Cabin published in book form
Franklin Pierce elected president

▼**1854**
Gadsden Purchase ratified
Kansas-Nebraska Act opens territories to slavery
Ostend Manifesto

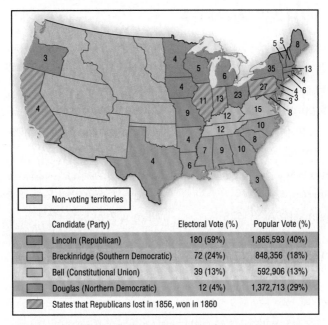

Candidate (Party)	Electoral Vote (%)	Popular Vote (%)
Lincoln (Republican)	180 (59%)	1,865,593 (40%)
Breckinridge (Southern Democratic)	72 (24%)	848,356 (18%)
Bell (Constitutional Union)	39 (13%)	592,906 (13%)
Douglas (Northern Democratic)	12 (4%)	1,372,713 (29%)
States that Republicans lost in 1856, won in 1860		

Map 13–5   The Election of 1860 By 1860, no presidential candidate could appeal to voters in both the North and the South. By then, the northern population had grown so rapidly that a united North could elect Lincoln to the presidency without any southern support.

prosperous slave economy depended on a system of commercialized agriculture in which laborers were commodities as much as the cash crops they produced. The political tensions arising from these differences finally pushed the nation into civil war. And as the war progressed, the same fundamental differences would shape the destiny of the Union and Confederate forces.

▼**1856**
"Bleeding Kansas"
Sumner-Brooks affray
James Buchanan elected
    president

▼**1857**
Dred Scott decision
Lecompton constitution in
    Kansas reopens slavery
    controversy

▼**1858**
Lincoln-Douglas debates

▼**1859**
John Brown's raid on
    Harpers Ferry

▼**1860**
Abraham Lincoln elected
    first Republican
    president
South Carolina declares its
    independence

WHO, WHAT, WHERE

REVIEW QUESTIONS

1. What were the major differences between the northern and southern economies by the 1850s?

2. How did the war with Mexico provoke a conflict over slavery?

3. What did the Republican Party stand for?

4. What was the Kansas-Nebraska Act and why was it so important?

5. What were the major issues in the Lincoln-Douglas debates?

CRITICAL-THINKING QUESTIONS

1. Was the slavery battle primarily a conflict between two different economic systems, or was it more of a moral issue?

2. Which congressional action in this period did the most to push the nation toward civil war (the Wilmot Proviso, the Compromise of 1850, the Kansas-Nebraska Act, the debate over the Lecompton Constitution)? Explain your answer.

3. How did developments that first appeared to be victories for the South end up benefiting the antislavery cause in the long run?

4. Violence played a role in the debate over slavery even before the first shots of the Civil War. In your opinion, was John Brown's violent crusade justified? Why or why not?

SUGGESTED READINGS

Fehrenbacher, Don. *The Slaveholding Republic: An Account of the United States Government's Relations to Slavery*. New York: Oxford University Press, 2001.

Freehling, William W. *The Road to Disunion. Volume 1: Secessionists at Bay, 1776–1854*. New York: Oxford University Press, 1990.

Richards, Leonard L. *The Slave Power: The Free North and Southern Domination, 1780–1861*. Baton Rouge: Louisiana State University Press, 2000.

For further review materials and resource information, please visit www.oup.com/us/ofthepeople

CHAPTER 13:   The Politics of Slavery, 1848–1860
Primary Sources

13.1   JOHN GREENLEAF WHITTIER, "THE HASCHISH" (1854)

New England's great Quaker poet John Greenleaf Whittier wrote on many subjects, but before and during the war, he also turned his pen to fervent antislavery appeals and critiques of the North's complicity in human bondage. His poem "The Haschish" compared the hallucinogenic drugs of the East to the self-deluding qualities that profits from the sale of cotton had given to public figures. Its references incidentally suggest the arcane knowledge about Middle Eastern society that poets assumed the general reading public enjoyed.

Of all that Orient lands can vaunt
Of marvels with our own competing,
The strangest is the Haschish plant,
And what will follow on its eating.

What pictures to the taster rise,
Of Dervish or of Almeh dances!
Of Eblis, or of Paradise,
Set all aglow with Houri glances!

The poppy visions of Cathay,
The heavy beer-trance of the Suabian;
The wizard lights and demon play
Of nights Walpurgis and Arabian!

The Mullah and the Christian dog
Change place in mad metempsychosis;
The muezzin climbs the synagogue,
The Rabbi shakes his beard at Moses!

The Arab by his desert well
Sits choosing from some Caliph's daughters,
And hears his single camel's bell
Sound welcome to his regal quarter.

The Koran's reader makes complaint
Of Shitan dancing on and off it;
The robber offers alms, the saint
Drinks Tokay and blasphemes the Prophet.

Such scenes that Eastern plant awakes;
But we have one ordained to beat it,
The Haschish of the West, which makes
Or fools or knaves of all who eat it.

The preacher eats, and straight appears
His Bible in a new translation;
Its angels negro overseers,
And Heaven itself a snug plantation!

The man of peace, about whose dreams
The sweet millennial angels cluster,
Tastes the mad weed, and plots and schemes,
A raving Cuban filibuster!

The noisiest Democrat, with ease,
It turns to Slavery's parish beadle;
The shrewdest statesman eats and sees
Due southward point the polar needle.

The Judge partakes, and sits erelong
Upon his bench a railing blackguard;
Decides off-hand that right is wrong,
And reads the ten commandments backward.

O potent plant! So rare a taste
Has never Turk or Gentoo gotten;
The hempen Haschish of the East
Is powerless to our Western Cotton!

Source: John Greenleaf Whittier, *The Complete Poetical Works of John Greenleaf Whittier* (Boston: Hough-
ton, Osgood & Company, 1879), pp. 201–202.

13.2   THE FUGITIVE SLAVE LAW CLAIMS A VICTIM (1852)

Nothing brought home the travesty that slavery made of due process, where Blacks
were concerned, like the practical operations of the Fugitive Slave Law in the North.
In April 1852 the New York Tribune reported one such case, the seizing of Horace
Preston, alleged to have escaped his master five years before he settled in New York,
found work, and married.

The case was conducted before Hon. George W. Morton, United States commissioner, and
we can truly say that more extraordinary legal proceedings were never heard of in a civilized country. The duty of the commissioner, as he himself stated it, was to satisfy himself whether there was sufficient evidence to prove the man a slave. The process consisted
simply in hearing the testimony on one side only; in allowing the witness on whose affidavit the arrest was made, to refuse to answer on cross-examination, and to withhold all facts
that may have been in his knowledge bearing on the right of the prisoner to his freedom;
in declining to take any measures to compel the attendance of an important witness for the
defence; in refusing to hear the evidence of witnesses in attendance on that side, although
the respectable counsel declared it to be of vital consequence; and in finally deciding the
case, and hurrying the man off into slavery with that evidence unheard and unconsidered.

This is a plain and simple statement of the matter, confirmed by the card of Messrs. Jay
and Culver, the counsel for the defence, which we publish in another column.

It will be remembered, and so the evidence on the trial shows, that Preston, the alleged fugitive, was arrested late in the afternoon of Tuesday last, on the pretended charge of stealing; that his master in Baltimore was immediately telegraphed that his man was caught; that, on the same evening, he appointed Mr. Busteed, of this city, his agent to pursue and claim the fugitive for him; that the claimant's son came on the next day. He arrived here in the evening, went to Busteed's about eleven o'clock, and had an interview with him. Busteed, net morning, made an affidavit swearing positively and unequivocally to the slavery, the title, and the escape, making out the whole case.

Preston, the "fugitive," was taken by officer Martin to the Tombs, and locked up in the sixth ward cells. He could not, nor could Mr. Culver, his counsel, learn that any complaint had been preferred against him, or any warrant issued, or any examination had, or any commitment made out. He was kept locked up in that place, as he says, till twelve or one o'clock at night, (mark the hour!) then taken out and conducted to the second ward station-house. There he was held till the claimant's son arrived, when, it appears, he, together with Busteed and martin, held a consultation at the second ward station-house. Preston's wife, his counsel, and several of his friends had been untiring in their pursuit of, and inquiry for him, but could learn nothing whatever until a man halloed to the wife in the Park, that they had just taken her husband into the United States court-room. Preston's counsel and wife hurried with all speed to the court-room, but on arriving found a witness sworn and giving evidence. At this stage our reporter had taken up the case and kept our readers advised on the subject.

When the case was adjourned on Friday afternoon to Saturday morning, it was with the avowed understanding on the part of Preston's counsel, and assented to by the commissioner, that if the latter should deny the motion made and argued by Mr. Jay to quash or dismiss the proceedings, then the counsel should go into their defence on the merits. To that end, several witnesses were in attendance; others had process out for them, to be served as soon as found. Some of these witnesses had known Preston in Baltimore, and were prepared to prove the declarations of his former mistress as to his freedom, and the provisions in her will to that effect. By others it was proposed to show the admission of the claimant and others, to contradict Busteed's affidavit and prove a conspiracy.

The commissioners, instead of deciding the preliminary motion of Mr. Jay, and then stopping, took the counsel, the prisoner, and the audience by surprise. He decided the whole case—had his certificate in his hand—delivered it over in the twinkling of an eye—gathered up his papers, and retreated toward the back door of the room. Busteed hardly had time to kiss the Bible held out to him by the commissioner. It was all in vain that Messrs. Jay, Emmet, and Culver jumped upon the floor, asking the commissioner to hear them—urging their surprise, and the injustice done their client. Their efforts were all fruitless. The commissioner refused to hear anything further.

Mr. Culver was drawing an affidavit for Preston to attach a witness. His client, however, was taken suddenly from him and removed to a back room in the marshal's office. Mr. Culver at once applied to the marshal for permission to go to the room and see his client, to have him sign an affidavit for a *habeas corpus*. His request was sternly denied—nor could he get sight of Preston again till he was brought out to be started off south.

Preston's counsel then applied to Judge Judson for a *habeas corpus*, but he could not hear the application.

Meantime the condemned man was got ready. His wife went in and had her last sad interview with him. Her cries and sobs were heard by the multitude outside.

We doubt if a more touching exhibition of the workings of the fugitive-slave law has ever been witnessed. This man's wife stood by her husband for three days, with a devotion and tenderness unparalleled. Whenever permitted to sit near him, she had fast hold of his hand in both of hers, wringing herself in the most intense, half-suppressed agony. Near the time of the final separation, Busteed, the lawyer, to console her, gave her an orange, or peeled one for her!

About 12 o'clock, the procession appeared from the back room, Gen. Henry F. Tallmadge, United States marshal, in front; his sons, one on the right and the other on the left of the fugitive, and two sturdy deputies of foreign birth behind. Each seemed satisfied with the honorable post he was permitted to take in doing the slaveholder's work. The fugitive was conducted out at the back door into Chambers street, where a covered carriage was in readiness, into which he was put. The crowd, chiefly of colored people, rushed around to catch their last view of their friend—some running to the carriage door to shake hands, and bid good-bye, some in tears, some in suppressed murmurs, some calling on God to avenge the wrong, and one devotional old woman was heard crying, "God'll punish 'em! God'll punish 'em!"

The carriage left at the time of writing this article. Horace Preston is back into slavery for life. A woman robbed of her husband, and a little girl four years old of her father. So ends the fourth fugitive slave case in New York.

Source: "The Late Slave Case," from the *New York Tribune*, April 5, 1852.

13.3   LETTER FROM EDWARD BRIDGMAN ABOUT KANSAS WARFARE (1856)

Massachusetts-raised, Edward Bridgman (1834–1915) came to Kansas just as the conflict over slavery reached a fighting pitch. One of his letters captured the violence on both sides: "border ruffians" sacking the city of Lawrence, and John Brown slaughtering proslavery settlers.

Kansas May 25, 1856

Dear Cousin Sidney

I write now to let you know my present situation and a little about the affairs of Kansas. . . . In some small towns the men are called up nearly every night to hold themselves in readiness to meet the worst as scouting parties of Alabamians Georgians and Missourians are around continually, plundering clothes yards, horses and cattle, and everything they can lay hold of. A few miles from Lawrence a man was plowing. [A] party of Southerners came along and being hungry killed his best ox, ate what they wanted, took away some and left the rest. Such like occurrences are almost daily taking place. Last Thursday, news came from Lawrence that he was in the hands of the Ruffians, and that they had demolished the free state Hotel, burned Robinson's house, and destroyed the two printing presses. Almost immediately a company of 30 was raised. There was no reason why I could not go for one, so I borrowed a rifle and ammunition and joined them. The thought of engaging in battle is not a pleasing one, but the free state men are compelled to. Why should I not do [so] as wall as others, I have nothing to hinder me and my life is no dearer to me than the lives of others are to them. At sundown we divided into 2 divisions and took turns in walking. It was really affecting to see husbands and wives bid each other good bye—not knowing as they would ever see each other again. yet the sympathies of the women are as much enlisted in the cause as the men. It is nothing uncommon to see them running bullets and making catriges [*sic.*] One woman yesterday told me that she had often been called up nights to make them. . . .

Tuesday [May] 27. Since I wrote the above the Osawatomie company has returned to O. as news came that we could do nothing immediately, so we returned back. On our way back we heard that 5 men had been killed by Free State men. The men were butchered—ears cut off and the bodies thrown into the river [.] the murdered men (Proslavery) had thrown out threats and insults, yet the act was barbarous and inhuman whoever committed by [.] we met the men going when we were going up and knew that they were on a secret expedition, yet didn't know what it was. Tomorrow something will be done to arrest them. there were

8 concerned in the act. perhaps they had good motives, some think they had, how that is I don't know. The affairs took place 8 miles from Osawatomie. The War seems to have commenced in real earnest. Horses are stolen on all sides whenrver [sic] they can be taken....

Weds eve. Since yesterday I have learned that those men who committed those murders were a party of Browns. One of them was formerly in the wool business in Springfield, John Brown[.] his son (Jn) has been taken today, tho he had no hand in the act, but was knowing to it, but when I write to Maria I will give further particulars [.] Osawatomie is in much fear and excitement [.] News came tonight that a co. of Georgians and Alabamians were coming to make this their headquarters. All work is nearly suspended, the women are in constant fear [.] It was really pleasing to witness the reception of our co., by the women after they came in to O. It was a little after dark. A longline of women and children stood by the roadside to greet us and joy was depicted on every countenance. Hands were heartily shaken and congratulations offered [.] but I must close....

Yours truly, E

It wont be best for me to write my name so you must guess who wrote this [.] but very few now attach their full name to a letter.

Source: "Notes and Documents," *Mississippi Valley Historical Review*, 6 no. 4 (1920): 557–560.

13.4 JAMES H. HAMMOND, "SPEECH ON THE ADMISSION OF KANSAS" (1858)

A South Carolina lawyer and editor who married into money, James Henry Hammond ended up as successful in politics as he had in planting. The legislature elected him governor twice; he served in the House and then in the Senate. Although he was by no means one of the "fire-eater" extremists in the state, he earned that reputation up north in his taunting reply to a speech by Senator William Seward of New York in March 1858.

No, you dare not make war on cotton. No power on earth dares to make war upon it. Cotton is king. Until lately the Bank of England was king; but she tried to put her screws as usual, the fall before the last, upon the cotton crop, and was utterly vanquished. The last power has been conquered. Who can doubt, that has looked at recent events, that cotton is supreme? When the abuse of credit had destroyed credit and annihilated confidence; when thousands of the strongest commercial houses in the world were coming down, and hundreds of millions of dollars of supposed property evaporating in thin air; when you came to a dead lock, and revolutions were threatened, what brought you up? Fortunately for you it was the commencement of the cotton season, and we have poured in upon you one million six hundred thousand bales of cotton just at the crisis to save you from destruction. That cotton, but for the bursting of your speculative bubbles in the North, which produced the whole of this convulsion, would have brought us $100,000,000. We have sold it for $65,000,000, and saved you. Thirty-five million dollars we, the slaveholders of the South, have put into the charity box for your magnificent financiers, your "cotton lords," your "merchant princes."

But, sir, the greatest strength of the South arises from the harmony of her political and social institutions. This harmony gives her a frame of society, the best in the world, and an extent of political freedom, combined with entire security, such as no other people ever enjoyed upon the face of the earth....We threw off a Government not adapted to our social system, and made one for ourselves. The question is, how far have we succeeded? The South, so far as that is concerned, is satisfied, harmonious, and prosperous, but demands to be let alone.

In all social systems there must be a class to do the menial duties, to perform the drudgery of life. That is, a class requiring but a low order of intellect and but little skill. Its requisites are vigor, docility, fidelity. Such a class you must have, or you would not have that other class which leads progress, civilization, and refinement. It constitutes the very mud-sill of society and of political government; and you might as well attempt to build a house in the air, as to build either the one or the other, except on this mud-sill. Fortunately for the South, she found a race adapted to that purpose to her hand. A race inferior to her own, but eminently qualified in temper, in vigor, in docility, in capacity to stand the climate, to answer all her purposes. We use them for our purpose, and call them slaves. . . . I will not characterize that class at the North by that term; but you have it; it is there; it is everywhere; it is eternal.

The Senator from New York said yesterday that the whole world had abolished slavery. Aye, the *name*, but not the *thing*; all the powers of the earth cannot abolish that. God only can do it when he repeals the fiat, "the poor ye always have with you"; for the man who lives by daily labor, and scarcely lives at that, and who has to put out his labor in the market, and take the best he can get for it; in short, your whole hireling class of manual laborers and "operatives," as you call them, are essentially slaves. The difference between us is, that our slaves are hired for life and well compensated; there is no starvation, no begging, no want of employment among our people, and not too much employment either. Yours are hired by the day, not cared for, and scantily compensated, which may be proved in the most painful manner, at any hour in any street in any of your large towns. Why, you meet more beggars in one day in any single street of the city of New York, than you would meet in a lifetime in the whole South. We do not think that whites should be slaves either by law or necessity. Our slaves are black, of another and inferior race. The *status* in which we have placed them is an elevation. They are elevated from the condition in which God first created them, by being made our slaves. None of that race on the whole face of the globe can be compared with the slaves of the South. They are happy, content, unaspiring, and utterly incapable, from intellectual weakness, ever to give us any trouble by their aspirations. Yours are white, of your own race; you are brothers of one blood. They are your equals in natural endowment of intellect, and they feel galled by their degradation. Our slaves do not vote. We give them no political power. Yours do vote, and, being the majority, they are the depositaries of all your political power. If they knew the tremendous secret, that the ballot-box is stronger than "an army with banners," and could combine, where would you be? Your society would be reconstructed, your government overthrown, your property divided, not as they have mistakenly attempted to initiate such proceedings by meeting in parks, with arms in their hands, but by the quiet process of the ballot-box. You have been making war upon us to our very hearthstones. How would you like for us to send lecturers and agitators North, to teach these people this, to aid in combining and to lead them?

… Transient and temporary causes have thus far been your preservation. The great West has been open to your surplus population, and your hordes of semibarbarian immigrants, who are crowding in year by year. They make a great movement, and you call it progress. Whither? It is progress; but it is progress towards Vigilance Committees. The South have sustained you in a great measure. You are our factors. You fetch and carry for us. One hundred and fifty million dollars of our money passes annually through your hands. Much of it sticks; all of it assists to keep your machinery together and in motion. Suppose we were to discharge you; suppose we were to take our business out of your hands;—we should consign you to anarchy and poverty. You complain of the rule of the South; that has been another cause that has preserved you. We have kept the Government conservative to the great purposes of the Constitution. We have placed it, and kept it, upon the Constitution; and that has been the cause of your peace and prosperity. The Senator from New York says that that is about to be at an end; that you intend to take the Government from us; that it will pass from our hands into yours. Perhaps what he says is true; it may be; but do not forget—it can never be forgotten—it is written on the brightest page of human history— that we, the slaveholders of the South, took our country in her infancy, and, after ruling her for sixty out of the seventy years of her existence, we surrendered her to you without a stain upon her honor, boundless in prosperity, incalculable in her strength, the wonder and the admiration of the world. Time will show what you will make of her; but no time can diminish our glory or your responsibility.

Source: "Speech on the Admission of Kansas," US Senate, March 4, 1858, in *Selections from the Letters and Speeches of the Hon. James H. Hammond, of South Carolina* (New York: John F. Trow & Co., 1866), pp. 317–322, from *Congressional Globe*, 35th Congress 1st session, 961–992.

13.5 ABRAHAM LINCOLN, SPEECH AT SPRINGFIELD, ILLINOIS (1857)

Troubled by the Dred Scott decision that no Black person could become a US citizen and its denial of the power of either Congress or local governments to forbid slavery in the territories, Abraham Lincoln challenged both the Supreme Court's assumptions and those of Senator Stephen A. Douglas, author of the Kansas-Nebraska bill, in a speech on June 26, 1857. At the same time, he made clear that while Republicans opposed slavery's extension, this did not make them abolitionists or supporters of full racial equality. On the contrary, Lincoln emphasized his belief in separation of the races and ultimate colonization of Black Americans—a view that he abandoned only as his own outlook changed in wartime. He also used the speech to counter one of the standard Democratic arguments: that if Black people were set free, they would intermarry with whites.

[Judge Douglas] makes an occasion for lugging it in from the opposition to the Dred Scott decision. He finds the Republicans insisting that the Declaration of Independence includes ALL MEN, black as well as white; and forthwith he boldly denies that it includes negroes at all, and proceeds to argue gravely that all who contend it does, do so only because they want to vote, and eat, and sleep, and marry with negroes. He will have it that they cannot be consistent else. Now I protest against that counterfeit logic which concludes that, because I do not want a black woman for a *slave* I must necessarily want her for a *wife*. I need not have her for either, I can just leave her alone. In some respects she certainly is not my equal; but in her natural right to eat the bread she earns with her own hands without asking leave of any one else, she is my equal, and the equal of all others.

Chief Justice Taney, in his opinion in the Dred Scott case, admits that the language of the Declaration is broad enough to include the whole human family, but he and Judge Douglas argue that the authors of that instrument did not intend to include negroes, by the fact that they did not at once, actually place them on an equality with the whites.... I think the authors of that notable instrument intended to include *all* men, but they did not intend to declare all men equal *in all respects*. They did not mean to say all were equal in color, size, intellect, moral developments, or social capacity. They defined with tolerable distinctness, in what respects they did consider all men created equal—equal in "certain inalienable rights, among which are life, liberty, and the pursuit of happiness." This they said, and this meant. They did not mean to assert the obvious untruth, that all were then actually enjoying that equality, nor yet, that they were about to confer it immediately upon them. In fact they had no power to confer such a boon. They meant simply to declare the *right*, so that the *enforcement* of it might follow as fast as circumstances should permit.... The assertion that "all men are created equal" was of no practical use in effecting our separation from Great Britain; and it was placed in the Declaration, not for that, but for future use. Its authors meant it to be, thank God, it is now proving itself, a stumbling block to those who in after times might seek to turn a free people back into the hateful paths of despotism. They knew the proneness of prosperity to breed tyrants, and they meant when such should re-appear in this fair land and commence their vocation they should find left for them at least one hard nut to crack.

...

Now let us hear Judge Douglas' view of the same subject, as I find it in the printed report of his late speech....

"They were speaking of British subjects on this continent being equal to British subjects born and residing in Great Britain!" Why according to this, not only negroes but white people outside of Great Britain and America are not spoken of in that instrument. The English, Irish and Scotch, along with white Americans, were included to be sure, but the French, Germans and other white people of the world are all gone to pot along with the Judge's inferior races.

I had thought the Declaration promised something better than the condition of British subjects; but no, it only meant that we should be *equal* to them in their own oppressed and *unequal* condition. According to that, it gave no promise that having kicked off the King and Lords of Great Britain, we should not at once be saddled with a King and lords of our own.

....

I understand you are preparing to celebrate the "Fourth," tomorrow week. What for? The doings of that day had no reference to the present; and quite half of you are not even descendants of those who were referred to at that day. But I suppose you will celebrate; and will even go so far as to read the Declaration. Suppose after you read it once in the old fashioned way, you read it once more with Judge Douglas' version. It will then run thus: "We hold these truths to be self-evident that all British subjects who were on this continent eighty-one years ago, were created equal to all British subjects born and *then* residing in Great Britain."

And now I appeal to all—to Democrats as well as others,—are you really willing that the Declaration shall be thus frittered away?—thus left no more at most, than an interesting memorial of the dead past? thus shorn of vitality, and practical value; and left without the *germ* or even the *suggestion* of the individual rights of man in it?

But Judge Douglas is especially horrified at the thought of the mixing blood by the white and black races: agreed for once—a thousand times agreed. There are white men enough to marry all the white women, and black men enough to marry all the black women; and so let them be married. On this point we fully agreed with the Judge; and when he shall show that his policy is better adapted to prevent amalgamation than ours we shall drop ours, and adopt his.... A separation of the races is the only perfect preventive of amalgamation but as an immediate separation is impossible the next best thing is to *keep* them apart *where* they are not already together. If white and black people never get together in Kansas, they will never mix blood in Kansas. That is at least one self-evident truth.

This very Dred Scott case afford[s] a strong test as to which party most favors amalgamation, the Republicans or the dear Union-saving Democracy. Dred Scott, his wife and two daughters were all involved in the suit. We desired the court to have held that they were citizens so far at least as to entitle them to a hearing as to whether they were free or not; and then, also, that they were in fact and in law really free. Could we have had our way, the chances of these black girls, ever mixing their blood with that of white people, would have been diminished at least to the extent that it could not have been without their consent. But Judge Douglas is delighted to have them decided to be slaves, and not human enough to have a hearing, even if they were free, and thus left subject to the forced concubinage of their masters, and liable to become the mothers of mulattoes in spite of themselves—the very state of case that produces the nine tenths of all the mulattoes—all the mixing of blood in the nation.

Source: Roy P. Basler, ed., *The Collected Works of Abraham Lincoln* (New Brunswick, NJ: Rutgers University Press, 1953), vol. 2, 405–409.

A War for Union and Emancipation

1861–1865

< Confederate soldiers, 1861

Laura M. Towne and the Sea Island Invasion

Late in 1861, Union gunboats took control of the flat marshy Sea Islands off the South Carolina coast near Port Royal. Plantation owners fled at the first gunfire, leaving behind 10,000 African Americans, who were enslaved no longer. Union commanders wanted to put them to work making cotton for northern mills. Thus began the "Port Royal experiment," in which the formerly enslaved worked land abandoned by plantation owners. The program proved that African Americans worked hard and well in freedom. But northern missionaries, who had come south to spread the Gospel, wrote home of multitudes of ill-clothed, ill-fed, and ill-housed African Americans. They needed as much care for their bodies as their souls. Among the volunteers that a Philadelphia relief committee sent in the spring of 1862 to aid the formerly enslaved was Laura Towne.

Born in 1825 in Pittsburgh and trained as a teacher and in homeopathic medicine, Laura Towne was a firm abolitionist. For Towne, the war offered a chance not only to save the Union but also to give it a second chance to live up to its ideals. It was not just men's work but women's as well, and in that war, Towne enlisted, as it turned out, for life. At first working as a healer, Towne and her close friend Ellen Murray began teaching in a plantation mansion. By New England standards, the formerly enslaved lacked all self-discipline. "They had no idea of sitting still, of giving attention, of ceasing to talk aloud," she wrote. "They got up by the dozen, made their curtsies, and walked off to the neighboring field for blackberries, coming back to their seats with a curtsy when they were ready. They evidently did not understand me, and I could not understand them, and after two hours and a half of effort I was thoroughly exhausted." But Towne and Murray also found the community eager and able to learn. Classes moved into a prefabricated schoolhouse, and the Penn School was established as a school for the freed enslaved. It would last well into the next century and Towne would teach there until she died in 1901.

Towne was just one among many "Yankee school marms" who came south during or after the war. Northern congregations paid their wages, which were paltry at best; Towne lived off her small inheritance. Even before the war ended, benevolent associations in Boston, Philadelphia, and New York were raising money to feed and clothe southerners of both races. Towne spent much of her time distributing supplies to the destitute and visiting the sick. Like many northerners, she became an unofficial adviser to freedpeople, a moral counselor, and a public health officer. A more perfect Union, to her, meant giving the formerly enslaved a freedom worth keeping. That meant more than fostering the Penn School's mission as the only institution for Black secondary education in South Carolina and one of the foremost training centers for Black teachers. It meant imparting Christianity, devotion to the nation, and an understanding of its history as Republicans had always defined it, a belief in racial equality and cleanliness, both moral and physical.

Laura Towne's career shows one of the many ways in which the Civil War depended on women's actions as well as men's, and how the Civil War's original goal of restoring the nation would change. Towne's work also serves as a reminder that no battlefield settlement could create the more perfect Union that reformers envisioned. Towne exemplified that very radicalism that Confederates had feared from the start, in a North where none of the boundaries confining women's roles or those of African Americans would stand fast for long.

LIBERTY AND UNION

The four-month period between Lincoln's election and his inauguration must have seemed the longest and worst interval Americans had ever known. Within six weeks, South Carolina dissolved its connection to the Union. Scarcely two months later, it became part of a new nation, stretching from the Atlantic to the Rio Grande. Cheering crowds waved palmetto leaves and set off fireworks to celebrate the parting. Military companies paraded. "We are divorced, North and South, because we have hated each other so," a senator's wife wrote. Cooler heads did not join the celebration. They knew that this divorce would be contested bitterly. "They have … set a blazing torch to the temple of Constitutional liberty," a Carolinian warned his compatriots, "and, please God, we shall have no more peace forever." What followed would be a war more horrible than the celebrating crowds dreamed, with results more tremendous than most Americans expected. Why, then, did so many white southerners feel **secession** was necessary? And what made so many Americans accept war rather than a disunited country?

For secessionists, a Republican presidency seemed the last in a long line of insults against slavery, but also the first move in a conspiracy against their liberty, specifically the right to hold enslaved people. Far from betraying the American Revolution, they claimed to follow its example. They, too, were breaking free from would-be tyrants to protect a social system dependent on slave labor. Secessionists warned that Republican rule meant slave insurrections, laws keeping slave owners from selling their property across state lines, a welcome mat put out to every runaway come north, and a Supreme Court packed with antislavery zealots. Republicanism would encourage every southern critic of slavery, now cowed into silence and kept from voting his opinions. It would make thousands of new ones among nonslaveholders. In time, the West would furnish enough free states to amend the Constitution. Then slavery would end everywhere. Set free, African Americans would set off a war of races, with the blessing of northern fanatics. If slaveholders craved safety, they must part the Union at once, before the shackles were laid on their limbs.

For most northerners, the Union had become too intertwined with American liberty to surrender. Taught to see America as a lighthouse of liberty in a world of tyranny, they warned that if government based on the consent of the governed perished, it would carry "the last best hope" for oppressed peoples throughout the world with it. As one state after the other seceded, all doubt about what to do vanished. Retiring President Buchanan may have been hesitant and defeatist, but he shared a universal northern belief that no state had the right to secede and that the Confederate government had no legal standing. Each day brought another abject surrender to insurrectionary forces: Fort Pulaski on the Savannah River, military installations in Texas, the arsenal in Augusta. Northerners cried that each retreat must be the last. Long before the government called for a single volunteer, communities across the North were raising military companies. When Buchanan sent an abortive relief mission to save **Fort Sumter** in Charleston Harbor, the whole North applauded him. Northerners blamed the slaveholding elite for the war, telling themselves that most white southerners had been stampeded out of a Union they still loved. Most Democrats would have welcomed, and most Republicans accepted, a reunion leaving slavery intact in states that had it. But a growing number of Unionists were prepared to destroy slavery if the Union could be saved no other way. And abolitionists and the more radical Republicans insisted there was no other way.

The Deep South Secedes

South Carolina's secession on December 20, 1860, added momentum to the movement in its neighbors across the Cotton South. Dissenting voices, denounced as cowards and "submissionists," often risked their lives by standing in white public opinion's way. Within weeks, Mississippi, Florida, Alabama, Georgia, Louisiana, and Texas announced their separation (see Map 14–1). Meeting in Montgomery, Alabama, in early February 1861, secessionists drafted a basic charter for their new government, the Confederate States of America. They selected as president an experienced administrator and planter, Senator **Jefferson Davis** of Mississippi.

The Confederate constitution differed from the US Constitution in only a few provisions, but these were key. The Confederate chief executive served a single, six-year term and had a line-item veto. More important, while the constitution emphasized the states' "sovereign and independent character," it wrote slavery's protection into fundamental law. The new nation's "cornerstone" was "the great truth that the negro is not equal to the white man," Confederate Vice President Alexander Stephens announced, "that slavery, subordination to the superior race, is his natural and normal condition." Optimists spoke of a republic spreading to the California coast and possibly even the ultimate absorption of states north of the Ohio River.

The Upper South Makes Its Choice

Then, as quickly as it had begun, the secession movement stalled. Even in the lower South many whites, among them Texas governor Sam Houston, had seen no immediate threat in Lincoln's election. In Louisiana, the secessionists had just barely won. Elsewhere farmers in counties where slavery was comparatively rare had shown much less eagerness for quitting the Union. Many had been "cooperationists," wanting the whole South to secede together, or making their eventual support for secession conditional on some northern overt act. In the more heavily

Map 14-1 The Secession of the Southern States The South seceded in two stages. During the "secession winter" of 1860–1861, the lower South states seceded in reaction to the election of Abraham Lincoln. The following spring, the upper South seceded in response to Lincoln's raising troops to uphold federal authority. The border slave states of Maryland, Delaware, Kentucky, and Missouri never left the Union.

white states of the upper South, where robust two-party systems survived, outright Unionists joined cooperationists in opposing hasty action.

Lincoln and many Republicans hoped that if they moved cautiously, they could keep the upper South in the Union and thereby derail the secession movement. But **cooperationism** made a shaky foundation for a rebuilt Union, particularly when so many of its supporters opposed any government action enforcing its laws in Confederate territory, which was viewed as coercion, and insisted on northern concessions as the price of future loyalty.

Democrats and upper South Unionists generally hoped to halt secession permanently with one last deal, a series of constitutional amendments proposed by Kentucky senator John J. Crittenden. The Crittenden Compromise would have restored the Missouri Compromise line and guaranteed federal protection of slavery south of that line in all territories currently held or later acquired by the United States. It would have barred Congress from abolishing slavery in Washington, DC, and from regulating the interstate slave trade. Finally, it called for the compensation of masters unable to recover fugitive enslaved people from the North.

Republicans balked. They were ready to promise enforcement of the Fugitive Slave Law and willing to consider admitting New Mexico as a slave state, or even an amendment protecting slavery in the states from federal interference. But they refused to surrender the program on which they had won. Lincoln would not agree to let slavery spread. As opponents warned, a South able to extort concessions on threats of breaking up the Union would not stop there. Every crisis would bring

Struggles For Democracy continued

so that when the shooting ceased, their bodies could be identified.

All the same, this remained a democratic war, dependent on the people's consent, even that of enlistees. Lincoln's generals included not just West Point professionals but politicians, Democratic and Republican, whose influence with members of their party made them dangerous to dismiss.

As for the soldiers, they continued to think like civilians, if on a lethal holiday. Nearly all of them would muster out eagerly at war's end, some of them before the official dismissal came. And in 1864, still in the service, the Union volunteers voted for president the same as ever, except in one particular. Most of them, even onetime Democrats, cast their ballots for Lincoln.

If Union soldiers blamed slavery for the war, few of them started out aiming for its destruction. That came only as the cost of saving the nation mounted and their own bitterness against the enemy and commitment to the cause intensified. By the end of the conflict, most northern soldiers believed that to restore the Union and destroy the Confederacy they would have to abolish slavery as well.

MOBILIZING FOR WAR

A long war required very different things from both sides than a brief test of strength. By the end of the war, approximately 2.1 million men had served in the Union armed forces and another 900,000 in the Confederacy. To raise and sustain such numbers was an immense political and social problem. To feed, clothe, and arm them was an equally immense technological problem. To pay for such armed forces was an immense economic problem. The Civil War became a test of the competing economies of the North and the South (see Figure 14–1).

The Military Scorecard

In an even fight, Confederates declared, Federal soldiers stood no chance. "Just throw three or four shells among those blue-bellied Yankees and they'll scatter like sheep," a North Carolinian predicted. They learned differently soon enough, but on both sides a myth took hold that southerners made better natural soldiers. Unlike northern city boys, they had been virtually born in the saddle with a musket grafted to their hand. When it came to shooting accurately, riding, or taking orders, they would have a distinct advantage. There was some truth in the stereotyping. More southerners had gone to military academies, and their West Point officers brought skill and discipline to the Confederate army that the Union's West Pointer alumni struggled to match.

According to secessionists, slavery provided another advantage. Slave labor manned the arms factories and the Tredegar Iron Works, dug lead for bullets, did teamster duty, and built the entrenchments that Confederates stood behind.

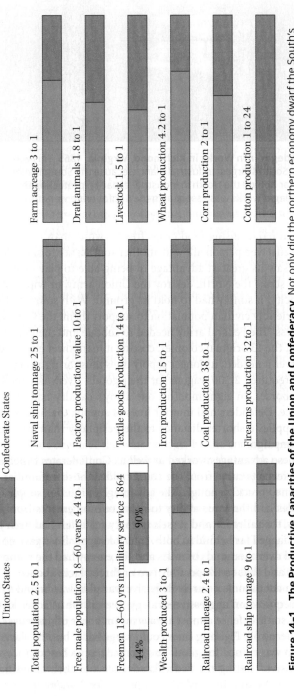

Figure 14-1 The Productive Capacities of the Union and Confederacy Not only did the northern economy dwarf the South's industrial capacity, it also outpaced southern agricultural production in everything but cotton.

Union States

Confederate States

Total population 2.5 to 1

Free male population 18–60 years 4.4 to 1

Freemen 18–60 yrs in military service 1864

44%

90%

Wealth produced 3 to 1

Railroad mileage 2.4 to 1

Railroad ship tonnage 9 to 1

Naval ship tonnage 25 to 1

Factory production value 10 to 1

Textile goods production 14 to 1

Iron production 15 to 1

Coal production 38 to 1

Firearms production 32 to 1

Farm acreage 3 to 1

Draft animals 1.8 to 1

Livestock 1.5 to 1

Wheat production 4.2 to 1

Corn production 2 to 1

Cotton production 1 to 24

the *Monitor*, arrived from New York. For most of the next day the "battle of the ironclads" raged, with neither vessel dominating. In reality, the threat that the *Virginia* posed was an illusion because ironclads could not navigate the deep waters where blockade ships waited. After the battle, the *Virginia* slipped up the James River to help defend Richmond. Two months later, the Confederates destroyed it to keep it from capture. The Union, on the other hand, turned out 50 more "monitors," in an effort to increase their naval supremacy.

King Cotton's Failed Diplomacy

The conviction that commerce ruled the world came naturally to the leaders of southern slave society. At the start of the war, Confederate strategists believed they could bring their enemies to heel by starving them of cotton. By keeping their most valuable cash crop from the market, they would bring northern industry to its knees and force England to recognize Confederate independence.

Southerners, however, assumed wrong. They overestimated England's dependence on American cotton and underestimated the strength of Britain's economic ties to the North. With their eyes fixed on European dangers, British leaders had no intention of risking an American war by breaking the Union blockade or granting the Confederacy diplomatic recognition, not even when three in every four cotton-mill workers had lost their jobs or been put on part-time employment. Egypt, India, even Brazil, could help satisfy Britain's needs. Union demand kept flax and woolen manufactories going full-blast, and England did a thriving business in saltpeter, which the North needed for making gunpowder.

Union diplomats like Charles Francis Adams, minister to Great Britain, worked hard to cut off the flow of ships built in British ports as blockade runners or privateers for the Confederates. Late in 1861, a Union navy captain waylaid a British ship, the *Trent*, in Havana, Cuba, and arrested two Confederate commissioners heading for Europe. A gust of anger rose across the Atlantic. Hastily, the Union administration let both men go and disclaimed any responsibility for the seizure. The commissioners got a hero's welcome, but not the foreign recognition of the Confederate government that they had come for. By the time the Confederacy started shipping cotton again in 1863, it had much less to offer. Thanks to the blockade, the 1 million bales of cotton that the Confederacy exported in the last three years of the war were miniscule in comparison to the 10 million they had shipped out in the last three years of peace.

The Political Economy of Total War

Total war required a total commitment of government resources and, for both sides, a broad expansion of authority from what Americans had experienced during peacetime. For all its homage to the idea of states' rights, even the Confederacy built a command economy of unprecedented size.

In the North, unhindered by southern opposition, a Republican Congress pushed through several measures to speed up economic development. The Morrill "War Tariff" raised needed revenue but also raised a wall against foreign competition with American industry. The Morrill Land-Grant College Act aided the establishment of "agricultural and mechanic" institutions, among which would be the nation's largest state university systems. A Homestead Act provided 160 acres of public land free to actual settlers. The Pacific Railroad Act issued a charter and gave money and 100 million acres in land to the Union Pacific and Central Pacific railroads to build a transcontinental line from the Missouri River to California—the first of several endowed and a seven-year task that required 20,000 workers.

To pay for the war, Congress augmented the Morrill tariff with taxes on liquor and tobacco, license taxes on almost every profession, stamp taxes, inheritance and property taxes, and the country's first progressive income tax. It also gave the Treasury authority to issue bonds. With skilled marketing by Jay Cooke's banking house, $2 billion of them were sold. The government also printed over $400 million in paper money, "greenbacks," to meet expenses. A Legal Tender Act declared them good for all debts and payments. In 1863, Congress set up a system for creating nationally chartered banks, empowered to issue bank notes as currency.

Confederate plans to finance the war worked less well. The Richmond government also passed an income tax but found it unenforceable. It levied a property tax and left the states to collect it; the states didn't. With planters objecting to any tax code that fell on them and European investors refusing to lend the new nation any money, the Confederate Congress left the Treasury no option but to grind out $1.5 billion in paper currency. Shinplasters, small-denomination notes, could be found in 250 different varieties, one southerner complained, "and not one dime in silver to be seen." Prices climbed at 10 percent per month. Eventually, Confederate dollars fell to one-hundredth of its face value. To supply the army, the government had to commandeer farmers' crops, mules, hogs, and horses and pay them in worthless currency.

Filling the Ranks—and the Jails

As the war dragged on, volunteering lagged. State governments offered bounties for new enlistees, but by April 1862, the Confederacy had to introduce **conscription**, compulsory enlistment for military service, covering all males from ages 18 to 35. Five months later, it was extended it to age 45. The Union imposed the draft in early 1863. In each case, conscription stirred deep resentments. Northern draftees could buy their way out of service by paying a $300 commutation fee—a year's income for a day laborer—or hiring someone to enlist in their place. Confederate soldiers fumed when their government unilaterally extended conscription. The southern statute contained a "planter's exemption" freeing one white male from service entirely for every 20 enslaved person who served. Plantation overseers and planters' sons benefited as a result of this law. The "twenty-Negro law" incensed small farmers, who complained that the Civil War was a "rich man's war but a poor man's fight." In the North, among those drafted, only 7 percent actually served. Employers bought exemptions to keep their labor supply and draft-insurance societies marketed policies that would hire substitutes. In some working-class districts, 98 percent of eligible men paid their way out of service. But that pay helped subsidize the bounty system, where potential draftees enlisted for as much as $1,000 in state, local, and national incentives.

To carry on the war, the Union and Confederate governments arrested people without warrant and jailed without trial. To crush armed rebellion and dissent, the Confederate army arrested Unionists and executed guerillas after a military court martial. In the first month of the war, Lincoln secured Maryland by suspending the writ of habeas corpus, by which an accused had the right to release unless specific charges were preferred, and by putting suspected secessionists under lock and key at Fort McHenry. Later, the War Department's provost-marshals rounded up draft resisters. Federal authorities locked up several newspaper editors and even a few judges for discouraging enlistments. Unionist mob violence put antiwar papers out of business, with soldiers smashing the presses and strewing the type in the streets. One speech denouncing federal tyranny led to former Ohio Congressman Clement Vallandigham being arrested, tried by military tribunal, and exiled across Confederate lines. None of these actions suppressed free speech much, however. Most of the thousands of arrests took place near the battlefront, in the Border South, and few political prisoners stayed behind bars for long. In the case of Ex parte *Milligan* (1866), the Supreme Court declared military trials illegal where civil courts were open—well after the war was over. Further from the danger zone, Lincoln's critics felt free to accuse him of despotism, call for his assassination, and inform readers that he actually was African American himself.

Sinews of War

At the start of the war, the Union had twice as many railroads per square mile as the Confederacy. It made 97 percent of the country's firearms and more than 90 percent of its boots, shoes, cloth, and pig iron. The South could raise more than enough food to feed its armies and civilian population; it just couldn't deliver it. Its rail system, never as comprehensive as the Union's, started off inadequate and only became more so as the war continued. Rails wore out. Locomotives broke down. Nobody could afford to replace them, nor could anyone in the South make them. With food rotting in warehouses, Confederate soldiers made the Commissary-General "the most cussed and vilified man in the Confederacy," but that did not fill their rucksacks.

Only in firepower did the Confederacy hold its own to the war's end. As head of the Ordnance Bureau that handled the supply of arms and ammunition, Josiah Gorgas proved a wizard of improvisation. From Europe came Enfield rifles, while at home small foundries and armories sprang up. Church bells were melted down for bronze to forge cannons, distilleries gave up their copper to manufacture rifle percussion caps, and Confederates combed battlefields for lead to make new bullets.

Union supplies started out almost as badly. Contractors produced cloth for uniforms so poor that it tore to rags in a heavy rain and shoes barely a week old fell apart, giving the term "shoddy" its present meaning. Thanks to Quartermaster-General Montgomery Meigs, uniforms improved dramatically, even as Confederate ones wore into shreds and patches. Stoves, ambulances, underwear, carts, forage for animals—Meigs came up with them all. In terms of infrastructural strength, the United States Military Railroads agency took over captured southern railroads, refitted them, ran them, and built new ones. By 1865, it was the largest single railroad company in the world, with 419 engines and 2,105 miles of track.

Soldiers on both sides grumbled about food. They talked about beef so full of maggots that they ran it away before cooks could desecrate it and "hardtack" crackers that had to be softened with musket butts before being eaten; others preferred to crumble them into the soup, thus allowing the weevils that managed to infiltrate it to float to the surface and properly cook. As the state of Confederate provisions worsened, however, Union diets improved. Salt pork, dried beans, "hardtack" crackers, and coffee "strong enough to float an iron wedge" were varied with potatoes, fresh meat, dried apples, and molasses. From Gail Borden's plant, cans of condensed milk by the thousands made their way to the front. Canneries sprouted up to provide tinned vegetables. By 1865, the Union army was the best supplied and best fed in the world. As a result, there was less sickness and, among the wounded, higher recovery rates.

The Union had one more intangible asset: its president. Lincoln's homespun humor and lack of polish made many underestimate him, though they usually liked him. Soldiers' nicknames suggested that he was as common as if he were family: "Old Abe," "Uncle Abe," and "Father Abraham." Indeed, the most famous mascot of the war was a Wisconsin regiment's bald eagle, "Old Abe" (who, name aside, was actually a female). Intimates glimpsed anguish behind the laughter and sharp instincts about how far public opinion would let him go. No one thought him a statesman, but he was what the war needed: a flexible politician with a gift for expressing ideas in clear, familiar language and an ability to grasp the larger picture. Patient and self-effacing, Lincoln had the ability to get along with Congress and his Cabinet of prima donnas that Jefferson Davis lacked. Lincoln's first Secretary of War, an unscrupulous, incompetent hack, was forced out, so Lincoln chose one of Buchanan's former Cabinet officers, Edwin M. Stanton. Stanton was a rude, hot-tempered bully; his contempt for Lincoln was no secret. But Lincoln saw Stanton's ruthlessness, aggressiveness, and administrative skill as what the war effort needed. When it came to policy, radicals like Senator Charles Sumner lamented how slowly the president struck blows at slavery, but they knew that the door was always open for them to make their case. Sometimes they convinced themselves that their words had converted him. If Lincoln grew in office, abolitionist Wendell Phillips once said, it was "because they had watered him." When Lincoln lay dying, Sumner and Stanton were among those grieving at his bedside, and it was Stanton who pronounced the epitaph: "Now he belongs to the ages."

THE CIVIL WAR AS SOCIAL REVOLUTION

By 1862, the North and the South had built up powerful military machines. At the same time, the North's war aims were shifting to include universal emancipation and the destruction of the southern social system. In the earliest months of the war, Republicans in Congress and the Lincoln administration adopted the view that emancipation was a military necessity, but they restricted emancipation to enslaved people coming voluntarily into Union lines. Within a year they would shift to a policy of universal emancipation as part of an emerging policy of **hard war**, with the seizure or destruction of anything of military value to the enemy. Throughout the South, a civil war erupted within the Civil War.

Union Victories in the West

Across the Appalachians, the Union's war went very well. Confederate forces were driven out of Missouri, and, at the battle of Pea Ridge, much of Arkansas, too. A Texas expedition to conquer New Mexico was beaten; only a straggling remnant made it home. Kentucky had tried not to join either side, but when a Confederate

northerners, particularly Democrats, protested making slavery's destruction a war aim. Most Union soldiers shared the mindset of one Illinois volunteer. He and his comrades liked "the Negro no better now than we did then," he allowed, "but we hate his master worse and I tell you when Old Abe carries out his Proclamation he kills this Rebellion and not before."

The Turn of the Tide—Gettysburg and Vicksburg

In vain, Lincoln sought an eastern commander matching the boldness of Lee and Jackson. Weary of McClellan's excuses and delays, Lincoln dismissed him and put Ambrose Burnside at the head of the Army of the Potomac. On December 13, 1862, Burnside threw his forces against Lee's well-entrenched army behind Fredericksburg, Virginia. A terrible, futile slaughter followed. To make matters worse, Burnside moved his men upriver to find a way behind Lee's lines in deep winter. So many soldiers became sick and died in the "Mud March" that the offensive was cancelled. One sufferer spoke for all his fellow soldiers when he complained that thanks to that winter's mishaps, "patriotism has oozed out through the pores." Only "the thought of their families," another wrote, "keeps them from suicide."

With the Army nearly dissolved, Lincoln gave command to "Fighting Joe" Hooker, brave, cocky, and hard-drinking, who may have saved the Army. He restored its morale, improved its food and housing, and imposed discipline. He made the Union cavalry the Confederates' match. One of his officers devised the lights-out bugle call known as "Taps." But in May 1863, moving against Confederate forces, Hooker lost his nerve at Chancellorsville. Lee and Jackson not only bluffed him into yielding the initiative, but in a daring move, they smashed the far end of his lines. With all the fight drained from him, Hooker ordered a retreat, but Lee's victory came at high cost. General Stonewall Jackson was among the thousands killed.

Hoping to deal a fatal blow to the Union's will to fight or at least supply his troops off the fat of the land, Lee crossed the Potomac in June and headed north. Seizing livestock, shoes, and kidnapping free Blacks to sell as enslaved, Confederates may have aimed to take Harrisburg or Baltimore. The Union army, however, now under General George Meade, caught up with them first, on July 1, in southern Pennsylvania (see Map 14–4) for what proved to be a decisive battle. Pushed south of **Gettysburg** that first day, Union forces made their stand on a line of hills. They chose their ground well. Confederate forces could neither flank nor dislodge them. On the third day of fighting, Lee gambled on an all-out drive on his enemy's center at Cemetery Ridge. That charge across nearly a mile of open ground broke against Union lines, at such cost of life that Lee had to retreat to Virginia. With more than a third of his force lost, his army would never recover. To Lincoln's perplexity, Meade's exhausted forces were unable to cut off the enemy's escape.

Even as Lee forded the Potomac River, the Confederacy lost its last important bastion along the Mississippi River. After months of effort and a prolonged siege, Grant starved **Vicksburg** into surrender, taking an entire 30,000-man army prisoner. When Port Hudson gave up soon after, the entire river fell into Union hands. Midwesterners could ship their crops out, federal troops landed anywhere along both shore, and Confederate forces in the West were helpless to aid their eastern comrades. Much of Mississippi and nearly two-thirds of Tennessee were irretrievably lost.

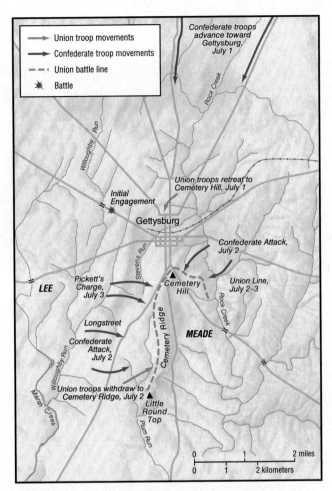

Map 14–4   The Battle of Gettysburg, July 1–3, 1863 In three extraordinary days in Gettysburg, Pennsylvania, the Union army turned back Lee's second invasion of the North. The Union victory, combined with equally important successes in the West at the same time, turned the tide of the war in the North's favor. At the dedication of a military cemetery at Gettysburg a few months later, Lincoln articulated his most profound justification for waging war against the South.

Despite his disappointment with Meade's failure to pursue and destroy the Army of Northern Virginia, Lincoln grasped the significance of the Union victories. In November, he dedicated a military cemetery at the Gettysburg battlefield. There he articulated a profound justification of the Union war effort. The Civil War, Lincoln said, had become a great test of democracy and of the principle of human equality. The soldiers who died at Gettysburg had dedicated their lives to those principles, the president noted. It remained only "for us the living" to similarly "resolve that these dead shall not have died in vain—that this nation, under God,

Gettysburg—The Aftermath The bodies of dead soldiers littered the battlefield at Gettysburg. Shortly thereafter, workers rushed to bury the corpses in time for the dedication of the battlefield as a military cemetery.

shall have a new birth of freedom—and that government of the people, by the people, for the people, shall not perish from the earth."

Emancipation in Practice

That new birth of freedom showed itself clearest in the breakdown of slavery. By the time Lincoln issued the Emancipation Proclamation on January 1, 1863, the Union had been freeing enslaved people and enslaved people had been freeing themselves for more than a year, but the pace quickened at once. Instead of entering Union lines by the hundreds, "contrabands" arrived by the thousands. Commanders built sprawling camps across the South to house them. With food and shelter lacking at first and epidemics in abundance, newcomers often fell sick. Some died and a few made their way back home again. Gradually, the army improved conditions. Across the Potomac from Washington, DC, the Arlington estate formerly owned by Robert E. Lee's family housed "Freedman's Village," a model camp with a school, hospital, and cemetery that would later become Arlington National Cemetery. Most of the camps proved to be way stations on the route to other destinations. Some freedpeople headed north to work Midwestern fields. Far more moved to Union-occupied plantation country to work as contract labor raising the cotton that northern mills required.

Young Black men had another option: they could don the blue uniform of the Union. Black men had served in the American Revolution and the War of 1812, but the army had refused their services. Now it welcomed them. By war's end, 186,000 Black men had signed up, with 134,411 recruited in the South. That equated to about 1 Union soldier in 10. After initial doubts, Lincoln quickly discovered their worth. "The bare sight of 50,000 armed and drilled Black soldiers upon the banks of the Mississippi," he said in March 1863, "would end the rebellion at once." He was wrong, but their numbers tipped the balance of forces decisively in favor of the Union army, contributing to the Confederate disadvantage.

Black soldiers suffered unequal treatment in the army. At first, they received less pay than whites: ten dollars a month with three deducted for their clothing, rather than thirteen with a clothing allowance included. They fought under white commissioned officers almost exclusively. Some Federal soldiers never got used to serving with African Americans. One general let them spearhead a hopeless charge, explaining, "We may as well get rid of them one time as another." Confederates were likelier to kill them than take prisoners, and they enslaved many that they captured. Still, for Black soldiers, fighting for their race's emancipation was exhilarating. Northerners were moved at the courage they showed before the entrenchments of Port Hudson and Fort Wagner, where two in every five were killed or wounded. "A shell would explode and clear a space of twenty feet," a survivor recalled, and "our men would close up again." Black soldiers were an edifying spectacle for those still enslaved, but to white southerners, their worst nightmare had come true. Confederate prisoners confessed, "it was the hardest stroke that there cause has received. ... Not a few of them [said] that they would rather fight two Regiments of White Soldiers than one of Niggers. Rebel Citizens fear them more than they would fear Indians." By the end of the war, 15 Black soldiers and 8 Black sailors had earned the Congressional Medal of Honor.

Company E, 4th United States Colored Infantry, at Fort Lincoln, Washington, DC, 1865 Black people serving in the Union army symbolized the revolutionary turn the Civil War took with emancipation as the policy of the North. Despite overwhelming loss of life by the Black troops, their bravery impressed many northerners and helped change white attitudes about the goals of the Civil War.

THE WAR AT HOME

African American troops could not end the rebellion "at once," as Lincoln hoped. The war persisted for two more years. As body counts rose and hardships mounted, civilians in the North and the South began to register their discontent.

The "Butcher's Bill"

Bad generalship cost some lives, but the new technology of war did much more. Instead of the old smoothbore musket, soldiers carried rifled muskets; instead of the round ball that guns once fired, they shot a grooved, oblong bullet, the Minie Ball, that could be pushed down the barrel loose and spun out tight. Those two innovations made muskets more accurate and powerful enough to kill at half a mile, rather than the 100-yard range they had had up until then. The old charge across an open field became far more lethal, and against defenders behind walls or standing in trenches, suicidal. "It was not war, it was *murder*," one general commented after a failed assault on Union positions at Malvern Hill. More than half the Confederate generals were wounded or killed. Two days at Shiloh cost as many casualties as in the country's last three major wars combined. Over 50,000 were killed or wounded at Gettysburg, 35,000 at Chickamauga, and nearly 25,000 at Murfreesboro. In every encounter the "butcher's bill," as newspapers called it, was agonizingly high.

Disease, however, killed far more soldiers than combat. Crowded into camps, recruits fell prey to every contagious disease: measles, mumps, and influenza. Malaria and dysentery were also major killers. Soldiers gave diarrhea joking names like "the Richmond Quick-Step," but it often debilitated and sometimes killed. Unacquainted with germ theory or the need for sterilization, overworked medics found themselves overstretched in tending to the wounded while the battle raged. Injured men might lie on the field for five days before help reached them. A bone-shattering bullet wound carried almost certain infection and probably gangrene as the flesh rotted—invariably fatal. Only immediate amputation could save a life, usually with no anesthetic stronger than whiskey and no surgical tool but a lumberman's saw. Many patients died.

Despite the circumstances, medical conditions improved, more in the North than in the South. At the war's outbreak, the Union had 98 medical officers and the Confederacy had 24. Four years later, 15,000 surgeons tended the armies and over 350 general hospitals handled their care. Many women volunteered their services as nurses. The United States Sanitary Commission, a private organization led by men but inspired by Elizabeth Blackwell, the first woman physician in America, and staffed by thousands of other women, supplied meals and lodging for convalescent soldiers. It sent commissioners to regimental camps to advise them about drainage and keeping the water supply clean. General McClellan is credited with setting up the first ambulance corps to carry the wounded from the field, which became a model for other nations. These medical reforms improved conditions notably. In the Mexican war, disease killed seven soldiers for every one killed in fighting. Now, the ratio was two to one (see Figure 14–2).

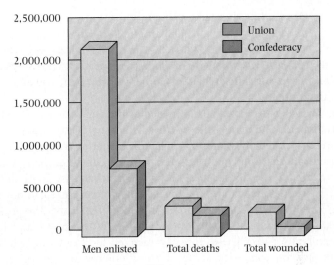

Figure 14–2   Casualties of War

Discontent on Both Sides

The longer the war went on, the louder criticism grew on either side, and military setbacks gave it real urgency. In the North, Democrats splintered. Some War Democrats like Senator Andrew Johnson of Tennessee and General Benjamin Butler supported the administration, emancipation included. Most members of the party blamed Republicans for not making the compromises that would have prevented a war. When Lincoln claimed the right to suspend the writ of **habeas corpus** and institute a draft, Democrats protested bitterly. Every new power the government took carried the country further from the "farmer's republic" that Thomas Jefferson had made, based on liberty and local control. Copperheads, as Peace Democrats were known, went further. In Lincoln they saw a would-be tyrant, in his government a plundering expedition, and in emancipation a deliberate strategy to prolong the war indefinitely while privileged interests lined their pockets at farmers' expense. War, Copperheads argued, only deepened the bitterness between Americans. Negotiation alone could restore the Union. In the 1862 off-year elections, Democrats made gains in Congress and carried Midwestern legislatures. There, enemies of the war threatened to withhold troops.

With inflation outpacing their wages and Blacks competing for their jobs, day laborers and unskilled workers resented a draft that the rich could pay their way out of; in their view, unprivileged whites were forced to die in order to make Blacks free. Riots erupted in Boston and other cities, the worst of which took place in New York City on July 13, 1863, and lasted four days. Protestors wrecked recruiting stations and draft offices. As the disorder continued, the crowd's composition changed and so did its targets. Mobs went after well-dressed "$300 men" (in reference to the $300 commutation fee men could pay to avoid conscription). They smashed the job-destroying, grain-loading elevators. Irish Catholics burned Protestant churches and missions. Only newly invented Gatling machine guns saved Horace Greeley's New York *Tribune* building from attack. Blaming Blacks for the war, whites beat or killed any that crossed their path. At least 12 African Americans were lynched and the Colored Orphan Asylum went up in flames. Troops had to be called in to quell the New York City **draft riots**. By the time order was restored, over 100 people had died, 74 of them rioters.

In the Confederacy, hardships deepened as the war went on. Due to lack of funds, rural schools and many colleges closed. Short on usable paper, newspapers cut their size or printed on whatever was handy, including wallpaper. The 80 percent inflation rate that the Union suffered over the course of the war was manageable compared to the Confederacy's 9,000 percent increase. With flour selling for $425 a barrel, potatoes for $25 a bushel, and a ham for $350, once-affluent people just barely scraped by, and poorer ones faced real want. The prosperity of the profiteers only made the contrast more glaring. With wheat scarce for bakeries and abundant for distilleries, angry women led food riots in Richmond and Mobile, taking army supplies for themselves. Women wrote desperate letters to their husbands and sons in the Confederate armies, begging them to come home and rescue their families from the threat of starvation. Soldiers "cannot be expected to fight for the government that permits their wives and children to starve," one officer warned.

For the most part, however, they did fight. Ill-equipped and beleaguered, Confederate troops signed up willingly when their enlistments ran out. "No amount of poverty seems to shake their faith," a Union general marveled. Most whites blamed the North for their sufferings, and Lincoln's emancipation policy only reinforced their belief that their very lives depended on victory. Some, Jefferson Davis and Robert E. Lee among them, took the cause so to heart that by early 1865 they were prepared to arm enslaved people and promise them their freedom if they would "fight for their homes and country."

Even so, the Confederate government faced intense, often crippling criticism. Southerners protested every infringement on states' rights. Planters seethed when authorities burned private stores of cotton and impressed enslaved people into service without payment. Farmers despaired, as their own army raided the countryside, collecting fodder, mules, and crops for the war effort. It left behind fistfuls of documents acknowledging debt not worth the paper they were printed on. When, faced with swelling resistance, Davis suspended the writ of habeas corpus, the same cries of tyranny that greeted Lincoln rose against Confederate authority.

Conscription and centralization stoked fierce conflict and several state governors, in particular Joseph E. Brown of Georgia and Zebulon Vance of North Carolina, took matters into their own hands. Brown and Vance were loyal Confederates. They mobilized the state's power to relieve civilian want, and like most states, taxed property and enslaved people to do it, but their complaints gave the Confederate president endless headaches. Jefferson Davis received more blame than he deserved for Confederate failures, while Lee got the credit for its successes. With no robust two-party system like the North's to compel discipline, Congress bickered, dithered, and undermined Cabinet officials' credibility. As a result, Davis went through four secretaries of state, six secretaries of war, and five attorneys-general in four years.

Draft resistance in the Confederacy went beyond anything the Union had experienced. In eastern Tennessee, one newspaper reported that of over 25,000 conscripts enrolled, only 6,000 showed up at roll call. In Alabama, the governor confessed enforcement of the conscript law "a humbug and a farce." Nor did the North face any resistance movement openly supporting the other side. In the mountains of eastern Tennessee and western North Carolina, where hostility to the Confederacy was widespread, savage guerrilla warfare erupted. Partisan bands burned bridges, and bushwhacked Confederate cavalry that had been sent to hunt down deserters.

UNION VICTORY AT TERRIBLE COST

A crippled Confederacy nonetheless sought desperately to maintain itself. At the same time, northern society seemed stronger than ever. Amid the most ferocious fighting ever witnessed on North American soil, the commander in chief ran for reelection to the presidency and won.

Grant Takes Command

During the summer of 1863, Union forces under William S. Rosecrans pushed Braxton Bragg's Confederate troops out of central Tennessee. Bragg retreated east to Chattanooga, a critical rail terminal. On September 19, the two armies met at Chickamauga Creek. The name, meaning "River of Death," earned its name over the next two bloody days, before Union forces were routed, nearly destroyed, and penned up in Chattanooga. Put in charge of all the Union's western armies, Grant opened supply routes to feed a starving army and in November launched an attack on Bragg's defensive line along the crest of Missionary Ridge. Thrown off the high ground, Confederates had no defensible position left in Tennessee. They were pushed into Georgia, with most of the cotton kingdom west of that virtually out of the fight.

In Grant, Lincoln saw the indomitable spirit he had been looking for. In March 1864, he gave the general charge of the entire Union army. Grant decided on a co-ordinated strategy, national in scope: heading the Army of the Potomac, he would confront Lee's Army of Northern Virginia while **William T. Sherman** took on Joseph E. Johnston's troops in Georgia. If he could not beat his opponent, he could keep him from reinforcing Johnston's army.

No Turning Back: Hard War in an Election Year

The "Overland campaign" that spring was like nothing Americans had ever seen, with hard marching and fighting every day. Grant and Lee's forces first collided on May 5 and 6, 1864, in the thick woods and clearings near Chancellorsville. Appropriately called the Wilderness, the terrain made it difficult to see for any distance and impossible for armies to maintain strict lines. Entire brigades got lost. In some places, shellfire set the woods aflame and wounded men burned to death. Two days of fighting cost the Union 17,000 casualties and the Confederates 11,000.

American Landscape

"Burnwell": Sherman's March from the Sea and the Long-Term Cost of Devastation

Any southerner who thought William Tecumseh Sherman's troops had done their worst in Georgia learned differently when they moved into South Carolina. There, every house was fair game. Lone chimneys, "Sherman's sentinels," stood on emptied landscapes. Iron rails, heated in a fire of railroad ties, were twisted around telegraph poles to make "Sherman's hairpins." "How shall I let you know where I am?" a cavalry officer asked the general. "Oh," he was told, "just burn a barn or something." The town of Barnwell, after the army passed through, was nicknamed "Burnwell." If Confederates started the fire that burned Columbia, and, as Sherman later protested, "God Almighty sent the wind," Sherman's men fed the blaze. Here, if anywhere, total war reached its utter fulfillment.

Where the Confederacy's enemies did not wreck it, its friends did. At war's end, Charleston was, in one traveler's words, "a city of ruins, of desolation, of vacated houses, of widowed women, of rotting wharves, of deserted warehouses, of weed-wild houses, of miles of grass-grown streets, of acres of pitiful and voiceful barrenness." The blockade brought the decay. Parting Confederates started the fire that caused the ruins. They did the same in Richmond. The South had lost most of its railroad cars and engines. Depots were gone, along with trestles and bridges. Farmers had lost their fences because one army or the other had needed firewood, but they could take bitter comfort in knowing that the cattle would not get out for they had been commandeered, too. No longer did southern banks need to operate on reserves of nearly worthless Confederate bonds and paper: the surrender made them completely worthless.

That story of a proud civilization, gone with the wind, became a lasting myth, but that was all it was. Within a year, an Atlanta bustling and booming more than ever rose out of the embers Sherman had left. Within two years, every railroad was running again and some were raising money to expand. Many planters, sure that slavery's fall had ruined them, discovered that they could get along almost as well or even better on freedpeople's labor, so much so that many persuaded themselves that slavery had been a burden on them and they gloried in throwing it off. By 1880, the South grew more cotton than ever before the war, and by 1900 it was home to thriving iron and textile industries as well.

Sherman's march illustrated not just the concept of hard war, but its

April 2, 1865. The Confederate government fled and Grant's forces pursued Lee's. Cornered near Appomattox Court House and facing a fight against hopeless odds, Lee accepted Grant's terms of an unconditional surrender. Joseph F. Johnston's army in North Carolina would not surrender to Sherman until a fortnight later, but Appomattox meant the real end of the war.

Atlanta in Ruins Much of Atlanta lay in ruins after General Sherman captured and burned the city. The northern general had made a conscious decision to make war "hell" by destroying the property of the southern civilians who supported the war.

limits. The wholesale slaughter of civilians, the free rein given to rape and other atrocities, commonplace in the next century, had no place on either side—against white people. Against Indians or Hispanics out west or southern Blacks, soldiers threw off restraints. Many formerly enslaved people following Sherman's troops through Georgia died, some from neglect, others killed almost casually. For all the general's infamy, white southerners had it easy compared to the western Indians he turned his wrath against after **Appomattox**. Contemporaries knew Sherman as outspoken in his sympathy for the people he had defeated. Not surprisingly, 15 years after the burning of Atlanta, civic leaders threw a banquet in his honor. He received a warm welcome even if, as the city's leading editor, Henry Grady, would quip, he had been "a mite careless about fire."

From Emancipation to Abolition

By the end of the war, military emancipation had freed approximately half a million of the South's 4 million enslaved people. Lincoln and the Republicans believed that those enslaved people "practically" freed by the war could never be reenslaved, but the fate of the vast majority still in service remained unclear. Under intense pressure from Washington, six states had abolished slavery, but they could always reinstate it. Slavery remained legal in the rest of the states, including Kentucky and Delaware. If the institution survived the war, the plantations would simply restock themselves with laborers, just as they had after the American Revolution. A legal challenge to Lincoln's power to set anyone free by military authority was a virtual certainty, and the slave owners might even win.

For all these reasons, by 1864 Republicans concluded that only a constitutional amendment could end slavery for good. War Democrats helped carry it through the Senate, but it fell short of the required two-thirds in the House. With the Republican platform endorsing the Thirteenth Amendment, the election gave voters a chance not only to pass on Lincoln but on abolition. His landslide victory gave the administration momentum; and persuasion, pressure, and patronage helped round up the Democratic support it needed. On January 30, 1865, the House passed the Thirteenth Amendment, which formally abolished slavery. Northern states ratified it at once, and so did several southern ones. That December, Secretary of State Seward announced the Amendment's ratification.

The Meaning of the Civil War

Despite wartime inflation and terrible loss of life, the Civil War years had only strengthened the North's economy. Mechanization allowed northern farmers to increase wheat production, despite losing one-third of the farm labor force to the army. Huge orders for military rations propelled the growth of the canned-food industry. The railroad boom of the 1850s persisted. By contrast, the slave economy was crushed. Much of the South lay in ruins. Thousands of miles of railroad track had been destroyed. One-third of the livestock had been killed; one-fourth of the young white men were dead. In 1860, the North and the South had identical per

TIME LINE

▼1860

South Carolina declares its independence

▼1861

Lower South announces itself out of the Union

Abraham Lincoln inaugurated

First shots fired at Fort Sumter

Upper South passes secession ordinances, Border South remains

Union declares runaway enslaved people "contraband"

First battle of Bull Run

McClellan takes command of Army of the Potomac

First Confiscation Act

Trent affair

▼1862

Battles of Fort Henry and Fort Donelson

"Battle of the ironclads"

Battle of Shiloh

Union capture of New Orleans

Slavery abolished in Washington, DC

Homestead Act

Confederacy establishes military draft

Peninsula campaign

Slavery prohibited in western territories

Second Confiscation Act passed by northern Congress

Second battle of Bull Run

capita incomes and nearly identical per capita wealth. By 1870, the North was 50 percent wealthier than the South.

The redistribution of political power was equally dramatic. Until 1860, slaveholders and their allies had controlled the Supreme Court, dominated the presidency, and exercised disproportionate influence in Congress. For the rest of the century, every elected president but one had a Union war record. Most justices, Speakers of the House, and all the commanders in the army and navy came from Union states. Until 1861, most people referred to the United States itself as the Union, something more than a federation of sovereignties, but less than a consolidated entity.

Some 750,000 men—maybe as many as 850,000—died during the Civil War. If anything beyond preserving the Union justified such loss, abolition did. In the sacrifices Lincoln glimpsed dimly the divine will, not on the Union's side, but on freedom's, and the war as a chastisement not just of the South but of all Americans for the wrong that slavery had done. "Fondly do we hope, fervently do we pray, that this mighty scourge of war may speedily pass away," he told his listeners. "Yet, if God wills that it continue until all the wealth piled by the bondsman's two hundred and fifty years of unrequited toil shall be sunk, and until every drop of blood drawn with the lash shall be paid by another drawn with the sword, as was said three thousand years ago, so still it must be said 'the judgments of the Lord are true and righteous altogether.'"

CONCLUSION

The president who had led the nation through the Civil War would not oversee the nation's reconstruction. On the evening of April 14, 1865, actor John Wilkes Booth, believing that he was rescuing America from tyranny and "nigger equality,"

Battle of Antietam
Preliminary Emancipation Proclamation
Battle of Fredericksburg

▼1863
Emancipation Proclamation
Union establishes military draft
Battle of Chancellorsville
Battle of Gettysburg
Vicksburg surrenders
New York City draft riots
Battle of Chickamauga
Gettysburg Address

▼1864
Wilderness campaign
Battle of Cold Harbor
Siege of Petersburg begins
Sherman captures Atlanta
Philip Sheridan raids Shenandoah Valley
Lincoln reelected
Sherman burns part of Atlanta and marches to the sea
Battles of Franklin and Nashville

▼1864–1865
Sherman's march through the Carolinas

▼1865
House of Representatives approves Thirteenth Amendment (January)
Lincoln's second inauguration
Lee surrenders to Grant at Appomattox
Lincoln assassinated
Thirteenth Amendment ratified (December)

assassinated Abraham Lincoln at Ford's Theater in Washington, DC. Only luck and misgivings kept his coconspirators from murdering other top government figures as well. Lincoln had puzzled over how to bind the nation anew, but he and Congress had not yet agreed on any particular plan. Would the Union simply be restored as swiftly as possible? Or would the South be refashioned, continuing the revolution begun during the Civil War? Upon Lincoln's death, those questions remained unanswered. That would come as the freedpeople in the South pressed to expand the meaning of that undelivered "new birth of freedom."

WHO, WHAT, WHERE

REVIEW QUESTIONS

1. What reasons did white southerners give for seceding?

2. What were the relative military advantages of the Union and the Confederacy at the beginning of the war?

3. What made emancipation a military necessity?

4. How much antiwar sentiment was there in the Union and the Confederacy?

CRITICAL-THINKING QUESTIONS

1. What role did the different economic systems of the free and slave states play in the Civil War?

2. Both the Union and Confederacy suspended civil liberties during the conflict. In your opinion, did the stakes of the war justify such measures? Explain your answer.

3. What were the military merits of Sherman's hard war in Georgia and South Carolina? Did the nature of the conflict warrant such a course of action?

SUGGESTED READINGS

Channing, Stephen A. *Crisis of Fear: Secession in South Carolina.* New York: Norton, 1970.

McPherson, James. *Battle-Cry of Freedom: The Civil War Era.* New York: Oxford University Press, 1988.

Mohr, Clarence L. *On the Threshold of Freedom: Masters and Slaves in Civil War Georgia.* Baton Rouge: Louisiana State University Press, 1986.

For further review materials and resource information, please visit www.oup.com/us/ofthepeople

CHAPTER 14:   A War for Union and Emancipation, 1861–1865
Primary Sources

14.1   JOHN SHERMAN, A LETTER ON THE CRISIS TO PHILADELPHIANS (1860)

Beginning a career that would carry him into the Senate, make him secretary of the treasury and later secretary of state, and credit him with some of the most important legislation in the latter part of the nineteenth century, John Sherman had already become one of the Republican moderates' most respected spokesmen. His letter to a public meeting in late 1860 explained why no new compromise could restore the Union, and why disunion inevitably must bring on war. On January 6, 1861, he sent a copy to his brother, William Tecumseh Sherman, who was even more conservative than he, but would prove the temper of his Unionism in quite a different way.

Washington, December 22, 1860.

Gentlemen:—Your note of the 15th inst., inviting me to attend a public dinner in your city, on Friday evening next, was duly received.

Fidelity to principle is demanded by the highest patriotism. The question is not whether this or that policy should prevail; but whether we shall allow the government to be broken into fragments, by disappointed partisans, condemned by four-fifths of the people. It is the same question answered by General Jackson in his proclamation of 1833. It is the same question answered by Henry Clay in the Senate in 1850. It is the same question answered by Madison and Jefferson, and recently by Wade and Johnson. It is a question which, I feel assured, every one of you will answer, in the patriotic language of General Jackson—"*The Union, it must be preserved.*"

   . . . .

The people, alarmed, excited, yet true to the Union and the constitution, are watching with eager fear, lest the noble government, baptized in the blood of the Revolution, shall be broken into fragments, before the President elect shall assume the functions of his office.

What pretext is given for this alarming condition of affairs?—for every treasonable act has its pretext. We are told that the people of the southern states *apprehend* that Mr. Lincoln will deprive them of their constitutional rights. It is not claimed that, as yet, their rights have been invaded, but upon an *apprehension* of evil, they will break up the most prosperous government the providence of God ever allowed to man.

We know very well how groundless are their apprehensions, but we are not even allowed to say so to our fellow-citizens of the south. So wild is their apprehension, that even such statesmen as Stephens, Johnson, Hill, Botts and Pettigrew, when they say, "wait, wait, till we see what this Republican party will attempt," are denounced as Abolitionists—Submissionists. You know very well that we do not propose to interfere in the slightest degree with slavery in the states. We know that our leader, for whose election you rejoice has, over and over again, affirmed his opposition to the abolition of slavery in the District of Columbia, except upon conditions that are not likely to occur; or to any interference with the interstate slave trade, and that he will enforce the constitutional right of the citizens of the slave states to recapture their fugitive slaves when they escape from service into the free states. We know very well that the great objects which those who elected Mr. Lincoln expect him to accomplish will be to secure to free labor its just right to the territories of the United States; to protect, as far as practicable, by wise revenue laws, the labor of our people; to secure the public lands to actual settlers, instead of non-resident speculators; to develop the internal resources of the country, by opening new means of communication between the Atlantic and the Pacific, and to purify the administration of the government from the pernicious influences of jobs, contracts, and unreasoning party warfare.

But some of you may say, all this is very well, but what will you do to save the Union? Why don't you compromise?

Gentlemen, remember that we are just recovering from the dishonor of breaking a legislative compromise. We have been struggling, against all the powers of the government, for six years, to secure practically what was expressly granted by a compromise. We have succeeded. Kansas is now free. The Missouri restriction is now practically restored by the incipient constitution of Kansas, and safer yet, by the will of her people. The baptism of strife through which she has passed has only strengthened the prohibition. There let it stand.

But our political opponents, who have dishonored the word compromise, who trampled, without a moment's hesitation, upon a compromise, when they expected to gain by it, now ask us to again compromise, by securing slavery south of a geographical line. To this we might fairly say: There is no occasion for compromise. We have done no wrong; we have no apologies to make, and no concessions to offer. You chose your ground, and we accepted your issue. We have beaten you, and you must submit, as we have done in the past, and as we would have done if the voice of the people had been against us. As good citizens, you must obey the laws, and respect the constituted authorities. But we will meet new questions of administration with a liberal spirit. Without surrendering our convictions in the least, we may now dispose of the whole territorial controversy by the exercise of unquestioned congressional power.

. . . .

The struggle to establish slavery in Kansas; the frequent murders and mobbings, in the south, of northern citizens; the present turbulence and violence of southern society; the manifest fear of the freedom of speech and of the press; the danger of insurrection; and now the attempt to subvert the government rather than submit to a constitutional election—these events, disguise it as you may, have aroused a counter irritation in the north that will not allow its representatives to yield merely for peace, more than is prescribed by the letter and spirit of the constitution. Every guarantee of this instrument ought to be faithfully and religiously observed. But when it is proposed to change it, to secure new guarantees to slavery, to extend and protect it, you invoke and arouse the antislavery feeling of the north to war against slavery everywhere.

… If the personal-liberty bills of any state infringe upon the constitution, they should at once be repealed. Most of them have slumbered upon the statute book for years. They are now seized upon, by those who are plotting disunion, as a pretext. We should give them no pretext. It is always right and proper for each state to apply to state laws the test of the constitution.

It is a remarkable fact that neither of the border free states—New Jersey, Pennsylvania, Ohio, Indiana, Illinois, nor Iowa—have any such upon their statute books. The laws of these states, against kidnapping, are similar to those of Virginia and Kentucky. The laws of other states, so-called, have never operated to release a single fugitive slave, and may be regarded simply as a protest of those states against the harsh features of the fugitive slave law. So far as they infringe upon the constitution, or impair, in the least, a constitutional right, they are void and ought to be repealed.

I venture the assertion that there have been more cases of kidnapping of free negroes in Ohio, than of peaceable or unlawful rescue of fugitive slaves in the whole United States.

It has been shown that the law of recapture and the penalties of rescue have been almost invariably executed. Count up all the cases of rescue of negroes in the north, and you can find in your newspapers more cases of unlawful lynching and murder of white men in the south.

....

Can a separation take place without war? If so, where will be the line? Who shall possess this magnificent capital, with all its evidences of progress and civilization? Shall the mouth of the Mississippi be separated from its sources? Who shall possess the territories? Suppose these difficulties to be overcome; suppose that in peace we should huckster and divide up our nationality, our flag, our history, all the recollections of the past; suppose all these difficulties overcome, how can two rival republics of the same race of men, divided only by a line of a river for thousands of miles, and with all the present difficulties aggravated by separation, avoid forays, disputes, and war? How can we travel on our future march of progress in Mexico, or on the high seas, or on the Pacific slope, without collision? It is impossible. To peacefully accomplish such results we must change the nature of man. Disunion is war! God knows, I do not threaten it, for I will seek to prevent it in every way possible. I speak but the logic of facts, which we should not conceal from each other. It is either hostilities between the government and the seceding states; or, if separation is yielded peaceably, it is a war of factions—a rivalry of insignificant communities, hating each other, and contemned by the civilized world. If war results, what a war it will be! Contemplate the north and south, in hostile array against each other. If these sections do not know each other *now* they will *then*.

.... With great respect, I remain, very truly,

Your obedient servant,

John Sherman.

Source: Rachel Sherman Thorndike, ed., *The Sherman Letters* (New York: Charles Scribner's and Sons, 1894), pp. 92–104.

14.2 JULIA WARD HOWE, "THE BATTLE HYMN OF THE REPUBLIC" (1862)

Julia Ward Howe, wife of antislavery reformer Samuel Gridley Howe, came up with "The Battle Hymn of the Republic" after touring an army camp near Washington, DC. The minister accompanying her suggested "some good words" for the tune of "John Brown's Body." That night, "the long lines of the desired poem began to twine themselves in my mind," she wrote. The *Atlantic Monthly* paid her $4 for the submission, which became one of the most celebrated war hymns of the Union.

Mine eyes have seen the glory of the coming of the Lord
He is trampling out the vintage where the grapes of wrath are stored,
He has loosed the fateful lightening of His terrible swift sword
His truth is marching on.

Glory! Glory! Hallelujah!
Glory! Glory! Hallelujah!
Glory! Glory! Hallelujah!
His truth is marching on.

I have seen Him in the watch-fires of a hundred circling camps
They have builded Him an altar in the evening dews and damps

I can read His righteous sentence by the dim and flaring lamps
His day is marching on.
Chorus: Glory! Glory! Hallelujah! &c.

I have read a fiery gospel writ in burnish'd rows of steel,
"As ye deal with my contemners, So with you my grace shall deal;"
Let the Hero, born of woman, crush the serpent with his heel
Since God is marching on.
Chorus: Glory! Glory! Hallelujah! &c.

He has sounded forth the trumpet that shall never call retreat
He is sifting out the hearts of men before His judgment-seat
Oh, be swift, my soul, to answer Him! be jubilant, my feet!
Our God is marching on.
Chorus: Glory! Glory! Hallelujah! &c.

In the beauty of the lilies Christ was born across the sea,
With a glory in His bosom that transfigures you and me:
As He died to make men holy, let us die to make men free,
While God is marching on.
Chorus: Glory! Glory! Hallelujah! &c.

Source: *Atlantic Monthly*, February 1862, quoted in Henry Steele Commager, ed., *The Blue and the Gray: The Story of the Civil War as Told by Participants* (Indianapolis: Bobbs-Merrill, 1950), vol. 1, pp. 561–563, 571–573.

14.3 LOUISA MAY ALCOTT NURSES THE WOUNDED (1863)

Women, too, gave the last full measure of devotion in the war. Among those volunteering to tend the wounded and dying soldiers was the Massachusetts author Louisa May Alcott, who later would write the best-selling and semiautobiographical novel *Little Women*.

The first thing I met was a regiment of the vilest odors that ever assaulted the human nose, and took it by storm. Cologne, with its seven and seventy evil savors, was a posy-bed to it; and the worst of this affliction was, every one had assured me that it was a chronic weakness of all hospitals, and I must bear it. I did, armed with lavender water, with which I so besprinkled myself and premises, that, like my friend Sairy, I was soon known among my patients as "the nurse with the bottle." Having been run over by three excited surgeons, bumped against by migratory coal-hods, water-pails, and small boys, nearly scalded by an avalanche of newly-filled tea-pots, and hopelessly entangled in a knot of colored sisters coming to wash, I progressed by slow stages up stairs and down, till the main hall was reached, and I paused to take breath and a survey. There they were! "our brave boys," as the papers justly call them, for cowards could hardly have been so riddled with shot and shell, so torn and shattered, nor have borne suffering for which we have no name, with an uncomplaining fortitude, which made one glad to cherish each as a brother. In they came, some on stretchers, some in men's arms, some feebly staggering along propped on rude crutches, and one lay stark and still with covered face, as a comrade gave his name to be recorded before they carried him away to the dead house. All was hurry and confusion; the hall was full of these wrecks of humanity, for the most exhausted could not reach a bed till duly ticketed and registered; the walls were lined with rows of such as could sit, the floor covered with the more disabled, the steps and doorways filled with helpers and lookers on; the sound of many feet and voices made that usually quiet hour as noisy as noon; and, in the midst of it all, the matron's motherly face brought more comfort to many a poor soul, than the cordial draughts she administered, or the cheery words that welcomed all, making of the hospital a home.

The sight of several stretchers, each with its legless, armless, or desperately wounded occupant, entering my ward, admonished me that I was there to work, not to wonder or weep; so I corked up my feelings, and returned to the path of duty, which was rather "a hard road to travel" just then. The house had been a hotel before hospitals were needed, and many of the doors still bore their old names; some not so inappropriate as might be imagined, for my ward was in truth a *ball-room*, if gun-shot wounds could christen it. Forty beds were prepared, many already tenanted by tired men who fell down anywhere, and drowsed till the smell of food roused them. Round the great stove was gathered the dreariest group I ever saw–ragged, gaunt and pale, mud to the knees, with bloody bandages untouched since put on days before; many bundled up in blankets, coats being lost or useless; and all wearing that disheartened look which proclaimed defeat, more plainly than any telegram of the Burnside blunder. I pitied them so much, I dared not speak to them, though, remembering all they had been through since the route at Fredericksburg, I yearned to serve the dreariest of them all. Presently, Miss Blank tore me from my refuge behind piles of one-sleeved shirts, odd socks, bandages and lint; put basin, sponge, towels, and a block of brown soap into my hands, with these appalling directions:

"Come, my dear, begin to wash as fast as you can. Tell them to take off socks, coats and shirts, scrub them well, put on clean shirts, and the attendants will finish them off, and lay them in bed."

If she had requested me to shave them all, or dance a hornpipe on the stove funnel, I should have been less staggered; but to scrub some dozen lords of creation at a moment's notice, was really–really–. However, there was no time for nonsense, and, having resolved when I came to do everything I was bid, I drowned my scruples in my wash-bowl, clutched my soap manfully, and, assuming a business-like air, made a dab at the first dirty specimen I saw, bent on performing my task *vi et armis* if necessary.

… All having eaten, drank, and rested, the surgeons began their rounds; and I took my first lesson in the art of dressing wounds. It wasn't a festive scene, by any means; for Dr P., whose Aid I constituted myself, fell to work with a vigor which soon convinced me that I was a weaker vessel, though nothing would have induced me to confess it then. He had served in the Crimea, and seemed to regard a dilapidated body very much as I should have regarded a damaged garment; and, turning up his cuffs, whipped out a very unpleasant looking housewife, cutting, sawing, patching and piecing, with the enthusiasm of an accomplished surgical seamstress; explaining the process, in scientific terms, to the patient, meantime; which, of course, was immensely cheering and comfortable. There was an uncanny sort of fascination in watching him, as he peered and probed into the mechanism of those wonderful bodies, whose mysteries he understood so well. The more intricate the wound, the better he liked it. A poor private, with both legs off, and shot through the lungs, possessed more attractions for him than a dozen generals, slightly scratched in some "masterly retreat;" and had any one appeared in small pieces, requesting to be put together again, he would have considered it a special dispensation.

… Then came the doctor's evening visit; the administration of medicines; washing feverish faces; smoothing tumbled beds; wetting wounds; singing lullabies; and preparations for the night. By twelve, the last labor of love was done; the last "good night" spoken; and, if any needed a reward for that day's work, they surely received it, in the silent eloquence of those long lines of faces, showing pale and peaceful in the shaded rooms, as we quitted them, followed by grateful glances that lighted us to bed, where rest, the sweetest, made our pillows soft, while Night and Nature took our places, filling that great house of pain with the healing miracles of Sleep, and his diviner brother, Death.

Source: Louisa May Alcott, *Hospital Sketches* (Boston: James Redpath, 1863).

14.4 JOHN BEAUCHAMP JONES OBSERVES THE DETERIORATION ON THE CONFEDERATE HOME FRONT (1863–1864)

John Beauchamp Jones, a clerk in the Confederate War Department, kept a detailed diary of events. By mid-1863, he was chronicling the woes of a government unable to keep its armies fed or to control its faltering economy, and along with it the rising discontent, even rebelliousness, of state authorities that had lost faith in Jefferson Davis's government to perform basic functions.

OCTOBER 22D [1863].—Gen. Wheeler has taken 700 of the enemy's cavalry in East Tennessee, 6 cannon, 50 wagons, commissary stores, etc. *Per contra*, the steamer Venus, with bacon, from Nassau, got aground trying to enter the port of Wilmington, and ship and cargo were lost. There is a rumor that Gen. Taylor, trans-Mississippi, has captured Gen. Banks, his staff, and sixteen regiments. This, I fear, is not well authenticated.

A poor woman yesterday applied to a merchant in Carey Street to purchase a barrel of flour. The price he demanded was $70.

"My God!" exclaimed she, "how can I pay such prices? I have seven children; what shall I do?"

"I don't know, madam," said he, coolly, "unless you eat your children."

Such is the power of cupidity—it transforms men into demons. And if this spirit prevails throughout the country, a just God will bring calamities upon the land, which will reach these cormorants, but which, it may be feared, will involve all classes in a common ruin.

NOVEMBER 11TH.—No news. I saw, to-day, Gen. Lee's letter of the 7th instant, simply announcing the capture of Hoke's and Haye's brigades. They were on the north side of the river, guarding the *pont de tete*. There is no excuse, no palliation. He said it was likely Meade's entire army would cross. This had been sent by the Secretary to the President, who indorsed upon it as follows: "If it be possible to reinforce, it should be done promptly. Can any militia or local defense men be made available?—J. D." …

I have written Custis Lee, the President's aid, that but one alternative now remains: for the President, or some *one* else, to assume all power, temporarily, and crush the speculators. This I think is the only chance of independence. I may be mistaken—but we shall see.

Capt. Warner, who feeds the 13,000 prisoners here, when he has the means of doing so, says Col. Northrop, the Commissary, does not respond to his requisitions for meat. He fears the prisoners will take or destroy the city, and talks of sending his family out of it.

I condemned the reign of martial law in this city, in 1862, as it was not then necessary, and because its execution was intrusted to improper and obnoxious men. But now I am inclined to think it necessary not only here, but everywhere in the Confederacy. Many farmers refuse to get out their grain, or to sell their meat, because they say they have enough Confederate money! money for the redemption of which their last negro and last acre are responsible. So, if they be permitted to maintain this position, neither the army nor the non-producing class of the population can be subsisted; and, of course, all classes must be

De oberseer he made us trubbel,
An' he dribe us round a spell;
We lock him up in de smoke-house cellar,
Wid de key trown in de well.
De whip is lost, de hand-cuff's broken,
But de massa'll hab his pay.
He's ole enough, big enough, ought to known better
Dan to went an' run away.

Source: "Kingdom Coming," from Louis A. Banks, ed., *Immortal Songs of Camp and Field* (Cleveland, OH: 1899), pp. 140–144, quoted in William Benton, publ., *The Annals of America. Volume 9, 1858–1865: The Crisis of the Union* (Chicago: Encyclopedia Britannica, Inc., 1968), pp. 400–401.

14.6 ABRAHAM LINCOLN, SECOND INAUGURAL ADDRESS (1865)

On March 4, 1865, at the start of his second term, President Lincoln gave what remains the shortest inaugural address in history. In it, he strove to explain how a merciful God could have allowed so cruel a war and how, from the first, the saving of the Union had been bound up with the destruction of slavery.

Fellow-Countrymen:

At this second appearing to take the oath of the presidential office there is less occasion for an extended address than there was at the first. Then a statement, somewhat in detail, of a course to be pursued, seemed fitting and proper. Now, at the expiration of four years, during which public declarations have been constantly called forth on every point and phase of the great contest which still absorbs the attention, and engrosses the energies of the nation, little that is new could be presented. The progress of our arms, upon which all else chiefly depends, is as well known to the public as to myself; and it is, I trust, reasonably satisfactory and encouraging to all. With high hope for the future, no prediction in regard to it is ventured.

On the occasion corresponding to this four years ago, all thoughts were anxiously directed to an impending civil war. All dreaded it—all sought to avert it. While the inaugural address was being delivered from this place, devoted altogether to *saving* the Union without war, urgent agents were in the city seeking to *destroy* it without war—seeking to dissolve the Union and divide effects, by negotiation. Both parties deprecated war, but one of them would *make* war rather than let the nation survive; and the other would *accept* war rather than let it perish. And the war came.

One-eighth of the whole population were colored slaves, not distributed generally over the Union, but localized in the Southern part of it. These slaves constituted a peculiar and powerful interest. All knew that this interest was, somehow, the cause of the war. To strengthen, perpetuate, and extend this interest was the object for which the insurgents would rend the Union, even by war; while the government claimed no right to do more than to restrict the territorial enlargement of it. Neither party expected for the war, the magnitude, or the duration, which it has already attained. Neither anticipated that the *cause* of the conflict might cease with, or even before, the conflict itself should cease. Each looked for an easier triumph, and a result less fundamental and astounding. Both read the same Bible, and pray to the same God; and each invokes His aid against the other. It may seem strange that any men should dare to ask a just God's assistance in wringing their bread from the sweat of other men's faces; but let us judge not that we be not judged. The prayers of both could not be answered; that of neither has been answered fully. The Almighty has His own purposes. "Woe unto the world because of offences! for it must needs be that offences come; but woe to that man by whom the offence cometh!" If we shall suppose that American Slavery is one of those offences which, in the providence of God, must needs come, but which, having continued through His appointed time, He now wills to remove, and that He gives to both North and South this terrible war as the woe due to those by whom the offence came, shall we discern therein any departure from those divine attributes which the believers in a Living God always ascribe to Him? Fondly do we hope—fervently do we pray—that this mighty scourge of war may speedily pass away. Yet, if God wills that it continue, until all the wealth piled by the bond-man's two hundred and fifty years of unrequited toil shall be sunk, and until every drop of blood drawn with the lash shall be paid by another drawn with the sword, as was said three thousand years ago, so still it must be said "the judgments of the Lord are true and righteous altogether."

With malice toward none; with charity for all; with firmness in the right as God gives us to see the right, let us strive on to finish the work we are in; to bind up the nation's wounds; to care for him who shall have borne the battle, and for his widow and his orphan—to do all which may achieve and cherish a just, and a lasting peace, among ourselves, and with all nations.

Source: Abraham Lincoln, "Second Inaugural Address," from Roy P. Basler, ed., *The Collected Works of Abraham Lincoln* (New Brunswick, NJ: Rutgers University Press, 1953), vol. 8, pp. 332–333.

Reconstructing a Nation
1865–1877

< White supremacists fire upon Black men, women, and children, Choctaw County, Alabama, 1874

483

John Dennett Visits a Freedmen's Bureau Court

John Richard Dennett arrived in Liberty, Virginia, on August 17, 1865, on a tour of the South reporting for the magazine *The Nation*. The editors wanted accurate weekly accounts of conditions in the recently defeated Confederate states, and Dennett was the kind of man they could trust: a Harvard graduate, a firm believer in the sanctity of the Union, and a member of the class of elite Yankees who thought of themselves as the "best men" the country had to offer.

At Liberty, Dennett was accompanied by a Freedmen's Bureau agent. The **Freedmen's Bureau** was a branch of the US Army established by Congress to assist the freedpeople, as the formerly enslaved were known. Dennett and the agent went to the courthouse because one of the Freedmen's Bureau's functions was to adjudicate disputes between the freedpeople and southern whites.

The first case was that of an old white farmer who complained that two Black people who worked on his farm were "roamin' about and refusin' to work." He wanted the agent to help find the men and bring them back. Both men had wives and children living on his farm and eating his corn, the old man complained. "Have you been paying any wages?" the Freedmen's Bureau agent asked. "Well, they get what the other niggers get," the farmer answered. "I a'n't payin' great wages this year." There was not much the agent could do, but one of his soldiers volunteered to go and tell the men that "they ought to be at home supporting their wives and children."

A well-to-do planter came in to see if he could fire the Black people who had been working on his plantation since the beginning of the year. Warned not to beat his workers the way he would enslaved people, the planter complained that they were unmanageable without what he considered proper punishment. Under the circumstances, the planter wondered, "Will the Government take them off our hands?" The agent suspected that the planter was looking for a way to dismiss his workforce unpaid at the end of the growing season. "If they've worked on your crops all the year so far," the agent told the planter, "I guess they've got a claim on you to keep them a while longer."

Next came a "good-looking mulatto man" representing a number of African Americans worried that they would be forced into five-year contracts with their employers. "No, it a'n't true," the agent said. Could they rent or buy land to work themselves? "Yes, rent or buy," the agent said. But with no horses, mules, or plows, the formerly enslaved people wanted to see "if the Government would help us out after we get the land." All that the agent could offer was a note from the bureau authorizing them to acquire farms of their own.

The last case involved a field hand whose master had beaten him with a stick. The agent sent the field hand back to work. "Don't be sassy, don't be lazy when you've got work to do; and I guess he won't trouble you." A minute later, the worker returned to procure a letter to his master "enjoining him to keep the peace, as he feared the man would shoot him, he having on two or three occasions threatened to do so."

Most of the cases Dennett witnessed centered on labor relations, which often spilled over into other matters, including the family lives of the formerly enslaved, their civil rights, and their ability to buy land. The freedpeople preferred to work their own land but lacked the resources to rent or buy farms. Black workers and white owners who negotiated wage contracts had trouble figuring out each other's rights and responsibilities. The former masters clung to all their old authority that they could. Freedpeople wanted as free a hand as possible.

The Freedmen's Bureau was in the middle of these conflicts. Generally, agents tried to see to it that freedpeople had written contracts guaranteeing their essential right to work as free laborers, uncoerced by whip, club, or gun. Southern whites resented any intrusion with people they still saw as essentially property, and they let civil authorities know it. The Freedmen's Bureau became a lightning rod for the political conflicts of the Reconstruction period.

Conditions in the South elicited sharply different responses from lawmakers in Washington. At one extreme was President Andrew Johnson, who believed in small government and a speedy readmission of the southern states and looked on the Freedmen's Bureau with suspicion. At the other extreme were radical Republicans calling on the federal government to redistribute confiscated land to former enslaved people, give African American men the vote, and take it away from whites who were not loyal to the United States during the war. In between, there were moderate Republicans who at first tried to work with the president and were content simply to guarantee African Americans' basic civil rights. But as reports of violence and the abusive treatment of the freedpeople reached Washington, Republicans shifted in more radical directions.

Back and forth it went: events in the South triggered policy decisions in Washington, which in turn shaped events in the South. What John Dennett saw in Liberty, Virginia, was a good example of this. Policies set in Washington shaped what the Freedmen's Bureau agent could do for former masters and enslaved people. However, those policies shifted when the Bureau's reports and those of journalists, like Dennett, exposed just how troubled southern conditions were. From this interaction the politics of Reconstruction, and with it a "New South," slowly emerged.

WARTIME RECONSTRUCTION

Even as emancipation began, the US government began experimenting with reconstructing the Union. The two goals merged: by creating new, loyal southern states and making their abolition of slavery a condition for reunion, Lincoln could enact emancipation there without court challenge. Through a generous policy of pardons, he could encourage Confederates to make their peace with the Union, speeding the war's end.

Despite the chorus of cries for hanging Jefferson Davis from a sour-apple tree, few northerners wanted to pursue bloody punishments for the million Confederate soldiers who were technically guilty of treason. In the end, Confederate generals went home unharmed to become lawyers, businessmen, and planters; General Robert E. Lee became a college president. No civil leader was hanged for treason, not even Jefferson Davis. Two years after his arrest, he walked out of prison, thanks to bail put up by northerners like editor Horace Greeley. In later years, former Confederates became senators, governors, and federal judges. Months before the war ended, northerners were raising money to rebuild the southern economy and feed its destitute people. What the North wanted was not vengeance, but guarantees of lasting loyalty and a meaningful freedom. Questions arose with no easy answers: What did it take to reunite America? Should it be restored, or reconstructed, and if the latter, how drastically? How far could yesterday's enemies be trusted? What did freedom mean, and what rights should the "freedpeople" enjoy? In reconstructing society, how far did the government's power go?

Lincoln's Ten Percent Plan Versus the Wade-Davis Bill

Lincoln moved to shape a postwar South based on free labor and to replace military control, Banks's included, with new civil governments. However, wartime Reconstruction had to take Confederate resistance into account. Any terms the president set would need to draw as much white southern support as it could and hold out an inducement to those at war with the United States to return to their old loyalties. In December 1863, Lincoln issued a Proclamation of Amnesty and Reconstruction, offering a full pardon and the restoration of civil rights to all those who swore loyalty to the Union, excluding only a few high-ranking Confederate military and political leaders. When the number of loyal whites in a former Confederate state reached 10 percent of the 1860 voting population, they could organize a new state constitution and government. But Lincoln's **"Ten Per Cent Plan"** also required that the state abolish slavery, just as Congress had demanded before admitting West Virginia earlier that year. Attempts to coax Confederate states back to loyalty foundered, but circumstances in Union-occupied bits of Louisiana proved more promising. Under General Nathaniel Banks's guidance, Free State whites met in New Orleans in 1864 and produced a new state constitution abolishing slavery.

By that time, however, radical Unionists were expecting more. Propertied and well educated, the free Black community in New Orleans pleaded that without equal rights to education and the vote, mere freedom would not be enough. Impressed by their argument, Lincoln hinted to Louisiana authorities that he would welcome steps opening the vote for at least some Blacks. The hints were ignored.

Black spokesmen found a friendlier audience among radical Republicans in Congress, among them Thaddeus Stevens of Pennsylvania and Charles Sumner of Massachusetts. Believing that justice required lowering the color bar for suffrage and setting a more rigorous standard of loyalty for white southerners than Lincoln's plan offered, they shared a much wider concern that any new government must rest on statutory law, not presidential proclamations and military commanders' decrees. They agreed that secession had thrown the political character of the states so far out of kilter that they could not reconstruct themselves unaided—that the federal government must decide what it would take to restore them to proper functioning (a judgment that the Supreme Court would confirm in *Texas v. White* later). But they were not at all prepared to treat Lincoln's "loyal" states as fit to return to Congress—not when so much of Louisiana and Arkansas remained in Confederate hands and was barred from the new constitution-making—not when a speckling of enclaves pretended to speak for the state of Virginia.

As doubts grew about Louisiana's Reconstruction, Congress edged away from Lincoln's program. In mid-1864, Senator Benjamin F. Wade of Ohio and Congressman Henry Winter Davis of Maryland advanced a different plan, requiring a majority of a state's white voters to swear allegiance to the Union before Reconstruction could begin. Slavery must also be abolished and African Americans given full equality before the law. Lincoln pocket-vetoed the Wade-Davis bill to protect the governments that were already under way toward reform. However, he could not make Congress admit a single one of his newly reconstructed states.

The Meaning of Freedom

"We was glad to be set free," a former enslaved person remembered years afterward. "I didn't know what it would be like. It was just like opening the door and lettin' the bird fly out. He might starve, or freeze, or be killed pretty soon but he just felt good because he was free." Blacks' departure came as a terrible shock to masters lulled into believing that their "servants" appreciated their treatment. Some former slave owners persuaded themselves that they were the real gainers of slavery's abolition. "I was glad and thankful—on my own account—when slavery ended and I ceased to belong, body and soul, to my negroes," a Virginia woman later insisted. Forced to do their own cooking or washing, other mistresses fumed at Blacks' ingratitude. In fact, many African Americans left, not out of unkindness, but simply to prove that they could get along on their own. White fears that Blacks, once free, would murder their masters proved groundless.

Leaving the plantation was the first step in a long journey for African Americans. Many took to the roads, some of them returning to their old homes near the coasts, from which masters had evacuated as Union armies approached. Others went searching for family members, parted from them during slavery. For 20 years, Black newspapers carried advertisements, begging for news of a husband or wife long since lost. Those who had not been separated went out of their way to have their marriages secured by law. That way, their children could be made legitimate and their vows made permanent. Once married, men sought work contracts that allowed their families to live with them on plantations. Because Black women across the South had become what the law called "domestic dependents," husbands could refuse employers their wives' services and keep them home. In fact, freedwomen were likelier to work outside the home than white women. They tended the family garden, raised children, hired out as domestics, and, as cotton prices fell, shared the work of hoeing and picking in the fields just so the family could make ends meet.

The end of slavery meant many things to freedpeople. It meant that they could move about their neighborhoods without passes, and that they did not have to step aside to let whites pass them on the street. They could own dogs or carry canes, both among the master's exclusive privileges. They could dress as they pleased or choose their own names, including, for the first time, a surname.

Freedom liberated African Americans from the white minister's take on Christianity. No longer were large portions of the Bible closed off to them. Most southern Blacks withdrew from white churches and established their own congregations, particularly in the Methodist and Baptist faith. In time, the church emerged as a central institution in the southern Black community, the meeting place, social center, and source of comfort that larger society denied them. A dozen years after the war, South Carolina had a thousand ministers of the African Methodist Episcopal Church alone.

To read the Gospel, however, freedpeople needed schooling. One former enslaved man remembered his master's parting words on this matter: "Charles, you is a free man they say, but Ah tells you now, you is still a slave and if you lives to be a hundred you'll STILL be a slave, 'cause you got no education, and education is what makes a man free!" Even before the war ended, northern teachers poured into the South to set up schools. When the fighting stopped, the US Army helped recruit and organize thousands of northern women as teachers, but they could never send enough. Old and young spared what time they had from work, paying teachers in eggs or produce when coin was scarce. Black classes met wherever they could: in mule stables and cotton houses, even the slave pen in New Orleans, where the old auction block became a globe stand. Due to a lack of schoolbooks, they read dictionaries and almanacs. On meager resources, hundreds of thousands of southern Blacks learned to read and write over the next generation. The first Black colleges would be founded in the postwar years, including Hampton Institute in Virginia and Howard University in Washington, DC. The American Missionary Association established seven, Atlanta and Fisk Universities among them.

Finally, freedom allowed freedpeople to congregate, to celebrate the Fourth of July or Emancipation Day, or to petition for equal rights before the law. Memorial Day may have begun with Blacks gathering to honor the Union dead whose sacrifices had helped make them free.

Experiments with Free Labor

Many whites insisted that Blacks would never work in freedom and foresaw a South ruined forever. Freedpeople proved just the opposite. When Union troops landed on the Sea Islands off South Carolina in November 1861, the landlords fled, leaving behind between 5,000 and 10,000 enslaved people. Within months the abandoned plantations of the Sea Islands were being reorganized. Eventually Black families were given small plots of their own to till. In return for their labor they received a "share" of the year's crop. When the masters returned after the war to reclaim their lands, the labor system had already proven itself. Much modified, it would form the basis for the arrangement known as **sharecropping**.

The sugar and cotton plantations around New Orleans provided another opportunity to shape the future of free labor. When the Union army came to occupy New Orleans in 1862, the tens of thousands of field hands on these plantations were no longer enslaved, but the landowners still held possession of the land. Unlike the Sea Islands, these plantations could not be broken up. And sugar plantations could not be effectively organized into small sharecropping units.

Hoping to stem the flow of Black refugees to Union lines and cut the loss of Black lives in the contraband camps, Union general Nathaniel Banks issued stringent regulations to put the freedpeople back to work quickly in Louisiana. At the time, Banks was the commander of the Department of the Gulf during the occupation of New Orleans and his policy, known as the Banks Plan, required freedpeople to sign yearlong contracts to work on their former plantations. Workers would be paid either 5 percent of the proceeds of the crop or three dollars per month. The former masters would provide food and shelter, and African American workers were forbidden to leave the plantations without permission. Established planters welcomed the plan, but many critics protested that Banks had simply replaced one form of slavery with another; however, most freedpeople knew the difference and accepted the work conditions. The Banks Plan became the model for plantations throughout the lower Mississippi Valley.

Understandably, freedpeople wanted land of their own. Only then could they avoid working for their old masters on any terms. "The labor of these people had for two hundred years cleared away the forests and produced crops that brought millions of dollars annually," H. C. Bruce explained. "It does seem to me that a Christian Nation would, at least, have given them one year's support, 40 acres of land and a mule each." As the war ended, many African Americans expected the government's help in becoming landowners. Union general William Tecumseh Sherman heard an appeal from freedpeople on the Sea Islands. "The way we can best take care of ourselves is to have land," they argued, "and turn it out and till it by our own labor." Convinced, Sherman issued Special Field Order No. 15 granting them captured land. By June, 400,000 acres had been distributed to 40,000 former enslaved people.

Congress did not leave matters there. In March 1865, the Republicans established the Bureau of Refugees, Freedmen, and Abandoned Lands, commonly known as the Freedmen's Bureau. In the area of labor relations, the Bureau sometimes sided with landowners against the interests of the freedpeople. But it also provided immediate relief for thousands of people of both races. Indeed, of more than 18 million rations distributed over three years, more than 5 million went to whites in need. The Bureau joined with northern religious groups in creating some 4,000 Black schools. It ran charity hospitals and provided medical services. Freedpeople came to Bureau agents for justice when white-dominated courts denied it and took counsel when labor contracts were to be negotiated. Some agents sided instinctively with the former masters. Most courted white hostility by protecting freedpeople from violence, settling their complaints, advising them on labor contracts, and seeing that employers paid as promised.

The Freedmen's Bureau also became involved in the politics of land redistribution and controlled the disposition of 850,000 acres of confiscated and abandoned Confederate lands. In July 1865, General Oliver Otis Howard, the head of the Bureau, directed his agents to rent the land to the freedpeople in 40-acre plots that they could eventually buy. Many agents believed that to reeducate them in the values of thrift and hard work, the freedpeople should be encouraged to save money and acquire land for themselves. A Freedman's Savings Bank helped many do just that.

Moderate and radical Republicans alike were resolved to press for more than a nominal freedom for Blacks. Equally important, Congress made it clear that it would insist on being consulted in any Reconstruction policy.

PRESIDENTIAL RECONSTRUCTION, 1865–1867

Andrew Johnson took office in April 1865 as a great unknown. Born in a log cabin and too poor to attend school, he began his career on a tailor's bench where he had shown grit and enterprise. In time he had risen to moderate wealth in the eastern Tennessee hill country, enough to own enslaved people, but he never forgot his humble beginnings. Before the war, he had defended slavery and the common man, called for taxpayer-supported public schools, and free homesteads. A courageous Union Democrat in wartime, he had run roughshod over Tennessee Confederates as military governor. He hated treason and the rich planters that he blamed for the war. Johnson deserved much of the credit for Tennessee abolishing slavery; however, he alarmed some radicals along the way who found more pardons than penalties in his policies. Convinced that a lasting reunion of the states could only come by earning white southerners' good will and determined to see the Thirteenth Amendment ratified quickly, the president started Reconstruction six months before Congress convened and left it wholly in white hands. In doing so, he offended not only the radicals favoring a color-blind suffrage but also the moderates who felt that Reconstruction must be done by law and not executive order.

The Political Economy of Contract Labor

Presidential Reconstruction began in late May 1865, when President Johnson offered amnesty and the restoration of property to white southerners who swore loyalty to the Union, excluding only high-ranking Confederate military and political leaders and very rich planters. He named provisional governors in seven seceded states and told them to summon constitutional conventions. For readmission to the Union and restoration of their full privileges, conventions must adopt the Thirteenth Amendment, void their secession ordinances, and repudiate their Confederate war debt. Most of the constitutional conventions met those conditions, though with grumbling and legal quibbling. Many made clear that they still thought the South had been right all along and only bowed to military force. "We have for breakfast salt-fish, fried potatoes, and treason," a lodger at a Virginia boarding house wrote. "Fried potatoes, treason, and salt-fish for dinner. At supper the fare is slightly varied, and we have treason, salt-fish, fried potatoes, and a little more treason."

Elections under these new constitutions would then choose civil governments to replace provisional authority. Only white men covered by the amnesty proclamation or subsequent pardons could vote, but by September Johnson was signing pardons wholesale. Secessionists flocked to the polls. Freshly pardoned Confederates won some of the top offices, former Confederate Vice President Alexander Stephens among them.

White southerners welcomed Johnson's leniency. Once pardoned, they petitioned for restoration of their confiscated or abandoned properties. In September 1865, Johnson ordered the lands returned to their former owners. By late 1865, former enslaved people were being forced off the 40-acre plots that the government agency had given them.

No sooner did conservative legislatures meet than they fashioned **Black Codes** defining, or rather confining, Blacks' new freedom. Some states ordered different punishments: fines for whites and whipping or sale for Black offenders. Elsewhere, lawmakers forbade freedpeople from renting land, owning guns, or buying liquor. Vagrancy laws gave police wide discretion to collar any Black and subject him or her to forced labor, sometimes for an old master. Apprenticeship statutes let the courts take away Black children without parents' consent and bind them out to years of unpaid labor. Blacks were allowed to testify only in certain cases. They were taxed to pay for white schools; the Johnsonian state governments provided them with none of their own.

Landowners gave their Black employees as little as they could. With the legal machinery backing them up, they forced them into labor contracts that stipulated what they could do with their private time. One planter required his Black workers to "go by his direction the same as in slavery time." Other landowners denied them the right to leave the plantation without their "master's" consent. Some arrangements allotted as little as a tenth of the crop in wages, and many employers found an excuse to turn their field hands off unpaid as soon as the crop was in. No wonder many freedmen saw contract labor as slavery under a new name, or that thousands refused to sign any terms at the year's end.

Resistance to Presidential Reconstruction

An undercurrent of violence underlay conservative control. In North Carolina, a resident wrote, the Negro was "sneered at by all and informed daily yes hourly that he is incompetent to care for himself—that his race is now doomed to perish from off the face of the Earth—that he will not work—that he is a thief by nature[,] that he lies more easily and naturally than an honest man breathes." Blacks were assaulted for not showing proper deference to whites, for disputing the terms of labor contracts, or for failing to meet the standards that white employers demanded. Black churches were burned, rebuilt, and burned again. A Bureau agent in Kentucky classified the incidents in just a few counties: twenty-three "cases of severe and inhuman beating and whipping of men; four of beating and shooting; two of robbing and shooting; three of robbing; five men shot and killed; two shot and wounded; four beaten to death; one beaten and roasted; three women assaulted and ravished; four women beaten, two women tied up and whipped until insensible; two men and their families beaten and driven from their homes, and their property destroyed; two instances of burning of dwellings and one of the inmates shot." White witnesses refused to acknowledge what they knew to be true, white judges dismissed cases involving Black defendants, and white juries invariably acquitted offenders. If Johnson expressed content with the speedy restoration of loyalty in the South, a growing chorus of complaints from freedpeople and Unionists down South told a different story.

Congress Clashes with the President

Troubled by presidential Reconstruction's failings, a Republican Congress refused to readmit former Confederate states without investigation. A Joint Committee on Reconstruction was formed to examine their loyalty and the safety of white and Black Unionists' rights. At the same time, moderate Republicans also wanted to design a program for readmission that Johnson would support. By expanding the power of the Freedmen's Bureau and proposing a Civil Rights bill, they thought they had the makings of a compromise.

The first extended the Bureau's life, strengthened its powers, and let it set up courts that allowed Black testimony. The second overturned the Dred Scott decision, by granting United States citizenship to American men regardless of race. This marked the first time that the federal government intervened in states' rights to guarantee due process and basic civil rights.

To Republicans' amazement, Johnson vetoed both bills and in terms that made no compromise possible. Hinting that Congress had no right to reconstruct until the southern states were readmitted and doubting Blacks' fitness to enjoy the same civil rights as whites, the president declared Reconstruction completed. Unable to override the Freedmen's Bureau bill veto, Congress did pass the Civil Rights bill, which served as the foundation for section one of the Fourteenth Amendment, and later carried a new Freedmen's Bureau bill.

Origins of the Fourteenth Amendment

During the spring of 1866, the Joint Committee on Reconstruction proposed a **Fourteenth Amendment** to the Constitution, outlining the conditions that Republicans thought were essential for a just and lasting peace. Provisions guaranteed payment of the national debt and prevented payment of the Confederate one. Confederates who had held public office before the war were barred from office until Congress removed their disabilities. Replacing the Constitution's three-fifths clause, which counted enslaved people as three-fifths of a person for the purpose of taxation and representation, representation in Congress would now be based on a state's voting population. If freed Blacks entitled southern states to additional House seats, that representation entitled Blacks to the right to vote (see Table 15–1). "Happy will our disappointment be if this dry stalk shall bud and blossom into Impartial Suffrage," one radical wrote, doubtfully. Even if it did not, the South would return to Congress weaker in strength than it had left. But the crucial provision wrote civil rights guarantees into fundamental law, guaranteeing citizenship to all American-born males. Few of its authors could foresee how, over the century to come, its promise would expand the national commitment to furthering equality, not just for men but for women and other disadvantaged groups; nor could they see how far it could be used to expand the government's authority to set things right.

Deserted by the party that had elected him, Johnson fought on. He launched the National Union movement, a bipartisan coalition of conservatives whose goal was to defeat Republicans at the midterm elections. A railroad tour to Chicago and back to Washington allowed him to make his case to the American people. However, the National Union movement fizzled; hardly any Republican thought the proposed Amendment presented unfair terms for a defeated South. Johnson's "Swing Around the Circle" tour ended in crowds trading insults with the president.

Anti-Freedmen's Bureau Poster Led by President Andrew Johnson, attacks on the Freedmen's Bureau became more and more openly racist in late 1865 and 1866. This Democratic Party broadside was circulated during the 1866 election.

Two incidents confirmed northern fears that presidential Reconstruction had left southern Unionists defenseless. On May 1, 1866, after two drivers—one Black, one white—had a traffic accident, Memphis police arrested the Black one. A group of Black veterans tried to prevent the arrest, and as a result, a white crowd gathered. A riot broke out. Over the next three days, white mobs burned hundreds of homes, destroyed churches, and attacked Black schools. Five Black women were raped; nearly fifty people, all but two of them Black, were killed.

Three months later, violence of an explicitly political dimension broke out in New Orleans. Alarmed at former Confederates' return to power in Louisiana, "Free Staters" sought to recall the state's 1864 constitutional convention. They may have meant to open voting rights to some Blacks or cut "rebels" out, but they never got the chance. On July 30, 1866, when a few dozen delegates assembled at Mechanics' Institute, white mobs set on the convention's supporters, who were mostly Black. Led by police and firemen, many of them Confederate veterans, rioters opened fire on a Black parade and broke into the convention hall. "The floor was covered with blood," one victim remembered, "and in walking downstairs the blood splashed under the soles of my boots." Blacks trying to surrender were gunned down. By the time the attackers dispersed, 34 Blacks and 3 white supporters had been killed, and another 100 had been injured.

Table 15–1 Reconstruction Amendments, 1865–1870

Amendment	Main Provisions	Congressional Passage (two-thirds majority in each house required)	Ratification Process (three-quarters of all states including ex-Confederate states required)
13	Slavery prohibited in the United States	January 1865	December 1865 (27 states, including 8 southern states)
14	1. National citizenship for all men and women born in the United States	June 1866	Rejected by 12 southern and border states, February 1867
	2. State representation in Congress reduced proportionally to number of voters disfranchised		Radicals make readmission of southern states hinge on ratification
	3. Former high-ranking Confederates denied right to hold office until Congress removes disabilities		Ratified July 1868
	4. Confederate debt repudiated		
15	Denial of franchise because of race, color, or past servitude explicitly prohibited	February 1869	Ratification required for readmission of Virginia, Texas, Mississippi, and Georgia; ratified March 1870

CONGRESSIONAL RECONSTRUCTION

The elections of 1866 became a referendum on whether Johnson's policies had gone far enough to assure the permanent safety of the Union. But they also posed competing visions of what American democracy should mean. For President Johnson, "democracy" meant government by local majorities, which often meant white supremacy. For African Americans and a growing number of Republicans in Congress, genuine democracy demanded a firm foundation of equal civil and political rights. The sweep that followed brought in an even more solidly Republican Congress than before and doomed presidential Reconstruction. Congressional Reconstruction would be far different. It was an extraordinary series of events, second only to emancipation in its impact on the history of the United States.

The South Remade

Republicans had agreed on the Fourteenth Amendment's provisions as a final settlement of the war's issues. Southern states that ratified it would be readmitted, whether they enfranchised Blacks or not. Tennessee ratified the amendment and was readmitted to Congress immediately. But in the remaining southern states, conservatives rejected the amendment by wide margins, and with the president's encouragement. As unpunished assaults on Unionists and freedpeople continued, Congress lost patience. In the short run, the army could keep order, but a long-term solution was needed. Moderate Republicans came to agree with radicals: only by putting loyal men, regardless of race, in charge could a loyal, just South come into being. The only other alternative would be an open-ended national commitment to rule the South by force.

Although they were far from what radical Republicans had hoped for, in March 1867, Congress passed two Reconstruction Acts. Leaving the Johnsonian state governments in office, the acts declared them provisional and their officeholders subject to removal if they hamstrung the Reconstruction process. Ten ex-Confederate states were divided into five military districts and placed under army supervision (see Map 15–1). The army would register voters, both white and Black, except for the comparatively small number disqualified by the not-yet-ratified Fourteenth Amendment. To regain congressional representation, each state must call a constitutional convention and draw up a new constitution providing for equal civil and political rights. Voters then must ratify it, and the newly elected governments must adopt the Fourteenth Amendment. Military oversight would end as civil authority replaced it. Thus, most white southern men had a say in constructing the new political order, and when those states were readmitted, they were granted the same rights as others. For all the laws' limits, remaking state governments and requiring a broader male suffrage promised a Radical Reconstruction indeed.

The Impeachment and Trial of Andrew Johnson

Johnson could not stop congressional Reconstruction. But he could temper it. Battling now to protect the executive's powers, Johnson shared Democrats' fears that Congress had veered far from the Constitution, placing military authority above civil authority and overturning what he saw as the natural order of society, where Blacks were kept in subordination.

In vain, radical Republicans called for Johnson's impeachment. Instead, Congress tried to restrain him by law. The **Tenure of Office Act** kept the president from removing officials who had been appointed in his administration with Senate confirmation. Another law required that every presidential order to the military pass through General **Ulysses S. Grant**. Johnson could still dismiss district commanders (and did when they interpreted their powers differently than he did), but as long as Grant headed the army and Edwin M. Stanton the War Department, Republicans felt that they had safeguarded the Reconstruction Acts against a potential coup.

Provoked by these challenges to his authority, Johnson issued interpretations of the Reconstruction Acts to permit wider conservative registration, forcing Congress into special session to revise the law with a Third Reconstruction Act. He issued broader amnesty proclamations for former Confederates, forced the dismissal of Republican officers, and, abiding by the Tenure of Office Act, suspended Stanton in August 1867. When the Senate reinstated him the following winter, Johnson ordered him ejected. "What good did your moderation do you?" radical Republican Thaddeus Stevens taunted moderates. "If you don't kill the beast, he will kill you." With the law seemingly broken, the House impeached Johnson.

**Map 15–1
Reconstruction and
Redemption** By
1870, Congress had
readmitted every
southern state to the
Union. In most cases
the Republican Party
retained control of
the "reconstructed"
state governments for
only a few years.

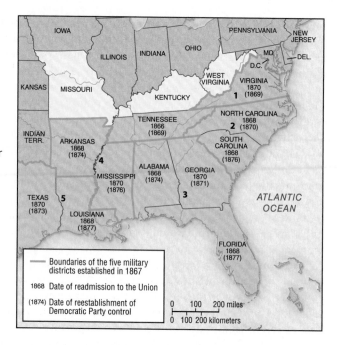

The expected removal never happened. Rejecting Stevens's argument that presidential obstruction was enough for conviction, senators required an intentional violation of law. The Tenure of Office Act's wording was so unclear that it may not have applied to Stanton. When the president promised to restrain himself and chose a successor to Stanton that moderates trusted, the impeachment process lost momentum. In May, the Senate fell one vote short of the two-thirds needed to convict. Within a month, Congress had readmitted seven southern states, thus limiting Johnson's power to stymie Reconstruction in those states; with Grant's election to the presidency that fall, the new governments had whatever backing the army could afford them.

Radical Reconstruction in the South

With the help of Union Leagues, auxiliaries of the Republican Party whose goal was to mobilize and educate Black voters, and with military protection against conservative violence in place, **Radical Reconstruction** transformed the Cotton South dramatically. Within six months, 735,000 Blacks and 635,000 whites had registered to vote. Blacks formed electoral majorities in South Carolina, Florida, Mississippi, Alabama, and Louisiana. In most states they found white support in the so-called scalawags, white Southerners who supported Reconstruction and Republican policies. Wartime Unionists, hill farmers neglected by planter-dominated governments, debtors seeking relief, development-minded businessmen seeking a new, more diversified South, and even some Confederate leaders and planters all welcomed Radical Reconstruction. Carpetbaggers, northerners who had come south to farm, invest, preach, or teach, were few in numbers, but they took a front rank among the leaders in Black-majority states.

Starting in the fall of 1867, ten states called constitutional conventions, heavily Republican and predominantly, but not exclusively, white. The results of these conventions' so-called Black and Tan constitutions guaranteed a color-blind right to suffrage, mandated public school systems, and overhauled the tax structure. They also included a right to bear arms in their bills of rights. Only a few states shut any Confederates out of the vote, and most of those that did removed the electoral disabilities before a year was out.

Achievements and Failures of Radical Government

Later caricatured as a dire era of "bayonet" and "negro rule," Radical Reconstruction was neither. The Republican governments won in fairer elections and with greater turnouts than any that the South had known up until that time. Republican leadership remained overwhelmingly white and southern born. While some 700 Blacks served in state legislatures, only in South Carolina and possibly Louisiana did they ever outnumber whites. No state elected a Black governor, while only 16 Blacks served in Congress, 2 of whom were senators. Still, the contrast between what had been and what would follow was revolutionary. These Reconstruction legislatures were more representative of their constituents than most legislatures in nineteenth-century America (see Figure 15–1). While some African American officeholders were indeed illiterate, former enslaved people who did not own land, a disproportionate number came from the tiny prewar free African American elite of ministers, teachers, and small business owners. Freedpeople also filled hundreds of county offices. They served as sheriffs, bailiffs, judges, and jurors, offering the promise, at least, of a fair hearing in court for Black defendants and litigants. Sharing power locally meant a greater chance for Black communities to share in the benefits of public expenditures.

Republican rule delivered on its promises. The whipping post and debtor's prison vanished. The new governments funded insane asylums, roads, and prisons.

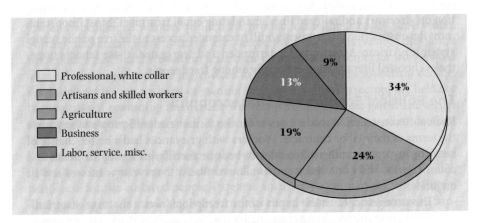

Professional, white collar
Artisans and skilled workers
Agriculture
Business
Labor, service, misc.

9%
13%
34%
19%
24%

Figure 15–1   Occupations of Black Officeholders During Reconstruction
Although former enslaved people were underrepresented among Black officeholders, the Reconstruction governments were among the most broadly representative legislatures in US history.

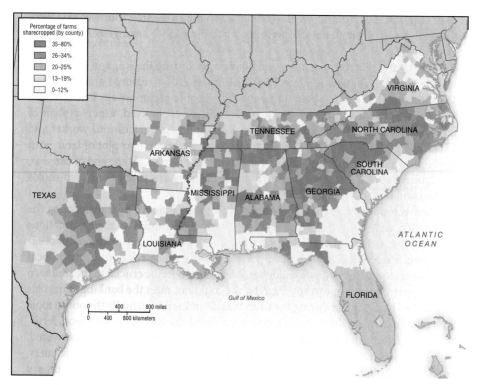

Map 15-2 Sharecropping By 1880, the sharecropping system had spread across the South. It was most common in the inland areas, where primarily cotton and tobacco plantations existed before the Civil War.

marriages had no legal standing. With emancipation, these patriarchal assumptions of American family law shaped the lives of freed men and women. Once married, women often found that their property belonged to their husbands. The sharecropping system further assumed that as head of the household the husband made the economic decisions for the entire family. Men signed most labor contracts, and most contracts assumed that the husband would take his family to work with him.

Sharecropping shaped the social system of the postwar South. It influenced the balance of power between men and women. It established the balance of power between landowners and sharecroppers. It tied the southern economy to agriculture, in particular to cotton production, impeding the region's overall economic development.

The Gospel of Prosperity

Only a diversified economy could break the planters' hold over a Black labor force; railroads could lower farmers' shipping costs and tap the South's coal and iron resources. Economic development might even give the South an independence worth having: it was no longer required to look north for its investment capital or finished goods. A program that made all classes prosper seemed ready-made to recruit more whites for a party and push racial issues into the background. Republicans

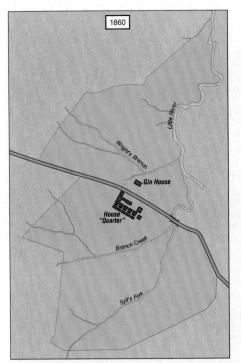
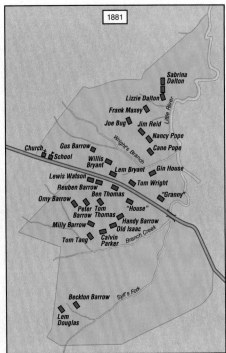

Map 15-3   The Effect of Sharecropping in the South: The Barrow Plantation in Oglethorpe County, Georgia Sharecropping cut large estates into small landholdings worked by sharecroppers and tenants, changing the landscape of the South.

preached a "gospel of prosperity" that would use government aid to build a richer South and benefit ordinary white southerners. Reconstruction governments committed the states' credit and funds to building its industrial base.

The strategy had big drawbacks. Diverting scarce resources to railroads and corporations left less for Black constituencies' needs, especially school systems. Investors hesitated to invest in bonds issued by governments at risk of violent overthrow. Hungry corporations hounded the legislature for favors and made bribery their clinching argument. State-owned railroads were sold to private firms for a song—and a payoff. States already spending heavily to repair the damage of the war and to build new state services on a much-reduced tax base obligated themselves for millions more. As taxes soared, white farmers became increasingly receptive to Democratic claims that they were being robbed, their money wasted by swag-grabbing outsiders and ignorant Black upstarts in office. The passage of civil rights bills, ending discrimination in public transportation, only alienated former scalawags further and stirred conservatives to bring the stay-at-homes to the polls. Everywhere, Republicans split over how far to trust former Confederates. That division cost Virginia and Tennessee to the "Redeemers," conservative white Democrats, in 1869. In Arkansas, two Republicans claimed the governorship in 1872. Two years later they raised armies to fight it out. The "Brooks-Baxter war" ended with the Democrat-backed contestant winning and a new constitution that put both Republicans out for good.

"A COMPANY OF WHITES LAY IN AMBUSH FOR A PARTY OF NEGROES RETURNING FROM CHURCH, KILLED TEN, AND WOUNDED THIRTEEN."

Reconstruction Violence Terrorism against Republican governments targeted churches, schools, and Black landowners, not just the politically active. In this engraving, a band of white supremacists fire upon a group of Black people returning from church services in Choctaw County, Alabama, August 1, 1874.

A Counterrevolution of Terrorism and Economic Pressure

Republicans' policy failures alone did not destroy them. Terrorism and economic pressure did. Everywhere planters used their power to keep Black tenants from voting. White radicals found themselves shunned by society. They were denied credit or employment unless they left politics. As early as 1867, secret organizations were arising, bent on Reconstruction's overthrow and the restoration of white dominance, which, effectively, meant bringing Democrats into power by threats, beatings, and killings. From the Carolinas to Texas, the **Ku-Klux Klan** and similar organizations shot Republican lawmakers and burned Black schools and

America In The World
Reconstructing America's Foreign Policy

As the Civil War approached, slavery's expansionists tainted manifest destiny for everyone but Democrats. Republicans had no intention of spreading an empire of the unfree—nor of letting any European power do so. In Mexico, the French emperor had installed a puppet state headed by Maximilian, the Austrian archduke. The Johnson administration helped force France to withdraw its troops. Unbacked, Maximilian's regime collapsed. Spreading the republic's bounds would only spread liberty. It might even give Black southerners a place free of race prejudice where they could fulfill their potential. Secretary of State William Seward dreamed of all North America, perhaps even most of the Caribbean, as one vast federation; Senator Charles Sumner suggested that the United States ease Canada into the Union.

Nothing of the kind happened. Seward's biggest success came in 1867, in purchasing Alaska from Russia. A few months later, however, the Senate

rejected a treaty buying the Virgin Islands from Denmark and held off on leasing a naval base in Santo Domingo. A treaty with Colombia giving the United States exclusive rights to build a canal across the Isthmus of Panama came to nothing. Canadians showed no interest in joining the Union and instead forged a union of their own separate provinces.

Not all the wealth of the West Indies could carry the United States beyond trade to the taking of territory. Slavery's end killed most of the zest for annexing Cuba; the fact that its people were Catholics and racially diverse alarmed even some Republicans. When a rebellion broke out there in 1868, Congress did nothing about it. Similar inhibitions thwarted Grant's plan to annex Santo Domingo in 1870. As head of the Senate Foreign Relations Committee, Sumner's opposition doomed the treaty and, ironically, himself; as a result, Grant and Fish forced the Senate to depose him from his chairmanship.

churches, often in broad daylight. Black landowners and renters were targeted. African American employees or tenants who complained about being cheated faced flogging or death for "insolence." Teachers, party organizers, and white wartime Unionists all fell victim. Politically active Blacks were threatened, driven from their homes, whipped, or shot. Their wives were raped and their homes plundered while Democratic newspapers defamed the victims. In a single year, authorities counted well over 500 killings in Georgia alone—and just about no arrests, much less indictments. Witnesses refused to testify, cowed juries dared not convict, and sheriffs dared not arrest. In Arkansas, Texas, and Tennessee, Republican governors mustered a white militia that broke the terrorist movement. Elsewhere they found themselves powerless or outgunned. Terrorism carried North Carolina, Alabama, and Georgia for the Democrats in 1870, crippling Reconstruction in the first state and effectively ending it in the other two. By 1872, Redeemers had regained the

Charles Russell, *Buffalo Hunt* More devastating to Plains nations than military attacks were the slaughter of the buffalo herds that fed and clothed them and were used in every aspect of their culture.

sporadic, and ugly. The ugliest came at **Wounded Knee, South Dakota,** in 1890. Fearing that the Ghost Dance religious revival movement would stir up rebellion, soldiers gunned down over 200 Native American men, women, and children. Sitting Bull did not live to see it. He had been shot resisting arrest days before.

Reforming Native American Tribes out of Existence

Sharing none of the settlers' fear of and less of their contempt for Indians, reformers hoped that reservations would function not just as holding pens, but as schools and civilizers. Lincoln's commissioner of Indian Affairs, William P. Dole, believed that "Indians are capable of attaining a high degree of civilization." Like other reformers, Dole equated civilization with a belief in individual property rather than communal holdings, Christian values rather than native religions, and the discipline of the regular hours that farmers and workers, rather than hunters, observed. Accordingly, reformers set out, as one of them put it, to destroy the Indian and save the person. They introduced government schools on reservations to teach the virtues of private property, individual achievement, and social mobility.

The reformers' influence peaked in 1887 when Congress passed the Dawes Severalty Act, the most important Indian legislation of the century, and the very kind of confiscation never done on freedpeoples' behalf. Reservation land was broken up into separate plots and distributed among individual families. The goal was to force Indians to live like white farmers, or as one reformer would put it later, killing the Indian and saving the man. But the lands allotted were generally so poor, and the plots so small, that their owners quickly sold them. Large tracts were kept in trust by the government and gradually sold off, purportedly to pay for uplifting and assimilating the Indians. By the early twentieth century only a few, sharply diminished reservations remained outside the desert Southwest. Native American cultures endured, but many Native Americans did not. Poverty, overcrowding, and epidemic disease brought their population to its lowest point. For many eastern onlookers, those conditions only proved how unworthy the race was to compete in the struggle for life—a conclusion all too many had drawn about African Americans from Reconstruction's downfall.

THE RETREAT FROM REPUBLICAN RADICALISM

A series of makeshift laws and improvisations, congressional Reconstruction had stirred misgivings among moderate Republicans who were fearful of stretching the Constitution too far and uneasy with using the expanded authority that war had given them in peacetime. New steps, such as confiscating planters' property, say, or a nationally funded school system, were out of the question. Even the Freedmen's Bureau was cut back, and except for education, closed down completely when reconstructed states were readmitted to Congress. Public backlash against radicalism gave Democrats heavy gains in the 1867 elections. In order to survive, Reconstruction had to consolidate its gains and leave the new state governments to meet its promises.

Republicans Become the Party of Moderation

By then, the 1868 presidential campaign was under way. Running the war hero General Ulysses S. Grant for president, Republicans could offer a candidate above politics. His slogan, "Let us have peace," emphasized that the party meant to restore the Union, rather than advance radicalism. The platform endorsed congressional Reconstruction and defended Black voting in the South, but it left states not covered by Reconstruction to decide the issue of suffrage for themselves. Positioning themselves as protectors of the war's accomplishments came all the more easily after Democrats nominated former New York governor Horatio Seymour on a platform declaring the Reconstruction Acts as illegal, null, and void. Their fiercest spokesmen swore that if Democrats won, they would overturn the newly elected southern governments and install white conservative ones. Voiding those governments would invalidate the Fourteenth Amendment, ratified by southern legislatures; some partisans even argued that every measure passed since southern congressmen walked out in 1861 had no legal force. Bondholders, fearful that Democrats would turn their national securities into waste paper or pay them in depreciated "greenbacks," thought Grant the safer choice, even without Republicans' shouting that Seymour's election would reward traitors and bring on civil war again.

Northern voters got a taste of what Democratic rule would mean in an epidemic of violence across the South. Riots and massacres in Louisiana and Georgia kept Republicans from voting and carried both states for Seymour. For Northern voters, those outrages may have been decisive in electing Grant. Carrying the electoral college by a huge margin, he won the popular vote more narrowly with just 53 percent, and then only because of a heavy Black turnout in his favor.

RECONSTRUCTING THE NORTH

Although Reconstruction was aimed primarily at the South, the North was affected as well, especially by the struggle over the Black vote. The transformation of the North was an important chapter in the history of Reconstruction.

The Fifteenth Amendment and Nationwide African American Suffrage

Segregated into separate facilities or excluded entirely, denied the right to vote in nearly every state outside of New England, Blacks in wartime fought to end discrimination in the North. Biracial efforts chipped away at many states' discriminatory Black Laws and the Fourteenth Amendment eliminated the rest nationwide. Streetcar lines in some cities stopped running separate cars, Black testimony was admitted on the same terms as white, and in a few northern communities, Black children began attending white schools. Ending the color bar on voting and jury service proved to be more difficult: when impartial suffrage went on the ballot, most northern states voted against it (though most Republicans favored it and Congress mandated it in the territories and the District of Columbia).

The shocking electoral violence of 1868 persuaded Republicans that equal suffrage in the South needed permanent protection. In 1869, Congress added a **Fifteenth Amendment** to the Constitution forbidding the use of "race, color, or previous condition of servitude" as a bar to suffrage in the North as well as the South. For those states not yet readmitted to the Union (Virginia, Mississippi, and Texas), it made ratification of the amendment an additional condition. On March 30, 1870, the Fifteenth Amendment became part of the Constitution.

Revolutionary as it was, the Fifteenth Amendment had serious limitations that would weaken its impact later. As the Supreme Court would note, it conferred no right to vote on anybody. It simply limited the grounds on which it could be denied. States could impose property or taxpaying qualifications or a literacy test if they pleased, as long as the restrictions made no distinction on the basis of race. They could set up residency requirements or limit the vote to naturalized citizens, or to men.

Women and Suffrage

The issue of Black voting added to tensions among northern radicals. Feminists and abolitionists had worked together in the struggle for emancipation, but signs of trouble appeared as early as May 1863 at the convention of the Woman's National Loyal League in New York City. The League had been organized to assist in defeating the slave South. One of the convention's resolutions declared that "there never can be a true peace in this Republic until the civil and political rights of all citizens of African descent and all women are practically established." For some delegates, this went too far. They argued that it was inappropriate to inject the issue of women's rights into the struggle to restore the Union.

With the war's end, the radical crusade for Black suffrage intensified debate among reformers. **Elizabeth Cady Stanton** and others pointed out the injustice of letting "Patrick and Sambo and Hans and Yung Tung" vote while propertied, educated women were denied suffrage. The Fourteenth Amendment, by privileging male inhabitants' right to vote explicitly, appalled Stanton, and the Fifteenth Amendment's failure to address gender discrimination at the polls only confirmed her suspicion that what one abolitionist called "the Negro's hour" would never give way to one for women. Friendly to women's suffrage though they were, abolitionists like Frederick Douglass and suffragists like Lucy Stone argued that the critical issue was the protection of the freedpeople. "When women, because they are women, are dragged from their homes and hung upon lamp-posts," Douglass reminded an audience, "when their children are torn from their arms and their brains dashed to the pavement; when they are the objects of insult and outrage at every turn; when they are in danger of having their homes burnt down over their heads; when their children are not allowed to enter schools; then they will have an urgency to obtain the ballot." In 1869, radical and abolitionist allies parted ways. The women's suffrage movement divided into rival organizations, Stanton's National Woman Suffrage Association and Stone's American Woman Suffrage Association.

Some radicals, Charles Sumner among them, favored women's suffrage. Most Republicans did not. The territories of Wyoming and Utah enfranchised women. Elsewhere, lawmakers let women participate in school-board elections, but voting reform went no further. Most states refused even to put the issue on the ballot. When they did so, it was voted down. Denying women's appeal that as citizens they were entitled to vote, the Supreme Court declared that the Fourteenth Amendment's right of citizenship carried no such right with it.

THE END OF RECONSTRUCTION

Events outside the South helped speed Reconstruction's collapse. Reform-oriented Republicans felt alarm at the spread of political corruption after the war. Convinced, too, that full reconciliation must come, now that the war's goals had been met, they broke with the party and abandoned their support for federal intervention in southern affairs. Additionally, a depression took voters' minds off Reconstruction issues. By 1876, **Redemption** had carried white Democrats to power in all but a few southern states. Yet a hotly disputed presidential election and divided power would doom even those.

Corruption Is the Fashion

Never before had corruption loomed so large in the United States. With more money to spend, more favors to give, and more functions to perform, both state and federal governments found themselves besieged by supplicants, and office-holders found opportunities to turn a dishonest penny where none had existed before. In New York City, infamous state senator William M. Tweed used the **Tammany Hall** political machine to steal tens of millions of dollars. Senators bought their seats in Kansas and South Carolina, while Tennessee congressmen sold appointments to West Point. The Standard Oil Company did everything with the Pennsylvania legislature except refine it. As Henry Clay Warmoth, the governor of Louisiana put it, corruption was "the fashion." He, incidentally, was very fashionable himself.

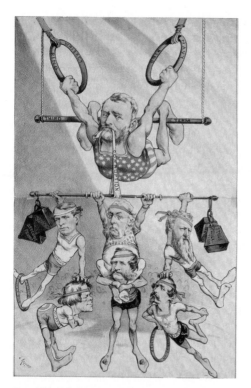

President Grant as a Strong Man Despite solid accomplishments and his own honesty, Ulysses S. Grant would be remembered for scandals in just about every department. Here he upholds various corrupt "rings" and the thieves and hacks that mulcted the War and Navy Departments, the government of the District of Columbia, and the custom-house service.

With an honest but credulous chief executive, Grant's administration became notoriously corrupt. Customs collectors shook down merchants and used their employees to manage party conventions. With help from administration insiders, the notorious speculators Jay Gould and Jim Fisk tried to corner the nation's gold supply and brought on a brief, ruinous panic on Wall Street. Grant's private secretary was even exposed as a member of the "Whiskey Ring," a group of distillers and revenue agents who cheated the government out of millions of dollars in taxes. Charges of making money by swindling the Indians forced the Secretary of Interior out of office. Months later, the Secretary of War quit when investigators traced kickbacks to his wife. Having overcharged the government for supplies while building the Union Pacific Railroad, the fraudulent Credit Mobilier contracting firm shared mammoth profits with nearly a dozen top congressmen. The Republican platform, one critic snarled, was just a conjugation of the verb "to steal."

Southern corruption reflected national patterns. In the worst states, both parties stole, bribed, and profited. But in the South, Democrats blamed such action on ignorant Black voters and nonlandowning white Republicans. Shifting the issue from equal rights to honest government, they insisted that clean, cheap government, run by society's natural leaders (white and well-heeled), would benefit all races. Every scandal discredited Republican rule further, including the many upright and talented leaders, both Black and white, that fought against corruption. This helped galvanize the opposition, destroying Republican hopes of attracting white voters and weakening support for Reconstruction. By 1875, northerners assumed the worst of any carpetbagger, even one fighting to cut taxes and block cheats.

Liberal Republicans Revolt

Voicing widely held concerns, a small, potent group of northern Republican intellectuals, editors, and activists challenged a political system that, in their view, rested on greed, selfishness, partisanship, and politicians' keeping war hatreds alive. Known as **liberal Republicans**, they viewed bosses and political machines, which were out to loot the Treasury, and special interests as detrimental to good government. They were weary of railroads receiving land grants, of steamship lines receiving subsidies, and government clerkships given to cronies. Decrying corruption and disenchanted with Reconstruction, they called for reform: a lower tariff, a stable currency system based on gold, a merit-based civil service system for appointments to office, and full, universal amnesty for former Confederates.

When Democrats announced a "New Departure," accepting the three constitutional amendments, liberal Republicans took them at their word. Despairing of preventing Grant's renomination, they nominated the eccentric, reform-minded editor **Horace Greeley** for president in 1872. The platform promised to remove all political disabilities and reconcile North and South, in essence by ending all federal intervention on Black southerners' behalf. Desperate to win, Democrats endorsed the editor, their lifelong enemy, but thousands stayed home on Election Day rather than vote for him. Having cut the tariff and restored the office-holding rights of all but a handful of ex-Confederates, Republicans won many reformers back. Greeley lost in a landslide and died in a sanitarium less than a month later.

Grant's reelection bought Reconstruction time; it could not do more than that. Northerners, even Republican ones, became increasingly alarmed every time the national government used its power to act on behalf of Reconstruction governments and deal with issues that should be handled by local authorities. As a result, the president found it increasingly hard to justify intervening on the behalf of Black voters.

"Redeeming" the South

In September 1873, America's premier financial institution, Jay Cooke & Company, went bankrupt after overextending itself on investments in the Northern Pacific Railroad. Within weeks, hundreds of banks and thousands of businesses failed. The country sank into a depression that lasted five years. Unemployment rose to 14 percent as corporations slashed wages. Bitter strikes in textile plants, coal fields, and on the railroad lines ended in failure and violence. As America turned its attention to issues of corruption, labor unrest, and economic depression, Reconstruction took a backseat.

Between the corruption scandals buffeting the Grant administration and the economic crisis, northern voters' interest in Reconstruction plummeted. Those who had favored government intervention to keep "Rebels" from coming to power no longer saw the need. Former Confederates stood by the flag as earnestly as Unionists. In the 1874 elections, Democrats made a dramatic comeback. For the first time since 1859, they carried the House, guaranteeing a deadlocked Congress. Outgoing Republicans made one last advance, passing Charles Sumner's civil rights bill, which outlawed discrimination in public places. The law left segregated schools and cemeteries alone, and most southern establishments ignored even those provisions that did pass. But with Congress's adjournment in March 1875, Republicans no longer had any chance of bolstering Reconstruction with legislation, or even funding an army big enough to protect a fair vote at the polls.

Supreme Court rulings made implementing Reconstruction legislation harder still. In the 1873 *Slaughterhouse* cases, a majority decided that the Fourteenth Amendment's protection of equal rights under the law covered only those rights associated with national citizenship. Rights affiliated with state citizenship—for

forced most scalawags to drop out of politics, making it easier to draw a sharp color line. Paramilitaries then applied violence and intimidation to keep Blacks from the polls. By the fall of 1874, they were overthrowing local governments in Mississippi and Louisiana. White Leagues took over the streets in New Orleans and briefly ousted the governor. Terrorism helped "redeem" Alabama that November, among other places.

That left two securely Republican states, both with considerable Black majorities: South Carolina and Mississippi. In 1875, Democrats in the latter mounted the most flagrant show of force yet. Governor Adelbert Ames begged for federal help and was told to look to his own resources first. The election that followed was as quiet as White League shotguns could make it. In the end, enough Blacks were disfranchised and enough scalawags voted their racial prejudices to hand power to the Democrats. Within months they forced Ames's resignation. In 1876, South Carolina whites adopted the "Mississippi Plan" with an even more open commitment to violent overthrow of the Republican majority. Mounted, armed men broke up Republican rallies. In Hamburg, white paramilitaries besieged local Black militiamen and, after their surrender, killed seven of them. "We write to tell you that our people are being shot down like dogs, and no matter what democrats may say," one South Carolinian wrote the president, "unless you help us our folks will not dare go to the polls." In Louisiana, Redeemer violence may have been worse still.

The Twice-Stolen Election of 1876

Amid a serious economic depression, and with an electorate tired of Reconstruction, the Democrats stood a good chance of winning the presidency in 1876. The Democratic candidate, New York governor Samuel J. Tilden, had won a reputation for fighting thieves in his own party. On election night, Tilden won 250,000 more votes than his equally reform-minded Republican opponent, Ohio governor Rutherford B. Hayes (see Map 15–5). But Republican "returning boards" in three southern states—Florida, South Carolina, and Louisiana—counted Hayes in to a one-electoral vote victory.

Democrats swore that they had been cheated out of the presidency, though even without white violence and vote-rigging, Hayes probably would have won not just in the three disputed states but elsewhere in the South. As Congress deadlocked on the electoral count, cries of "Tilden or Blood" rang in the air. In the end, both sides compromised by choosing a special electoral commission to settle the matter. In an eight-to-seven vote, it awarded Hayes every disputed state. House Democrats could not stop "His Fraudulency" from being sworn in, but their southern members, cutting the best deal they could, agreed to drop their obstruction in return for assurances that Hayes would not prop up the last two Reconstruction governments. A month after taking office, Hayes withdrew the regiments guarding Republican statehouses in South Carolina and Louisiana; by then Redeemer Democrats had full control of the states anyway. So Reconstruction met its symbolic end. Hereafter, the president would emphasize goodwill between the North and South and trust Redeemers' promises to protect Black rights—a trust speedily betrayed, and nowhere more so than on the farms where most freedpeople worked for a white landowner.

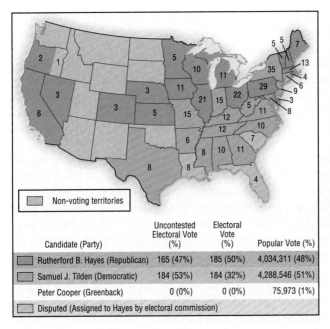

Map 15–5   The Presidential Election, 1876 In 1876, the Democratic presidential candidate, Samuel Tilden, won what popular vote white southern Democrats permitted to be cast, but he was denied the presidency because Republicans claimed that a fair count gave Louisiana, South Carolina, Oregon, and Florida to their candidate, Rutherford B. Hayes.

Candidate (Party)	Uncontested Electoral Vote (%)	Electoral Vote (%)	Popular Vote (%)
Rutherford B. Hayes (Republican)	165 (47%)	185 (50%)	4,034,311 (48%)
Samuel J. Tilden (Democratic)	184 (53%)	184 (32%)	4,288,546 (51%)
Peter Cooper (Greenback)	0 (0%)	0 (0%)	75,973 (1%)
Disputed (Assigned to Hayes by electoral commission)			

Sharecropping Becomes Wage Labor

As the southern economy recovered from the devastation of the Civil War, many observers predicted a bright future for the region. Optimists saw a wealth of opportunities from untapped natural and human resources, a South freed from the inefficient slave labor system and ripe for investment.

Americans were building railroads at an exuberant clip, but southerners built them faster—with northern money. By 1890, steel mills lit the night skies of Birmingham, Alabama. Textile mills dotted the Piedmont Plateau (along the eastern foothills of the Appalachian Mountains from Virginia to Georgia). Southerners were migrating from the countryside to the towns, expanding cotton production into new areas, like the rich Mississippi delta soil. Yet ordinary southerners, especially African Americans, did not share in the New South's prosperity.

Redemption shifted the terms of the new labor relationship between landlords and sharecroppers in landowners' direction. The most important question was who owned the cotton crop at the end of the year: the sharecropper who raised it, the landlord who owned the farm, or the merchant who lent the supplies to bring the crop in.

Legal resolution in favor of the landlord came by the middle of the 1880s. The courts defined a sharecropper as a wage laborer. The landlord owned the crop and paid his workers a share of it as a wage. Landlords also won a stronger claim on the crop than the merchant creditors. Under the circumstances, merchants were reluctant to advance money to sharecroppers. Many left plantation districts and moved up-country, doing business with white yeomen farmers. Trapped in a cycle of debt, white farmers in the 1880s began losing their land and falling into tenancy. Meanwhile, in the "Black belt" (where most African Americans lived and most of the cotton was produced), successful landlords became merchants while successful merchants purchased land and hired sharecroppers of their own. By the mid-1880s, Black sharecroppers worked as wage laborers for the landlord-merchant class across much of the South.

Sharecropping differed in two critical ways from the wage work of industrial America. First, sharecropping was family labor, depending on a husband and father who signed the contract and delivered the labor of his wife and children to the landlord. Second, because sharecropping contracts were yearlong, the labor market was restricted to a few weeks at the end of each year. If croppers left before the end of the year, they risked losing everything.

The political economy of sharecropping impoverished the South by binding the region to cotton, a crop that steadily depleted the soil even as prices fell. Yet most southern Blacks found few alternatives. In time a few Black farmers purchased their own land, but their farms were generally tiny and the soil poor. The skilled Black artisans who had worked on plantations before the Civil War moved to southern cities, where they took unskilled, low-paying jobs. Northern factories were segregated, as were the steel mills of Birmingham, Alabama, and the Piedmont textile mills. Black women worked as domestic servants to supplement their husbands' meager incomes. Wage labor transformed southern Blacks' lives, but it brought no prosperity.

The **New South** of industry and diversified agriculture opened southern forests to northern timber companies and dotted southern rivers with textile mills, but it did not break the stranglehold that cash crops and plantations had over the economy. It made the region more dependent on northern capital and finished goods

TIME LINE

▼**1851**
Fort Laramie Treaty
  establishes Indian
  reservations

▼**1862**
Passage of Homestead Act

▼**1863**
Lincoln's Proclamation
  of Amnesty and
  Reconstruction

▼**1864**
Wade-Davis Bill

▼**1865**
Thirteenth Amendment
  adopted and ratified

Freedmen's Bureau
  established
Confederate armies
  surrender
Lincoln assassinated;
  Andrew Johnson
  becomes president
Johnson creates provisional
  governments in
  the South; new civil
  governments begin
Joint Committee on
  Reconstruction
  established by Congress

▼**1866**
Congress renews
  Freedmen's Bureau;
  Johnson vetoes it

Civil Rights Act vetoed
  by Johnson; Congress
  overrides veto
Congress passes
  Fourteenth Amendment
New Orleans and Memphis
  massacres
Republicans sweep
  midterm elections

▼**1867**
First, Second, and Third
  Reconstruction Acts
  passed
Tenure of Office Act
Medicine Lodge Treaty

than ever. Most of all, for the freedpeople outside a few large cities, it did not prove new at all. They found themselves excluded from juries and unprotected from white harassment and attack. White judges, white police, and white sheriffs guaranteed a white justice that treated every Black witness's testimony as suspect and turned petty larceny into an excuse for jail time and permanent disfranchisement. Black convicts stood more chance of serving on the chain gang, often hired out as cheap labor to employers who paid the state pennies a day for the work done. In the Deep South, lynchings became almost an everyday occurrence, and, to judge from the souvenir sellers and excursion trains bringing in viewers, a kind of obscene spectator sport. Prejudice closed the door to Blacks seeking to become professionals or craftsmen and guaranteed the skimpiest of funding for their schools. In a few states, the whipping post made a comeback. With the laws and the lawless working together to keep most Blacks from voting, freedom meant much less than it had in Reconstruction days. But now, there were few northerners willing to listen when Black southerners appealed for help.

Hoping to escape poverty and discrimination, some former enslaved people moved west. One group, the **Exodusters**, moved to the Kansas prairie during the mid-1870s. By 1880, more than 6,000 Blacks had joined them, searching for cheap land for independent farms. Like white farmers, the Exodusters fought with cattlemen. Blacks who settled in cow towns such as Dodge City and Topeka found the same discrimination they had known in the South. Still, some of the Exodusters did buy land and build farms.

▼**1868**
Second Fort Laramie Treaty
Washita River Massacre
Johnson fires Secretary of
 War Stanton
House of Representatives
 impeaches Johnson
Senate trial of Johnson
 ends in acquittal
Fourteenth Amendment
 ratified
Waves of Klan violence
 sweep Cotton South
Ulysses S. Grant elected
 president

▼**1869**
Congress passes Fifteenth
 Amendment

▼**1870**
Fifteenth Amendment
 ratified

▼**1872**
Liberal Republican revolt
Grant reelected

▼**1873**
Financial panic sets off
 depression

▼**1875**
Mississippi Plan succeeds
Civil Rights Act enacted

▼**1876**
Disputed presidential
 election of Rutherford

B. Hayes and Samuel J.
 Tilden
Custer's Last Stand at Little
 Bighorn

▼**1877**
Electoral commission
 counts in Rutherford B.
 Hayes as president
Last Reconstruction
 governments collapse

▼**1887**
Dawes Severalty Act

CONCLUSION

Inspired by a vision of society based on equal rights and free labor, Republicans expected emancipation to transform the South. Freed from the shackles of the slave power, the region might yet become a shining example of democracy and prosperity. Twenty years later, events seemed to mock that promise. The South was scarcely more industrial than before the war and, as far as former enslaved people were concerned, far from completely free. Cotton, sugar, rice, and tobacco still defined the South's economy far more than the hoped-for mines and mills. Only a small fraction of freedpeople had become landowners, and most of them would never escape poverty and dependence on propertied whites. After the Panic of 1873, sharecropping eliminated most Blacks' hope of real economic independence. As fears of a new rebellion dimmed, Republicans lost their zeal for federal intervention in the South. Republican state authorities could not save themselves, much less their Black constituents. Chastened by Reconstruction's defects, Americans began to turn their attention to the new problems of urban, industrial America and to the epic success story, as they saw it, of the "winning of the West."

Even so, the achievements of Reconstruction were monumental. In the West, it settled vast multitudes of people—and unsettled multitudes more. Over two generations, it created as many states as had gone into rebellion in 1861. Across the South, African Americans carved out a space in which their families could live more freely than before. Black and white men elected to office some of the most democratic state legislatures of the nineteenth century. Thousands of Black workers had escaped a stifling contract-labor system for the comparatively wider autonomy of sharecropping. Hundreds of thousands of former enslaved people learned to read and write and were able to worship in churches of their own making. Most important, Reconstruction added three important amendments to the Constitution that transformed civil rights and electoral laws throughout the nation. For the first time, the protections in the Bill of Rights would apply not just against national encroachment but that of the states as well. As a result of those changes in fundamental law, Reconstruction, then, was not so much a promise broken as one waiting to be fulfilled.

WHO, WHAT, WHERE

REVIEW QUESTIONS

1. What made congressional Reconstruction radical?
2. How did conditions for the readmission of states into the Union change over time?
3. How did Reconstruction change the South?
4. How did western Indians respond to westward expansion?
5. How did Reconstruction change the North?
6. What were the major factors that brought Reconstruction to an end?

CRITICAL-THINKING QUESTIONS

1. Compare and contrast wartime Reconstruction, presidential Reconstruction, and congressional (radical) Reconstruction. What were the key differences between the three phases?
2. How critical was the failure of land redistribution for Blacks? Was sharecropping an acceptable substitute for achieving economic freedom? Why or why not?
3. How did terrorism and economic pressure both hinder and help the Reconstruction of the South?

SUGGESTED READINGS

Foner, Eric. *Reconstruction: America's Unfinished Revolution, 1863–1877*. New York: Harper-Collins, 2014.

Hahn, Steven. *A Nation Under Our Feet: Black Political Struggles in the Rural South from Slavery to the Great Migration*. Cambridge, MA: Harvard University Press, 2003.

Litwack, Leon. *Been in the Storm So Long: The Aftermath of Slavery*. New York: Oxford University Press, 1979.

Summers, Mark Wahlgren. *The Ordeal of the Reunion: A New History of Reconstruction*. Chapel Hill: University of North Carolina Press, 2014.

For further review materials and resource information, please visit www.oup.com/us/ofthepeople

CHAPTER 15: Reconstructing a Nation, 1865–1877
Primary Sources

15.1 PETROLEUM V. NASBY [DAVID ROSS LOCKE], *A PLATFORM FOR NORTHERN DEMOCRATS* (1865)

David Ross Locke, the editor of the *Toledo Blade*, made his fortune under another name: Petroleum V. Nasby, a fictional postmaster and sometimes pastor, whose letters gave a Republican spoof of what Copperhead Democrats believed. Bad spelling was a common way of signaling to readers that a piece was meant to be humorous, though Locke also meant to show that Nasby's ideas were not only vicious and absurd but founded on a virtually illiterate ignorance.

Saint's Rest (wich is in the Stait uv Noo Jersey), June the 23d, 1865

These is the dark days uv the dimokrasy. The misforchoons that befell our armies in front uv Richmond, the fall uv our capital, follered by the surrender uv our armies to Grant and Sherman, hez hurt us. Our leaders are either pinin in loathsome dunguns, incarseratid by the hevin-defyin, man-destroyin, tyrannical edix uv our late lamented President, or are baskin in the free air uv Italy and Canady. We hev no way uv keepin our voters together. Opposin the war won't do no good, for before the next elecshun the heft uv our voters will hev diskiverd that the war is over. The fear uv drafts may do suthin in some parts uv Pennsylvany and suthern Illinoy, for sum time yuit, but that can't be depended on.

But we hev wun resource for a ishoo—ther will alluz be a dimokrasy so long as ther's a nigger.

Ther is a uncompromising dislike to the nigger in the mind uv a ginooine dimekrat. The Spanish bullfighter, when he wants to inflame the bull to extra cavortin, waves a red flag afore him. When yoo desire a dimekrat to froth at the mouth, yoo will find a Black face will anser the purpose. Therefore, the nigger is, today, our best and only holt. Let us use him.

For the guidance uv the faithful, I shel lay down a few plain rools to be observed, in order to make the most uv the capital we hev:

1. Alluz assert that the nigger will never be able to take care uv hisself, but will alluz be a public burden. He may, possibly, give us the lie by goin to work. In such a emergency, the dooty uv every dimekrat is plane. He must not be allowed to work. Associashens must be organized, pledged to neither give him employment, to work with him, to work for anyone who will give him work, or patronize any wun who duz. (I wood sejest that sich uv us ez hev bin forchoonit enuff to git credit, pay a trifle on account, so ez to make our patronage worth suthin.) This course, rigidly and persistently follered, will drive the best uv em to stealin, and the balance to the poorhouses, provin wat we hev alluz claimed, that they are a idle and vishus race. Think, my brethren, wat a inspirin effeck our poorhouses and jails full uv niggers wood hev on the people! My sole expands ez I contemplate the delitetful vision.

2. Likewise assert that the nigger will come North, and take all the good places, throwin all our skilled mechanics out uv work by underbiddin uv em. This mite be open to two objecshuns, to-wit: It crosses slitely rool the 1, and white men mite say, ef there's jist enuff labor for wat's here, why not perhibit furriners from comin?

I anser: It's the biznis uv the voter to reconcile the contraicshun—he may believe either or both. Ez to the second objeckshun, wher is the Dimekrat who coodent be underbid, and stand it even to starvashen, ef the underbiddin wux dun by a man uv the proud Caukashen race? And wher is the Dimekrat so lost to manhjood ez not to drink blood, ef the same underbiddin is dun by a nigger? The starving for work ain't the question—it's the color uv the cause uv the starvashen that makes the difference.

Nigger equality may be worked agin to advantage. All men, without distincshun uv sex, are fond uv flatrin theirselves that somebody's lower down in the scale uv humanity than they is. Ef 'twan't for niggers, what wood the dimokrasy do for sumbody to look down upon? It's also shoor to enlist wun style uv wimmen on our sides. In times gone by, I've notist gushin virgins uv forty-five, full sixteen hands high and tough ez wire, holdin aloft banners onto which wuz inscribd—"Save us from Nigger Equality." Yoo see it soothed em to hev a chase uv advertising, 1st, That they wuz frail, helplis critters; and, 2d, That, anshent and tough ez they wuz, some wun wuz still goin for em.

Ef ther ain't no niggers, central commities must furnish em. A half dozen will do for a ordinary county, ef they're hustled along with energy. Ef they won't steal, the central commities must do it theirselves. Show yer niggers in a township in the morning, an the same nite rob the clothes-lines and hen-roosts. Ever willin to sacrifice myself for the cause, I volunteer to do this latter dooty in six populous counties.

These ijees, ef follered, will, no doubt, keep us together until our enemies split, when we will reap the reward uv our constancy and fidelity. May the Lord hasten the day.

Petroleum V. Nasby

Lait Paster uv the Church uv the Noo Dispensashun

Source: David Ross Locke/Petroleum V. Nasby, *A Platform for Northern Democrats*, from Locke, *The Struggles, Social, Financial and Political of Petroleum V. Nasby* (Boston, 1888), quoted in William Benton, publ., *The Annals of America. Volume 9, 1858–1865: The Crisis of the Union* (Chicago: Encyclopedia Britannica, Inc., 1968), pp. 597–598.

15.2 A BLACK TENANT FARMER DESCRIBES WORKING CONDITIONS

Landless African Americans found few options in the late-nineteenth-century southern countryside. Their exploitation came in varying degrees of injustice, the worst of them a peonage not far from slavery. White society was rarely interested in their condition, and those who spoke out did so at their own physical peril. This account from a Black who chose to remain anonymous appeared in a religious periodical early in the twentieth century.

I am a negro and was born some time during the war in Elbert County, Ga., and I reckon by this time I must be a little over forty years old. My mother was not married when I was born, and I never knew who my father was or anything about him. Shortly after the war my mother died, and I was left to the care of my uncle. All this happened before I was eight years old, and so I can't remember very much about it. When I was about ten years old, my uncle hired me out to Captain—. I had already learned how to plow, and was also a good hand at picking cotton. I was told that the Captain wanted me for his house-boy, and that later on he was going to train me to be his coachman. To be a coachman in those days was considered a post of honor, and, young as I was, I was glad of the chance. But I had not been at the Captain's a month before I was put to work on the farm, with some twenty or thirty other negroes—men, women and children. From the beginning the boys had the polls or I would be met by 600 men on horses. So about six or eight hundred of us armed and went to the polls with our bayonets. That man that had told me that did not show up. So we voted, and voted for whom we wanted. At that time the Rebels who rebelled against this country could not vote and they said that these Negroes shouldn't vote but we showed them. Of course, they came down and stood and looked at us but they didn't bother us. We went there armed and prepared for fighting so that if they started anything, there would be trouble. When they mustered me out from the army, I brought my gun from Nashville right here to Clarksville and kept it twenty-five years. Finally I let an old soldier have it.

When I first came here we had no teachers here but white teachers. They would call the roll same as calling the roll for soldiers. They taught school in the churches before they had school houses. They used to go to school at night and work all day. Clarence C. White's father, Will White, was the first teacher or principal of the school here in Clarksville.

…

When the War was over some of the colored returned to their white folks, but I didn't want to be under the white folks again. I was glad to get out. Once, for fifteen years here, I run a saloon and livery stable. One time I worked on a boat. When I was on my first boat, one time I went to vote. A white man told me that if I voted Republican he would fire me, so I told him to fire me then. I just told him he could fire me right now for I didn't want to work anyway. I went on and voted the Republican ticket, and they told me they liked my principle and I could go on and go to work.

I still got my discharge from way back in 1866. I keeps it and I mean to keep it as long as I live. I am proud of it.

Source: George P. Rawick, ed. *The American Slave: A Composite Autobiography. Volume 18. Unwritten History of Slavery* (Fisk University) (Westport, CT: Greenwood, 1972), pp. 121–128.

15.5   A SOUTHERN UNIONIST JUDGE'S DAUGHTER WRITES THE PRESIDENT FOR HELP (1874)

Mrs. S. A. Wayne was the daughter of an Alabama Unionist, Judge James A. Abrahams. As the 1874 political campaign grew more violent, she wrote begging President Grant to send protection to Republicans like herself. Soon after the letter was sent, Abrahams was shot by persons unknown. Shortly after that, Grant sent troops to Livingston County. It was not enough to give Black and white voters the security they needed; Democratic Redeemers swept the election.

I feel more like addressing you as my dear Father & Friend for such you have proven to me & mine—but—Oh, my God! you have no conception of the trouble we are in—War is declared in our midst and though the U. S. troops are here the Ku Klux are worse than before they came—And who are they fighting? The poor defenseless negroes—Why? For voting or rather expressing their determination to vote the Republican ticket—This evening the lives of my husband—father & brother were threatened—with the intention of making them renounce their principles—God only knows what the end will be—I have seen the Capt & Lt stationed at this place—& they say the only hope is Martial law—& that is the only remedy—Since I last wrote you some four or five negroes have been killed in this County—& the Ku Klux are now at Belmont 16 miles from this place in force & will probably murder as many more—They are exasperated against the three white Republicans in this place because they refused to go with them on one of their raids last weeks—hence the threats against their lives—My Father left this evening & I pray God he may not return until Martial law is declared—Oh my dear Sir *you can save* the country—oh protect the Union loving men against those who despise it & are doing all to overthrow it—I write you this not thinking my enlisting in the cause will help it, but because I feel it my duty to let you know how great our trouble is—No excuse can be given by these murderers—for since the assassination of Mr Billings not one single Republican meeting has been held in this county—And this is what the Democrats are fighting for—Unless Martial law is declared hundreds of the poor negroes will be killed—even now they do not sleep in their houses & are hunted down like wild beasts by the Democracy because they will not vote their ticket—Oh! My dear Sir act & be our friends. God knows the innocent only suffer—& the blush of shame mantles my cheek when I read the pitiable excuses in the Democratic papers—apologizing for their cowardly deeds—No brave man is afraid of a few of them in open daylight but a hundred or two banded together; making night hideous with their demoniac yells is enough to make the stoutest heart quail—I have written you hurriedly—There is no security in the mails & I send this by a U.S. Paymaster who arrived here this afternoon & leaves to night—Again I beg you to help us in this dreadful emergency—No U.S. Marshall has been here & if they were to come they could not punish these murderers immediately—& they ought to be dealt with severely & immediately—This is private & I write as to my own dear Father & confide to you our troubles—We have lived in the midst of it since the war & it is more terrible now than ever—Every Union man will be killed if active steps are not taken by the Government to stop it—I am ever your true & loving Union woman.

Source: S. A. Wayne to Ulysses S. Grant, September 18, 1874, quoted in John Y. Simon, ed., *The Papers of Ulysses S. Grant: Volume 25: 1874* (Carbondale: Southern Illinois University Press, 2003), pp. 195–196.

15.6 RED CLOUD PLEADS THE PLAINS INDIANS' POINT OF VIEW AT COOPER UNION (1870)

As one of the foremost leaders of the Teton Sioux, Red Cloud had kept the US Army at bay for several years. The war, as his speech pointed out, had never been his own doing. He, like many other Indians, sought a fair peace; like them, he found that all the power to define what peace meant and how it would be enforced lay in the hands of the indifferent, the ill-informed, and the insatiable.

My brethren and my friends who are here before me this day, God Almighty has made us all, and He is here to bless what I have to say to you today. The Good Spirit made us both. He gave you lands and He gave us lands; He gave us these lands; you came in here, and we respected you as brothers. God Almighty made you but made you all white and clothed you; when He made us He made us with red skins and poor; now you have come.

When you first came we were very many, and you were few; now you are many, and we are getting very few, and we are poor. You do not know who appears before you today to speak. I am a representative of the original American race, the first people of this continent. We are good and not bad. The reports that you hear concerning us are all on one side. We are always well-disposed to them. You are here told that we are traders and thieves, and it is not so. We have given you nearly all our lands, and if we had any more land to give we would be very glad to give it. We have nothing more. We are driven into a very little land, and we want you now, as our dear friends, to help us with the government of the United States.

The Great Father made us poor and ignorant—made you rich and wise and more skillful in these things that we know nothing about. The Great Father, the Good Father in Heaven, made you all to eat tame food—made us to eat wild food—gives us the wild food. You ask anybody who has gone through our country to California; ask those who have settled there and in Utah, and you will find that we have treated them always well. You have children; we have children. You want to raise your children and make them happy and prosperous; we want to raise and make them happy and prosperous. We ask you to help us to do it.

At the mouth of the Horse Creek, in 1852, the Great Father made a treaty with us by which we agreed to let all that country open for fifty-five years for the transit of those who were going through. We kept this treaty; we never treated any man wrong; we never committed any murder or depredation until afterward the troops were sent into that country, and the troops killed our people and ill-treated them, and thus war and trouble arose; but before the troops were sent there we were quiet and peaceable, and there was no disturbance. Since that time there have been various goods sent from time to time to us, the only ones that ever reached us, and then after they reached us (very soon after) the government took them away. You, as good men, ought to help us to these goods.

Colonel Fitzpatrick of the government said we must all go to farm, and some of the people went to Fort Laramie and were badly treated. I only want to do that which is peaceful, and the Great Fathers know it, and also the Great Father who made us both. I came to Washington to see the Great Father in order to have peace and in order to have peace continue. That is all we want, and that is the reason why we are here now.

In 1868 men came out and brought papers. We are ignorant and do not read papers, and they did not tell us right what was in these papers. We wanted them to take away their forts, leave our country, would not make war, and give our traders something. They said we had bound ourselves to trade on the Missouri, and we said, no, we did not want that. The interpreters deceived us. When I went to Washington I saw the Great Father. The Great Father showed me what the treaties were; he showed me all these points and showed me that the interpreters had deceived me and did not let me know what the right side of the treaty was. All I want is right and justice. ... I represent the Sioux Nation; they will be governed by what I say and what I represent. ...

Look at me. I am poor and naked, but I am the Chief of the Nation. We do not want riches, we do not ask for riches, but we want our children properly trained and brought up. We look to you for your sympathy. Our riches will ... do us no good; we cannot take away into the other world anything we have—we want to have love and peace. ... We would like to know why commissioners are sent out there to do nothing but rob [us] and get the riches of this world away from us?

I was brought up among the traders and those who came out there in those early times. I had a good time for they treated us nicely and well. They taught me how to wear clothes and use tobacco, and to use firearms and ammunition, and all went on very well until the Great Father sent out another kind of men—men who drank whisky. He sent out whisky-men, men who drank and quarreled, men who were so bad that he could not keep them at home, and so he sent them out there. I have sent a great many words to the Great Father, but I don't know that they ever reach the Great Father. They were drowned on the way, therefore I was a little offended with it. The words I told the Great Father lately would never come to him, so I thought I would come and tell you myself.

And I am going to leave you today, and I am going back to my home. I want to tell the people that we cannot trust his agents and superintendents. I don't want strange people that we know nothing about. I am very glad that you belong to us. I am very glad that we have come here and found you and that we can understand one another. I don't want any more such men sent out there, who are so poor that when they come out there their first thoughts are how they can fill their own pockets.

We want preserves in our reserves. We want honest men, and we want you to help to keep us in the lands that belong to us so that we may not be a prey to those who are viciously disposed. I am going back home. I am very glad that you have listened to me, and I wish you good-bye and give you an affectionate farewell.

Source: *New York Times*, July 17, 1870, cited in William Benton, publ., *Annals of America, Volume 10: Re-construction and Industrialization* (Chicago: Encyclopedia Britannica, Inc., 1968), 242–244.

Appendix A

HISTORICAL DOCUMENTS
The Declaration of Independence

When in the course of human events, it becomes necessary for one people to dissolve the political bands which have connected them with another, and to assume, among the powers of the earth, the separate and equal station to which the Laws of Nature and of Nature's God entitle them, a decent respect to the opinions of mankind requires that they should declare the causes which impel them to the separation.

We hold these truths to be self-evident, that all men are created equal, that they are endowed by their Creator with certain unalienable Rights, that among these are life, liberty and the pursuit of happiness. That to secure these rights, governments are instituted among men, deriving their just powers from the consent of the governed; that whenever any form of government becomes destructive of these ends, it is the right of the people to alter or to abolish it, and to institute new Government, laying its foundation on such principles and organizing its powers in such form, as to them shall seem most likely to effect their safety and happiness. Prudence, indeed, will dictate that Governments long established should not be changed for light and transient causes; and, accordingly, all experience hath shown, that mankind are more disposed to suffer, while evils are sufferable, than to right themselves by abolishing the forms to which they are accustomed. But when a long train of abuses and usurpations, pursuing invariably the same object evinces a design to reduce them under absolute despotism, it is their right, it is their duty, to throw off such government, and to provide new guards for their future security. Such has been the patient sufferance of these colonies; and such is now the necessity which constrains them to alter their former systems of government. The history of the present King of Great Britain is a history of repeated injuries and usurpations, all having in direct object the establishment of an absolute tyranny over these States. To prove this, let facts be submitted to a candid world:

He has refused his assent to laws, the most wholesome and necessary for the public good.

He has forbidden his governors to pass laws of immediate and pressing importance, unless suspended in their operation till his assent should be obtained; and, when so suspended, he has utterly neglected to attend to them.

He has refused to pass other laws for the accommodation of large districts of people, unless those people would relinquish the right of representation in the legislature, a right inestimable to them and formidable to tyrants only.

He has called together legislative bodies at places unusual, uncomfortable, and distant from the depository of their public records, for the sole purpose of fatiguing them into compliance with his measures.

He has dissolved representative houses repeatedly, for opposing with manly firmness his invasions on the rights of the people.

He has refused for a long time, after such dissolutions, to cause others to be elected; whereby the legislative powers, incapable of annihilation, have returned to the People at large for their exercise; the State remaining in the mean time exposed to all the dangers of invasion from without, and convulsions within.

He has endeavored to prevent the population of these States; for that purpose obstructing the laws for naturalization of foreigners; refusing to pass others to encourage their migrations hither, and raising the conditions of new appropriations of lands.

He has obstructed the administration of justice, by refusing his assent to laws for establishing judiciary powers.

He has made judges dependent on his will alone, for the tenure of their offices, and the amount and payment of their salaries.

He has erected a multitude of new offices, and sent hither swarms of officers to harass our people, and eat out their substance.

He has kept among us, in times of peace, standing armies without the consent of our legislatures.

He has affected to render the Military independent of, and superior to, the civil power.

He has combined with others to subject us to a jurisdiction foreign to our constitution and unacknowledged by our laws; giving his assent to their acts of pretended legislation:

For quartering large bodies of armed troops among us;

For protecting them, by a mock trial, from punishment for any murders which they should commit on the inhabitants of these States;

For cutting off our trade with all parts of the world;

For imposing taxes on us without our Consent;

For depriving us, in many cases, of the benefits of Trial by Jury;

For transporting us beyond Seas to be tried for pretended offences;

For abolishing the free System of English Laws in a neighbouring Province, establishing therein an Arbitrary government, and enlarging its Boundaries so as to render it at once an example and fit instrument for introducing the same absolute rule into these colonies;

For taking away our charters, abolishing our most valuable laws, and altering fundamentally the forms of our governments;

For suspending our own legislatures, and declaring themselves invested with power to legislate for us in all cases whatsoever.

He has abdicated government here, by declaring us out of his protection and waging war against us.

He has plundered our seas, ravaged our coasts, burnt our towns, and destroyed the lives of our people.

He is at this time transporting large armies of foreign mercenaries to complete the works of death, desolation and tyranny, already begun with circumstances of cruelty and perfidy scarcely paralleled in the most barbarous ages, and totally unworthy the head of a civilized nation.

He has constrained our fellow citizens taken captive on the high seas to bear arms against their country, to become the executioners of their friends and brethren, or to fall themselves by their hands.

He has excited domestic insurrections amongst us, and has endeavored to bring on the inhabitants of our frontiers, the merciless Indian savages, whose known rule of warfare, is an undistinguished destruction of all ages, sexes and conditions.

In every stage of these oppressions we have petitioned for redress in the most humble terms; our repeated petitions have been answered only by repeated injury. A prince whose character is thus marked by every act which may define a tyrant, is unfit to be the ruler of a free people.

Nor have we been wanting in attentions to our British brethren. We have warned them from time to time of attempts by their legislature to extend an unwarrantable jurisdiction over us. We have reminded them of the circumstances of our emigration and settlement here. We have appealed to their native justice and magnanimity, and we have conjured them by the ties of our common kindred to disavow these usurpations, which, would inevitably interrupt our connections and correspondence. They, too, have been deaf to the voice of justice and of consanguinity. We must, therefore, acquiesce in the necessity, which denounces our separation, and hold them, as we hold the rest of mankind, enemies in war, in peace friends.

We, therefore, the representatives of the United States of America, in general Congress, assembled, appealing to the Supreme Judge of the world for the rectitude of our intentions, do, in the name, and by the authority of the good people of these colonies, solemnly publish and declare, that these united colonies are, and of right ought to be free and independent states; that they are absolved from all allegiance to the British Crown, and that all political connection between them and the state of Great Britain, is and ought to be totally dissolved; and that, as free and independent states, they have full power to levy war, conclude peace, contract alliances, establish commerce, and to do all other acts and things which independent states may of right do. And for the support of this declaration, with a firm reliance on the protection of Divine Providence, we mutually pledge to each other our lives, our fortunes and our sacred honor.

The Constitution of the United States of America

We the People of the United States, in Order to form a more perfect Union, establish Justice, insure domestic Tranquility, provide for the common defence, promote the general Welfare, and secure the Blessings of Liberty to ourselves and our Posterity, do ordain and establish this Constitution for the United States of America.

Article I
Section 1

All legislative Powers herein granted shall be vested in a Congress of the United States, which shall consist of a Senate and House of Representatives.

Section 2

The House of Representatives shall be composed of Members chosen every second Year by the People of the several States, and the Electors in each State shall have the Qualifications requisite for Electors of the most numerous Branch of the State Legislature.

No Person shall be a Representative who shall not have attained to the Age of twenty five Years, and been seven Years a Citizen of the United States, and who shall not, when elected, be an Inhabitant of that State in which he shall be chosen.

Representatives and direct Taxes shall be apportioned among the several States which may be included within this Union, according to their respective Numbers, which shall be determined by adding to the whole Number of free Persons, including those bound to Service for a Term of Years, and excluding Indians not taxed, three fifths of all other Persons. The actual Enumeration shall be made within three Years after the first Meeting of the Congress of the United States, and within every subsequent Term of ten Years, in such Manner as they shall by Law direct. The Number of Representatives shall not exceed one for every thirty Thousand, but each State shall have at Least one Representative; and until such enumeration shall be made, the State of New Hampshire shall be entitled to choose three, Massachusetts eight, Rhode-Island and Providence Plantations one, Connecticut five, New York six, New Jersey four, Pennsylvania eight, Delaware one, Maryland six, Virginia ten, North Carolina five, South Carolina five, and Georgia three.

When vacancies happen in the Representation from any State, the Executive Authority thereof shall issue Writs of Election to fill such Vacancies.

The House of Representatives shall choose their Speaker and other Officers; and shall have the sole Power of Impeachment.

Section 3

The Senate of the United States shall be composed of two Senators from each State, chosen by the Legislature thereof for six Years; and each Senator shall have one Vote.

Immediately after they shall be assembled in Consequence of the first Election, they shall be divided as equally as may be into three Classes. The Seats of the Senators of the first Class shall be vacated at the Expiration of the second Year, of the second Class at the Expiration of the fourth Year, and of the third Class at the Expiration of the sixth Year, so that one third may be chosen every second Year; and if Vacancies happen by Resignation, or otherwise, during the Recess of the Legislature of any State, the Executive thereof may make temporary Appointments until the next Meeting of the Legislature, which shall then fill such Vacancies.

No Person shall be a Senator who shall not have attained to the Age of thirty Years, and been nine Years a Citizen of the United States, and who shall not, when elected, be an Inhabitant of that State for which he shall be chosen.

The Vice President of the United States shall be President of the Senate, but shall have no Vote, unless they be equally divided.

The Senate shall choose their other Officers, and also a President pro tempore, in the Absence of the Vice President, or when he shall exercise the Office of President of the United States.

The Senate shall have the sole Power to try all Impeachments. When sitting for that Purpose, they shall be on Oath or Affirmation. When the President of the United States is tried, the Chief Justice shall preside: And no Person shall be convicted without the Concurrence of two thirds of the Members present.

Judgment in Cases of Impeachment shall not extend further than to removal from Office, and disqualification to hold and enjoy any Office of honor, Trust or

New York
Alexander Hamilton

New Jersey
Wil: Livingston
David Brearley
Wm. Paterson
Jona: Dayton

Pennsylvania
B Franklin
Thomas Mifflin
Robt. Morris
Geo. Clymer
Thos. FitzSimons
Jared Ingersoll
James Wilson
Gouv Morris

Articles

In addition to, and Amendment of the Constitution of the United States of America, proposed by Congress, and ratified by the Legislatures of the several States, pursuant to the fifth Article of the original Constitution.

(The first ten amendments to the U.S. Constitution were ratified December 15, 1791, and form what is known as the "Bill of Rights.")

AMENDMENT I

Congress shall make no law respecting an establishment of religion, or prohibiting the free exercise thereof; or abridging the freedom of speech, or of the press; or the right of the people peaceably to assemble, and to petition the Government for a redress of grievances.

AMENDMENT II

A well regulated Militia, being necessary to the security of a free State, the right of the people to keep and bear Arms, shall not be infringed.

AMENDMENT III

No Soldier shall, in time of peace be quartered in any house, without the consent of the Owner, nor in time of war, but in a manner to be prescribed by law.

AMENDMENT IV

The right of the people to be secure in their persons, houses, papers, and effects, against unreasonable searches and seizures, shall not be violated, and no Warrants shall issue, but upon probable cause, supported by Oath or affirmation, and particularly describing the place to be searched, and the persons or things to be seized.

AMENDMENT V

No person shall be held to answer for a capital, or otherwise infamous crime, unless on a presentment or indictment of a Grand Jury, except in cases arising in the land or naval forces, or in the Militia, when in actual service in time of War or public danger; nor shall any person be subject for the same offence to be twice put in jeopardy of life or limb; nor shall be compelled in any criminal case to be a witness against himself, nor be deprived of life, liberty, or property, without due process of law; nor shall private property be taken for public use, without just compensation.

AMENDMENT VI

In all criminal prosecutions, the accused shall enjoy the right to a speedy and public trial, by an impartial jury of the State and district wherein the crime shall have been committed, which district shall have been previously ascertained by law, and to be informed of the nature and cause of the accusation; to be confronted with the witnesses against him; to have compulsory process for obtaining witnesses in his favor, and to have the Assistance of Counsel for his defence.

AMENDMENT VII

In Suits at common law, where the value in controversy shall exceed twenty dollars, the right of trial by jury shall be preserved, and no fact tried by a jury, shall be otherwise re-examined in any Court of the United States, than according to the rules of the common law.

AMENDMENT VIII

Excessive bail shall not be required, nor excessive fines imposed, nor cruel and unusual punishments inflicted.

AMENDMENT IX

The enumeration in the Constitution, of certain rights, shall not be construed to deny or disparage others retained by the people.

AMENDMENT X

The powers not delegated to the United States by the Constitution, nor prohibited by it to the States, are reserved to the States respectively, or to the people.

AMENDMENT XI

Passed by Congress March 4, 1794. Ratified February 7, 1795.

Note: Article III, Section 2, of the Constitution was modified by Amendment XI.

The Judicial power of the United States shall not be construed to extend to any suit in law or equity, commenced or prosecuted against one of the United States by Citizens of another State, or by Citizens or Subjects of any Foreign State.

AMENDMENT XII

Passed by Congress December 9, 1803. Ratified June 15, 1804.

Note: A portion of Article II, Section 1, of the Constitution was superseded by the Twelfth Amendment.

The Electors shall meet in their respective states and vote by ballot for President and Vice-President, one of whom, at least, shall not be an inhabitant of the same state with themselves; they shall name in their ballots the person voted for as President, and in distinct ballots the person voted for as Vice-President, and they shall make distinct lists of all persons voted for as President, and of all persons voted for as Vice-President, and of the number of votes for each, which lists they shall sign and certify, and transmit sealed to the seat of the government of the United States, directed to the President of the Senate;—the President of the Senate shall, in the presence of the Senate and House of Representatives, open all the certificates and the votes shall then be counted;—The person having the greatest number of votes for President, shall be the President, if such number be a majority of the whole number of Electors appointed; and if no person have such majority, then from the persons having the highest numbers not exceeding three on the list of those voted for as President, the House of Representatives shall choose immediately, by ballot, the President. But in choosing the President, the votes shall be taken by states, the representation from each state having one vote; a quorum for this purpose shall consist of a member or members from two-thirds of the states, and a majority of all the states shall be necessary to a choice. [And if the House of Representatives shall not choose a President whenever the right of choice shall devolve upon them, before the fourth day of March next following, then the Vice-President shall act as President, as in case of the death or other constitutional disability of the President.—]* The person having the greatest number of votes as Vice-President, shall be the Vice-President, if such number be a majority of the whole number of Electors appointed, and if no person have a majority, then from the two highest numbers on the list, the Senate shall choose the Vice-President; a quorum for the purpose shall consist of two-thirds of the whole number of Senators, and a majority of the whole number shall be necessary to a choice. But no person constitutionally ineligible to the office of President shall be eligible to that of Vice-President of the United States.

AMENDMENT XIII

Passed by Congress January 31, 1865. Ratified December 6, 1865.

Note: A portion of Article IV, Section 2, of the Constitution was superseded by the Thirteenth Amendment.

Section 1

Neither slavery nor involuntary servitude, except as a punishment for crime whereof the party shall have been duly convicted, shall exist within the United States, or any place subject to their jurisdiction.

Section 2

Congress shall have power to enforce this article by appropriate legislation.

AMENDMENT XIV

Passed by Congress June 13, 1866. Ratified July 9, 1868.

Note: Article I, Section 2, of the Constitution was modified by Section 2 of the Fourteenth Amendment.

---

*Superseded by Section 3 of the Twentieth Amendment.

Section 1

All persons born or naturalized in the United States, and subject to the jurisdiction thereof, are citizens of the United States and of the State wherein they reside. No State shall make or enforce any law which shall abridge the privileges or immunities of citizens of the United States; nor shall any State deprive any person of life, liberty, or property, without due process of law; nor deny to any person within its jurisdiction the equal protection of the laws.

Section 2

Representatives shall be apportioned among the several States according to their respective numbers, counting the whole number of persons in each State, excluding Indians not taxed. But when the right to vote at any election for the choice of electors for President and Vice-President of the United States, Representatives in Congress, the Executive and Judicial officers of a State, or the members of the Legislature thereof, is denied to any of the male inhabitants of such State, being twenty-one years of age,* and citizens of the United States, or in any way abridged, except for participation in rebellion, or other crime, the basis of representation therein shall be reduced in the proportion which the number of such male citizens shall bear to the whole number of male citizens twenty-one years of age in such State.

Section 3

No person shall be a Senator or Representative in Congress, or elector of President and Vice-President, or hold any office, civil or military, under the United States, or under any State, who, having previously taken an oath, as a member of Congress, or as an officer of the United States, or as a member of any State legislature, or as an executive or judicial officer of any State, to support the Constitution of the United States, shall have engaged in insurrection or rebellion against the same, or given aid or comfort to the enemies thereof. But Congress may by a vote of two-thirds of each House, remove such disability.

Section 4

The validity of the public debt of the United States, authorized by law, including debts incurred for payment of pensions and bounties for services in suppressing insurrection or rebellion, shall not be questioned. But neither the United States nor any State shall assume or pay any debt or obligation incurred in aid of insurrection or rebellion against the United States, or any claim for the loss or emancipation of any slave; but all such debts, obligations and claims shall be held illegal and void.

Section 5

The Congress shall have the power to enforce, by appropriate legislation, the provisions of this article.

---

*Changed by Section 1 of the Twenty-sixth Amendment.

AMENDMENT XV

Passed by Congress February 26, 1869. Ratified February 3, 1870.

Section 1

The right of citizens of the United States to vote shall not be denied or abridged by the United States or by any State on account of race, color, or previous condition of servitude.

Section 2

The Congress shall have the power to enforce this article by appropriate legislation.

AMENDMENT XVI

Passed by Congress July 2, 1909. Ratified February 3, 1913.

Note: Article I, Section 9, of the Constitution was modified by Amendment XVI.

The Congress shall have power to lay and collect taxes on incomes, from what-ever source derived, without apportionment among the several States, and without regard to any census or enumeration.

AMENDMENT XVII

Passed by Congress May 13, 1912. Ratified April 8, 1913.

Note: Article I, Section 3, of the Constitution was modified by the Seventeenth Amendment.

The Senate of the United States shall be composed of two Senators from each State, elected by the people thereof, for six years; and each Senator shall have one vote. The electors in each State shall have the qualifications requisite for electors of the most numerous branch of the State legislatures.

When vacancies happen in the representation of any State in the Senate, the executive authority of such State shall issue writs of election to fill such vacancies: Provided, That the legislature of any State may empower the executive thereof to make temporary appointments until the people fill the vacancies by election as the legislature may direct.

This amendment shall not be so construed as to affect the election or term of any Senator chosen before it becomes valid as part of the Constitution.

AMENDMENT XVIII

Passed by Congress December 18, 1917. Ratified January 16, 1919. Repealed by Amendment XXI.

Section 1

After one year from the ratification of this article the manufacture, sale, or trans-portation of intoxicating liquors within, the importation thereof into, or the

Table App B-1 *continued*

	President	Vice President	Political Party	Term
25	William McKinley	Garret A. Hobart Theodore Roosevelt	Republican	1897–1901
26	Theodore Roosevelt	Charles W. Fairbanks	Republican	1901–1909
27	William Howard Taft	James S. Sherman	Republican	1909–1913
28	Woodrow Wilson	Thomas R. Marshall	Democratic	1913–1921
29	Warren Gamaliel Harding	Calvin Coolidge	Republican	1921–1923
30	Calvin Coolidge	Charles G. Dawes	Republican	1923–1929
31	Herbert Clark Hoover	Charles Curtis	Republican	1929–1933
32	Franklin Delano Roosevelt	John Nance Garner Henry A. Wallace Harry S. Truman	Democratic	1933–1945
33	Harry S. Truman	Alben W. Barkley	Democratic	1945–1953
34	Dwight David Eisenhower	Richard Milhous Nixon	Republican	1953–1961
35	John Fitzgerald Kennedy	Lyndon Baines Johnson	Democratic	1961–1963
36	Lyndon Baines Johnson	Hubert Horatio Humphrey	Democratic	1963–1969
37	Richard Milhous Nixon	Spiro T. Agnew Gerald Rudolph Ford	Republican	1969–1974
38	Gerald Rudolph Ford	Nelson Rockefeller	Republican	1974–1977
39	James Earl Carter Jr.	Walter Mondale	Democratic	1977–1981
40	Ronald Wilson Reagan	George Herbert Walker Bush	Republican	1981–1989
41	George Herbert Walker Bush	J. Danforth Quayle	Republican	1989–1993
42	William Jefferson Clinton	Albert Gore Jr.	Democratic	1993–2001
43	George Walker Bush	Richard Cheney	Republican	2001–2009
44	Barack Hussein Obama	Joseph Biden	Democratic	2009–2016
45	Donald J. Trump	Michael R. Pence	Republican	2017–2021
46	Joseph R. Biden	Kamala D. Harris	Democratic	2021–

cost-plus contract This style of contract provides manufacturers with a guarantee of costs of research and production and a profit. During World War I, to incentivize wartime industry, the United States government offered cost-plus contracts to industries that switched to production of wartime goods.

coverture A legal principle according to which a married woman's rights and even identity are subsumed under those of her husband.

crop lien The first right to the proceeds of a harvested crop, given by farmers to their creditors. At the beginning of the growing season, farmers paid on credit for seeds, supplies, and food to get them through the year. They repaid these debts when the crop was sold.

cultural mediator A figure able to translate one culture to another, literally and figuratively.

deindustrialization The reverse of industrialization, as factory shutdowns decreased the size of the manufacturing sector. Plant closings began to plague the American economy in the 1970s, prompting fears that the nation would lose its industrial base.

Democratic Republicans One of the two parties to make up the first American party system. Following the fiscal and political views of Jefferson and Madison, Democratic Republicans generally advocated a weak federal government and opposed federal intervention in the economy of the nation.

deregulation Term popularized in the 1970s for the repeal of government controls on business, labor, and the environment.

détente This French term for the relaxation of tensions was used to describe the central foreign policy innovation of the Nixon administration—a new, less confrontational relationship with Communism. In addition to opening a dialogue with the People's Republic of China, Nixon sought a more stable, less confrontational relationship with the Soviet Union.

disfranchisement The act of depriving a person or group of voting rights. In the nineteenth century the right to vote was popularly known as the franchise. The Fourteenth Amendment of the Constitution affirmed the right of adult male citizens to vote, but state-imposed restrictions and taxes deprived large numbers of Americans—particularly African Americans—of the vote from the 1890s until the passage of the Voting Rights Act of 1965.

domino theory The idea that the fall of one country to Communism would lead to the fall of others. The theory was one of the chief justifications for US intervention in Vietnam in the 1950s and 1960s.

downsizing American corporations' layoffs of both blue- and white-collar workers in an attempt to become more efficient and competitive. Downsizing was one of the factors that made Americans uneasy about the economy in the 1990s, despite the impressive surge in the stock market.

draft riots Uprisings in New York City, Buffalo, and elsewhere in 1863 in protest of conscription.

Dred Scott decision An 1857 Supreme Court decision that declared the Missouri Compromise or any Congressional ban on slavery in the territories unconstitutional and denied African Americans from becoming citizens of the United States.

Dust Bowl Across much of the Great Plains, decades of wasteful farming practices combined with several years of drought in the early 1930s to produce a series of massive dust storms that blew the topsoil across hundreds of miles. The area in Texas and Oklahoma affected by these storms became known as the Dust Bowl.

e-commerce Short for "electronic commerce," this was the term for the internet-based buying and selling that was one of the key hopes for the computer-driven postindustrial economy. The promise of e-commerce was still unfulfilled by the start of the twenty-first century.

Electoral College   Created by the US Constitution as the mechanism for choosing the president and vice president. Voters do not cast votes directly for presidential and vice presidential candidates, but instead for slates of electors pledged to support one presidential ticket or another.

emancipation   Literally, the act of freeing someone from slavery. Emancipation movements began in the North shortly after the American Revolution.

encomienda   A system of labor developed by the Spanish in the New World in which Spanish settlers (*encomenderos*) compelled groups of Native Americans to work for them. The encomendero did not own the Indians who labored for him, but he had the unlimited right to compel a particular group of Indians to work for him. This system was unique to the New World; nothing precisely like it had existed in Europe or elsewhere.

Enlightenment   A shift in thinking that occurred in the eighteenth century valuing the natural rights of individuals over traditional hierarchy, and scientific rationalism over faith. The term is much debated today for a number of reasons, among them the fact that men who considered themselves proponents of the Enlightenment often remained slaveholders.

establishment   The elite of mainly Ivy League–educated, Anglo-Saxon, Protestant, male, liberal northeasterners that supposedly dominated Wall Street and Washington after World War II. The Establishment's support for corporations, activist government, and containment engendered hostility from opposite poles of the political spectrum—from conservatives and Republicans like Richard Nixon at one end and from the New Left and the movement at the other. Although many of the post–World War II leaders of the United States did tend to share common origins and ideologies, this elite was never as powerful, self-conscious, or unified as its opponents believed.

eugenics   The practice of attempting to solve social problems through the control of human reproduction. Drawing on the authority of evolutionary biology, eugenists enjoyed considerable influence in the United States, especially on issues of corrections and public health, from the turn of the century through World War II. Applications of this pseudoscience included the identification of "born" criminals by physical characteristics and "better baby" contests at county fairs.

family values   Rallying cry for conservatives and Republicans in the 1990s and after who believed that gay and women's rights, changing family structures, and popular culture were undermining traditional morality.

Farmers' Alliance   A group organized in the late nineteenth century to help farmers pool their knowledge and resources. By 1890, it had entered politics, endorsing candidates and building the political connections in the South and West that would lead to the Populist Party.

Federalists   One of the two political parties to make up the first American party system. Following the fiscal and political policies proposed by Alexander Hamilton, Federalists generally advocated the importance of a strong federal government, including federal intervention in the economy of the new nation.

feminism   An ideology insisting on the fundamental equality of women and men. The feminists of the 1960s differed over how to achieve that equality: while liberal feminists mostly demanded equal rights for women in the workplace and in politics, radical feminists more thoroughly condemned the capitalist system and male oppression and demanded equality in both private and public life.

feudalism   A social and political system that developed in Europe in the Middle Ages under which powerful lords offered less powerful noblemen protection in return for their loyalty. Feudalism also included the economic system of manorialism, under which dependent serfs worked on the manors controlled by those lords.

Fifteenth Amendment   An 1870 constitutional amendment forbidding discrimination in voting on the basis of race, color, or previous condition of servitude.

fire-eaters   Militant southerners who pushed for secession in the 1850s.

flexible response   The defense doctrine of the Kennedy and Johnson administrations. Abandoning the Eisenhower administration's heavy emphasis on nuclear weapons, flexible response stressed the buildup of the nation's conventional and special forces so that the president had a range of military options in response to Communist aggression.

Fordism   A system of mass production that relied on mass consumption, pioneered by and named for Henry Ford.

Fourteenth Amendment   An 1868 constitutional amendment defining national citizenship, mandating equal justice before the law, guaranteeing essential civil rights, redefining the basis on which seats in the House of Representatives would be apportioned, declaring the national debt inviolate, and disqualifying some Confederate leaders from holding office until Congress had removed their disabilities.

Freedmen's Bureau   The Bureau of Refugees, Freedmen, and Abandoned Lands, a government agency formed in 1865 and administered by the army, that afforded aid and protection to former enslaved people, among others.

front   Early-twentieth-century mechanized wars were fought along a battle line or "front" separating opposing sides. By World War II, tactical innovations—blitzkrieg, parachute troops, gliders, and amphibious landings—complicated warfare by breaking through, disrupting, or bypassing the front. The front thus became a more fluid boundary than the fortified trench lines of World War I. The term also acquired a political meaning, particularly for labor and the left. A coalition of parties supporting (or opposing) an agreed-upon line could be called a "popular front."

Fugitive Slave Act   A widely protested 1850 federal law that increased federal powers to capture people accused of being fugitives from slavery, convict them without a jury trial or the right to testify on their own behalf, and return them to their owners, even in free states.

fundamentalism   A conservative Christian doctrine that subscribed to the literal truths of the Bible. Uneasy with the changes of the 1920s, Fundamentalists rejected modern culture and instead advocated a dedication to traditional authority and religious beliefs.

Galveston Plan   A system of municipal government by appointed commissioners, each with responsibility for a utility or service. After a hurricane devastated Galveston, Texas, in 1900, unelected commissioners temporarily took charge to oversee relief and rebuilding efforts.

gentility   A term without precise meaning that represented all that was polite, civilized, refined, and fashionable. It was everything that vulgarity was not. Because the term had no precise meaning, it was always subject to negotiation, striving, and anxiety as Americans, beginning in the eighteenth century, tried to show others that they were genteel through their manners, their appearance, and their styles of life.

glass ceiling   The invisible barrier of discrimination that prevented female white-collar workers from rising to top executive positions in corporations.

globalization   This term first came into use during the 1980s to describe the web of technological, economic, military, political, and cultural developments binding people and nations ever more tightly together. America had been defined by its relationship to the world for centuries, but the coining of the term *globalization* reflected the emergence of closer international ties.

gold standard   The practice by which gold served as backing for all national currency.

Great Awakening   A period in which a large proportion of the populace becomes invested in evangelical revivalism. In American history, there have been a number of such periods, but the term is most often applied to the years of the 1730s through 1750s, and the 1820s and 1830s.

Great Society   President Lyndon Johnson's ambitious legislative program embodying the vision of the activist new liberalism of the 1960s. Enacted from 1965 to 1968, the Great Society sought to wipe out poverty, end segregation, and enhance the quality of life for all Americans.

greenbackers   Those who advocated currency inflation by keeping the type of money printed during the Civil War, known as "greenbacks," in circulation.

gridlock   Term for the political traffic jam that began tying up the federal government in the late 1980s and the 1990s. Gridlock developed from the inability of either major party to control both the presidency and Congress for any extended period of time. More fundamentally, gridlock reflected the inability of any party or president to win a popular mandate for a bold legislative program.

habeas corpus   The right to be released from jail unless you are notified of specific charges against you.

Half-Way Covenant   A policy solution developed by Puritan New England congregations in the second half of the seventeenth century which allowed the children and grandchildren of people who had not had a conversion experience to become partial members of the church.

hard war   A term used to describe the Civil War's transformation into a conflict in which cities and civilians, not just armies, became targets as a means of hastening victory.

headright   The system whereby a white male European settler was offered a certain number of acres of land for every family member or servant he brought with him to the New World.

Hog Island   Site of a shipyard near Philadelphia, which was hindered by the failure of railroads to deliver the materials needed for shipbuilding. The fiasco prompted Wilson to nationalize the railroads and then take a more active role in the economy through the creation of the War Industries Board.

Holocaust   Term for the Nazi murder of about six million European Jews during World War II.

Homestead Act   An 1862 law giving 160 acres of public land without cost to heads of households who would agree to settle and cultivate it for five years.

Hoovervilles   Makeshift settlements created on the outskirts of cities by those left homeless as a result of the Great Depression. Named for President Herbert Hoover, who many Americans believed to be indifferent to their suffering.

horizontal integration   Commonly known as "monopoly." An industry became "horizontally integrated" when a single company absorbed other firms and took control of virtually the entire market for a specific product.

Hudson River school   A movement among mid-nineteenth-century landscape painters. These artists were influenced by romanticism and sought inspiration in the idea of the sublime as embodied in America's natural terrain.

Hull House   After visiting Toynbee Hall in London, Jane Addams opened this settlement house in 1889 with the intent of providing aid to the impoverished population of Chicago's Near West Side.

human equality   The idea that all people are born with the same, unalienable rights.

immediatism   The variant antislavery sentiment that demanded immediate (as opposed to gradual) personal and federal action against the institution of slavery. This approach was most closely associated with William Lloyd.

Immigration Act of 1924   A Federal law that established quotas for immigrants from southern and eastern Europe, and prevented immigration from Asia, dramatically limiting immigration numbers from those regions.

imperialism   A process of extending dominion over territories beyond the national boundaries of a state. In the eighteenth century, Britain extended imperial control over North America through settlement, but in the 1890s, imperial influence was generally exercised through indirect rule. Subject peoples generally retained some local autonomy while the imperial power controlled commerce and defense. Few Americans went to the Philippines as settlers, but many passed through as tourists, missionaries, traders, and soldiers.

indentured servants   People who promised to work for a term of years (usually between two and seven) in exchange for passage to the New World.

Indian Territory   The portion of land "reserved" for forcibly relocated Native Americans. In 1834, Congress designated land west of the Mississippi as Indian Territory but gradually reduced it until Oklahoma statehood in 1907 marked its disappearance.

individualism   The social and political philosophy celebrating the central importance of the individual human being in society. Insisting on the rights of the individual in relationship to the group, individualism was one of the intellectual bases of capitalism and democracy. The resurgent individualism of the 1920s, with its emphasis on each American's freedom and fulfillment, was a critical element of the decade's emergent consumerism and Republican dominance.

industrious revolution   Beginning in the late seventeenth century in western Europe and extending to the North American colonies in the eighteenth century, a fundamental change in the way people worked, as they worked harder and organized their households to produce goods that could be sold, so they could have money to pay for the new consumer goods they wanted.

influenza   A severe respiratory illness, also known as "flu," that caused the deadly global pandemic of 1918-1919.

information economy   The postindustrial economy, gradually emerging in the mid- and late twentieth century, in which sophisticated communications, computing, biomedical technology, and services took the place of manufacturing.

initiative, recall, and referendum   First proposed by the People's Party's Omaha Platform (1892), along with the direct election of senators and the secret ballot, as measures to subject corporate capitalism to democratic controls. Progressives, chiefly in western and midwestern states, favored them as a check on the power of state officials. The initiative allows legislation to be proposed by petition. The recall allows voters to remove public officials, and the referendum places new laws or constitutional amendments on the ballot for the direct approval of the voters.

interest group   An association whose members organize to exert political pressure on officials or the public. Unlike political parties, whose platforms and slates cover nearly every issue and office, an interest group focuses on a narrower list of concerns reflecting the shared outlook of its members. With the decline of popular politics around the turn of the twentieth century, business, religious, agricultural, women's, professional, neighborhood, and reform associations created a new form of political participation.

internationalists   Those Americans opposed to isolationism and supportive of greater US involvement around the world, including trade agreements, international law conventions, and military alliances.

internment   Imprisonment, without trial, inspired by political justifications. During World War II, the United States government seized the property of, relocated, and imprisoned both Japanese immigrants and natural-born Japanese Americans based on the presumed threat this population posed to the nation.

isolationist   Between World War I and World War II, the United States refused to join the League of Nations, scaled back its military commitments abroad, and sought to maintain its independence of action in foreign affairs. These policies were called isolationist, although some historians prefer the term "independent internationalist," in recognition of the United States' continuing global influence. In the late 1930s, isolationists favored policies aimed at distancing the United States from European affairs and building a national defense based on air power and hemispheric security.

Jacksonian democracy   The style of politics associated with President Andrew Jackson, elimination of property requirements for voting on the state level and the promotion of white male equality, generally at the expense of minority populations.

Jim Crow laws   Statutes discriminating against nonwhite Americans, particularly in the South. The term specifically refers to regulations excluding Blacks from public facilities or compelling them to use ones separate from those allotted to whites.

jingoes   In the Gilded Age, those in favor of an aggressive, expansionist American foreign policy, including war with the Spain in 1898.

joint-stock company   A form of business organization that was a forerunner to the modern corporation. The joint-stock company was used to raise both capital and labor for New World ventures. Shareholders contributed either capital or their labor for a period of years.

Jones Mixer   Developed by Captain William R. Jones, a massive machine used for keeping molten iron hot, until it could be used with other ingredients to make steel.

judicial review   The principle of law that recognizes in the judiciary the power to review and rule on the constitutionality of laws. First established in *Marbury v. Madison* (1803) under Chief Justice John Marshall.

junk bonds   A corporation issues bonds in order to raise investment capital in return for a promise to pay regular interest to purchasers. Junk bonds are particularly risky promises of high interest that may never get paid.

Keynesian economics   The theory, named after the English economist John Maynard Keynes, that advocated the use of "countercyclical" fiscal policy. This meant that during good times the government should pay down the debt, so that during bad times, it could afford to stimulate the economy with deficit spending.

King Cotton diplomacy   Confederate efforts to use European dependence on cotton exports to win recognition as an independent nation.

Knights of Labor   The first national federation of trade unions, led by Terence V. Powderly. The Knights grew to its fullest size in the mid-1880s before a steep decline. The federation was based on the premise of a common interest of all producers (for example, farmers and industrial workers), and it supported reform as well as united action by workers.

liberalism   A body of political thought that traces its origins to John Locke and whose chief principles are consent, freedom of conscience, and property. Liberalism held that people could not be governed except by their own consent and that the purpose of government was to protect people as well as their property. Beginning in the late nineteenth century, liberals, including progressives, favored more government activism to protect rights and regulate the economy.

limited war   In the age of total war in the mid-twentieth century, limited war became a useful term to describe armed conflicts such as the Korean, Vietnam, Iraq, and Afghan wars in which a country did not fully mobilize its population, persistently attack civilians, and use its full arsenal, including nuclear weapons.

linked economic development   A form of economic development that ties together a variety of enterprises so that development in one stimulates development in others, for example, those that provide raw materials, parts, or transportation.

Longhorn cattle   Rangy, tough, resourceful cattle found on the southern Great Plains. They were ideal for long cattle drives like those along the Abilene Trail.

loyalists   Those who remained devoted to the British monarchical government during the Revolutionary War.

lyceum movement   A voluntary adult-education movement that swept New England and the mid-Atlantic states in the early and mid-nineteenth century, credited in large part to the efforts of Josiah Holbrook. Lyceum organizations hosted educational lectures in towns and cities. Lecturers included such prominent speakers as Ralph Waldo Emerson, Mark Twain, and Abraham Lincoln.

New France Term for the French colonies in the New World. An area encompassing trading outposts in Canada, the American Midwest, and Louisiana, New France ceased to exist with the signing of the Treaty of Paris in 1763.

New Left The radical student movement that emerged in opposition to the new liberalism in the 1960s. The New Left condemned the Cold War and corporate power and called for the creation of a true "participatory democracy" in the United States. Placing its faith in the radical potential of young, middle-class students, the New Left differed from the "old left" of the late nineteenth and early twentieth centuries, which believed workers would lead the way to socialism.

New Negro A term used to describe African Americans, many of whom had left the rural South during the first decades of the twentieth century, who challenged racial inequality and expressed racial pride.

New Netherland Term for the Dutch colony in the New World, located in the Hudson River Valley area, until conquest by the British in 1664.

New Right The conservative movement that swept Ronald Reagan into power in 1980 and sustained his presidency. The New Right was much like the new conservatism of the 1950s and 1960s, but with greater emphasis on social issues such as abortion.

New South The hope of elite white Southerners that the states of the former Confederacy would attract northern investment, increase industrial production, diversify agriculture, and generally modernize.

New Woman A term used to describe women of the late nineteenth century who advocated on behalf of their rights to equal educational, economic, and political opportunities. In the 1920s, this figure became increasingly linked to sexual liberation and the culture of fun.

New World Order With the end of the Cold War, President George H. W. Bush called for the United States to help ensure a world dominated by democracy, free trade, and peace.

nongovernmental organizations (NGOs) Private, nongovernmental, noncommercial organizations. NGOs such as Greenpeace, the International Red Cross, and the World Economic Forum played key roles in globalization in the late twentieth and early twenty-first centuries.

NSC-68 A secret document issued by President Truman's National Security Council in 1950 that detailed US military strategy, including the development of thermonuclear weapons, to counter the Soviet Union.

nullification The theory that a state could overturn federal law, which South Carolinians invoked to defy the US "tariff of abominations" beginning in 1828 and set off the nullification crisis.

Omaha Platform The Populist Party's program endorsed at the party's national convention in Omaha in 1892. Among its planks were government ownership of railroads and telegraph lines, the direct election of senators, a subtreasury system, and an expansion of the money supply.

Open Door The turn-of-the-twentieth-century American ideal for China, in which the country remained open to international trade. This model would allow the United States to expand its global economic reach without the responsibilities of maintaining an empire.

Oregon or Overland Trail The route from the Missouri River west to Oregon and California, begun in the early 1840s and eventually replaced by railroads after the Civil War.

Ostend Manifesto An 1854 declaration justifying the United States' need to buy Cuba, indicating a readiness to take it by force if Spain would not agree to sell it.

Pacifist Term for someone who opposes war.

Panama Canal The waterway, constructed between 1903 and 1914, that cuts through Central America and serves as a means of connecting the Atlantic and Pacific Oceans.

participatory democracy   Believing that the American political system did not heed the will of the people in the 1960s, Students for a Democratic Society called for a more truly participatory democratic politics that would empower ordinary Americans.

partisanship   The strong belief in a particular ideology, often that of a political party.

patent (for land)   An early form of land title, through which people could assert their ownership of land.

patriotism   Love of country. Ways of declaring and displaying national devotion underwent a change from the nineteenth to the twentieth centuries. Whereas politicians were once unblushingly called patriotic, after World War I the title was appropriated to describe the sacrifices of war veterans. Patriotic spectacle in the form of public oration and electoral rallies gave way to military-style commemorations of Armistice Day and the nation's martial heritage.

patronage   Term for the granting of governmental jobs to supporters of a winning candidate. The opposite of a merit-based system, such as that created by the Pendleton Act. *See* spoils system.

Peace Corps   Created by John F. Kennedy in 1961, the Peace Corps sent young Americans abroad to promote literacy, public health, and agriculture.

Pendleton Civil Service Act   1883 legislation that set up a merit system for hiring and promoting federal workers, and protecting them from forced political contributions. Covering only a small fraction of all government employees at first, its range expanded with each presidency.

perfectionism   The idea, associated with the Second Great Awakening, that people could first perfect themselves and then turn their efforts towards perfecting the world around them on the principles of Protestant Christianity.

political action committee (PAC)   Dating to the 1940s, organizations, not part of political parties, that have had greater and lesser freedom from the federal government to accept and spend unlimited donations on issues and candidates.

political economy   Traditionally, the study of the connections between economics and politics. In this text, political economy refers to the relationships among the economy, politics, and the daily lives of ordinary people. Use of the term underscores the importance of the economy in shaping American life and the importance of politics in shaping the economy. However, the economy and politics did not simply shape, but were in turn shaped by, the lives and cultural values of ordinary men and women.

political machine   An organization controlling a party, usually dominated by a "boss" and held together by loyalty and the distribution of rewards to those who had done the organization service.

popular sovereignty   A solution to the slavery controversy espoused by leading northern Democrats in the 1850s. It held that the inhabitants of western territories should be free to decide for themselves whether or not they wanted to have slavery. In principle, popular sovereignty would prevent Congress from either enforcing or restricting slavery's expansion into the western territories.

populism   The ideology of the People's (Populist) party in the 1890s, opposing the eastern economic elites and favoring government action to help producers in general and farmers in particular.

postindustrial economy   The service- and computer-based economy that was succeeding the industrial economy at the end of the twentieth century.

privateering   Piratical ventures authorized by a European government. A colonizing power might provide financial backing to captains who used their ships to attack the galleons or New World settlements belonging to a different colonial power.

producers ideology   The belief that all those who lived by producing goods shared a common political identity in opposition to those who lived off financial speculation, rent, or interest.

progressivism   Liberal ideology of late-nineteenth and early-twentieth-century mostly middle-class reformers who wanted to use politics, government, and private initiative to remake industrializing, diverse America in their own image. *See* liberalism.

propaganda   Information used to promote a particular cause or point of view. During the twentieth century, the United States' government attempted to persuade the American people to support various national efforts via text, image, radio, and film.

proprietary colony   Colony established by a royal grant to an individual or family. The proprietary colonies included Maryland, New York, New Jersey, Pennsylvania, and the Carolinas.

public opinion   Not quite democracy or consent, public opinion was a way of understanding the influence of the citizenry on political calculations. It emerged in the eighteenth century, when it was defined as a crucial source of a government's legitimacy. It was associated with the emergence of a press and a literate public free to discuss, and to question, government policy. In the twentieth century, Freudian psychology and the new mass media encouraged a view of the public as both fickle and powerful. Whereas the popular will (a nineteenth-century concept) was steady and rooted in national traditions, public opinion was variable and based on attitudes that could be aroused or manipulated by advertising.

Pueblos   Term for the indigenous group that inhabited New Mexico, the Pueblos were harshly treated by the Spanish and rebelled in in 1680.

Reagan Doctrine   Rejecting the Carter administration's emphasis on promoting human rights around the world in the 1970s, President Ronald Reagan contended in the 1980s that the United States should support authoritarian, antidemocratic regimes friendly to the United States.

Reaganomics   *See* supply-side economics.

Reconquista   Literally "reconquest." Between the eleventh and the fifteenth centuries, Christian nobles in Spain and Portugal fought to eject Muslim conquerors who had come from North Africa in the seventh and eighth centuries. In 1492, Ferdinand and Isabel defeated the last remaining Muslim ruler.

reconversion   The economic and social transition from the war effort to peacetime. Americans feared that reconversion might bring a return to the depression conditions of the 1930s.

Red Scare   The fear of a communist takeover of the United States following the Bolshevik Revolution of 1917. After World War I, the American government attempted to limit radicalism by suppressing the voices of communists, socialists, anarchists, and organized labor.

Redemption   A term used by southern Democrats for the undoing of Radical Reconstruction and the replacement of biracial regimes with conservative, white-dominated ones.

redemptioners   People who sold themselves into indentured servitude. At the end of the voyage to America, they were to be "redeemed" by those who paid the cost of their passage.

Religious Right   Conservative political movement by evangelical Protestants against abortion and for the Republican Party prominent in the 1980s and after.

Republic   A state in which the people, through their elected representatives, hold power. Distinguished in the Federalist Papers from a democracy, which, James Madison argued, would allow factions to gain too much power. In a republic, the people's representatives would guard against factional subversion.

republicanism   A set of doctrines rooted in classical antiquity that held that power is always grasping and dangerous and presents a threat to liberty. Republicanism supplied constitutionalism with a motive by explaining how a balanced constitution could be transformed into a tyranny as grasping men used their power to encroach on the liberty of citizens. In addition, republicanism held that people achieved fulfillment only through participation in public life, as citizens in a republic. Republicanism required the individual to display virtue by sacrificing his (or her) private interest for the good of the republic.

Requerimiento **(the Requirement)**   The statement of the Spanish Crown in 1513 declaring a legal basis for the enslavement of hostile Indians. Each conquistador was required to read a copy of the *Requerimiento* to each group of Indians he encountered. The *Requerimiento* promised friendship to all Indians who accepted Christianity, but threatened war and enslavement for all those who resisted.

reservations   Lands that the federal government reserved for Native American tribes as their homelands, either through limiting the domain that a tribe had claimed originally or through forcible relocation from the place where it already lived.

revivals   Large gatherings of people who come to hear evangelical preachers. Many experience their own Christian conversion and testify before the multitude.

royal colony   A colony owned and managed by the Crown (as opposed to a proprietary colony owned and managed by individual investors).

Rustbelt   Term for the deindustrializing states of Northeast and Midwest that lost jobs, population, and political clout during the 1970s.

safety-valve theory   An argument commonly made in the nineteenth century that the abundance of western land spared the United States from the social upheavals common to capitalist societies in Europe. In theory, as long as eastern workers had the option of migrating west and becoming independent farmers, they could not be subject to European levels of exploitation. Thus, the West was said to provide a "safety valve" against the pressures caused by capitalist development.

scabs   A derogatory term for those hired to take striking workers' places.

scalawag   A derogatory term referring to southern whites who supported the Republican party during Reconstruction.

scientific management   *See* Taylorism.

secession   A state's act in dissolving its allegiance to the United States government, as 11 southern states did in 1860 and 1861. The question of its legality formed the essential issue of the Civil War.

separate but equal   In 1896, *Plessy v. Ferguson* declared segregation was constitutional as long as the different accommodations provided for Blacks and whites were equivalent. The doctrine of "separate but equal" would allow legalized segregation throughout the South until the Supreme Court overturned the edict in 1954 with *Brown v. Board of Education.*

separation of powers   One of the chief innovations of the Constitution and a distinguishing mark of the American form of democracy, in which the executive, legislative, and judicial branches of government are separated so that they can check and balance each other.

sharecropping   The practice of a tenant farming the landlord's ground for a share of the crop, sold when the harvest came in. This became a common form of employment for former enslaved people in the post–Civil War South.

Sherman Anti-Trust Act   An 1890 federal law forbidding business combinations in restraint of trade, which gave the US government power to break up monopolies.

sit-in   An important tactic of grassroots, nonviolent civil disobedience, a sit-in is the occupation of a public place in order to protest and to demand change. The 1960 sit-in by the A&T Four to protest segregation at the Woolworth's lunch counter in Greensboro, North Carolina, popularized the tactic, which spread to the African American freedom struggle and inspired other protest movements for decades to come.

slave power   In the 1850s, northern Republicans explained the continued economic and political strength of slavery by claiming that a "slave power" had taken control of the federal government and used its authority to keep slavery alive artificially.

slave society   A society in which slavery is central to the economy and political structure, in contrast to a society with slaves, in which the presence of enslaved people does not alter the fundamental structures of the society.

slavery   A system of extreme social inequality distinguished by the definition of a human being as property, or chattel, and thus, in principle, totally subordinated to the slave owner.

Social Darwinism   Darwin's theory of natural selection transferred from biological evolution to human history. Social Darwinists argued that some individuals and groups, particularly racial groups, were better able to survive in the "race of life."

Social Security   Social insurance plan established in 1935 that required contributions from both employers and employees. The original legislation, though limited, provided Americans with workers' compensation, unemployment insurance, family aid, and old-age pensions.

spoils system   The practice of politicians giving offices and contracts on the basis of friendship and loyalty rather than merit.

stagflation   The unusual combination of stagnant growth and high inflation that plagued the American economy in the 1970s.

strict constructionism   The view that the Constitution has a fixed, explicit meaning which can be altered only through formal amendment. Loose constructionism is the view that the Constitution is a broad framework within which various interpretations and applications are possible without formal amendment.

subtreasury   A government-run bank in which farmers could get low-interest loans using their crops as collateral. The creation of subtreasuries formed a key plank in the Populist platform.

suburbanization   The spread of suburban housing developments and communities and, more broadly, of the suburban ideal.

suffrage   The right to vote in political elections. Women advocated for the right to vote from the mid-nineteenth century on and eventually secured the franchise via the Nineteenth Amendment in 1920.

supply-side economics   The controversial theory, associated with economist Arthur Laffer, that drove Reaganomics, the conservative economic policy of the Reagan administration. In contrast to liberal economic theory, supply-side economics emphasized that producers—the "supply side" of the economic equation—drove economic growth, rather than consumers—the "demand side." To encourage producers to invest more in new production, Laffer and other supply-siders called for massive tax cuts.

Tammany Hall   A fraternal organization in New York City that developed into a Democratic political machine, electing officials, mobilizing voters, and allotting contracts. Its enemies saw it as a symbol of corrupt, selfish, and incompetent government.

tariff   A tax on goods moving across an international boundary. Because the Constitution allows tariffs only on imports, as a political issue the tariff question has chiefly concerned the protection of domestic manufacturing from foreign competition. Industries producing mainly for American consumers have preferred a higher tariff, while farmers and industries aimed at global markets have typically favored reduced tariffs. Prior to the Civil War, the tariff was a symbol of diverging political economies in North and South. The North advocated high tariffs to protect growing domestic manufacturing ("protective tariffs"), and the South opposed high tariffs on the grounds that they increased the cost of imported manufactured goods.

Taylorism   A method for maximizing industrial efficiency by systematically reducing the time and motion involved in each step of the production process. The "scientific" system was designed by Frederick Taylor and explained in his book *The Principles of Scientific Management* (1911).

temperance   Moderation, or the use of something with restraint. In the Gilded Age, the temperance movement opposed the use of alcohol.

Ten Percent Plan   Abraham Lincoln's 1863 proposal for reconstructing former Confederate states, based on the creation of governments after 10 percent of the eligible voters had taken an oath of loyalty to the United States.

tenement   A multiapartment building in major cities, generally inhabited by the poor, often under the most squalid conditions.

Tennessee Valley Authority (TVA)   New Deal program that attempted to modernize the rural area along the Tennessee River via environmental control, the introduction of electricity, and the establishment of modern manufacturing.

Tenure of Office Act   Passed by Congress in 1867, the act forbade a president from removing any officer that he had appointed, without the consent of the Senate. Its violation became the central charge in Andrew Johnson's impeachment proceedings.

totalitarianism   An anti-democratic philosophy justifying citizens' submission to dictatorial government.

total war   Armed conflict that involves the complete mobilization of a nation's resources and population and that targets civilians as well as soldiers. A comparatively modern development, total war began in the United States with the Civil War, expanded in World War I with the introduction of bombers, submarines, and poison gas, and grew again in World War II with the strategic bombing of cities, the Holocaust, and the dropping of the first atomic bombs.

trusts   Corporate arrangements to unify action in production and distribution among different firms. Shareholders handed over control of their stock to a board that held the shares in trust and operated the combined concerns.

universalism   Enlightenment belief that all people are by their nature essentially the same.

vertical integration   The practice of taking control of every aspect of the production, distribution, and sale of a commodity. For example, Andrew Carnegie vertically integrated his steel operations by purchasing the mines that produced the ore, the railroads that carried the ore to the steel mills, the mills themselves, and the distribution system that carried the finished steel to consumers.

Victorian era   Literally, the reign of Queen Victoria's over the British empire, from 1837 to 1901. Applied to the United States, the term of dismissively signifies a dominant culture of public propriety, self-control, and starkly different gender roles.

virtual representation   British doctrine that said that all Britons, even those who did not vote, were represented by Parliament, if not "actually," by representatives they had chosen, then "virtually," because each member of parliament was supposed to act on behalf of the entire realm, not only his constituents or even those who had voted for him.

voluntarism   A style of political activism that took place largely outside of electoral politics. Voluntarism emerged in the nineteenth century, particularly among those Americans who were not allowed to vote. Thus, women formed voluntary associations that pressed for social and political reforms, even though women were excluded from electoral politics.

Wagner Act   1935 legislation that guaranteed workers' rights to bargain collectively with their employers, prohibited the firing of workers after a strike, and restricted other antiunion measures.

Waltham system   Named after the system used in early textile mills in Waltham, Massachusetts, the term refers to the practice of bringing all elements of production together in a single factory setting with the application of non-human-powered machinery.

wampum   Shell beads used by Indians of the Eastern Woodlands as jewelry, currency, and memorials of political agreements; later produced as currency in the trade networks established between Europeans and Indians.

War on Poverty   Declared by President Johnson in 1964, the war on poverty became the catch-all term for the Economic Opportunity Act of 1964 and the antipoverty legislation of the Democrats' Great Society.

Watergate   The name of the Washington, DC office and condominium complex where five men with ties to the presidential campaign of Richard Nixon were caught breaking into the headquarters of the Democratic National Committee in June 1972. "Watergate" became the catch-all term for the wide range of illegal practices of Nixon and his followers that were uncovered in the aftermath of the break-in.

The Wealth of Nations   The title of the most famous work of the renowned economist and philosopher, Adam Smith. Today the phrase is often used as shorthand for the core principles of classical economics.

Western Front   The main theater of action during World War I, traveling through France from the North Sea coast of Belgium to the Swiss border. Stretching approximately 440 miles, much of the front was comprised of an intricate system of trenches.

Whig Party   The political party founded by Henry Clay in the mid-1830s. The name derived from the seventeenth- and eighteenth-century British antimonarchical position and was intended to suggest that the Jacksonian Democrats (and Jackson in particular) sought despotic powers. In many ways the heirs of National Republicans, the Whigs supported economic expansion, but they also believed in a strong federal government to control the dynamism of the market. The Whig Party attracted many moral reformers.

Wilmot Proviso   An amendment to a military appropriations bill proposed in 1846 to keep slavery out of all territories taken in the Mexican War. Although it never passed, it excited four years of bitter sectional controversy.

Women's Christian Temperance Union (WCTU)   Women's reform organization founded in 1873 to discourage drinking and close down saloons, if possible, by prohibition of the sale or manufacture of alcohol.

women's rights movement   The antebellum organizing efforts of women on their own behalf, in the attempt to secure a broad range of social, civic, and political rights. This movement is generally dated from the convention of Seneca Falls in 1848. Only after the Civil War would women's rights activism begin to confine its efforts to suffrage.

Women's suffrage   *See* suffrage.

Photo Credits

Chapter 1: Wikipedia Commons; Photo by DeAgostini/Getty Images; Wikipedia Commons; Cahokia Mounds State Historic Site. Photo by Art Grossman; Sepia Times/Universal Images Group via Getty Images; Photo by DeAgostini/Getty Images; Granger – All rights reserved; Benson Latin American Collection, University of Texas, Austin; Photo by DeAgostini/Getty Images; DEA/SIOEN/Getty Images.

Chapter 2: Bridgeman Images; Indian in Body Paint (litho) White, John (fl. 1570-92) (after) Credit: Private Collection/Bridgeman Images; The Picture Art Collection/Alamy Stock Photo; Governor Peter Stuyvesant (1592-...) Couturier, Hendrick (fl. 1648-d.c...) Credit: Collection of the New York Historical Society, USA/Bridgeman Images; © John Carter Brown Library, Box 1894, Brown University, Providence, RI 02912; Bridgeman Images; © The Trustees of the British Museum/Art Resource, NY.

Chapter 3: Pilgrim Hall Museum, Plymouth, MA; National Portrait Gallery, Washington, D.C. (Photo by VCG Wilson/Corbis via Getty Images); Granger – All rights reserved; Photo 61085474 © Kclarksphotography | Dreamstime.com; Dennis MacDonald— AGE footstock; Pilgrim Hall Museum, Plymouth, MA.

Chapter 4: Kevin Fleming/Corbis/VCG/Getty; Photo by Briggs Co./George Eastman House/Getty Images; NYC Department of Records & Information Services; Plan et Scituation des Villages Tchikachas Plan and Situation of the Chicksaw Villages, Alexandre de Batz, 1737. French copy of a map made by a visitor to the Chicksaw; Plymouth County Commissioners, Plymouth Court House, Plymouth, MA/Dublin Seminar for New England Folklife, Concord, MA; Courtesy of The Newberry Library, Chicago. Call # Ayer MS map 30, Sheet 77; Kevin Fleming/Corbis/VCG/Getty; An American Indian Man and his M... Mexican School, (18th century) Credit: Museo de America, Madrid, Spain/Bridgeman Images.

Chapter 5: Granger – All rights reserved; Courtesy of the Library of Congress; Granger

– All rights reserved; Granger – All rights reserved; Mr. Peter Manigault and his Friends, 1854, By Louis Manigault (American, 1828-1899) after George Boone Roupell (1726-1794), Wash and ink on paper, Gift of Mr. Joseph e. Jenkins, 1968.005.0001, Image courtesy of the Gibbes Museum of Art/Carolina Art Association; GraphicaArtis/Getty Images; Granger – All rights reserved; Courtesy of the Library of Congress.

Chapter 6: Granger – All rights reserved; Frontispiece from *A Narrative of the Captivity of Mrs. Johnson* (Bowie, MD: Heritage Books, Inc. 1990), p. v, 181; Granger – All rights reserved; Benjamin West, 1738-1820 The Death of General Wolfe, 1770 oil on canvas 152.6 x 214.5 cm National Gallery of Canada Gift of the 2nd Duke of Westminster to the Canadian War Memorials, 1918, Transfer from the Canadian War Memorials, 1921; Granger – All rights reserved; Granger – All rights reserved.

Chapter 7: Yale University Art Gallery; Abigail Smith Adams, c 1766 (pastel on paper), Blyth, Benjamin (c. 1746-c. 1786)/Massachusetts Historical Society, Boston, MA, USA/Bridgeman Images; Granger – All rights reserved; Courtesy of the Library of Congress; Anonymous, 18th century English, after J.F. Renault: The British surrendering their arms to General Washington after their defeat at Yorktown in Virginia, October 1781. Colored engraving, Inv.: CFAc 295. © RMN-Grand Palais/Art Resource, NY; Granger – All rights reserved.

Chapter 8: Granger – All rights reserved; Courtesy Independence National Historical Park; Henry Francis Du Pont Winterthur Museum; Henry Francis Du Pont Winterthur Museum; Residence of Washington in High ... Breton, William L. (fl. 1830) Credit: Library Company of Philadelphia, PA, USA/Bridgeman Images; Granger – All rights reserved; Map located in the Military Journal of Major Ebenezer Denny, an officer in the Revolutionary and Indian Wars (J.B. Lippincott & Co., for the Historical Society of Pennsylvania, 1859), available via the Boston Public Library (E83.79.D4 1859x).

C-1

California Historical Society); ageFotostock; The Granger Collection; Courtesy of the Library of Congress; Courtesy of the Library of Congress; Courtesy of the Library of Congress.

Chapter 17: Bettmann/Getty Images; Nebraska State Historical Society; Puck. New York: Puck Publishing Co., 18771918; The Granger Collection; Bettmann/Getty Images; Image provided by GreatCaricatures.com © 2021; Courtesy of the Ohio History Connection; Art Resource, NY; Kansas State Historical Society; Jacob Riis (1849-1914).

Chapter 18: Courtesy of the Library of Congress; The Granger Collection; North Wind Picture Archives/Alamy Stock Photo; The Granger Collection; Courtesy of the Library of Congress; North Wind Picture Archives/Alamy Stock Photo; Courtesy of the Library of Congress.

Chapter 19: The Granger Collection; Tropical Press Agency/Getty Images; The Kheel Center at Cornell University; Courtesy of the Library of Congress; The University of Chicago Library, Special Collections Research Center, Photographic Archive apf1-08624; The Granger Collection; Chicago History Museum 139070_6f; Courtesy of the Library of Congress; Courtesy of the Library of Congress; Courtesy of the Library of Congress; Courtesy of the Library of Congress.

Chapter 20: "Emergency hospital in the midst of the influenza epidemic, Camp Funston, Kansas, circa 1918," (NCP 1603). OHA 250 New Contributed Photographs. Otis Historical Archives, National Museum of Health and Medicine; Courtesy of the Library of Congress; Courtesy of the Library of Congress; Credit: Courtesy of the Pennsylvania State Archives; The Art Archive/Art Resource; Wikimedia Commons; "Emergency hospital in the midst of the influenza epidemic, Camp Funston, Kansas, circa 1918," (NCP 1603). OHA 250 New Contributed Photographs. Otis Historical Archives, National Museum of Health and Medicine; Photo by NY Daily News Archive via Getty Images.

Chapter 21: Smith Collection/Gado/Getty Images; Courtesy of the Library of Congress; Hulton Archive/Getty Images; Pictorial Press Ltd/Alamy Stock Photo; Photo by Oklahoma Historical Society/Getty Images; Smith Collection/Gado/Getty Images; Duke University Libraries Ad Access, BH0714 Ann Elsner in honor of Allan Todd Sagraves.

Chapter 22: MPI/Stringer/Getty Images; Courtesy of the Library of Congress; Three Lions/Getty Images; Bettmann/Getty Images; MPI/Stringer/Getty Images; AP Photo; Bettman/Getty Images; Courtesy of the Library of Congress; Courtesy of the Library of Congress; Courtesy of the Library of Congress.

Chapter 23: HWRD Photo 136, University Archives & Manuscripts Department, University of Hawaii at Manoa Library; Getty Images; Bettmann/Getty Images; HWRD Photo 136, University Archives & Manuscripts Department, University of Hawaii at Manoa Library; Courtesy National Park Service Museum Management Program and Tuskegee Airmen National Historic Site, TUA131; Getty Images; Bettmann/Getty Images; Bettmann/Getty Images.

Chapter 24: Alamy Stock Photo; Courtesy Turchinetz family; British Cartoon Archive, University of Kent ILW1059; Photo by Galerie Bilderwelt/Getty Images; Bettmann/Getty Images; AP Photo/File; Alamy Stock Photo.

Chapter 25: Guy Gillette/Getty Images; CBS Photo Archive/Getty Images; AP Photos; Guy Gillette/Getty Images; Bettmann/Getty Images; Bettmann; AP Photos; Duke University Libraries Ad Access, T032 Ann Elsner in honor of Allan Todd Sagraves; Photo by Allan Grant/The LIFE Picture Collection via Getty Images; Photo by Grey Villet/The LIFE Picture Collection/Getty Images; A 1957 Herblock Cartoon, © The Herb Block Foundation; Dmitri Kessel/Getty Images.

Chapter 26: AP Photo/Robert W. Klein; GRANGER/GRANGER – All rights reserved; NASA Image and Video Library; Bob Adelman Archive; British Cartoon Archive, University of Kent ILW3584; AP Photo/Robert W. Klein; Bettmann/Getty Images.

Chapter 27: Bettmann/Getty Images; AP Photo/File; Bettmann/Getty Images; Allan Tannenbaum/Getty Images; Bettmann/Getty Images; Fred Ward; U.S. National Archives and Records Administration; Bettmann/Getty Images.

Chapter 28: Bettmann/Getty Images; Linda Chavez; Bettmann/Getty Images; Diana Walker/Getty Images; Bettmann/Getty Images; Getty Images; AP Photo/James A. Finley; AP Photo/Lionel Cironneau.

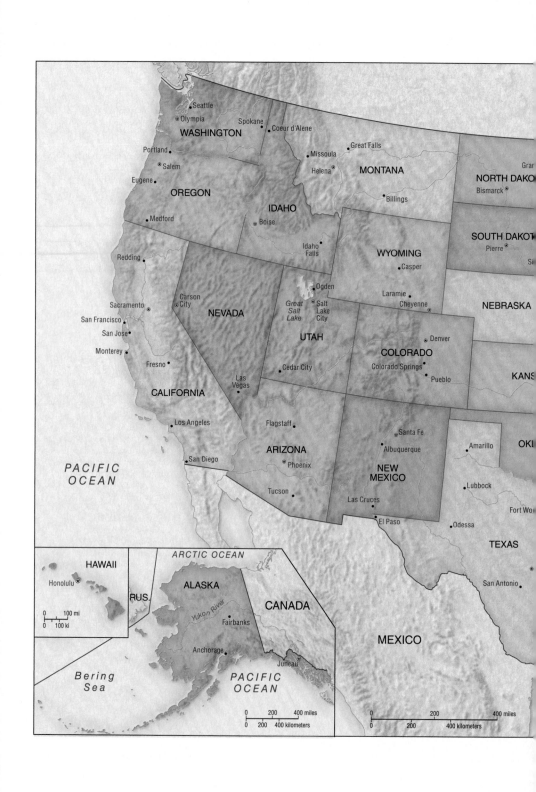

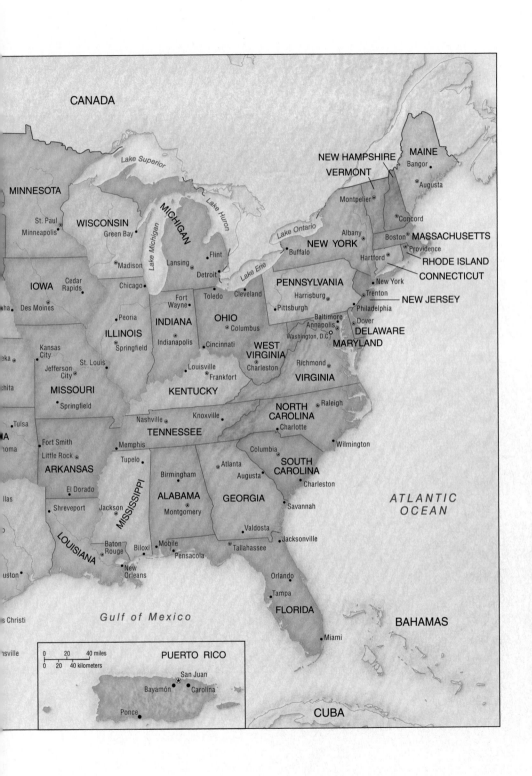